THE TENTH
Garfield
Fat Cat 3-Pack

JIM DAVIS

Ballantine Books • New York

A Ballantine Book
Published by The Ballantine Publishing Group

GARFIELD LIFE IN THE FAT LANE copyright © 1995 by Paws, Incorporated
GARFIELD TONS OF FUN copyright © 1996 by Paws, Incorporated
GARFIELD BIGGER AND BETTER copyright © 1996 by Paws, Incorporated
GARFIELD Comic Strips copyright © 1994, 1995, 1996 by Paws, Incorporated

www.randomhouse.com/BB/

Library of Congress Catalog Card Number: 98-96724

ISBN: 0-345-43458-7

Manufactured in the United States of America

First Edition: February 1999

10 9 8 7 6 5 4 3 2 1

Garfield
life in the fat lane

BY: JIM DAVIS

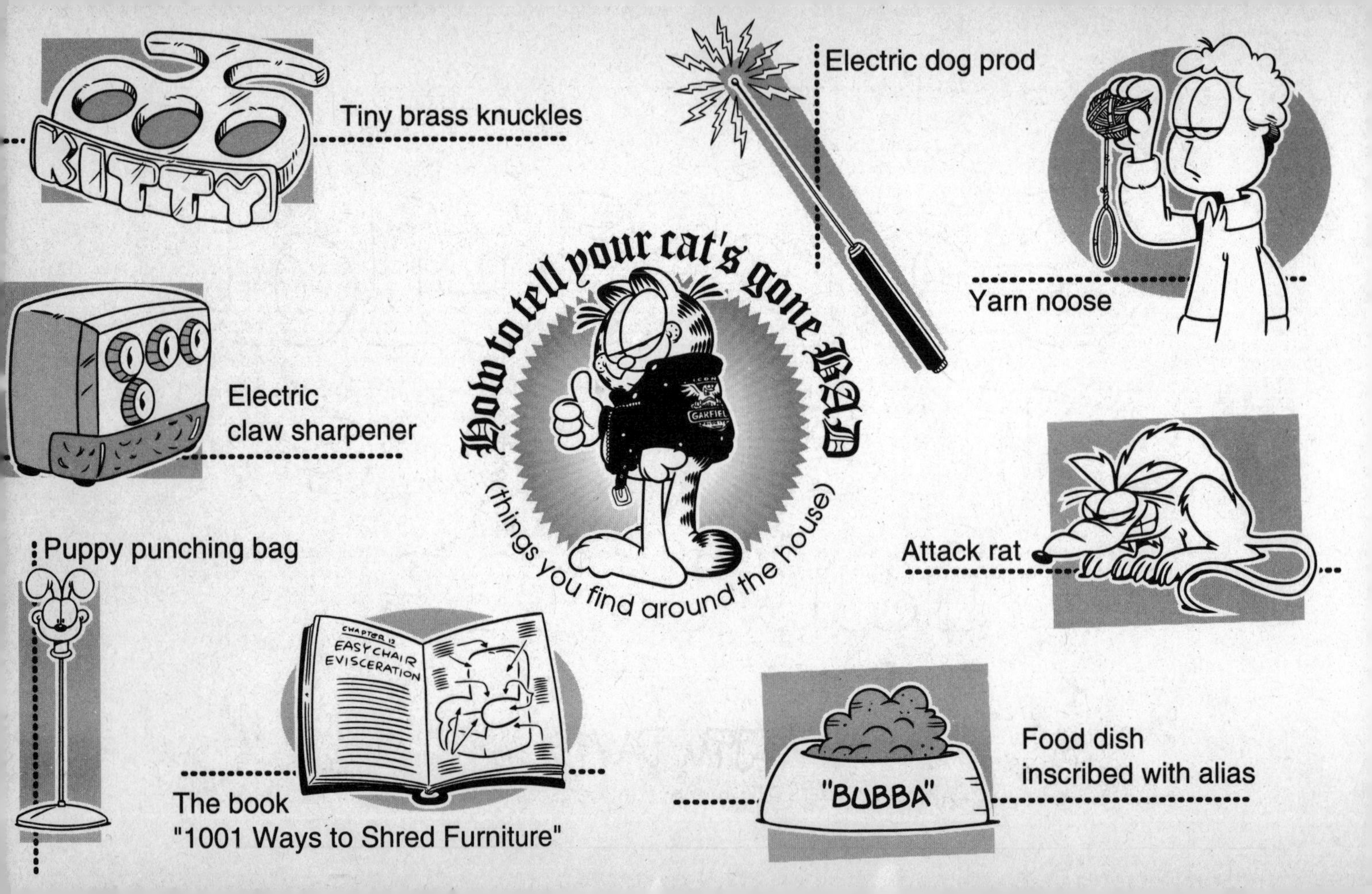
How to tell your cat's gone BAD
(things you find around the house)
Tiny brass knuckles
KITTY
Electric dog prod
Yarn noose
Electric
claw sharpener
GARFIELD
Attack rat
Puppy punching bag
CHAPTER 12
EASY CHAIR
EVISCERATION
The book
"1001 Ways to Shred Furniture"
Food dish
inscribed with alias
"BUBBA"

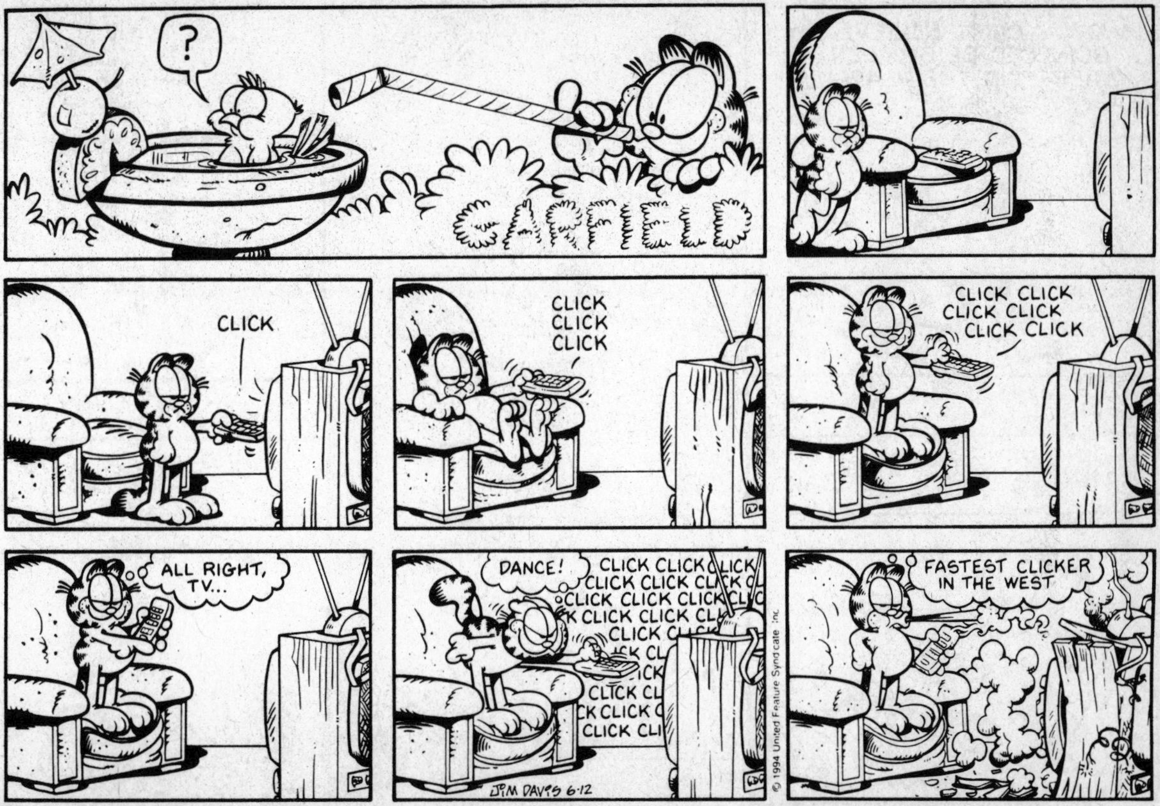
?
GARFIELD
CLICK
CLICK
CLICK
CLICK
CLICK CLICK
CLICK CLICK
CLICK CLICK
ALL RIGHT, TV...
DANCE!
CLICK CLICK CLICK CLICK CLICK CLICK CLICK CLICK CLICK CLICK CLICK CLICK CLICK CLICK CLICK CLICK CLICK CLICK CLICK CLICK
JIM DAVIS 6·12
FASTEST CLICKER IN THE WEST
© 1994 United Feature Syndicate, Inc.

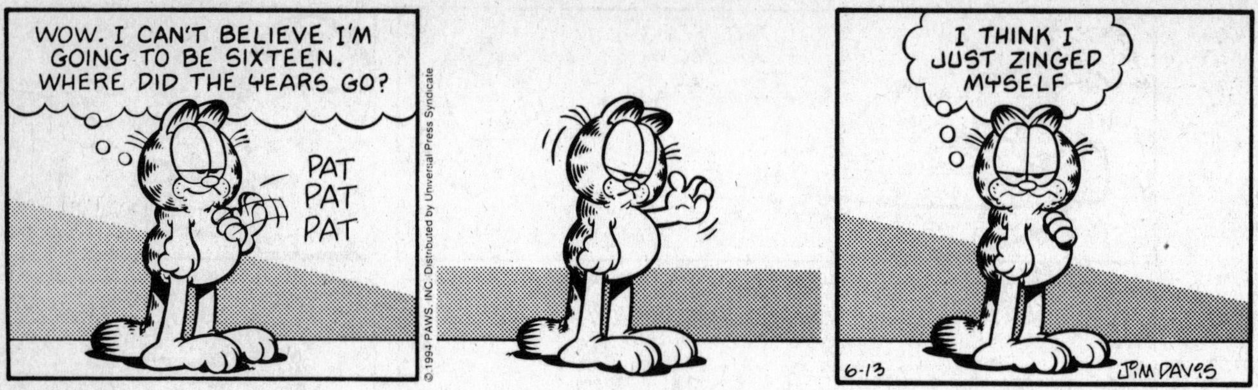
WOW. I CAN'T BELIEVE I'M GOING TO BE SIXTEEN. WHERE DID THE YEARS GO?
PAT PAT PAT
I THINK I JUST ZINGED MYSELF
6-13
JIM DAVIS

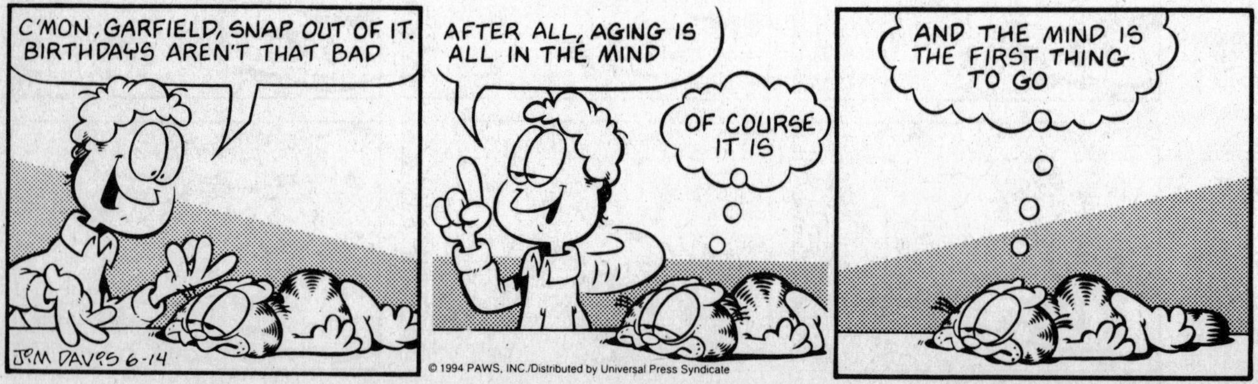
C'MON, GARFIELD, SNAP OUT OF IT. BIRTHDAYS AREN'T THAT BAD
JIM DAVIS 6-14
AFTER ALL, AGING IS ALL IN THE MIND
OF COURSE IT IS
AND THE MIND IS THE FIRST THING TO GO

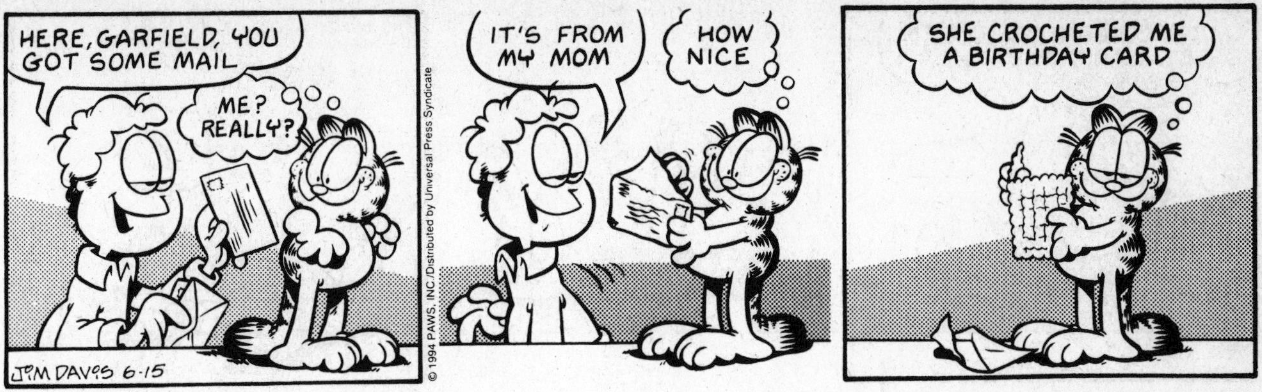
HERE, GARFIELD, YOU GOT SOME MAIL
ME? REALLY?
JIM DAVIS 6-15
IT'S FROM MY MOM
HOW NICE
SHE CROCHETED ME A BIRTHDAY CARD
© 1994 PAWS, INC./Distributed by Universal Press Syndicate

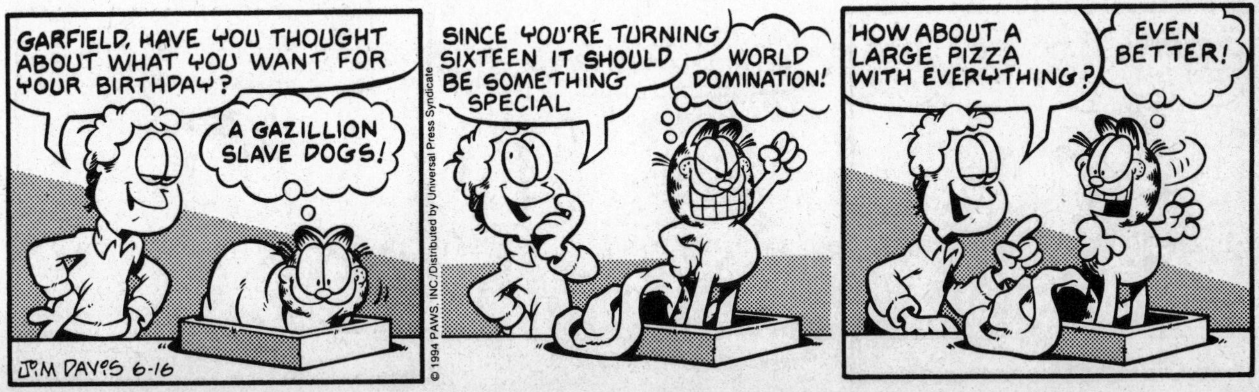
GARFIELD, HAVE YOU THOUGHT ABOUT WHAT YOU WANT FOR YOUR BIRTHDAY?
A GAZILLION SLAVE DOGS!
JIM DAVIS 6-16
SINCE YOU'RE TURNING SIXTEEN IT SHOULD BE SOMETHING SPECIAL
WORLD DOMINATION!
HOW ABOUT A LARGE PIZZA WITH EVERYTHING?
EVEN BETTER!
© 1994 PAWS, INC./Distributed by Universal Press Syndicate

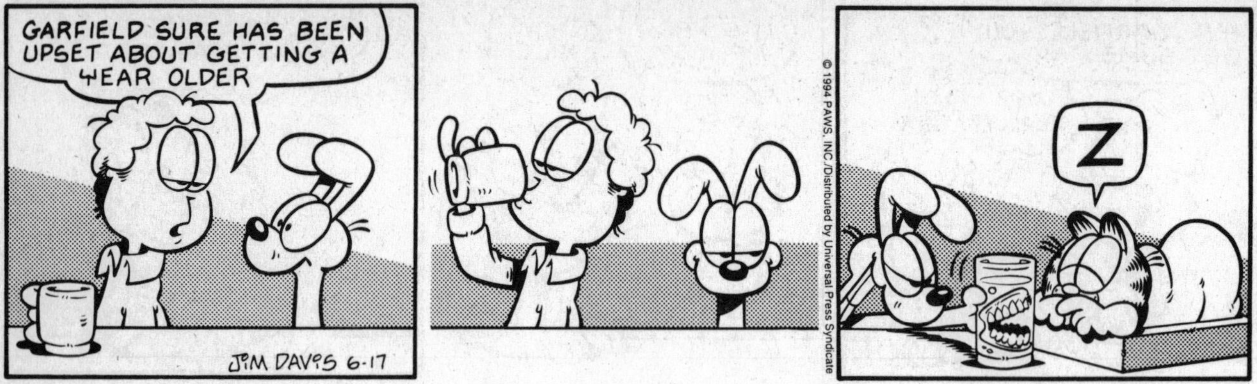
GARFIELD SURE HAS BEEN UPSET ABOUT GETTING A YEAR OLDER
Z
JIM DAVIS 6-17
© 1994 PAWS, INC./Distributed by Universal Press Syndicate

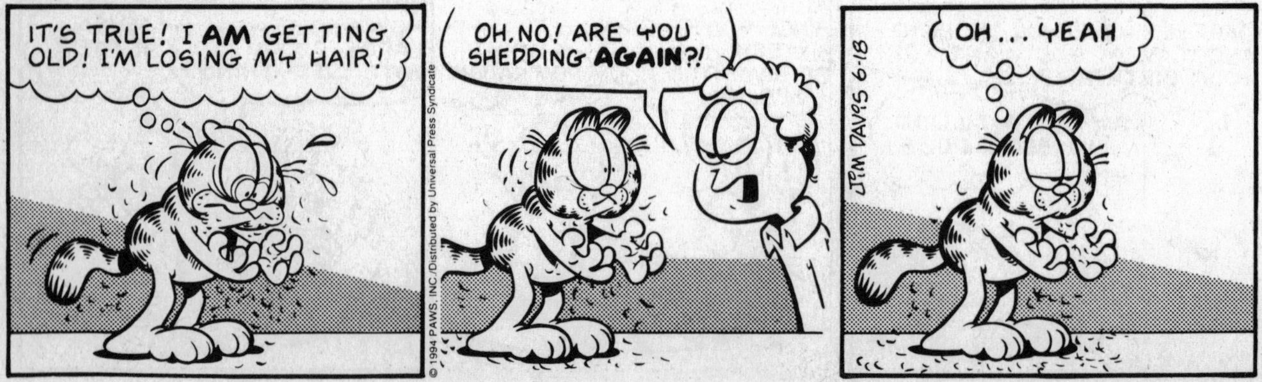
IT'S TRUE! I **AM** GETTING OLD! I'M LOSING MY HAIR!
OH, NO! ARE YOU SHEDDING **AGAIN**?!
OH... YEAH
JIM DAVIS 6-18
© 1994 PAWS, INC./Distributed by Universal Press Syndicate

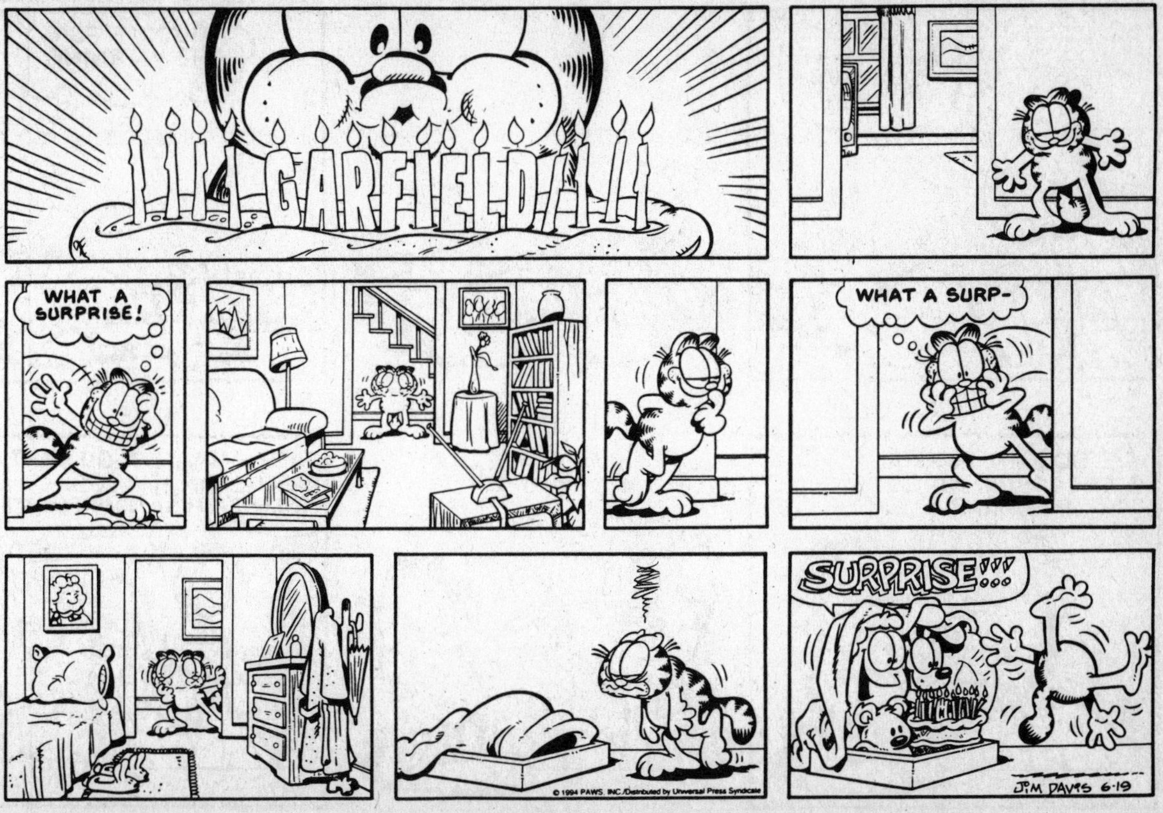
GARFIELD
WHAT A SURPRISE!
WHAT A SURP-
SURPRISE!!!
© 1994 PAWS, INC./Distributed by Universal Press Syndicate
JIM DAVIS 6-19

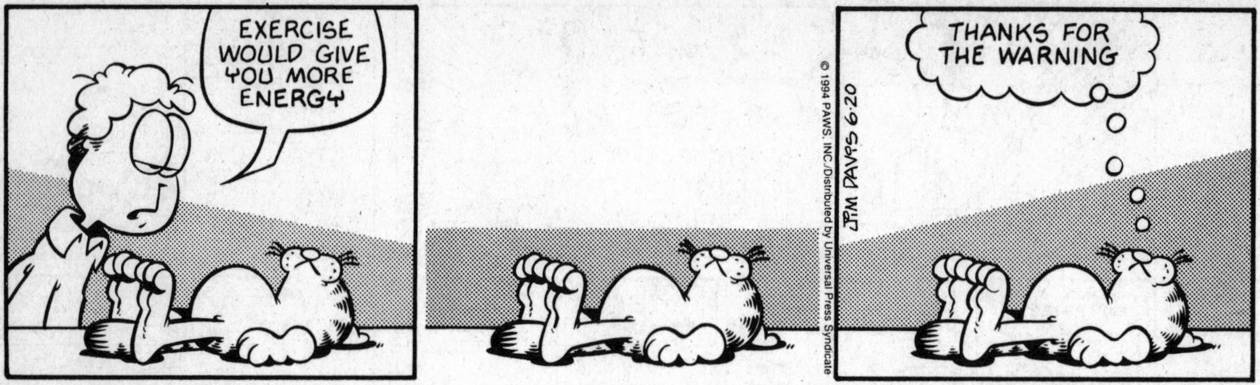
EXERCISE WOULD GIVE YOU MORE ENERGY
THANKS FOR THE WARNING
© 1994 PAWS, INC./Distributed by Universal Press Syndicate
JIM DAVIS 6-20

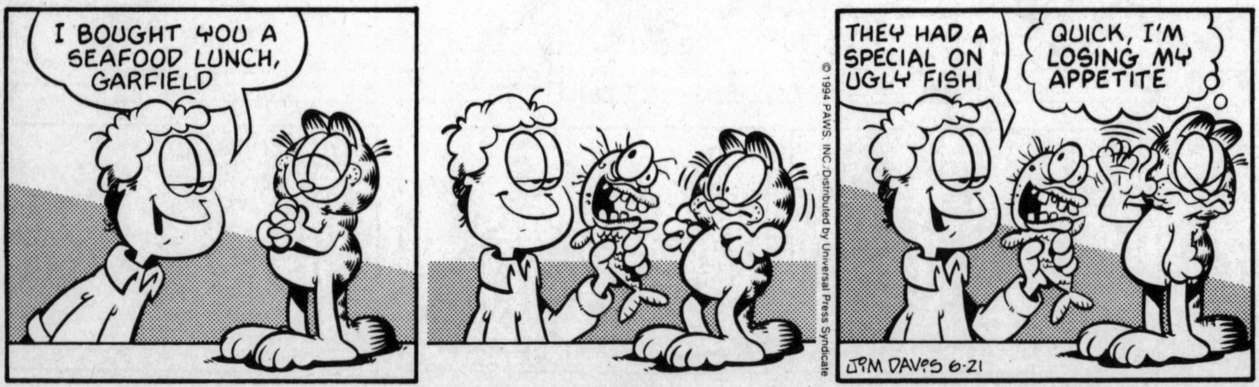
I BOUGHT YOU A SEAFOOD LUNCH, GARFIELD
THEY HAD A SPECIAL ON UGLY FISH
QUICK, I'M LOSING MY APPETITE
© 1994 PAWS, INC./Distributed by Universal Press Syndicate
JIM DAVIS 6-21

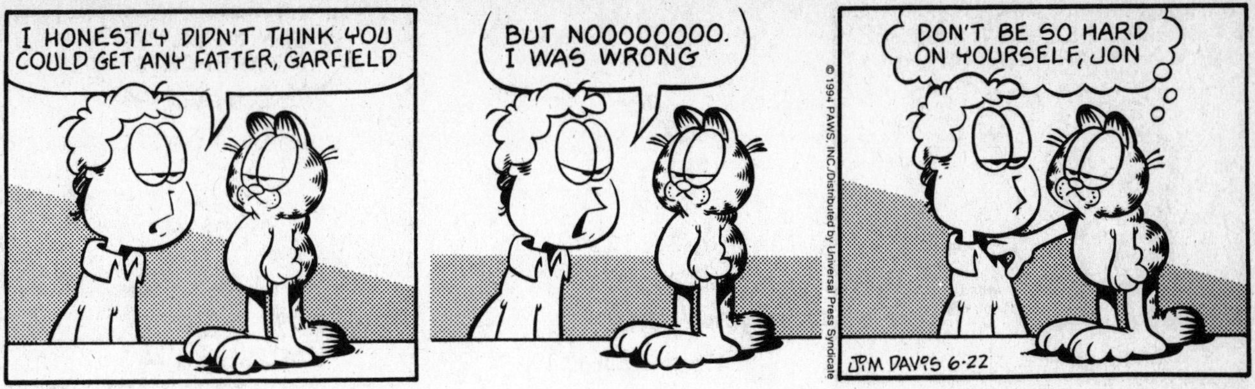
I HONESTLY DIDN'T THINK YOU COULD GET ANY FATTER, GARFIELD
BUT NOOOOOOOO. I WAS WRONG
DON'T BE SO HARD ON YOURSELF, JON
JIM DAVIS 6-22
© 1994 PAWS, INC./Distributed by Universal Press Syndicate

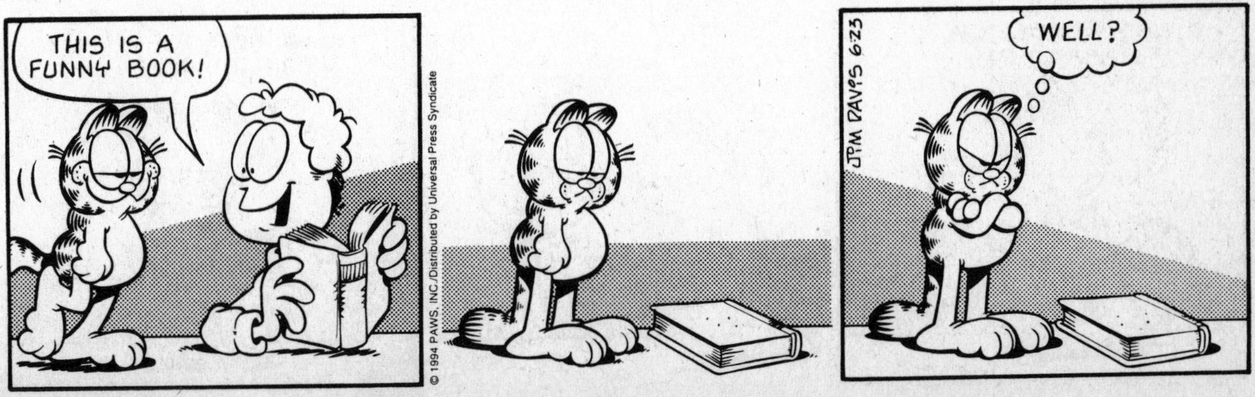
THIS IS A FUNNY BOOK!
WELL?
JIM DAVIS 6-23
© 1994 PAWS, INC./Distributed by Universal Press Syndicate

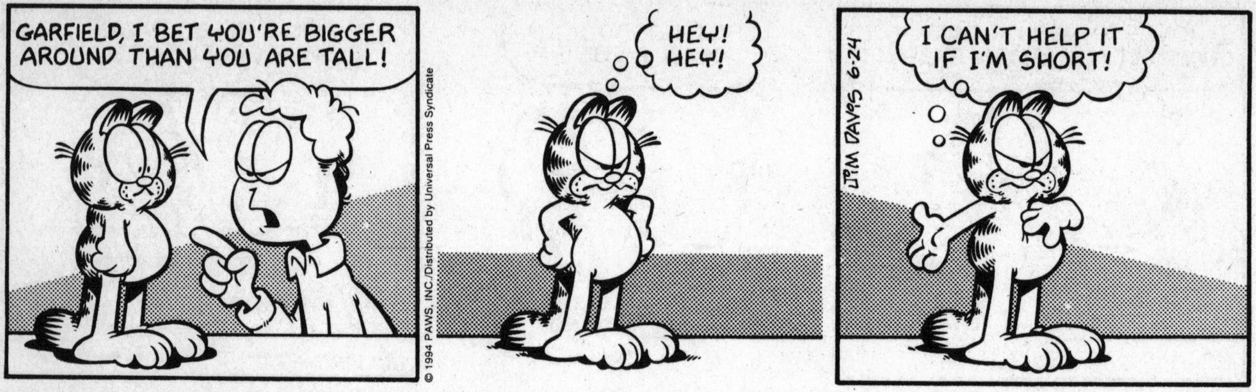
GARFIELD, I BET YOU'RE BIGGER AROUND THAN YOU ARE TALL!
HEY! HEY!
I CAN'T HELP IT IF I'M SHORT!
JIM DAVIS 6-24
© 1994 PAWS, INC./Distributed by Universal Press Syndicate

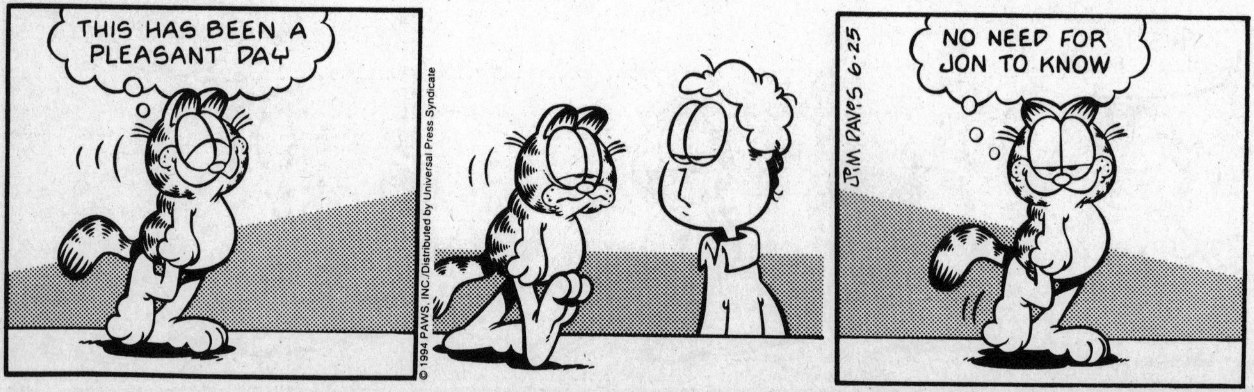
THIS HAS BEEN A PLEASANT DAY
NO NEED FOR JON TO KNOW
JIM DAVIS 6-25
© 1994 PAWS, INC./Distributed by Universal Press Syndicate

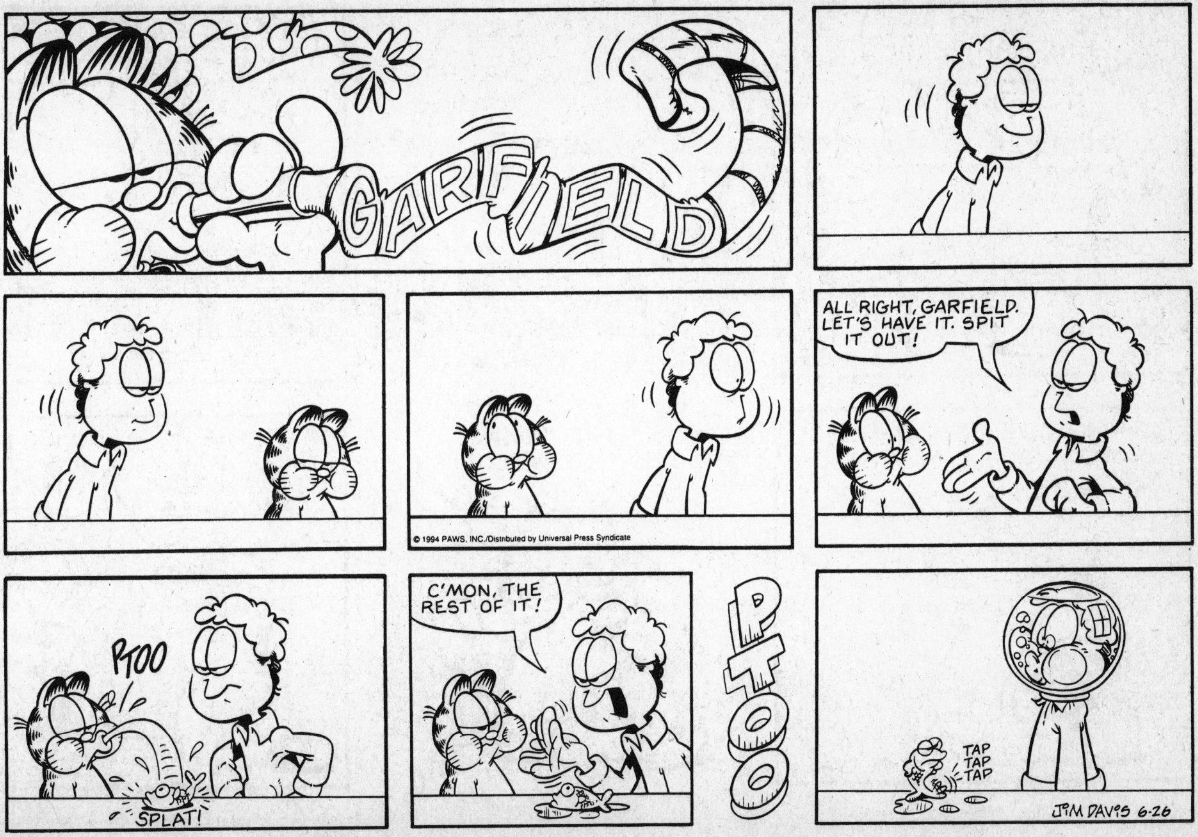
GARFIELD
ALL RIGHT, GARFIELD. LET'S HAVE IT. SPIT IT OUT!
© 1994 PAWS, INC./Distributed by Universal Press Syndicate
PTOO
SPLAT!
C'MON, THE REST OF IT!
PTOO
TAP TAP TAP
JIM DAVIS 6-26

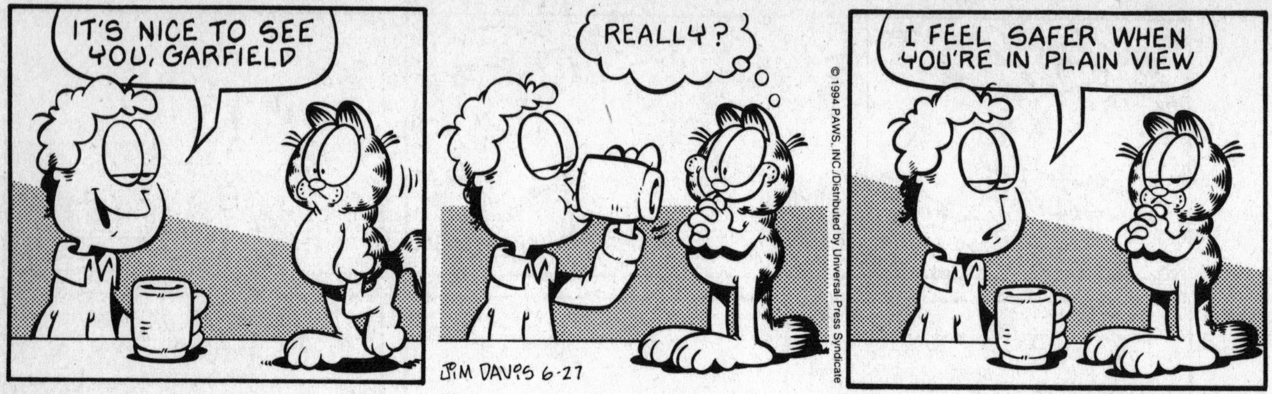
IT'S NICE TO SEE YOU, GARFIELD
REALLY?
I FEEL SAFER WHEN YOU'RE IN PLAIN VIEW
JIM DAVIS 6-27

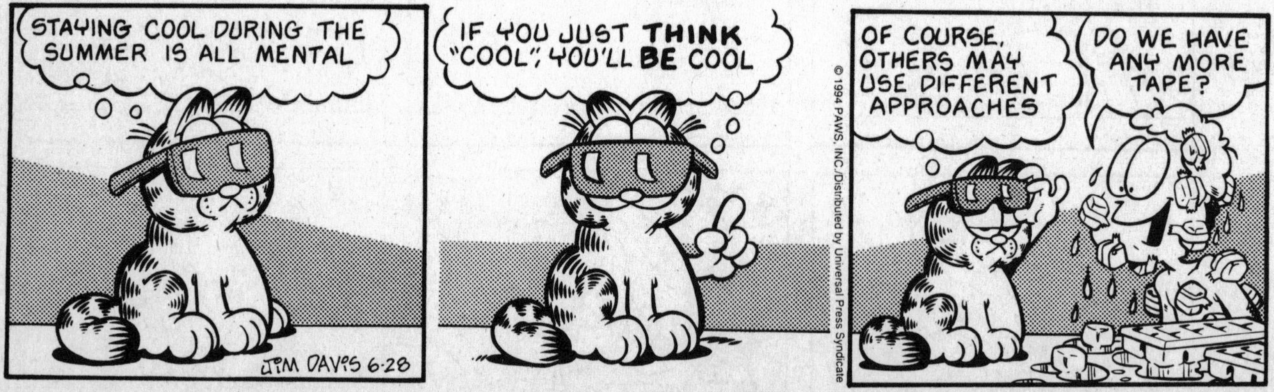
STAYING COOL DURING THE SUMMER IS ALL MENTAL
JIM DAVIS 6-28
IF YOU JUST **THINK** "COOL", YOU'LL **BE** COOL
OF COURSE, OTHERS MAY USE DIFFERENT APPROACHES
DO WE HAVE ANY MORE TAPE?

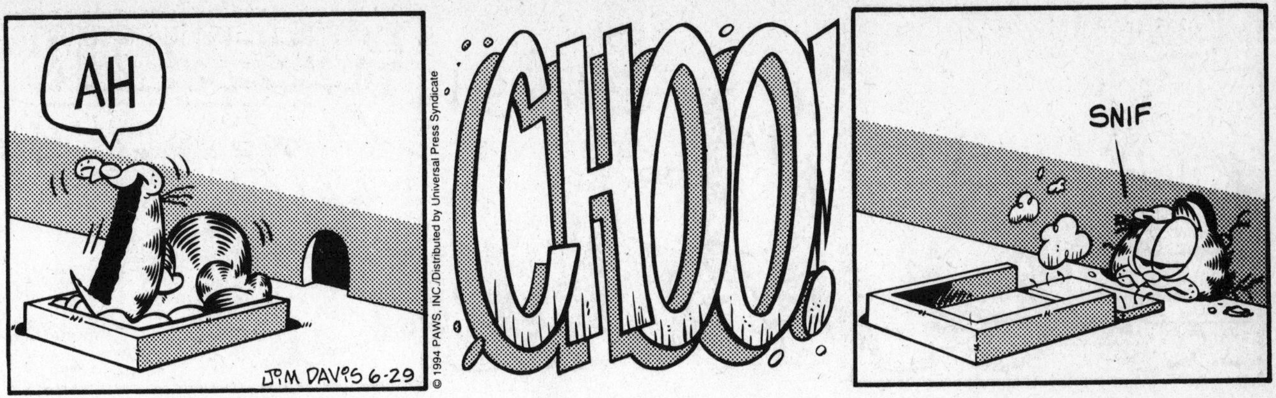
AH
CHOO!
SNIF
JIM DAVIS 6-29
© 1994 PAWS, INC./Distributed by Universal Press Syndicate

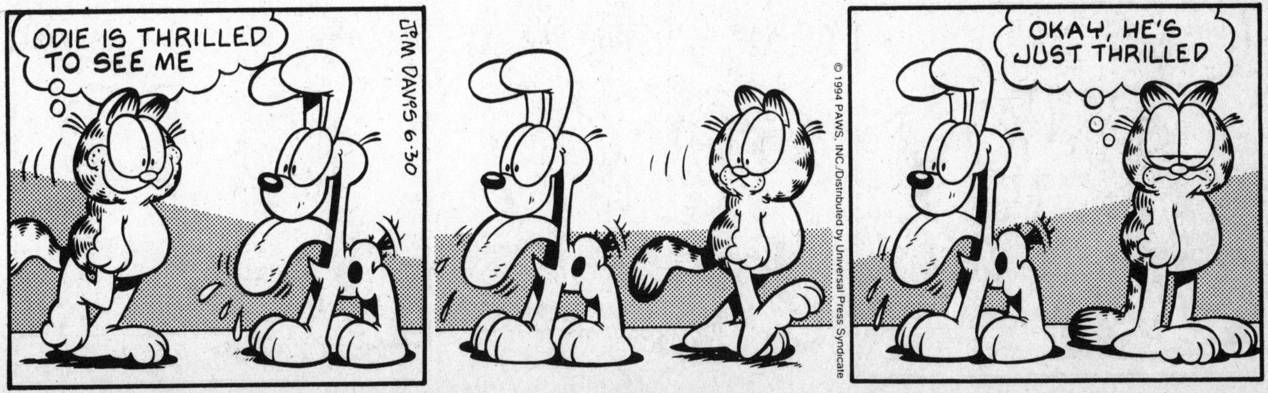
ODIE IS THRILLED TO SEE ME
JIM DAVIS 6-30
OKAY, HE'S JUST THRILLED
© 1994 PAWS, INC./Distributed by Universal Press Syndicate

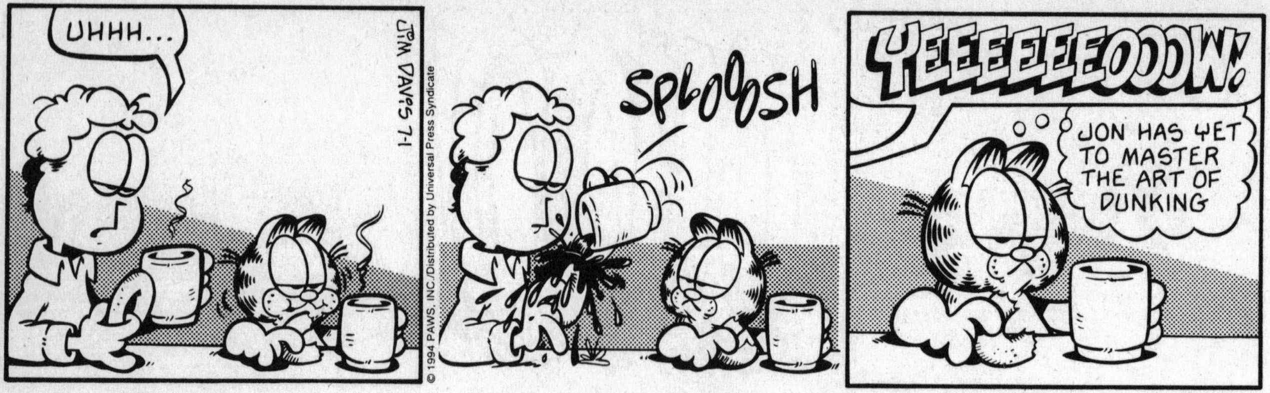
UHHH...
JIM DAVIS 7-1
© 1994 PAWS, INC./Distributed by Universal Press Syndicate
SPLOOOSH
YEEEEEEOOOOW!
JON HAS YET TO MASTER THE ART OF DUNKING

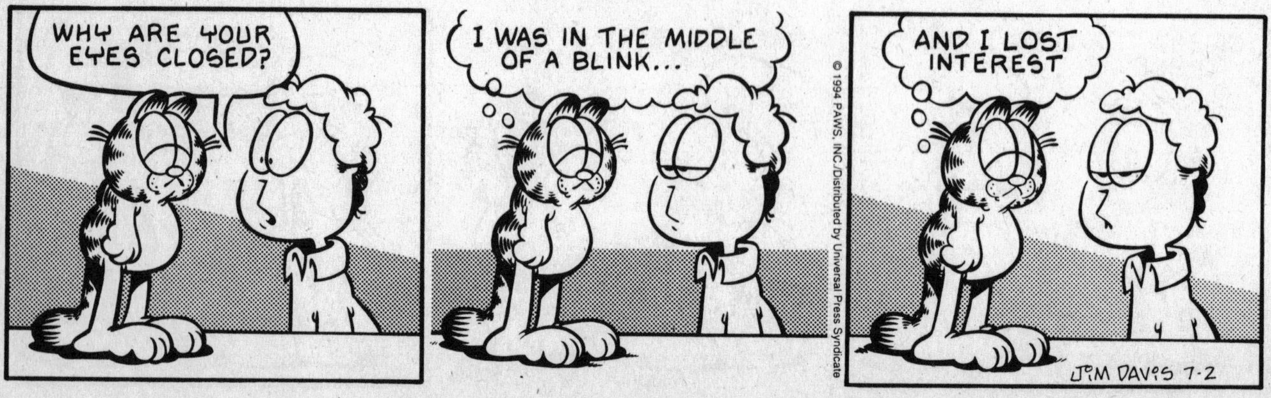
WHY ARE YOUR EYES CLOSED?
I WAS IN THE MIDDLE OF A BLINK...
© 1994 PAWS, INC./Distributed by Universal Press Syndicate
AND I LOST INTEREST
JIM DAVIS 7-2

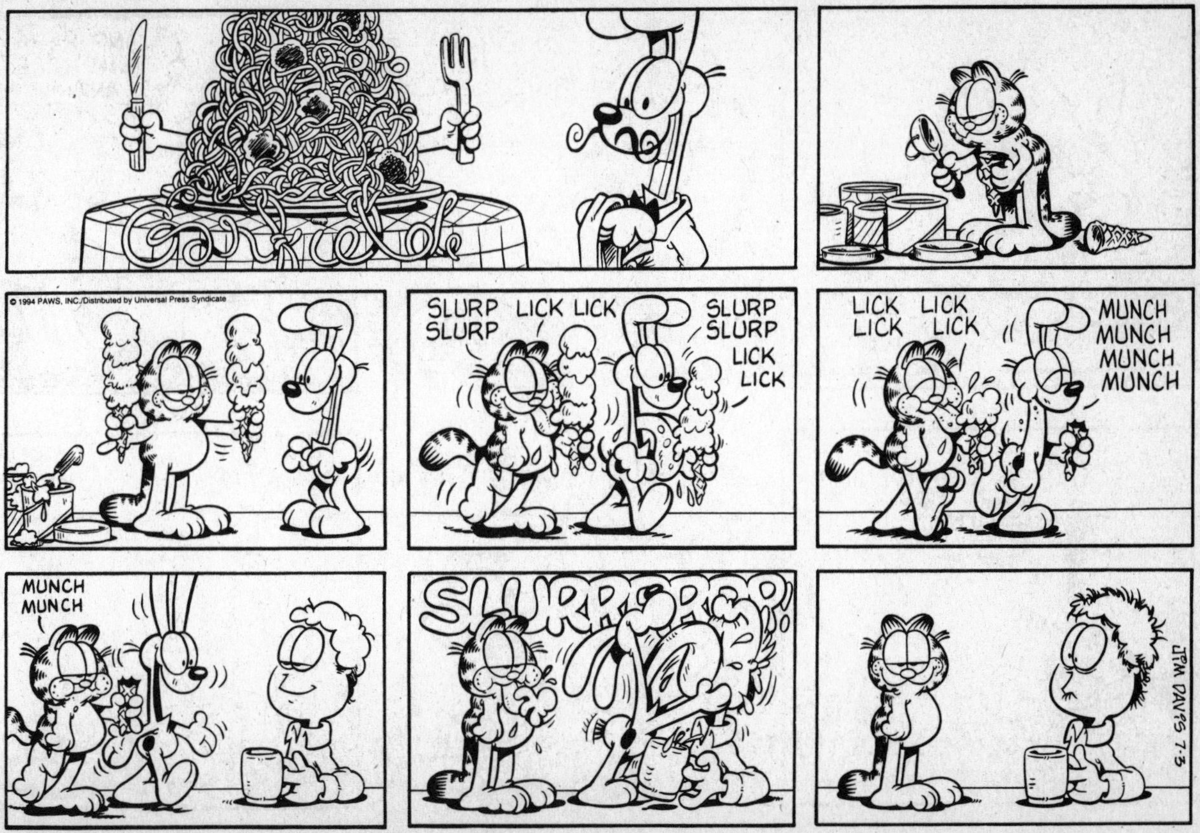
Garfield
SLURP SLURP
LICK LICK
SLURP SLURP
LICK LICK
LICK LICK
LICK LICK
MUNCH MUNCH MUNCH MUNCH
MUNCH MUNCH
SLURRRRRP!
JIM DAVIS 7-3

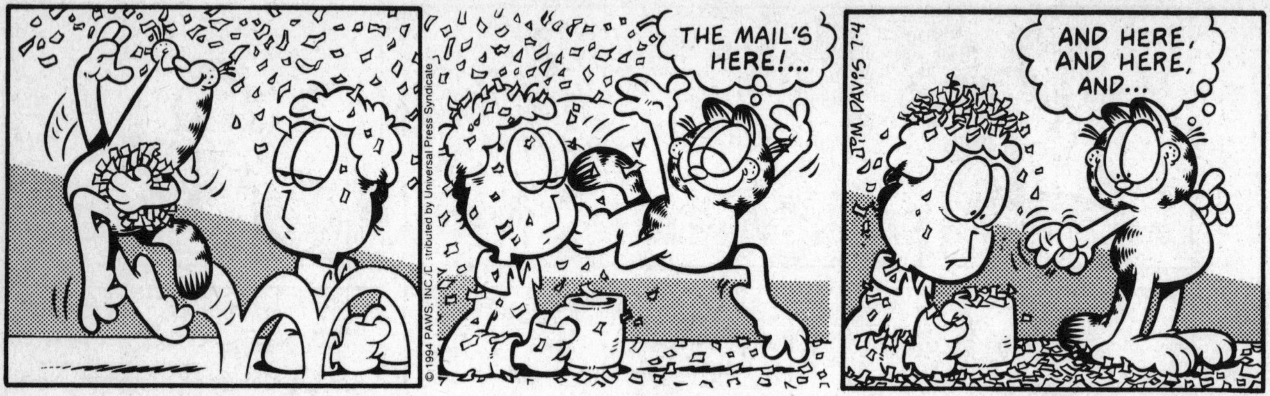
THE MAIL'S HERE!...
AND HERE, AND HERE, AND...
© 1994 PAWS, INC./Distributed by Universal Press Syndicate
JIM DAVIS 7-4

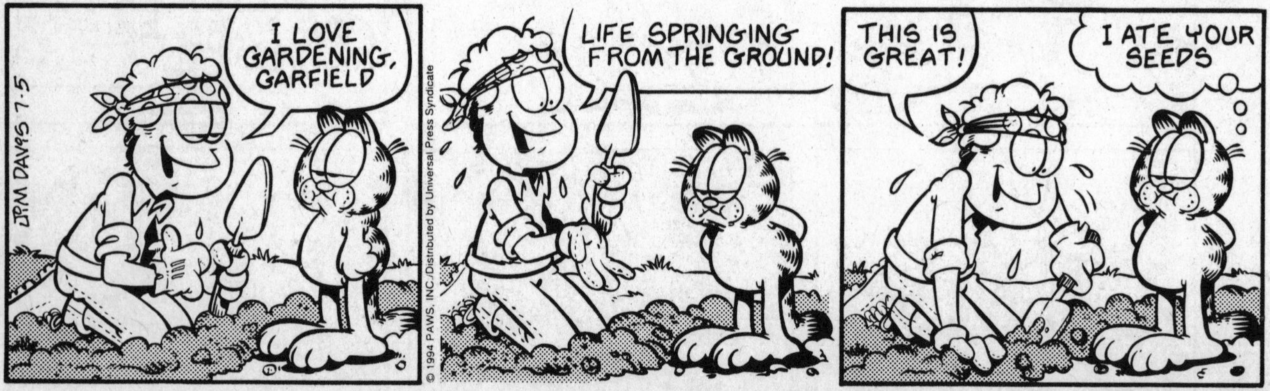
JIM DAVIS 7-5
I LOVE GARDENING, GARFIELD
LIFE SPRINGING FROM THE GROUND!
THIS IS GREAT!
I ATE YOUR SEEDS
© 1994 PAWS, INC./Distributed by Universal Press Syndicate

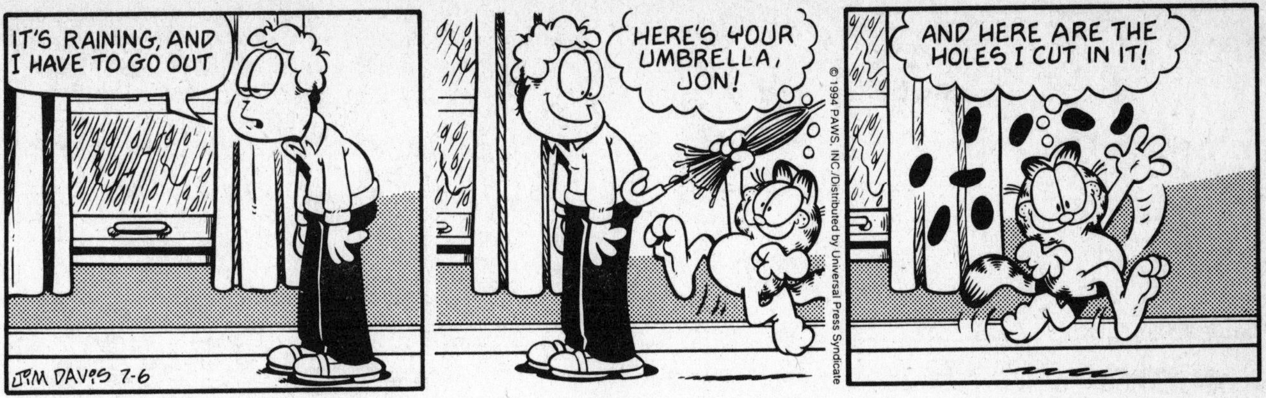
IT'S RAINING, AND I HAVE TO GO OUT
JIM DAVIS 7-6
HERE'S YOUR UMBRELLA, JON!
AND HERE ARE THE HOLES I CUT IN IT!
© 1994 PAWS, INC./Distributed by Universal Press Syndicate

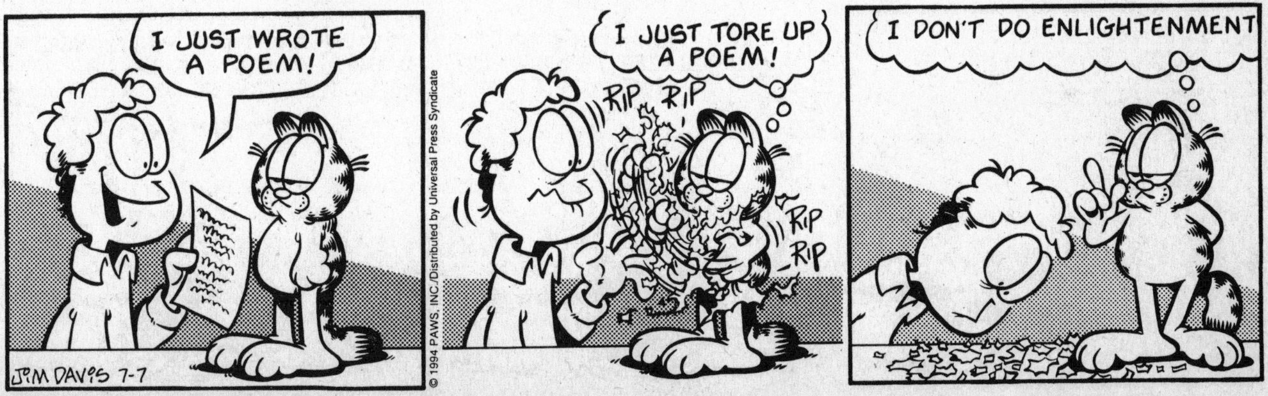
I JUST WROTE A POEM!
JIM DAVIS 7-7
© 1994 PAWS, INC./Distributed by Universal Press Syndicate
I JUST TORE UP A POEM!
RIP RIP
RIP
RIP
I DON'T DO ENLIGHTENMENT

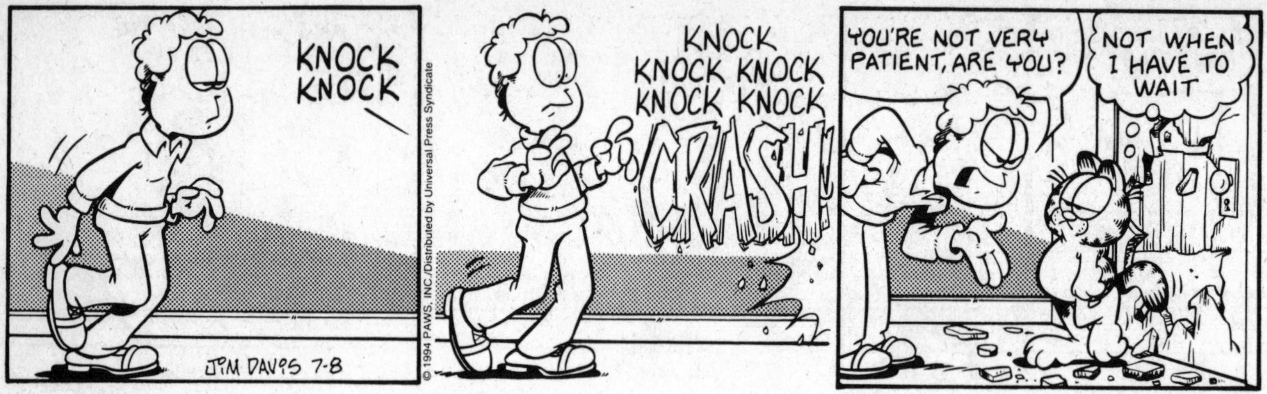
KNOCK KNOCK
JIM DAVIS 7-8
© 1994 PAWS, INC./Distributed by Universal Press Syndicate
KNOCK KNOCK KNOCK KNOCK KNOCK
CRASH
YOU'RE NOT VERY PATIENT, ARE YOU?
NOT WHEN I HAVE TO WAIT

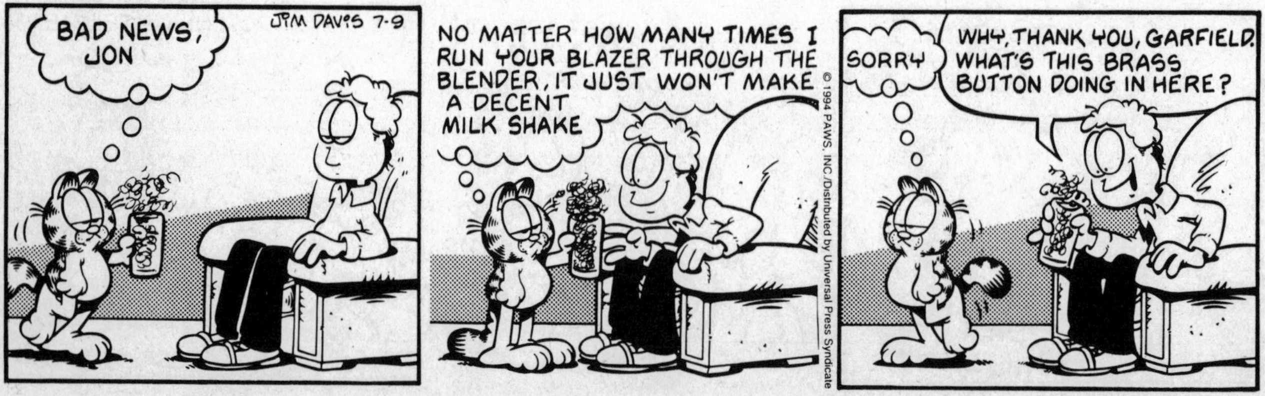
BAD NEWS, JON
JIM DAVIS 7-9
NO MATTER HOW MANY TIMES I RUN YOUR BLAZER THROUGH THE BLENDER, IT JUST WON'T MAKE A DECENT MILK SHAKE
© 1994 PAWS, INC./Distributed by Universal Press Syndicate
SORRY
WHY, THANK YOU, GARFIELD. WHAT'S THIS BRASS BUTTON DOING IN HERE?

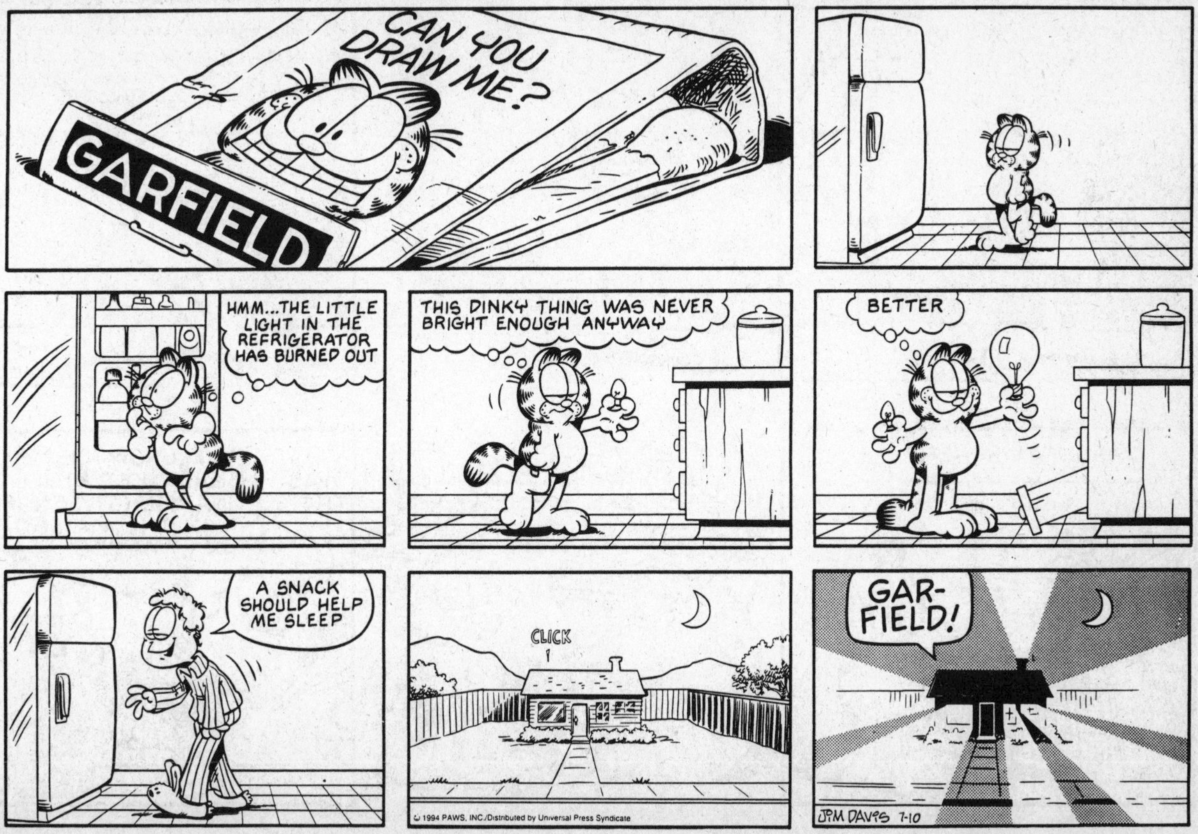

CAN YOU DRAW ME?
GARFIELD
HMM...THE LITTLE LIGHT IN THE REFRIGERATOR HAS BURNED OUT
THIS DINKY THING WAS NEVER BRIGHT ENOUGH ANYWAY
BETTER
A SNACK SHOULD HELP ME SLEEP
CLICK
GAR-FIELD!
© 1994 PAWS, INC./Distributed by Universal Press Syndicate
JIM DAVIS 7-10

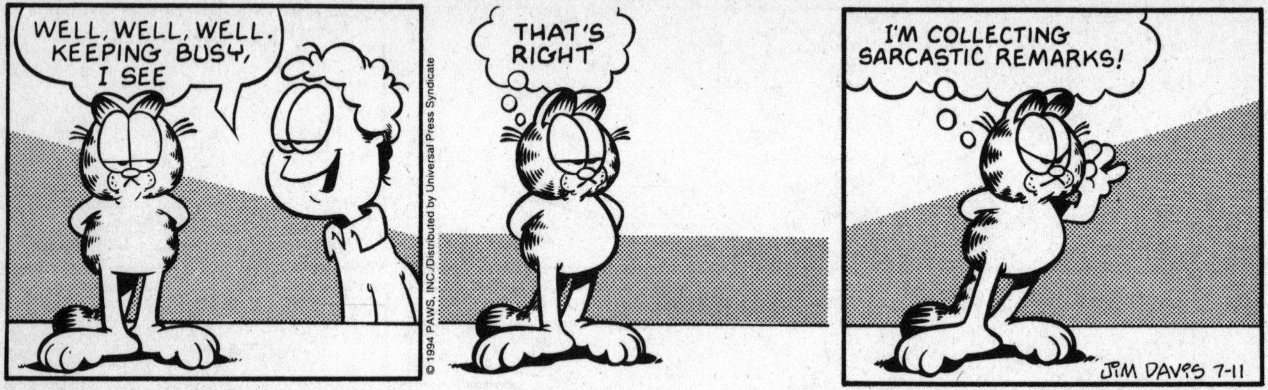
WELL, WELL, WELL. KEEPING BUSY, I SEE
THAT'S RIGHT
I'M COLLECTING SARCASTIC REMARKS!
JIM DAVIS 7-11
© 1994 PAWS, INC./Distributed by Universal Press Syndicate

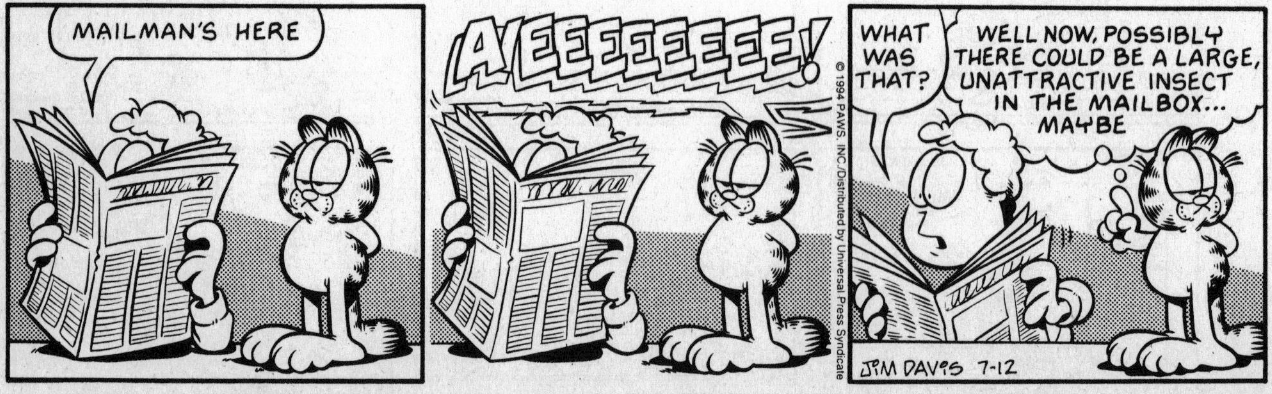
MAILMAN'S HERE
AIEEEEEEEEE!
WHAT WAS THAT?
WELL NOW, POSSIBLY THERE COULD BE A LARGE, UNATTRACTIVE INSECT IN THE MAILBOX... MAYBE
JIM DAVIS 7-12
© 1994 PAWS, INC./Distributed by Universal Press Syndicate

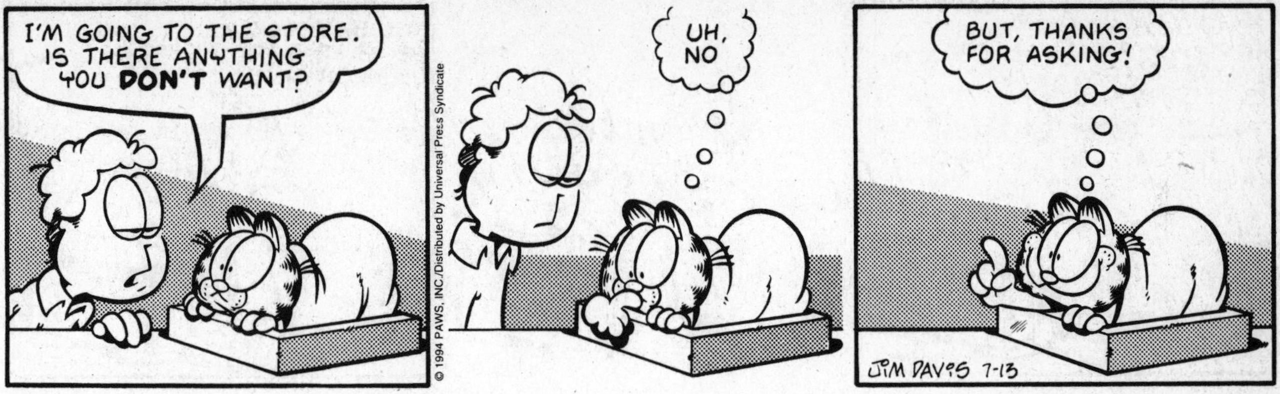
I'M GOING TO THE STORE. IS THERE ANYTHING YOU **DON'T** WANT?
UH, NO
BUT, THANKS FOR ASKING!
JIM DAVIS 7-13

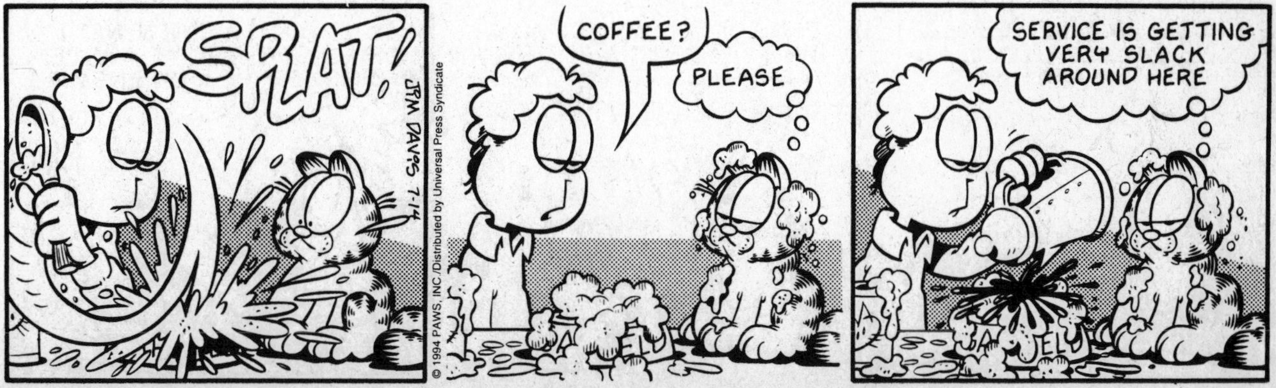
SPLAT!
JIM DAVIS 7-14
COFFEE?
PLEASE
SERVICE IS GETTING VERY SLACK AROUND HERE

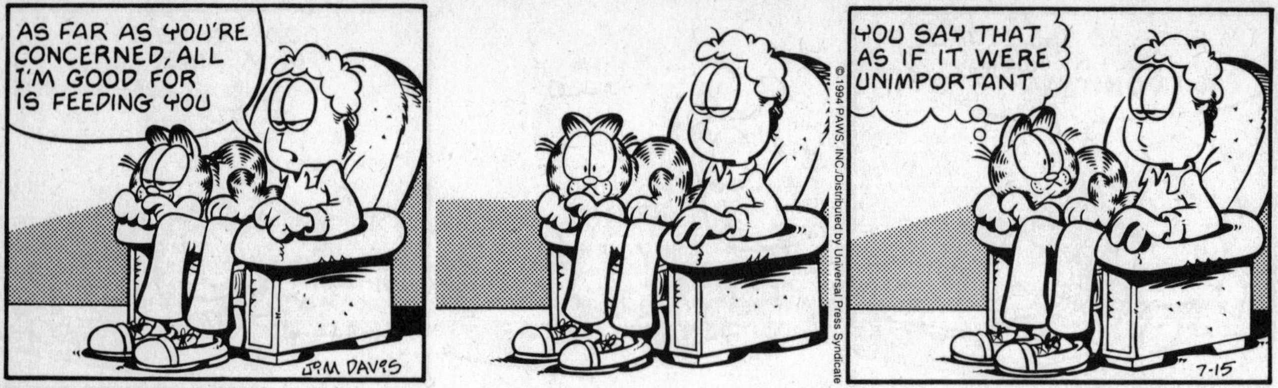
AS FAR AS YOU'RE CONCERNED, ALL I'M GOOD FOR IS FEEDING YOU
JIM DAVIS
YOU SAY THAT AS IF IT WERE UNIMPORTANT
7-15

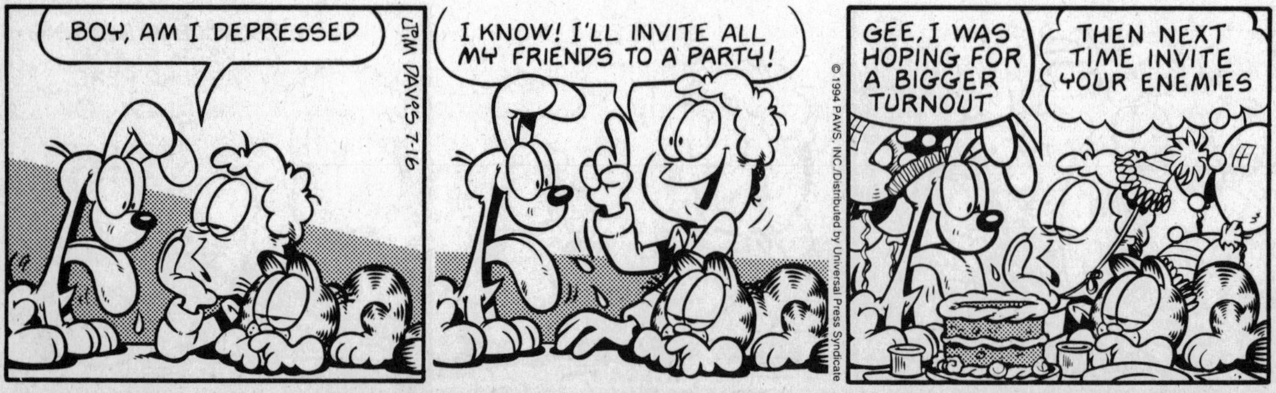
BOY, AM I DEPRESSED
JIM DAVIS 7-16
I KNOW! I'LL INVITE ALL MY FRIENDS TO A PARTY!
GEE, I WAS HOPING FOR A BIGGER TURNOUT
THEN NEXT TIME INVITE YOUR ENEMIES

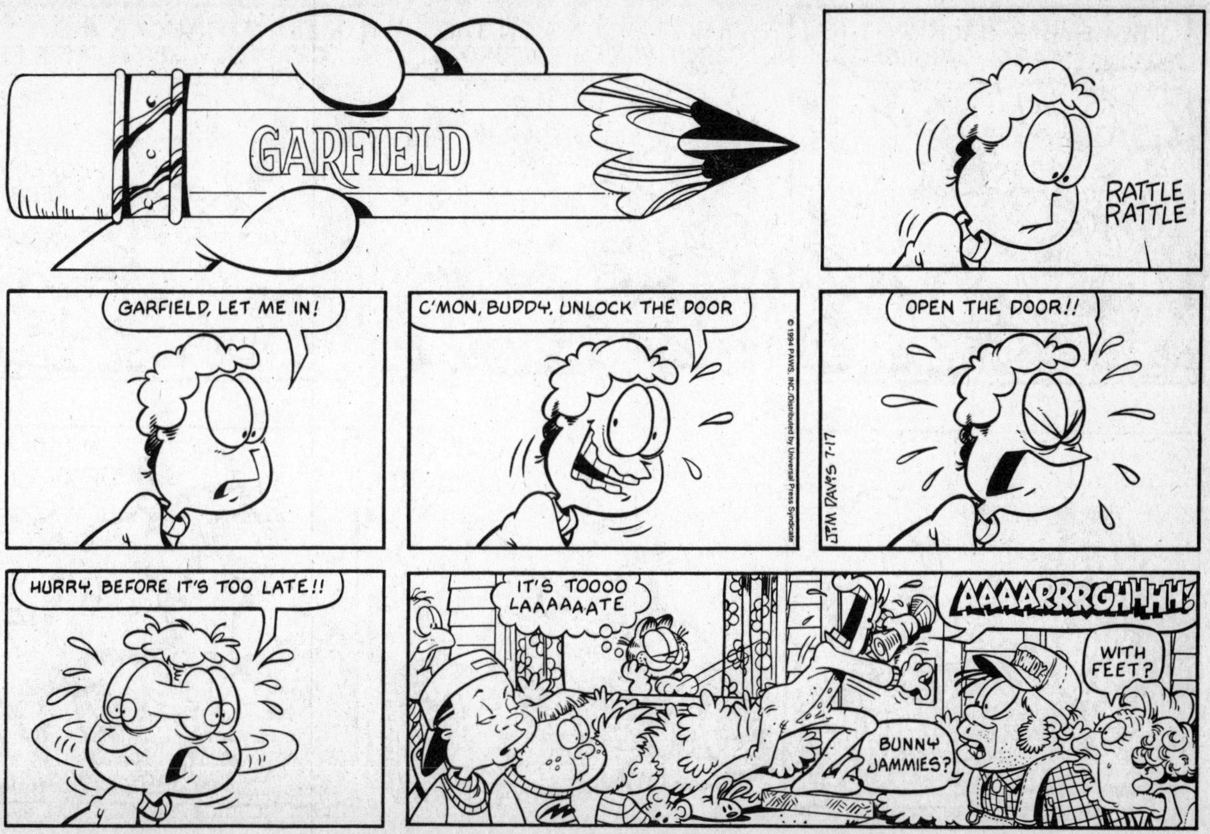
GARFIELD
RATTLE RATTLE
GARFIELD, LET ME IN!
C'MON, BUDDY. UNLOCK THE DOOR
© 1994 PAWS, INC./Distributed by Universal Press Syndicate
JPM DAVPS 7-17
OPEN THE DOOR!!
HURRY, BEFORE IT'S TOO LATE!!
IT'S TOOOO LAAAAAATE
AAAARRRGHHHH!
WITH FEET?
BUNNY JAMMIES?

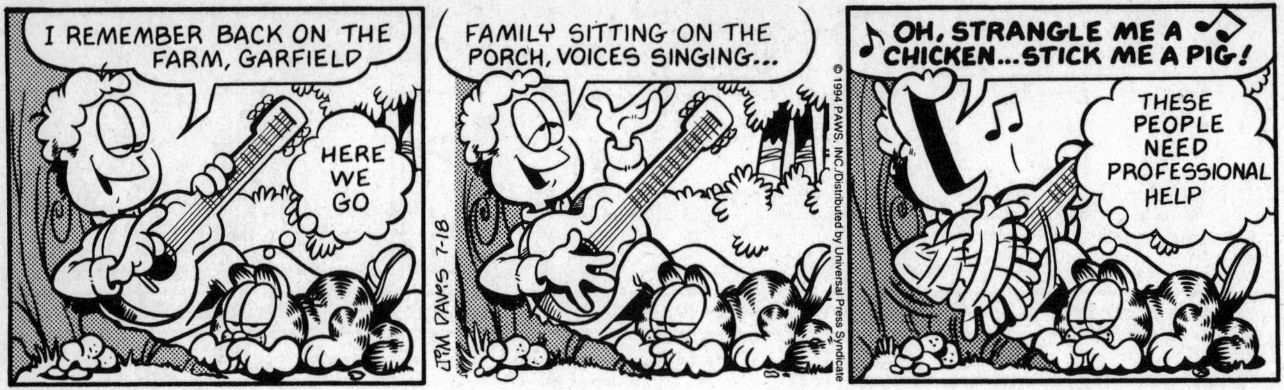
I REMEMBER BACK ON THE FARM, GARFIELD
HERE WE GO
JIM DAVIS 7-18
FAMILY SITTING ON THE PORCH, VOICES SINGING...
© 1994 PAWS, INC./Distributed by Universal Press Syndicate
♪ OH, STRANGLE ME A CHICKEN...STICK ME A PIG! ♫
THESE PEOPLE NEED PROFESSIONAL HELP

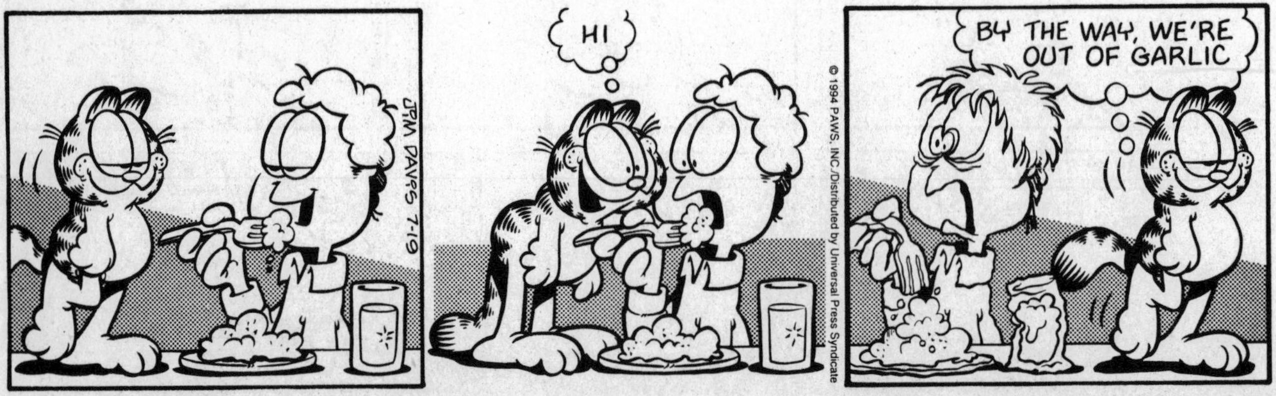
JIM DAVIS 7-19
HI
© 1994 PAWS, INC./Distributed by Universal Press Syndicate
BY THE WAY, WE'RE OUT OF GARLIC

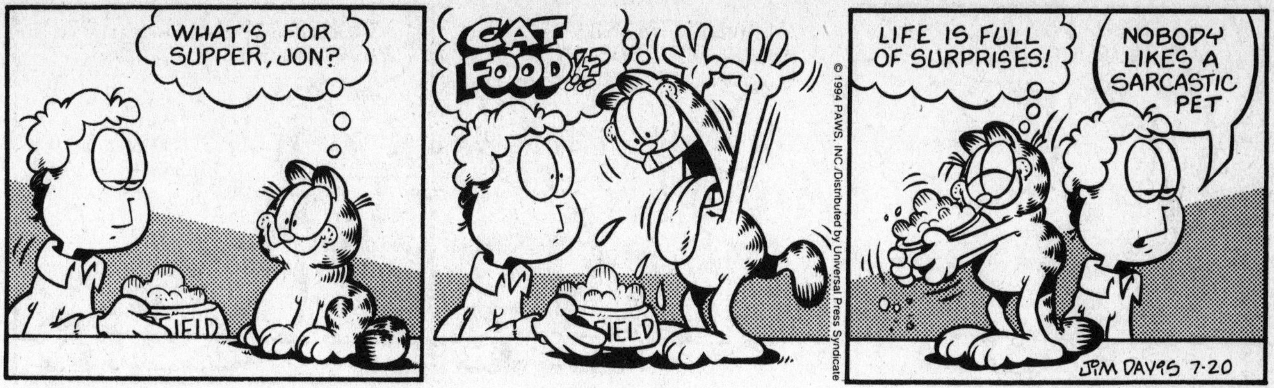
WHAT'S FOR SUPPER, JON?
CAT FOOD!?
LIFE IS FULL OF SURPRISES!
NOBODY LIKES A SARCASTIC PET
JIM DAVIS 7-20
© 1994 PAWS, INC./Distributed by Universal Press Syndicate

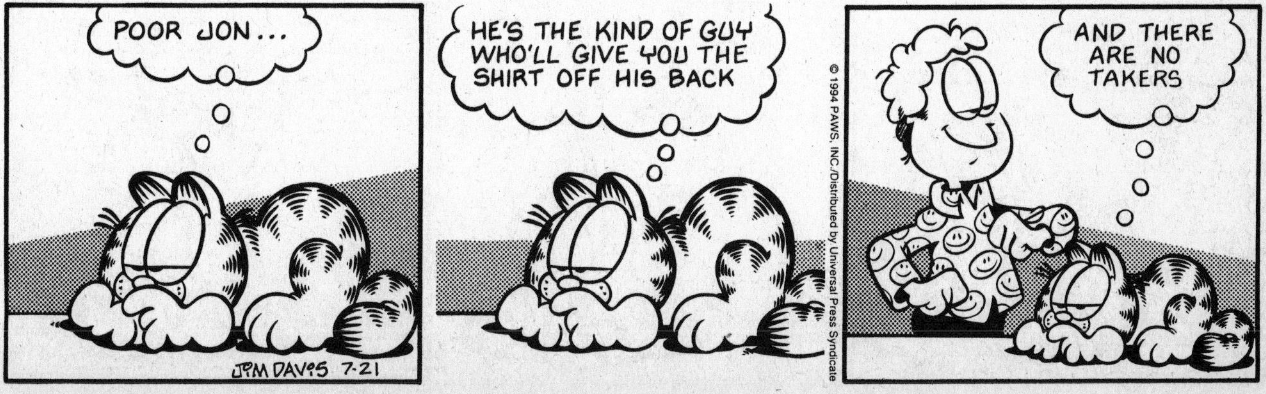
POOR JON...
HE'S THE KIND OF GUY WHO'LL GIVE YOU THE SHIRT OFF HIS BACK
AND THERE ARE NO TAKERS
JIM DAVIS 7-21
© 1994 PAWS, INC./Distributed by Universal Press Syndicate

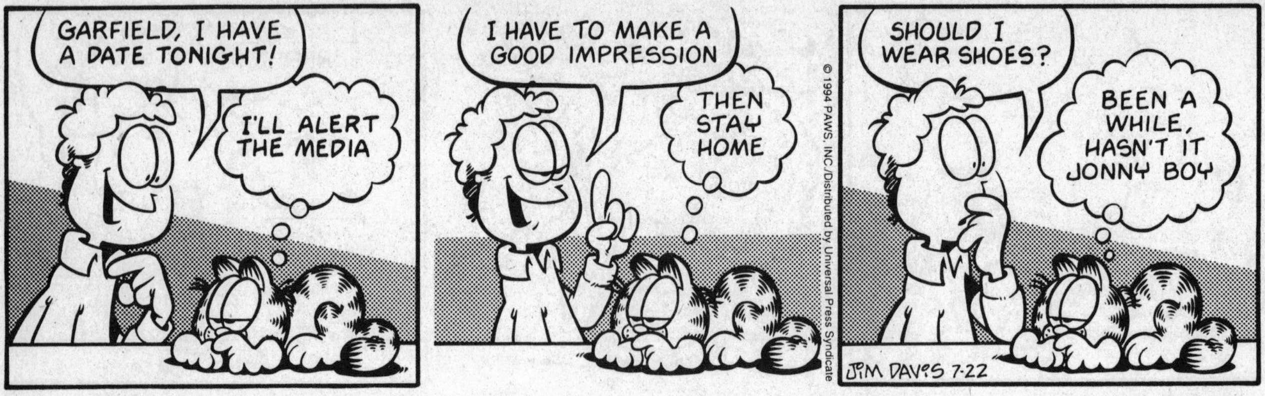
GARFIELD, I HAVE A DATE TONIGHT!
I'LL ALERT THE MEDIA
I HAVE TO MAKE A GOOD IMPRESSION
THEN STAY HOME
SHOULD I WEAR SHOES?
BEEN A WHILE, HASN'T IT JONNY BOY
JIM DAVIS 7-22

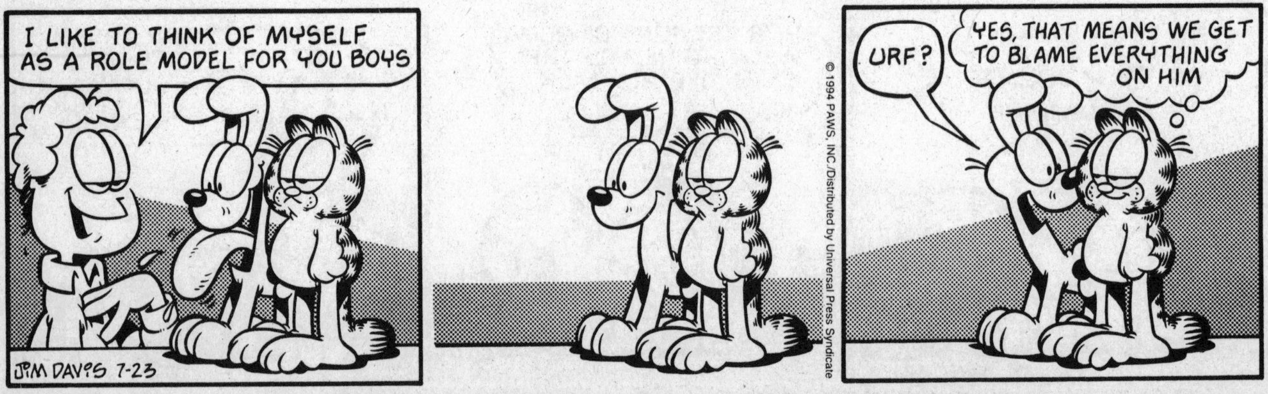
I LIKE TO THINK OF MYSELF AS A ROLE MODEL FOR YOU BOYS
JIM DAVIS 7-23
URF?
YES, THAT MEANS WE GET TO BLAME EVERYTHING ON HIM

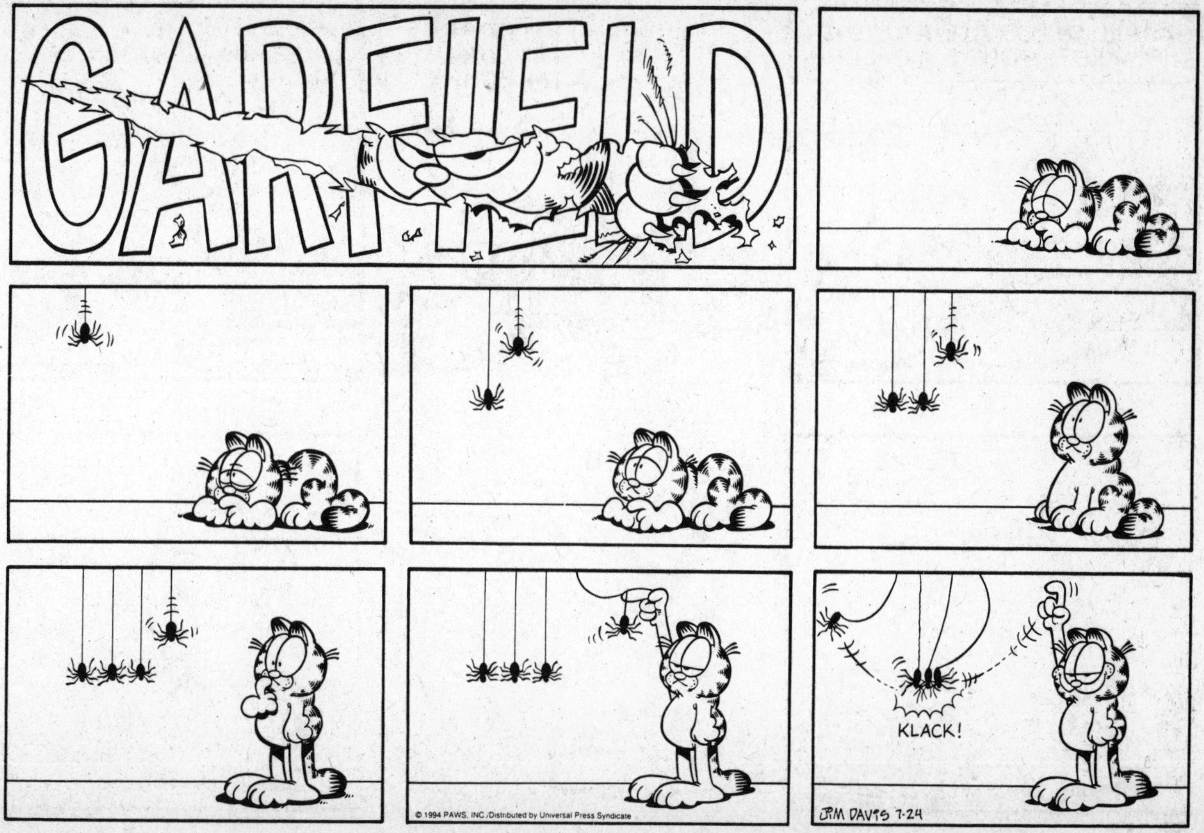
GARFIELD
KLACK!
JIM DAVIS 7-24

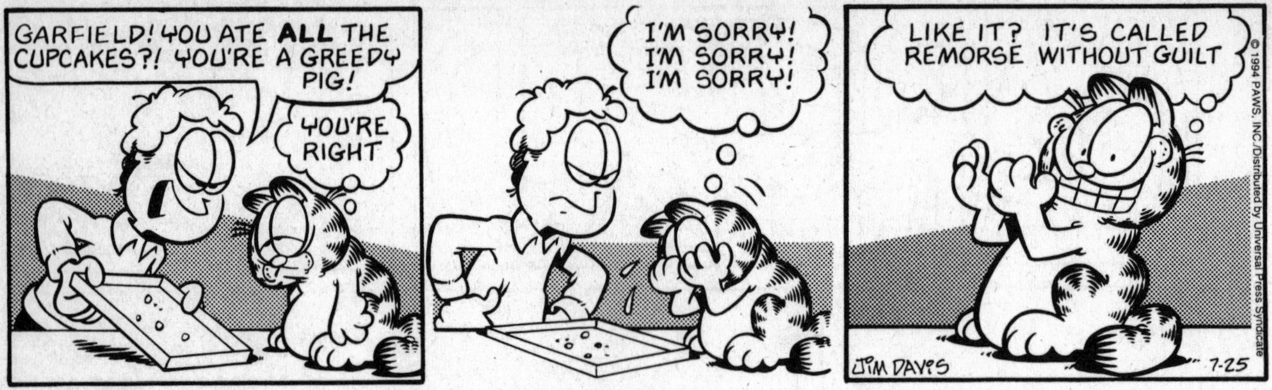
GARFIELD! YOU ATE ALL THE CUPCAKES?! YOU'RE A GREEDY PIG!
YOU'RE RIGHT
I'M SORRY! I'M SORRY! I'M SORRY!
LIKE IT? IT'S CALLED REMORSE WITHOUT GUILT
© 1994 PAWS, INC./Distributed by Universal Press Syndicate
JIM DAVIS 7-25

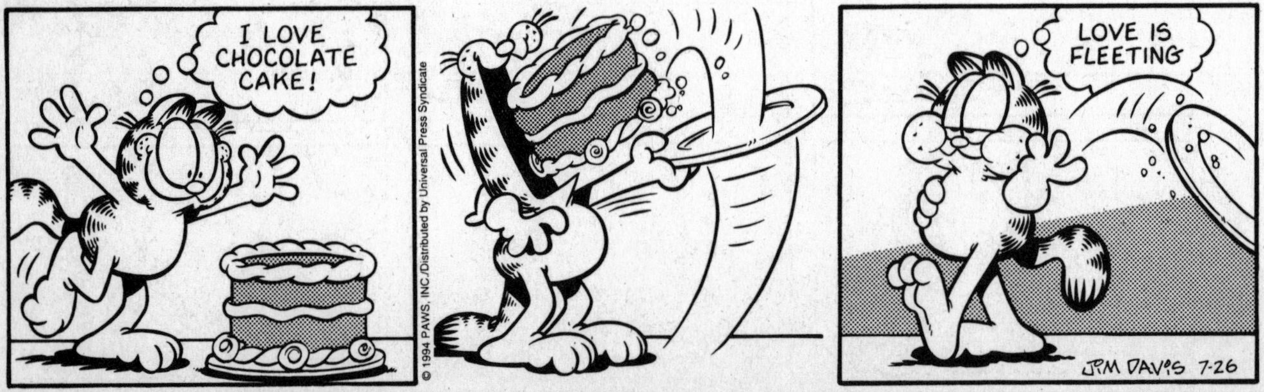
I LOVE CHOCOLATE CAKE!
© 1994 PAWS, INC./Distributed by Universal Press Syndicate
LOVE IS FLEETING
JIM DAVIS 7-26

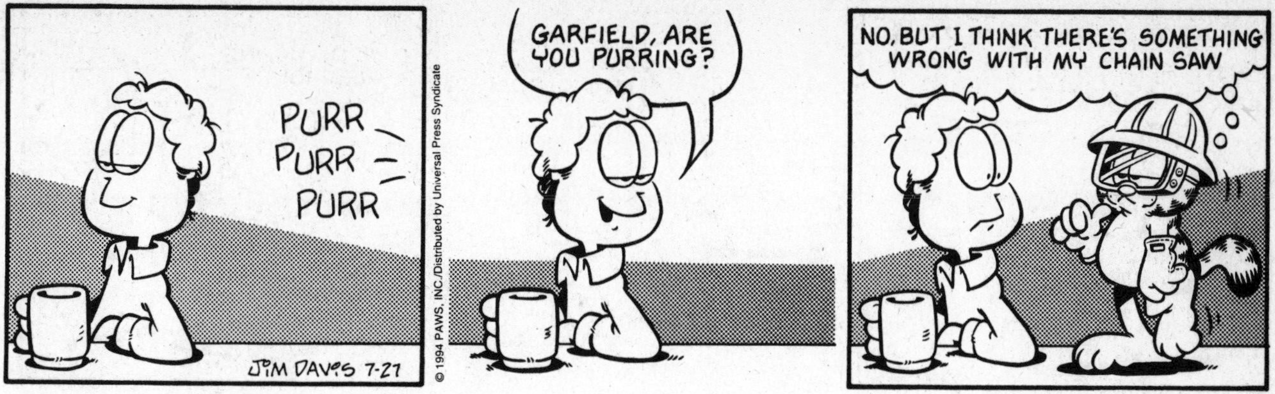
PURR
PURR
PURR
JIM DAVIS 7-27
© 1994 PAWS, INC./Distributed by Universal Press Syndicate
GARFIELD, ARE YOU PURRING?
NO, BUT I THINK THERE'S SOMETHING WRONG WITH MY CHAIN SAW

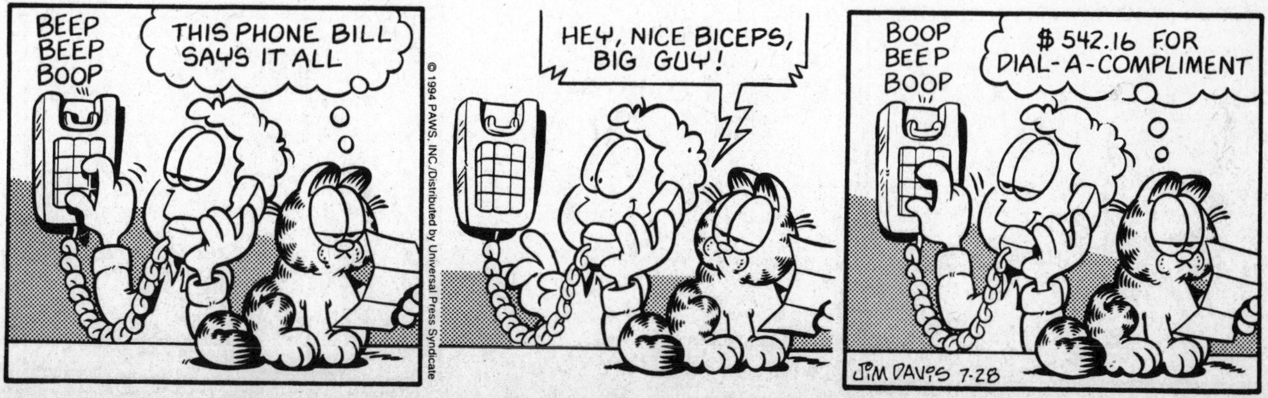
BEEP
BEEP
BOOP
THIS PHONE BILL SAYS IT ALL
© 1994 PAWS, INC./Distributed by Universal Press Syndicate
HEY, NICE BICEPS, BIG GUY!
BOOP
BEEP
BOOP
$ 542.16 FOR DIAL-A-COMPLIMENT
JIM DAVIS 7-28

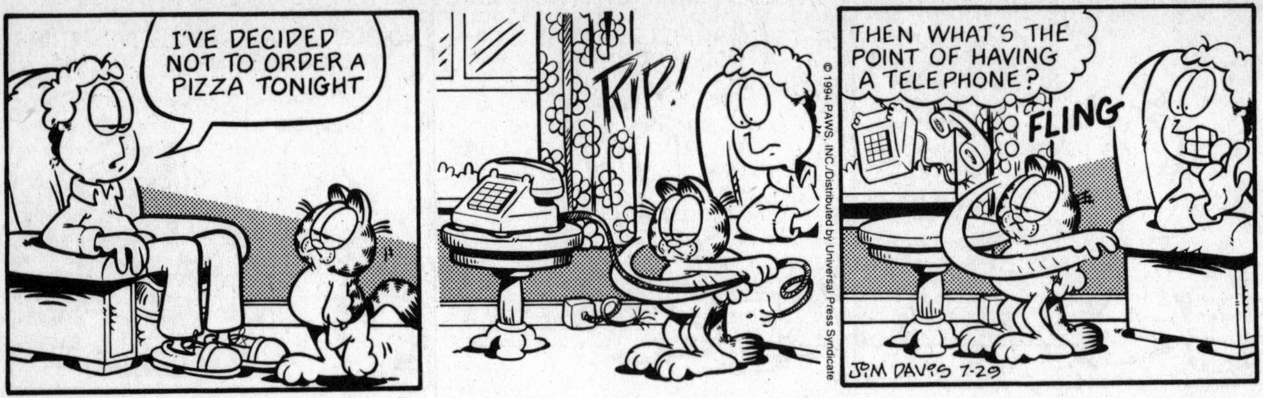
I'VE DECIDED NOT TO ORDER A PIZZA TONIGHT
RIP!
THEN WHAT'S THE POINT OF HAVING A TELEPHONE?
FLING
© 1994 PAWS, INC./Distributed by Universal Press Syndicate
JIM DAVIS 7-29

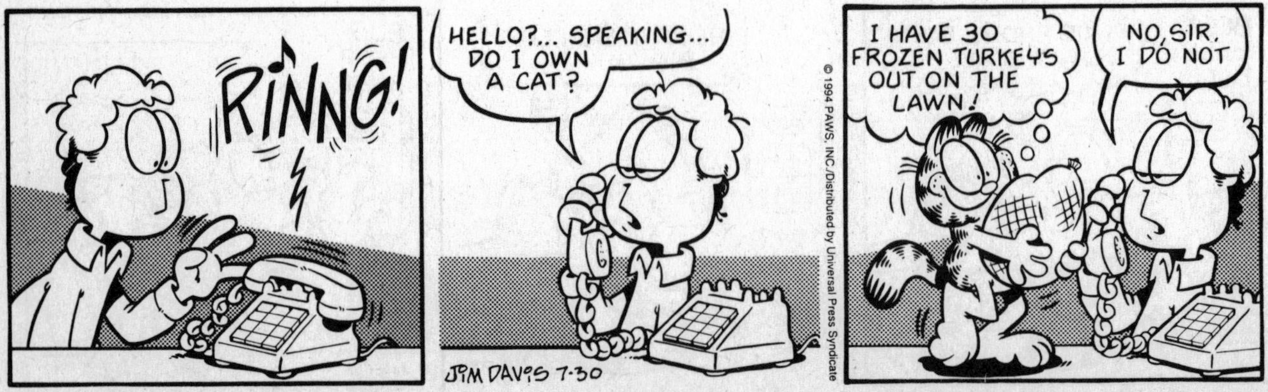
RINNG!
HELLO?... SPEAKING... DO I OWN A CAT?
JIM DAVIS 7-30
© 1994 PAWS, INC./Distributed by Universal Press Syndicate
I HAVE 30 FROZEN TURKEYS OUT ON THE LAWN!
NO, SIR, I DO NOT

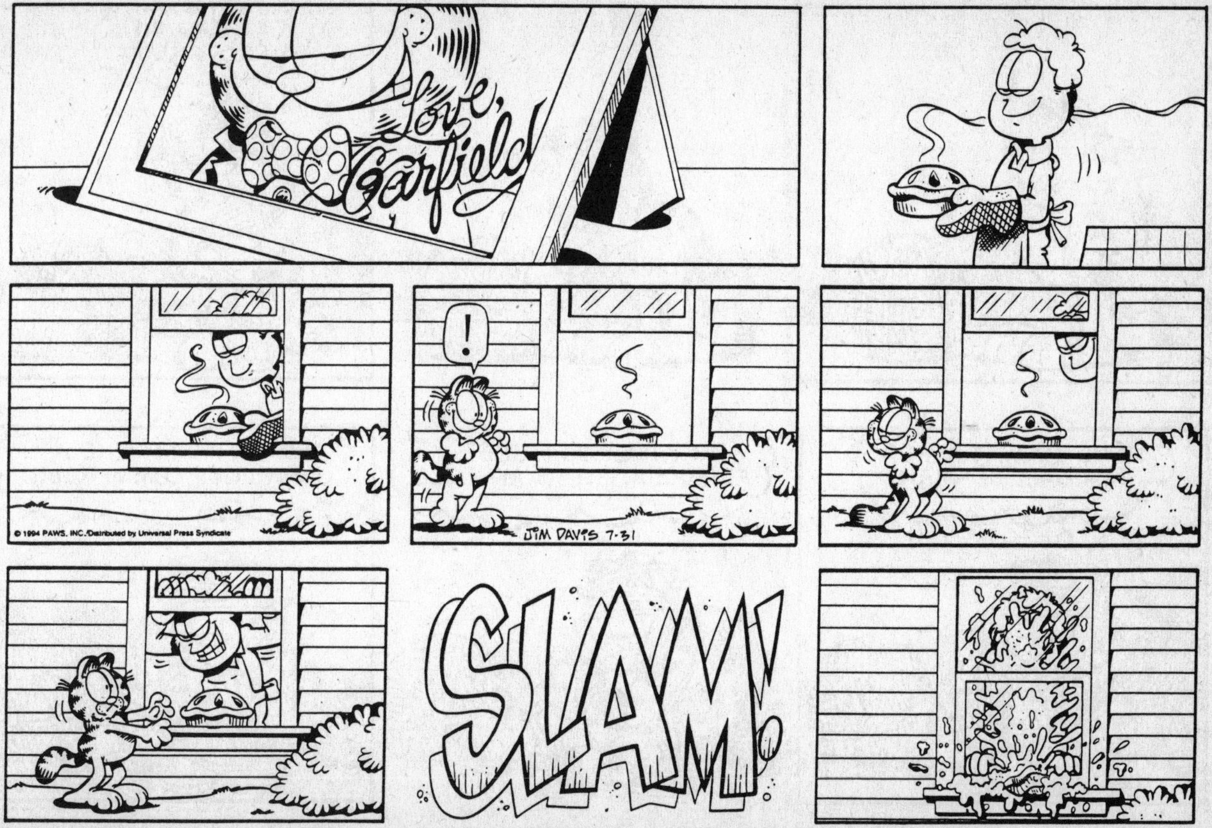

Love, Garfield
© 1994 PAWS, INC./Distributed by Universal Press Syndicate
!
JIM DAVIS 7-31
SLAM!

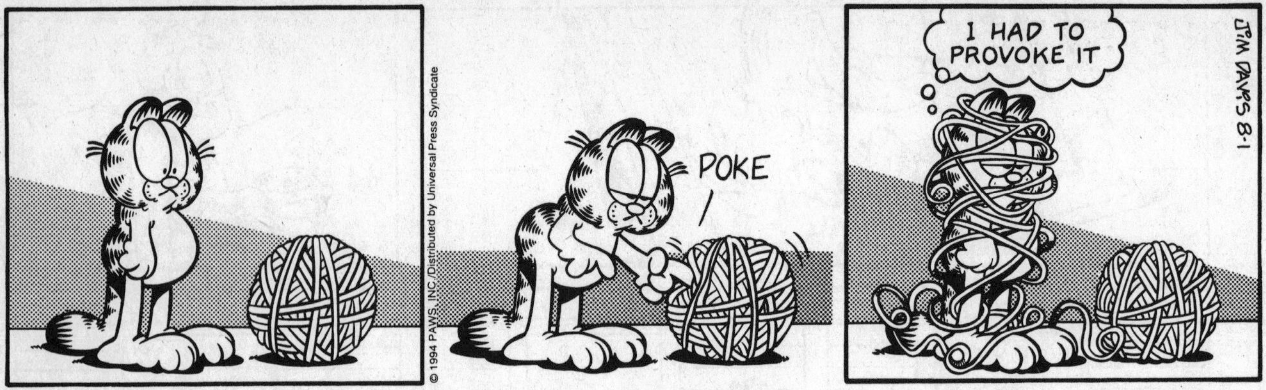
POKE
I HAD TO PROVOKE IT
JIM DAVIS 8-1
© 1994 PAWS, INC./Distributed by Universal Press Syndicate

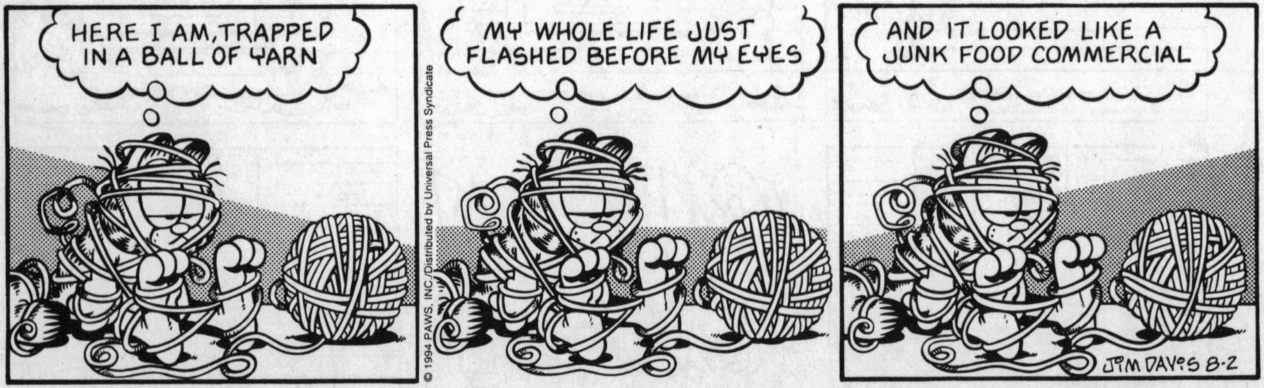
HERE I AM, TRAPPED IN A BALL OF YARN
MY WHOLE LIFE JUST FLASHED BEFORE MY EYES
AND IT LOOKED LIKE A JUNK FOOD COMMERCIAL
JIM DAVIS 8-2
© 1994 PAWS, INC./Distributed by Universal Press Syndicate

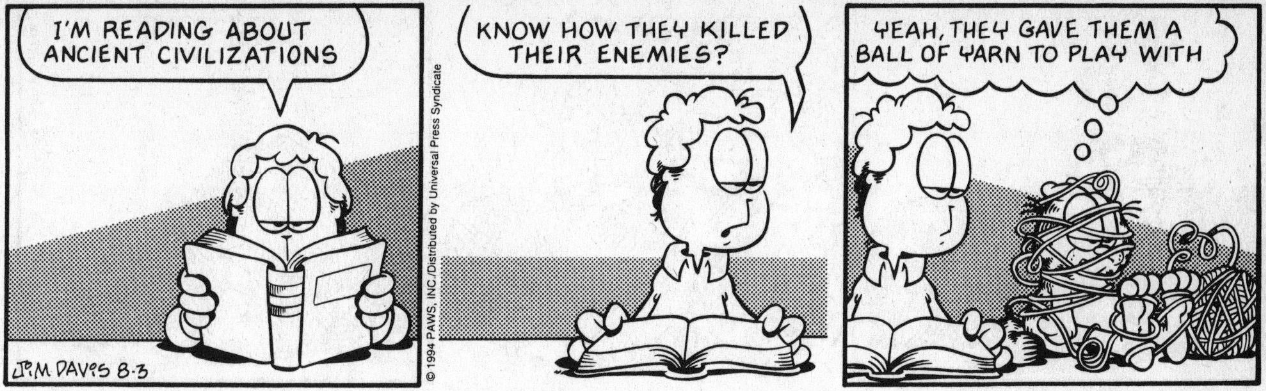
I'M READING ABOUT ANCIENT CIVILIZATIONS
JIM DAVIS 8-3
© 1994 PAWS, INC./Distributed by Universal Press Syndicate
KNOW HOW THEY KILLED THEIR ENEMIES?
YEAH, THEY GAVE THEM A BALL OF YARN TO PLAY WITH

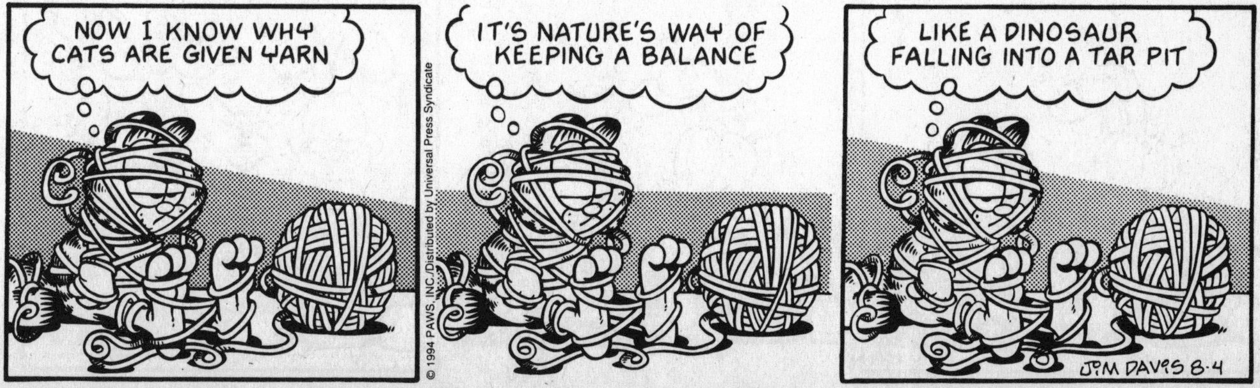
NOW I KNOW WHY CATS ARE GIVEN YARN
© 1994 PAWS, INC./Distributed by Universal Press Syndicate
IT'S NATURE'S WAY OF KEEPING A BALANCE
LIKE A DINOSAUR FALLING INTO A TAR PIT
JIM DAVIS 8-4

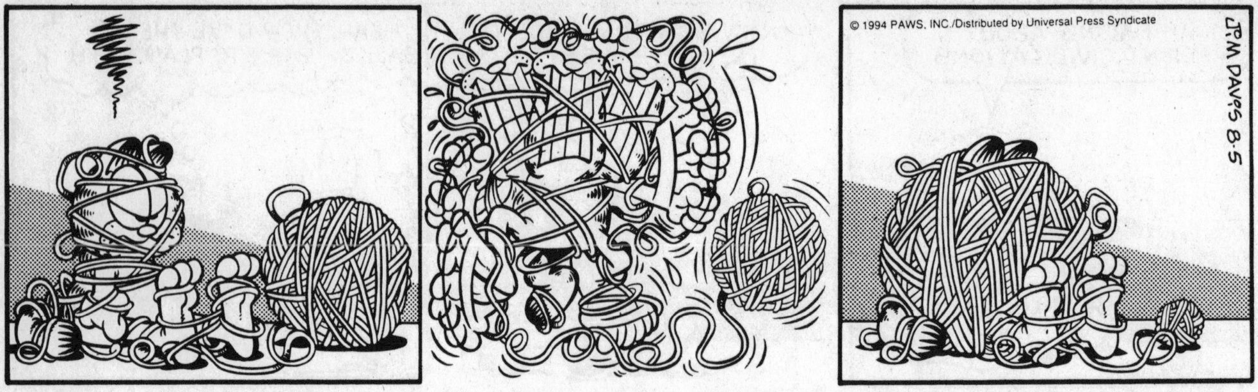
© 1994 PAWS, INC./Distributed by Universal Press Syndicate
JIM DAVIS 8-5

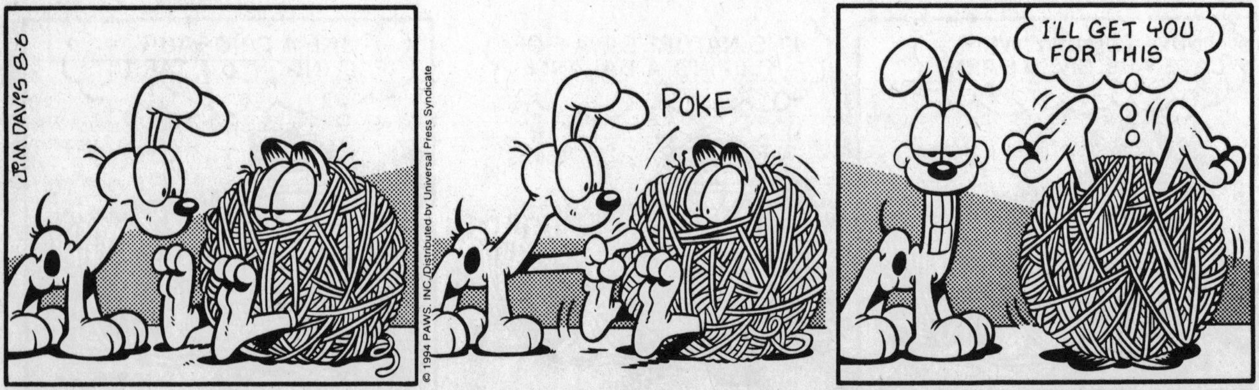
JIM DAVIS 8-6
© 1994 PAWS, INC./Distributed by Universal Press Syndicate
POKE
I'LL GET YOU FOR THIS

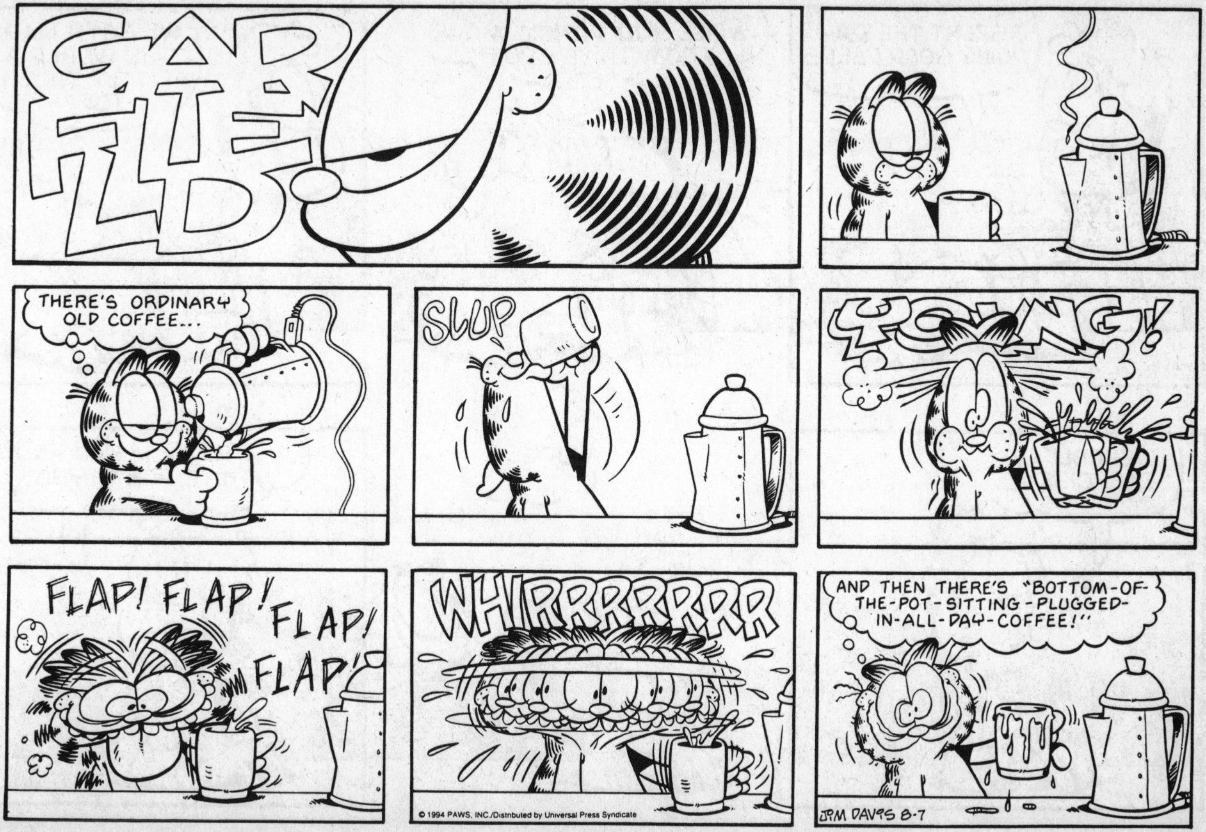
GARFIELD
THERE'S ORDINARY OLD COFFEE...
SLUP
YOWNG!
FLAP! FLAP! FLAP! FLAP!
WHIRRRRRRRR
AND THEN THERE'S "BOTTOM-OF-THE-POT-SITTING-PLUGGED-IN-ALL-DAY-COFFEE!"
© 1994 PAWS, INC./Distributed by Universal Press Syndicate
JIM DAVIS 8-7

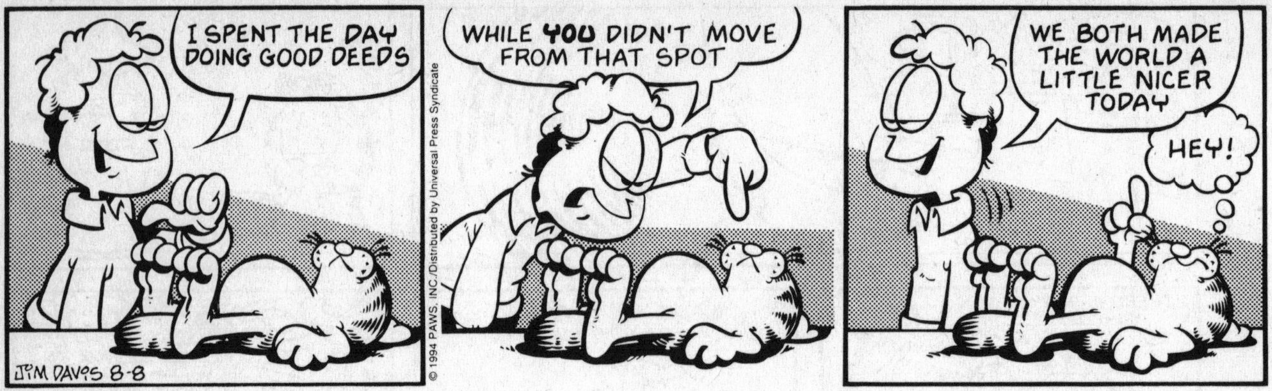
I SPENT THE DAY DOING GOOD DEEDS
JIM DAVIS 8-8
© 1994 PAWS, INC./Distributed by Universal Press Syndicate
WHILE YOU DIDN'T MOVE FROM THAT SPOT
WE BOTH MADE THE WORLD A LITTLE NICER TODAY
HEY!

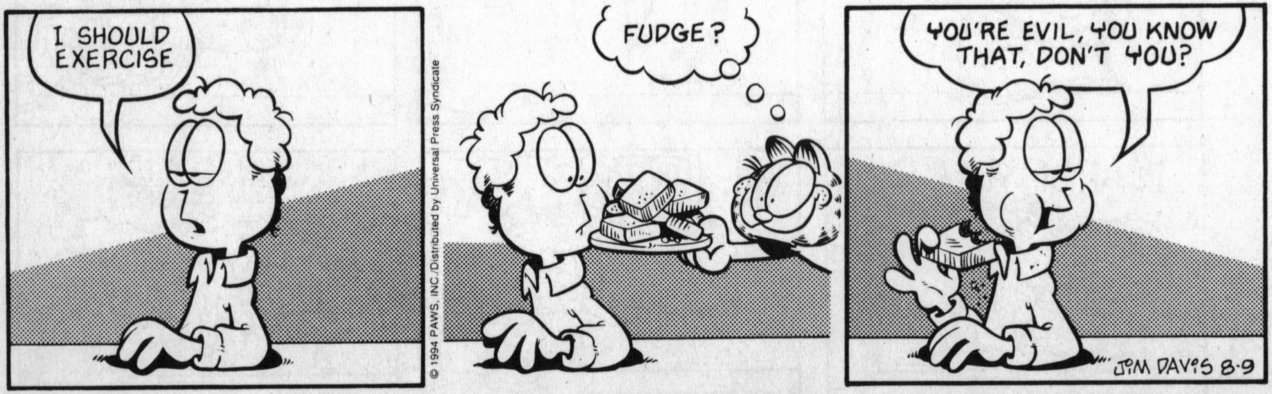
I SHOULD EXERCISE
© 1994 PAWS, INC./Distributed by Universal Press Syndicate
FUDGE?
YOU'RE EVIL, YOU KNOW THAT, DON'T YOU?
JIM DAVIS 8-9

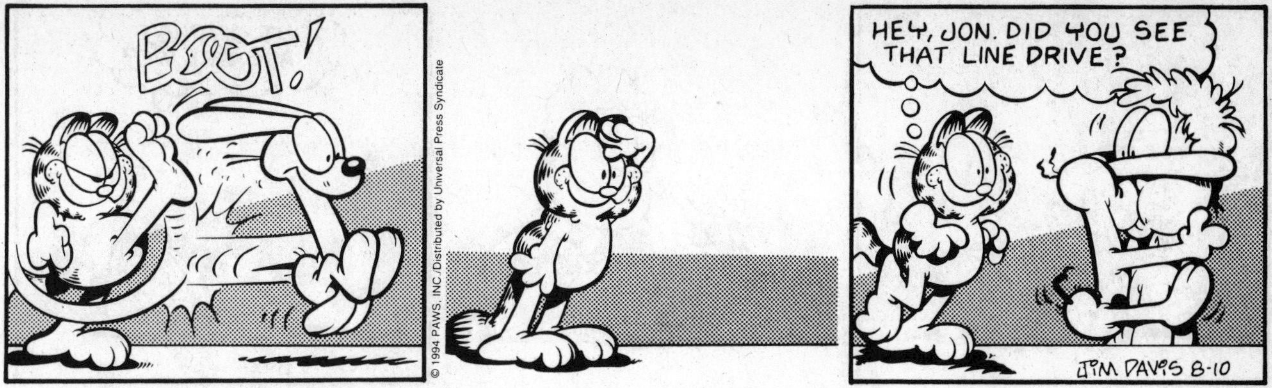
BOOT!
© 1994 PAWS, INC./Distributed by Universal Press Syndicate
HEY, JON. DID YOU SEE THAT LINE DRIVE?
JIM DAVIS 8-10

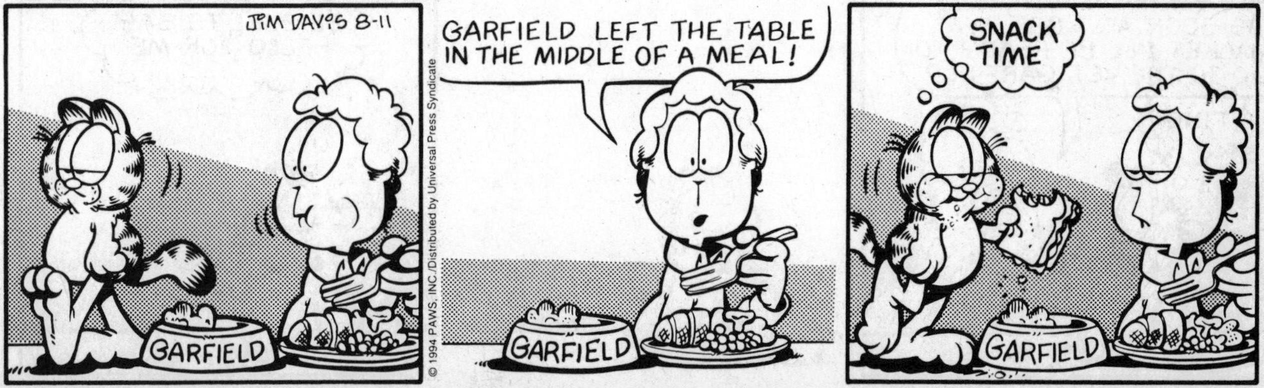
JIM DAVIS 8-11
GARFIELD
© 1994 PAWS, INC./Distributed by Universal Press Syndicate
GARFIELD LEFT THE TABLE IN THE MIDDLE OF A MEAL!
GARFIELD
SNACK TIME
GARFIELD

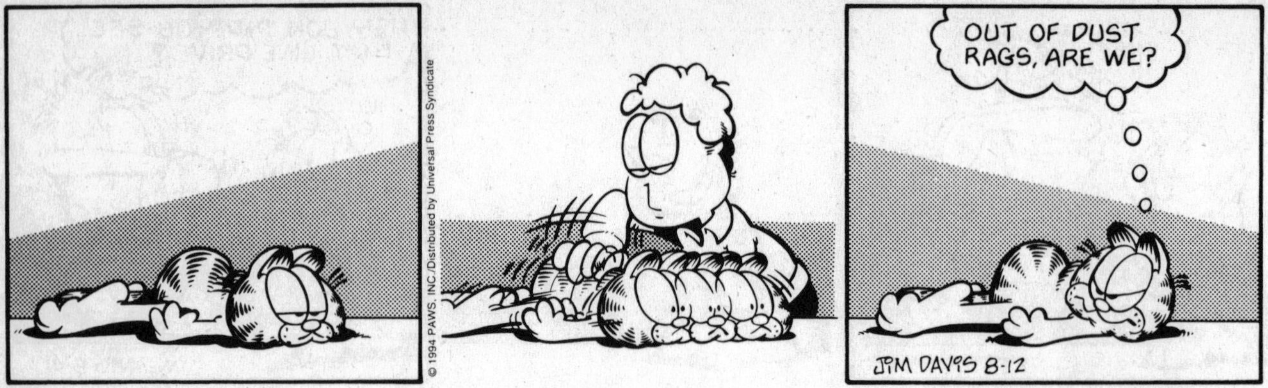
© 1994 PAWS, INC./Distributed by Universal Press Syndicate
OUT OF DUST RAGS, ARE WE?
JIM DAVIS 8-12

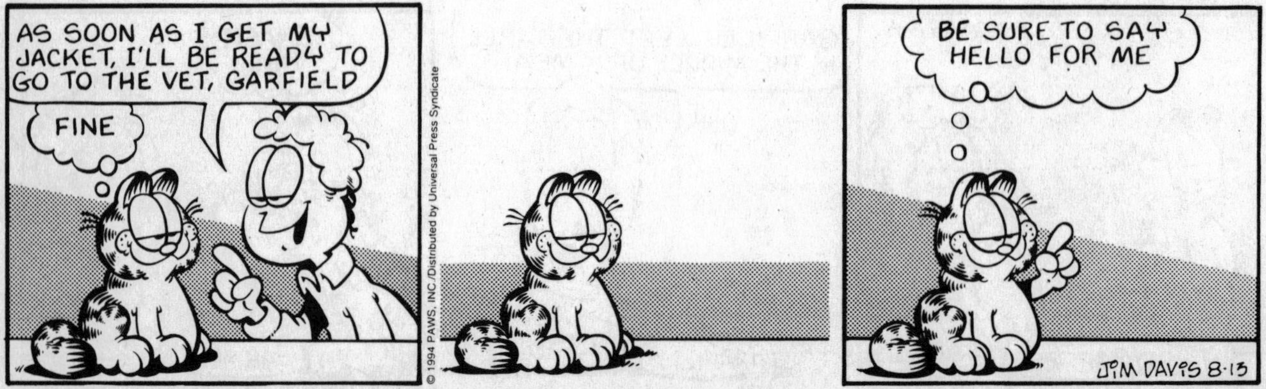
AS SOON AS I GET MY JACKET, I'LL BE READY TO GO TO THE VET, GARFIELD
FINE
© 1994 PAWS, INC./Distributed by Universal Press Syndicate
BE SURE TO SAY HELLO FOR ME
JIM DAVIS 8-13

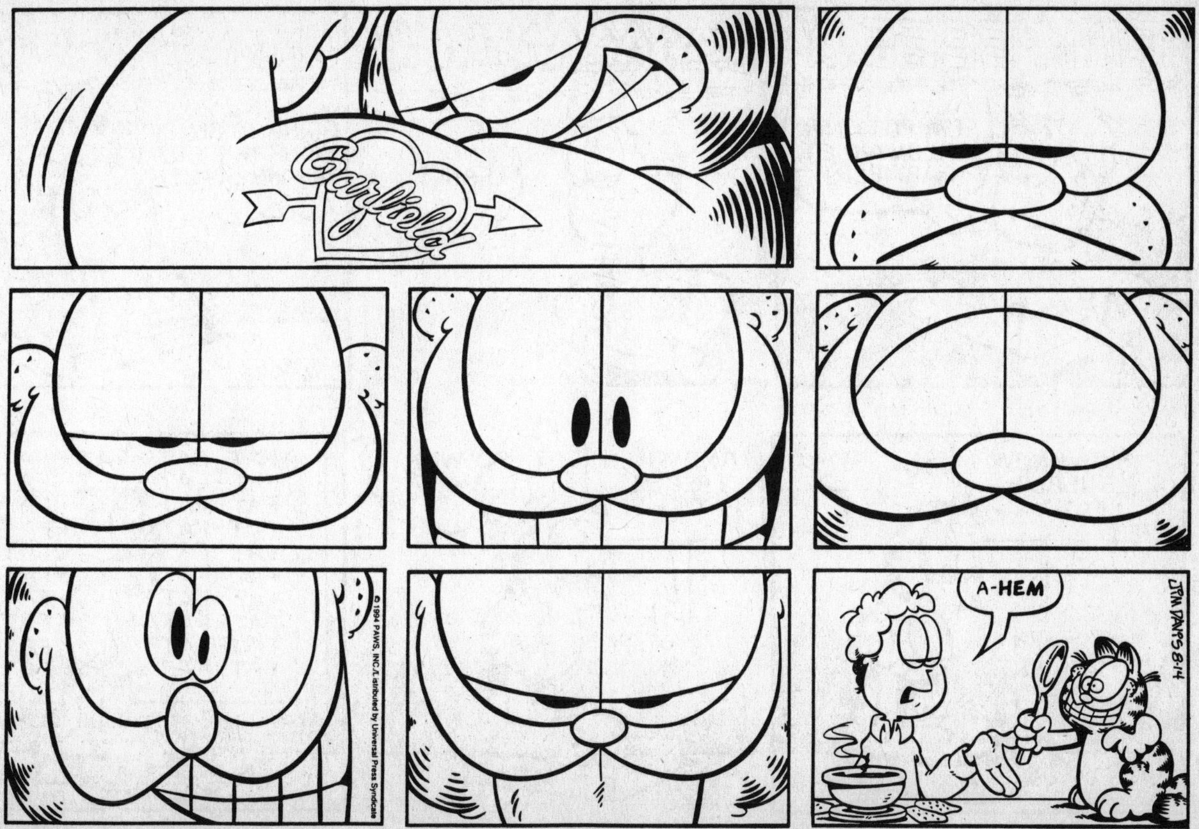

Garfield
© 1994 PAWS, INC./Distributed by Universal Press Syndicate
A-HEM
JPM DAVIS 8-14

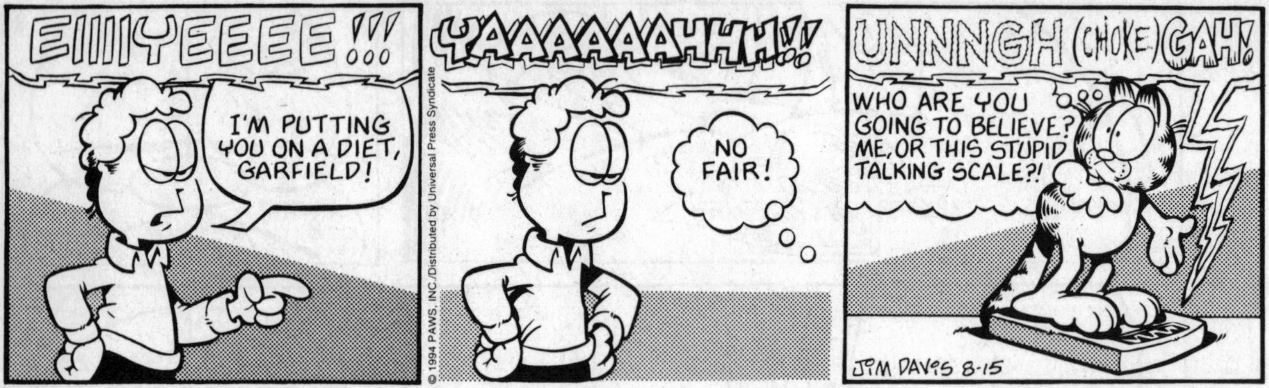
EIIIIYEEEEE!!!
I'M PUTTING YOU ON A DIET, GARFIELD!
YAAAAAAAHHH!!
NO FAIR!
UNNNGH (CHOKE) GAH!
WHO ARE YOU GOING TO BELIEVE? ME, OR THIS STUPID TALKING SCALE?!
JIM DAVIS 8-15

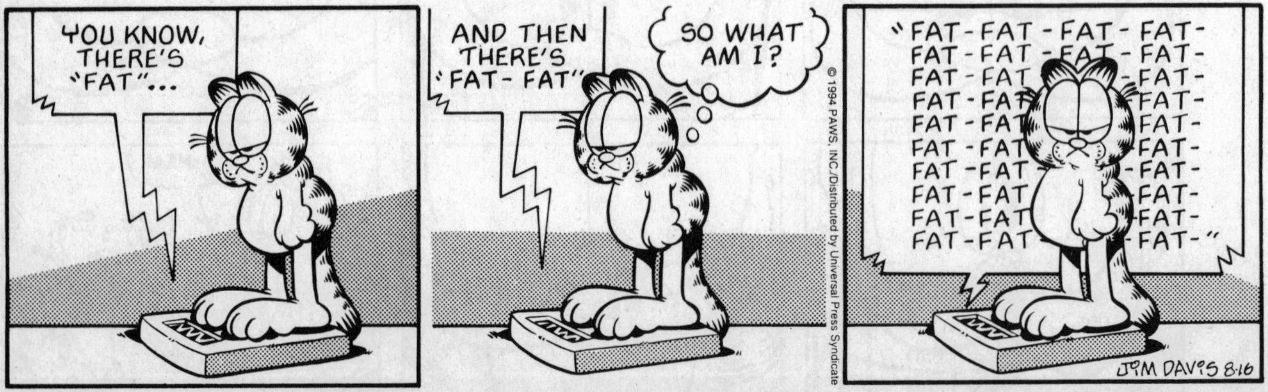
YOU KNOW, THERE'S "FAT"...
AND THEN THERE'S "FAT-FAT"
SO WHAT AM I?
"FAT-FAT-FAT-FAT-FAT-FAT-FAT-FAT-FAT-FAT-FAT-FAT-FAT-FAT-FAT-FAT-FAT-FAT-FAT-FAT-FAT-FAT-FAT-FAT-FAT-FAT-FAT-FAT-FAT-FAT-FAT-FAT-FAT-FAT-FAT-FAT-FAT-FAT-FAT-FAT-"
JIM DAVIS 8-16

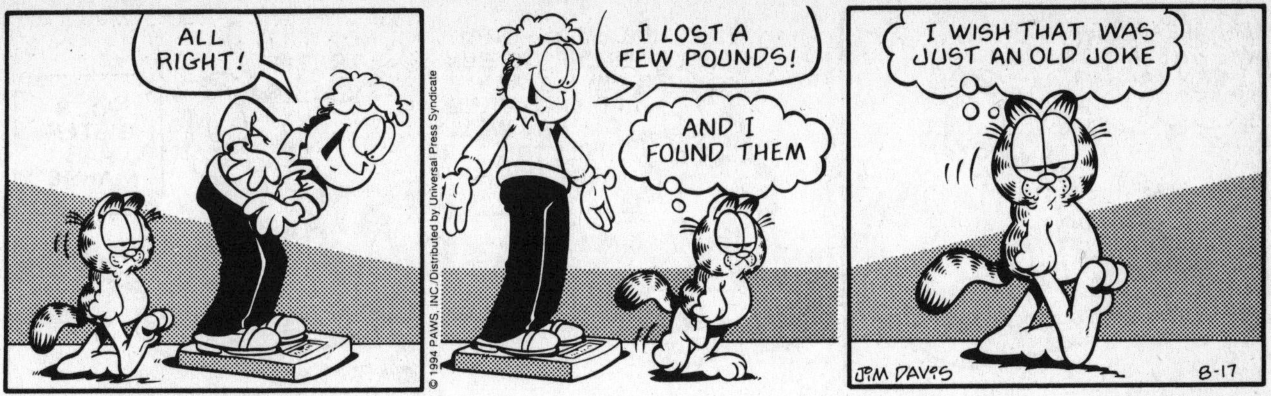
ALL RIGHT!
I LOST A FEW POUNDS!
AND I FOUND THEM
I WISH THAT WAS JUST AN OLD JOKE
JIM DAVIS 8-17
© 1994 PAWS, INC./Distributed by Universal Press Syndicate

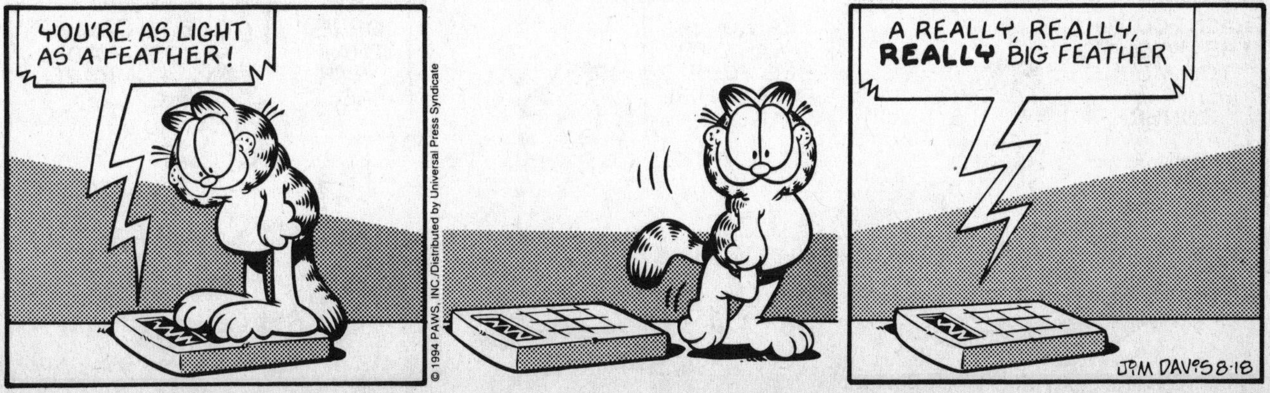
YOU'RE AS LIGHT AS A FEATHER!
A REALLY, REALLY, **REALLY** BIG FEATHER
JIM DAVIS 8-18
© 1994 PAWS, INC./Distributed by Universal Press Syndicate

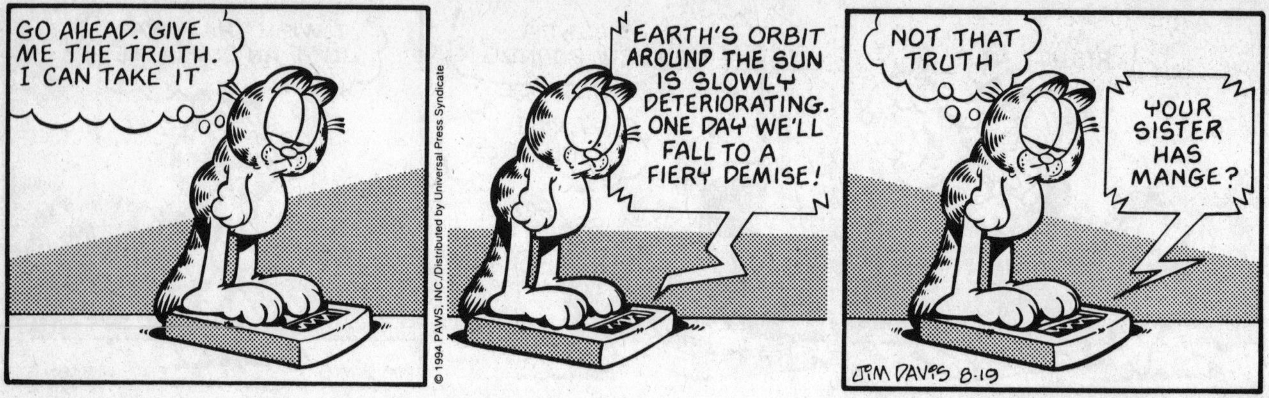
GO AHEAD. GIVE ME THE TRUTH. I CAN TAKE IT
EARTH'S ORBIT AROUND THE SUN IS SLOWLY DETERIORATING. ONE DAY WE'LL FALL TO A FIERY DEMISE!
NOT THAT TRUTH
YOUR SISTER HAS MANGE?
JIM DAVIS 8-19

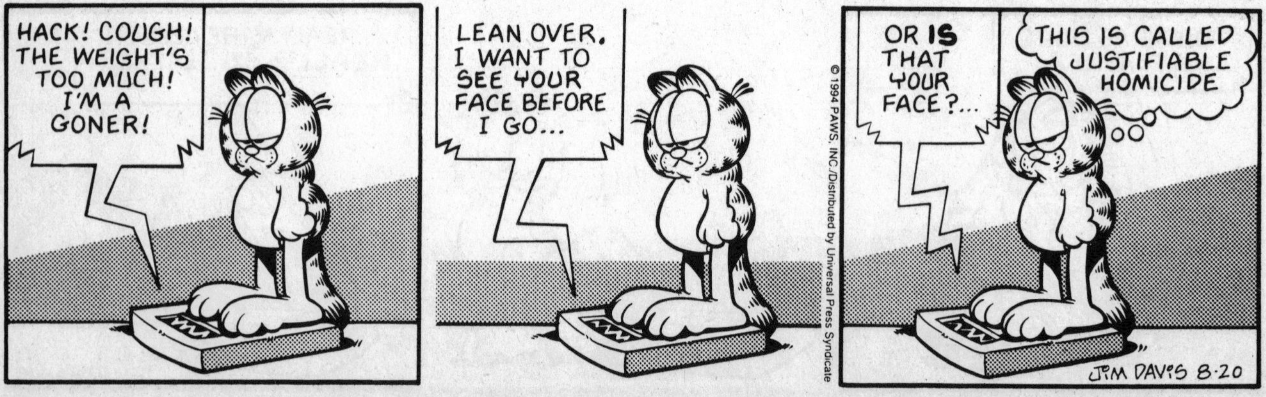
HACK! COUGH! THE WEIGHT'S TOO MUCH! I'M A GONER!
LEAN OVER. I WANT TO SEE YOUR FACE BEFORE I GO...
OR **IS** THAT YOUR FACE?...
THIS IS CALLED JUSTIFIABLE HOMICIDE
JIM DAVIS 8-20

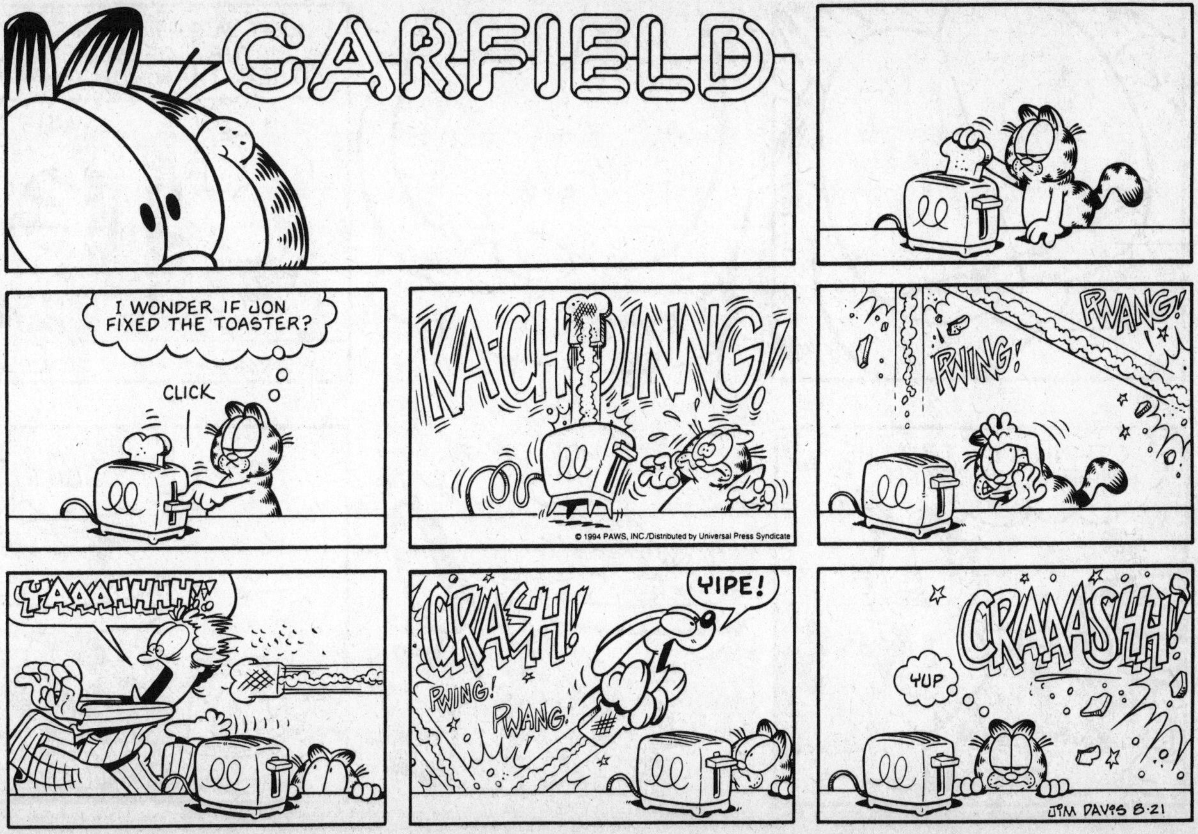
GARFIELD
I WONDER IF JON FIXED THE TOASTER?
CLICK
KA-CHOINNG!
© 1994 PAWS, INC./Distributed by Universal Press Syndicate
PWING!
PWANG!
YAAAHHHH!!
CRASH!
YIPE!
PWING!
PWANG!
CRAAASHH!
YUP
JIM DAVIS 8·21

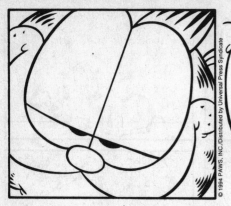

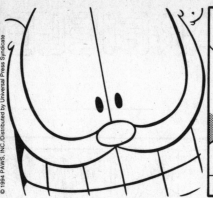

I JUST MIGHT WANT TO TAKE A PICTURE OF SOMETHING OTHER THAN YOU, GARFIELD

WHY?

JIM DAVIS 8-22

© 1994 PAWS, INC./Distributed by Universal Press Syndicate

I THINK I'LL TRY THE DIRECT APPROACH

JIM DAVIS 8-23

HOP IN!

© 1994 PAWS, INC./Distributed by Universal Press Syndicate

JUST A THOUGHT

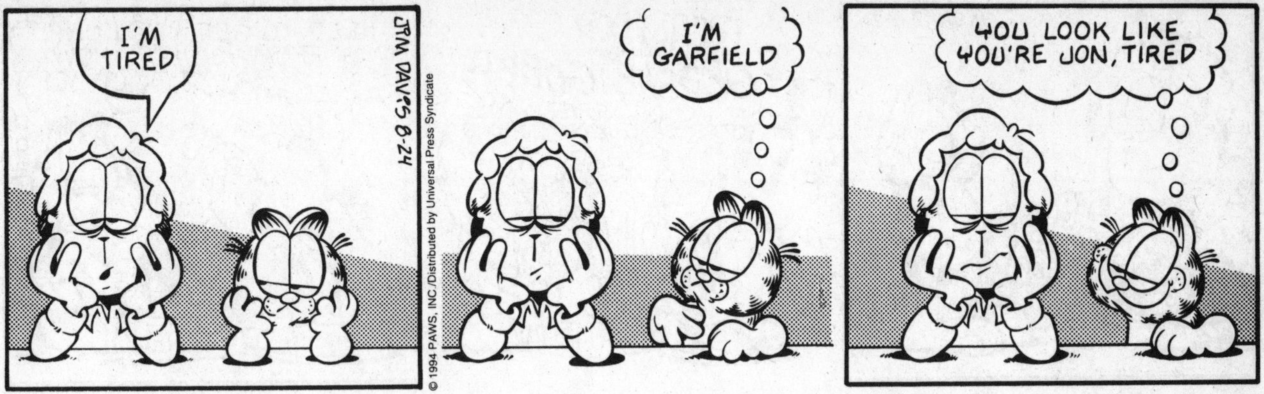
I'M TIRED
JIM DAVIS 8-24
© 1994 PAWS, INC./Distributed by Universal Press Syndicate
I'M GARFIELD
YOU LOOK LIKE YOU'RE JON, TIRED

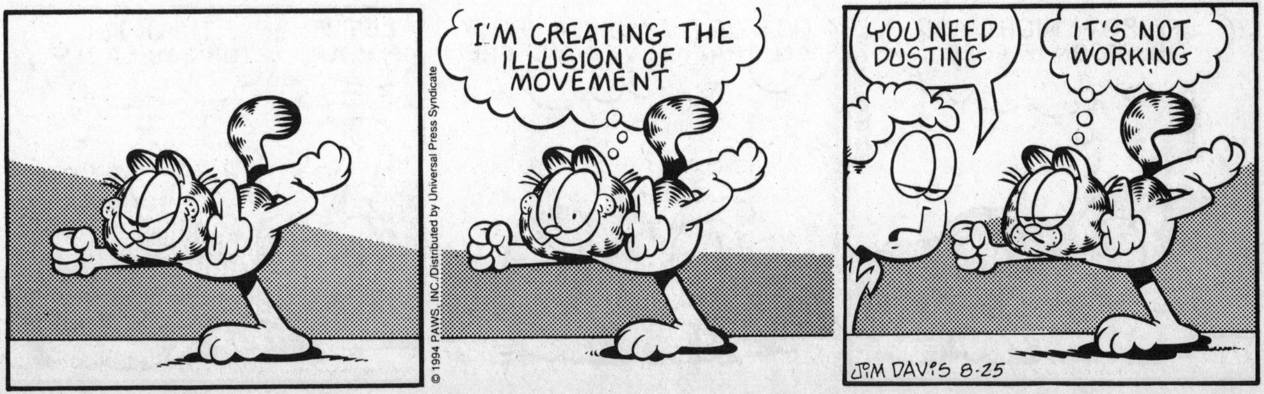
© 1994 PAWS, INC./Distributed by Universal Press Syndicate
I'M CREATING THE ILLUSION OF MOVEMENT
YOU NEED DUSTING
IT'S NOT WORKING
JIM DAVIS 8-25

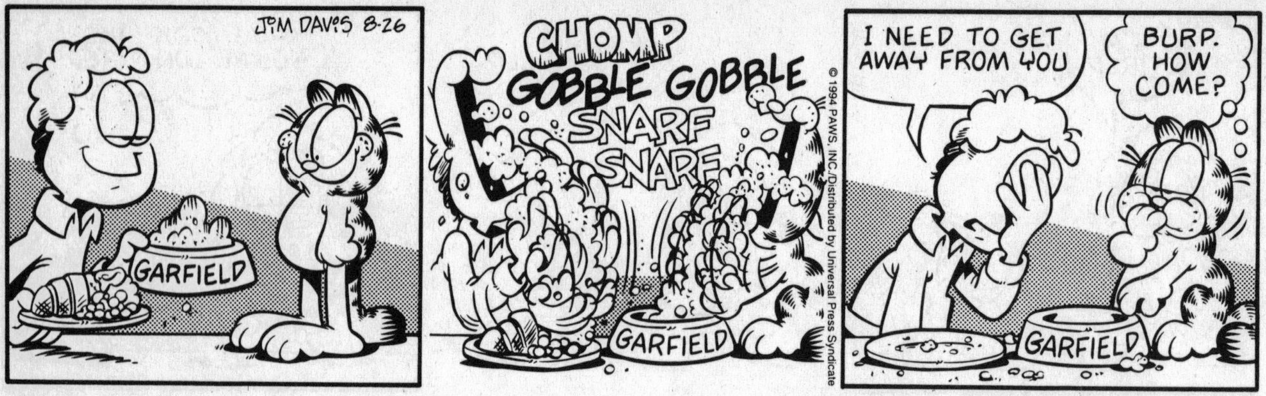
JIM DAVIS 8-26
GARFIELD
CHOMP
GOBBLE GOBBLE
SNARF
SNARF
GARFIELD
© 1994 PAWS, INC./Distributed by Universal Press Syndicate
I NEED TO GET AWAY FROM YOU
BURP. HOW COME?
GARFIELD

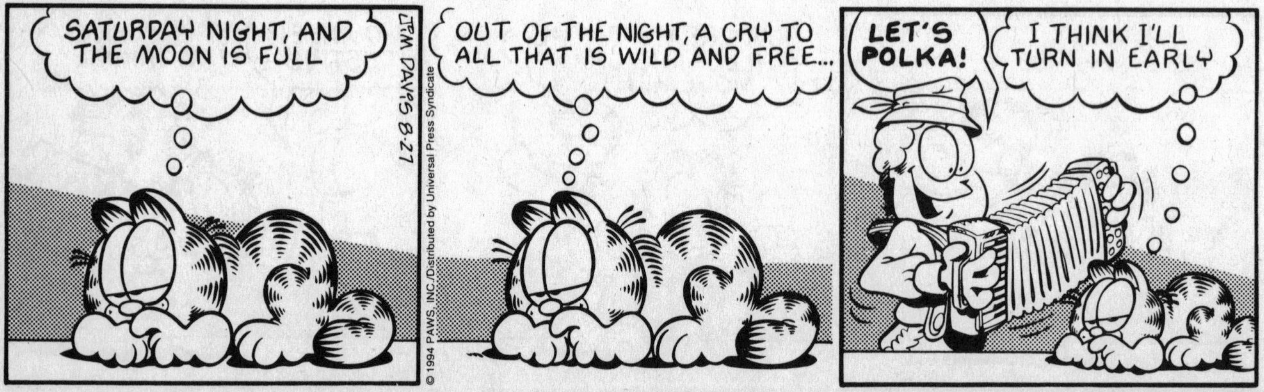
SATURDAY NIGHT, AND THE MOON IS FULL
JIM DAVIS 8-27
© 1994 PAWS, INC./Distributed by Universal Press Syndicate
OUT OF THE NIGHT, A CRY TO ALL THAT IS WILD AND FREE...
LET'S POLKA!
I THINK I'LL TURN IN EARLY

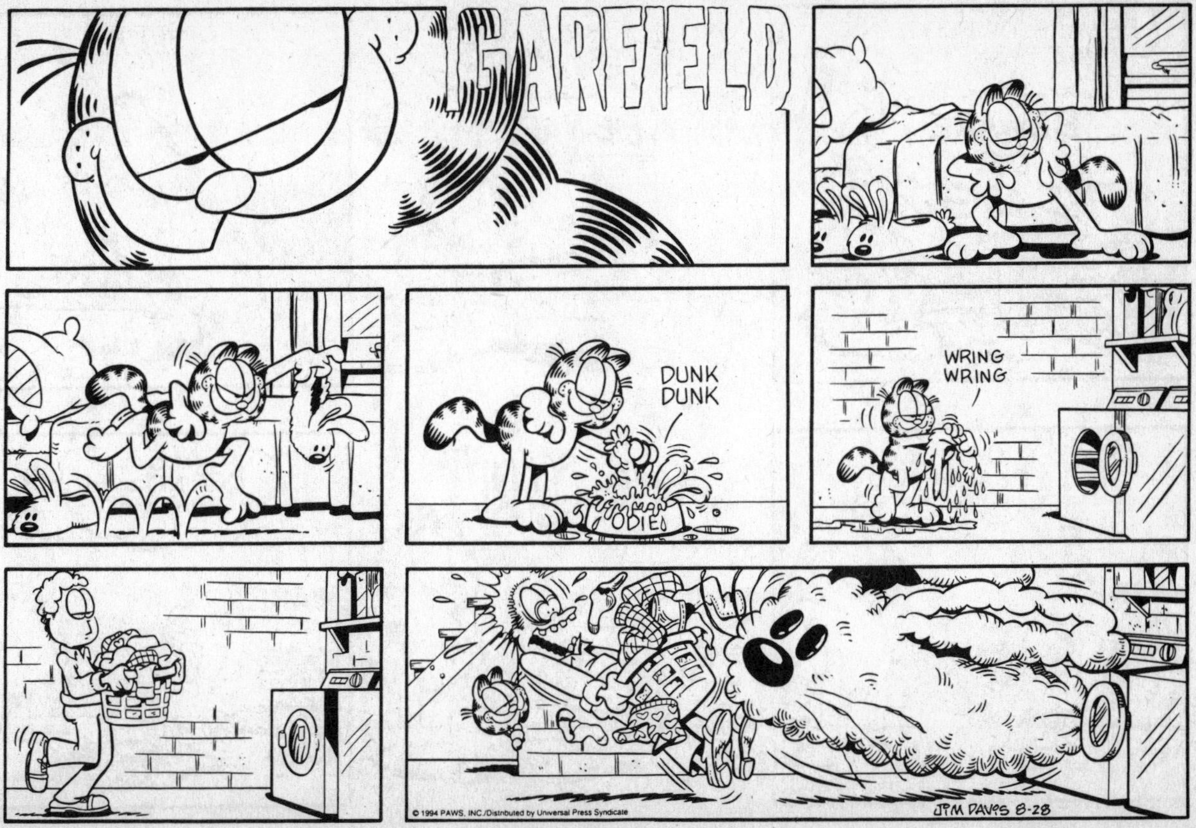
GARFIELD
DUNK
DUNK
ODIE
WRING
WRING
© 1994 PAWS, INC./Distributed by Universal Press Syndicate
JIM DAVIS 8-28

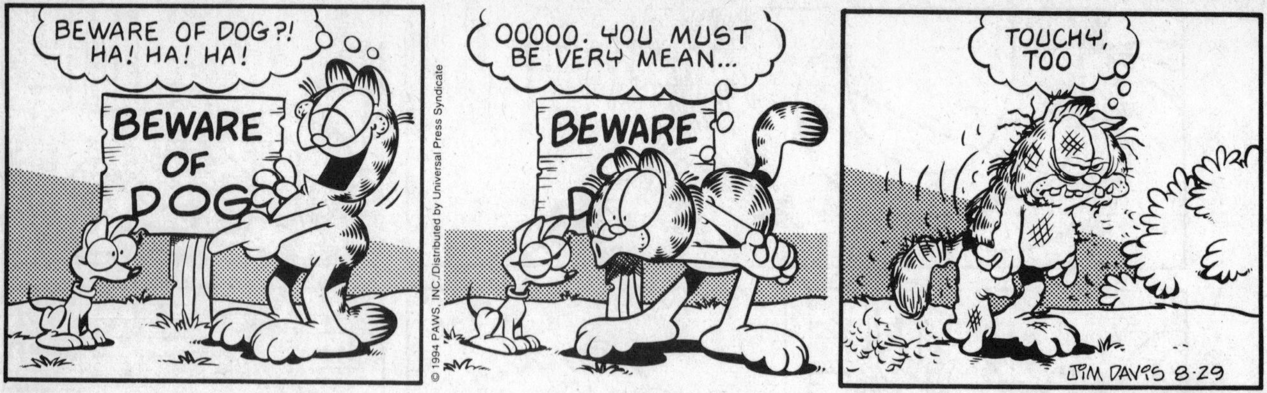
BEWARE OF DOG?! HA! HA! HA!
BEWARE OF DOG
OOOOO. YOU MUST BE VERY MEAN...
BEWARE
TOUCHY, TOO
JIM DAVIS 8-29

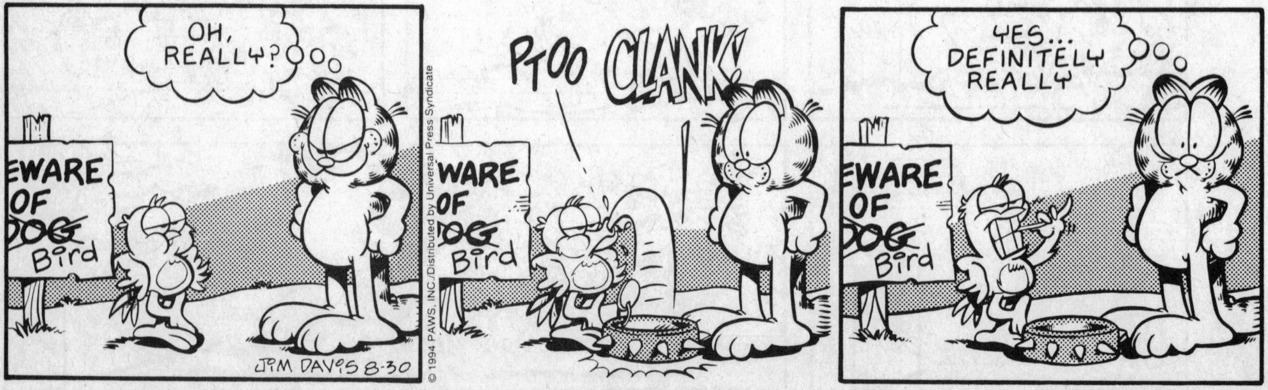
OH, REALLY?
EWARE OF DOG Bird
JIM DAVIS 8-30
PTOO CLANK!
WARE OF OG Bird
YES... DEFINITELY REALLY
EWARE OF OG Bird

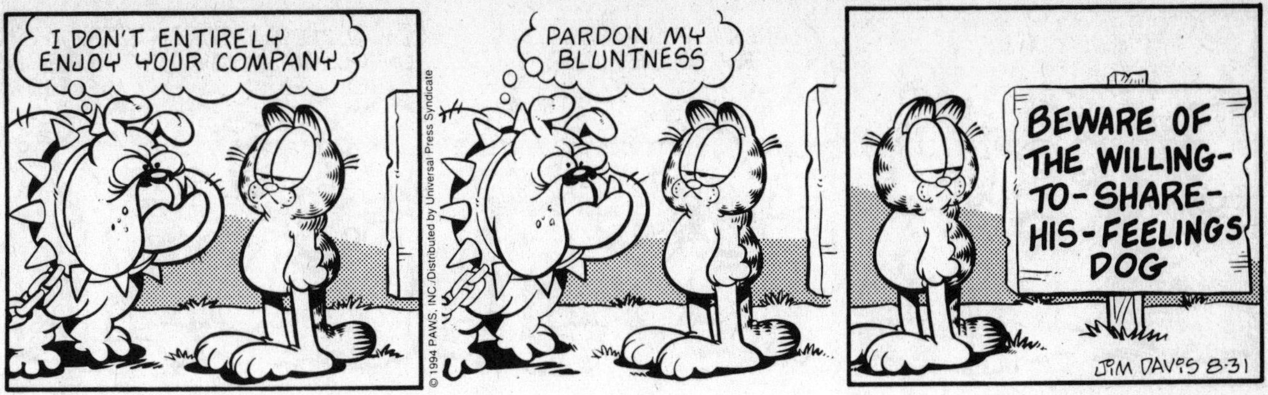
I DON'T ENTIRELY ENJOY YOUR COMPANY
PARDON MY BLUNTNESS
BEWARE OF THE WILLING-TO-SHARE-HIS-FEELINGS DOG
JIM DAVIS 8-31

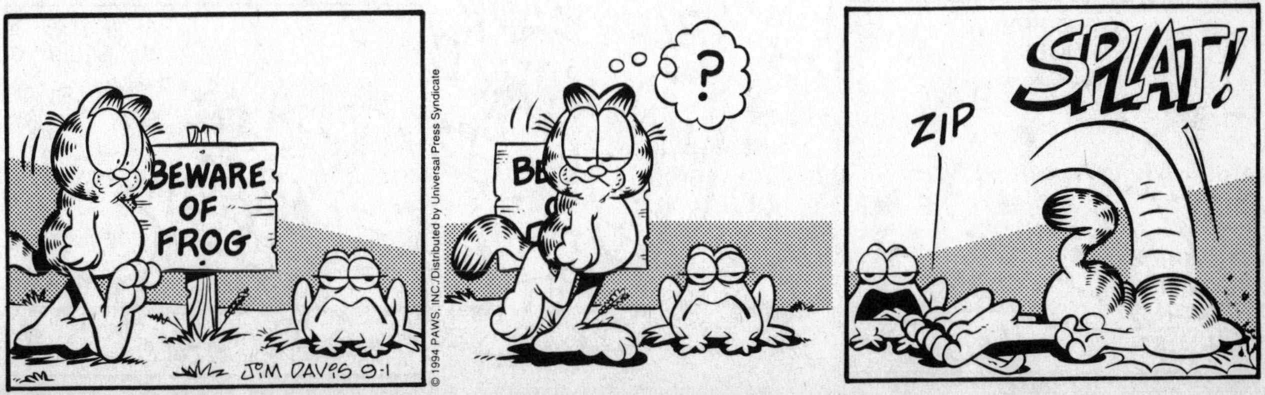
BEWARE OF FROG
JIM DAVIS 9-1
?
ZIP
SPLAT!

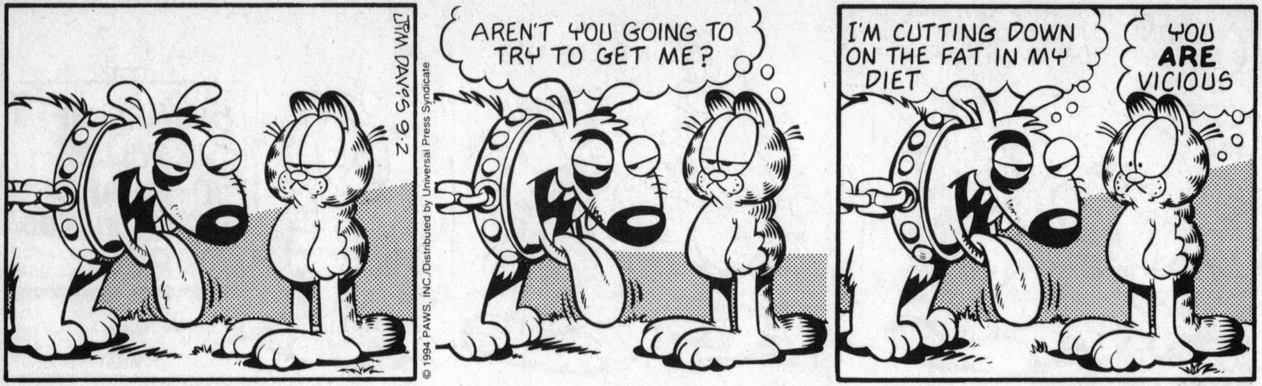
JIM DAVIS 9-2
© 1994 PAWS, INC./Distributed by Universal Press Syndicate
AREN'T YOU GOING TO TRY TO GET ME?
I'M CUTTING DOWN ON THE FAT IN MY DIET
YOU **ARE** VICIOUS

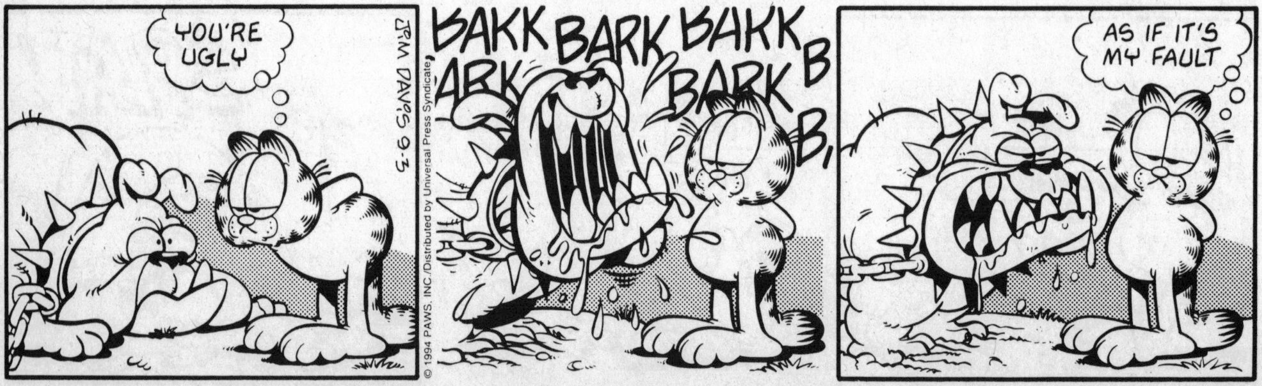
JIM DAVIS 9-3
© 1994 PAWS, INC./Distributed by Universal Press Syndicate
YOU'RE UGLY
BARK BARK BARK
BARK
B
BARK
AS IF IT'S MY FAULT

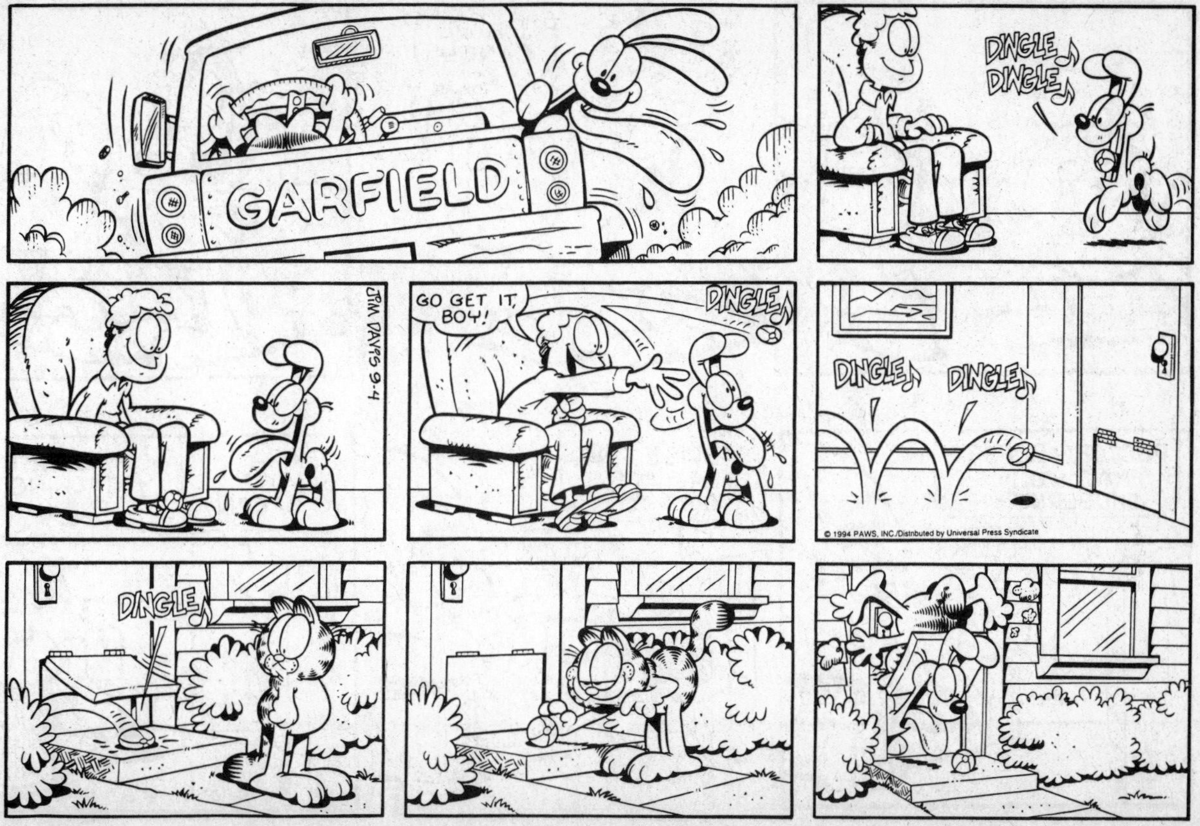
GARFIELD
DINGLE DINGLE
JPM DAVPS 9-4
GO GET IT, BOY!
DINGLE
DINGLE
DINGLE
© 1994 PAWS, INC./Distributed by Universal Press Syndicate
DINGLE

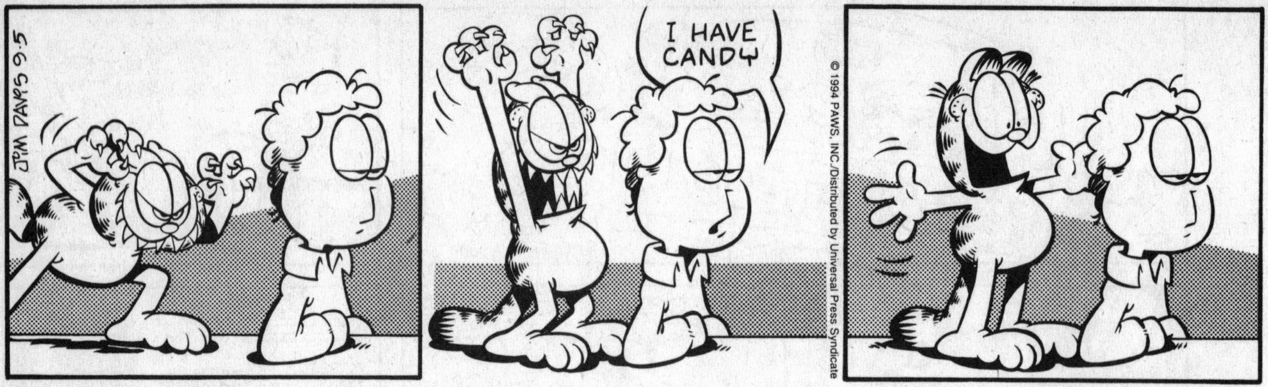
JIM DAVIS 9-5
I HAVE CANDY

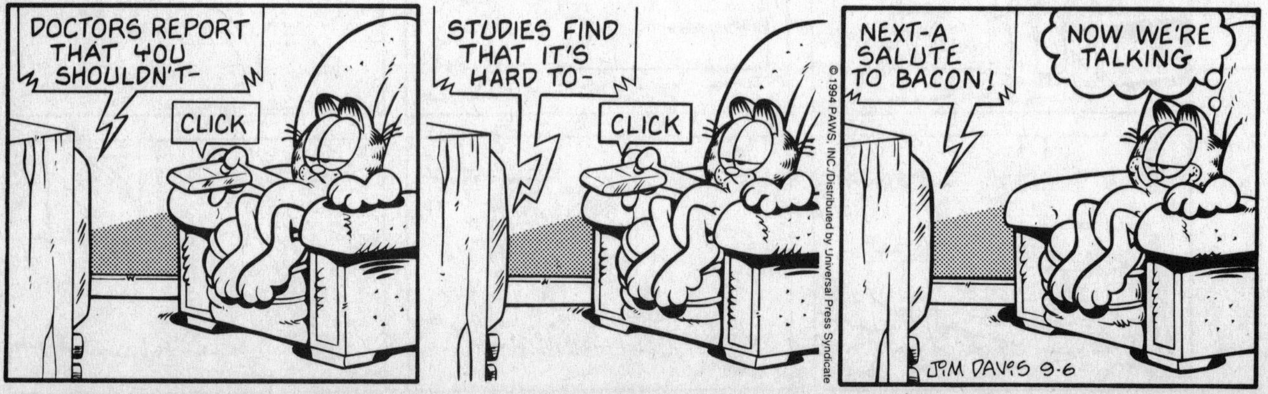
DOCTORS REPORT THAT YOU SHOULDN'T-
CLICK
STUDIES FIND THAT IT'S HARD TO-
CLICK
NEXT-A SALUTE TO BACON!
NOW WE'RE TALKING
JIM DAVIS 9-6

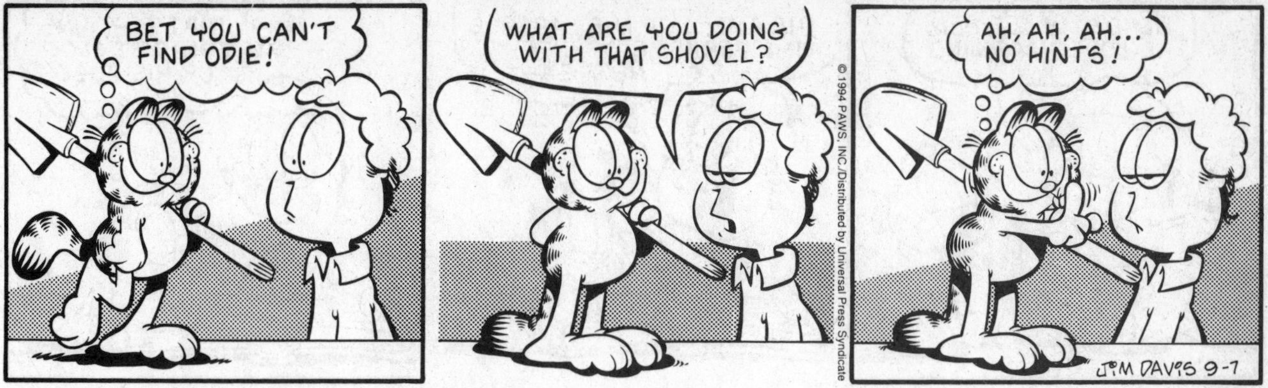
BET YOU CAN'T FIND ODIE!
WHAT ARE YOU DOING WITH THAT SHOVEL?
AH, AH, AH... NO HINTS!
JIM DAVIS 9-7

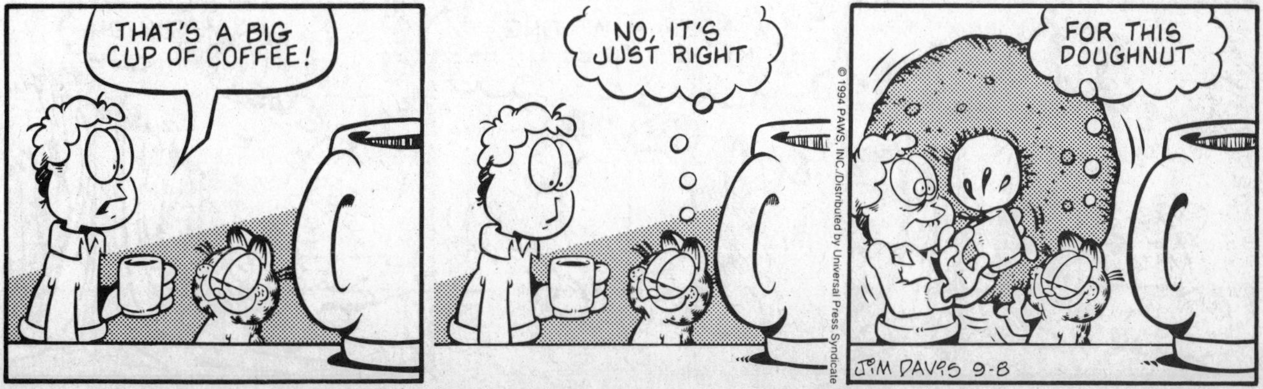
THAT'S A BIG CUP OF COFFEE!
NO, IT'S JUST RIGHT
FOR THIS DOUGHNUT
JIM DAVIS 9-8

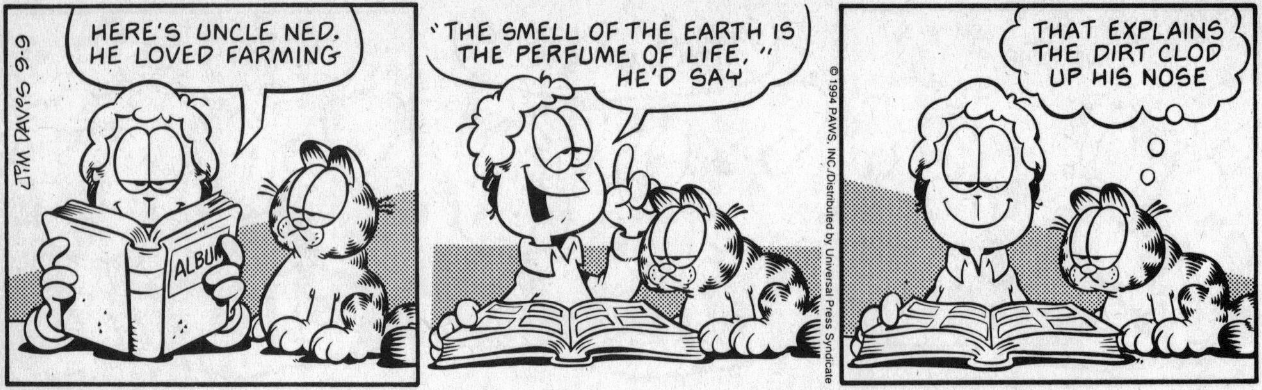
JIM DAVIS 9-9
HERE'S UNCLE NED. HE LOVED FARMING
ALBUM
"THE SMELL OF THE EARTH IS THE PERFUME OF LIFE," HE'D SAY
© 1994 PAWS, INC./Distributed by Universal Press Syndicate
THAT EXPLAINS THE DIRT CLOD UP HIS NOSE

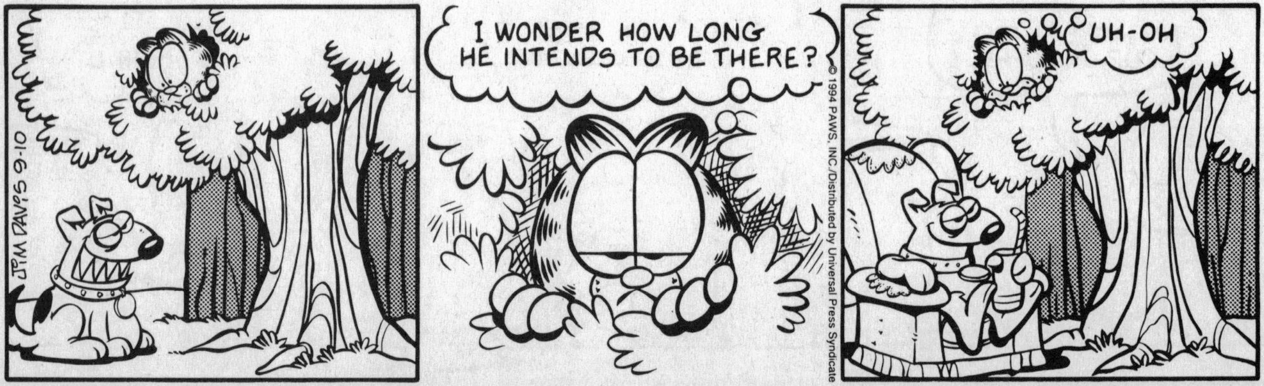
JIM DAVIS 9-10
I WONDER HOW LONG HE INTENDS TO BE THERE?
© 1994 PAWS, INC./Distributed by Universal Press Syndicate
UH-OH

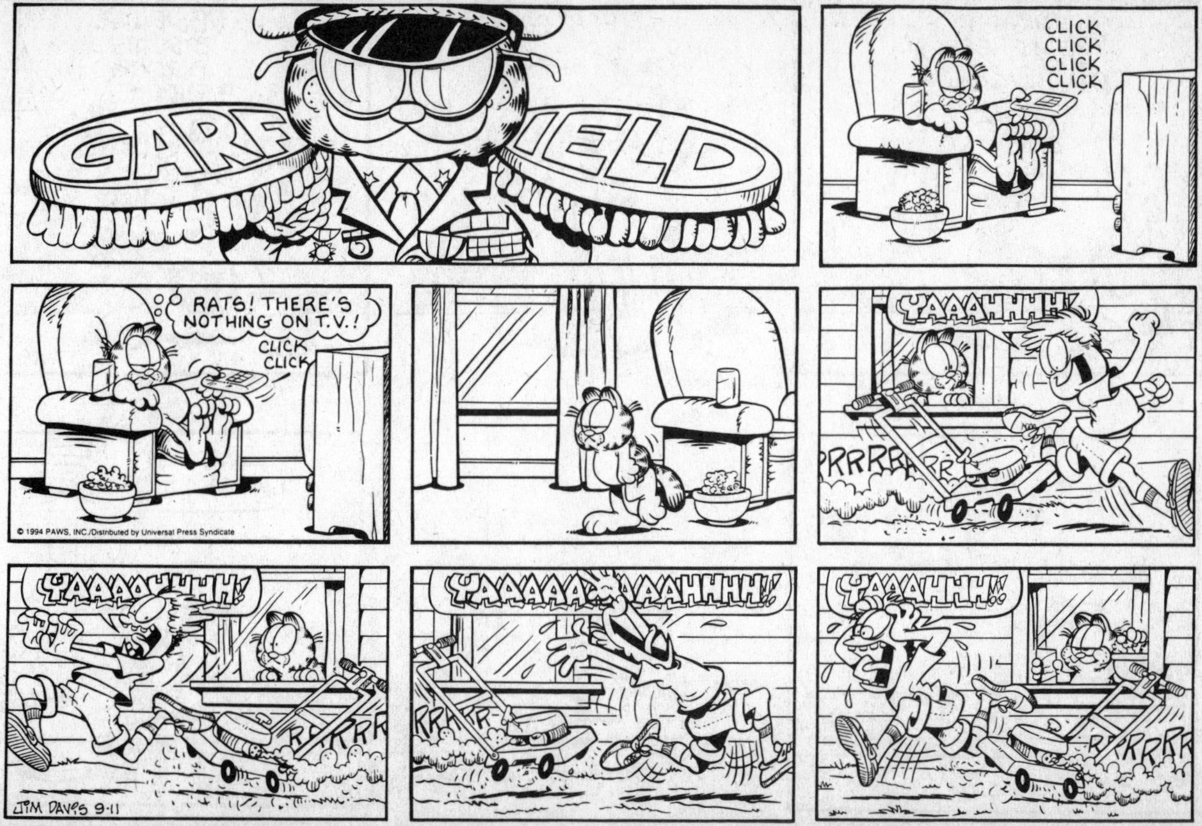
GARFIELD
CLICK
CLICK
CLICK
CLICK
RATS! THERE'S NOTHING ON T.V.!
CLICK
CLICK
YAAAHHH!
RRRRRRRR
YAAAAHHHH!
RRRRR
YAAAAAAAAHHHH!!
RRRR
YAAAHHH!!
RRRRR
JIM DAVIS 9-11

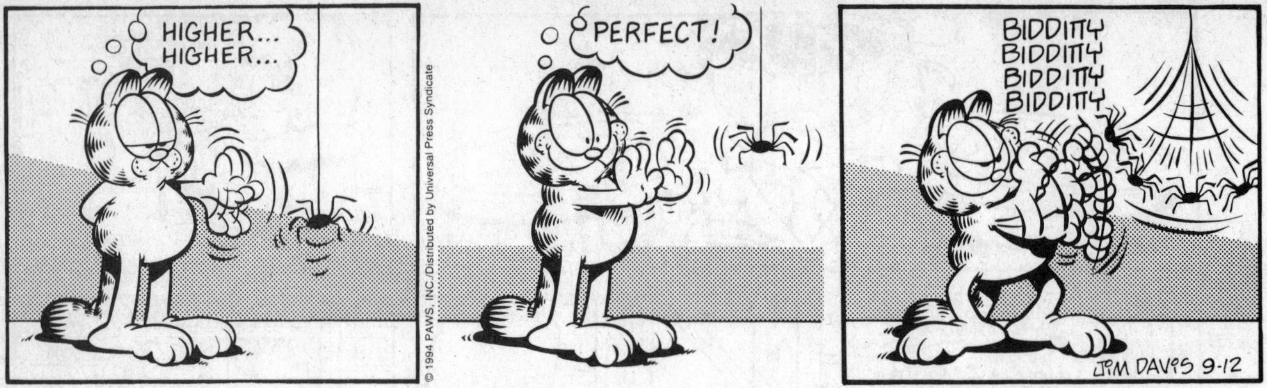
HIGHER... HIGHER...
PERFECT!
BIDDITTY
BIDDITTY
BIDDITTY
BIDDITTY
JIM DAVIS 9-12

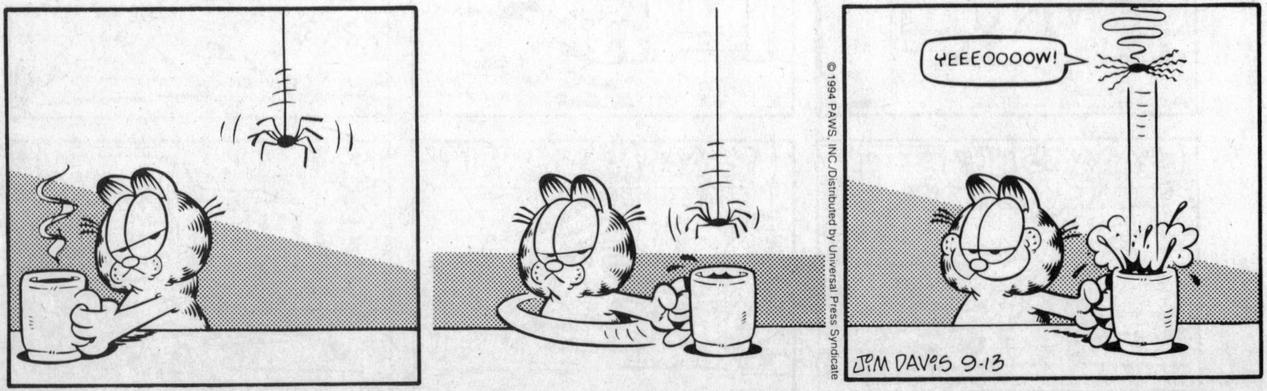
YEEEOOOOW!
JIM DAVIS 9-13

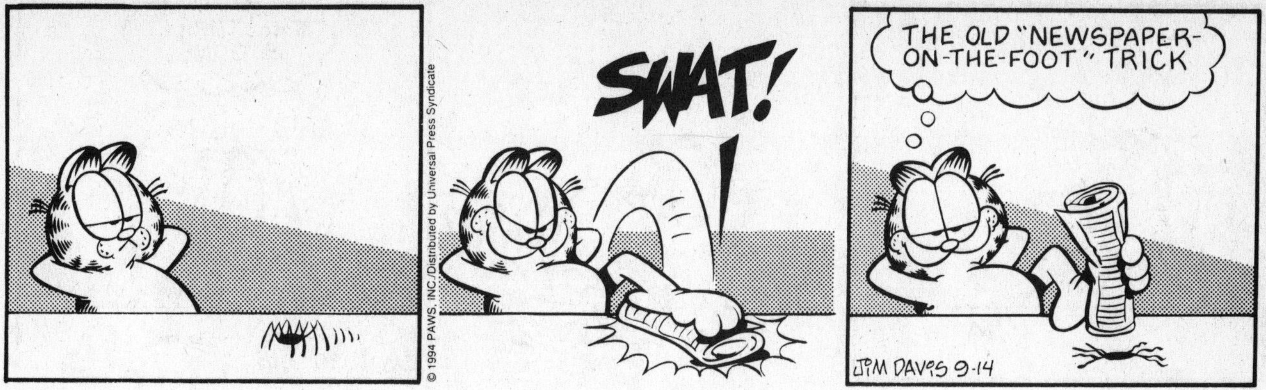
© 1994 PAWS, INC./Distributed by Universal Press Syndicate
SWAT!
THE OLD "NEWSPAPER-ON-THE-FOOT" TRICK
JIM DAVIS 9-14

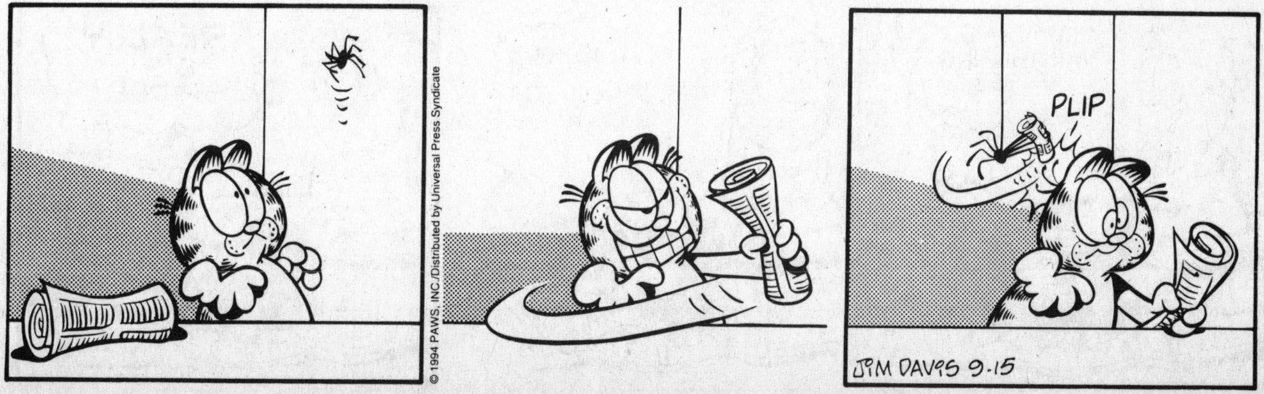
© 1994 PAWS, INC./Distributed by Universal Press Syndicate
PLIP
JIM DAVIS 9-15

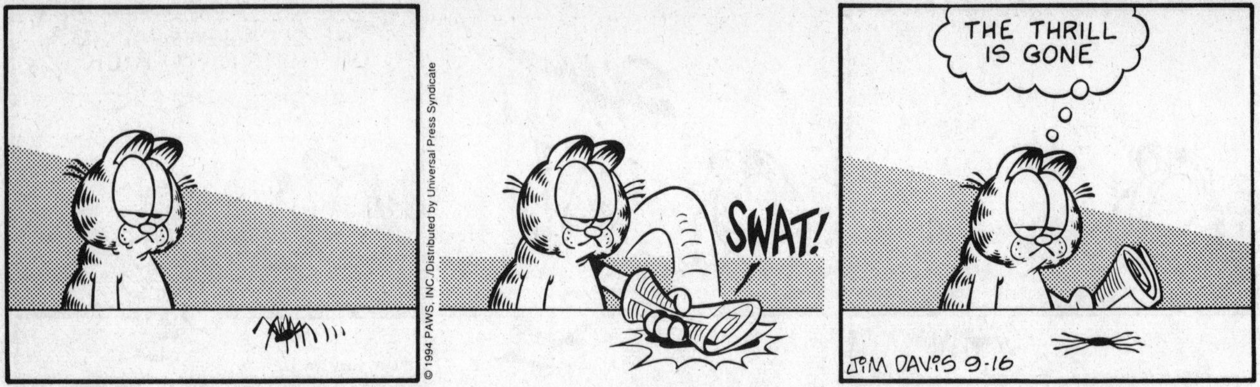
SWAT!
THE THRILL IS GONE
© 1994 PAWS, INC./Distributed by Universal Press Syndicate
JIM DAVIS 9-16

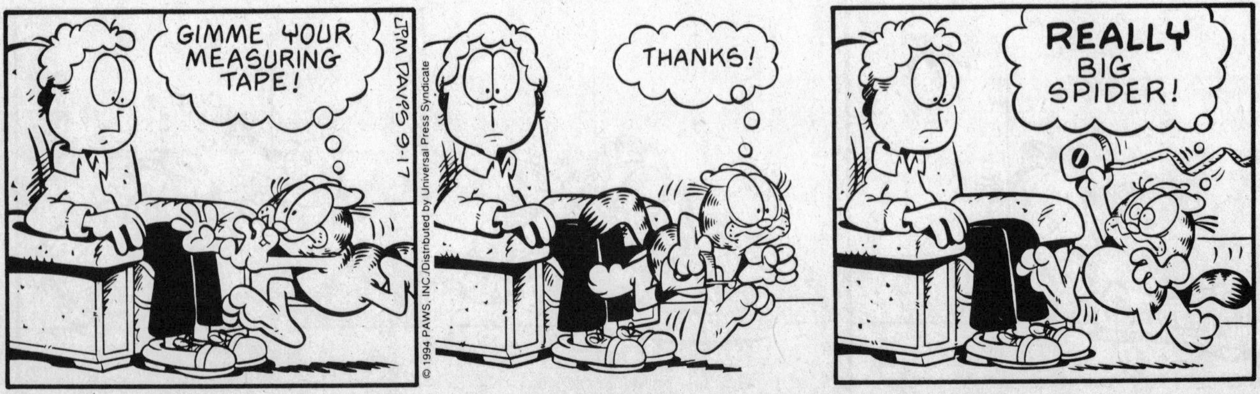
GIMME YOUR MEASURING TAPE!
THANKS!
REALLY BIG SPIDER!
JIM DAVIS 9-17
© 1994 PAWS, INC./Distributed by Universal Press Syndicate

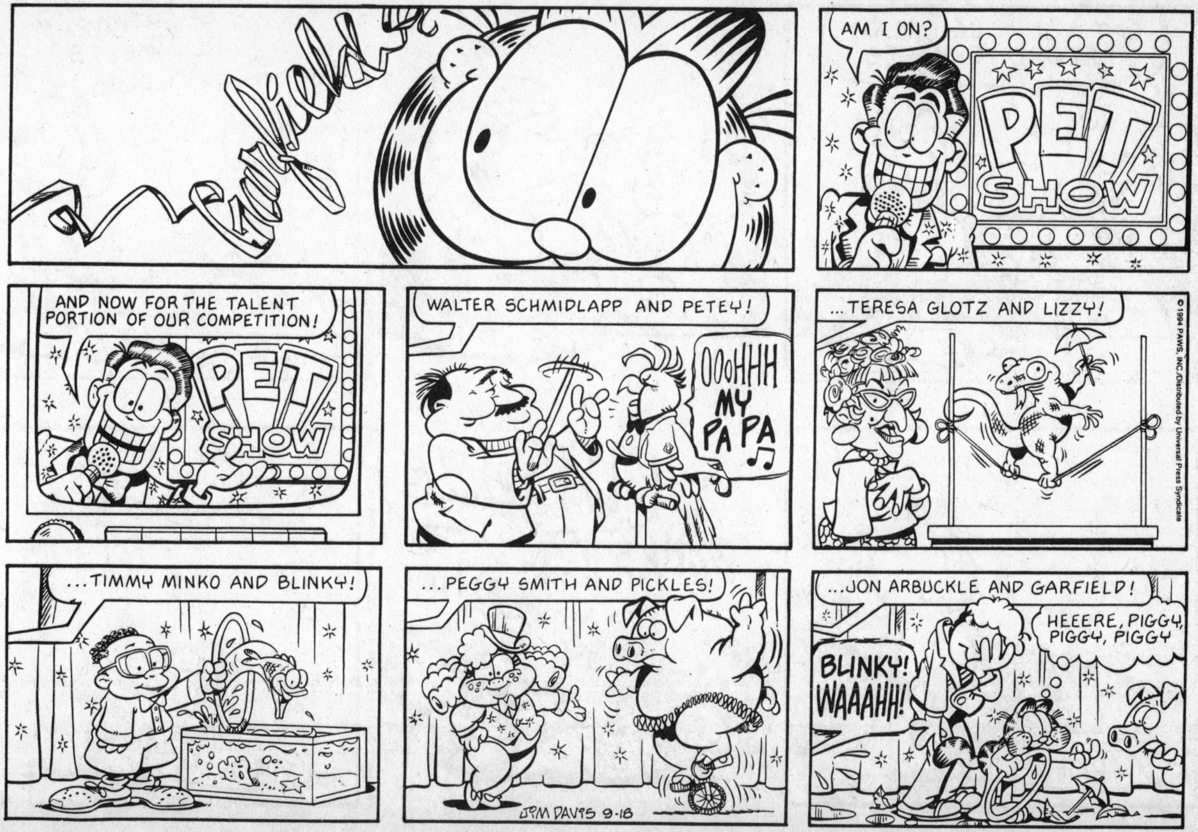
Garfield
AM I ON?
PET SHOW
AND NOW FOR THE TALENT PORTION OF OUR COMPETITION!
PET SHOW
WALTER SCHMIDLAPP AND PETEY!
OOOHHH MY PA PA
...TERESA GLOTZ AND LIZZY!
© 1994 PAWS, INC./Distributed by Universal Press Syndicate
...TIMMY MINKO AND BLINKY!
...PEGGY SMITH AND PICKLES!
JIM DAVIS 9-18
...JON ARBUCKLE AND GARFIELD!
HEEERE, PIGGY, PIGGY, PIGGY
BLINKY! WAAAHH!

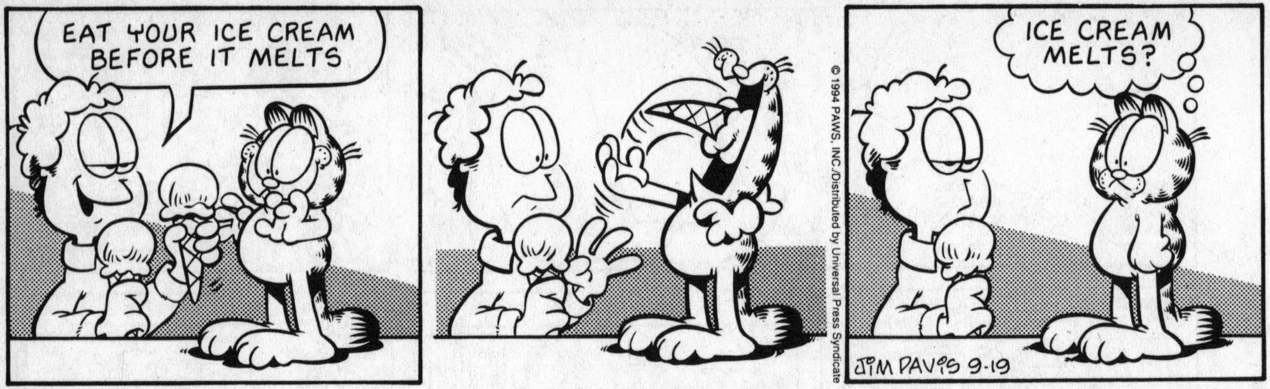
EAT YOUR ICE CREAM BEFORE IT MELTS
ICE CREAM MELTS?
JIM DAVIS 9-19
© 1994 PAWS, INC./Distributed by Universal Press Syndicate

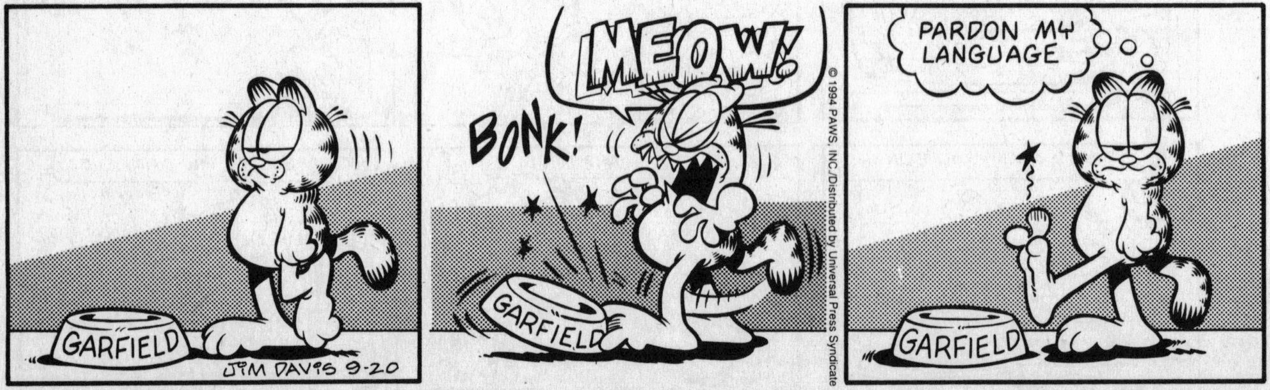
GARFIELD
JIM DAVIS 9-20
BONK!
MEOW!
GARFIELD
PARDON MY LANGUAGE
GARFIELD
© 1994 PAWS, INC./Distributed by Universal Press Syndicate

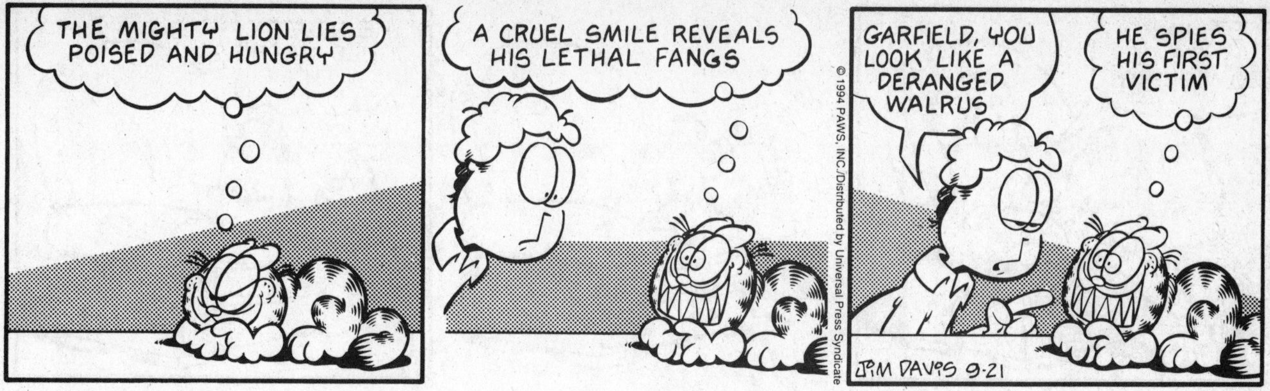
THE MIGHTY LION LIES POISED AND HUNGRY
A CRUEL SMILE REVEALS HIS LETHAL FANGS
GARFIELD, YOU LOOK LIKE A DERANGED WALRUS
HE SPIES HIS FIRST VICTIM
© 1994 PAWS, INC./Distributed by Universal Press Syndicate
JIM DAVIS 9-21

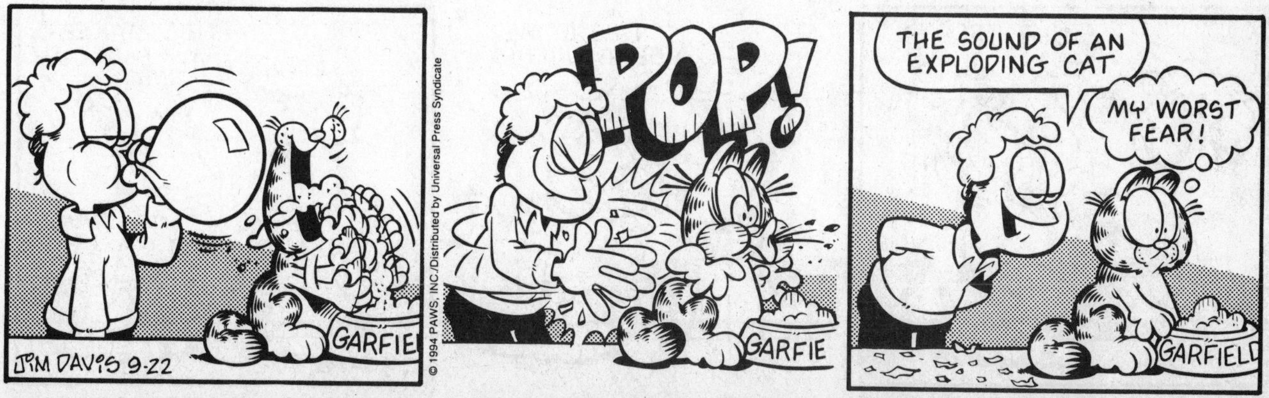
GARFIE
JIM DAVIS 9-22
© 1994 PAWS, INC./Distributed by Universal Press Syndicate
POP!
GARFIE
THE SOUND OF AN EXPLODING CAT
MY WORST FEAR!
GARFIELD

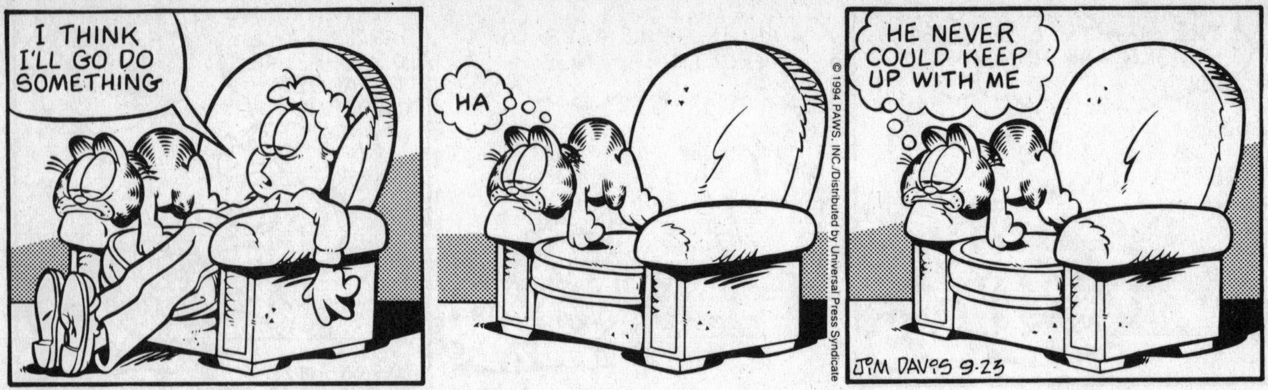
I THINK I'LL GO DO SOMETHING
HA
HE NEVER COULD KEEP UP WITH ME
© 1994 PAWS, INC./Distributed by Universal Press Syndicate
JIM DAVIS 9-23

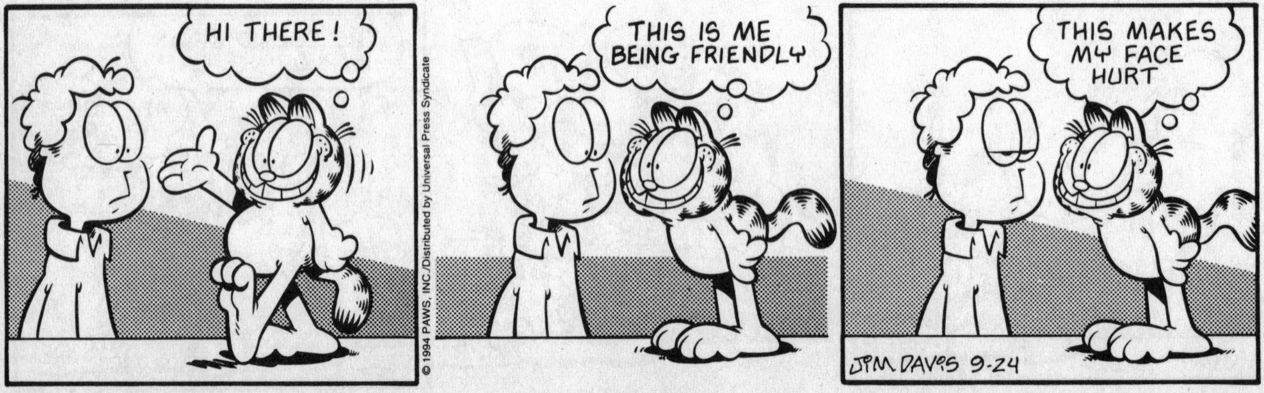
HI THERE!
© 1994 PAWS, INC./Distributed by Universal Press Syndicate
THIS IS ME BEING FRIENDLY
THIS MAKES MY FACE HURT
JIM DAVIS 9-24

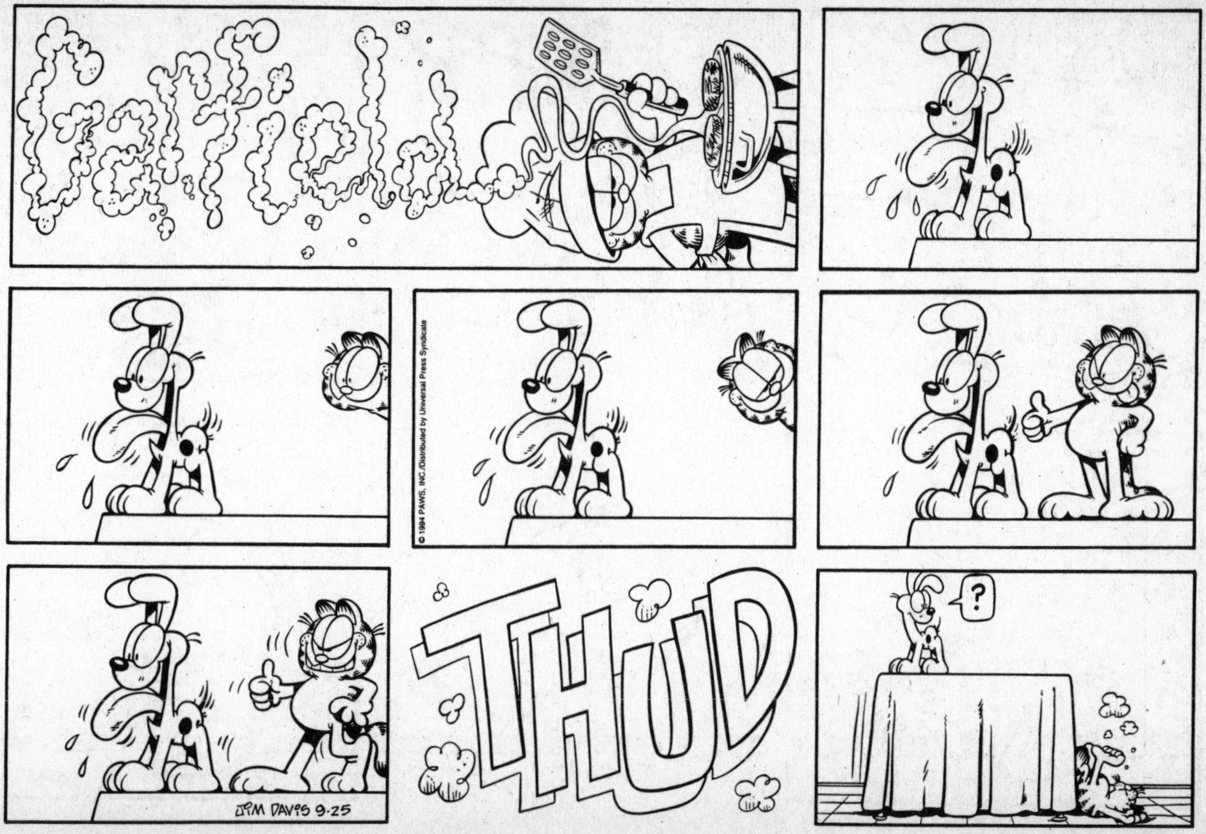
Garfield
© 1994 PAWS, INC./Distributed by Universal Press Syndicate
JIM DAVIS 9-25
THUD
?

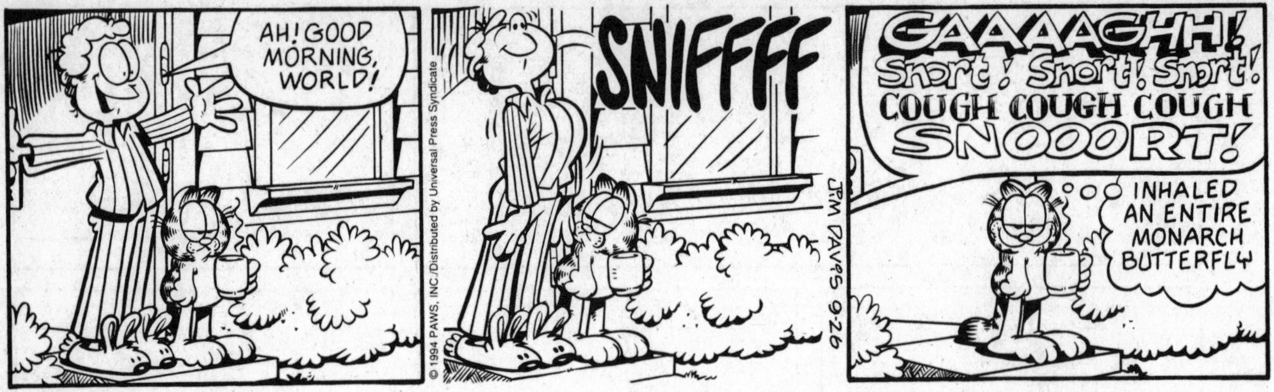
AH! GOOD MORNING, WORLD!
© 1994 PAWS, INC./Distributed by Universal Press Syndicate
SNIFFFF
JIM DAVIS 9-26
GAAAAGHH! Snort! Snort! Snort! COUGH COUGH COUGH SNOOORT!
INHALED AN ENTIRE MONARCH BUTTERFLY

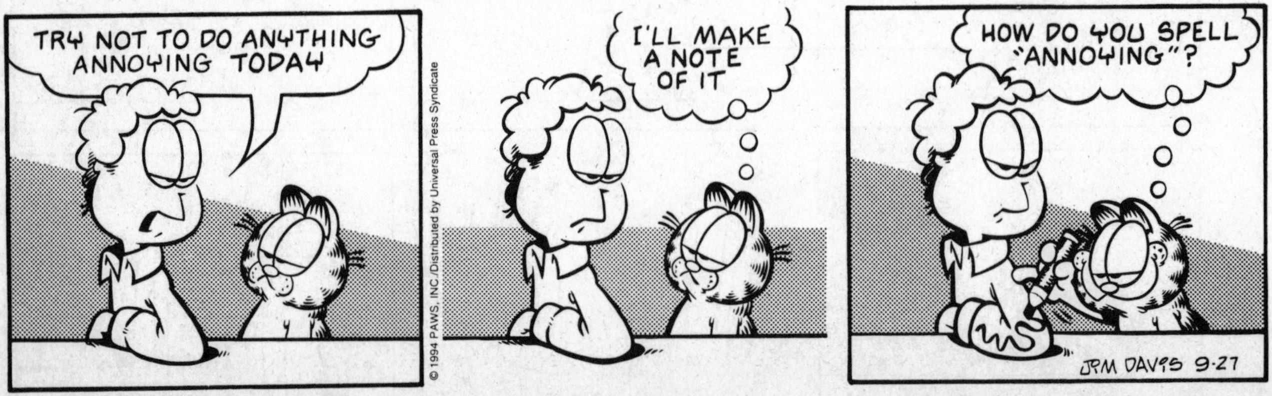
TRY NOT TO DO ANYTHING ANNOYING TODAY
© 1994 PAWS, INC./Distributed by Universal Press Syndicate
I'LL MAKE A NOTE OF IT
HOW DO YOU SPELL "ANNOYING"?
JIM DAVIS 9-27

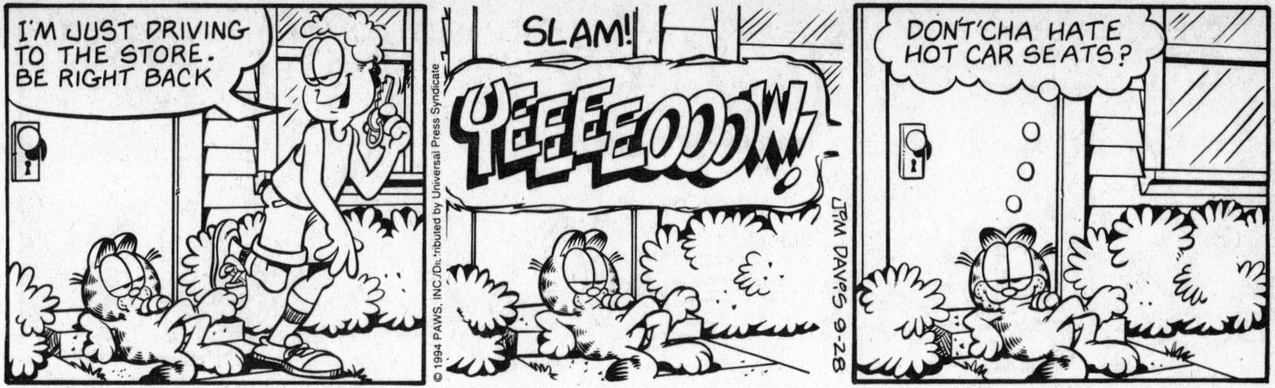
I'M JUST DRIVING TO THE STORE. BE RIGHT BACK
SLAM!
YEEEEOOOOW!
DON'T'CHA HATE HOT CAR SEATS?
JIM DAVIS 9-28
© 1994 PAWS, INC./Distributed by Universal Press Syndicate

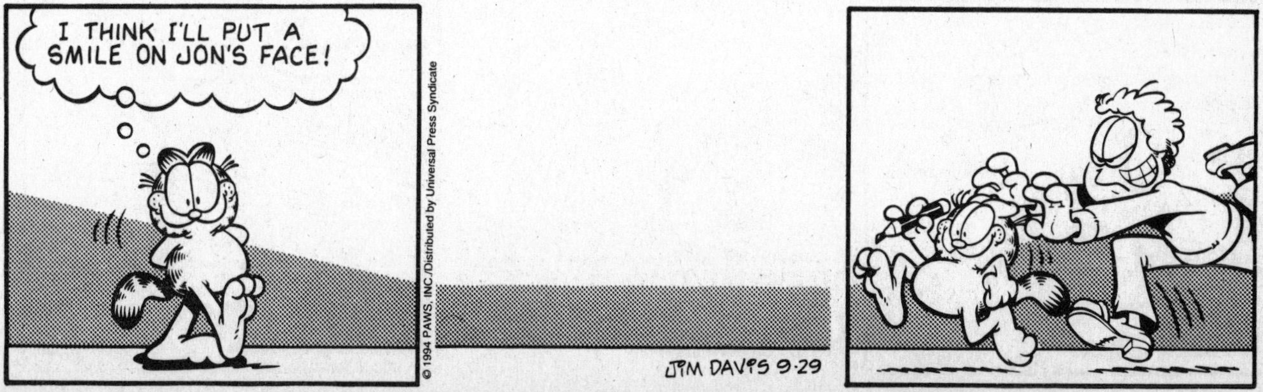
I THINK I'LL PUT A SMILE ON JON'S FACE!
JIM DAVIS 9-29
© 1994 PAWS, INC./Distributed by Universal Press Syndicate

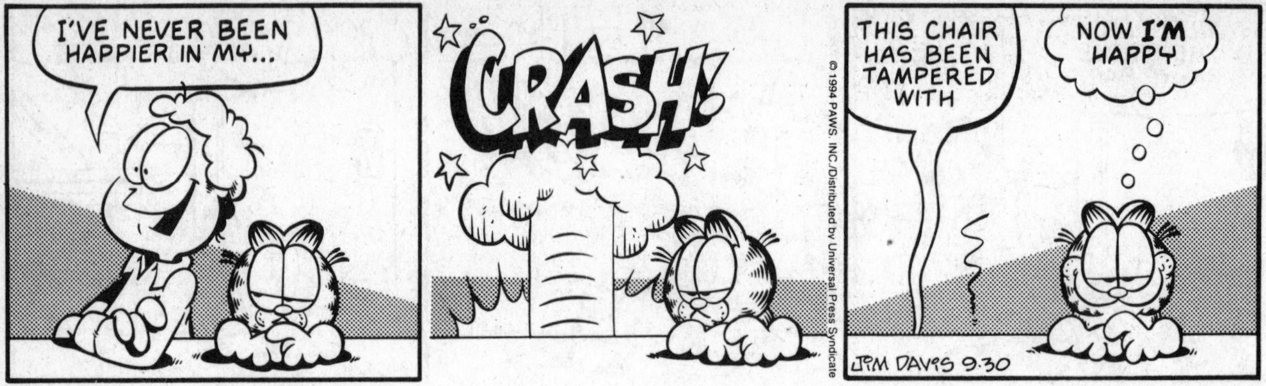

I'VE NEVER BEEN HAPPIER IN MY...
CRASH!
THIS CHAIR HAS BEEN TAMPERED WITH
NOW I'M HAPPY
JIM DAVIS 9·30
© 1994 PAWS. INC./Distributed by Universal Press Syndicate

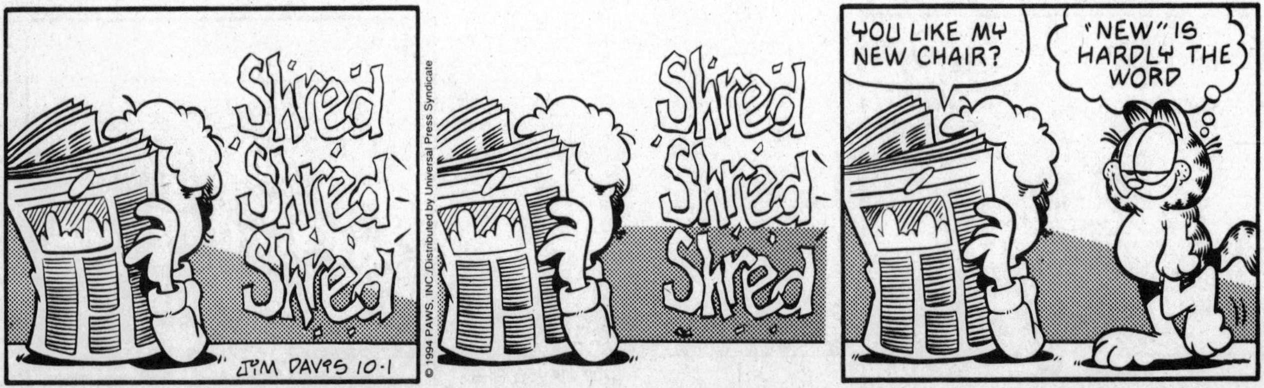

Shred Shred Shred
JIM DAVIS 10·1
© 1994 PAWS. INC./Distributed by Universal Press Syndicate
Shred Shred Shred
YOU LIKE MY NEW CHAIR?
"NEW" IS HARDLY THE WORD

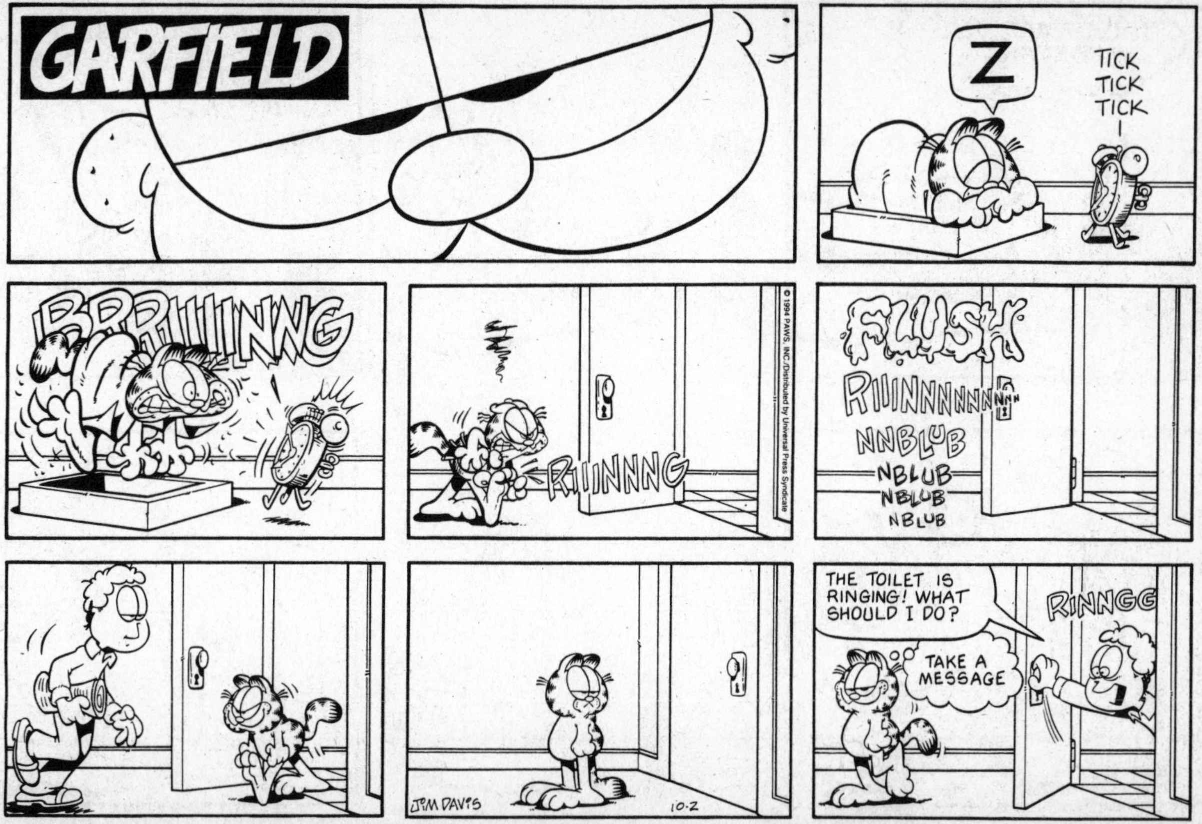
GARFIELD
Z
TICK
TICK
TICK
BRRIIIINNG
RIIINNNG
© 1994 PAWS, INC./Distributed by Universal Press Syndicate
FLUSH
RIIINNNNNNNN
NNBLUB
NBLUB
NBLUB
NBLUB
JIM DAVIS
10·2
THE TOILET IS RINGING! WHAT SHOULD I DO?
RINNGG
TAKE A MESSAGE

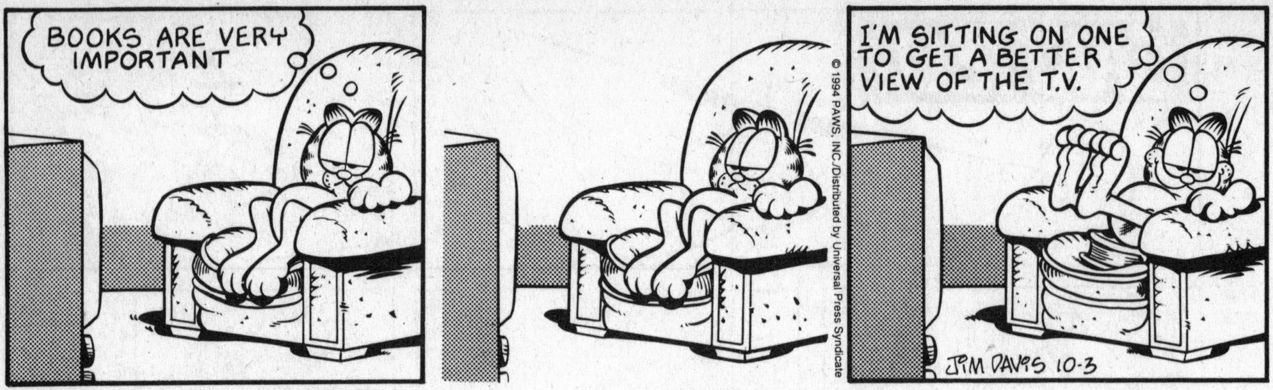
BOOKS ARE VERY IMPORTANT
I'M SITTING ON ONE TO GET A BETTER VIEW OF THE T.V.
JIM DAVIS 10-3
© 1994 PAWS, INC./Distributed by Universal Press Syndicate

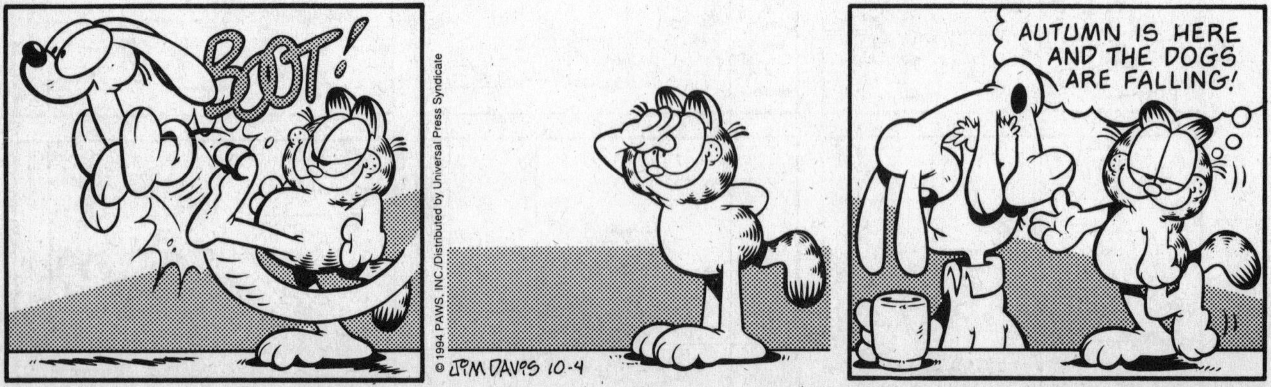
BOOT!
© 1994 PAWS, INC./Distributed by Universal Press Syndicate
JIM DAVIS 10-4
AUTUMN IS HERE AND THE DOGS ARE FALLING!

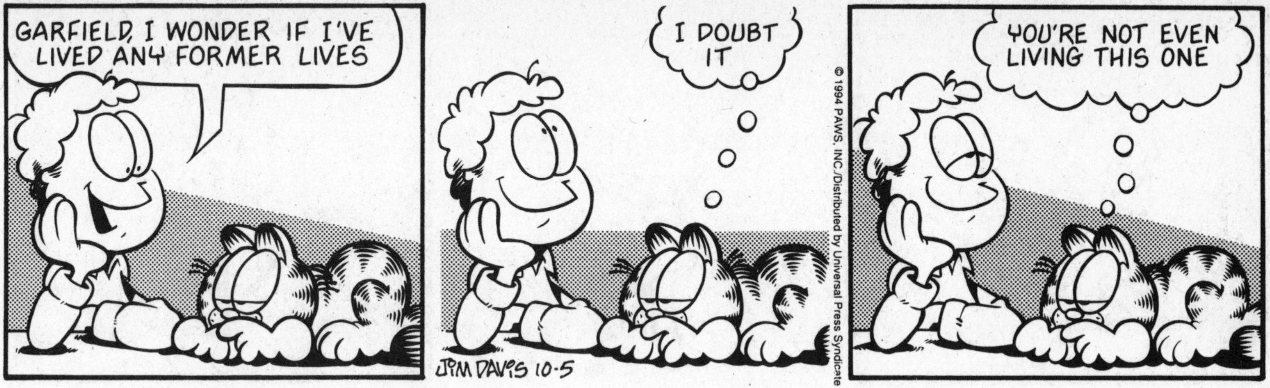
GARFIELD, I WONDER IF I'VE LIVED ANY FORMER LIVES
I DOUBT IT
YOU'RE NOT EVEN LIVING THIS ONE
JIM DAVIS 10-5
© 1994 PAWS, INC./Distributed by Universal Press Syndicate

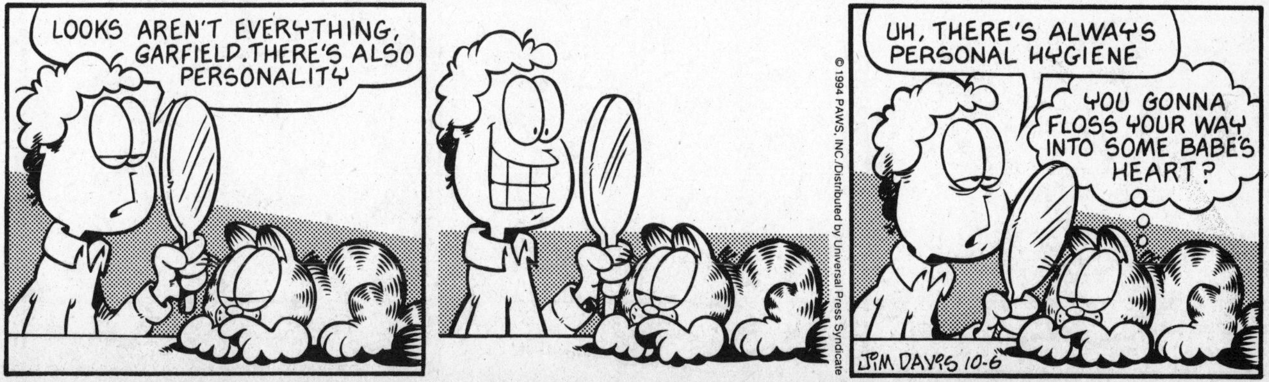
LOOKS AREN'T EVERYTHING, GARFIELD. THERE'S ALSO PERSONALITY
UH, THERE'S ALWAYS PERSONAL HYGIENE
YOU GONNA FLOSS YOUR WAY INTO SOME BABE'S HEART?
JIM DAVIS 10-6
© 1994 PAWS, INC./Distributed by Universal Press Syndicate

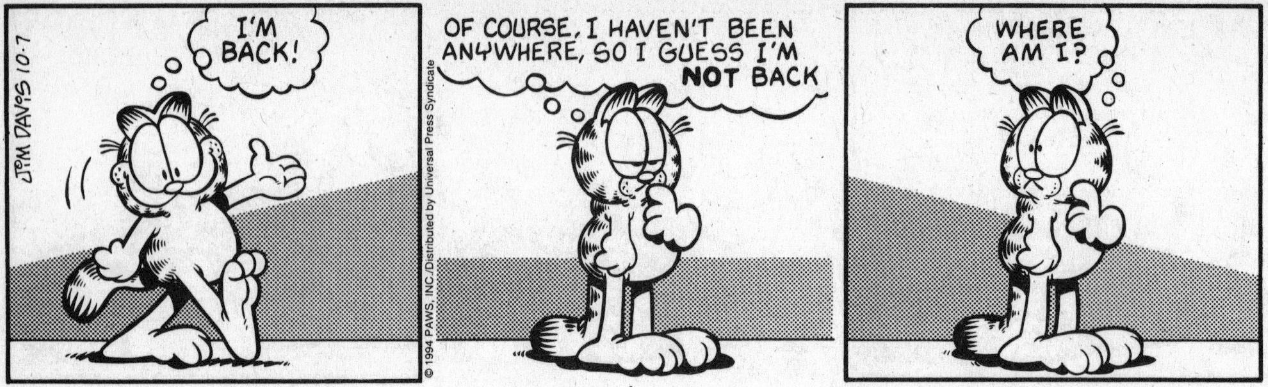
JIM DAVIS 10-7
I'M BACK!
OF COURSE, I HAVEN'T BEEN ANYWHERE, SO I GUESS I'M **NOT** BACK
WHERE AM I?

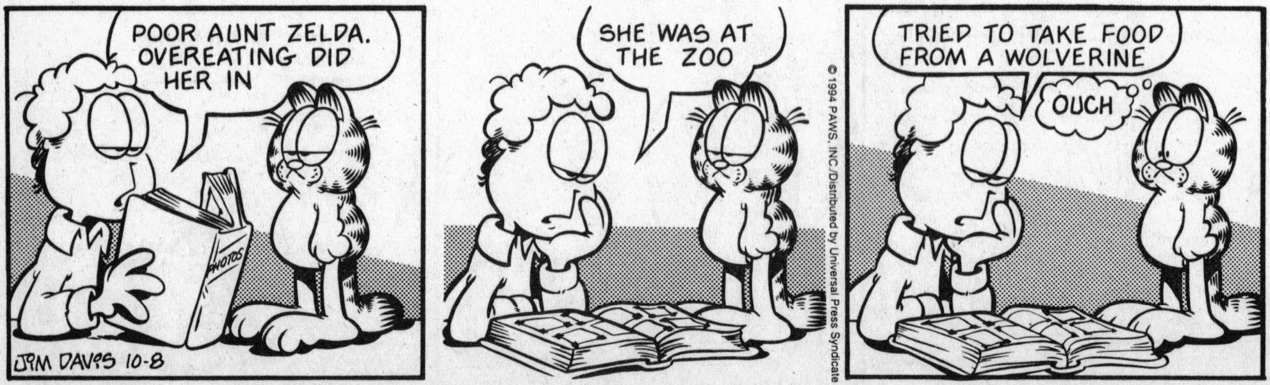
POOR AUNT ZELDA. OVEREATING DID HER IN
PHOTOS
JIM DAVIS 10-8
SHE WAS AT THE ZOO
TRIED TO TAKE FOOD FROM A WOLVERINE
OUCH

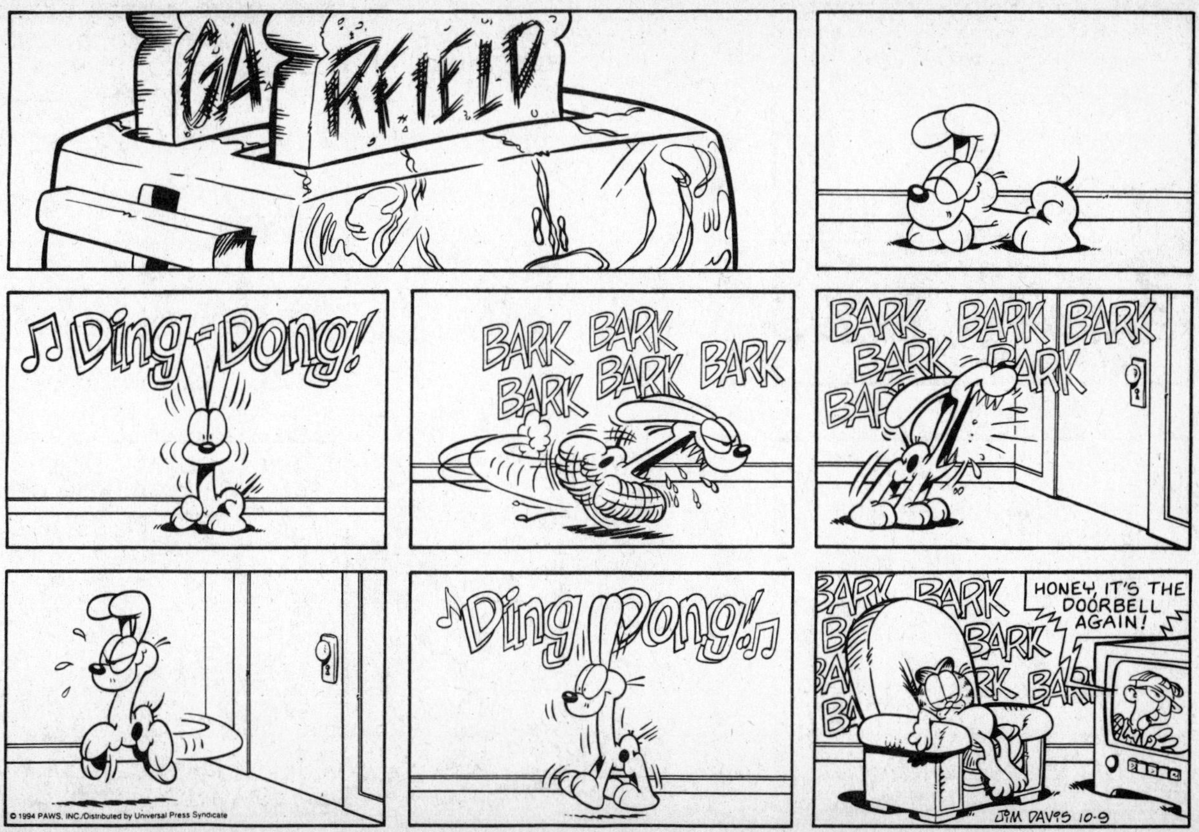
GARFIELD
Ding-Dong!
BARK BARK BARK BARK BARK BARK
BARK BARK BARK BARK BARK BARK
Ding Dong!
BARK BARK BARK BARK BARK
HONEY, IT'S THE DOORBELL AGAIN!
JIM DAVIS 10-9
© 1994 PAWS, INC./Distributed by Universal Press Syndicate

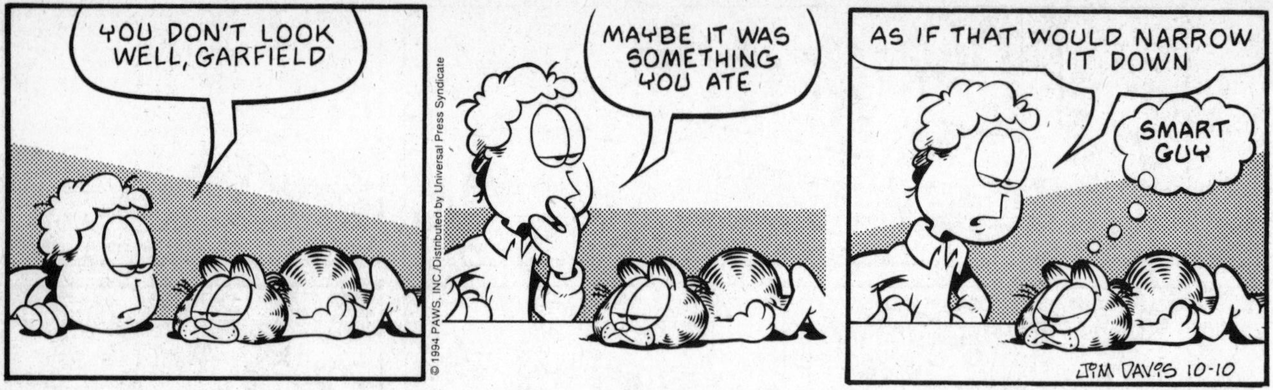
YOU DON'T LOOK WELL, GARFIELD
MAYBE IT WAS SOMETHING YOU ATE
AS IF THAT WOULD NARROW IT DOWN
SMART GUY
JIM DAVIS 10-10
© 1994 PAWS, INC./Distributed by Universal Press Syndicate

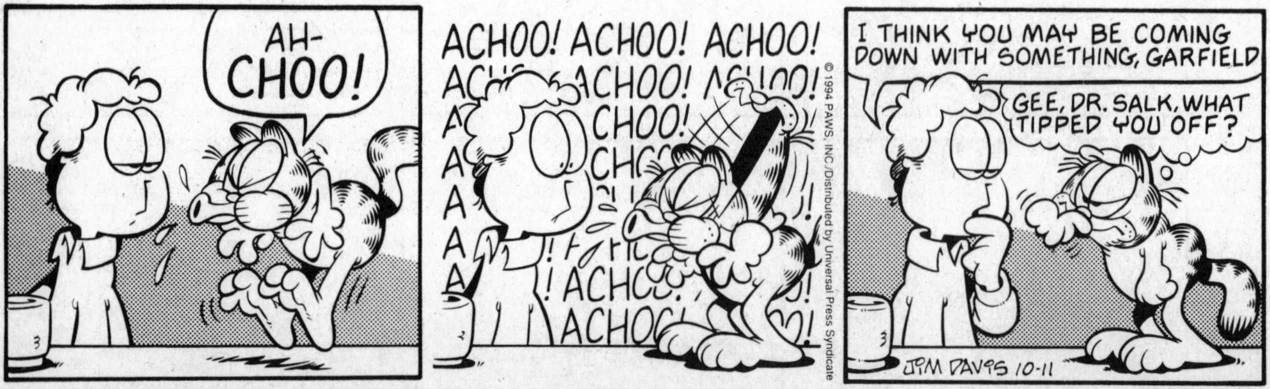
AH-CHOO!
ACHOO! ACHOO! ACHOO!
ACHOO!
CHOO!
I THINK YOU MAY BE COMING DOWN WITH SOMETHING, GARFIELD
GEE, DR. SALK, WHAT TIPPED YOU OFF?
JIM DAVIS 10-11
© 1994 PAWS, INC./Distributed by Universal Press Syndicate

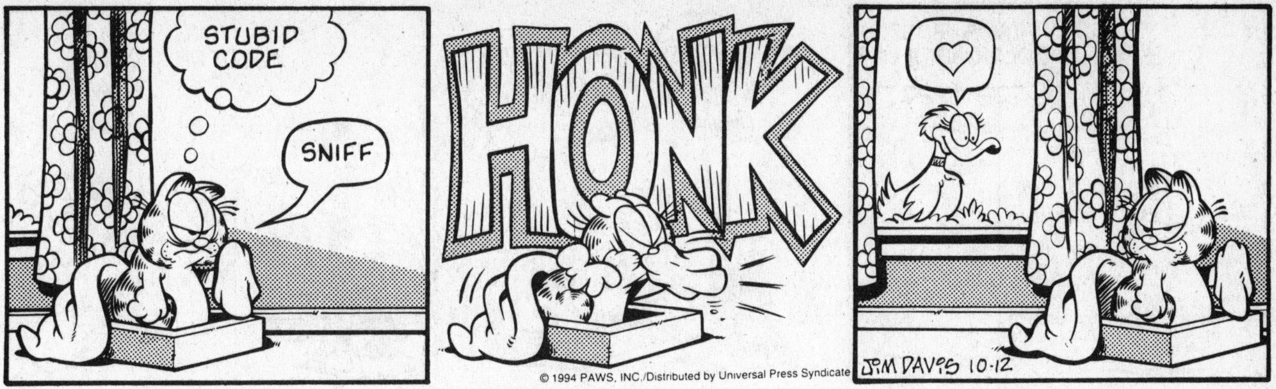
STUBID CODE
SNIFF
HONK
© 1994 PAWS, INC./Distributed by Universal Press Syndicate
JIM DAVIS 10-12

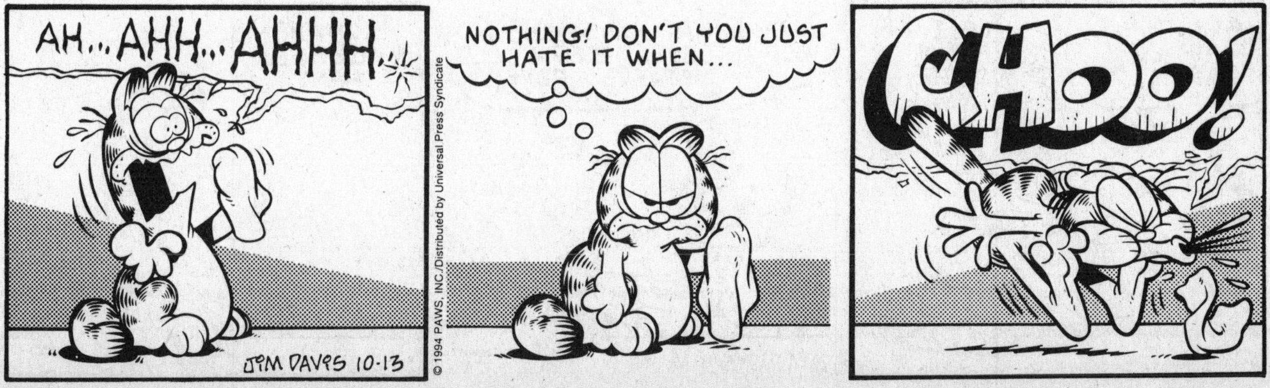
AH... AHH... AHHH...
JIM DAVIS 10-13
© 1994 PAWS, INC./Distributed by Universal Press Syndicate
NOTHING! DON'T YOU JUST HATE IT WHEN...
CHOO!

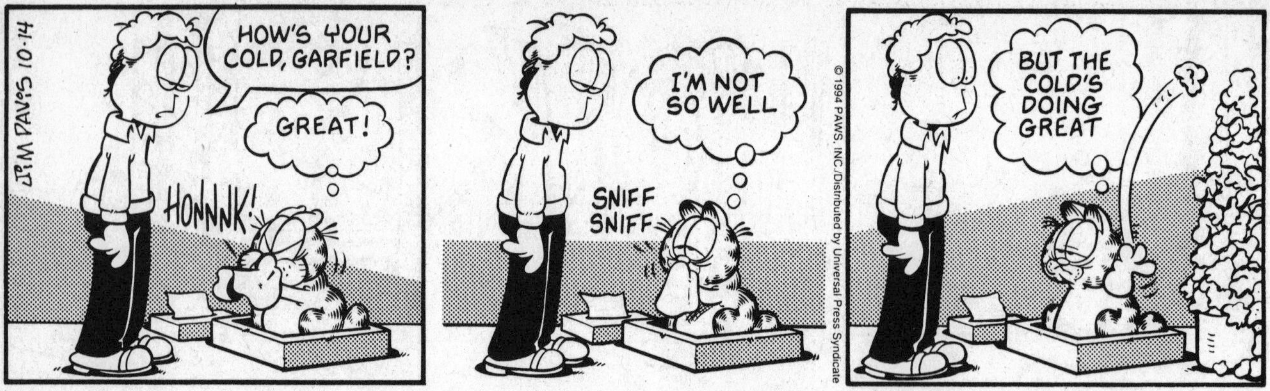
JIM DAVIS 10·14
HOW'S YOUR COLD, GARFIELD?
GREAT!
HONNNK!
I'M NOT SO WELL
SNIFF SNIFF
© 1994 PAWS, INC./Distributed by Universal Press Syndicate
BUT THE COLD'S DOING GREAT

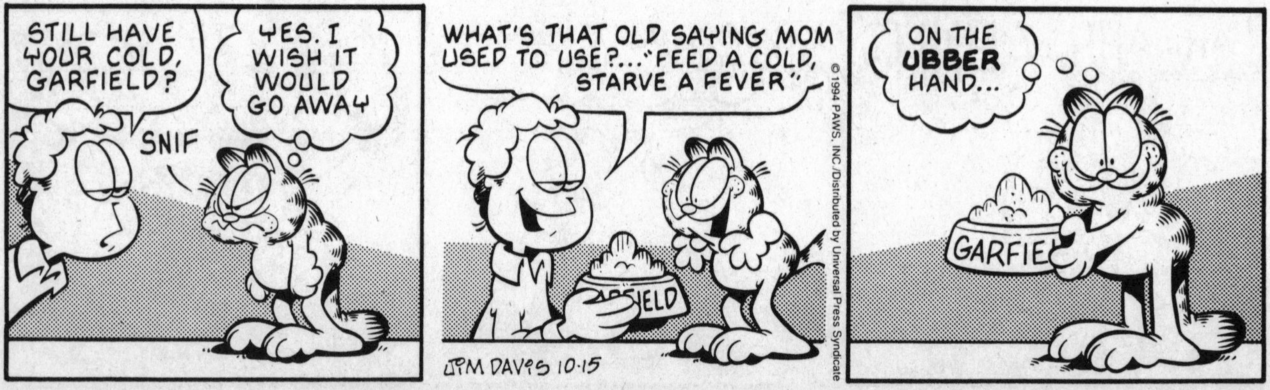
STILL HAVE YOUR COLD, GARFIELD?
YES. I WISH IT WOULD GO AWAY
SNIF
WHAT'S THAT OLD SAYING MOM USED TO USE?... "FEED A COLD, STARVE A FEVER"
JIM DAVIS 10·15
© 1994 PAWS, INC./Distributed by Universal Press Syndicate
ON THE **UBBER** HAND...
GARFIE

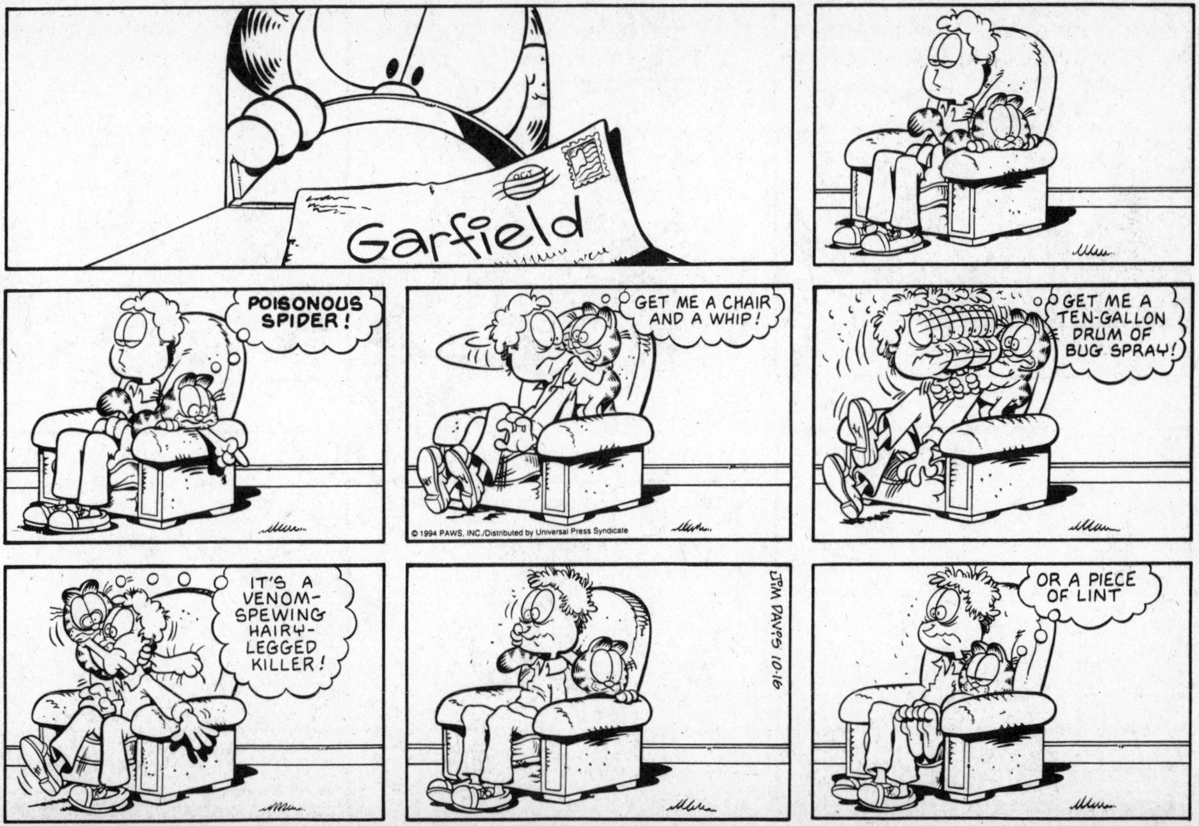
Garfield
POISONOUS SPIDER!
GET ME A CHAIR AND A WHIP!
GET ME A TEN-GALLON DRUM OF BUG SPRAY!
© 1994 PAWS, INC./Distributed by Universal Press Syndicate
IT'S A VENOM-SPEWING HAIRY-LEGGED KILLER!
JIM DAVIS 10-16
OR A PIECE OF LINT

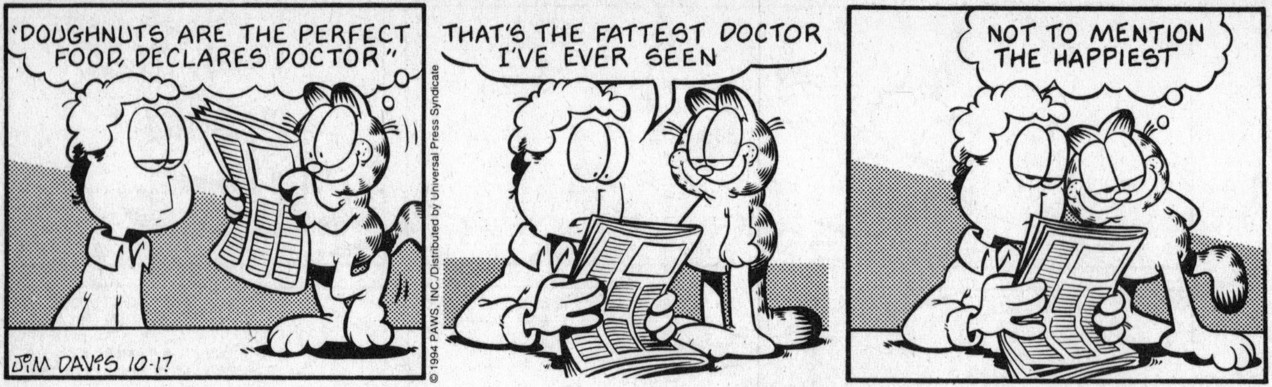
"DOUGHNUTS ARE THE PERFECT FOOD, DECLARES DOCTOR"
JIM DAVIS 10-17
© 1994 PAWS, INC./Distributed by Universal Press Syndicate
THAT'S THE FATTEST DOCTOR I'VE EVER SEEN
NOT TO MENTION THE HAPPIEST

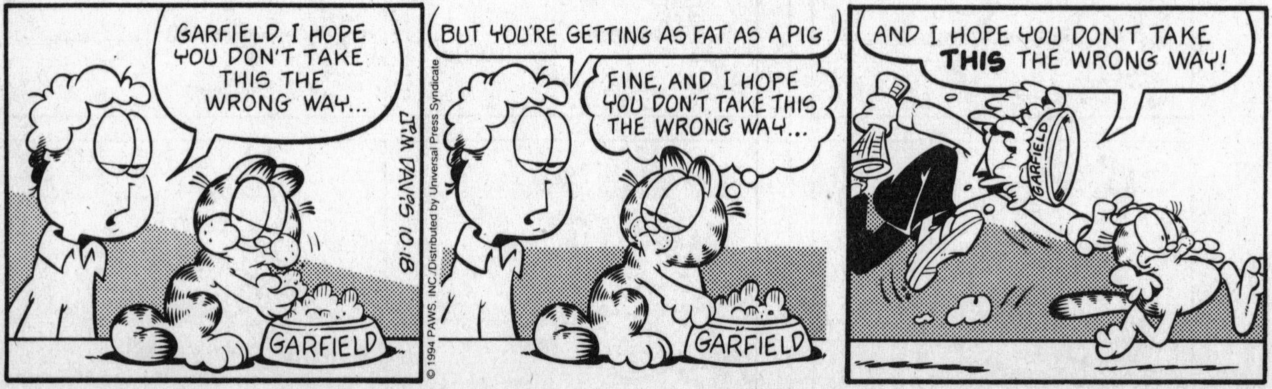
GARFIELD, I HOPE YOU DON'T TAKE THIS THE WRONG WAY...
JIM DAVIS 10-18
GARFIELD
© 1994 PAWS, INC./Distributed by Universal Press Syndicate
BUT YOU'RE GETTING AS FAT AS A PIG
FINE, AND I HOPE YOU DON'T TAKE THIS THE WRONG WAY...
GARFIELD
AND I HOPE YOU DON'T TAKE **THIS** THE WRONG WAY!
GARFIELD

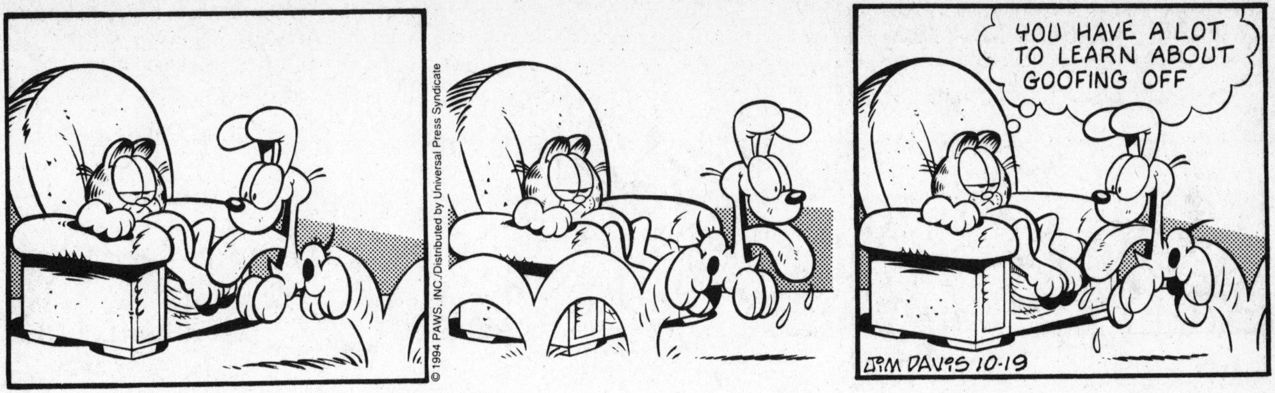
© 1994 PAWS, INC./Distributed by Universal Press Syndicate
YOU HAVE A LOT TO LEARN ABOUT GOOFING OFF
JIM DAVIS 10-19

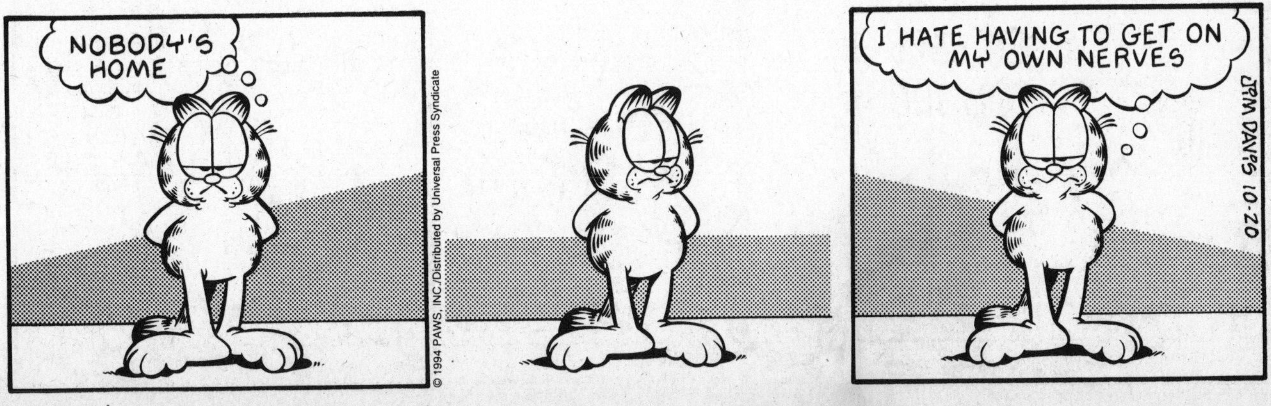
NOBODY'S HOME
© 1994 PAWS, INC./Distributed by Universal Press Syndicate
I HATE HAVING TO GET ON MY OWN NERVES
JIM DAVIS 10-20

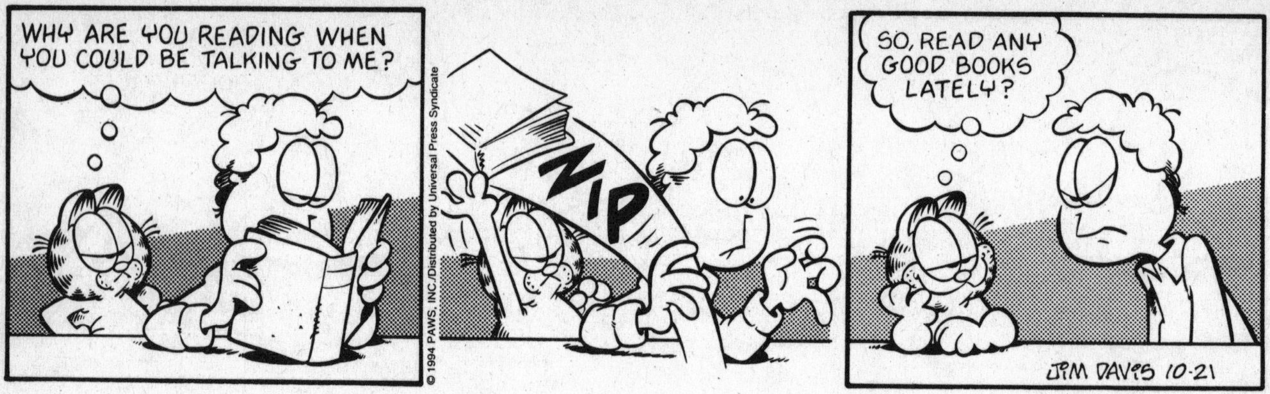
WHY ARE YOU READING WHEN YOU COULD BE TALKING TO ME?
RIP
SO, READ ANY GOOD BOOKS LATELY?
JIM DAVIS 10-21

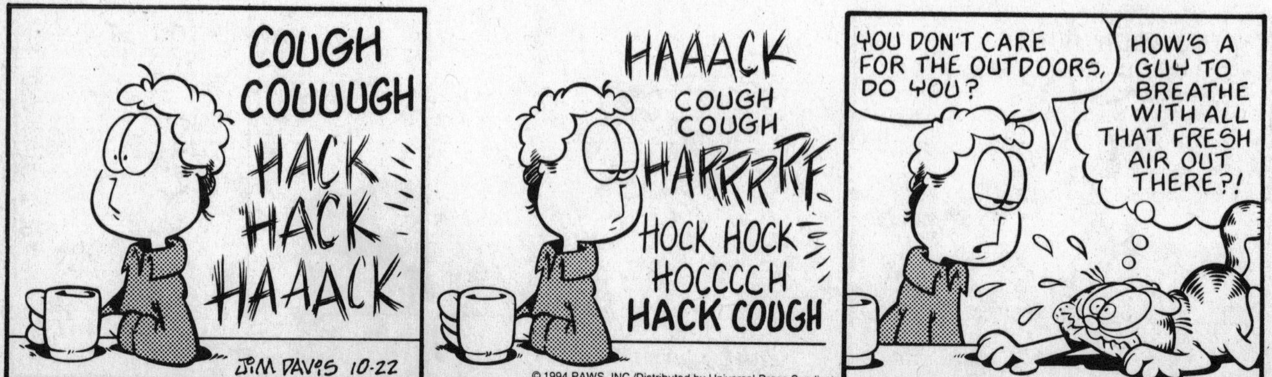
COUGH
COUUUGH
HACK
HACK
HAAACK
JIM DAVIS 10-22
HAAACK
COUGH
COUGH
HARRRRF
HOCK HOCK
HOCCCCH
HACK COUGH
YOU DON'T CARE FOR THE OUTDOORS, DO YOU?
HOW'S A GUY TO BREATHE WITH ALL THAT FRESH AIR OUT THERE?!

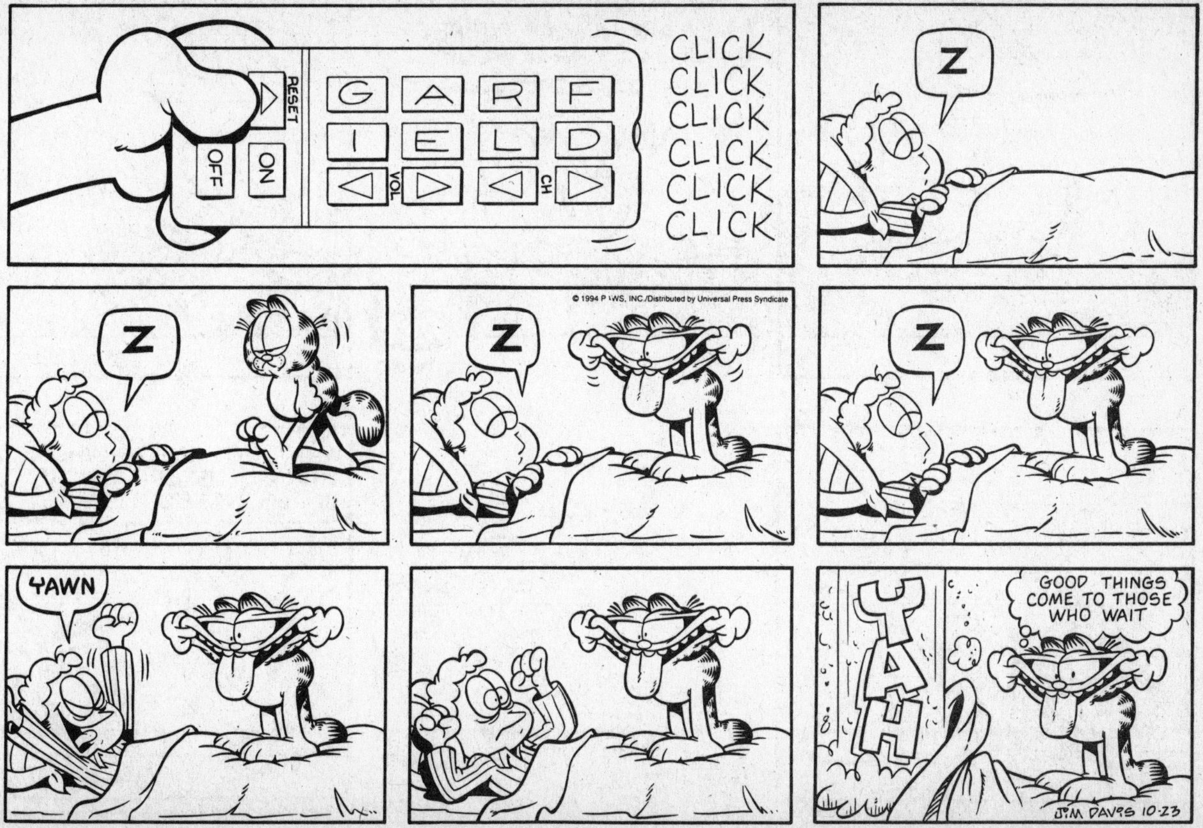
RESET
OFF
ON
GARF
IELD
VOL
CH
CLICK
CLICK
CLICK
CLICK
CLICK
CLICK
Z
Z
© 1994 PAWS, INC./Distributed by Universal Press Syndicate
Z
Z
YAWN
YAAH
GOOD THINGS COME TO THOSE WHO WAIT
JIM DAVIS 10-23

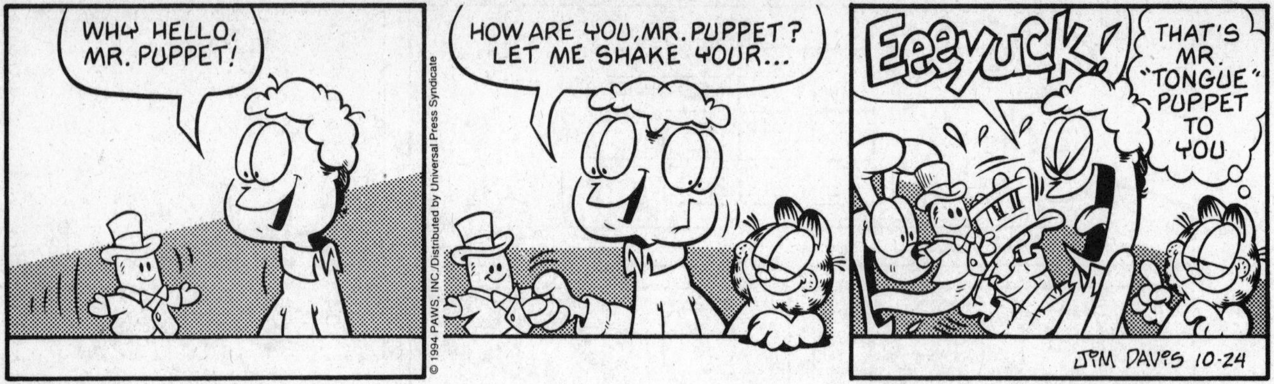
WHY HELLO, MR. PUPPET!
HOW ARE YOU, MR. PUPPET? LET ME SHAKE YOUR...
Eeeyuck!
THAT'S MR. "TONGUE" PUPPET TO YOU
JIM DAVIS 10-24

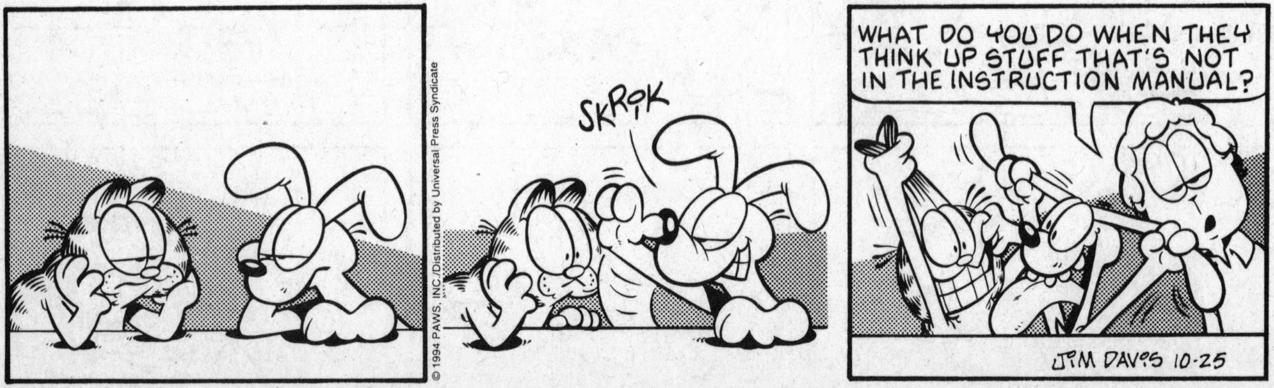
SKROIK
WHAT DO YOU DO WHEN THEY THINK UP STUFF THAT'S NOT IN THE INSTRUCTION MANUAL?
JIM DAVIS 10-25

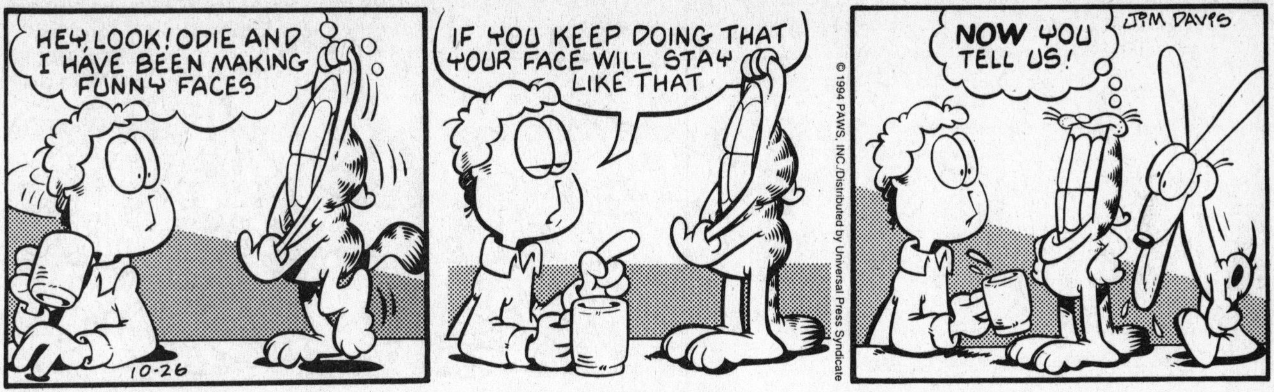
HEY, LOOK! ODIE AND I HAVE BEEN MAKING FUNNY FACES
10-26
IF YOU KEEP DOING THAT YOUR FACE WILL STAY LIKE THAT
© 1994 PAWS, INC./Distributed by Universal Press Syndicate
NOW YOU TELL US!
JIM DAVIS

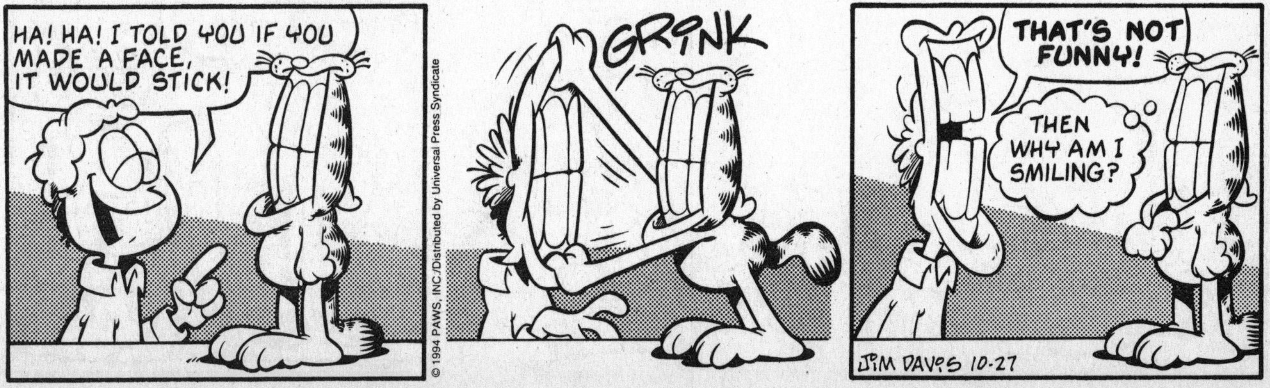
HA! HA! I TOLD YOU IF YOU MADE A FACE, IT WOULD STICK!
© 1994 PAWS, INC./Distributed by Universal Press Syndicate
GRINK
THAT'S NOT FUNNY!
THEN WHY AM I SMILING?
JIM DAVIS 10-27

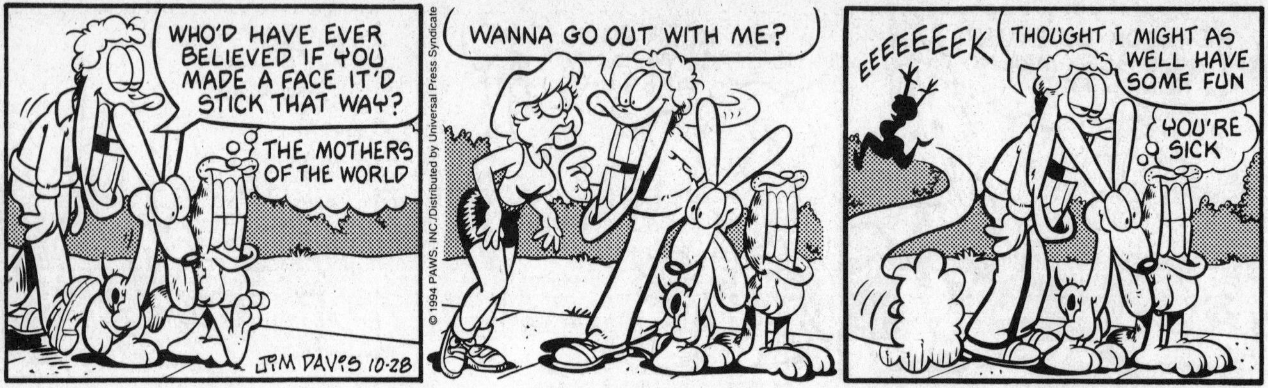
WHO'D HAVE EVER BELIEVED IF YOU MADE A FACE IT'D STICK THAT WAY?
THE MOTHERS OF THE WORLD
JIM DAVIS 10-28
© 1994 PAWS, INC./Distributed by Universal Press Syndicate
WANNA GO OUT WITH ME?
EEEEEEEK
THOUGHT I MIGHT AS WELL HAVE SOME FUN
YOU'RE SICK

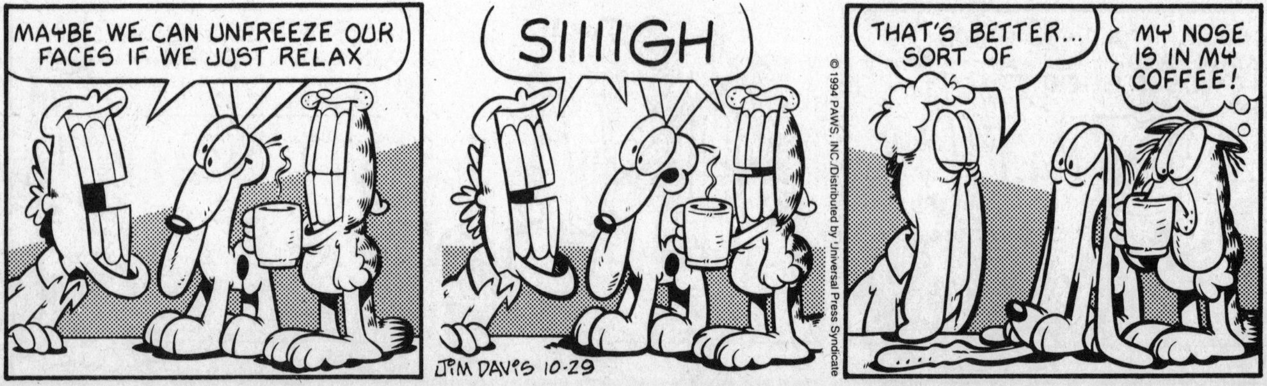
MAYBE WE CAN UNFREEZE OUR FACES IF WE JUST RELAX
SIIIIGH
JIM DAVIS 10-29
© 1994 PAWS, INC./Distributed by Universal Press Syndicate
THAT'S BETTER... SORT OF
MY NOSE IS IN MY COFFEE!

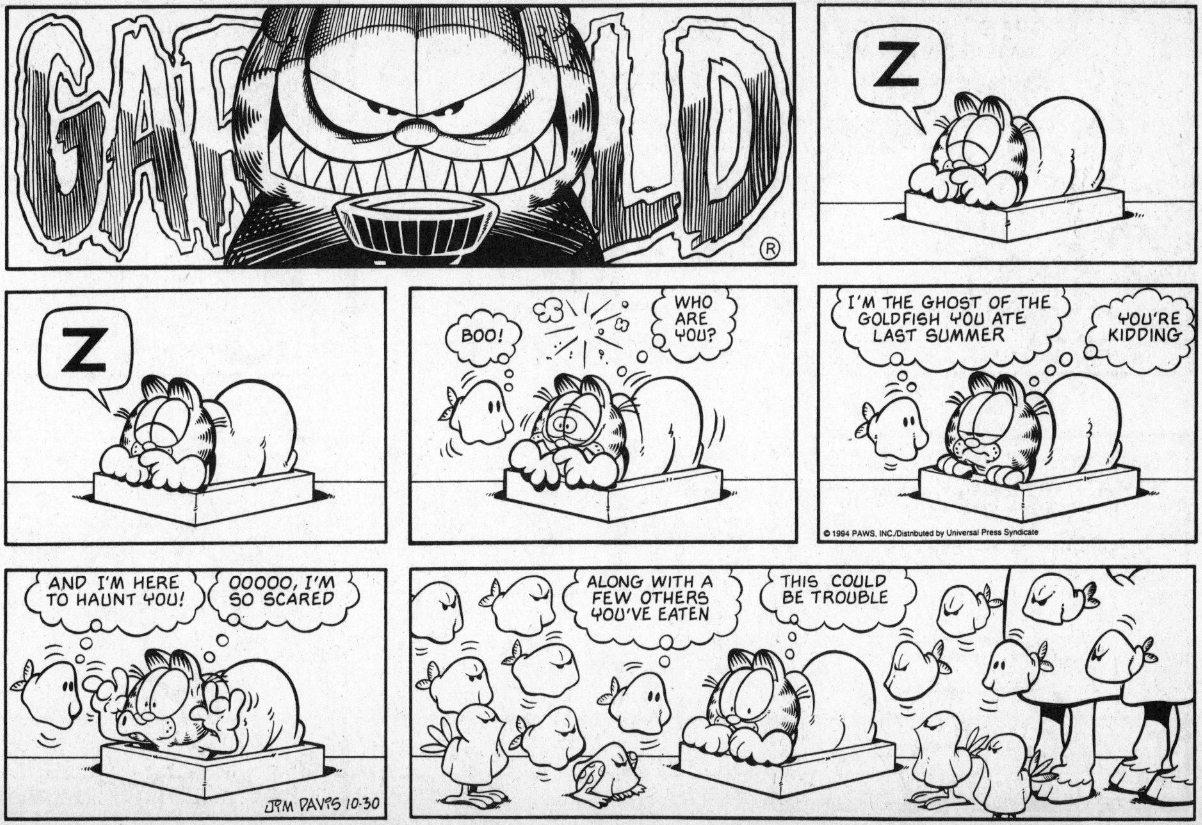

Z
Z
BOO!
WHO ARE YOU?
I'M THE GHOST OF THE GOLDFISH YOU ATE LAST SUMMER
YOU'RE KIDDING
© 1994 PAWS, INC./Distributed by Universal Press Syndicate
AND I'M HERE TO HAUNT YOU!
OOOOO, I'M SO SCARED
JIM DAVIS 10-30
ALONG WITH A FEW OTHERS YOU'VE EATEN
THIS COULD BE TROUBLE

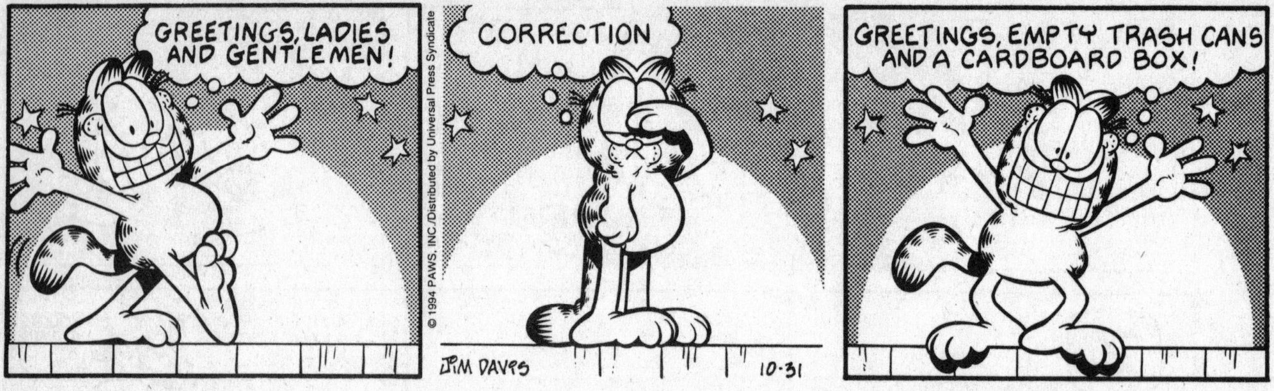
GREETINGS, LADIES AND GENTLEMEN!
© 1994 PAWS, INC./Distributed by Universal Press Syndicate
CORRECTION
JIM DAVIS
10-31
GREETINGS, EMPTY TRASH CANS AND A CARDBOARD BOX!

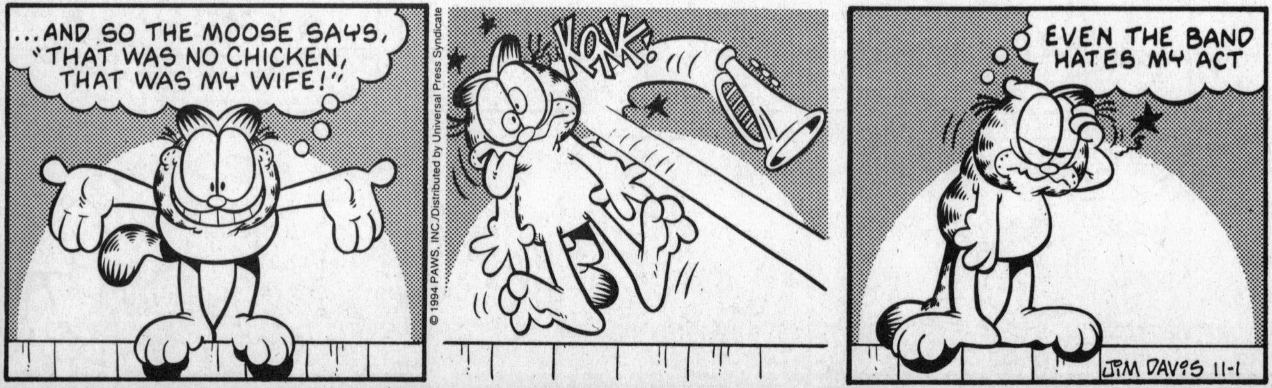
...AND SO THE MOOSE SAYS, "THAT WAS NO CHICKEN, THAT WAS MY WIFE!"
© 1994 PAWS, INC./Distributed by Universal Press Syndicate
KONK!
EVEN THE BAND HATES MY ACT
JIM DAVIS 11-1

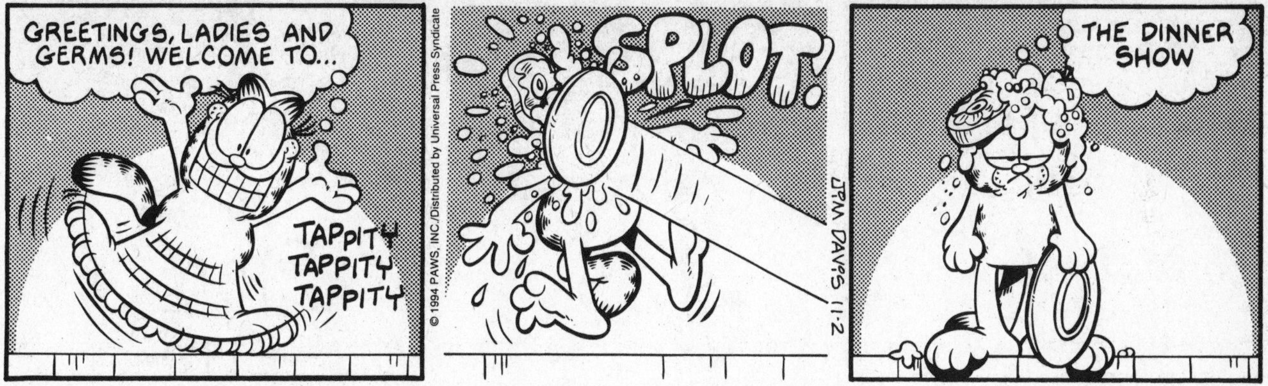

GREETINGS, LADIES AND GERMS! WELCOME TO...
TAPPITY TAPPITY TAPPITY
SPLOT!
THE DINNER SHOW
JIM DAVIS 11-2
© 1994 PAWS, INC./Distributed by Universal Press Syndicate

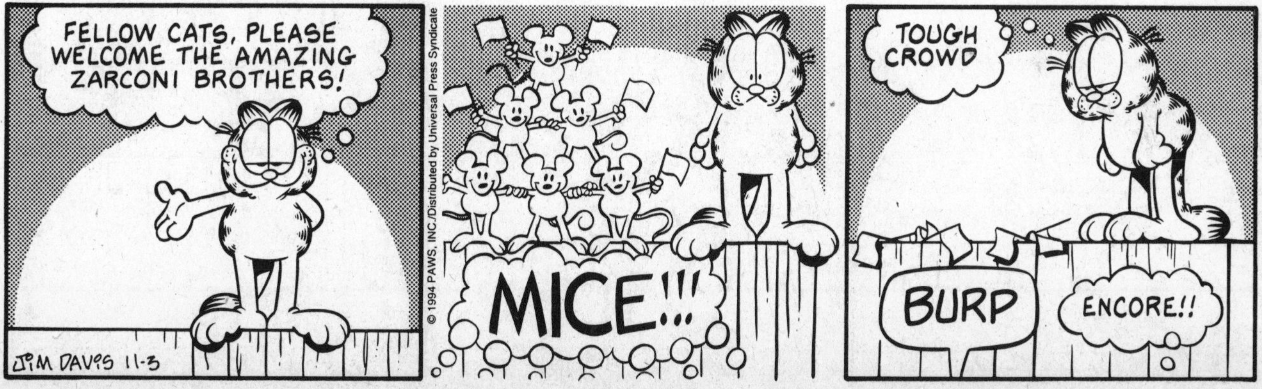

FELLOW CATS, PLEASE WELCOME THE AMAZING ZARCONI BROTHERS!
MICE!!!
TOUGH CROWD
BURP
ENCORE!!
JIM DAVIS 11-3
© 1994 PAWS, INC./Distributed by Universal Press Syndicate

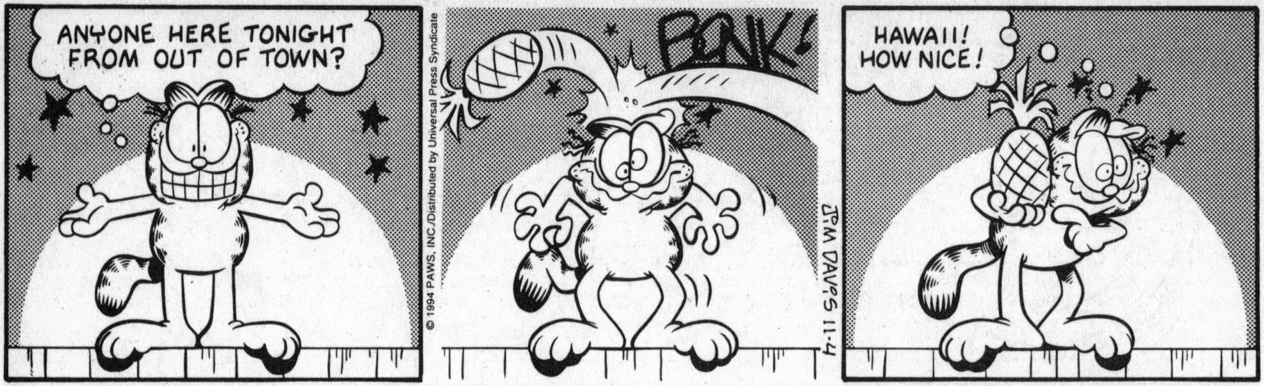
ANYONE HERE TONIGHT FROM OUT OF TOWN?
BONK!
HAWAII! HOW NICE!
© 1994 PAWS, INC./Distributed by Universal Press Syndicate
JIM DAVIS 11-4

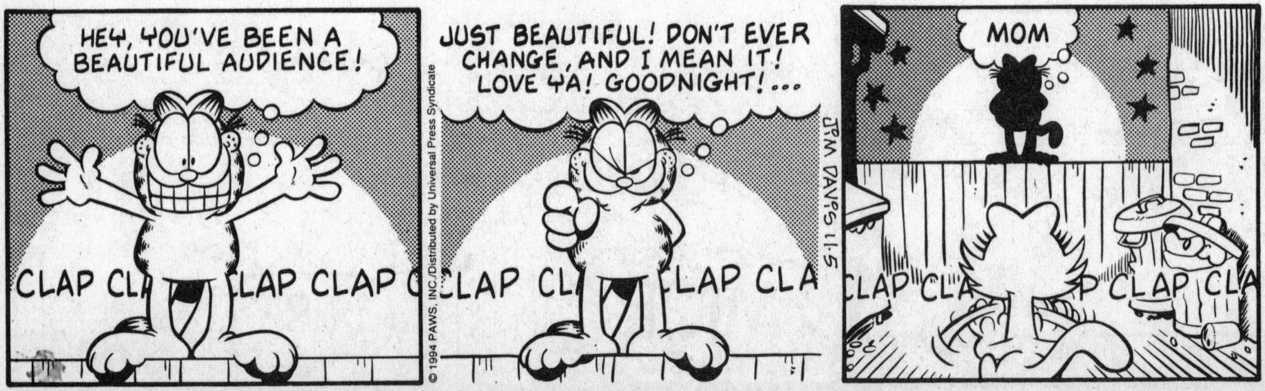
HEY, YOU'VE BEEN A BEAUTIFUL AUDIENCE!
CLAP CLAP CLAP CLAP
JUST BEAUTIFUL! DON'T EVER CHANGE, AND I MEAN IT! LOVE YA! GOODNIGHT!...
CLAP CLAP CLAP CLA
MOM
CLAP CLAP CLAP CLA
© 1994 PAWS, INC./Distributed by Universal Press Syndicate
JIM DAVIS 11-5

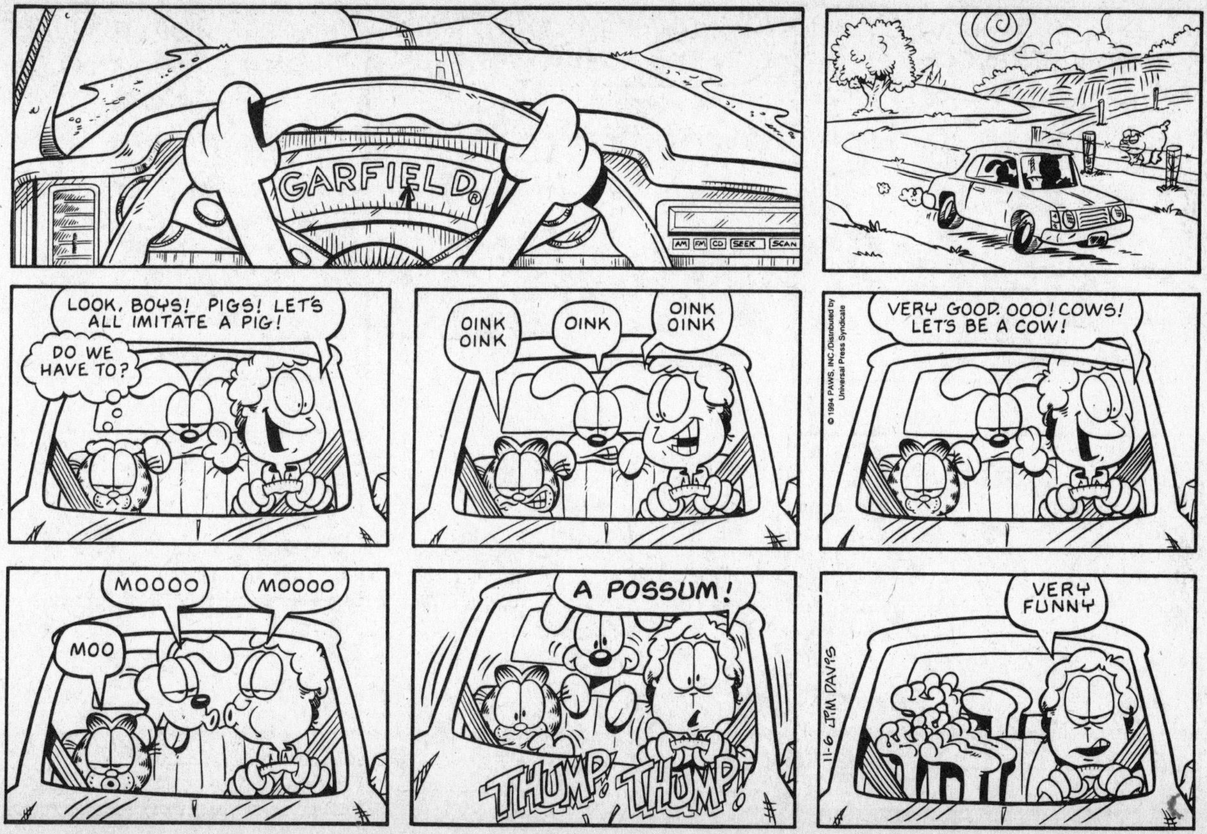
GARFIELD®
AM FM CD SEEK SCAN
LOOK, BOYS! PIGS! LET'S ALL IMITATE A PIG!
DO WE HAVE TO?
OINK OINK
OINK
OINK OINK
© 1994 PAWS, INC./Distributed by Universal Press Syndicate
VERY GOOD. OOO! COWS! LET'S BE A COW!
MOO
MOOOO
MOOOO
A POSSUM!
THUMP! THUMP!
11-6 JIM DAVIS
VERY FUNNY

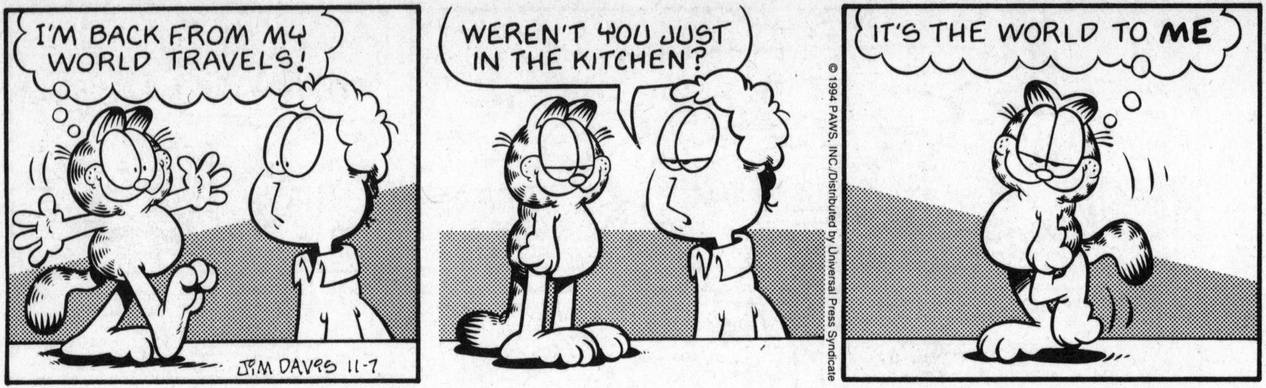
I'M BACK FROM MY WORLD TRAVELS!
JIM DAVIS 11-7
WEREN'T YOU JUST IN THE KITCHEN?
© 1994 PAWS, INC./Distributed by Universal Press Syndicate
IT'S THE WORLD TO **ME**

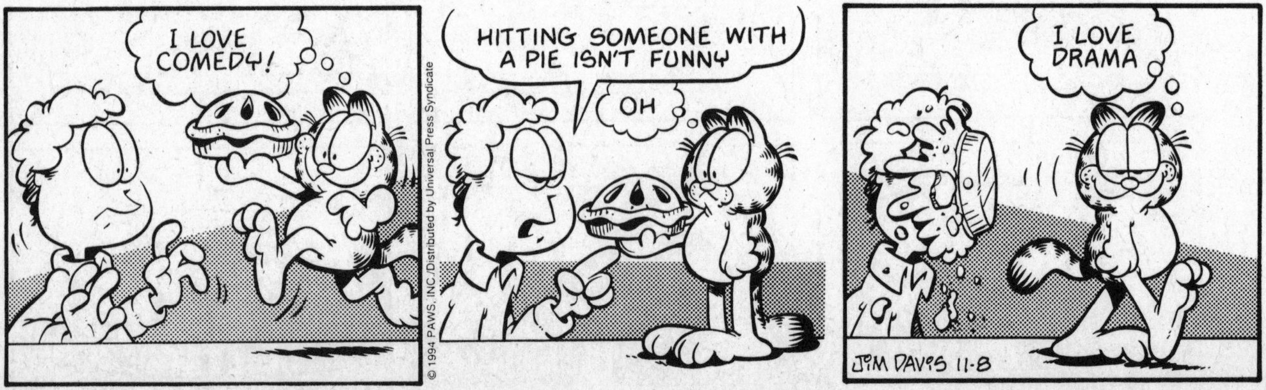
I LOVE COMEDY!
© 1994 PAWS, INC./Distributed by Universal Press Syndicate
HITTING SOMEONE WITH A PIE ISN'T FUNNY
OH
I LOVE DRAMA
JIM DAVIS 11-8

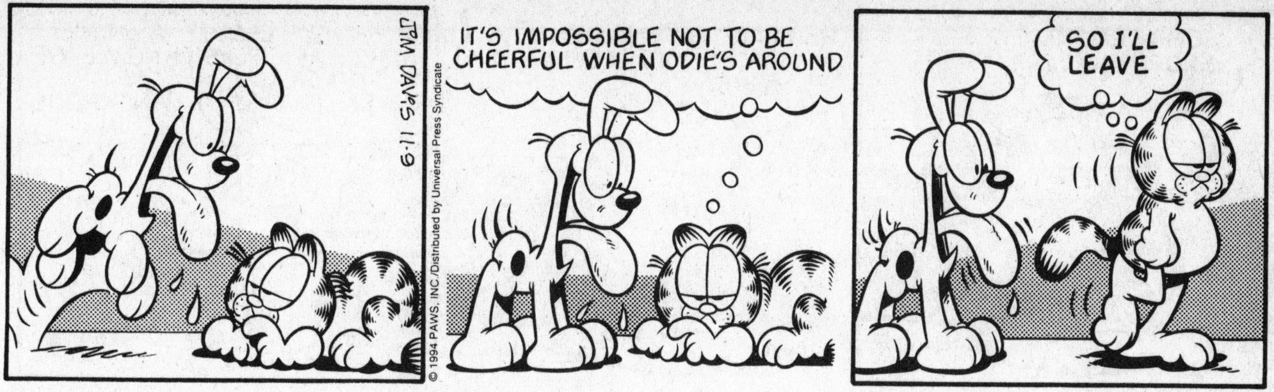
JPM DAVIS 11-9
© 1994 PAWS, INC./Distributed by Universal Press Syndicate
IT'S IMPOSSIBLE NOT TO BE CHEERFUL WHEN ODIE'S AROUND
SO I'LL LEAVE

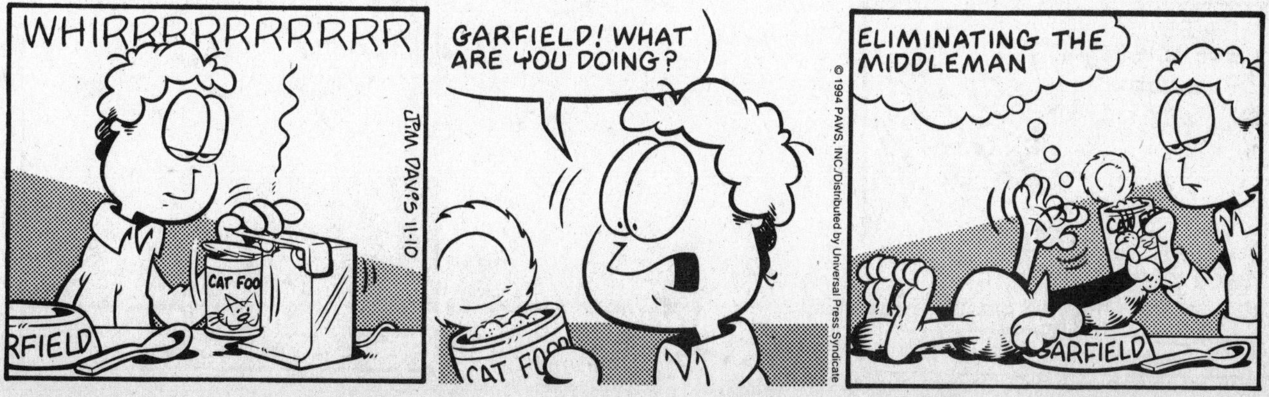
WHIRRRRRRRRRRR
JPM DAVIS 11-10
CAT FOO
RFIELD
GARFIELD! WHAT ARE YOU DOING?
CAT FO
ELIMINATING THE MIDDLEMAN
© 1994 PAWS, INC./Distributed by Universal Press Syndicate
ARFIELD

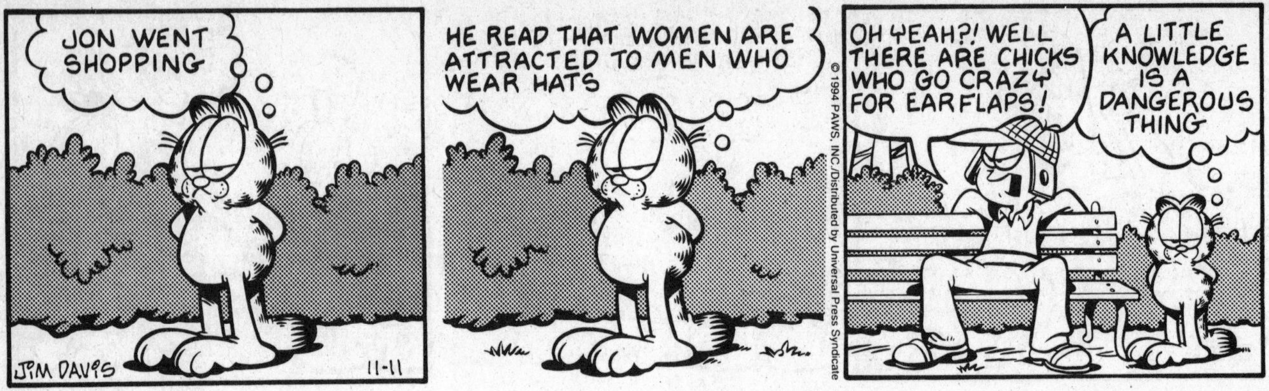
JON WENT SHOPPING
HE READ THAT WOMEN ARE ATTRACTED TO MEN WHO WEAR HATS
OH YEAH?! WELL THERE ARE CHICKS WHO GO CRAZY FOR EARFLAPS!
A LITTLE KNOWLEDGE IS A DANGEROUS THING
JIM DAVIS
11-11

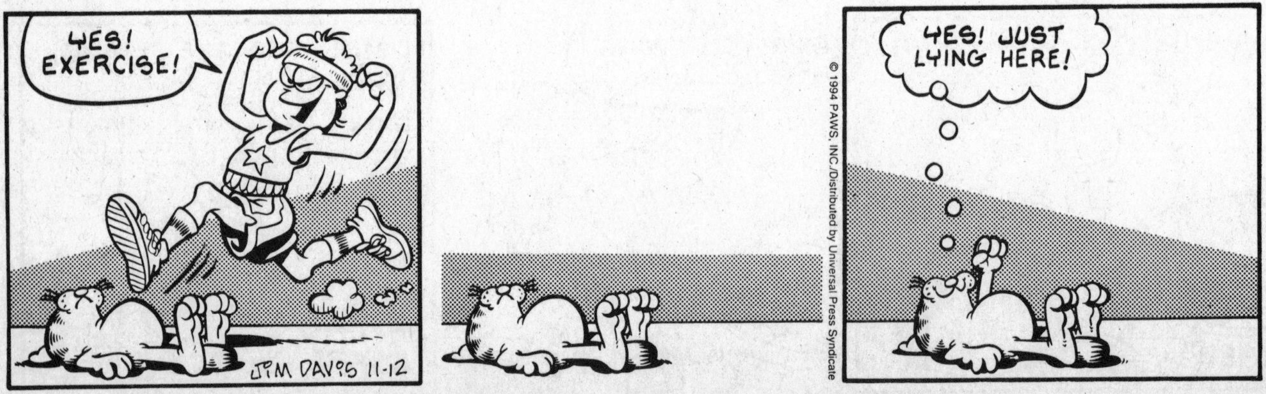
YES! EXERCISE!
JIM DAVIS 11-12
YES! JUST LYING HERE!

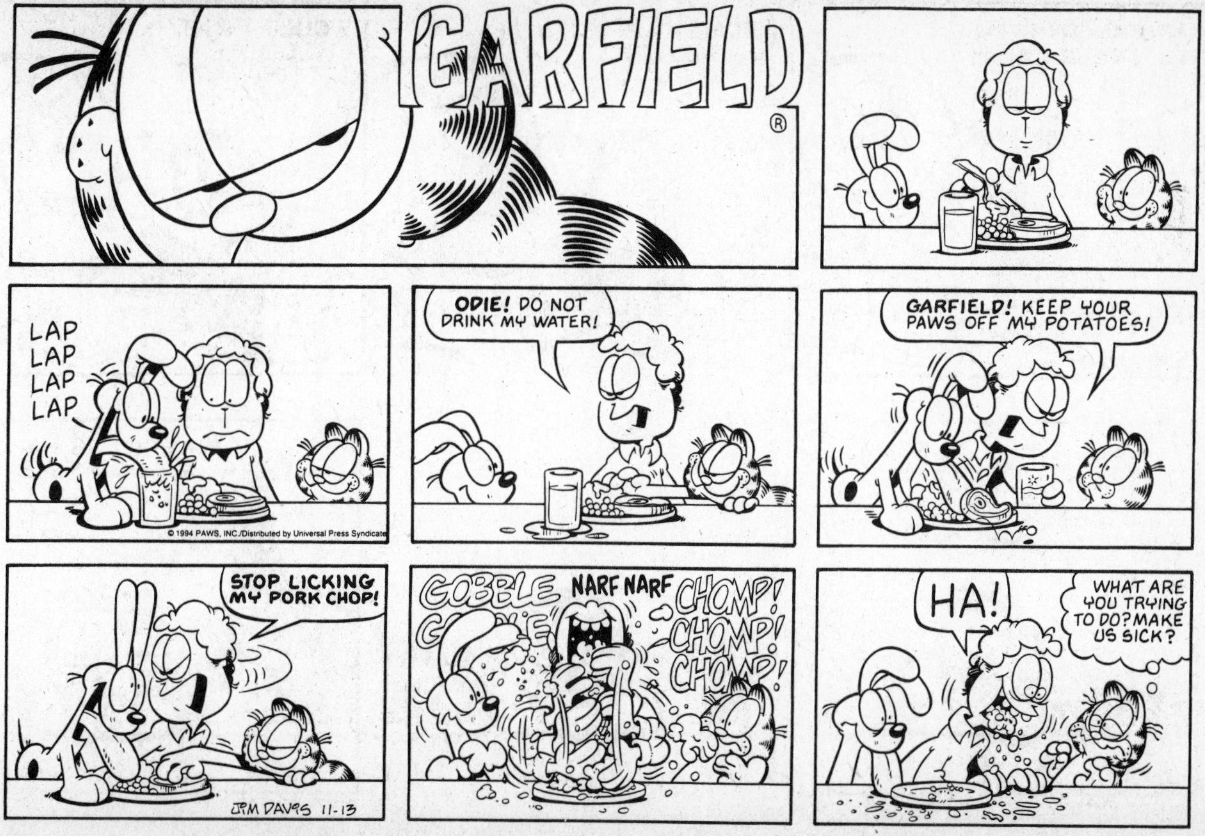
GARFIELD
LAP LAP LAP LAP
© 1994 PAWS, INC./Distributed by Universal Press Syndicate
ODIE! DO NOT DRINK MY WATER!
GARFIELD! KEEP YOUR PAWS OFF MY POTATOES!
STOP LICKING MY PORK CHOP!
JIM DAVIS 11-13
GOBBLE
NARF NARF
CHOMP! CHOMP! CHOMP!
HA!
WHAT ARE YOU TRYING TO DO? MAKE US SICK?

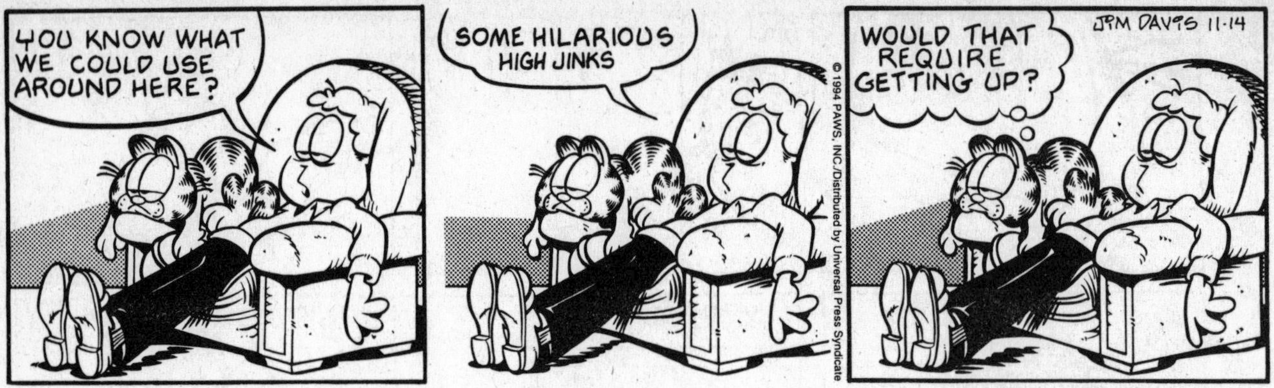
YOU KNOW WHAT WE COULD USE AROUND HERE?
SOME HILARIOUS HIGH JINKS
WOULD THAT REQUIRE GETTING UP?
JIM DAVIS 11-14
© 1994 PAWS, INC./Distributed by Universal Press Syndicate

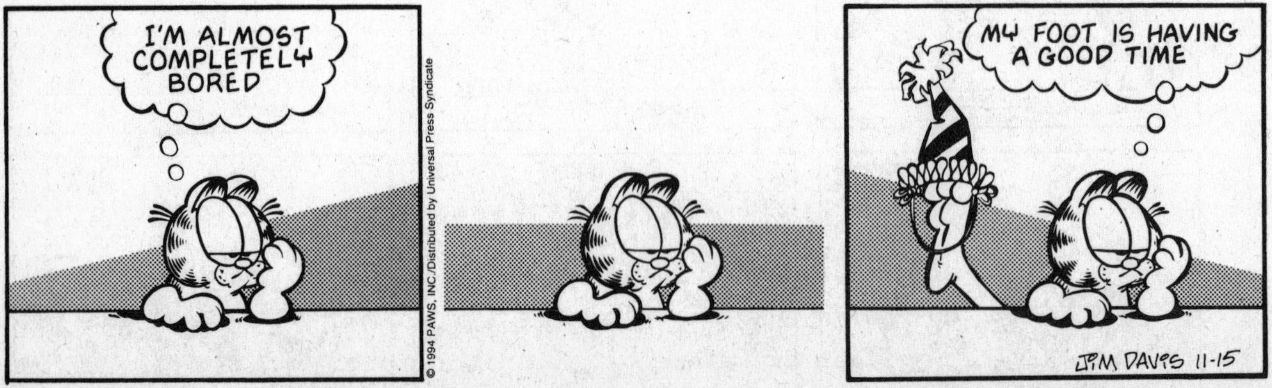
I'M ALMOST COMPLETELY BORED
MY FOOT IS HAVING A GOOD TIME
JIM DAVIS 11-15
© 1994 PAWS, INC./Distributed by Universal Press Syndicate

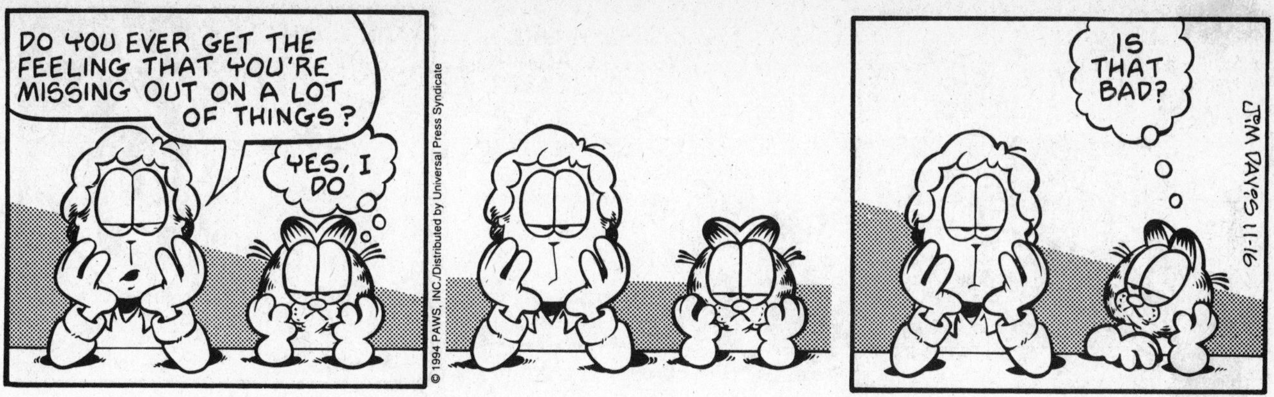
DO YOU EVER GET THE FEELING THAT YOU'RE MISSING OUT ON A LOT OF THINGS?
YES, I DO
© 1994 PAWS, INC./Distributed by Universal Press Syndicate
IS THAT BAD?
JIM DAVIS 11-16

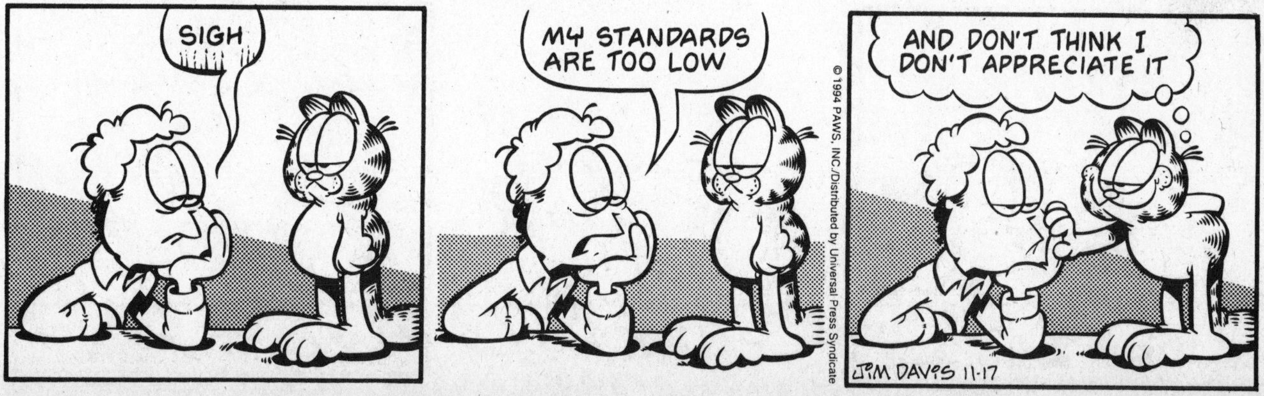
SIGH
MY STANDARDS ARE TOO LOW
© 1994 PAWS, INC./Distributed by Universal Press Syndicate
AND DON'T THINK I DON'T APPRECIATE IT
JIM DAVIS 11-17

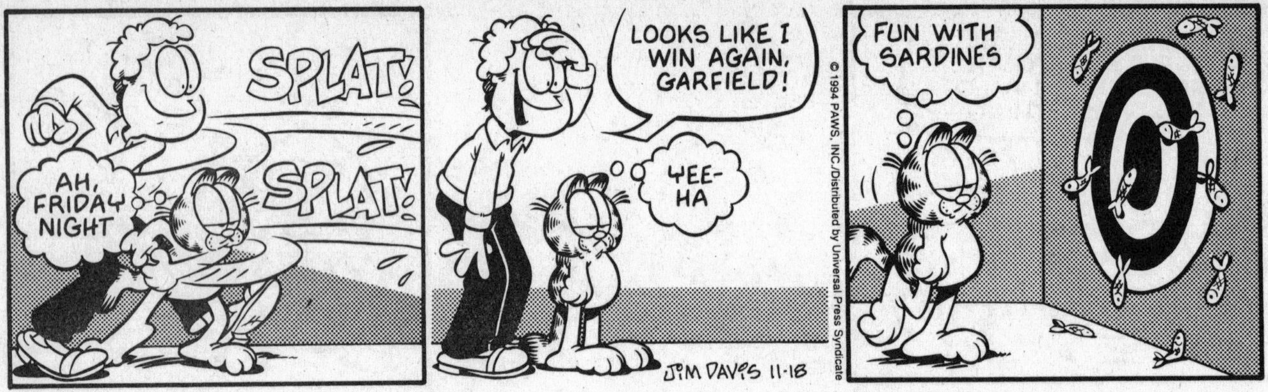
SPLAT!
SPLAT!
AH, FRIDAY NIGHT
LOOKS LIKE I WIN AGAIN, GARFIELD!
YEE-HA
FUN WITH SARDINES
JIM DAVIS 11-18
© 1994 PAWS, INC./Distributed by Universal Press Syndicate

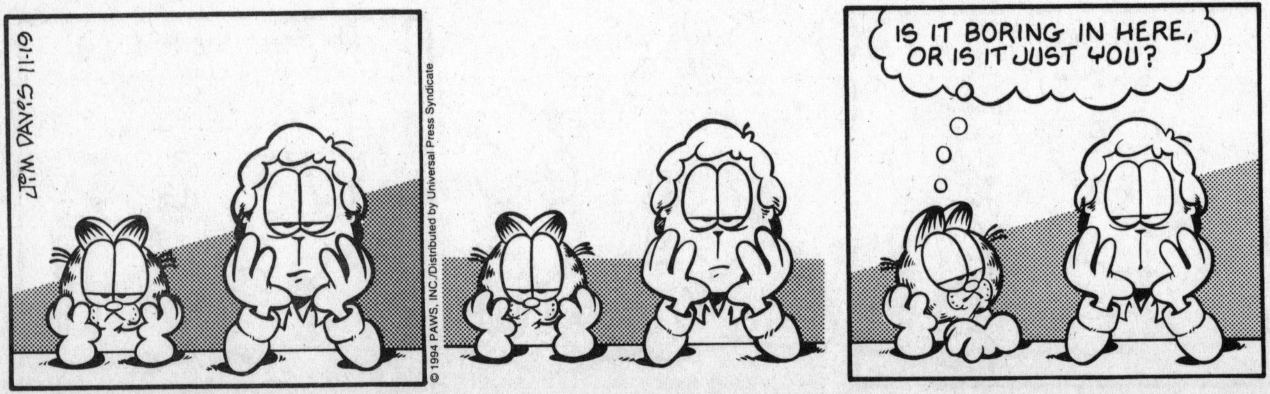
JIM DAVIS 11-19
© 1994 PAWS, INC./Distributed by Universal Press Syndicate
IS IT BORING IN HERE, OR IS IT JUST YOU?

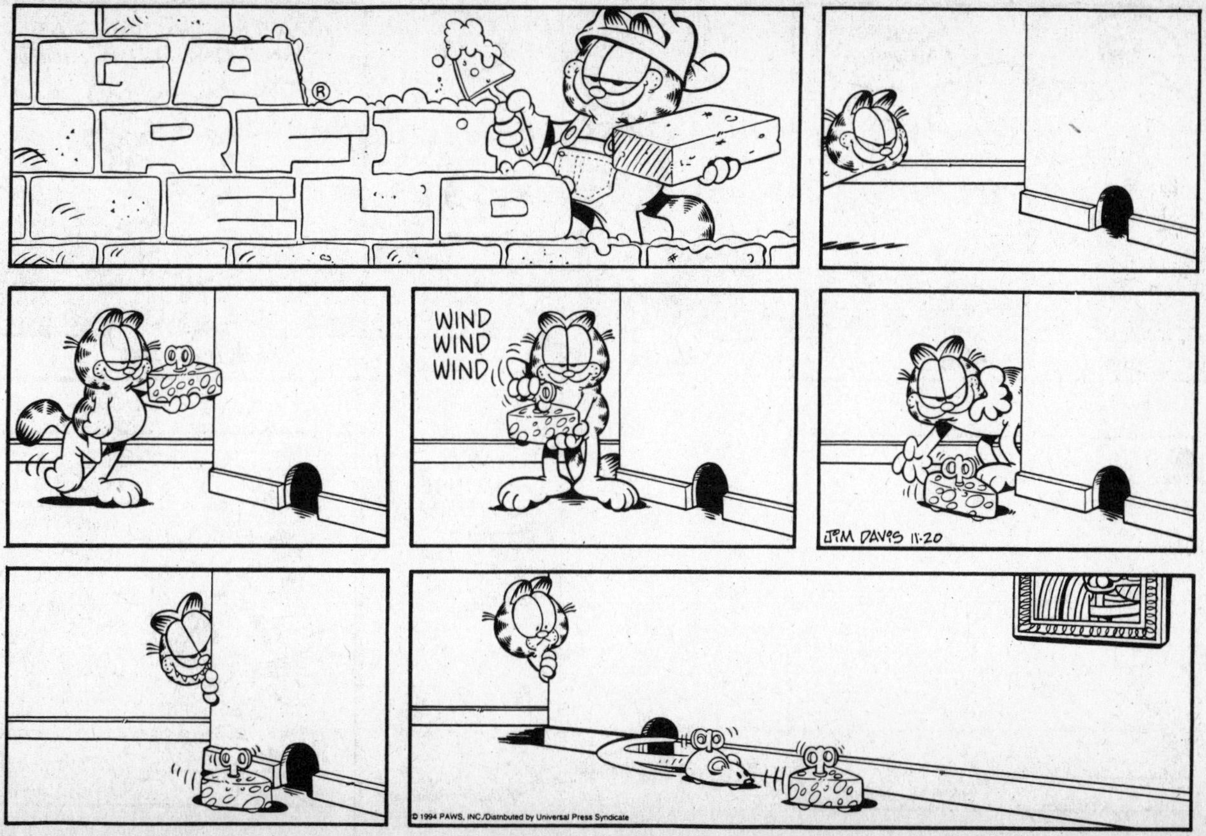

GARFIELD
WIND
WIND
WIND
JIM DAVIS 11-20

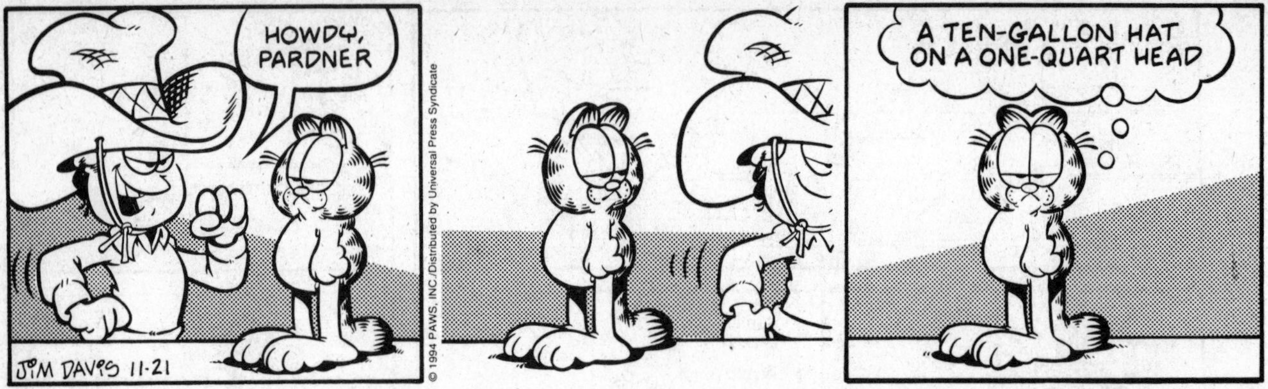
HOWDY, PARDNER
A TEN-GALLON HAT ON A ONE-QUART HEAD
JIM DAVIS 11-21

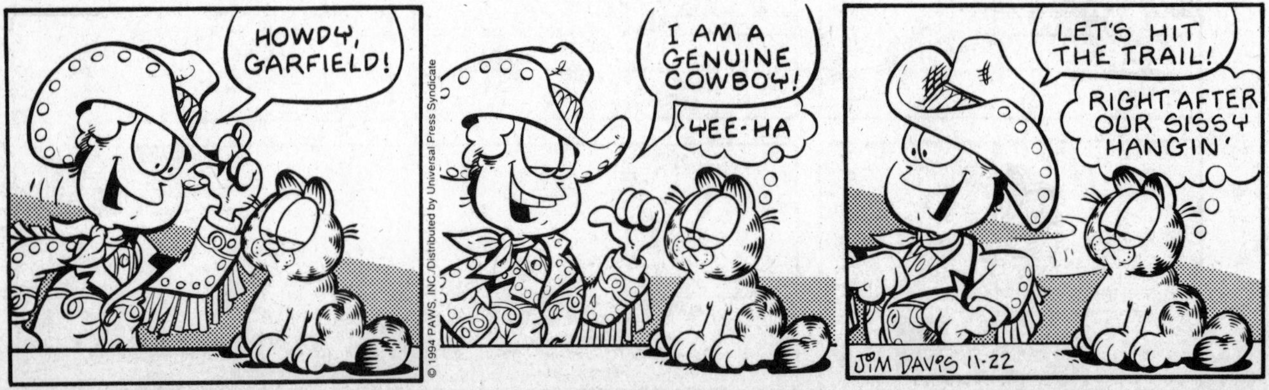
HOWDY, GARFIELD!
I AM A GENUINE COWBOY!
YEE-HA
LET'S HIT THE TRAIL!
RIGHT AFTER OUR SISSY HANGIN'
JIM DAVIS 11-22

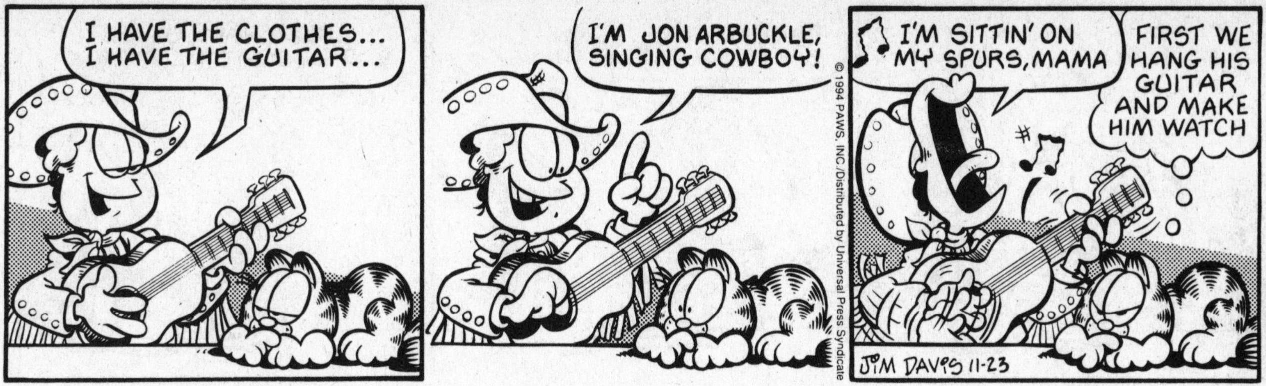
I HAVE THE CLOTHES...
I HAVE THE GUITAR...
I'M JON ARBUCKLE, SINGING COWBOY!
© 1994 PAWS, INC./Distributed by Universal Press Syndicate
I'M SITTIN' ON MY SPURS, MAMA
FIRST WE HANG HIS GUITAR AND MAKE HIM WATCH
JIM DAVIS 11-23

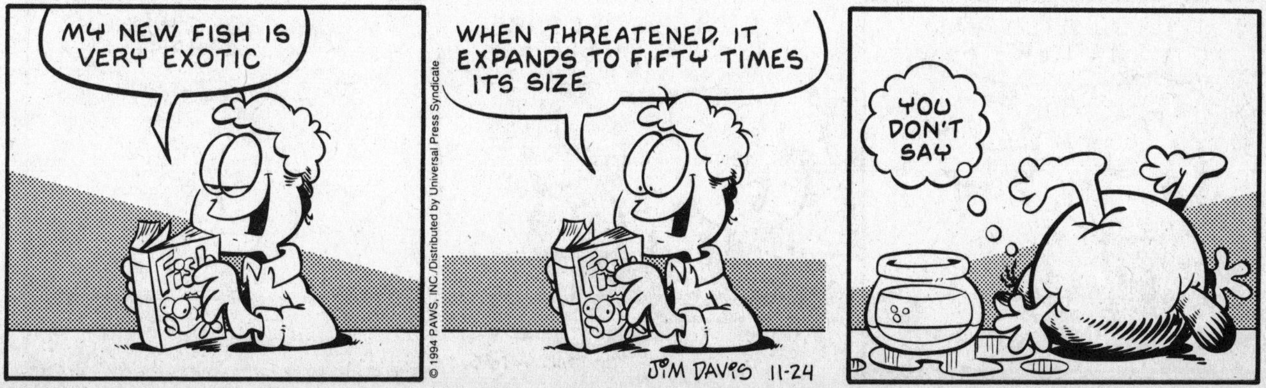
MY NEW FISH IS VERY EXOTIC
FISH
© 1994 PAWS, INC./Distributed by Universal Press Syndicate
WHEN THREATENED, IT EXPANDS TO FIFTY TIMES ITS SIZE
JIM DAVIS 11-24
YOU DON'T SAY

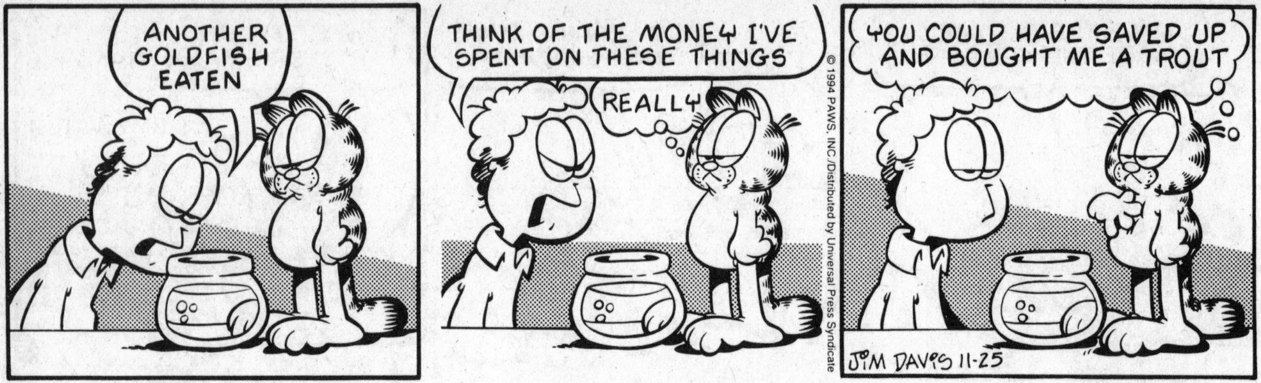
ANOTHER GOLDFISH EATEN
THINK OF THE MONEY I'VE SPENT ON THESE THINGS
REALLY
YOU COULD HAVE SAVED UP AND BOUGHT ME A TROUT
JIM DAVIS 11-25
© 1994 PAWS, INC./Distributed by Universal Press Syndicate

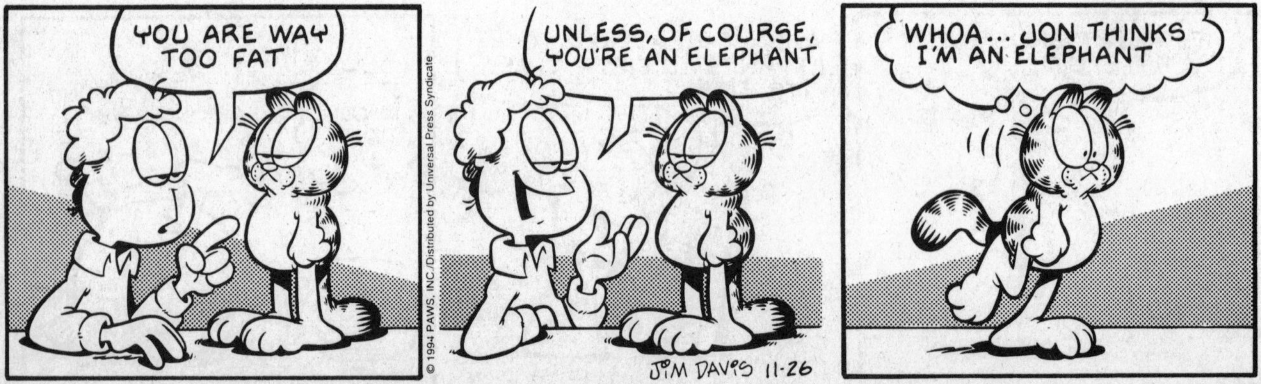
YOU ARE WAY TOO FAT
UNLESS, OF COURSE, YOU'RE AN ELEPHANT
WHOA... JON THINKS I'M AN ELEPHANT
JIM DAVIS 11-26
© 1994 PAWS, INC./Distributed by Universal Press Syndicate

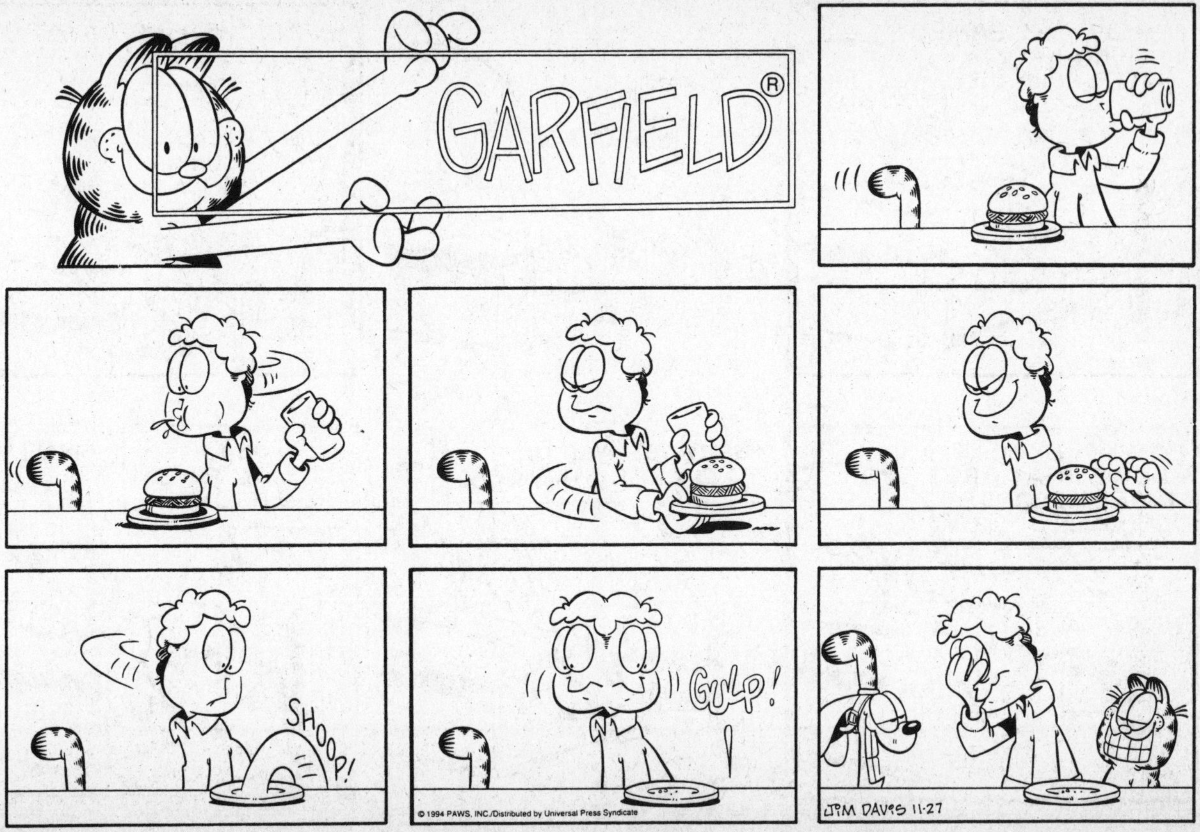
GARFIELD®
SHOOOP!
GULP!
© 1994 PAWS, INC./Distributed by Universal Press Syndicate
JIM DAVIS 11-27

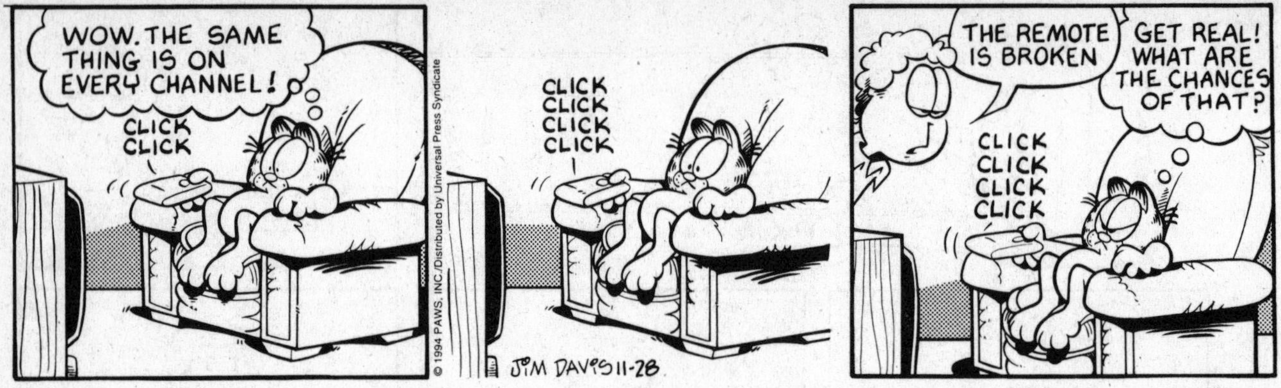
WOW. THE SAME THING IS ON EVERY CHANNEL!
CLICK CLICK
CLICK CLICK CLICK CLICK
THE REMOTE IS BROKEN
GET REAL! WHAT ARE THE CHANCES OF THAT?
CLICK CLICK CLICK CLICK
© 1994 PAWS, INC./Distributed by Universal Press Syndicate
JIM DAVIS 11-28

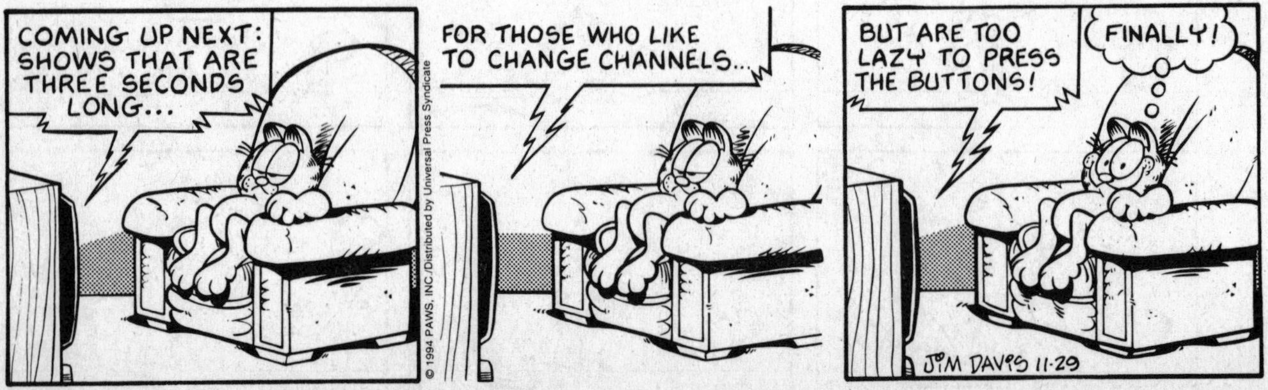
COMING UP NEXT: SHOWS THAT ARE THREE SECONDS LONG...
FOR THOSE WHO LIKE TO CHANGE CHANNELS...
BUT ARE TOO LAZY TO PRESS THE BUTTONS!
FINALLY!
© 1994 PAWS, INC./Distributed by Universal Press Syndicate
JIM DAVIS 11-29

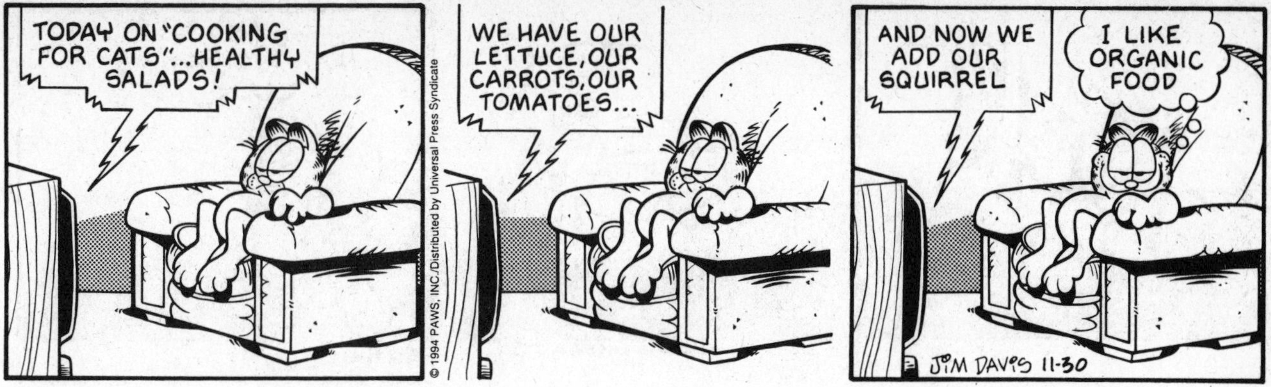
TODAY ON "COOKING FOR CATS"...HEALTHY SALADS!
© 1994 PAWS, INC./Distributed by Universal Press Syndicate
WE HAVE OUR LETTUCE, OUR CARROTS, OUR TOMATOES...
AND NOW WE ADD OUR SQUIRREL
I LIKE ORGANIC FOOD
JIM DAVIS 11-30

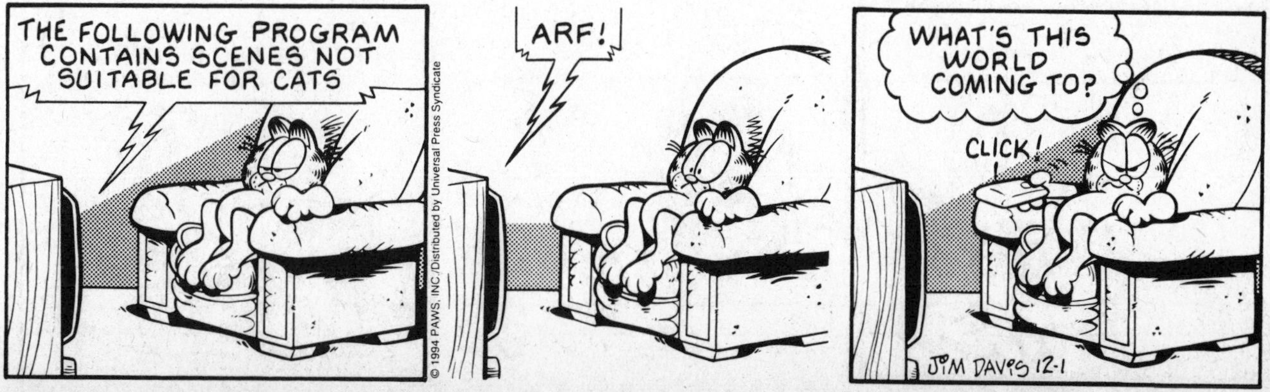
THE FOLLOWING PROGRAM CONTAINS SCENES NOT SUITABLE FOR CATS
© 1994 PAWS, INC./Distributed by Universal Press Syndicate
ARF!
WHAT'S THIS WORLD COMING TO?
CLICK!
JIM DAVIS 12-1

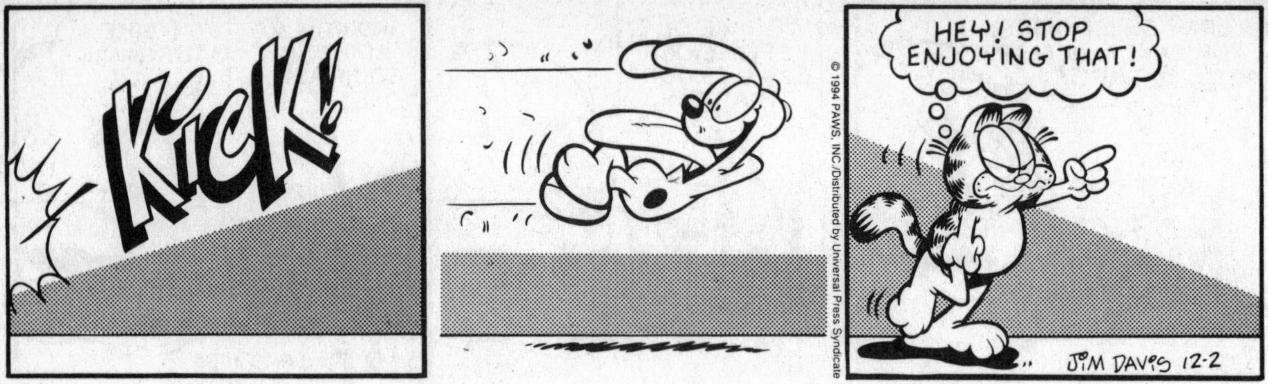
KICK!
HEY! STOP ENJOYING THAT!
© 1994 PAWS, INC./Distributed by Universal Press Syndicate
JIM DAVIS 12-2

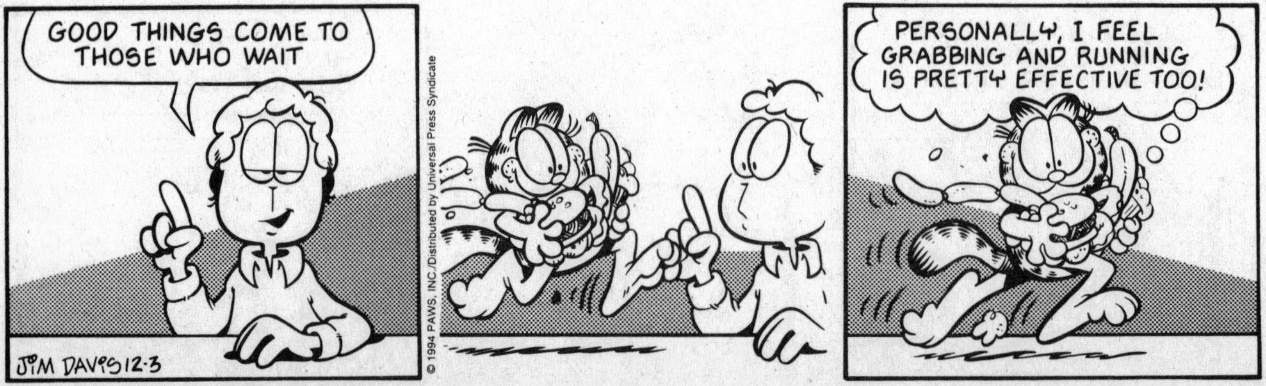
GOOD THINGS COME TO THOSE WHO WAIT
© 1994 PAWS, INC./Distributed by Universal Press Syndicate
PERSONALLY, I FEEL GRABBING AND RUNNING IS PRETTY EFFECTIVE TOO!
JIM DAVIS 12-3

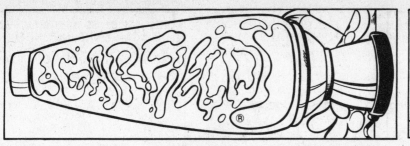

© 1994 PAWS, INC./Distributed by Universal Press Syndicate

GARFIELD

JIM DAVIS 12-4

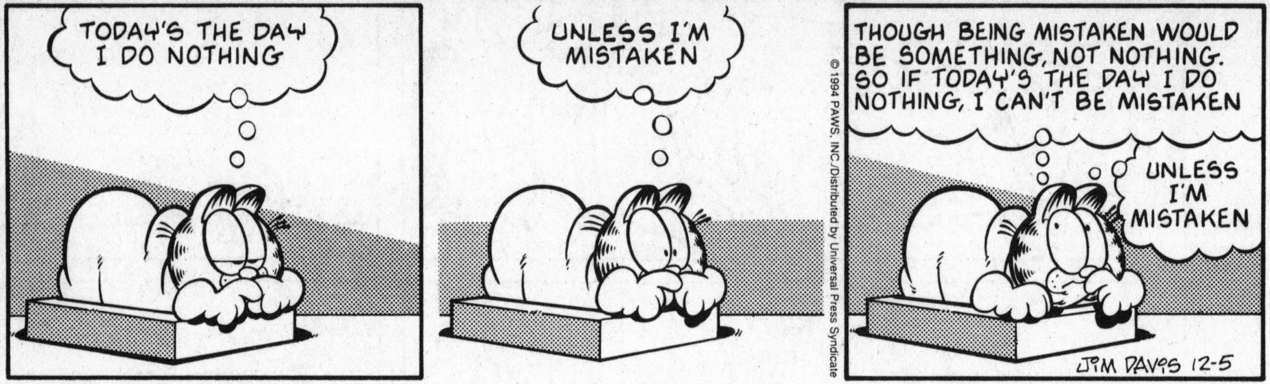
TODAY'S THE DAY I DO NOTHING
UNLESS I'M MISTAKEN
THOUGH BEING MISTAKEN WOULD BE SOMETHING, NOT NOTHING. SO IF TODAY'S THE DAY I DO NOTHING, I CAN'T BE MISTAKEN
UNLESS I'M MISTAKEN
JIM DAVIS 12-5

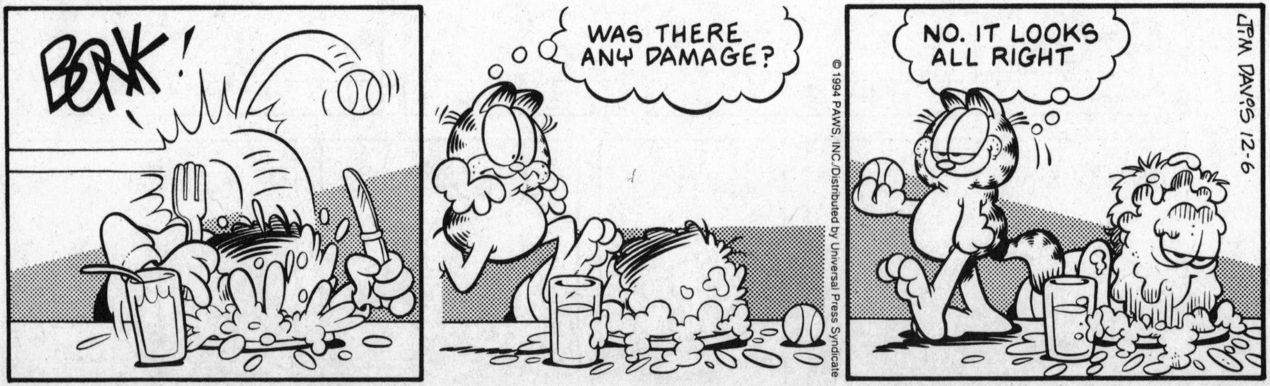
BONK!
WAS THERE ANY DAMAGE?
NO. IT LOOKS ALL RIGHT
JIM DAVIS 12-6

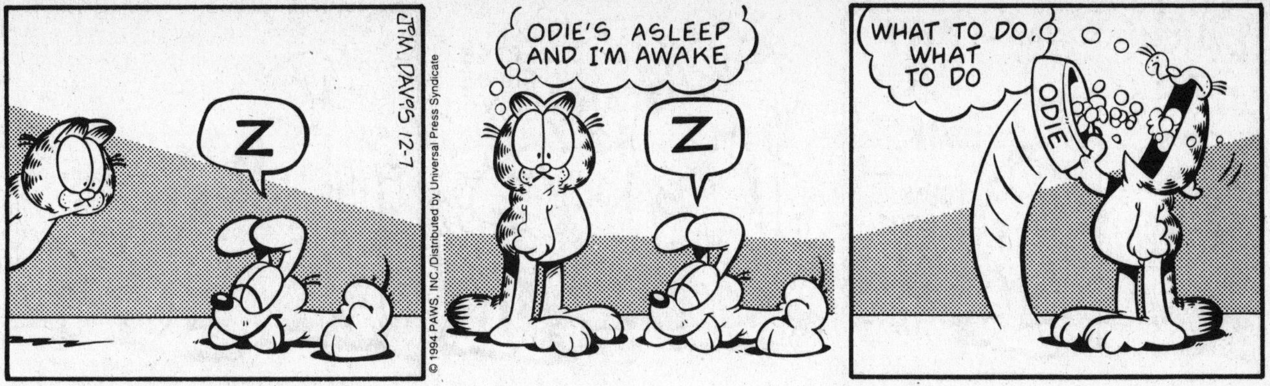
JIM DAVIS 12-7
Z
© 1994 PAWS, INC./Distributed by Universal Press Syndicate
ODIE'S ASLEEP AND I'M AWAKE
Z
WHAT TO DO, WHAT TO DO
ODIE

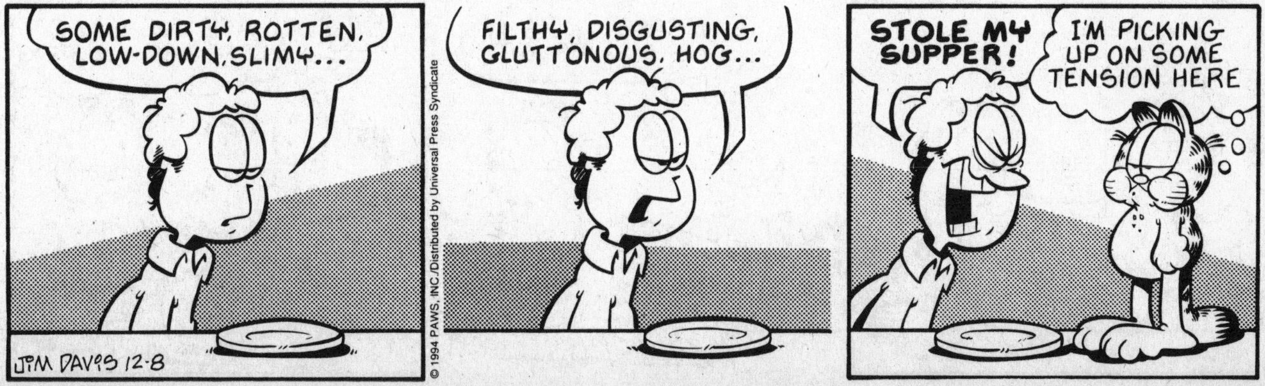
SOME DIRTY, ROTTEN, LOW-DOWN, SLIMY...
JIM DAVIS 12-8
© 1994 PAWS, INC./Distributed by Universal Press Syndicate
FILTHY, DISGUSTING, GLUTTONOUS, HOG...
STOLE MY SUPPER!
I'M PICKING UP ON SOME TENSION HERE

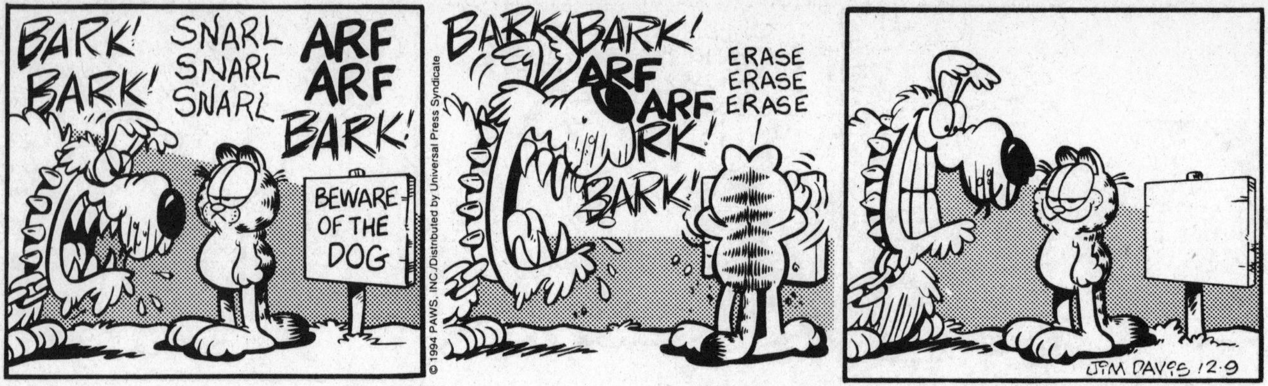
BARK! BARK!
SNARL SNARL SNARL
ARF ARF BARK!
BEWARE OF THE DOG
BARK! BARK!
ARF ARF
RK!
BARK!
ERASE ERASE ERASE
JIM DAVIS 12-9

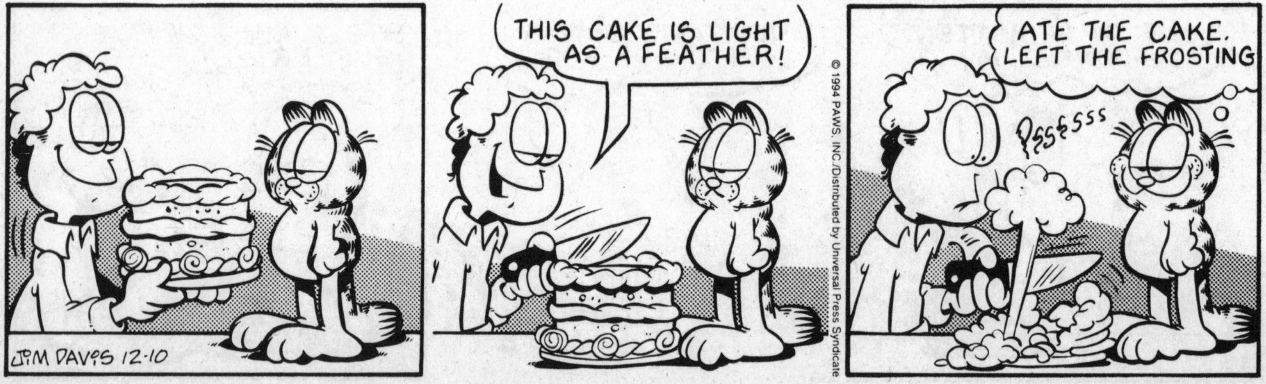
JIM DAVIS 12-10
THIS CAKE IS LIGHT AS A FEATHER!
PSSSSSSS
ATE THE CAKE. LEFT THE FROSTING

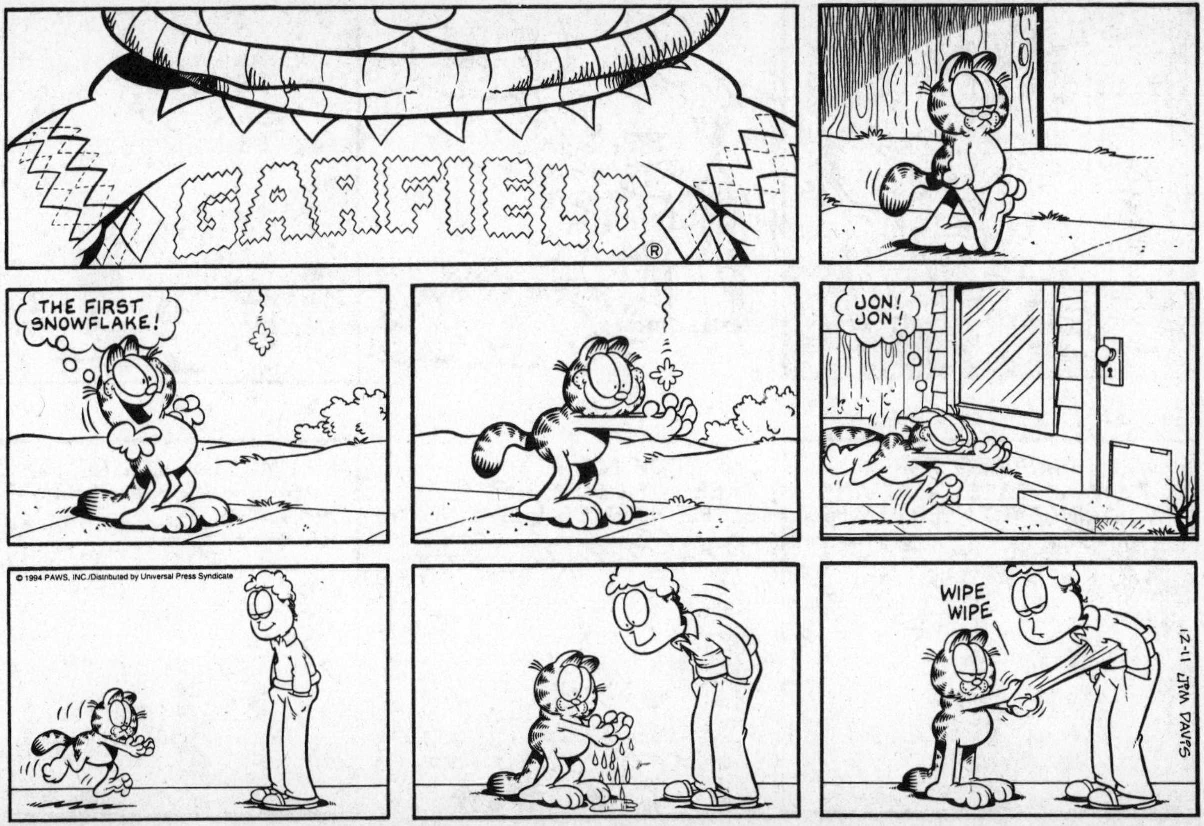

GARFIELD®
THE FIRST SNOWFLAKE!
JON! JON!
© 1994 PAWS, INC./Distributed by Universal Press Syndicate
WIPE WIPE
12-11 JIM DAVIS

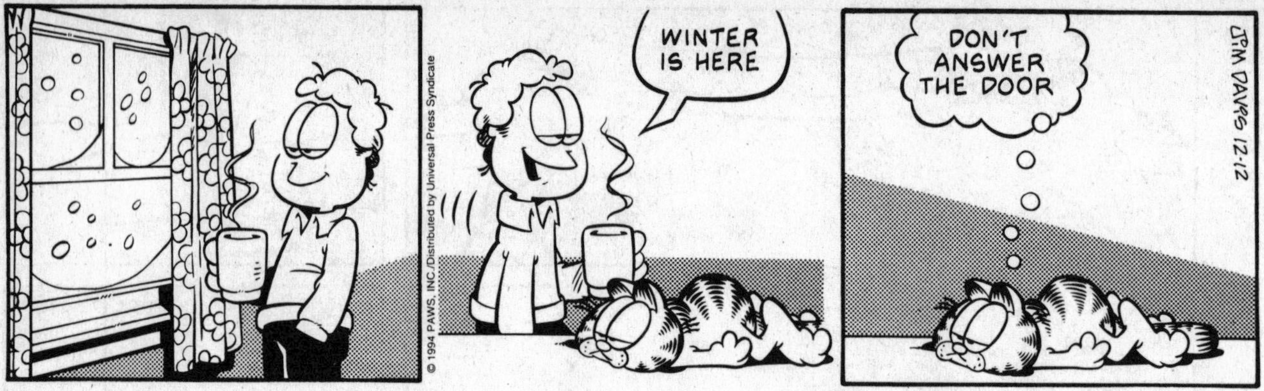
© 1994 PAWS, INC./Distributed by Universal Press Syndicate
WINTER IS HERE
DON'T ANSWER THE DOOR
JIM DAVIS 12-12

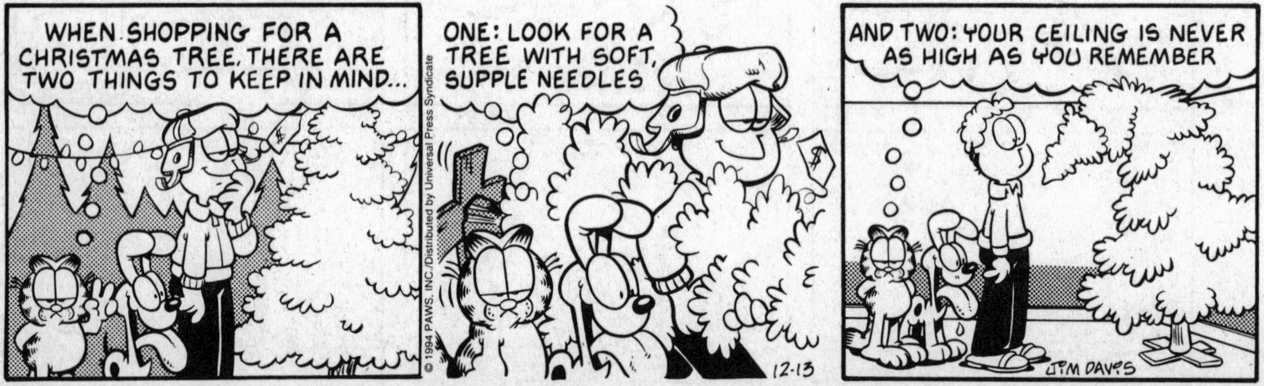
WHEN SHOPPING FOR A CHRISTMAS TREE, THERE ARE TWO THINGS TO KEEP IN MIND...
© 1994 PAWS, INC./Distributed by Universal Press Syndicate
ONE: LOOK FOR A TREE WITH SOFT, SUPPLE NEEDLES
12-13
AND TWO: YOUR CEILING IS NEVER AS HIGH AS YOU REMEMBER
JIM DAVIS

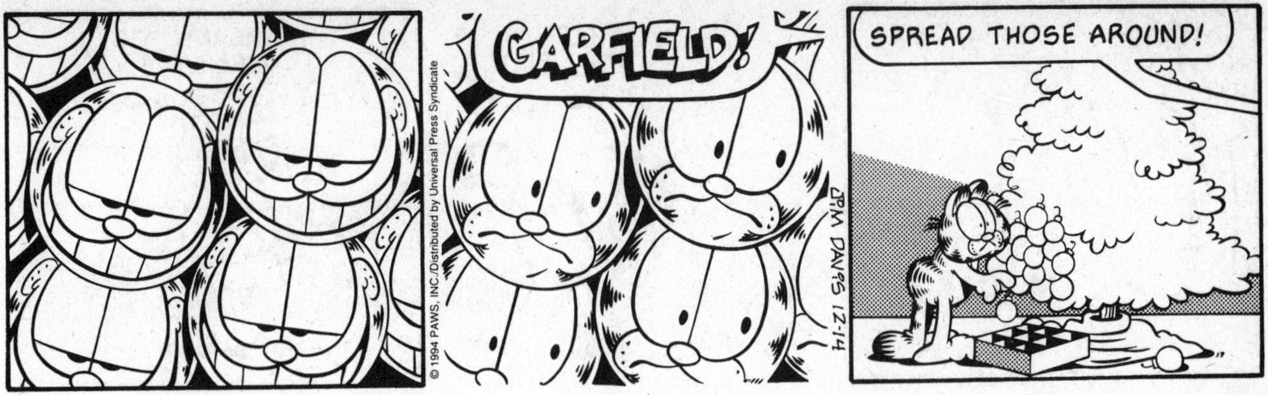
GARFIELD!
SPREAD THOSE AROUND!
© 1994 PAWS, INC./Distributed by Universal Press Syndicate
JIM DAVIS 12-14

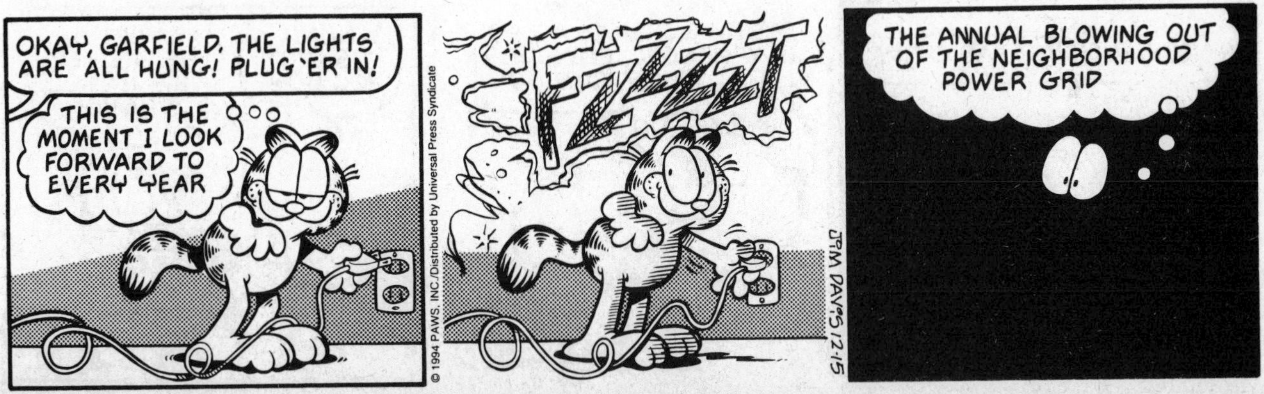
OKAY, GARFIELD. THE LIGHTS ARE ALL HUNG! PLUG 'ER IN!
THIS IS THE MOMENT I LOOK FORWARD TO EVERY YEAR
FZZZZT
THE ANNUAL BLOWING OUT OF THE NEIGHBORHOOD POWER GRID
© 1994 PAWS, INC./Distributed by Universal Press Syndicate
JIM DAVIS 12-15

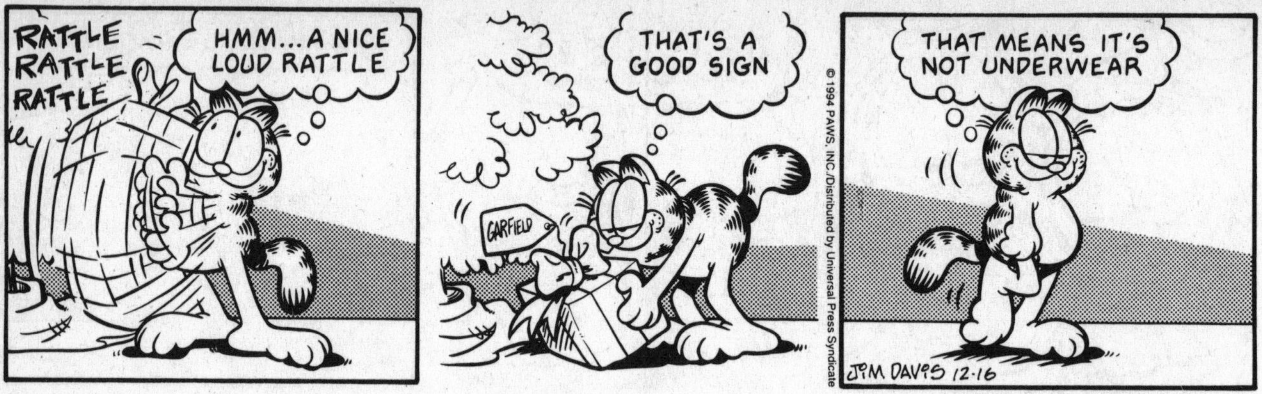
RATTLE RATTLE RATTLE
HMM... A NICE LOUD RATTLE
GARFIELD
THAT'S A GOOD SIGN
THAT MEANS IT'S NOT UNDERWEAR
© 1994 PAWS, INC./Distributed by Universal Press Syndicate
JIM DAVIS 12-16

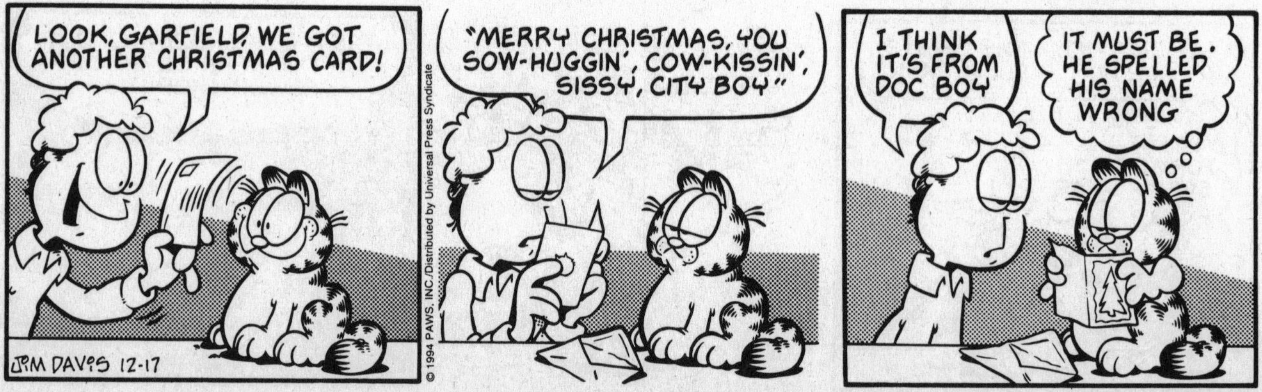
LOOK, GARFIELD, WE GOT ANOTHER CHRISTMAS CARD!
JIM DAVIS 12-17
© 1994 PAWS, INC./Distributed by Universal Press Syndicate
"MERRY CHRISTMAS, YOU SOW-HUGGIN', COW-KISSIN', SISSY, CITY BOY"
I THINK IT'S FROM DOC BOY
IT MUST BE. HE SPELLED HIS NAME WRONG

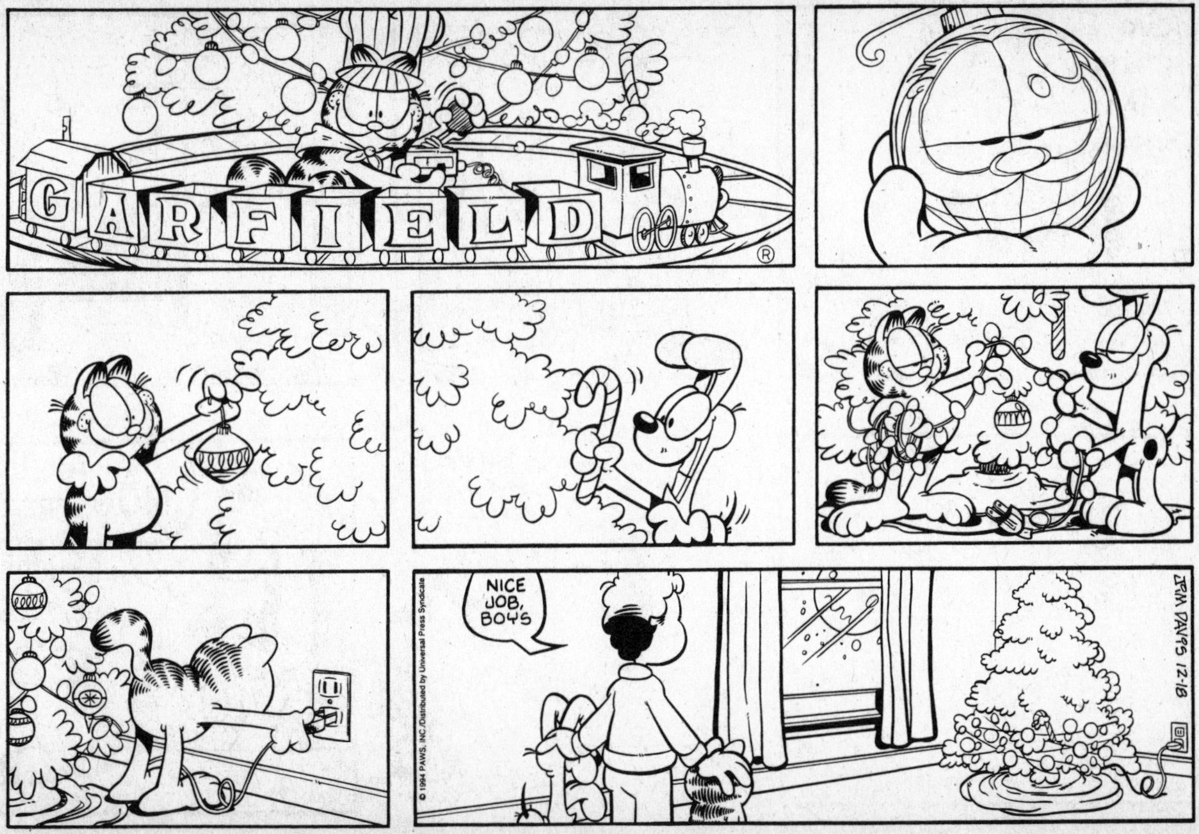
GARFIELD
NICE JOB, BOYS
© 1994 PAWS, INC./Distributed by Universal Press Syndicate
JPM DAVIS 12-18

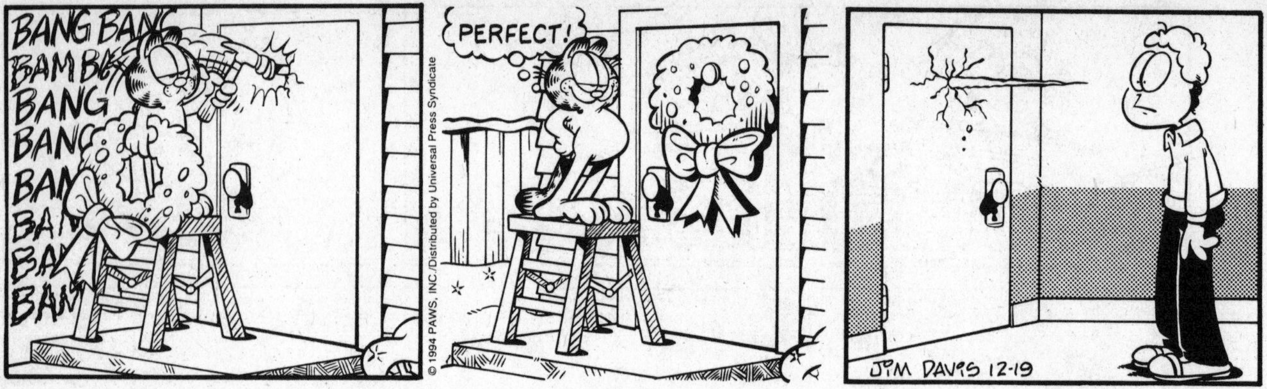
BANG BANG BAM BANG BANG BANG BAM BAM BAM BAM
PERFECT!
© 1994 PAWS, INC./Distributed by Universal Press Syndicate
JIM DAVIS 12-19

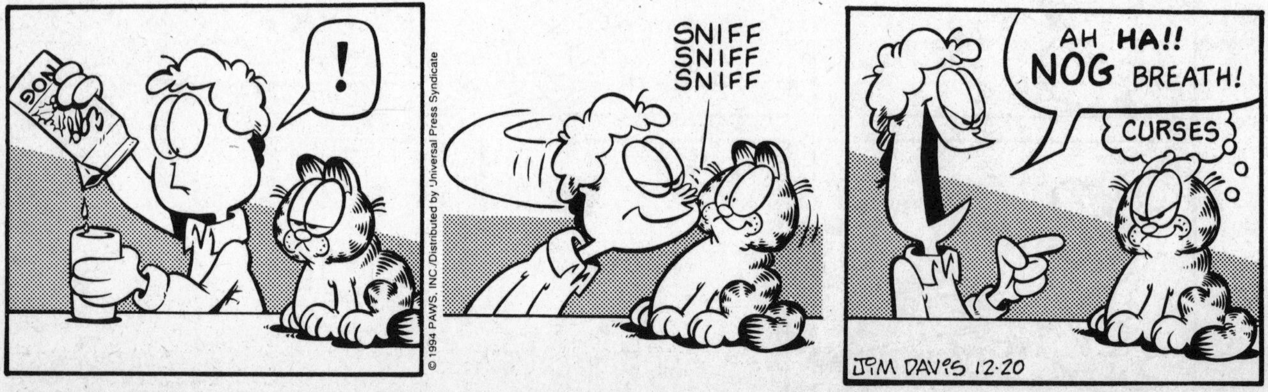
!
© 1994 PAWS, INC./Distributed by Universal Press Syndicate
SNIFF SNIFF SNIFF
AH HA!! NOG BREATH!
CURSES
JIM DAVIS 12-20

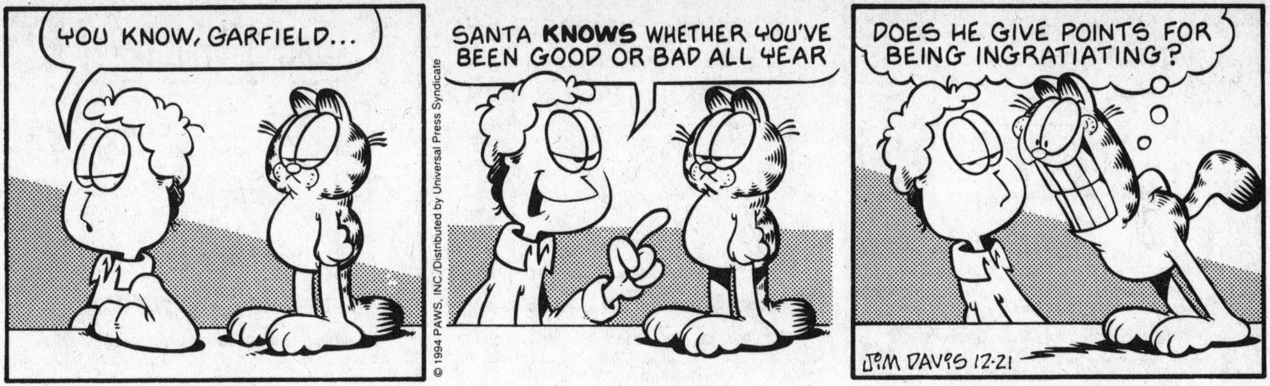
YOU KNOW, GARFIELD...
SANTA **KNOWS** WHETHER YOU'VE BEEN GOOD OR BAD ALL YEAR
DOES HE GIVE POINTS FOR BEING INGRATIATING?
JIM DAVIS 12-21
© 1994 PAWS, INC./Distributed by Universal Press Syndicate

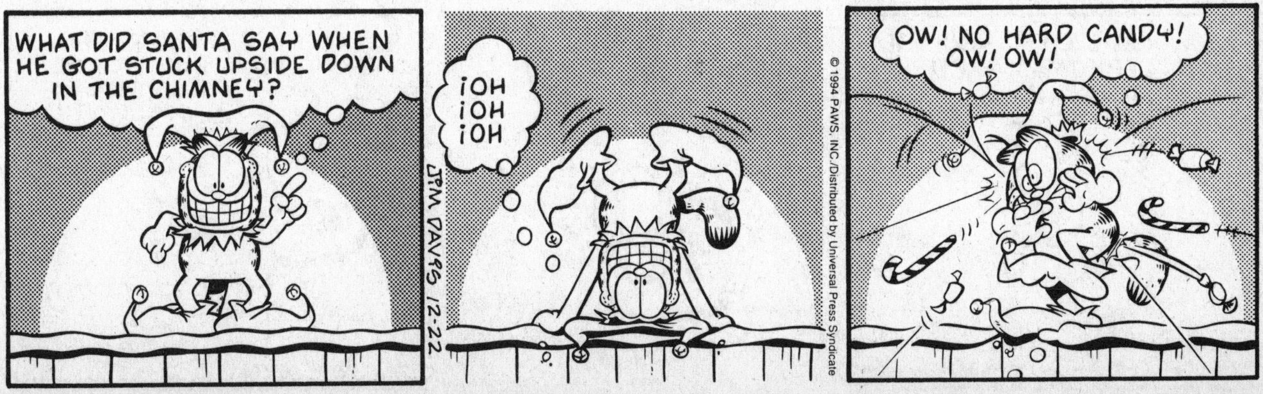
WHAT DID SANTA SAY WHEN HE GOT STUCK UPSIDE DOWN IN THE CHIMNEY?
¡OH ¡OH ¡OH
JIM DAVIS 12-22
OW! NO HARD CANDY! OW! OW!
© 1994 PAWS, INC./Distributed by Universal Press Syndicate

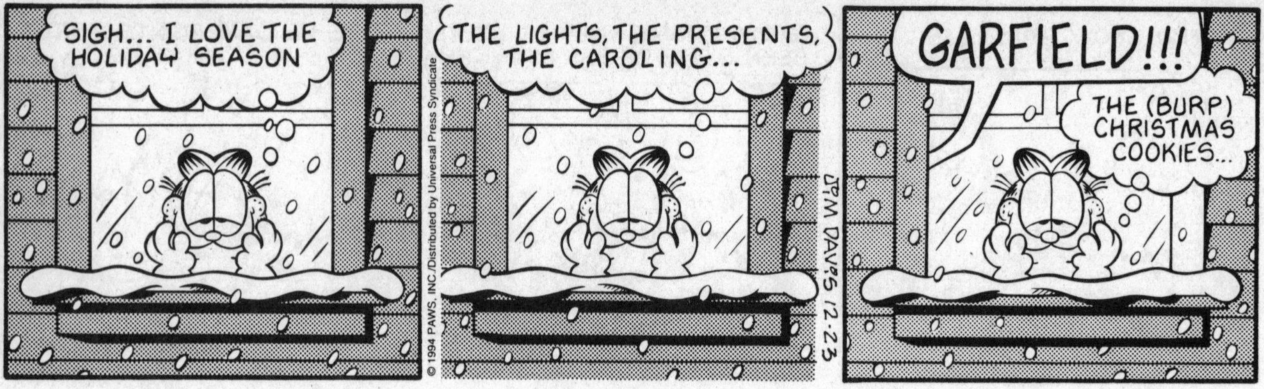

SIGH... I LOVE THE HOLIDAY SEASON
THE LIGHTS, THE PRESENTS, THE CAROLING...
GARFIELD!!!
THE (BURP) CHRISTMAS COOKIES...
JIM DAVIS 12-23
© 1994 PAWS, INC./Distributed by Universal Press Syndicate

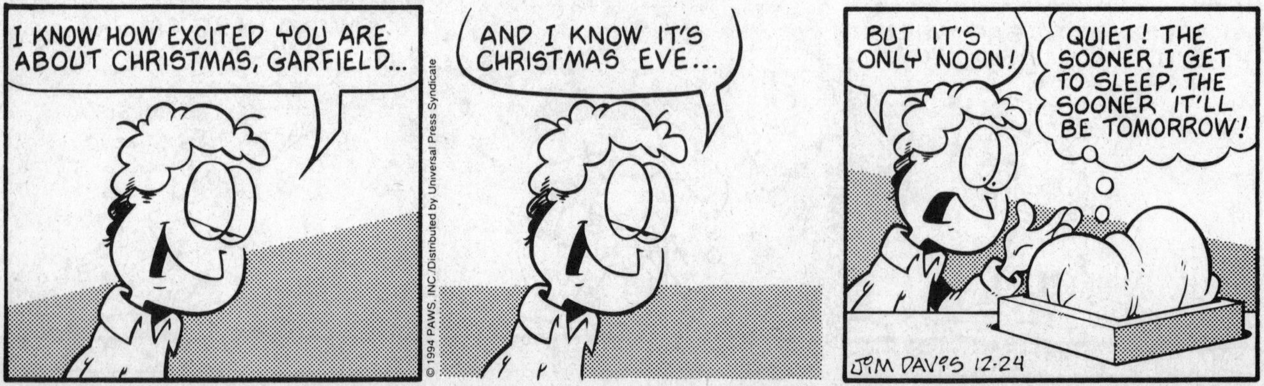

I KNOW HOW EXCITED YOU ARE ABOUT CHRISTMAS, GARFIELD...
AND I KNOW IT'S CHRISTMAS EVE...
BUT IT'S ONLY NOON!
QUIET! THE SOONER I GET TO SLEEP, THE SOONER IT'LL BE TOMORROW!
JIM DAVIS 12-24
© 1994 PAWS, INC./Distributed by Universal Press Syndicate

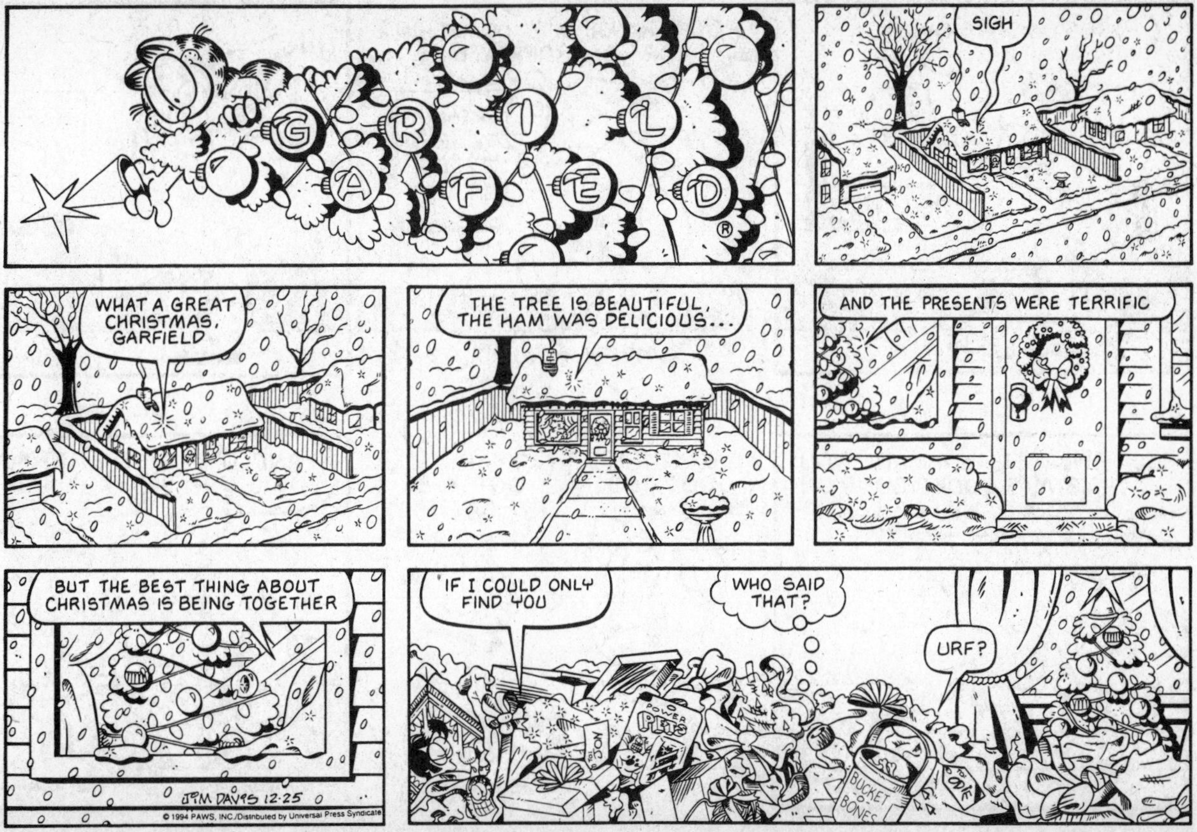

GARFIELD®
SIGH
WHAT A GREAT CHRISTMAS, GARFIELD
THE TREE IS BEAUTIFUL, THE HAM WAS DELICIOUS...
AND THE PRESENTS WERE TERRIFIC
BUT THE BEST THING ABOUT CHRISTMAS IS BEING TOGETHER
JIM DAVIS 12-25
© 1994 PAWS, INC./Distributed by Universal Press Syndicate
IF I COULD ONLY FIND YOU
WHO SAID THAT?
URF?
POWER PETS
TO: JON
BUCKET O BONES
TO: ODIE

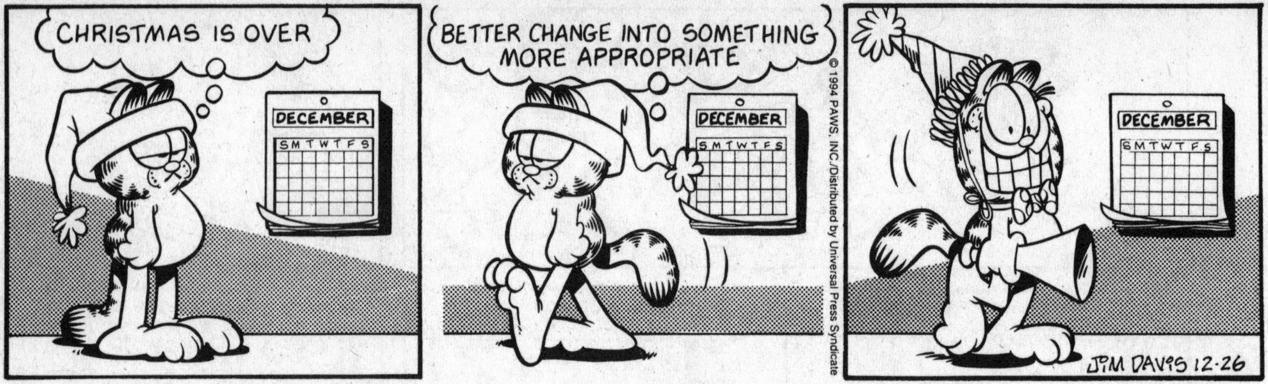
CHRISTMAS IS OVER
DECEMBER
S M T W T F S
BETTER CHANGE INTO SOMETHING MORE APPROPRIATE
DECEMBER
S M T W T F S
© 1994 PAWS, INC./Distributed by Universal Press Syndicate
DECEMBER
S M T W T F S
JIM DAVIS 12-26

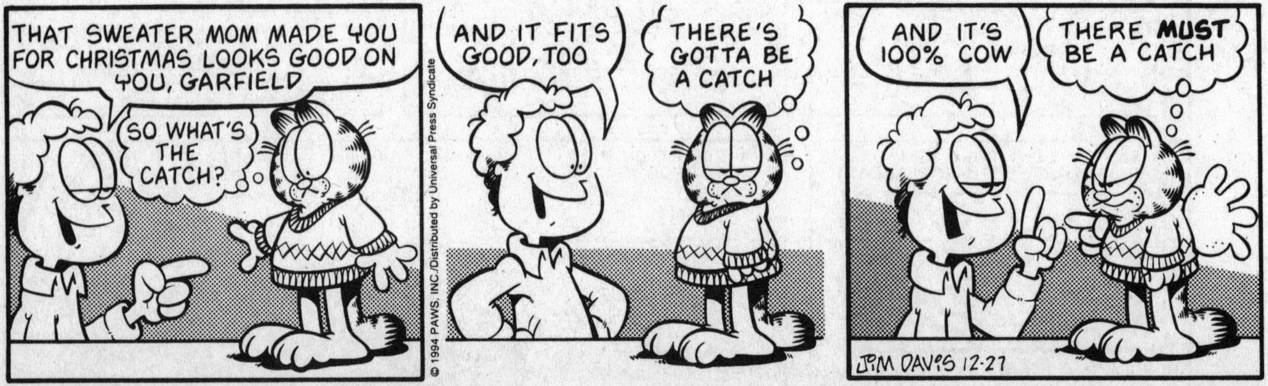
THAT SWEATER MOM MADE YOU FOR CHRISTMAS LOOKS GOOD ON YOU, GARFIELD
SO WHAT'S THE CATCH?
© 1994 PAWS, INC./Distributed by Universal Press Syndicate
AND IT FITS GOOD, TOO
THERE'S GOTTA BE A CATCH
AND IT'S 100% COW
THERE **MUST** BE A CATCH
JIM DAVIS 12-27

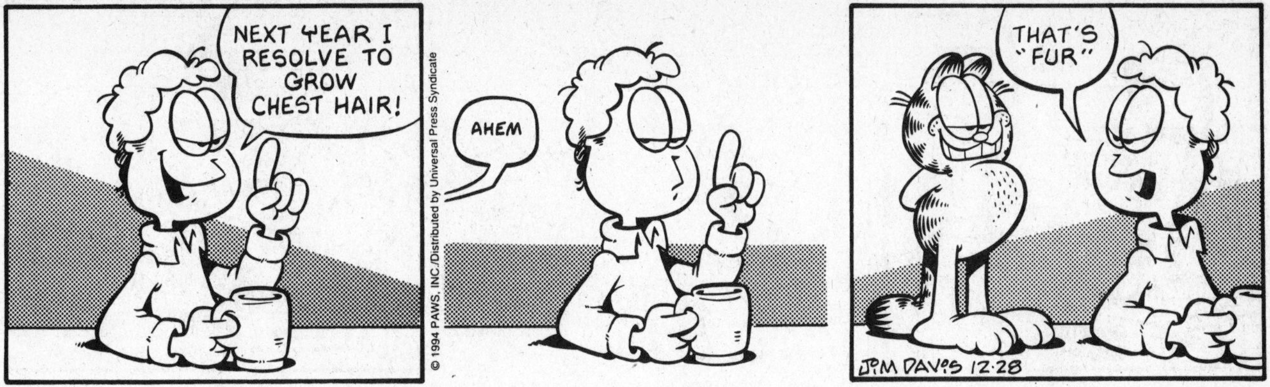
NEXT YEAR I RESOLVE TO GROW CHEST HAIR!
AHEM
THAT'S "FUR"
JIM DAVIS 12·28

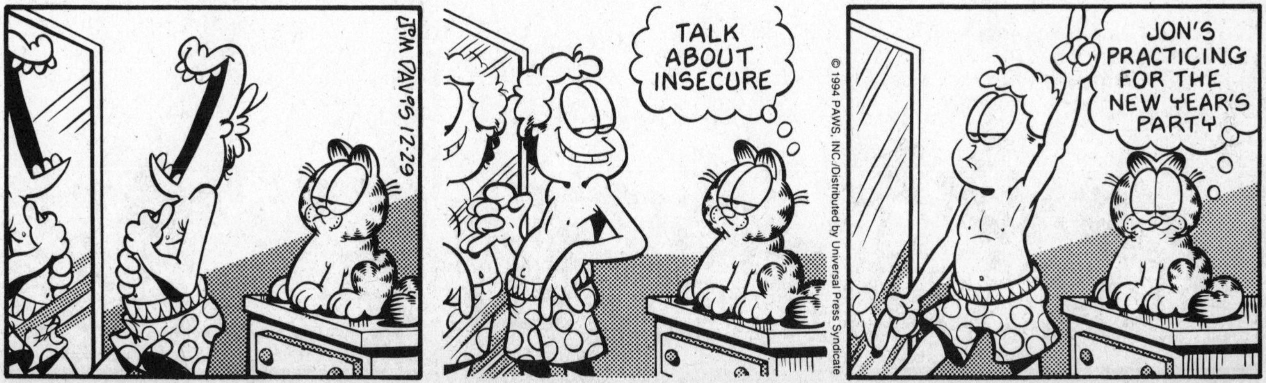
JIM DAVIS 12·29
TALK ABOUT INSECURE
JON'S PRACTICING FOR THE NEW YEAR'S PARTY

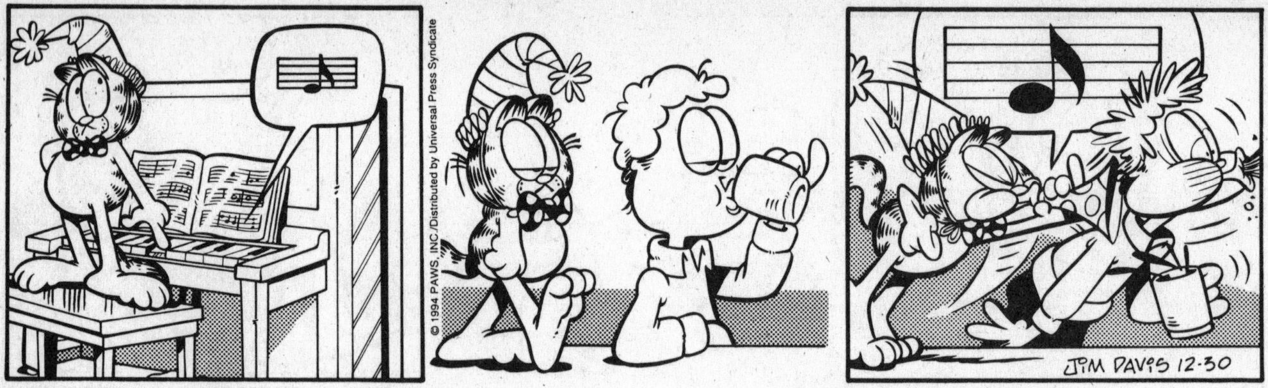
© 1994 PAWS, INC./Distributed by Universal Press Syndicate
JIM DAVIS 12-30

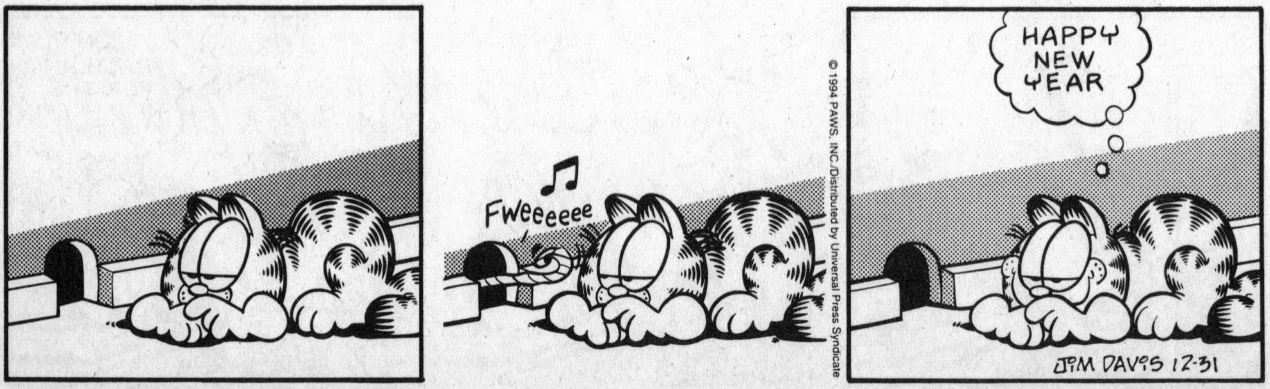
Fweeeeee
© 1994 PAWS, INC./Distributed by Universal Press Syndicate
HAPPY NEW YEAR
JIM DAVIS 12-31

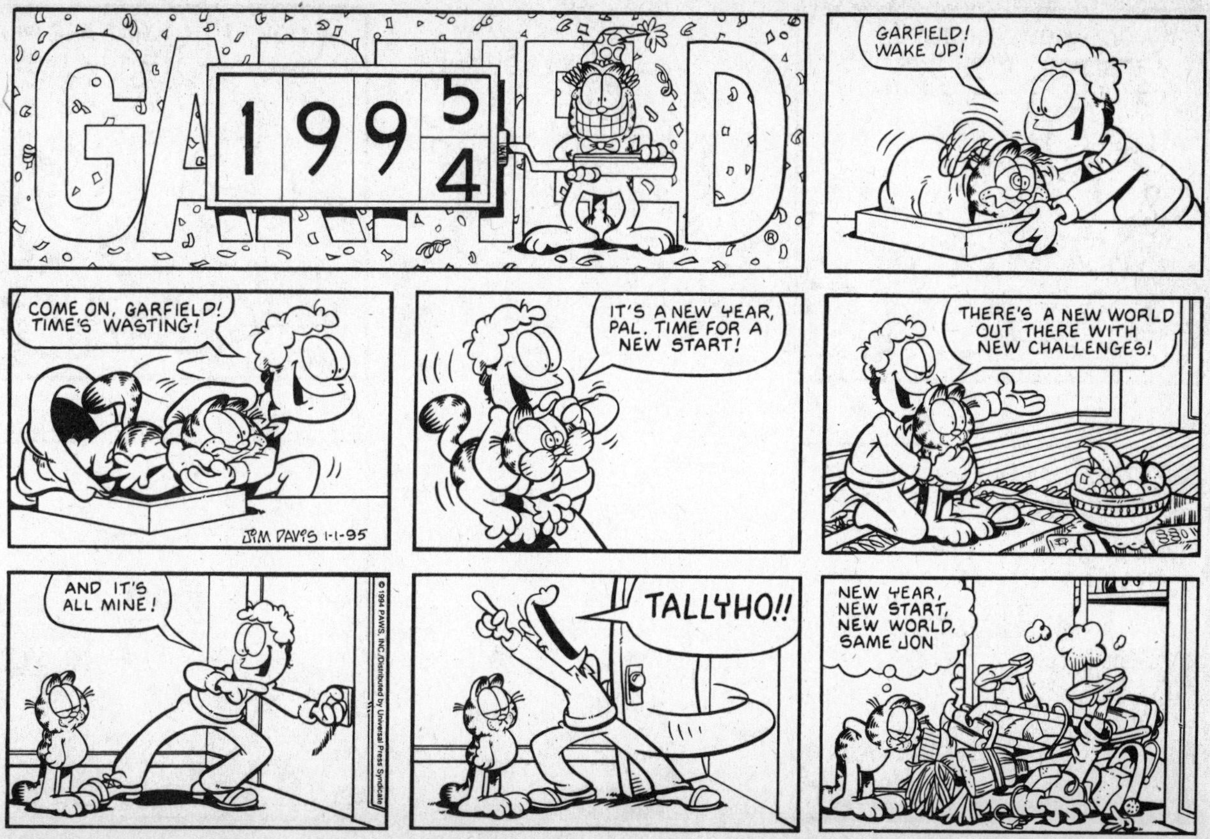
GARFIELD
1995
1994
GARFIELD! WAKE UP!
COME ON, GARFIELD! TIME'S WASTING!
JIM DAVIS 1-1-95
IT'S A NEW YEAR, PAL. TIME FOR A NEW START!
THERE'S A NEW WORLD OUT THERE WITH NEW CHALLENGES!
AND IT'S ALL MINE!
© 1994 PAWS, INC./Distributed by Universal Press Syndicate
TALLYHO!!
NEW YEAR, NEW START, NEW WORLD, SAME JON

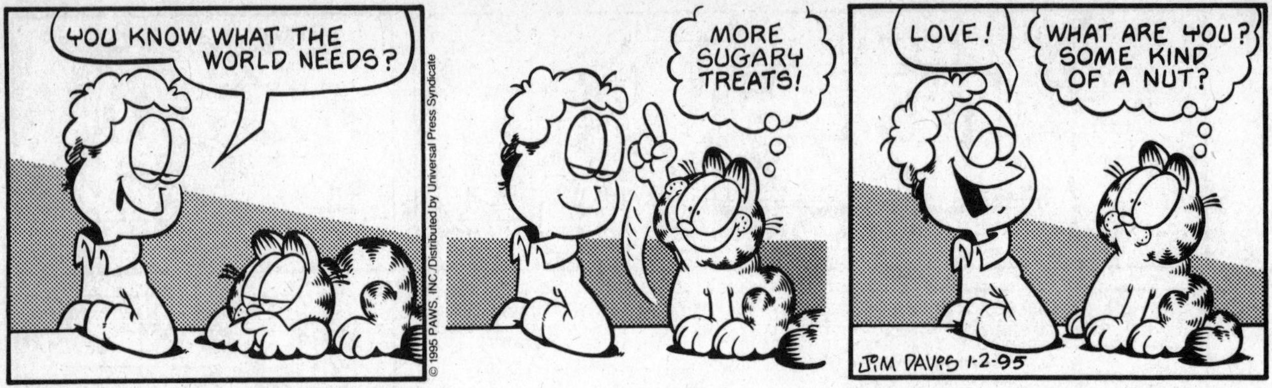
YOU KNOW WHAT THE WORLD NEEDS?
MORE SUGARY TREATS!
LOVE!
WHAT ARE YOU? SOME KIND OF A NUT?
JIM DAVIS 1-2-95
© 1995 PAWS, INC./Distributed by Universal Press Syndicate

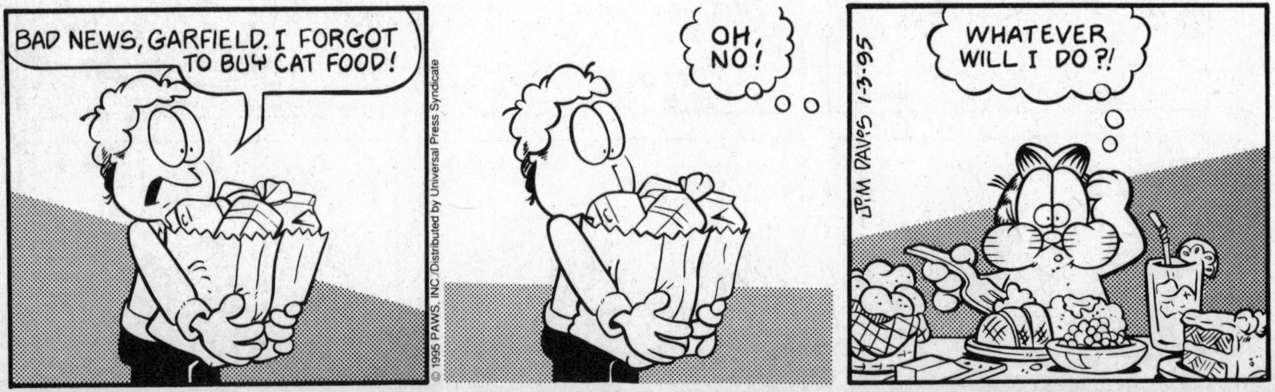
BAD NEWS, GARFIELD. I FORGOT TO BUY CAT FOOD!
OH, NO!
WHATEVER WILL I DO?!
JIM DAVIS 1-3-95
© 1995 PAWS, INC./Distributed by Universal Press Syndicate

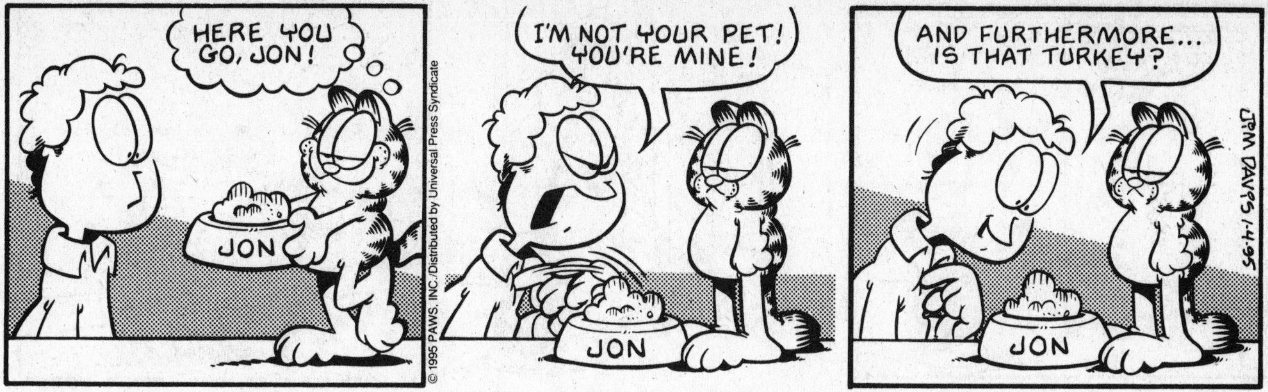
HERE YOU GO, JON!
JON
© 1995 PAWS, INC./Distributed by Universal Press Syndicate
I'M NOT YOUR PET! YOU'RE MINE!
JON
AND FURTHERMORE... IS THAT TURKEY?
JON
JIM DAVIS 1-4-95

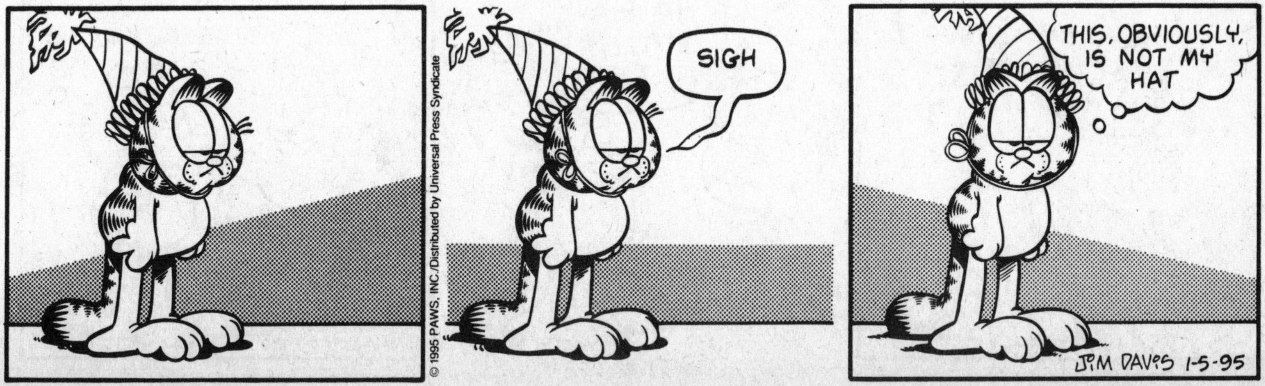
© 1995 PAWS, INC./Distributed by Universal Press Syndicate
SIGH
THIS, OBVIOUSLY, IS NOT MY HAT
JIM DAVIS 1-5-95

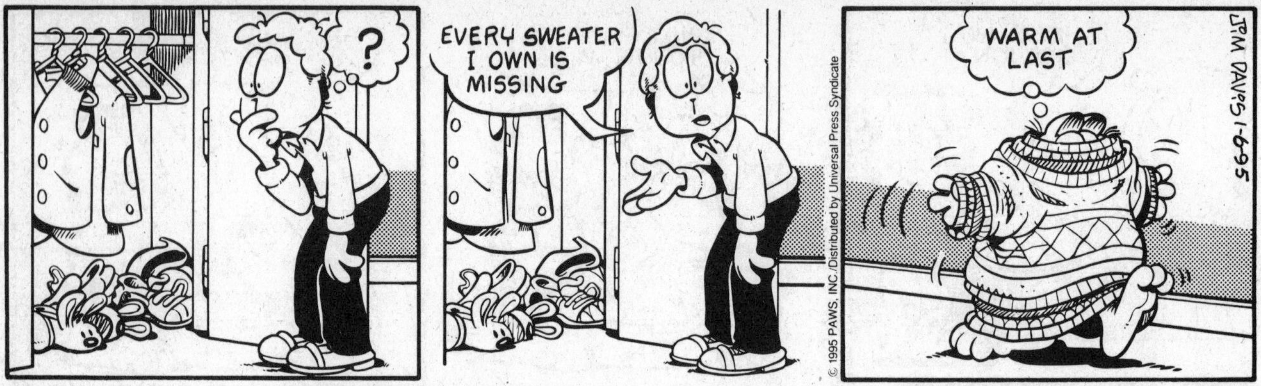
?
EVERY SWEATER I OWN IS MISSING
WARM AT LAST
JIM DAVIS 1-6-95
© 1995 PAWS, INC./Distributed by Universal Press Syndicate

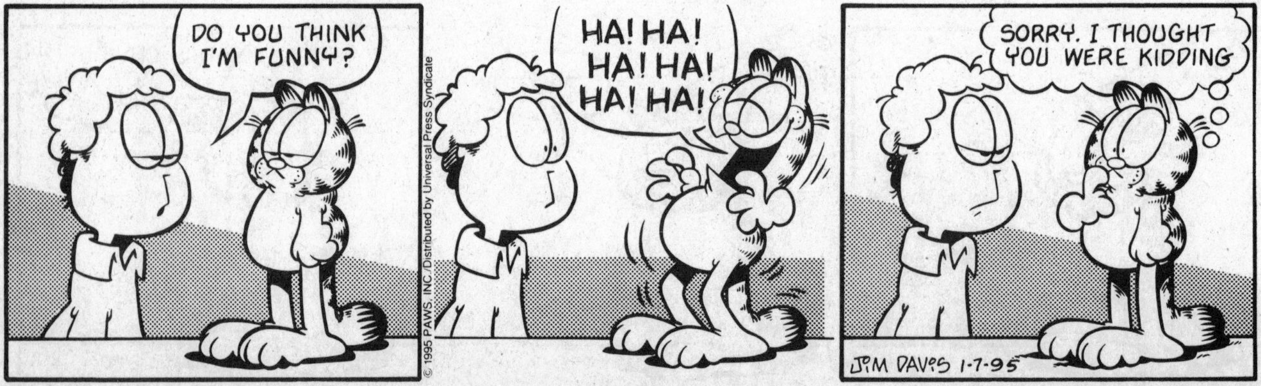
DO YOU THINK I'M FUNNY?
HA! HA! HA! HA! HA! HA!
SORRY. I THOUGHT YOU WERE KIDDING
JIM DAVIS 1-7-95
© 1995 PAWS, INC./Distributed by Universal Press Syndicate

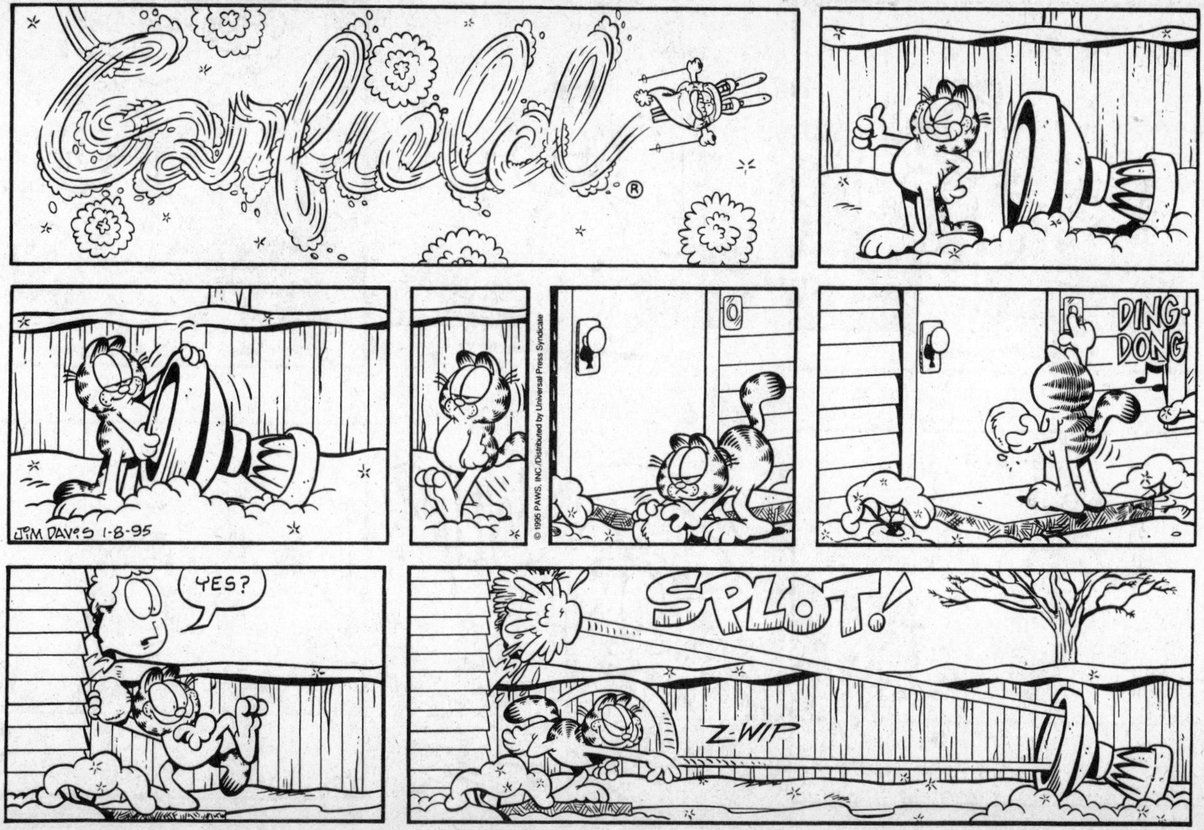
Garfield®
JIM DAVIS 1-8-95
© 1995 PAWS, INC./Distributed by Universal Press Syndicate
DING-DONG
YES?
SPLOT!
Z-WIP

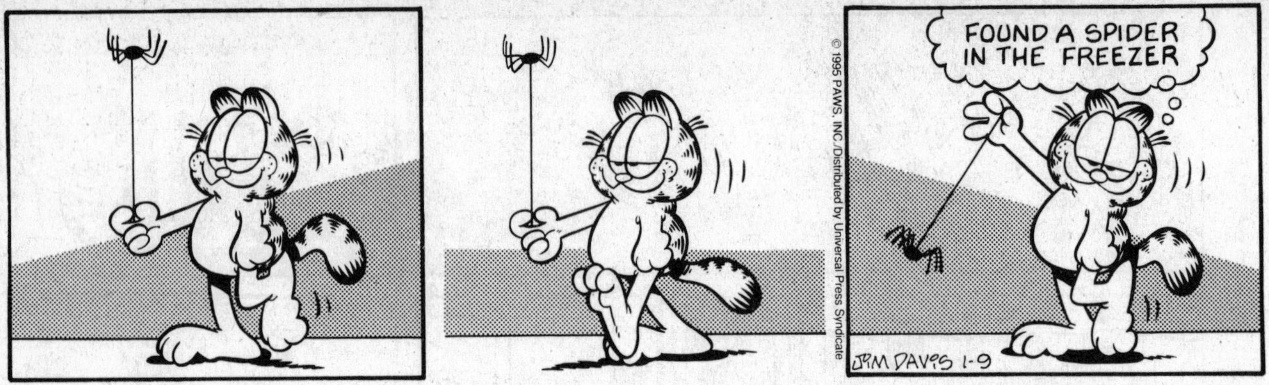
FOUND A SPIDER IN THE FREEZER
© 1995 PAWS, INC./Distributed by Universal Press Syndicate
JIM DAVIS 1-9

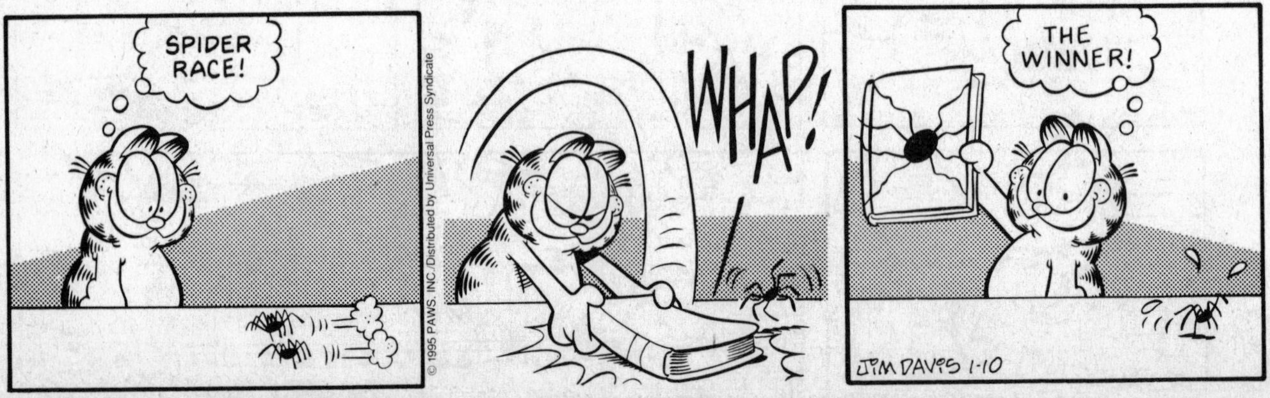
SPIDER RACE!
© 1995 PAWS, INC./Distributed by Universal Press Syndicate
WHAP!
THE WINNER!
JIM DAVIS 1-10

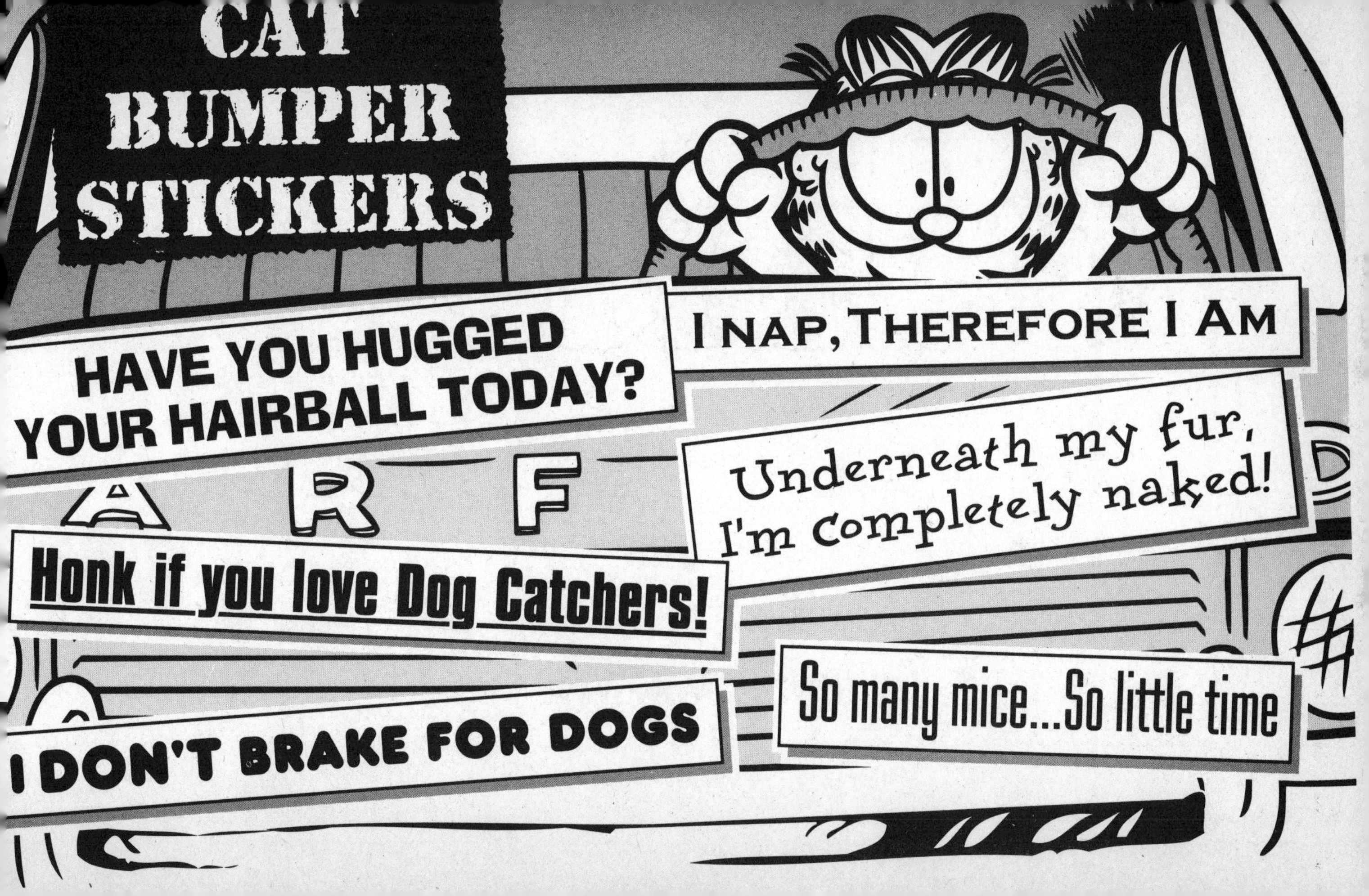
CAT BUMPER STICKERS
HAVE YOU HUGGED YOUR HAIRBALL TODAY?
I NAP, THEREFORE I AM
ARF
Underneath my fur, I'm completely naked!
Honk if you love Dog Catchers!
I DON'T BRAKE FOR DOGS
So many mice...So little time

Garfield

tons of fun

BY: JIM DAVIS

6 PRACTICAL USES FOR YOUR CAT

1 DOORSTOP

2 TV ANTENNA

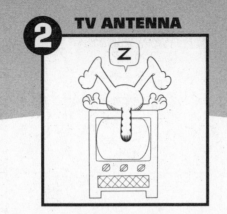

3 PAPERWEIGHT

4 HOOD ORNAMENT

5 LAP WARMER

6 HAT

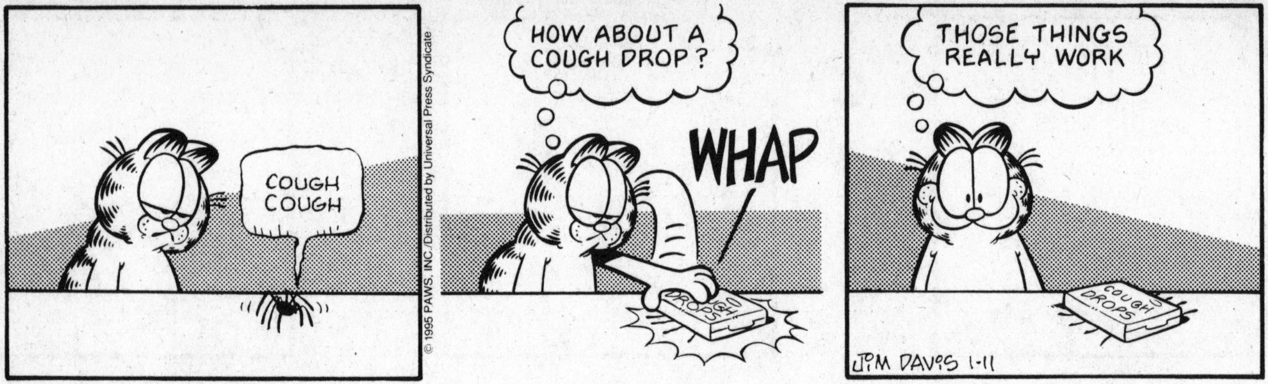
COUGH
COUGH
© 1995 PAWS, INC./Distributed by Universal Press Syndicate
HOW ABOUT A COUGH DROP?
WHAP
COUGH DROPS
THOSE THINGS REALLY WORK
COUGH DROPS
JIM DAVIS 1-11

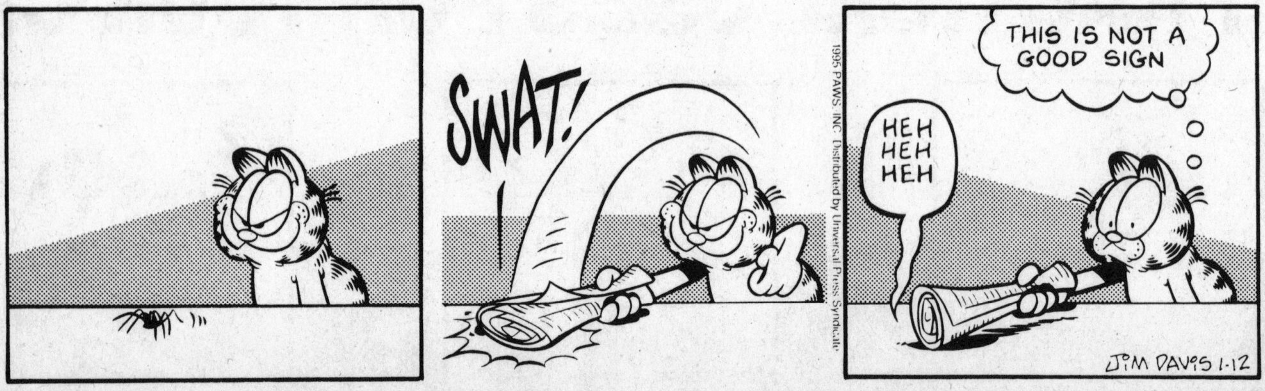
SWAT!
1995 PAWS. INC. Distributed by Universal Press Syndicate
HEH
HEH
HEH
THIS IS NOT A GOOD SIGN
JIM DAVIS 1-12

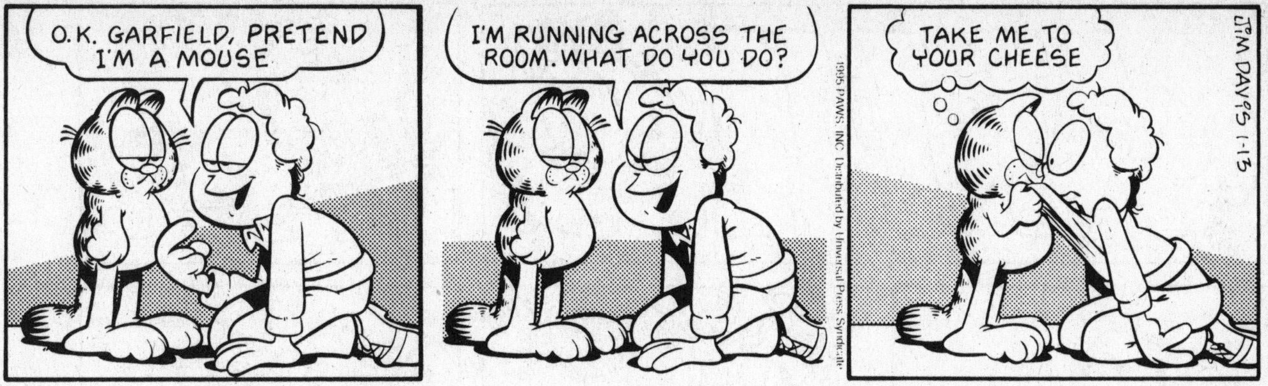
O.K. GARFIELD, PRETEND I'M A MOUSE
I'M RUNNING ACROSS THE ROOM. WHAT DO YOU DO?
© 1995 PAWS, INC. Distributed by Universal Press Syndicate
TAKE ME TO YOUR CHEESE
JIM DAVIS 1-13

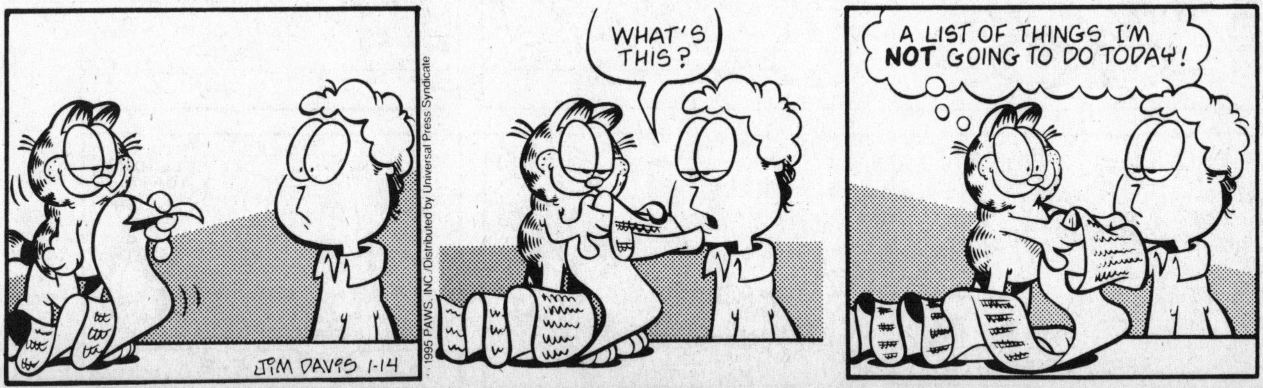
JIM DAVIS 1-14
© 1995 PAWS, INC./Distributed by Universal Press Syndicate
WHAT'S THIS?
A LIST OF THINGS I'M **NOT** GOING TO DO TODAY!

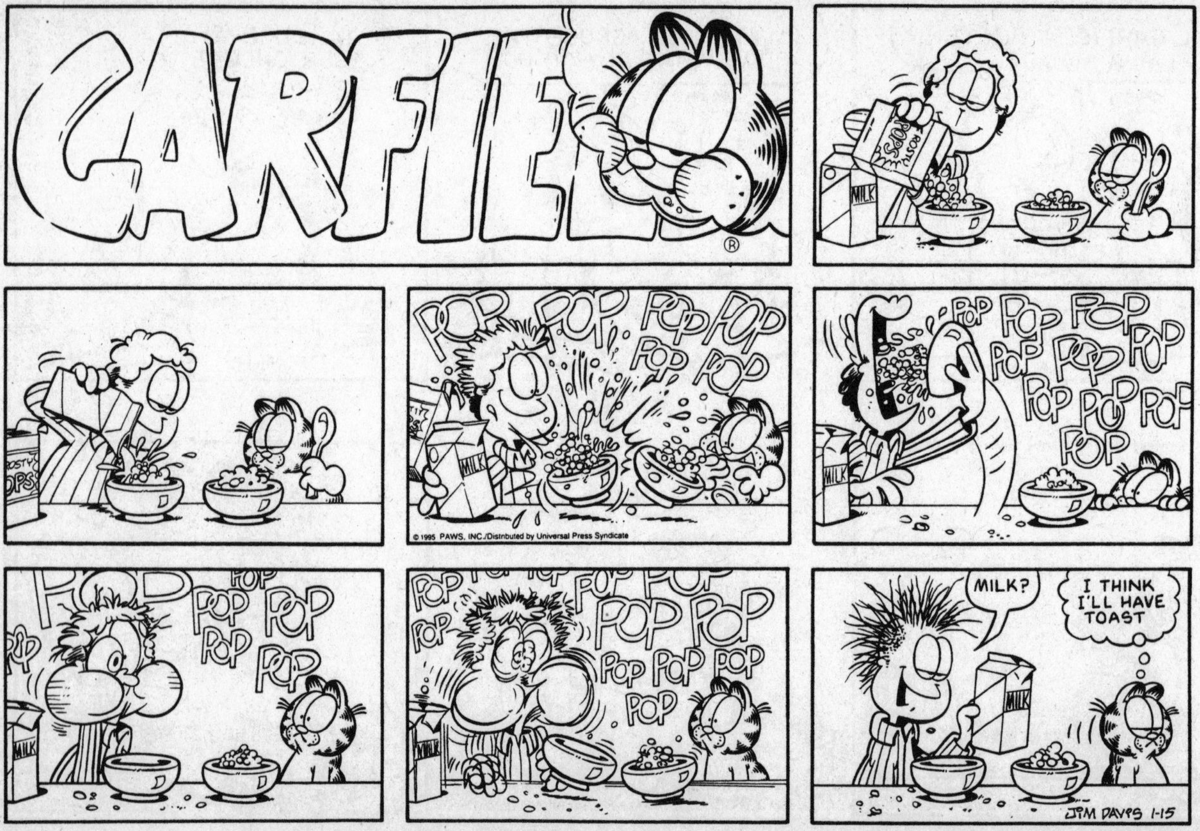
GARFIELD
FROSTY POPS
MILK
POP POP POP POP POP POP
© 1995 PAWS, INC./Distributed by Universal Press Syndicate
POP POP POP POP POP POP POP POP POP POP POP
POP POP POP POP POP
POP POP POP POP POP POP POP POP
MILK?
I THINK I'LL HAVE TOAST
JIM DAVIS 1-15

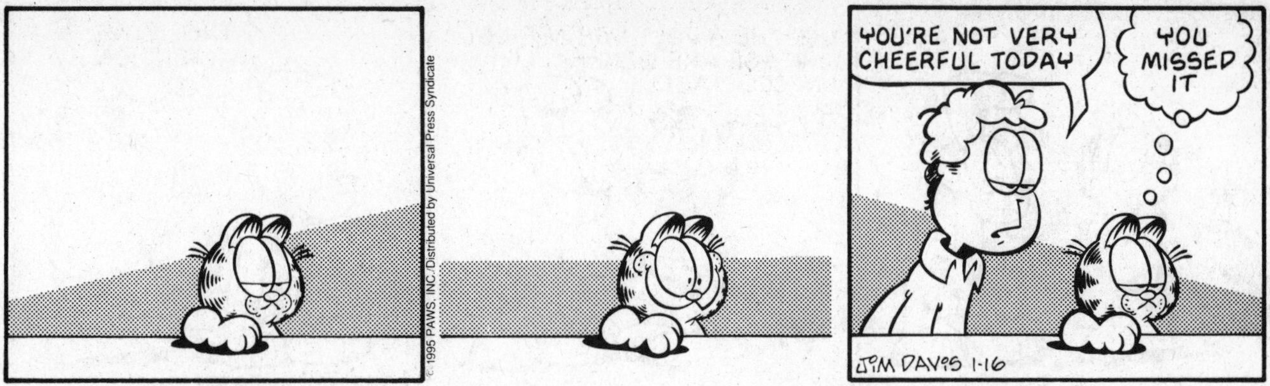
© 1995 PAWS, INC./Distributed by Universal Press Syndicate
YOU'RE NOT VERY CHEERFUL TODAY
YOU MISSED IT
JIM DAVIS 1-16

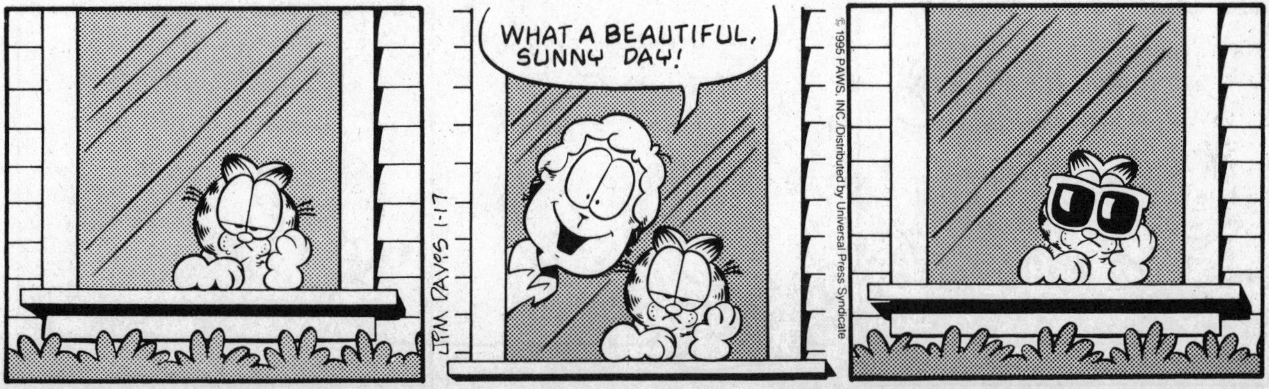
JIM DAVIS 1-17
WHAT A BEAUTIFUL, SUNNY DAY!
© 1995 PAWS, INC./Distributed by Universal Press Syndicate

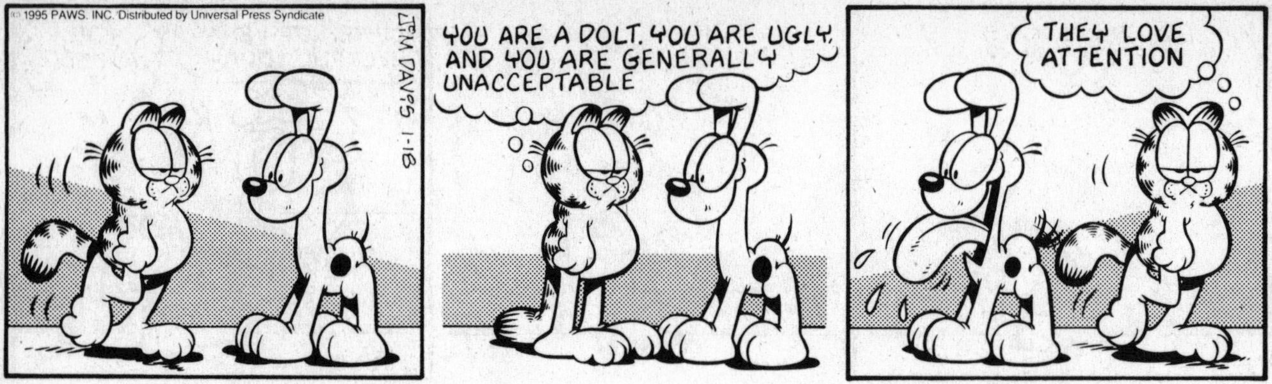
© 1995 PAWS. INC. Distributed by Universal Press Syndicate
JIM DAVIS 1-18
YOU ARE A DOLT. YOU ARE UGLY, AND YOU ARE GENERALLY UNACCEPTABLE
THEY LOVE ATTENTION

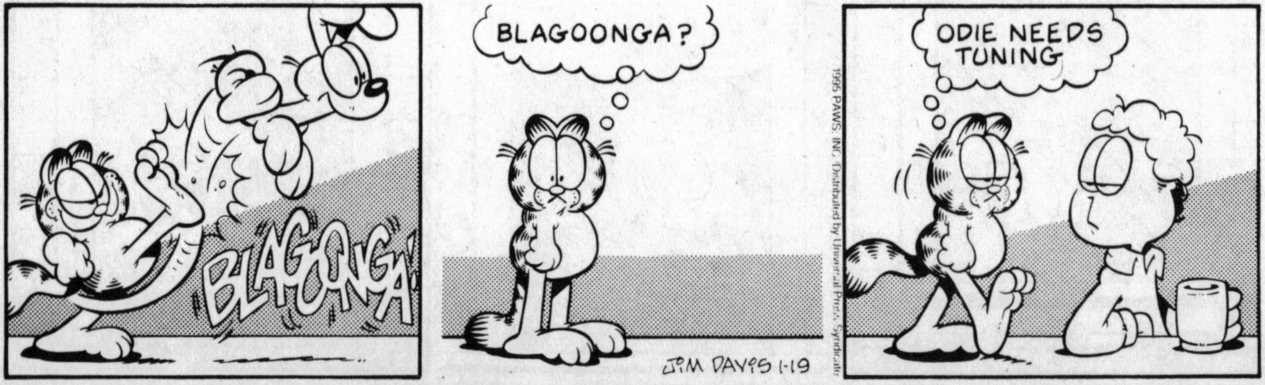
BLAGOONGA!
BLAGOONGA?
JIM DAVIS 1-19
1995 PAWS. INC. Distributed by Universal Press Syndicate
ODIE NEEDS TUNING

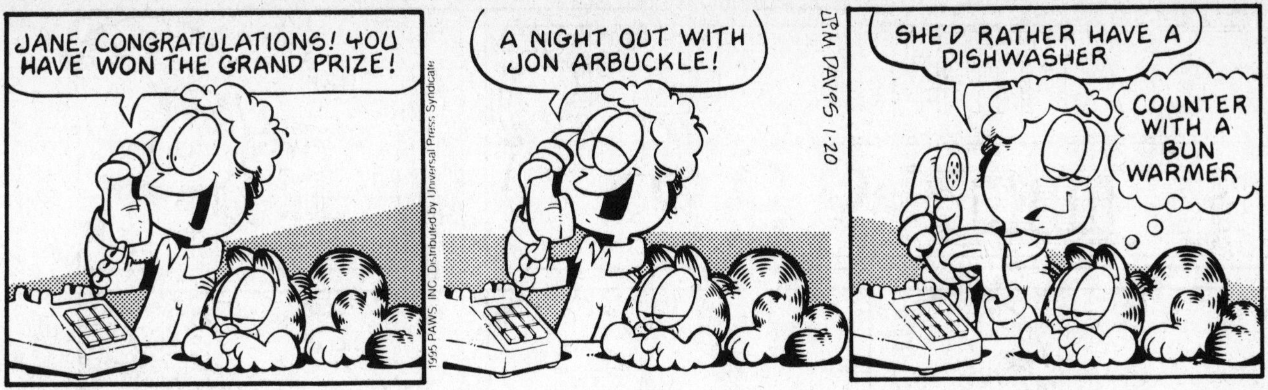
JANE, CONGRATULATIONS! YOU HAVE WON THE GRAND PRIZE!
A NIGHT OUT WITH JON ARBUCKLE!
SHE'D RATHER HAVE A DISHWASHER
COUNTER WITH A BUN WARMER
1995 PAWS, INC. Distributed by Universal Press Syndicate
JIM DAVIS 1-20

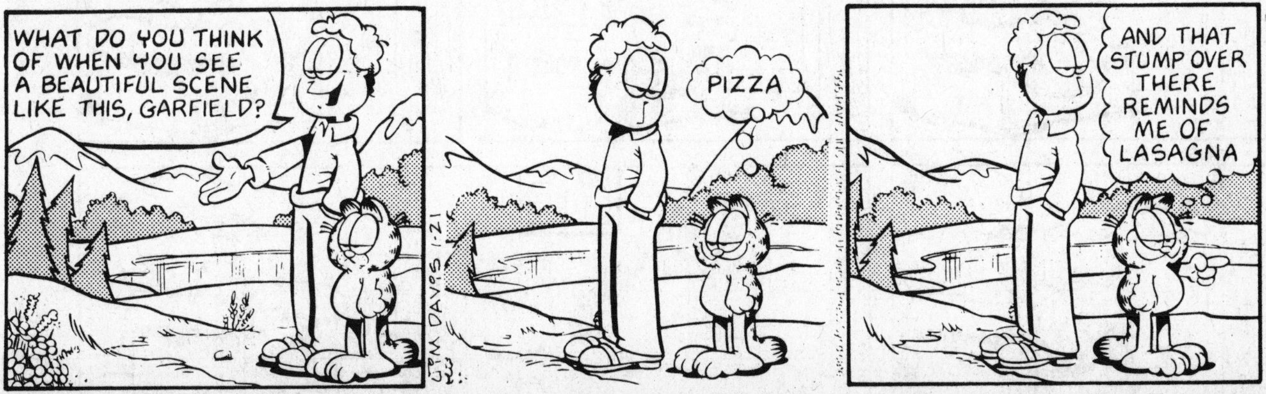
WHAT DO YOU THINK OF WHEN YOU SEE A BEAUTIFUL SCENE LIKE THIS, GARFIELD?
JIM DAVIS 1-21
PIZZA
AND THAT STUMP OVER THERE REMINDS ME OF LASAGNA

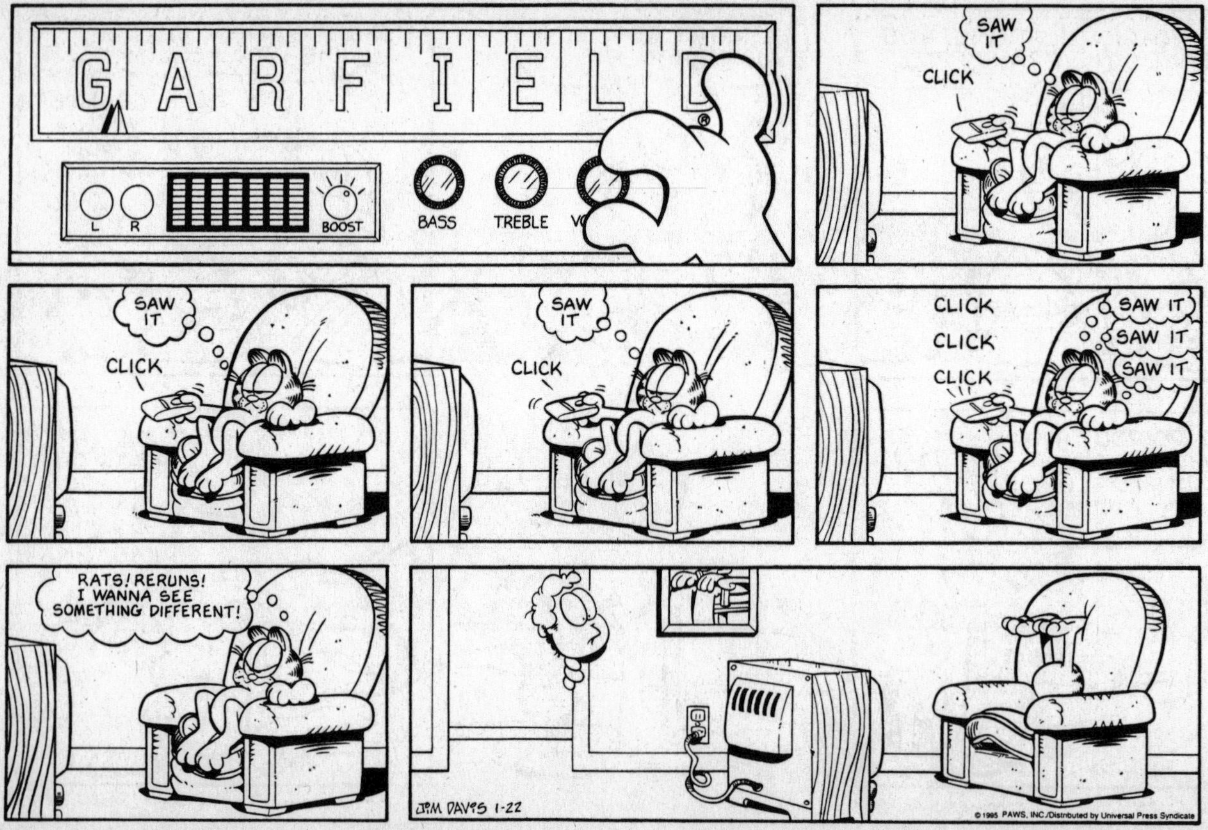
GARFIELD®
L
R
BOOST
BASS
TREBLE
CLICK
SAW IT
CLICK
SAW IT
CLICK
SAW IT
CLICK
CLICK
CLICK
SAW IT
SAW IT
SAW IT
RATS! RERUNS! I WANNA SEE SOMETHING DIFFERENT!
JIM DAVIS 1-22
© 1985 PAWS, INC./Distributed by Universal Press Syndicate

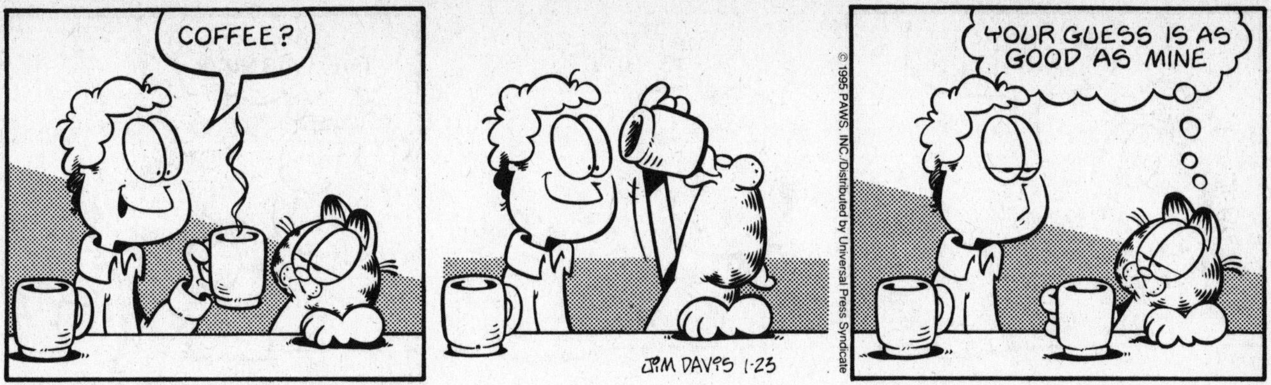
COFFEE?
YOUR GUESS IS AS GOOD AS MINE
JIM DAVIS 1-23
© 1995 PAWS, INC./Distributed by Universal Press Syndicate

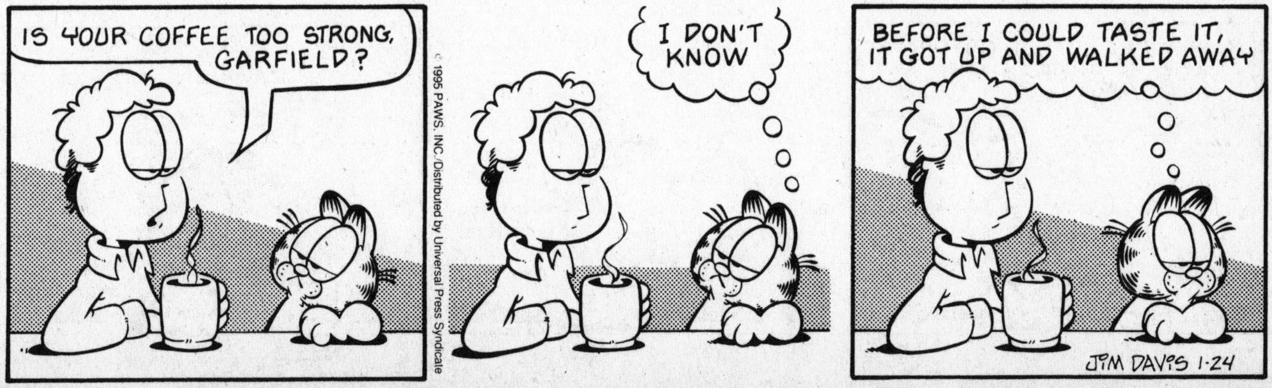
IS YOUR COFFEE TOO STRONG, GARFIELD?
I DON'T KNOW
BEFORE I COULD TASTE IT, IT GOT UP AND WALKED AWAY
JIM DAVIS 1-24
© 1995 PAWS, INC./Distributed by Universal Press Syndicate

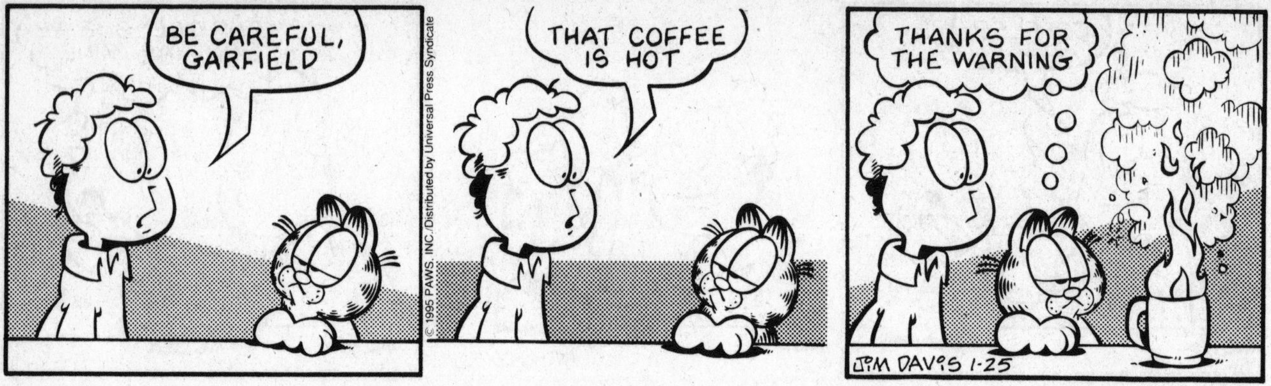
BE CAREFUL, GARFIELD
© 1995 PAWS, INC./Distributed by Universal Press Syndicate
THAT COFFEE IS HOT
THANKS FOR THE WARNING
JIM DAVIS 1-25

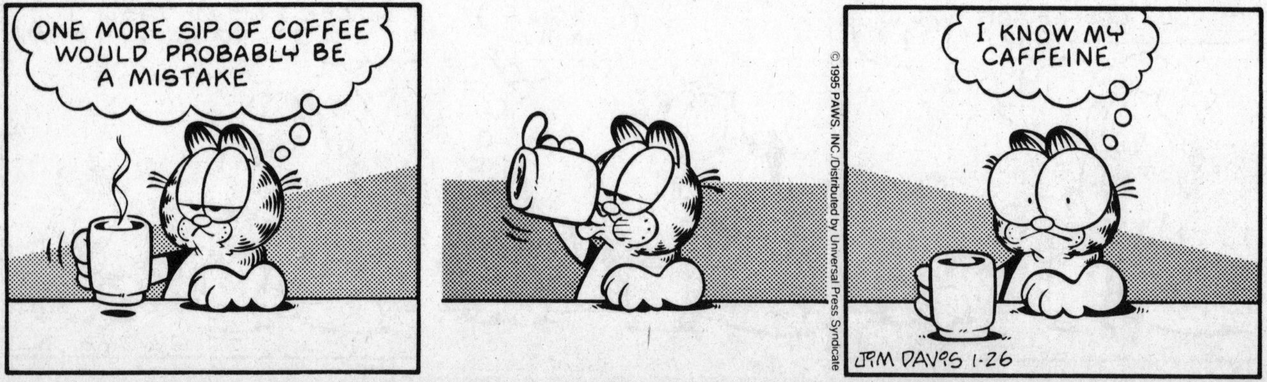
ONE MORE SIP OF COFFEE WOULD PROBABLY BE A MISTAKE
© 1995 PAWS, INC./Distributed by Universal Press Syndicate
I KNOW MY CAFFEINE
JIM DAVIS 1-26

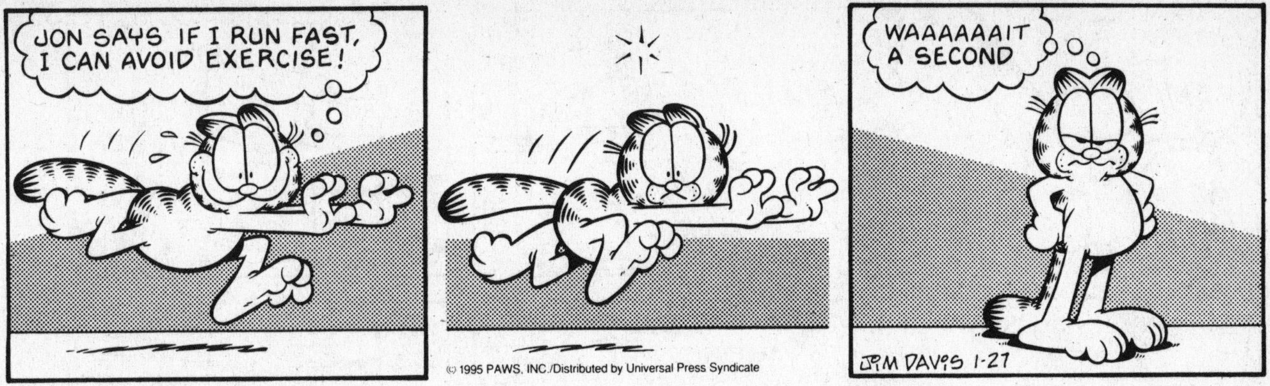
JON SAYS IF I RUN FAST, I CAN AVOID EXERCISE!
WAAAAAAIT A SECOND
JIM DAVIS 1-27

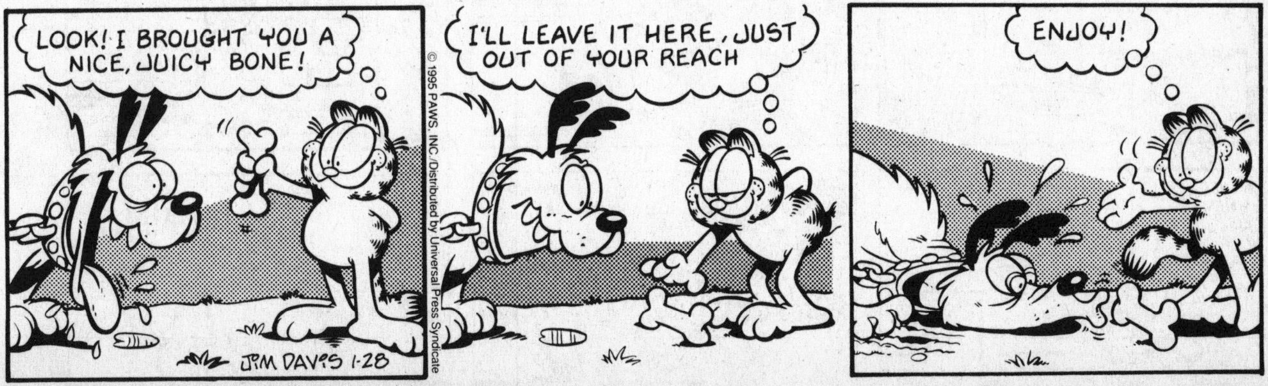
LOOK! I BROUGHT YOU A NICE, JUICY BONE!
I'LL LEAVE IT HERE, JUST OUT OF YOUR REACH
ENJOY!
JIM DAVIS 1-28

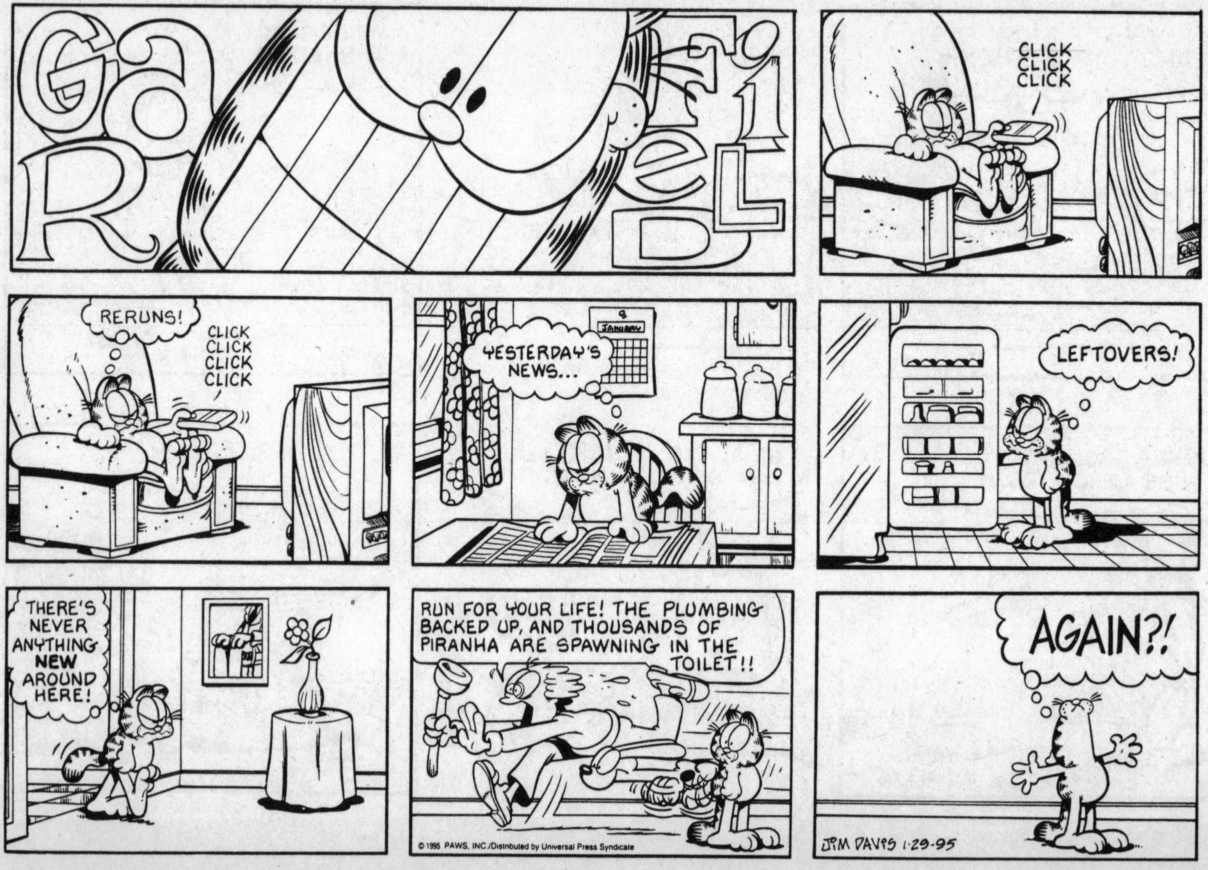
GARFIELD
CLICK CLICK CLICK
RERUNS!
CLICK CLICK CLICK CLICK
YESTERDAY'S NEWS...
LEFTOVERS!
THERE'S NEVER ANYTHING NEW AROUND HERE!
RUN FOR YOUR LIFE! THE PLUMBING BACKED UP, AND THOUSANDS OF PIRANHA ARE SPAWNING IN THE TOILET!!
AGAIN?!
JIM DAVIS 1·29·95
© 1995 PAWS, INC./Distributed by Universal Press Syndicate

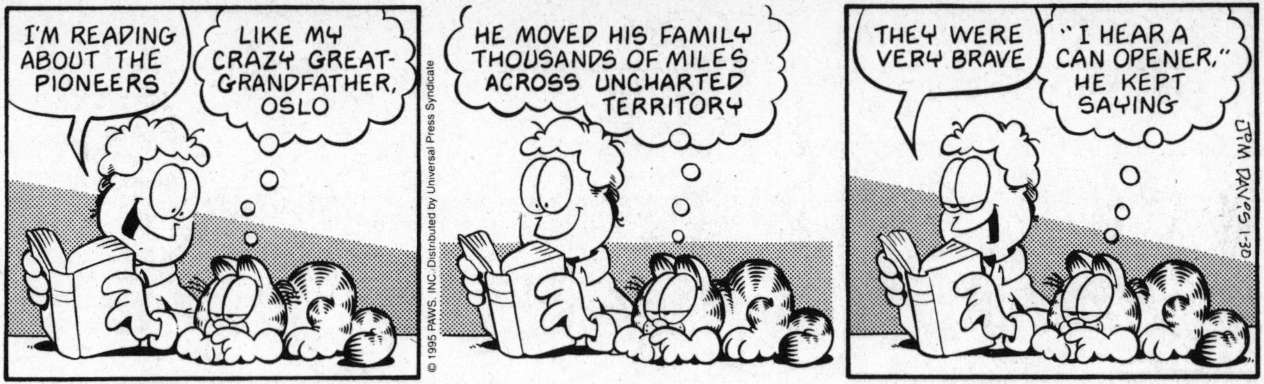
I'M READING ABOUT THE PIONEERS
LIKE MY CRAZY GREAT-GRANDFATHER, OSLO
HE MOVED HIS FAMILY THOUSANDS OF MILES ACROSS UNCHARTED TERRITORY
THEY WERE VERY BRAVE
"I HEAR A CAN OPENER," HE KEPT SAYING

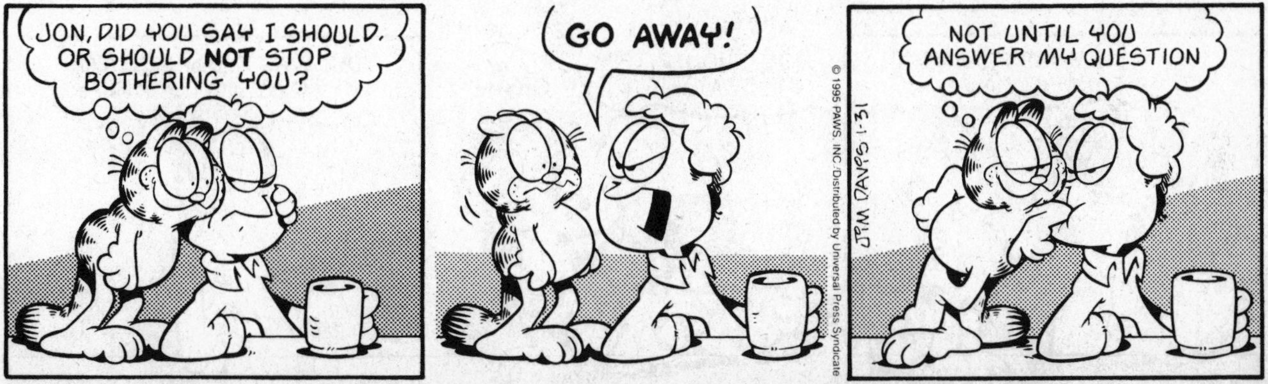
JON, DID YOU SAY I SHOULD, OR SHOULD **NOT** STOP BOTHERING YOU?
GO AWAY!
NOT UNTIL YOU ANSWER MY QUESTION

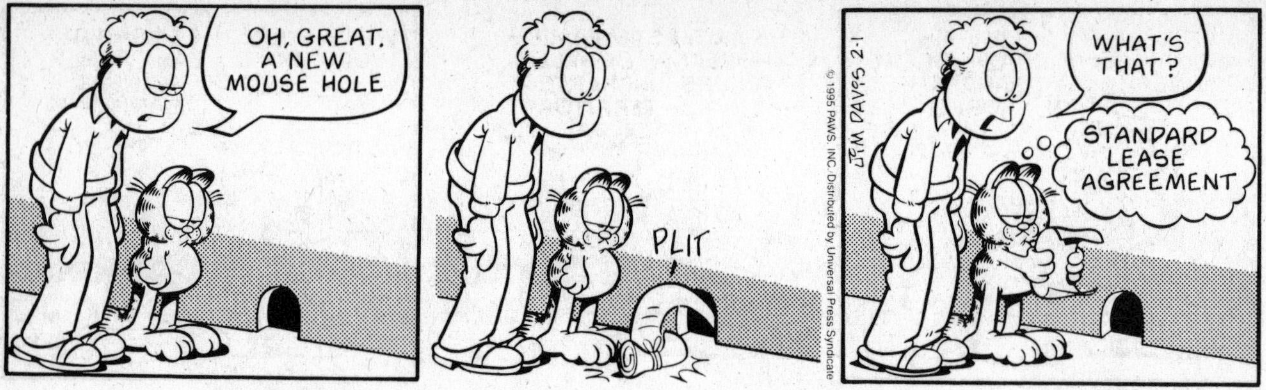
OH, GREAT. A NEW MOUSE HOLE
PLIT
WHAT'S THAT?
STANDARD LEASE AGREEMENT
JIM DAVIS 2-1

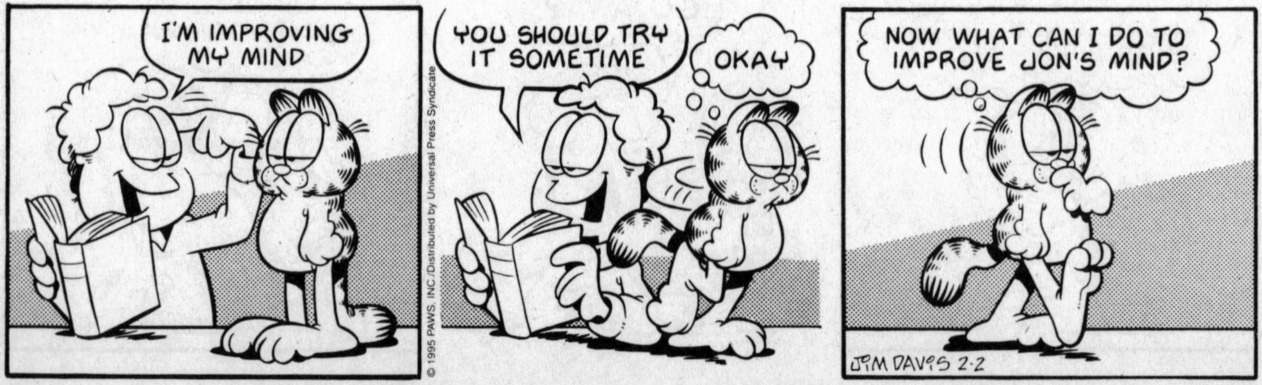
I'M IMPROVING MY MIND
YOU SHOULD TRY IT SOMETIME
OKAY
NOW WHAT CAN I DO TO IMPROVE JON'S MIND?
JIM DAVIS 2-2

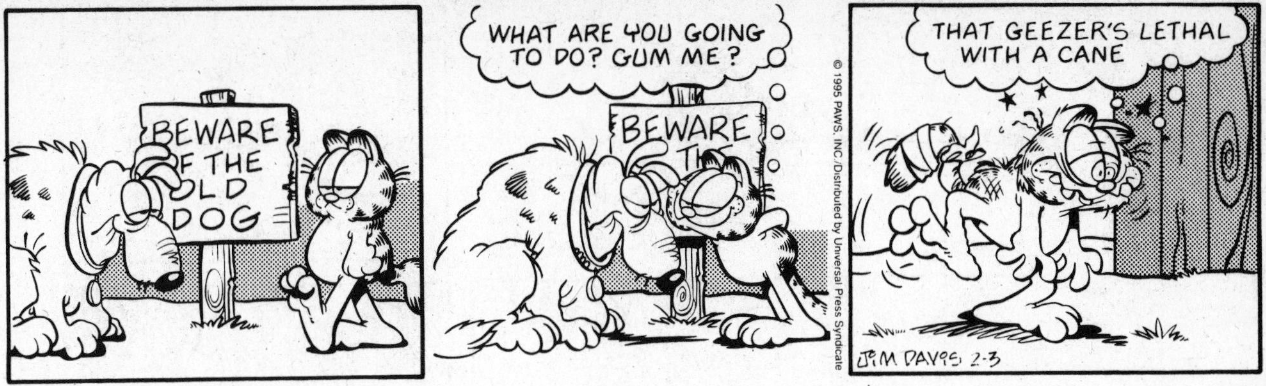
BEWARE
F THE
LD
DOG
WHAT ARE YOU GOING TO DO? GUM ME?
BEWARE
© 1995 PAWS, INC./Distributed by Universal Press Syndicate
THAT GEEZER'S LETHAL WITH A CANE
JIM DAVIS 2-3

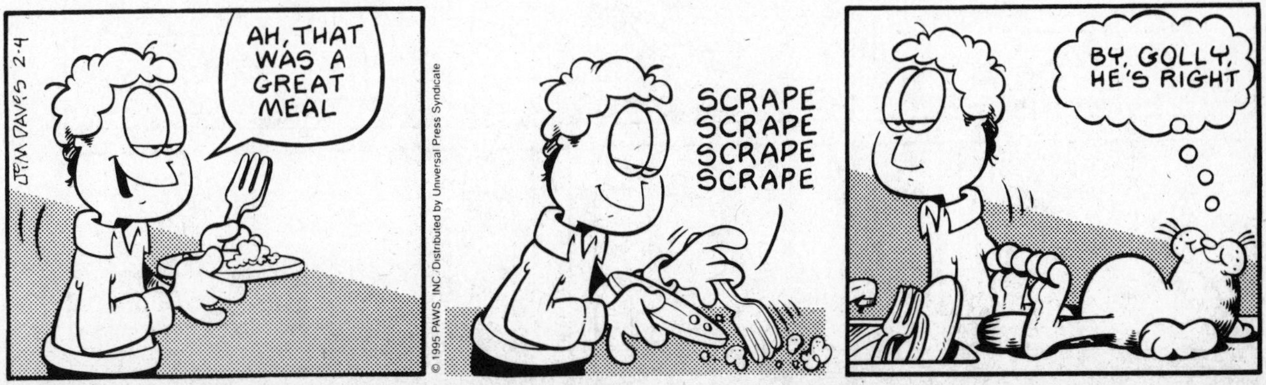
JIM DAVIS 2-4
AH, THAT WAS A GREAT MEAL
© 1995 PAWS, INC./Distributed by Universal Press Syndicate
SCRAPE SCRAPE SCRAPE SCRAPE
BY, GOLLY, HE'S RIGHT

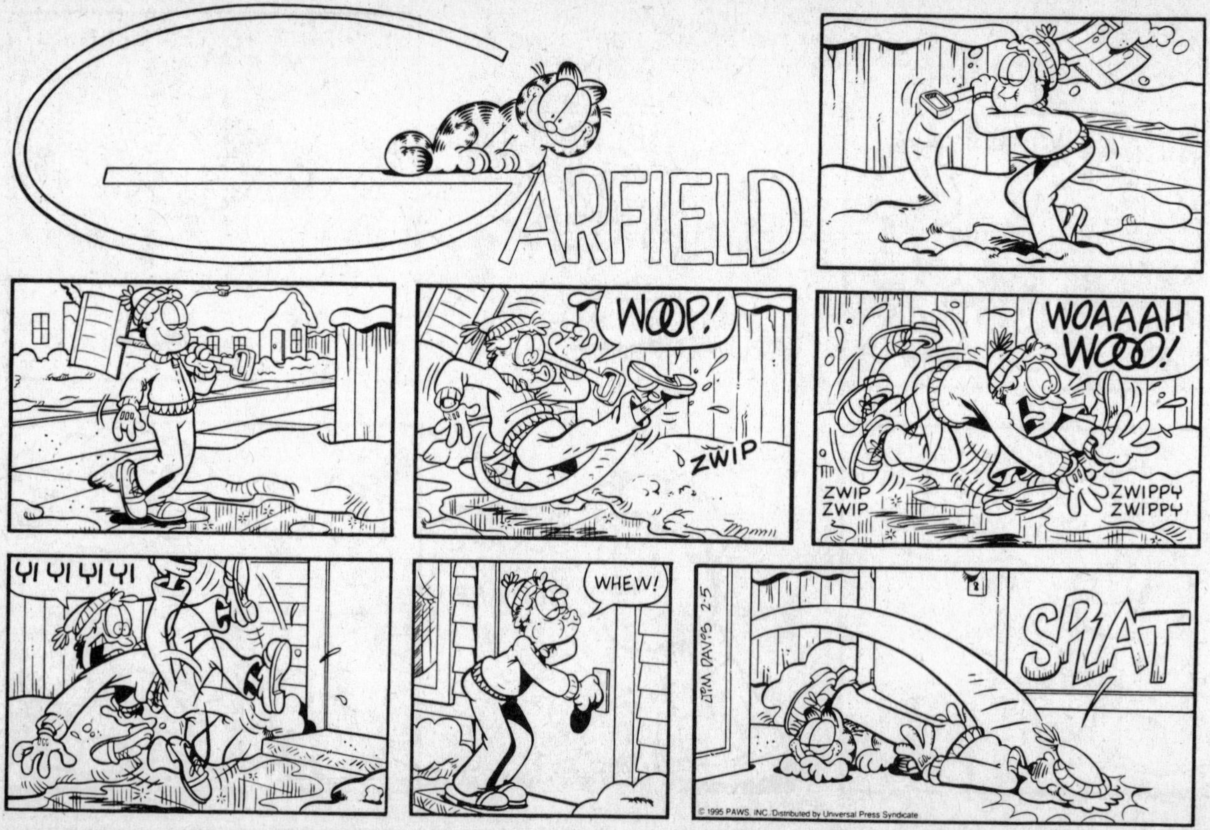
GARFIELD
WOOP!
ZWIP
WOAAAH WOOO!
ZWIP ZWIP
ZWIPPY ZWIPPY
YI YI YI YI
WHEW!
JPM DAVPS 2-5
SPLAT
© 1995 PAWS, INC. Distributed by Universal Press Syndicate

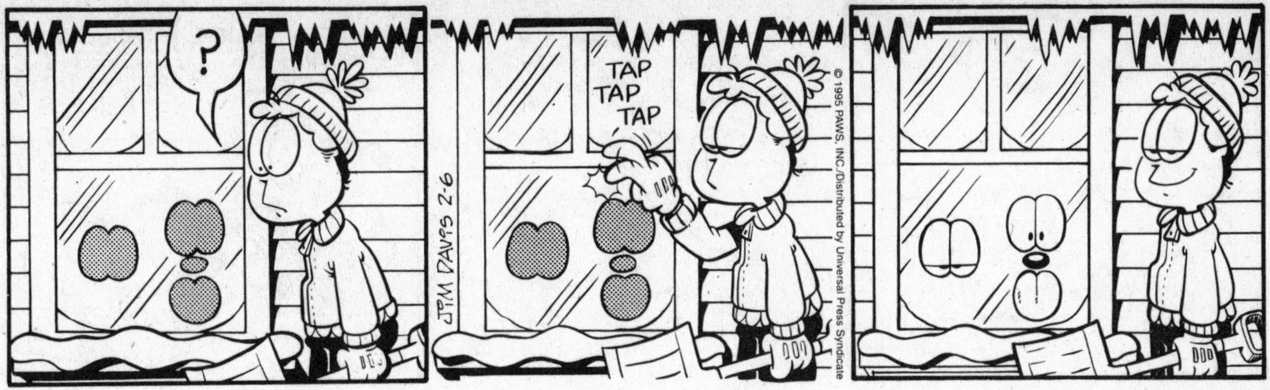
?
JIM DAVIS 2-6
TAP TAP TAP
© 1995 PAWS, INC./Distributed by Universal Press Syndicate

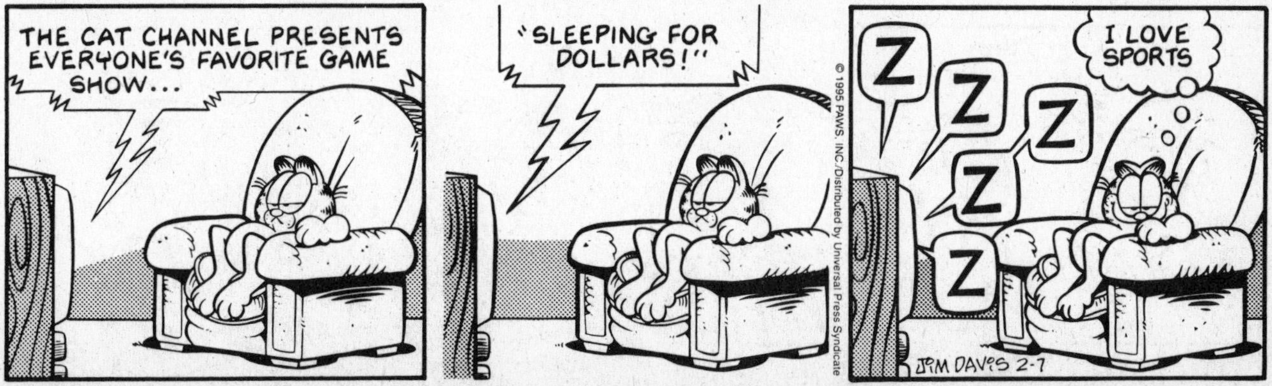
THE CAT CHANNEL PRESENTS EVERYONE'S FAVORITE GAME SHOW...
"SLEEPING FOR DOLLARS!"
© 1995 PAWS, INC./Distributed by Universal Press Syndicate
Z Z Z Z Z
I LOVE SPORTS
JIM DAVIS 2-7

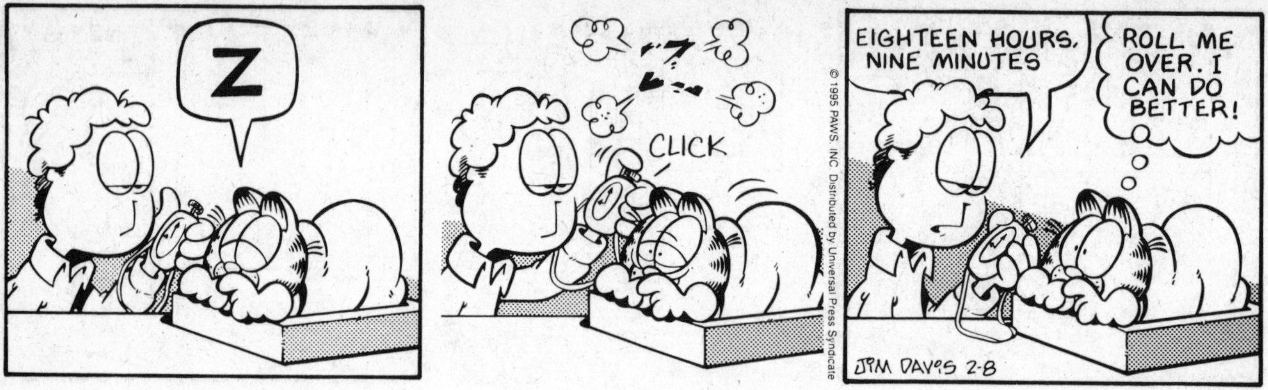
Z
CLICK
EIGHTEEN HOURS, NINE MINUTES
ROLL ME OVER. I CAN DO BETTER!
© 1995 PAWS, INC. Distributed by Universal Press Syndicate
JIM DAVIS 2-8

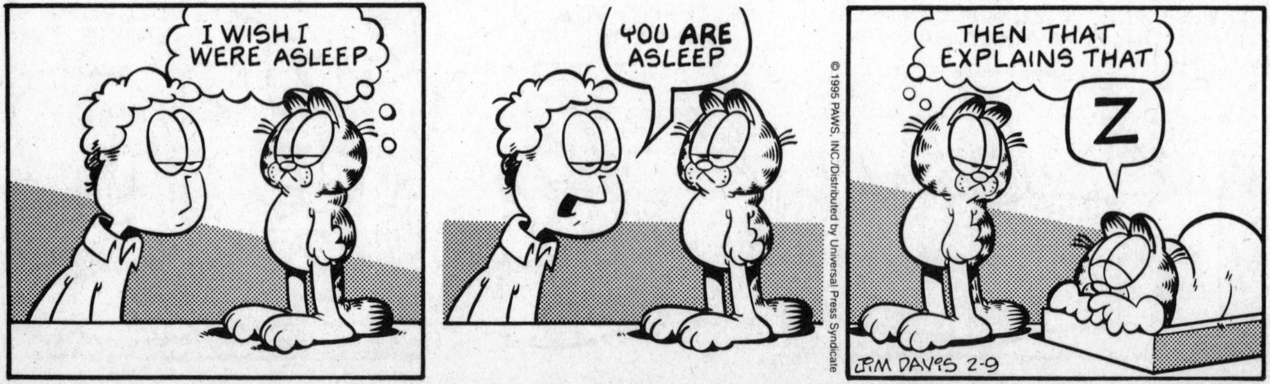
I WISH I WERE ASLEEP
YOU ARE ASLEEP
THEN THAT EXPLAINS THAT
Z
© 1995 PAWS, INC./Distributed by Universal Press Syndicate
JIM DAVIS 2-9

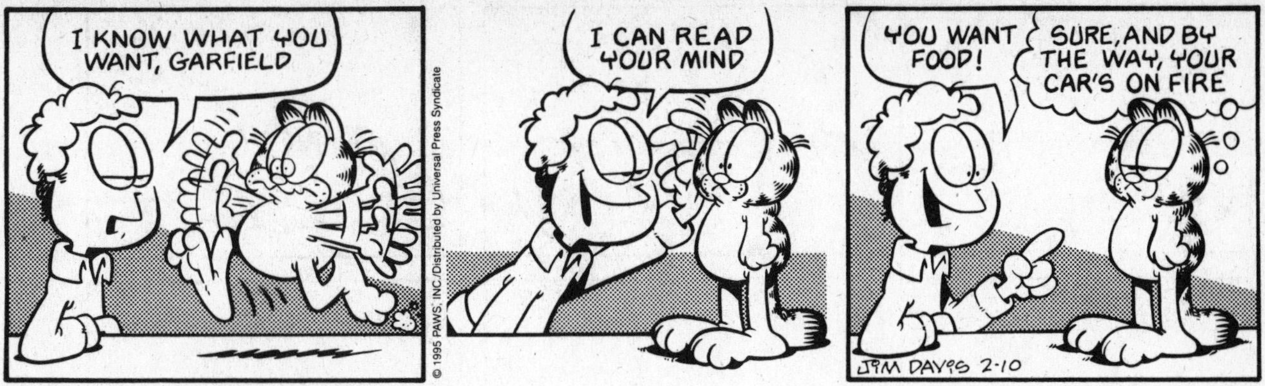
I KNOW WHAT YOU WANT, GARFIELD
I CAN READ YOUR MIND
YOU WANT FOOD!
SURE, AND BY THE WAY, YOUR CAR'S ON FIRE
JIM DAVIS 2-10
© 1995 PAWS, INC./Distributed by Universal Press Syndicate

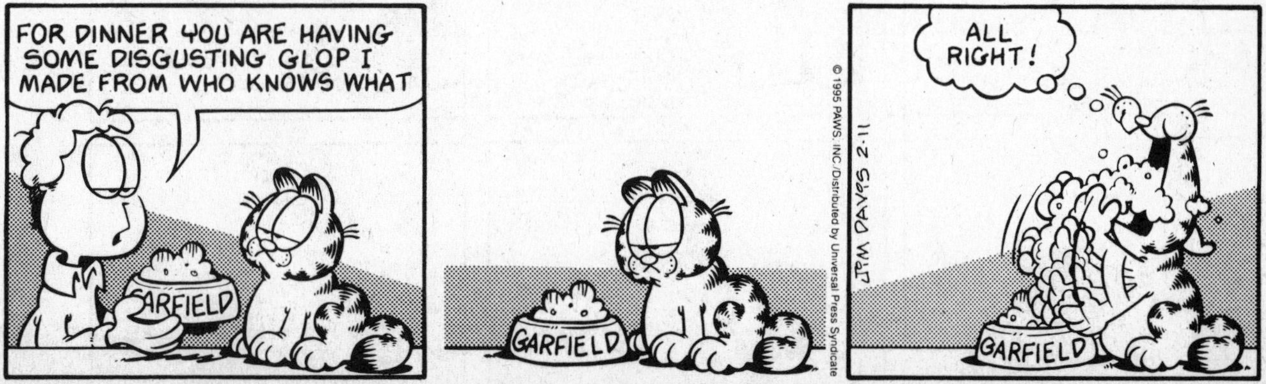
FOR DINNER YOU ARE HAVING SOME DISGUSTING GLOP I MADE FROM WHO KNOWS WHAT
GARFIELD
GARFIELD
ALL RIGHT!
GARFIELD
JIM DAVIS 2-11
© 1995 PAWS, INC./Distributed by Universal Press Syndicate

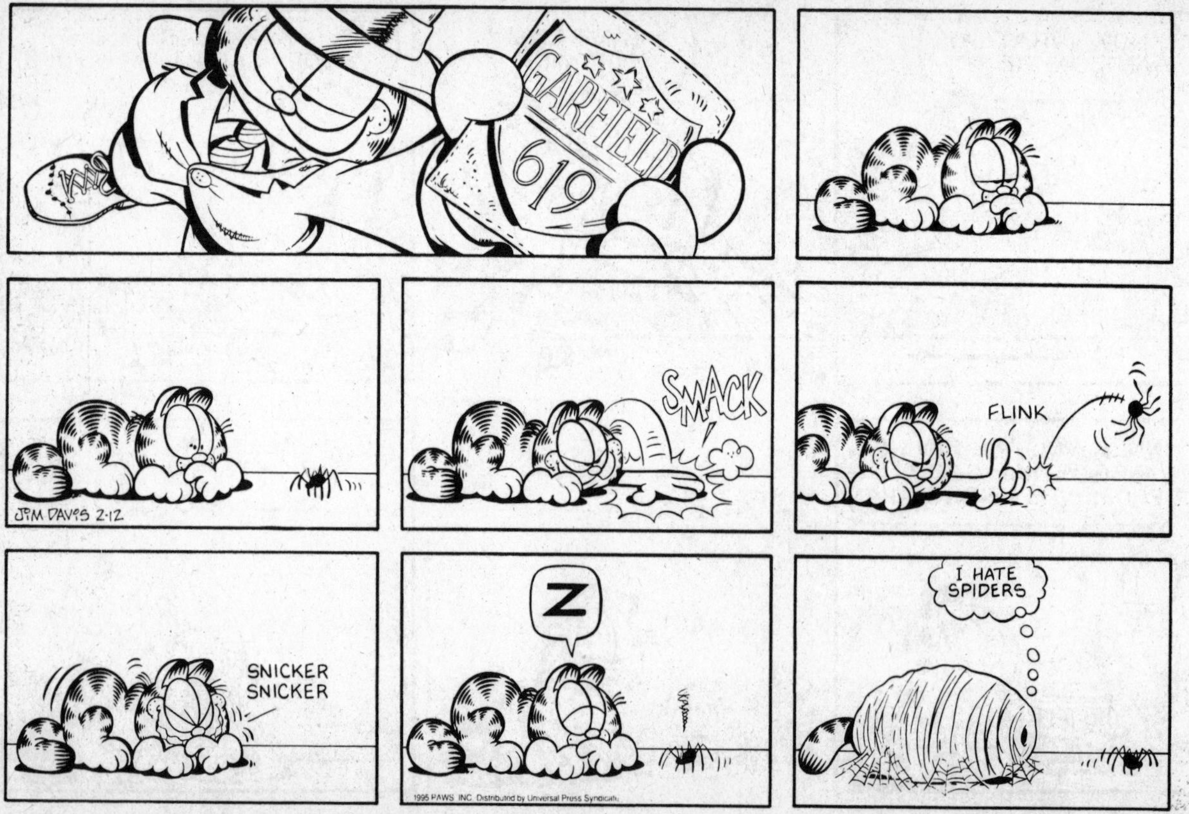
GARFIELD
619
JIM DAVIS 2-12
SMACK
FLINK
SNICKER
SNICKER
Z
1995 PAWS INC. Distributed by Universal Press Syndicate
I HATE
SPIDERS

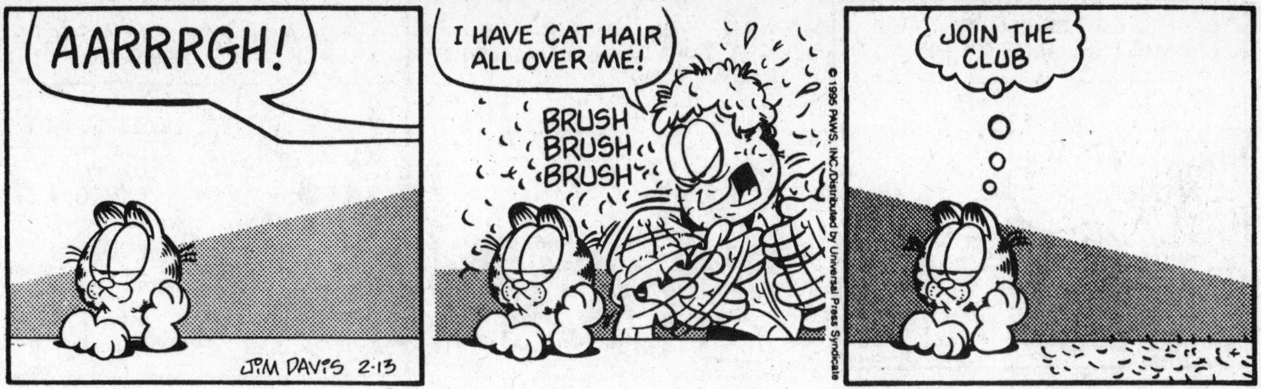
AARRRGH!
I HAVE CAT HAIR ALL OVER ME!
BRUSH BRUSH BRUSH
JOIN THE CLUB
JIM DAVIS 2-13
© 1995 PAWS, INC./Distributed by Universal Press Syndicate

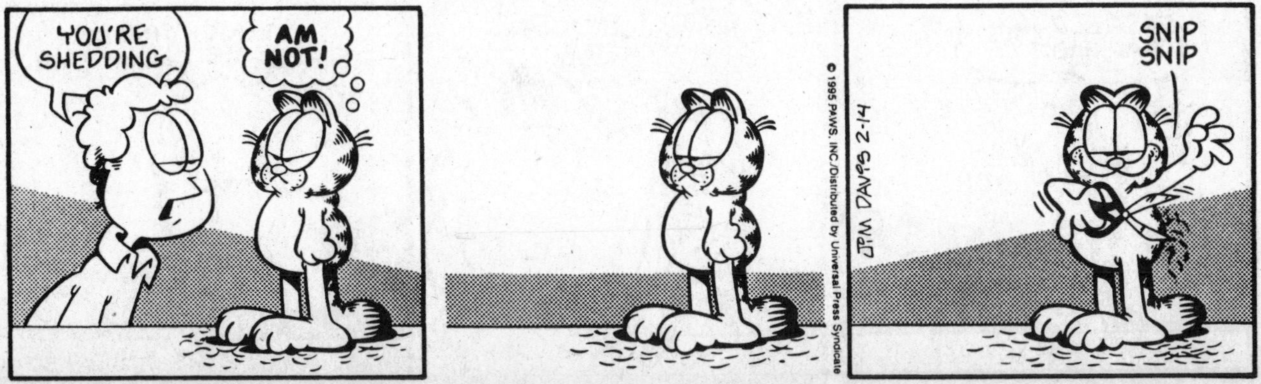
YOU'RE SHEDDING
AM NOT!
SNIP SNIP
JIM DAVIS 2-14
© 1995 PAWS, INC./Distributed by Universal Press Syndicate

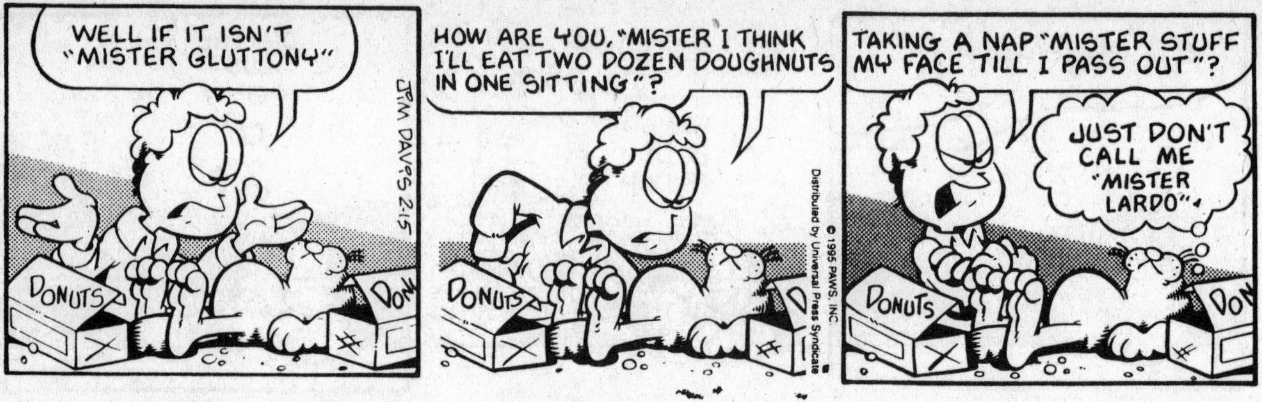
WELL IF IT ISN'T "MISTER GLUTTONY"
JIM DAVIS 2-15
HOW ARE YOU, "MISTER I THINK I'LL EAT TWO DOZEN DOUGHNUTS IN ONE SITTING"?
DONUTS
© 1995 PAWS, INC.
Distributed by Universal Press Syndicate
TAKING A NAP "MISTER STUFF MY FACE TILL I PASS OUT"?
JUST DON'T CALL ME "MISTER LARDO"
DONUTS

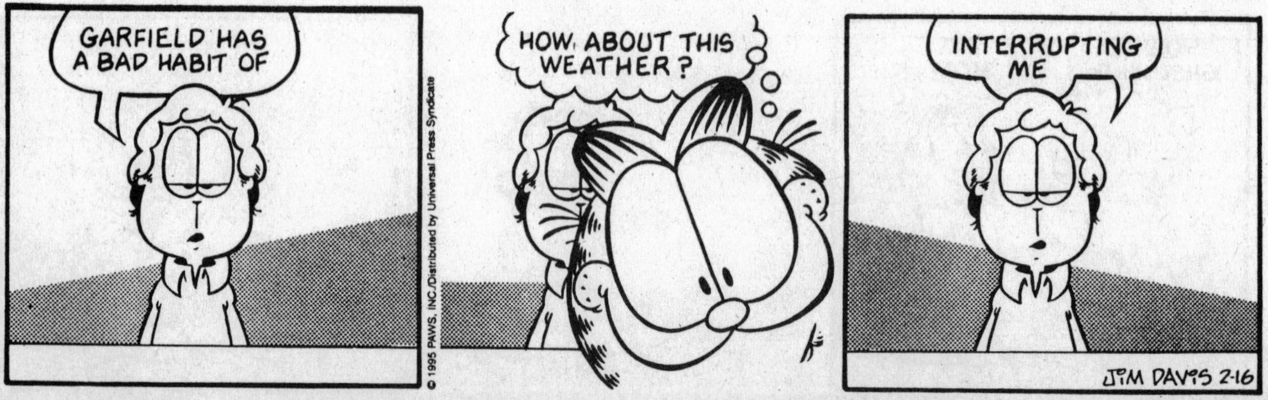
GARFIELD HAS A BAD HABIT OF
© 1995 PAWS, INC./Distributed by Universal Press Syndicate
HOW ABOUT THIS WEATHER?
INTERRUPTING ME
JIM DAVIS 2-16

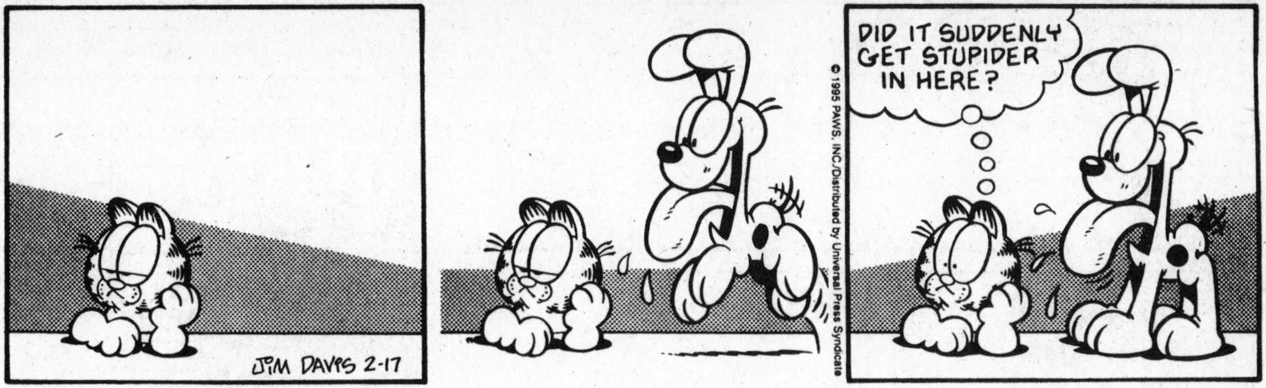
JIM DAVIS 2-17
© 1995 PAWS, INC./Distributed by Universal Press Syndicate
DID IT SUDDENLY GET STUPIDER IN HERE?

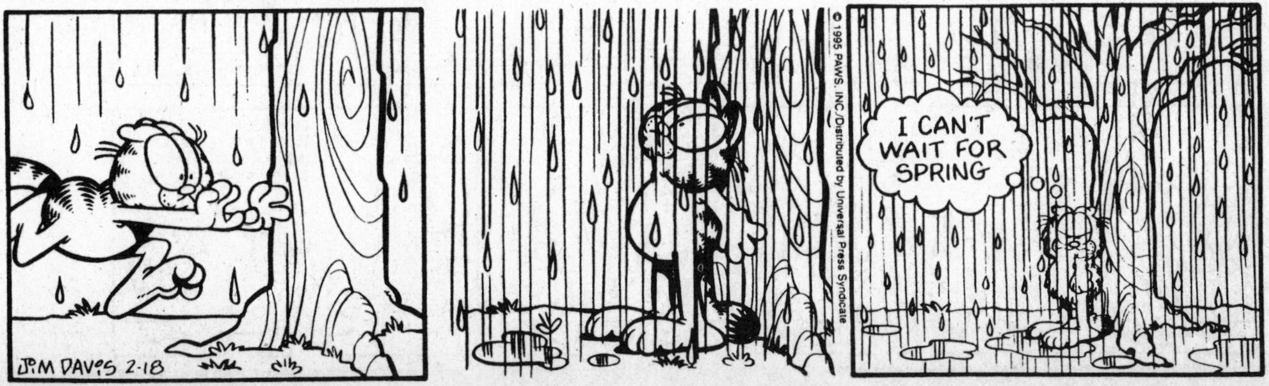
JIM DAVIS 2-18
© 1995 PAWS, INC./Distributed by Universal Press Syndicate
I CAN'T WAIT FOR SPRING

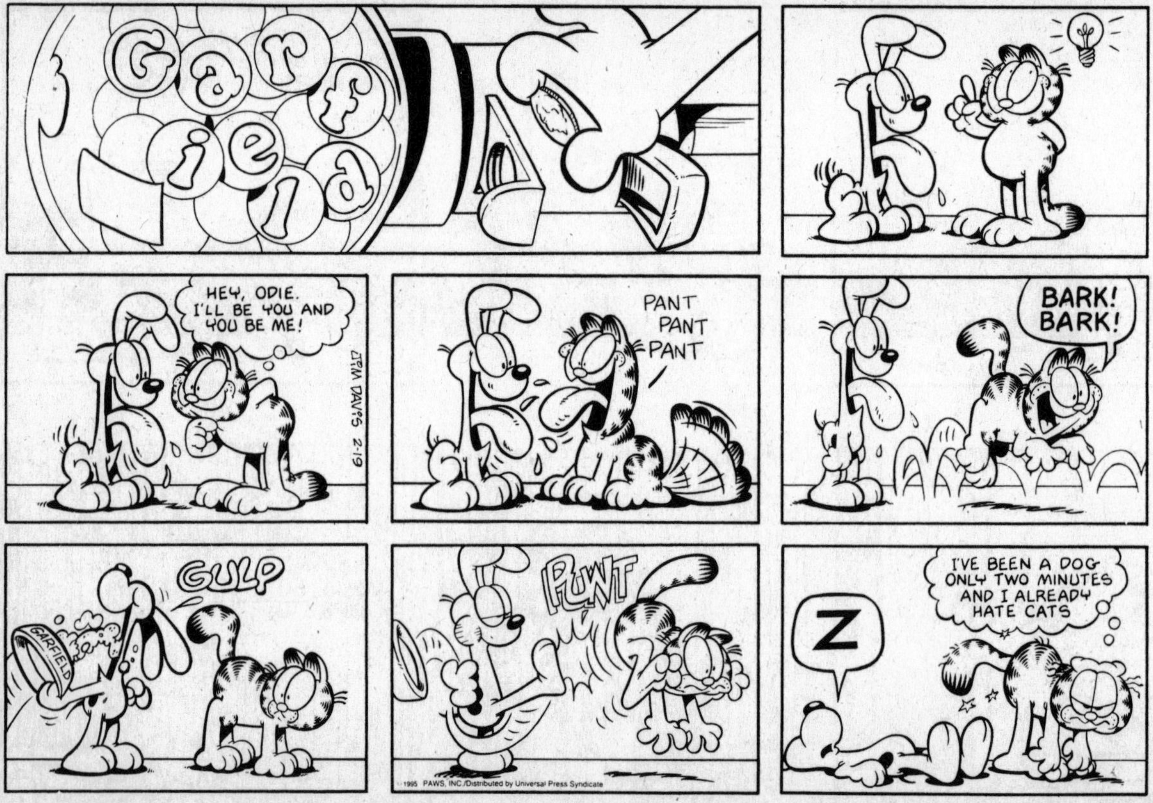
Garfield
HEY, ODIE. I'LL BE YOU AND YOU BE ME!
JIM DAVIS 2-19
PANT PANT PANT
BARK! BARK!
GULP
GARFIELD
PUNT
© 1995 PAWS, INC./Distributed by Universal Press Syndicate
Z
I'VE BEEN A DOG ONLY TWO MINUTES AND I ALREADY HATE CATS

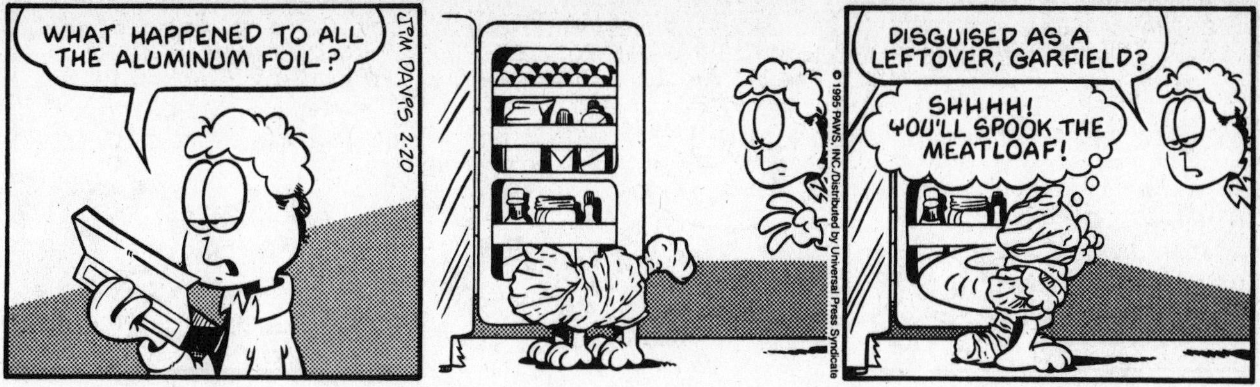

WHAT HAPPENED TO ALL THE ALUMINUM FOIL?
JIM DAVIS 2-20
© 1995 PAWS, INC./Distributed by Universal Press Syndicate
DISGUISED AS A LEFTOVER, GARFIELD?
SHHHHH! YOU'LL SPOOK THE MEATLOAF!

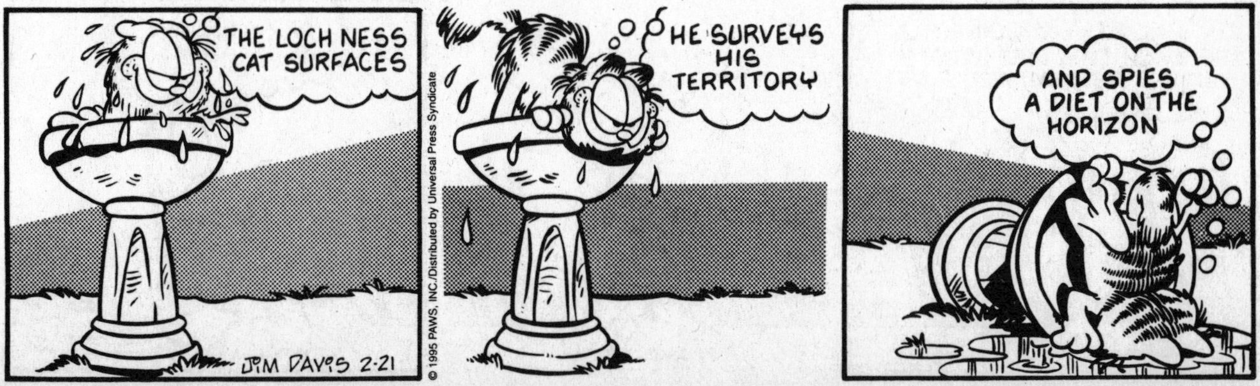

THE LOCH NESS CAT SURFACES
JIM DAVIS 2-21
© 1995 PAWS, INC./Distributed by Universal Press Syndicate
HE SURVEYS HIS TERRITORY
AND SPIES A DIET ON THE HORIZON

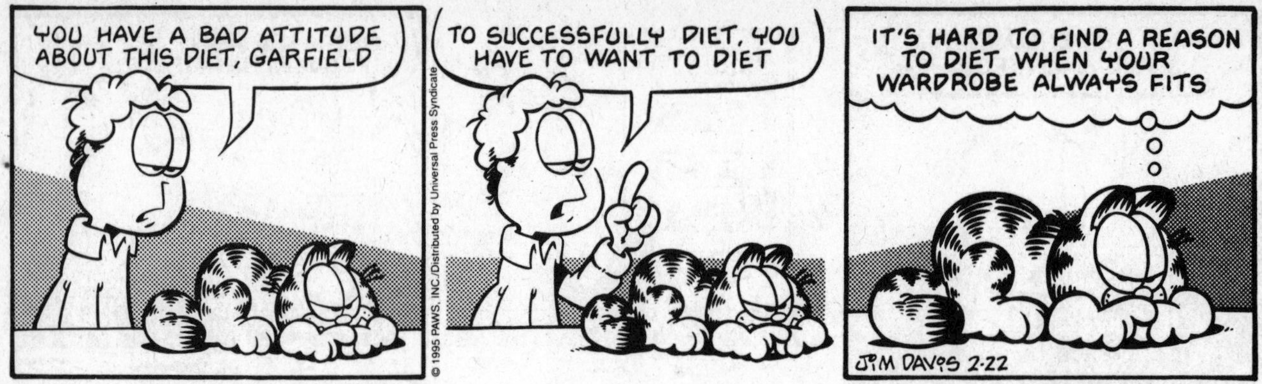
YOU HAVE A BAD ATTITUDE ABOUT THIS DIET, GARFIELD
TO SUCCESSFULLY DIET, YOU HAVE TO WANT TO DIET
IT'S HARD TO FIND A REASON TO DIET WHEN YOUR WARDROBE ALWAYS FITS
JIM DAVIS 2-22
© 1995 PAWS, INC./Distributed by Universal Press Syndicate

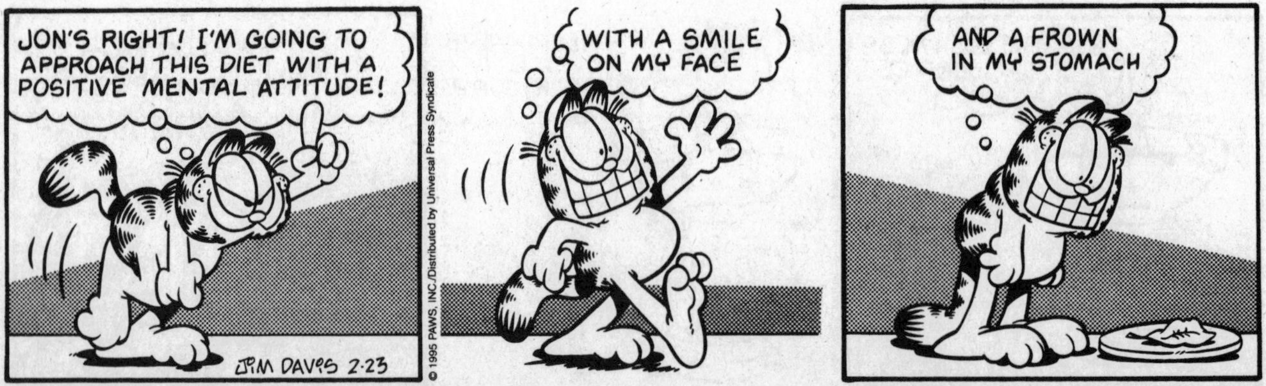
JON'S RIGHT! I'M GOING TO APPROACH THIS DIET WITH A POSITIVE MENTAL ATTITUDE!
JIM DAVIS 2-23
WITH A SMILE ON MY FACE
AND A FROWN IN MY STOMACH
© 1995 PAWS, INC./Distributed by Universal Press Syndicate

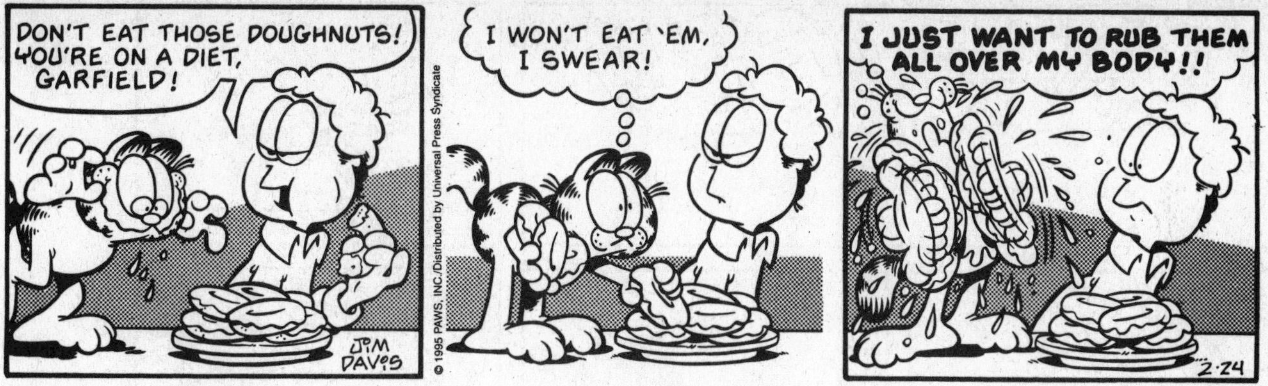
DON'T EAT THOSE DOUGHNUTS! YOU'RE ON A DIET, GARFIELD!
JIM DAVIS
© 1995 PAWS, INC./Distributed by Universal Press Syndicate
I WON'T EAT 'EM, I SWEAR!
I JUST WANT TO RUB THEM ALL OVER MY BODY!!
2·24

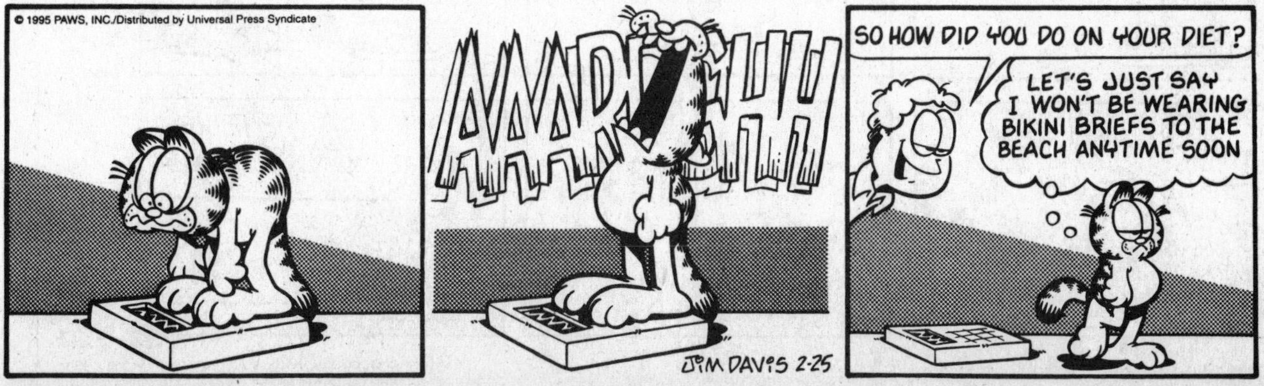
© 1995 PAWS, INC./Distributed by Universal Press Syndicate
AAAAAGHHH
JIM DAVIS 2·25
SO HOW DID YOU DO ON YOUR DIET?
LET'S JUST SAY I WON'T BE WEARING BIKINI BRIEFS TO THE BEACH ANYTIME SOON

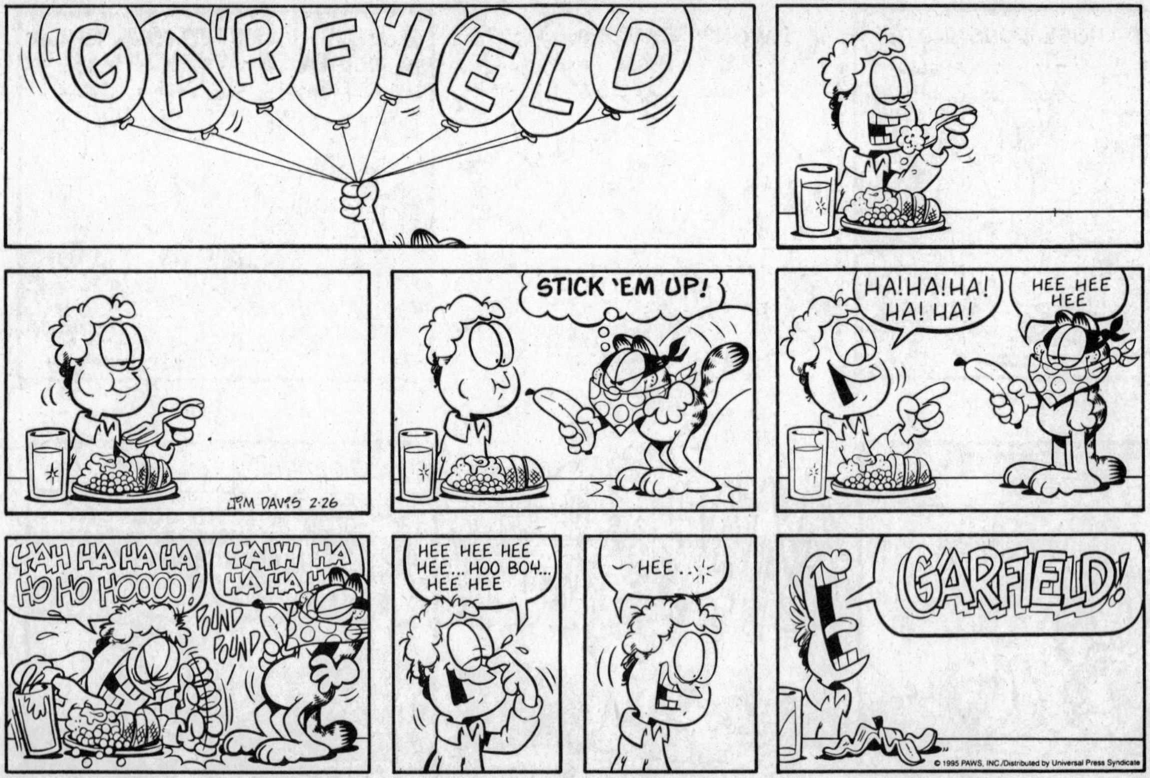
GARFIELD
JIM DAVIS 2·26
STICK 'EM UP!
HA! HA! HA! HA! HA!
HEE HEE HEE
YAH HA HA HA HO HO HOOOO!
YAHH HA HA HA H
POUND POUND
HEE HEE HEE HEE... HOO BOY... HEE HEE
HEE...
GARFIELD!
© 1995 PAWS, INC./Distributed by Universal Press Syndicate

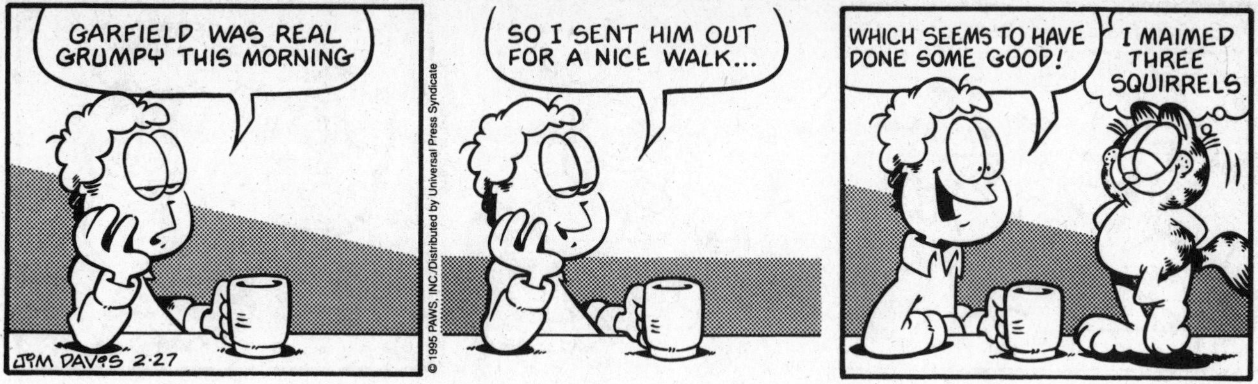
GARFIELD WAS REAL GRUMPY THIS MORNING
JIM DAVIS 2·27
SO I SENT HIM OUT FOR A NICE WALK...
WHICH SEEMS TO HAVE DONE SOME GOOD!
I MAIMED THREE SQUIRRELS
© 1995 PAWS, INC./Distributed by Universal Press Syndicate

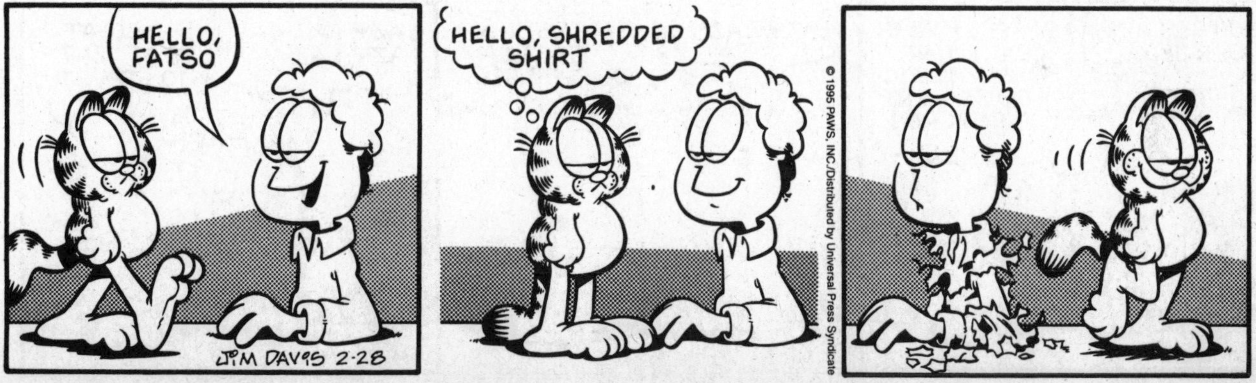
HELLO, FATSO
JIM DAVIS 2·28
HELLO, SHREDDED SHIRT
© 1995 PAWS, INC./Distributed by Universal Press Syndicate

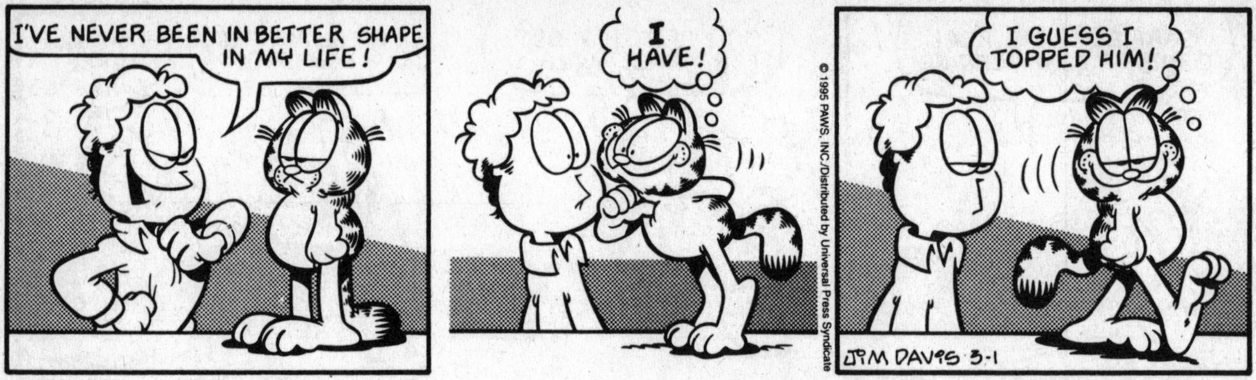
I'VE NEVER BEEN IN BETTER SHAPE IN MY LIFE!
I HAVE!
I GUESS I TOPPED HIM!
© 1995 PAWS, INC./Distributed by Universal Press Syndicate
JIM DAVIS 3-1

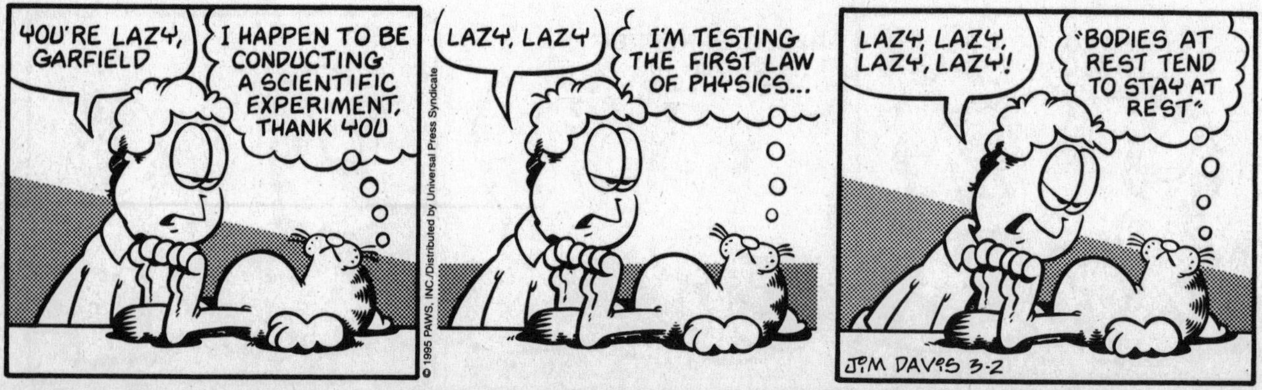
YOU'RE LAZY, GARFIELD
I HAPPEN TO BE CONDUCTING A SCIENTIFIC EXPERIMENT, THANK YOU
LAZY, LAZY
I'M TESTING THE FIRST LAW OF PHYSICS...
LAZY, LAZY, LAZY, LAZY!
"BODIES AT REST TEND TO STAY AT REST"
© 1995 PAWS, INC./Distributed by Universal Press Syndicate
JIM DAVIS 3-2

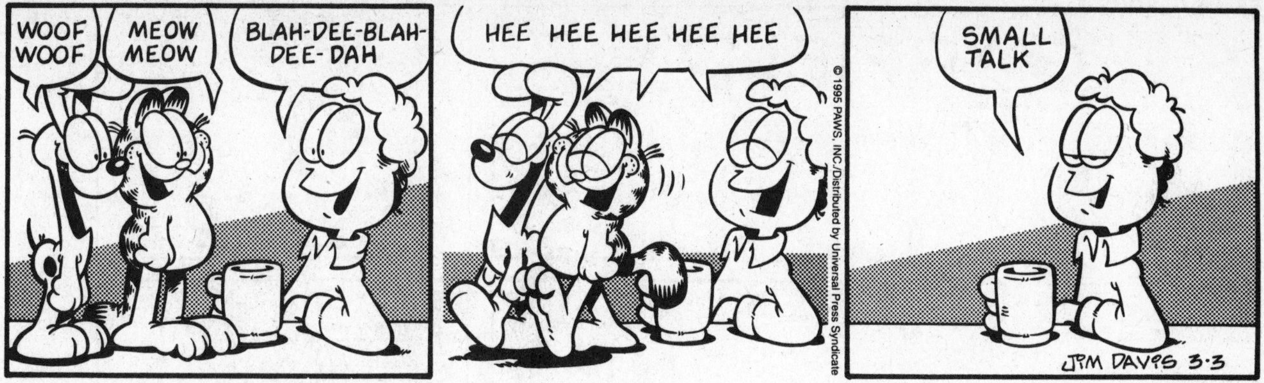
WOOF WOOF
MEOW MEOW
BLAH-DEE-BLAH-DEE-DAH
HEE HEE HEE HEE HEE
© 1995 PAWS, INC./Distributed by Universal Press Syndicate
SMALL TALK
JIM DAVIS 3-3

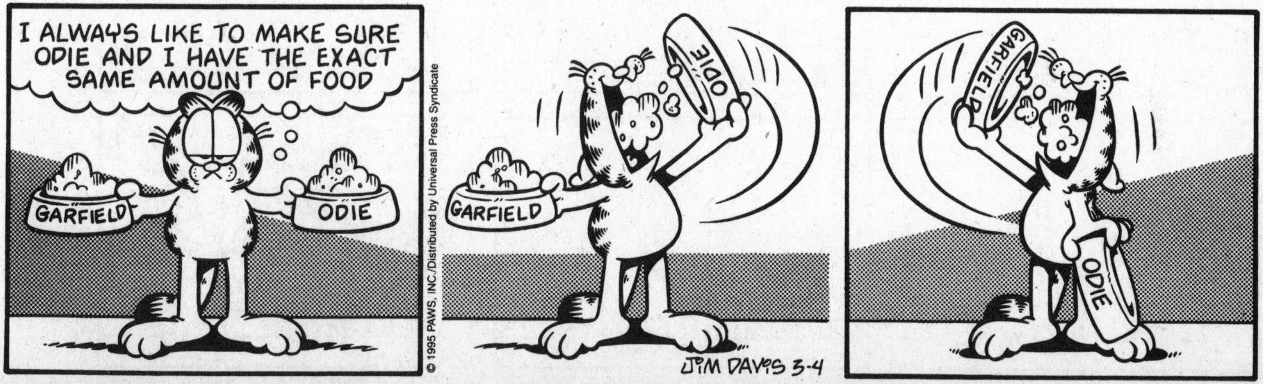
I ALWAYS LIKE TO MAKE SURE ODIE AND I HAVE THE EXACT SAME AMOUNT OF FOOD
GARFIELD
ODIE
© 1995 PAWS, INC./Distributed by Universal Press Syndicate
GARFIELD
ODIE
JIM DAVIS 3-4
GARFIELD
ODIE

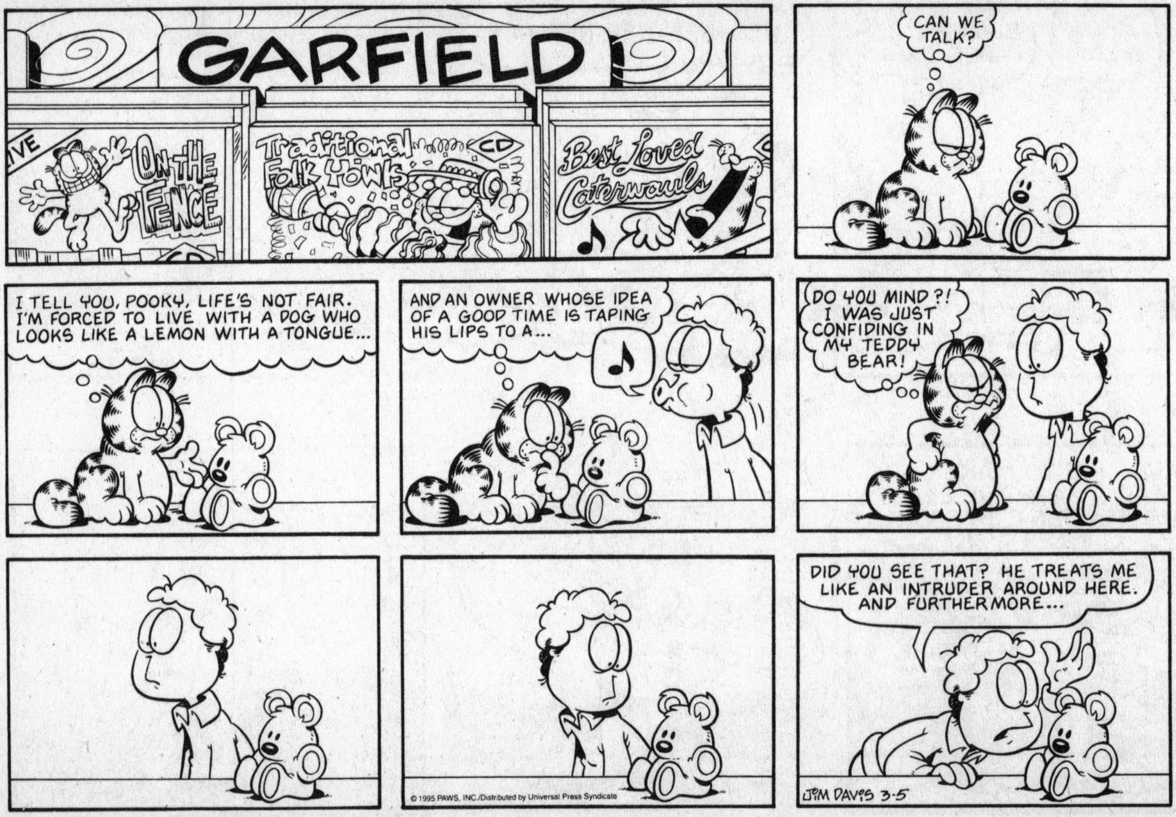
GARFIELD
LIVE
ON THE FENCE
CD
Traditional Folk Yowls
CD
Best Loved Caterwauls
CAN WE TALK?
I TELL YOU, POOKY, LIFE'S NOT FAIR. I'M FORCED TO LIVE WITH A DOG WHO LOOKS LIKE A LEMON WITH A TONGUE...
AND AN OWNER WHOSE IDEA OF A GOOD TIME IS TAPING HIS LIPS TO A...
DO YOU MIND?! I WAS JUST CONFIDING IN MY TEDDY BEAR!
© 1995 PAWS, INC./Distributed by Universal Press Syndicate
DID YOU SEE THAT? HE TREATS ME LIKE AN INTRUDER AROUND HERE. AND FURTHERMORE...
JIM DAVIS 3-5

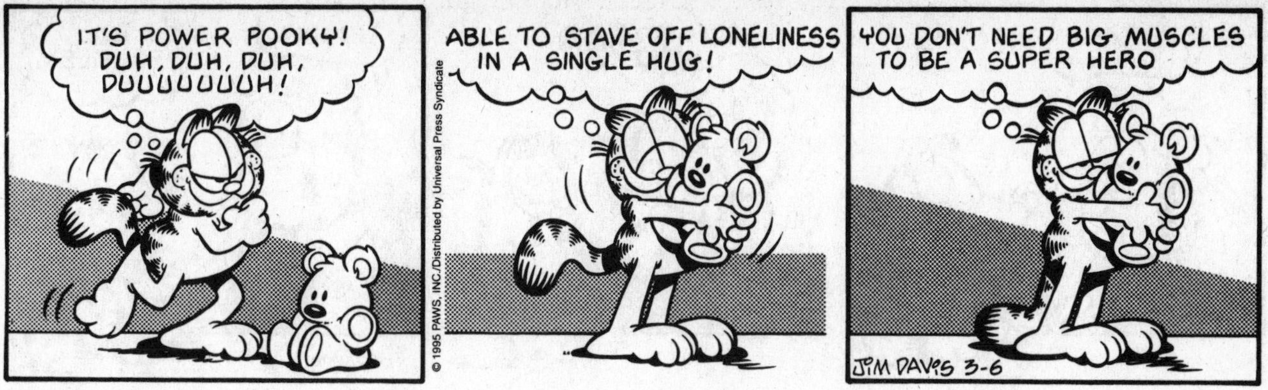
IT'S POWER POOKY! DUH, DUH, DUH, DUUUUUUUH!
ABLE TO STAVE OFF LONELINESS IN A SINGLE HUG!
© 1995 PAWS, INC./Distributed by Universal Press Syndicate
YOU DON'T NEED BIG MUSCLES TO BE A SUPER HERO
JIM DAVIS 3-6

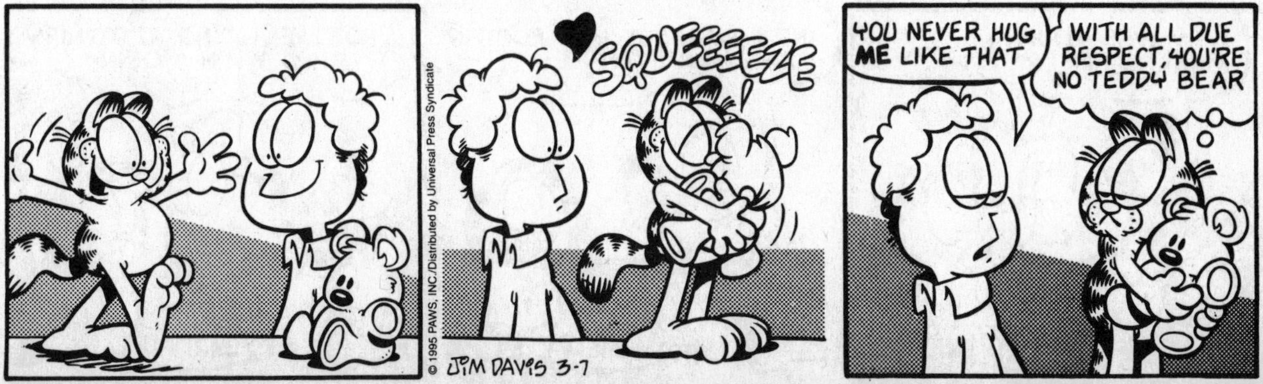
© 1995 PAWS, INC./Distributed by Universal Press Syndicate
SQUEEEEEZE
JIM DAVIS 3-7
YOU NEVER HUG **ME** LIKE THAT
WITH ALL DUE RESPECT, YOU'RE NO TEDDY BEAR

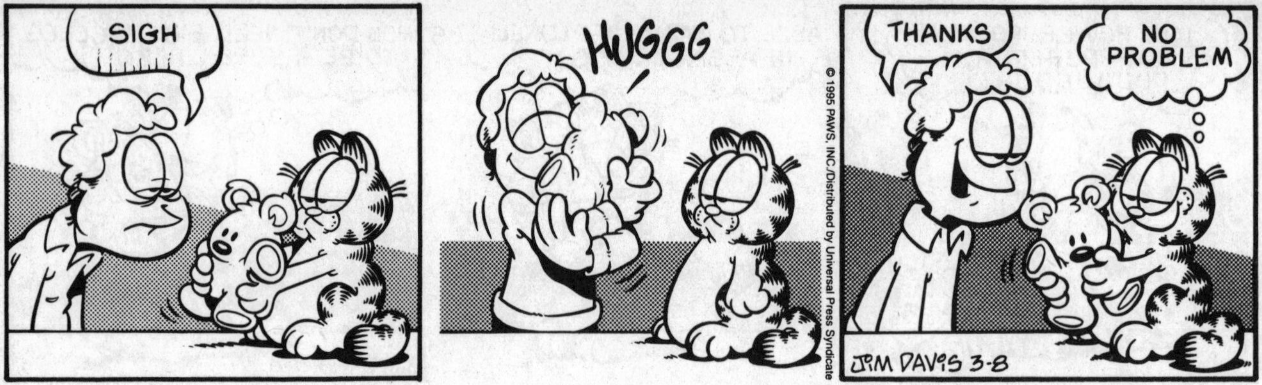
SIGH
HUGGG
© 1995 PAWS, INC./Distributed by Universal Press Syndicate
THANKS
NO PROBLEM
JIM DAVIS 3-8

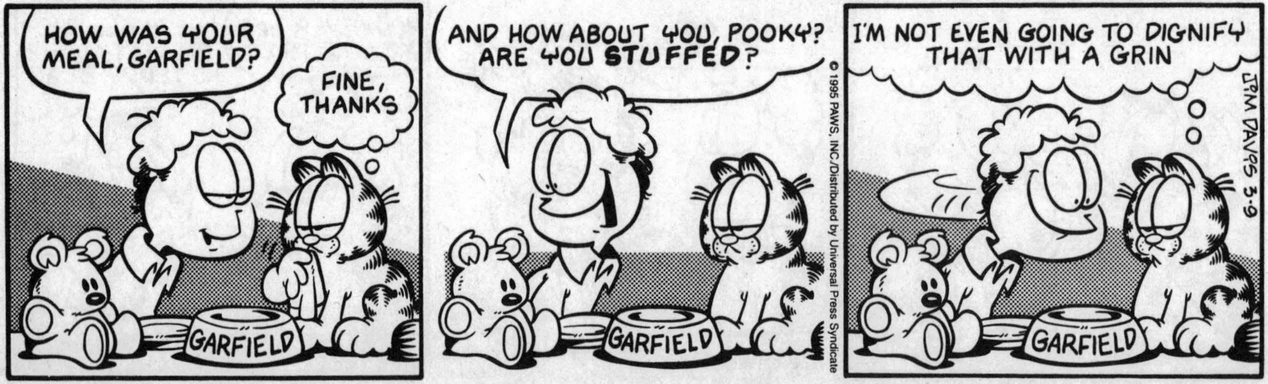
HOW WAS YOUR MEAL, GARFIELD?
FINE, THANKS
GARFIELD
AND HOW ABOUT YOU, POOKY? ARE YOU **STUFFED**?
GARFIELD
© 1995 PAWS, INC./Distributed by Universal Press Syndicate
I'M NOT EVEN GOING TO DIGNIFY THAT WITH A GRIN
JIM DAVIS 3-9
GARFIELD

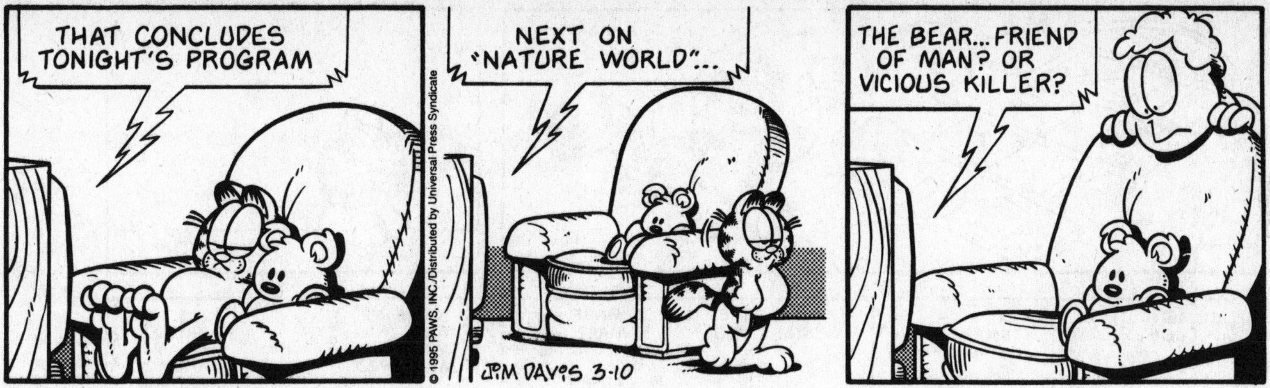
THAT CONCLUDES TONIGHT'S PROGRAM
NEXT ON "NATURE WORLD"...
THE BEAR... FRIEND OF MAN? OR VICIOUS KILLER?
© 1995 PAWS, INC./Distributed by Universal Press Syndicate
JIM DAVIS 3-10

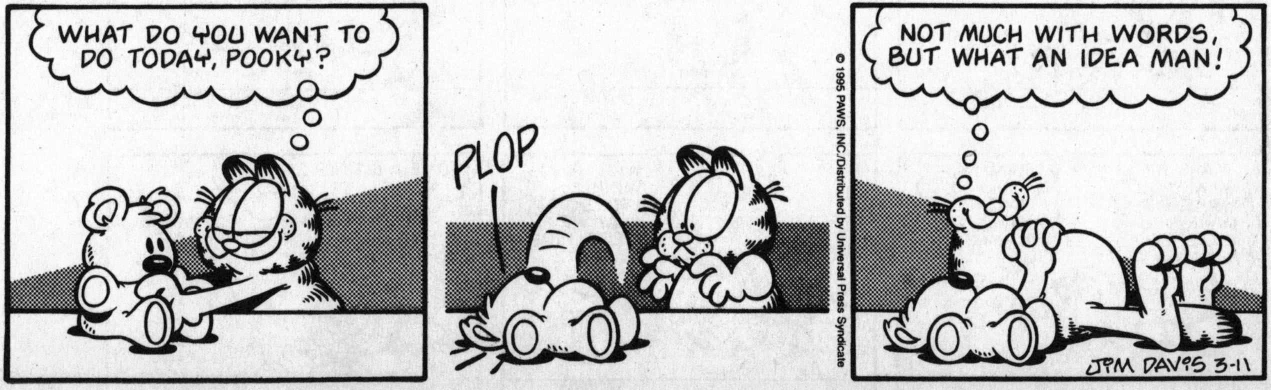
WHAT DO YOU WANT TO DO TODAY, POOKY?
PLOP
NOT MUCH WITH WORDS, BUT WHAT AN IDEA MAN!
© 1995 PAWS, INC./Distributed by Universal Press Syndicate
JIM DAVIS 3-11

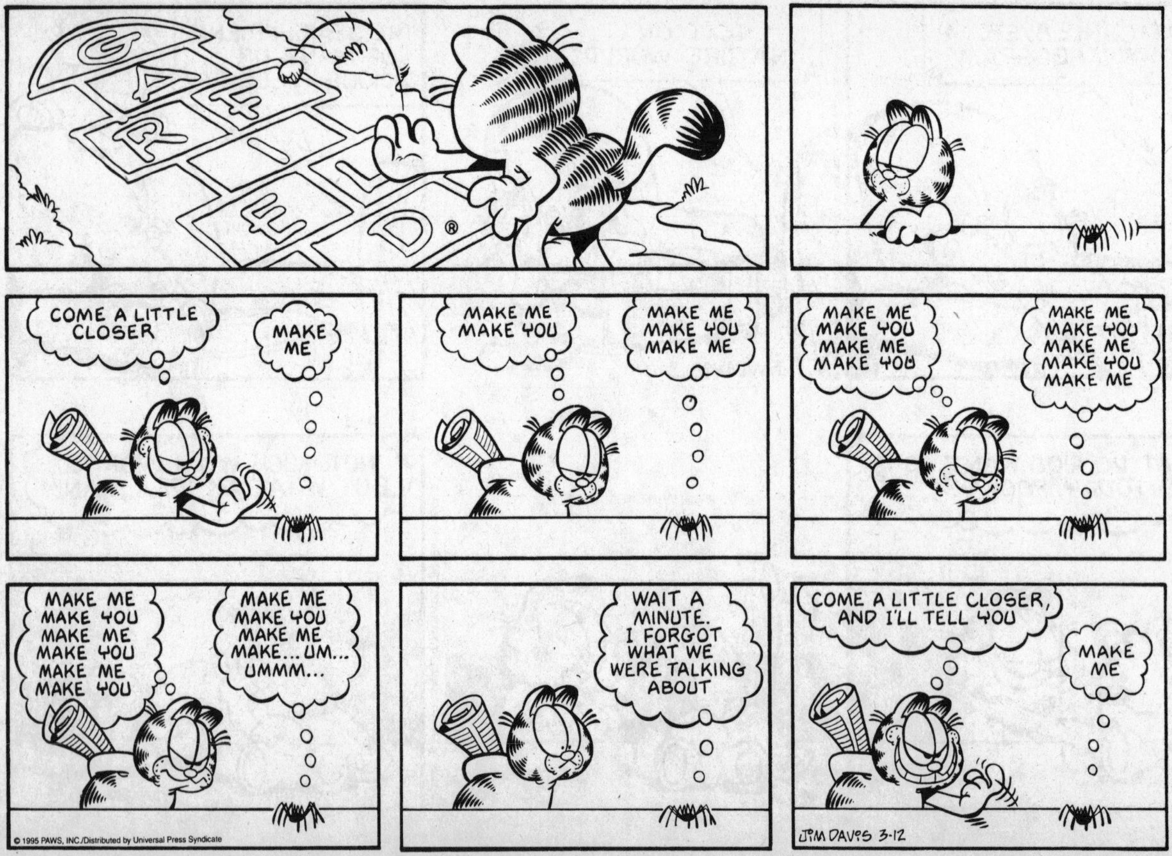
GARFIELD®
COME A LITTLE CLOSER
MAKE ME
MAKE ME MAKE YOU
MAKE ME MAKE YOU MAKE ME
MAKE ME MAKE YOU MAKE ME MAKE YOU
MAKE ME MAKE YOU MAKE ME MAKE YOU MAKE ME
MAKE ME MAKE YOU MAKE ME MAKE YOU MAKE ME MAKE YOU
MAKE ME MAKE YOU MAKE ME MAKE... UM... UMMM...
WAIT A MINUTE. I FORGOT WHAT WE WERE TALKING ABOUT
COME A LITTLE CLOSER, AND I'LL TELL YOU
MAKE ME
JIM DAVIS 3-12

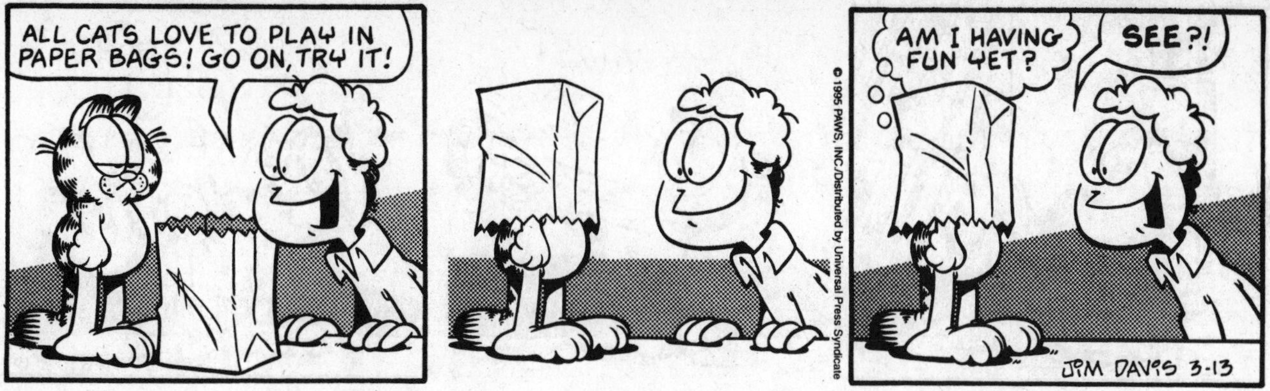
ALL CATS LOVE TO PLAY IN PAPER BAGS! GO ON, TRY IT!
AM I HAVING FUN YET?
SEE?!
JIM DAVIS 3-13
© 1995 PAWS, INC./Distributed by Universal Press Syndicate

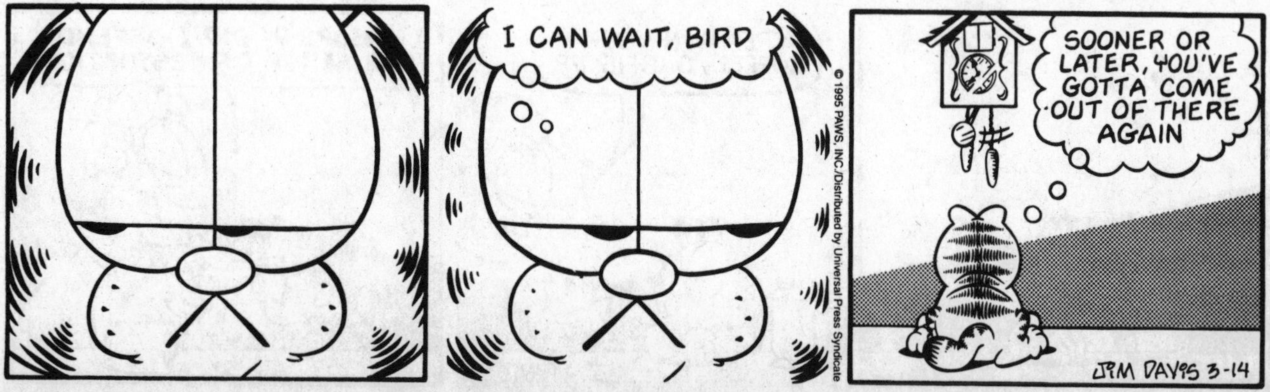
I CAN WAIT, BIRD
SOONER OR LATER, YOU'VE GOTTA COME OUT OF THERE AGAIN
JIM DAVIS 3-14
© 1995 PAWS, INC./Distributed by Universal Press Syndicate

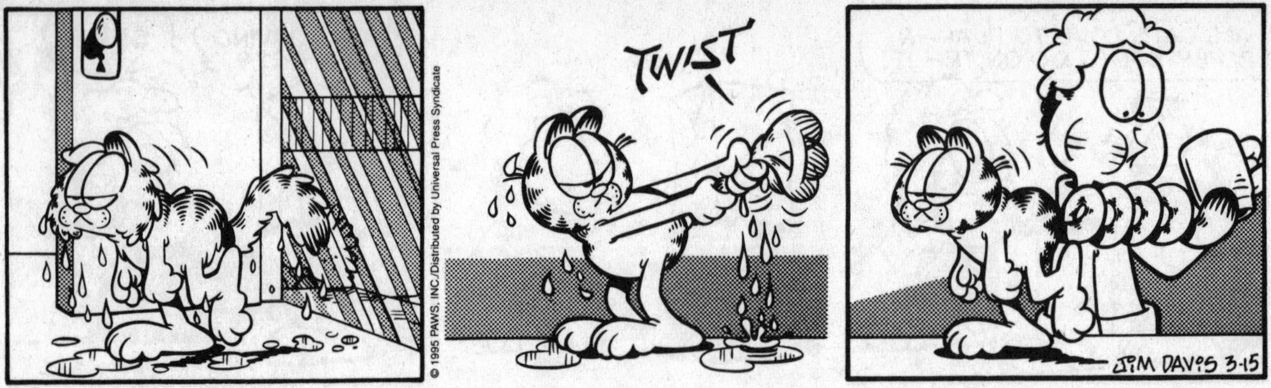

TWIST
© 1995 PAWS, INC./Distributed by Universal Press Syndicate
JIM DAVIS 3-15

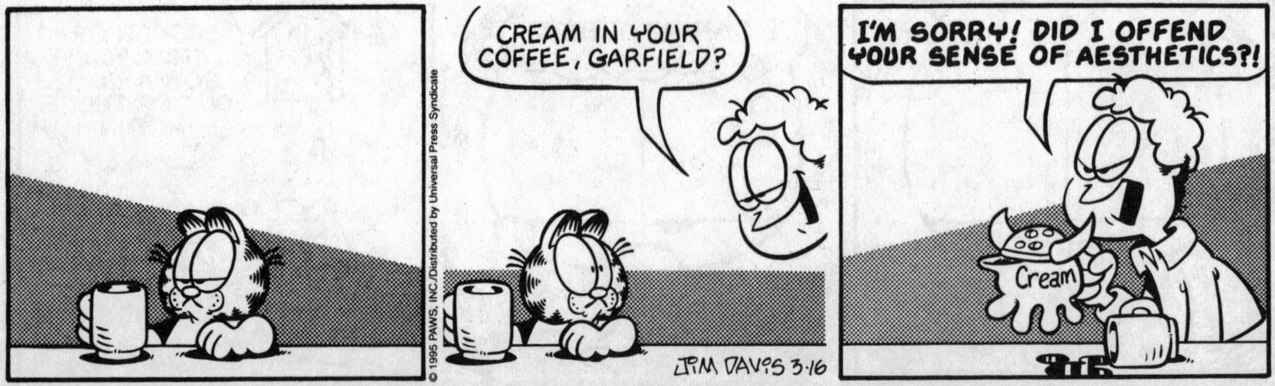

CREAM IN YOUR COFFEE, GARFIELD?
I'M SORRY! DID I OFFEND YOUR SENSE OF AESTHETICS?!
Cream
© 1995 PAWS, INC./Distributed by Universal Press Syndicate
JIM DAVIS 3-16

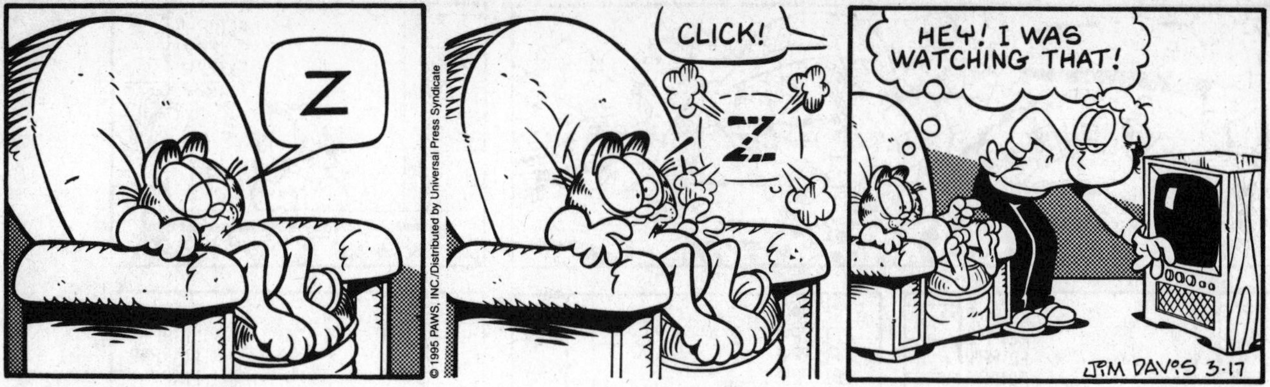
Z
© 1995 PAWS, INC./Distributed by Universal Press Syndicate
CLICK!
Z
HEY! I WAS WATCHING THAT!
JIM DAVIS 3-17

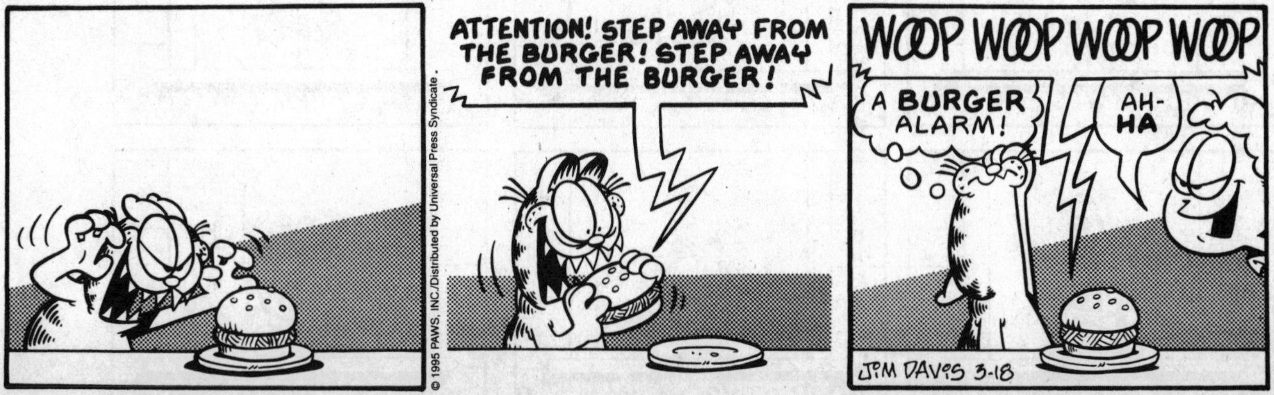
© 1995 PAWS, INC./Distributed by Universal Press Syndicate
ATTENTION! STEP AWAY FROM THE BURGER! STEP AWAY FROM THE BURGER!
WOOP WOOP WOOP WOOP
A BURGER ALARM!
AH-HA
JIM DAVIS 3-18

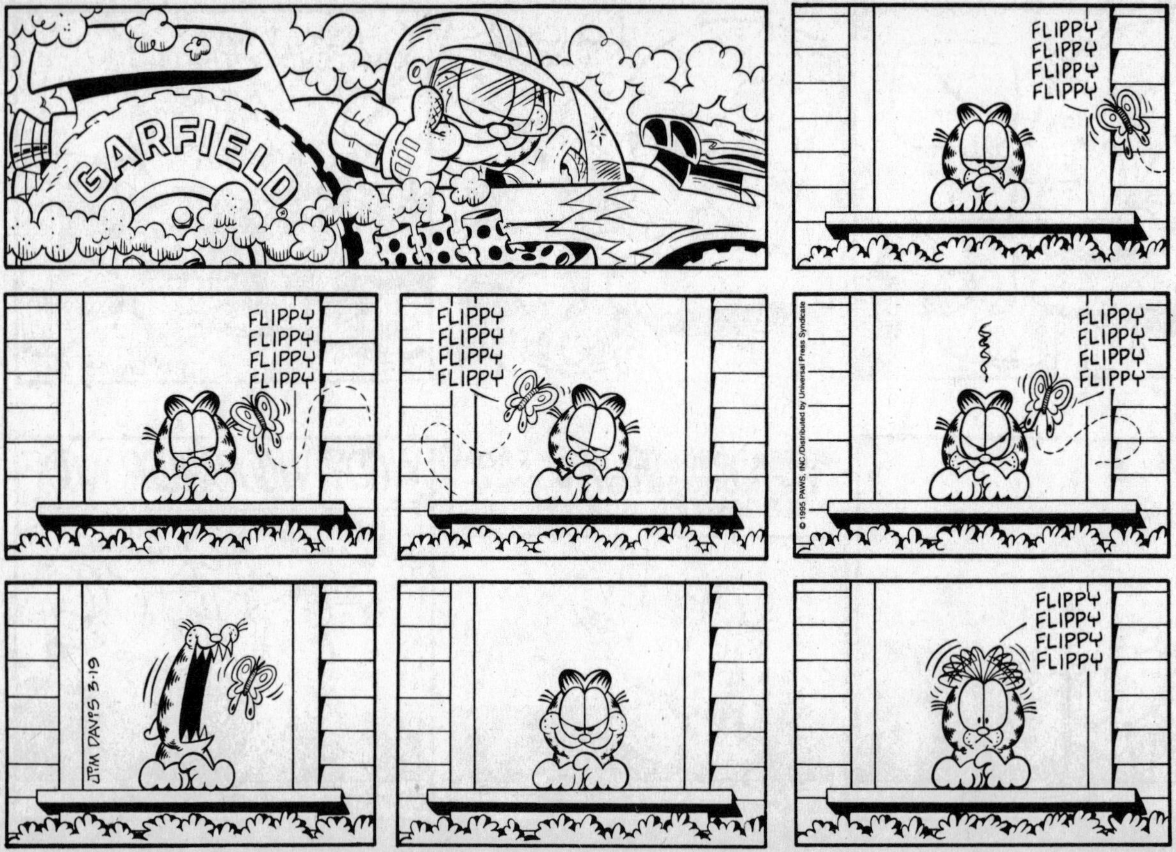
GARFIELD
FLIPPY FLIPPY FLIPPY FLIPPY
FLIPPY FLIPPY FLIPPY FLIPPY
FLIPPY FLIPPY FLIPPY FLIPPY
FLIPPY FLIPPY FLIPPY FLIPPY
© 1995 PAWS, INC./Distributed by Universal Press Syndicate
JPM DAVIS 3-19
FLIPPY FLIPPY FLIPPY FLIPPY

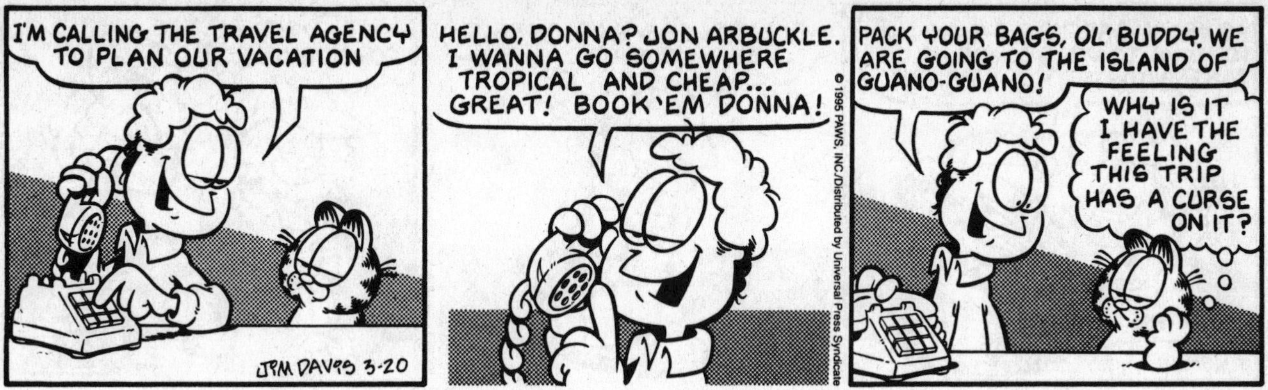
I'M CALLING THE TRAVEL AGENCY TO PLAN OUR VACATION
JIM DAVIS 3-20
HELLO, DONNA? JON ARBUCKLE. I WANNA GO SOMEWHERE TROPICAL AND CHEAP... GREAT! BOOK 'EM DONNA!
© 1995 PAWS, INC./Distributed by Universal Press Syndicate
PACK YOUR BAGS, OL' BUDDY. WE ARE GOING TO THE ISLAND OF GUANO-GUANO!
WHY IS IT I HAVE THE FEELING THIS TRIP HAS A CURSE ON IT?

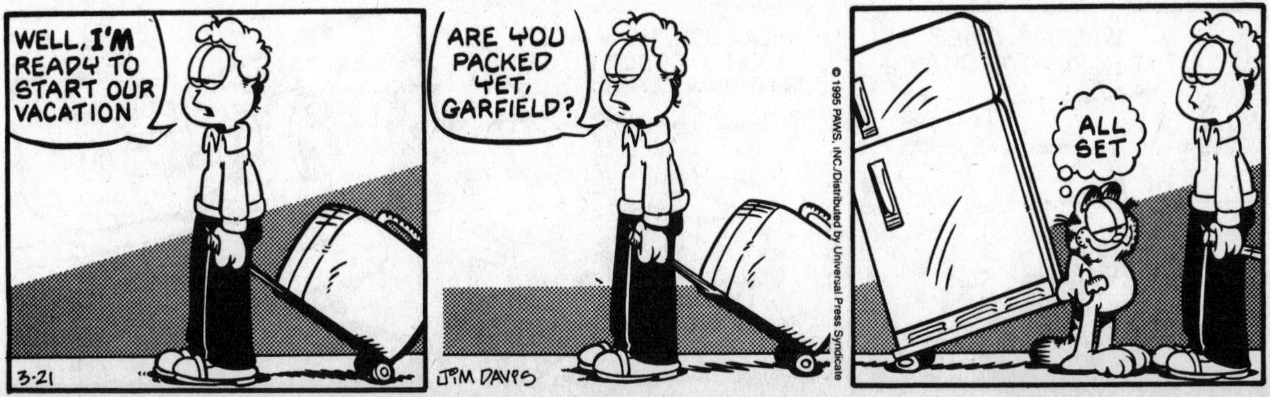
WELL, I'M READY TO START OUR VACATION
3-21
ARE YOU PACKED YET, GARFIELD?
JIM DAVIS
© 1995 PAWS, INC./Distributed by Universal Press Syndicate
ALL SET

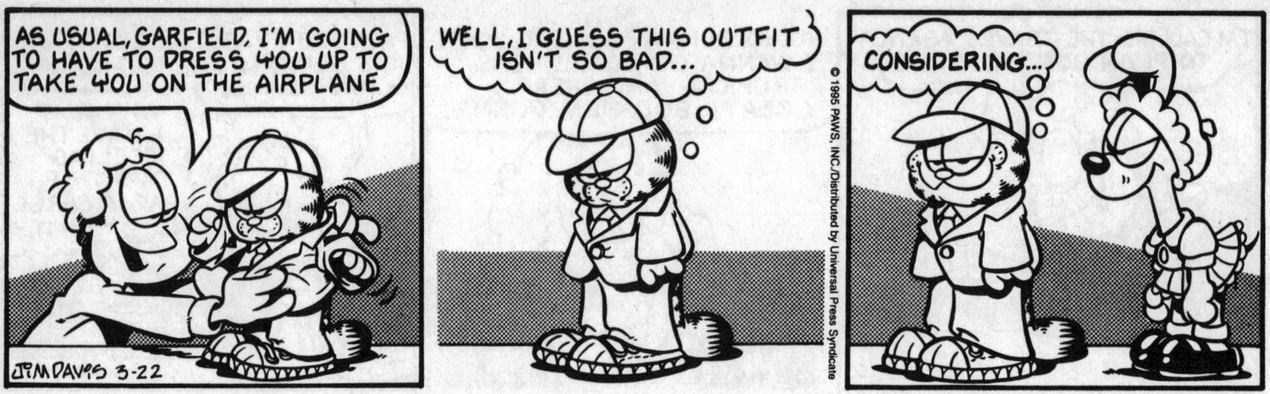
AS USUAL, GARFIELD, I'M GOING TO HAVE TO DRESS YOU UP TO TAKE YOU ON THE AIRPLANE
JIM DAVIS 3-22
WELL, I GUESS THIS OUTFIT ISN'T SO BAD...
© 1995 PAWS, INC./Distributed by Universal Press Syndicate
CONSIDERING...

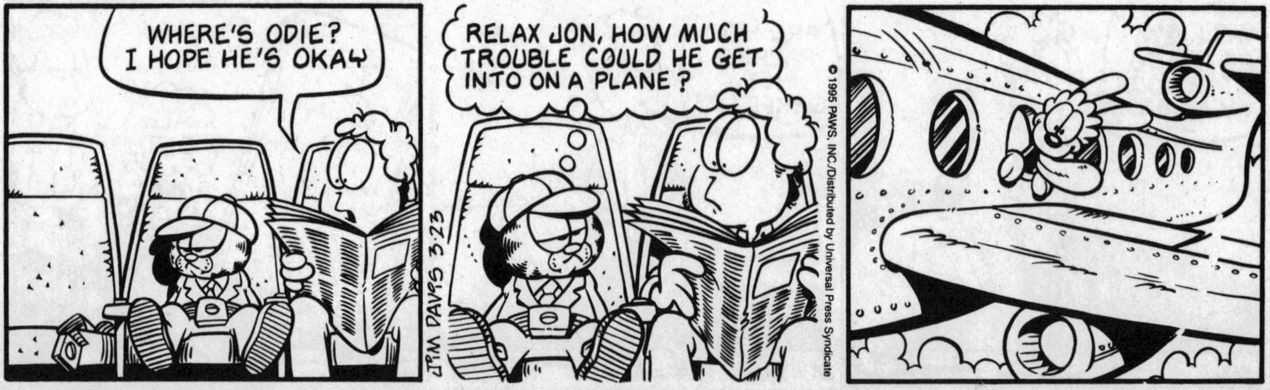
WHERE'S ODIE? I HOPE HE'S OKAY
JIM DAVIS 3-23
RELAX JON, HOW MUCH TROUBLE COULD HE GET INTO ON A PLANE?
© 1995 PAWS, INC./Distributed by Universal Press Syndicate

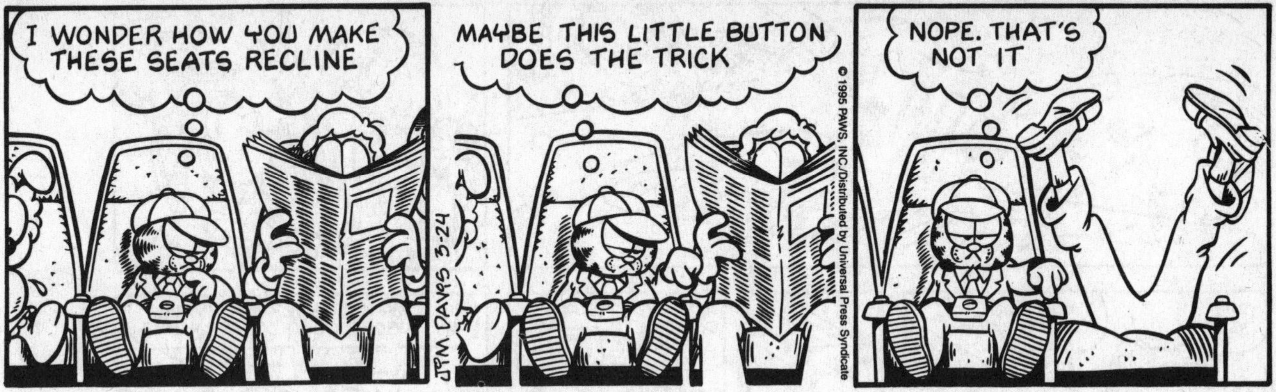
I WONDER HOW YOU MAKE THESE SEATS RECLINE
JIM DAVIS 3-24
MAYBE THIS LITTLE BUTTON DOES THE TRICK
© 1995 PAWS, INC./Distributed by Universal Press Syndicate
NOPE. THAT'S NOT IT

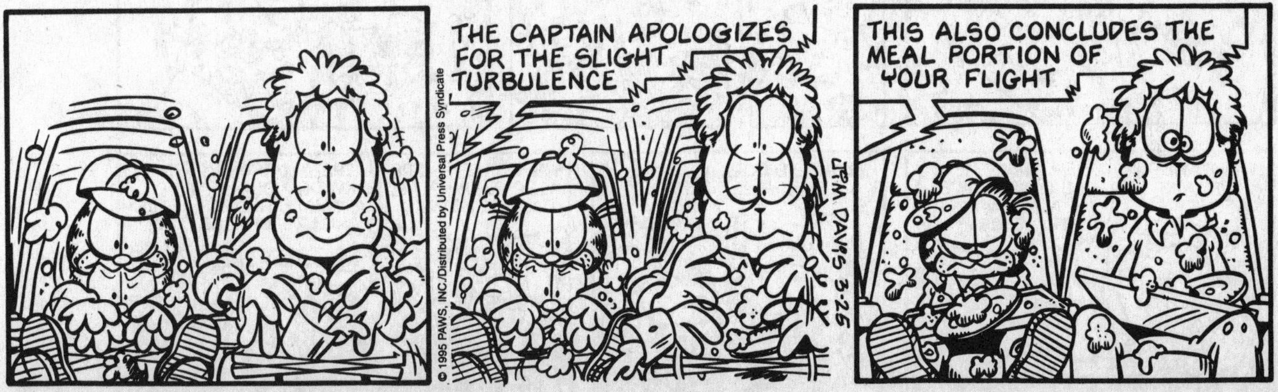
© 1995 PAWS, INC./Distributed by Universal Press Syndicate
THE CAPTAIN APOLOGIZES FOR THE SLIGHT TURBULENCE
JIM DAVIS 3-25
THIS ALSO CONCLUDES THE MEAL PORTION OF YOUR FLIGHT

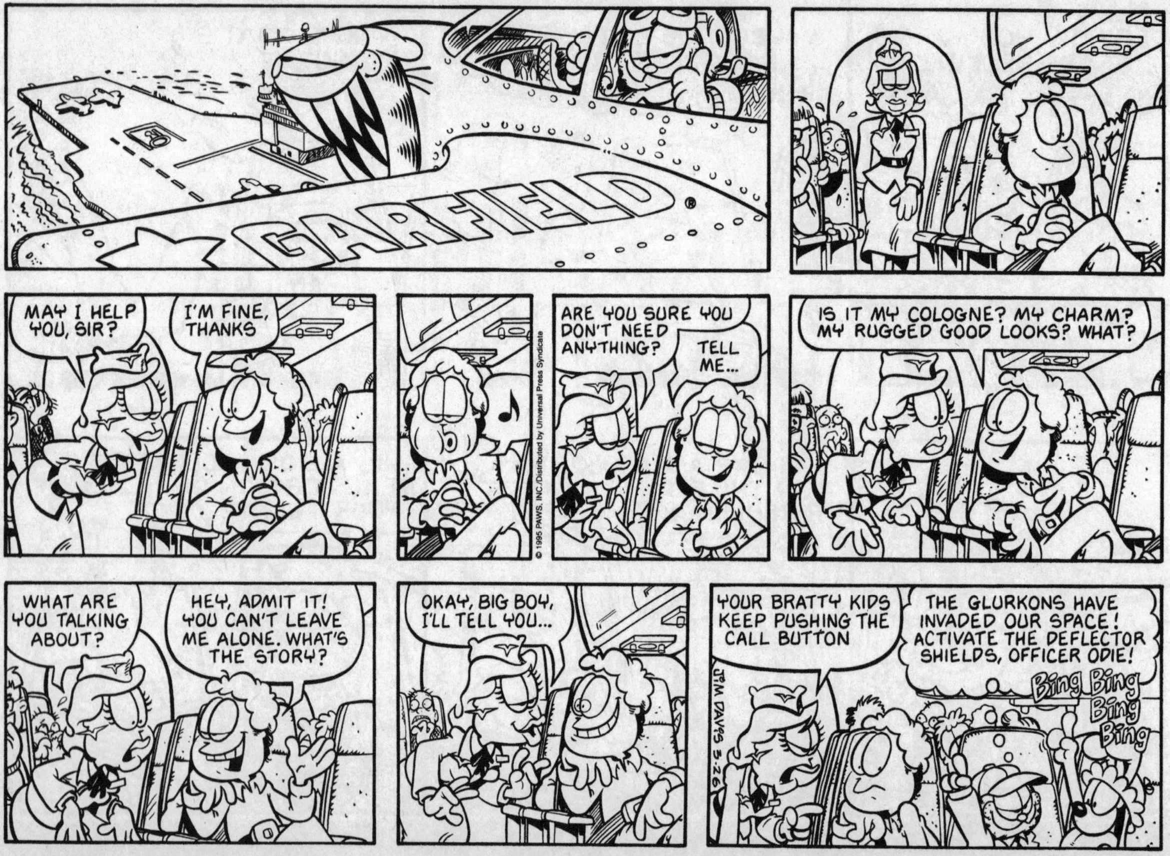
GARFIELD®
MAY I HELP YOU, SIR?
I'M FINE, THANKS
© 1995 PAWS, INC./Distributed by Universal Press Syndicate
ARE YOU SURE YOU DON'T NEED ANYTHING?
TELL ME...
IS IT MY COLOGNE? MY CHARM? MY RUGGED GOOD LOOKS? WHAT?
WHAT ARE YOU TALKING ABOUT?
HEY, ADMIT IT! YOU CAN'T LEAVE ME ALONE. WHAT'S THE STORY?
OKAY, BIG BOY, I'LL TELL YOU...
JIM DAVIS 3-26
YOUR BRATTY KIDS KEEP PUSHING THE CALL BUTTON
THE GLURKONS HAVE INVADED OUR SPACE! ACTIVATE THE DEFLECTOR SHIELDS, OFFICER ODIE!
Bing Bing Bing Bing

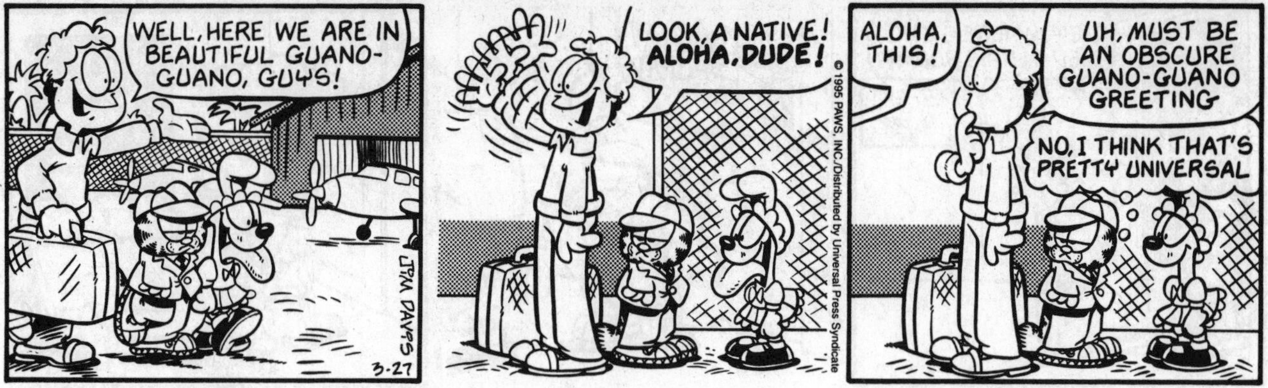
WELL, HERE WE ARE IN BEAUTIFUL GUANO-GUANO, GUYS!
JIM DAVIS 3-27
LOOK, A NATIVE! **ALOHA, DUDE!**
© 1995 PAWS, INC./Distributed by Universal Press Syndicate
ALOHA, THIS!
UH, MUST BE AN OBSCURE GUANO-GUANO GREETING
NO, I THINK THAT'S PRETTY UNIVERSAL

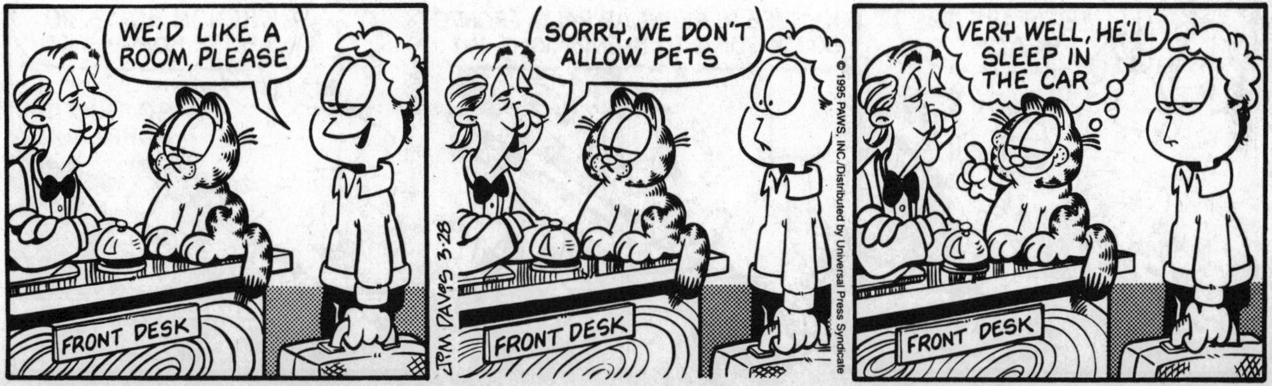
WE'D LIKE A ROOM, PLEASE
FRONT DESK
JIM DAVIS 3-28
SORRY, WE DON'T ALLOW PETS
FRONT DESK
© 1995 PAWS, INC./Distributed by Universal Press Syndicate
VERY WELL, HE'LL SLEEP IN THE CAR
FRONT DESK

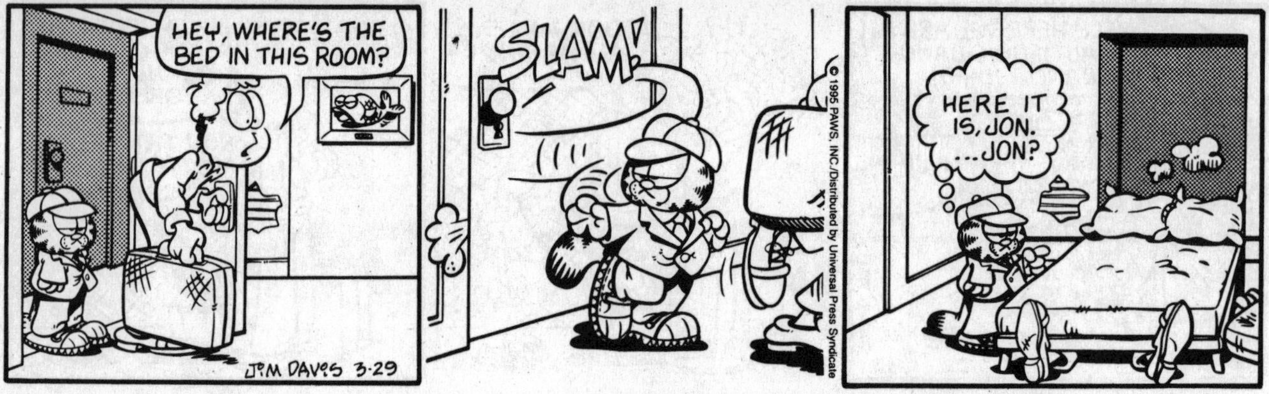
HEY, WHERE'S THE BED IN THIS ROOM?
JIM DAVIS 3-29
SLAM!
© 1995 PAWS, INC./Distributed by Universal Press Syndicate
HERE IT IS, JON. ...JON?

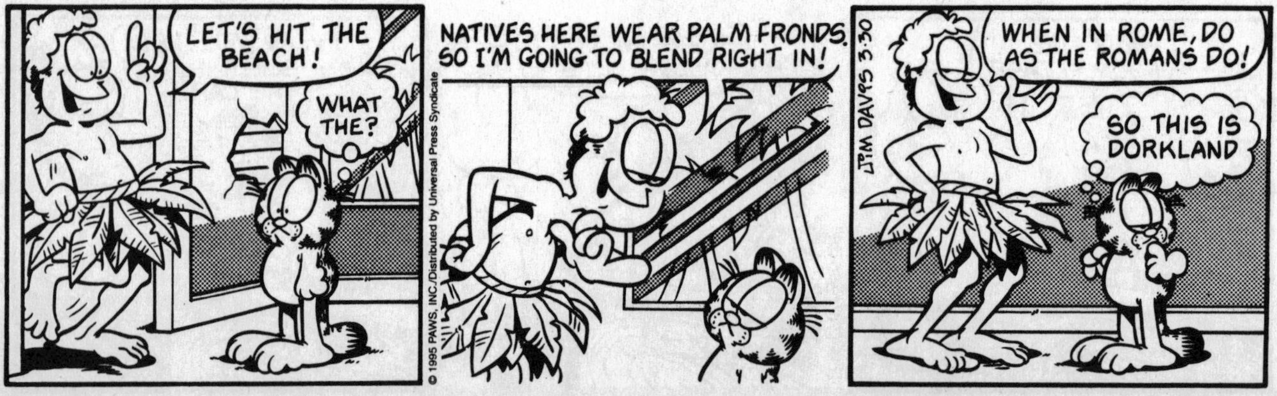
LET'S HIT THE BEACH!
WHAT THE?
© 1995 PAWS, INC./Distributed by Universal Press Syndicate
NATIVES HERE WEAR PALM FRONDS. SO I'M GOING TO BLEND RIGHT IN!
JIM DAVIS 3-30
WHEN IN ROME, DO AS THE ROMANS DO!
SO THIS IS DORKLAND

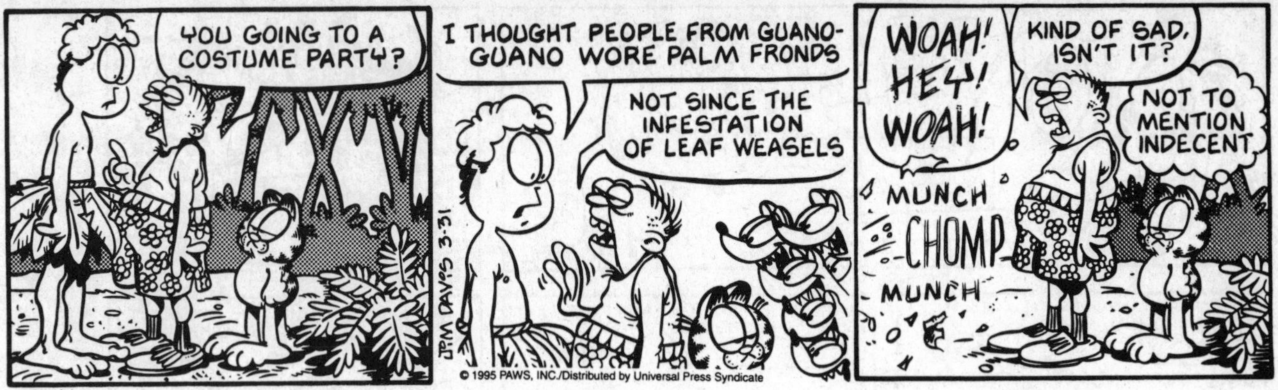
YOU GOING TO A COSTUME PARTY?
I THOUGHT PEOPLE FROM GUANO-GUANO WORE PALM FRONDS
NOT SINCE THE INFESTATION OF LEAF WEASELS
JPM DAVPS 3-31
© 1995 PAWS, INC./Distributed by Universal Press Syndicate
WOAH! HEY! WOAH!
MUNCH
CHOMP
MUNCH
KIND OF SAD, ISN'T IT?
NOT TO MENTION INDECENT

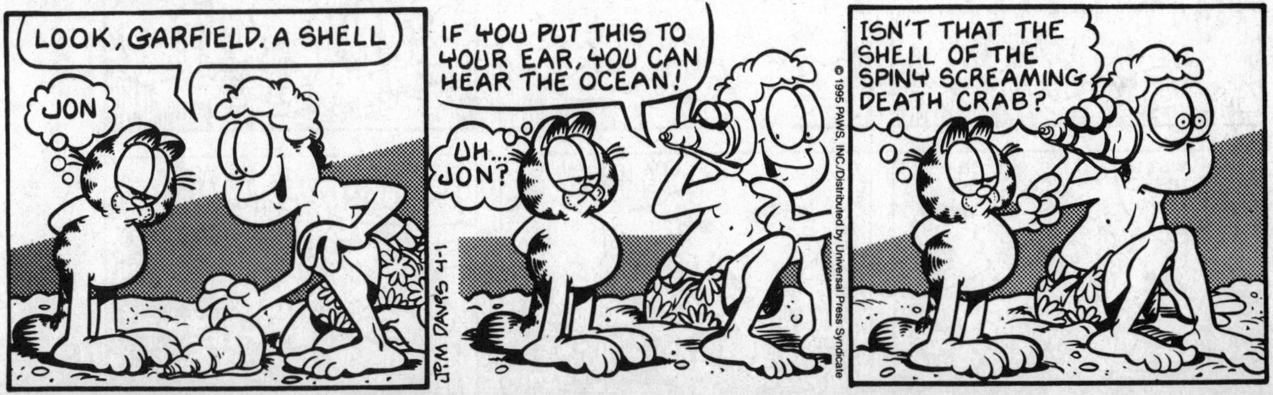
LOOK, GARFIELD. A SHELL
JON
JPM DAVPS 4-1
IF YOU PUT THIS TO YOUR EAR, YOU CAN HEAR THE OCEAN!
UH... JON?
© 1995 PAWS, INC./Distributed by Universal Press Syndicate
ISN'T THAT THE SHELL OF THE SPINY SCREAMING DEATH CRAB?

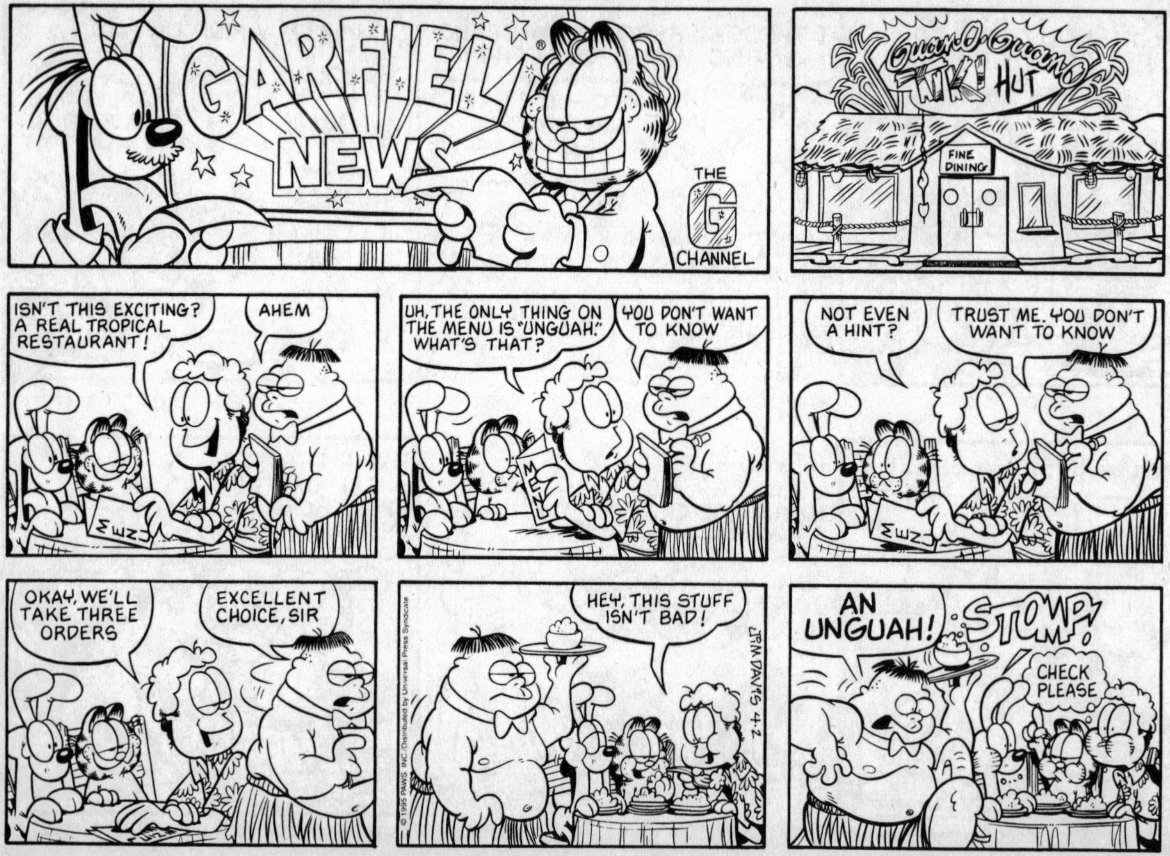
GARFIELD® NEWS
THE G CHANNEL
Guano-Guano TIKI HUT
FINE DINING
ISN'T THIS EXCITING? A REAL TROPICAL RESTAURANT!
AHEM
MENU
UH, THE ONLY THING ON THE MENU IS "UNGUAH." WHAT'S THAT?
YOU DON'T WANT TO KNOW
NOT EVEN A HINT?
TRUST ME. YOU DON'T WANT TO KNOW
OKAY, WE'LL TAKE THREE ORDERS
EXCELLENT CHOICE, SIR
© 1995 PAWS, INC./Distributed by Universal Press Syndicate
HEY, THIS STUFF ISN'T BAD!
JIM DAVIS 4-2
AN UNGUAH!
STOMP!
CHECK PLEASE

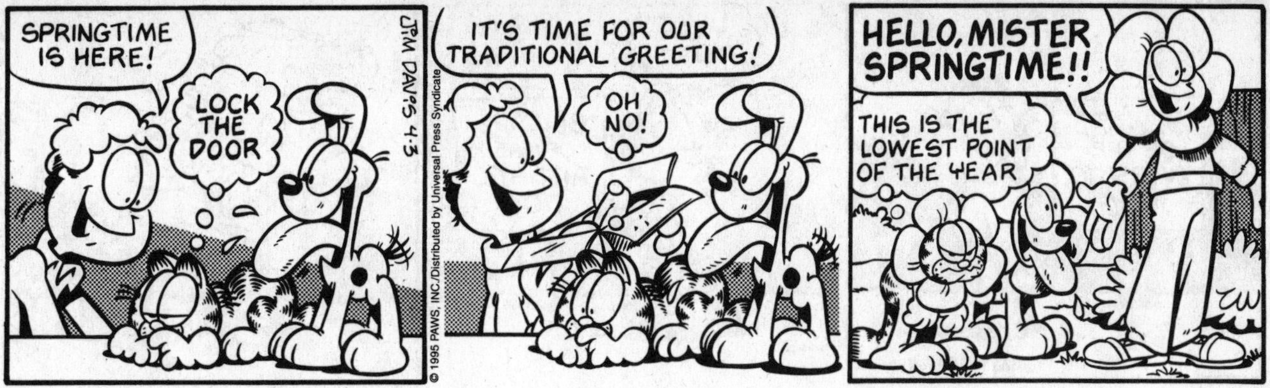
SPRINGTIME IS HERE!
LOCK THE DOOR
JIM DAVIS 4-3
© 1995 PAWS, INC./Distributed by Universal Press Syndicate
IT'S TIME FOR OUR TRADITIONAL GREETING!
OH NO!
HELLO, MISTER SPRINGTIME!!
THIS IS THE LOWEST POINT OF THE YEAR

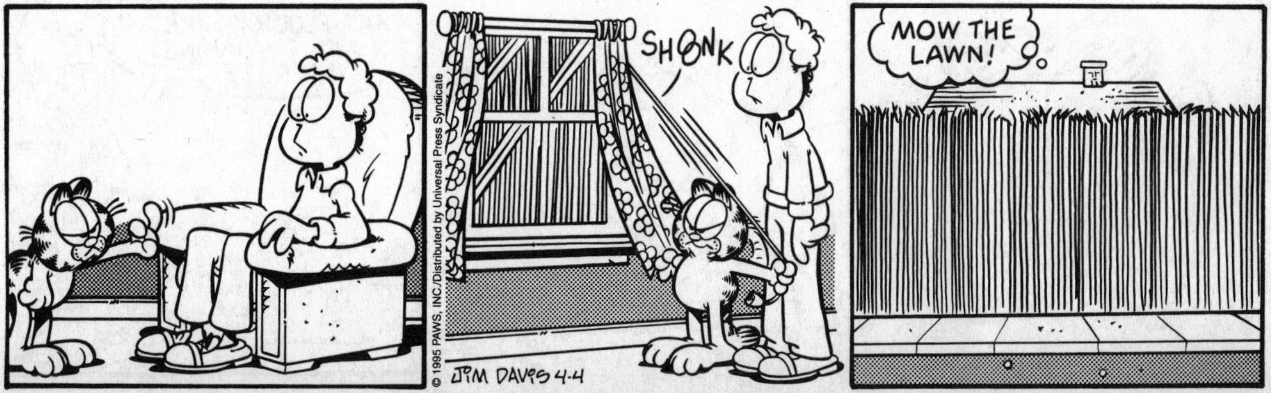
© 1995 PAWS, INC./Distributed by Universal Press Syndicate
SHONK
JIM DAVIS 4-4
MOW THE LAWN!

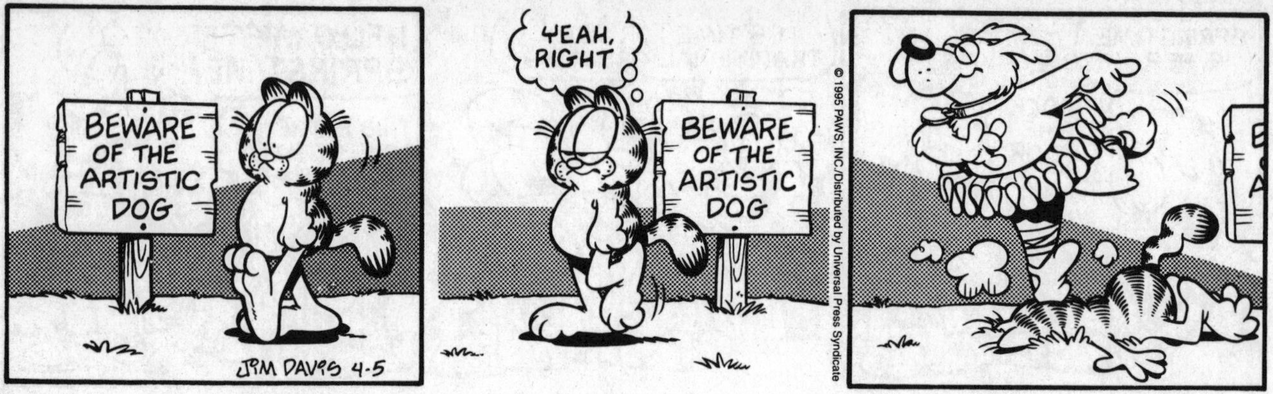
BEWARE OF THE ARTISTIC DOG
JIM DAVIS 4-5
YEAH, RIGHT
BEWARE OF THE ARTISTIC DOG
© 1995 PAWS, INC./Distributed by Universal Press Syndicate

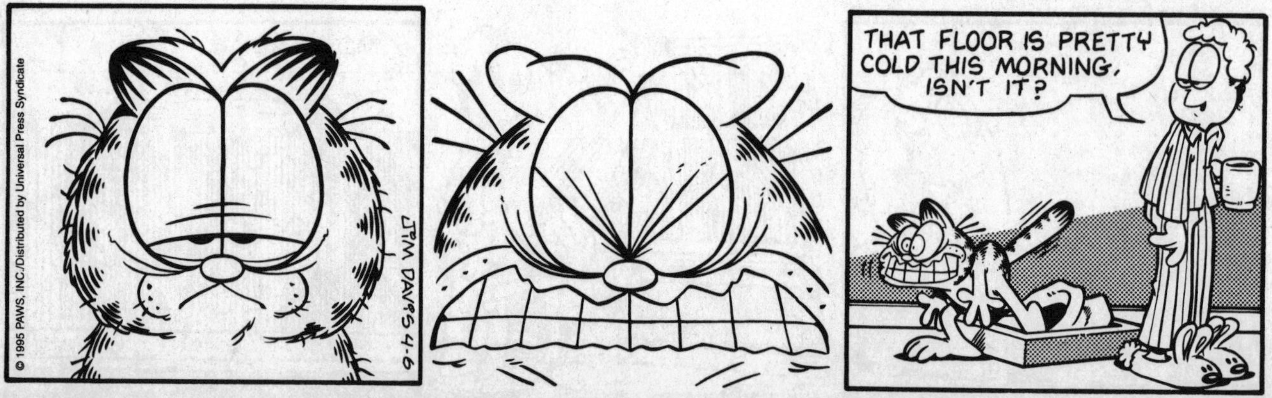
© 1995 PAWS, INC./Distributed by Universal Press Syndicate
JIM DAVIS 4-6
THAT FLOOR IS PRETTY COLD THIS MORNING, ISN'T IT?

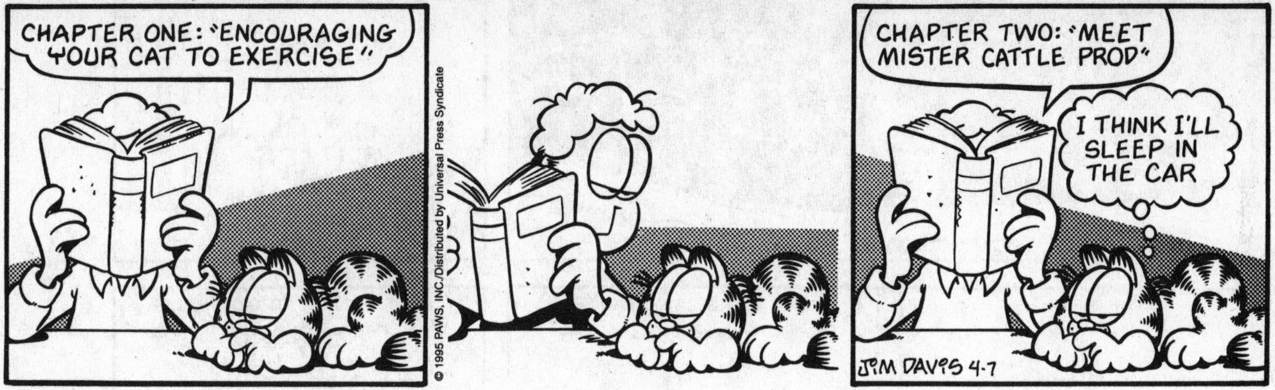
CHAPTER ONE: "ENCOURAGING YOUR CAT TO EXERCISE"
© 1995 PAWS, INC./Distributed by Universal Press Syndicate
CHAPTER TWO: "MEET MISTER CATTLE PROD"
I THINK I'LL SLEEP IN THE CAR
JIM DAVIS 4-7

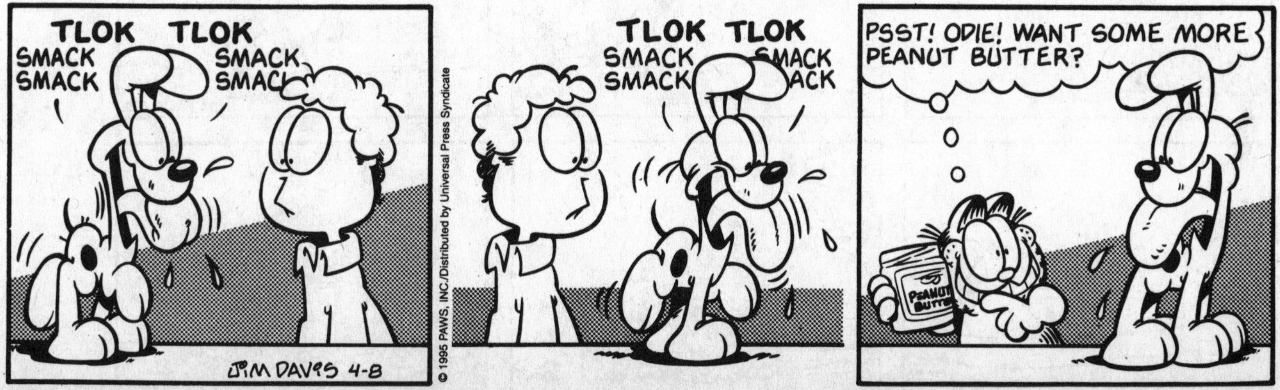
TLOK TLOK
SMACK SMACK
SMACK
JIM DAVIS 4-8
© 1995 PAWS, INC./Distributed by Universal Press Syndicate
TLOK TLOK
SMACK SMACK
PSST! ODIE! WANT SOME MORE PEANUT BUTTER?

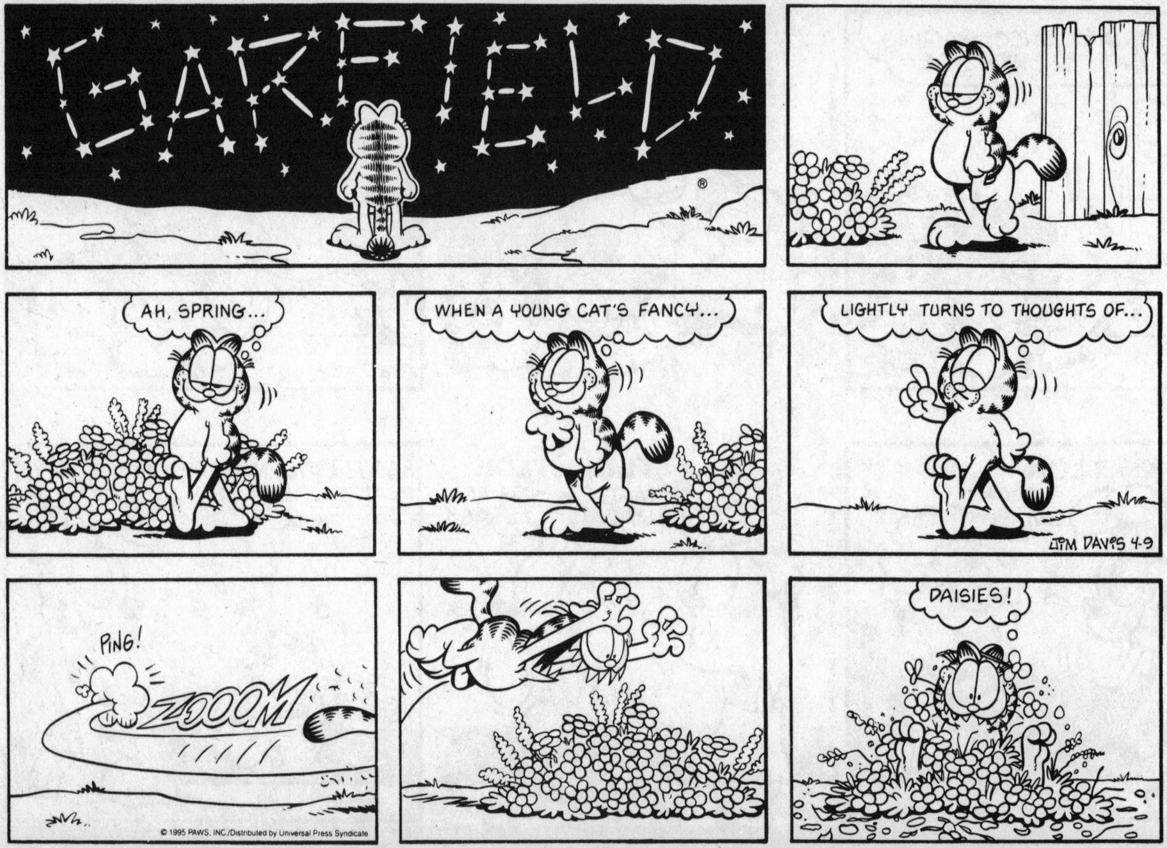
GARFIELD
AH, SPRING...
WHEN A YOUNG CAT'S FANCY...
LIGHTLY TURNS TO THOUGHTS OF...
JIM DAVIS 4-9
PING!
ZOOOM
© 1995 PAWS, INC./Distributed by Universal Press Syndicate
DAISIES!

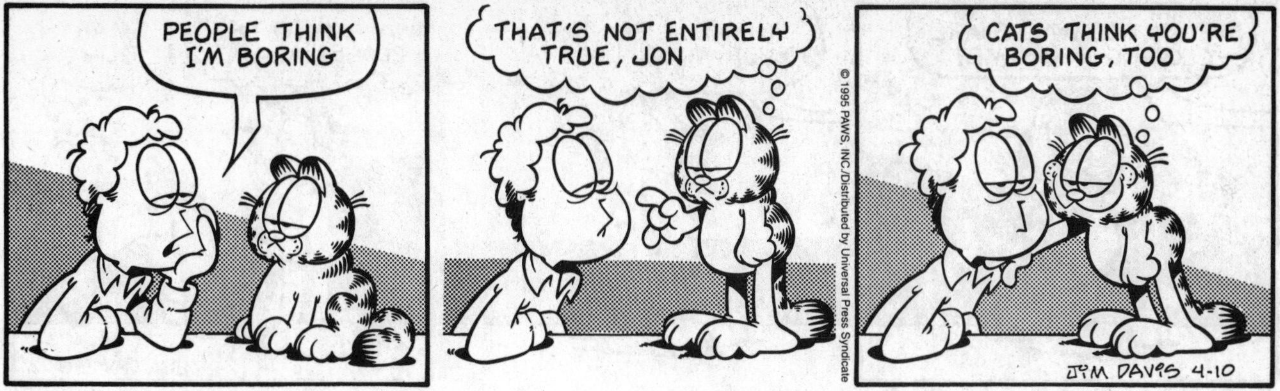
PEOPLE THINK I'M BORING
THAT'S NOT ENTIRELY TRUE, JON
CATS THINK YOU'RE BORING, TOO
© 1995 PAWS, INC./Distributed by Universal Press Syndicate
JIM DAVIS 4-10

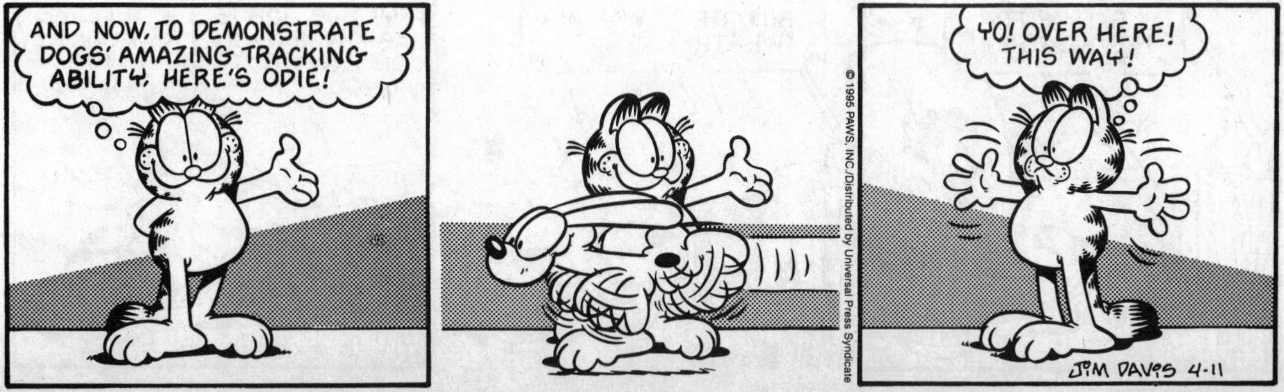
AND NOW, TO DEMONSTRATE DOGS' AMAZING TRACKING ABILITY, HERE'S ODIE!
YO! OVER HERE! THIS WAY!
© 1995 PAWS, INC./Distributed by Universal Press Syndicate
JIM DAVIS 4-11

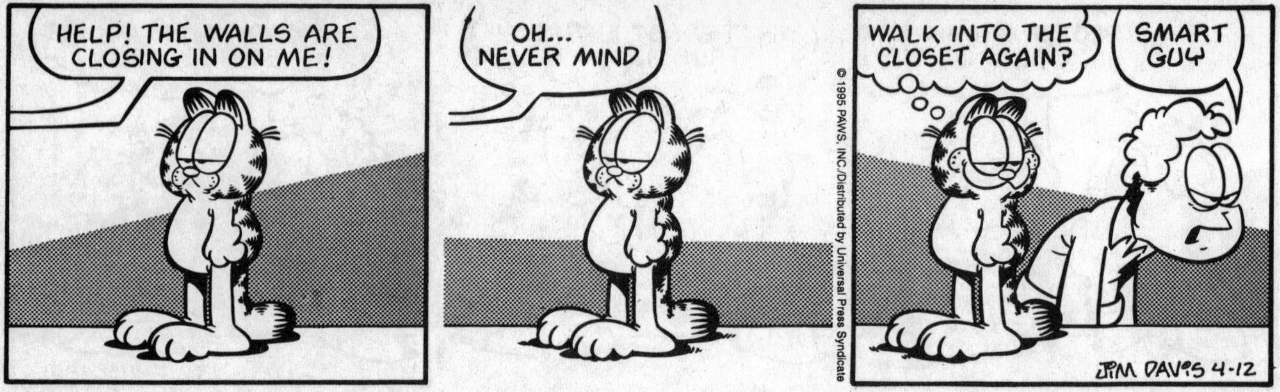
HELP! THE WALLS ARE CLOSING IN ON ME!
OH... NEVER MIND
WALK INTO THE CLOSET AGAIN?
SMART GUY
© 1995 PAWS, INC./Distributed by Universal Press Syndicate
JIM DAVIS 4-12

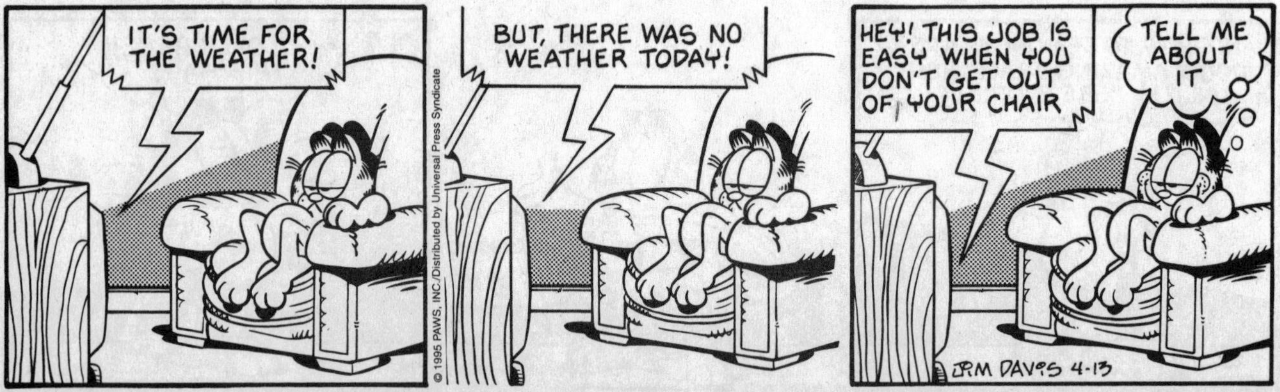
IT'S TIME FOR THE WEATHER!
BUT, THERE WAS NO WEATHER TODAY!
HEY! THIS JOB IS EASY WHEN YOU DON'T GET OUT OF YOUR CHAIR
TELL ME ABOUT IT
© 1995 PAWS, INC./Distributed by Universal Press Syndicate
JIM DAVIS 4-13

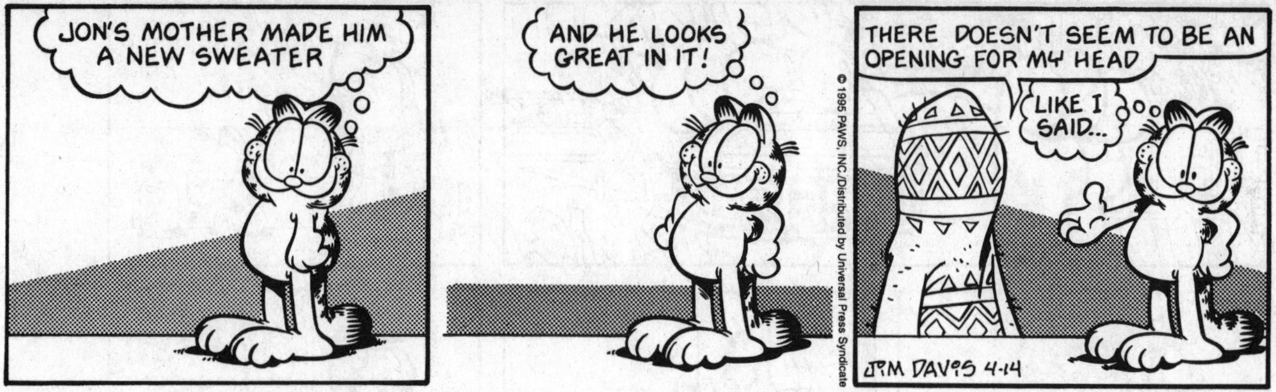
JON'S MOTHER MADE HIM A NEW SWEATER
AND HE LOOKS GREAT IN IT!
© 1995 PAWS, INC./Distributed by Universal Press Syndicate
THERE DOESN'T SEEM TO BE AN OPENING FOR MY HEAD
LIKE I SAID...
JIM DAVIS 4-14

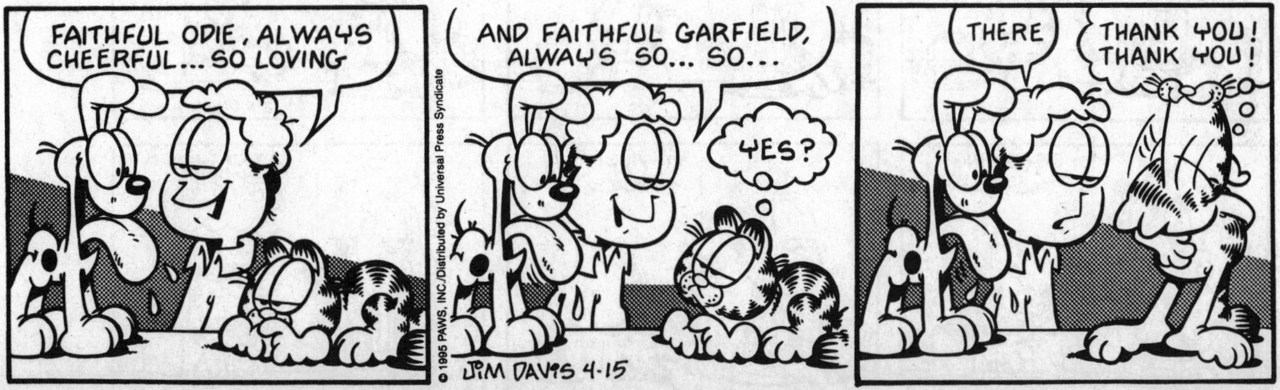
FAITHFUL ODIE, ALWAYS CHEERFUL... SO LOVING
© 1995 PAWS, INC./Distributed by Universal Press Syndicate
AND FAITHFUL GARFIELD, ALWAYS SO... SO...
YES?
JIM DAVIS 4-15
THERE
THANK YOU! THANK YOU!

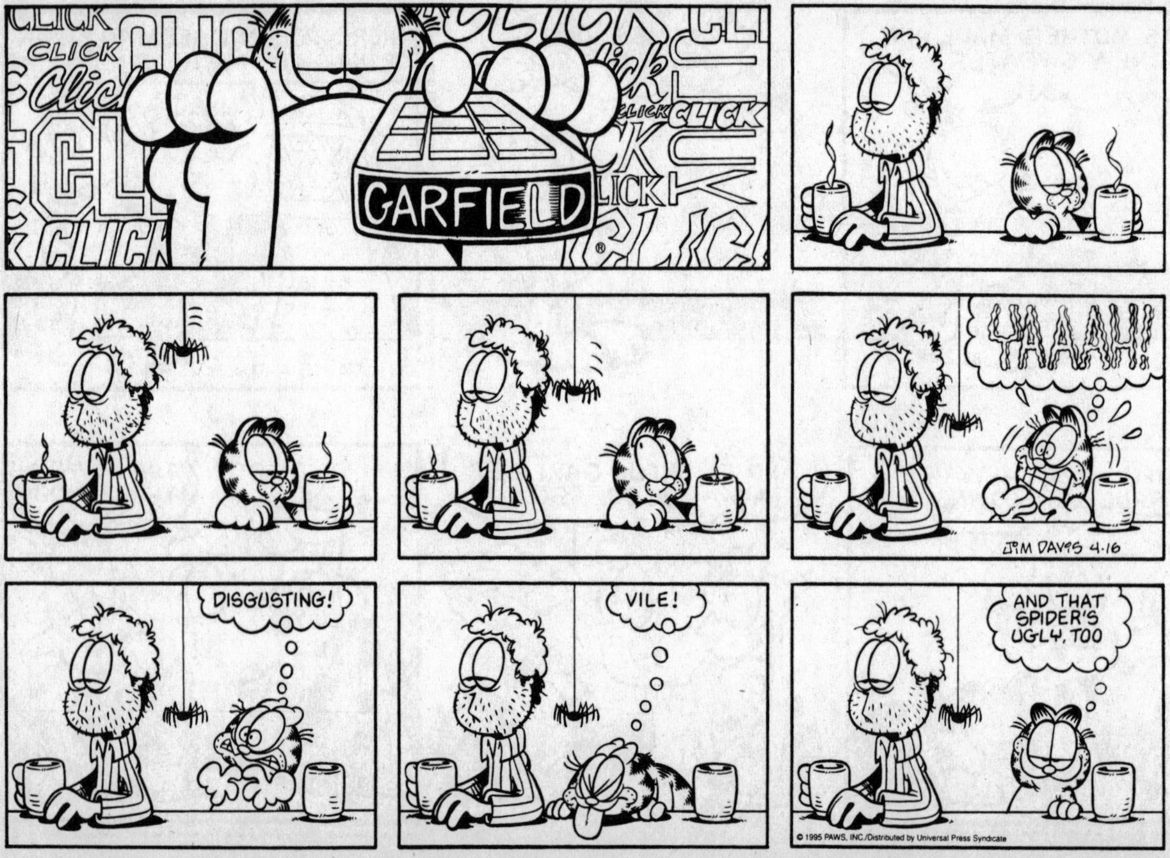
CLICK
GARFIELD
YAAAH!
DISGUSTING!
VILE!
AND THAT SPIDER'S UGLY, TOO
JIM DAVIS 4·16
© 1995 PAWS, INC./Distributed by Universal Press Syndicate

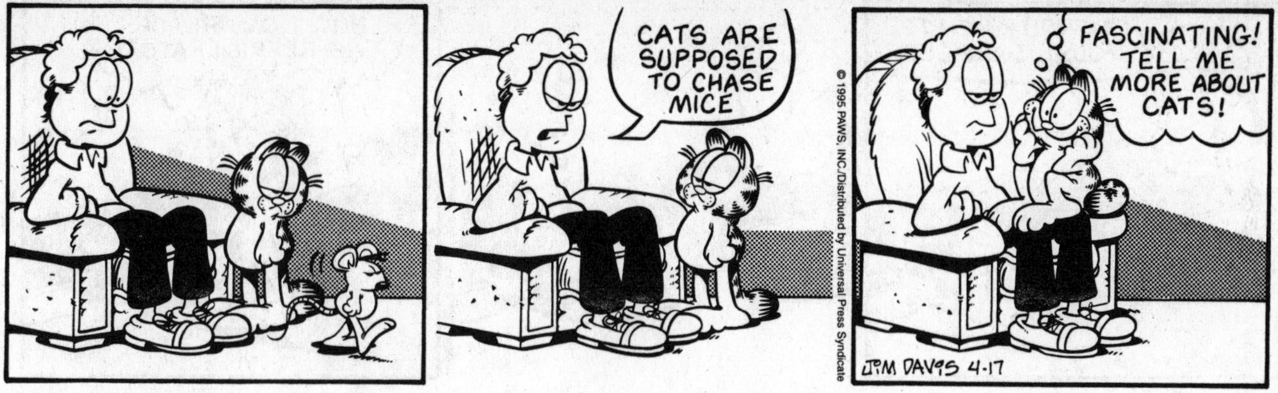
CATS ARE SUPPOSED TO CHASE MICE
FASCINATING! TELL ME MORE ABOUT CATS!
JIM DAVIS 4-17
© 1995 PAWS, INC./Distributed by Universal Press Syndicate

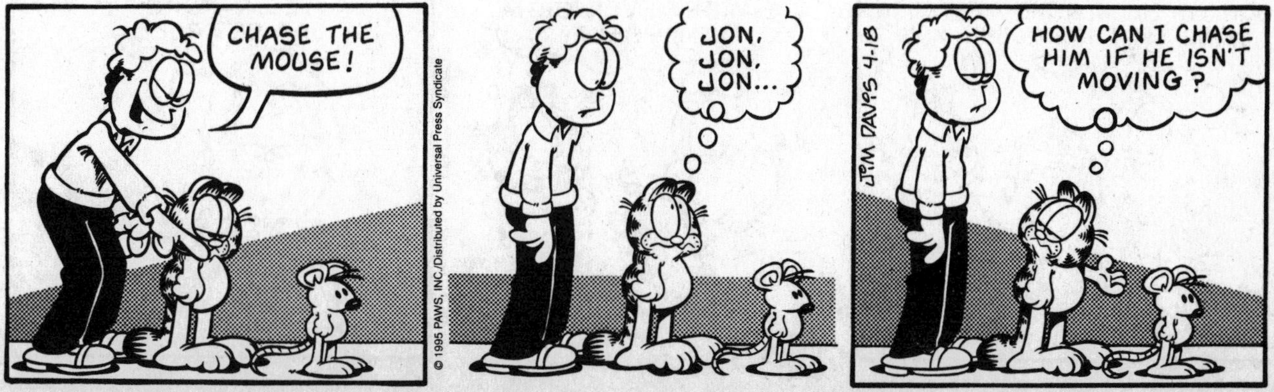
CHASE THE MOUSE!
© 1995 PAWS, INC./Distributed by Universal Press Syndicate
JON, JON, JON...
JIM DAVIS 4-18
HOW CAN I CHASE HIM IF HE ISN'T MOVING?

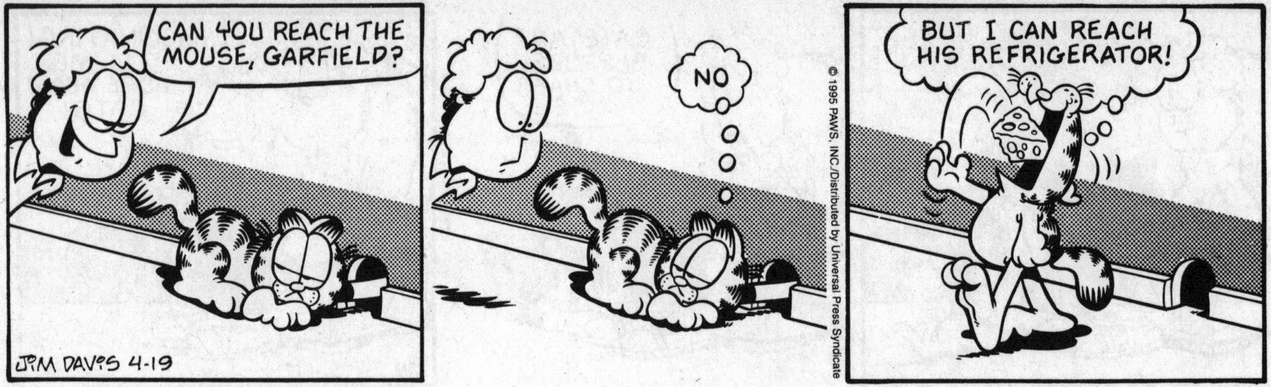
CAN YOU REACH THE MOUSE, GARFIELD?
NO
BUT I CAN REACH HIS REFRIGERATOR!
JIM DAVIS 4-19
© 1995 PAWS, INC./Distributed by Universal Press Syndicate

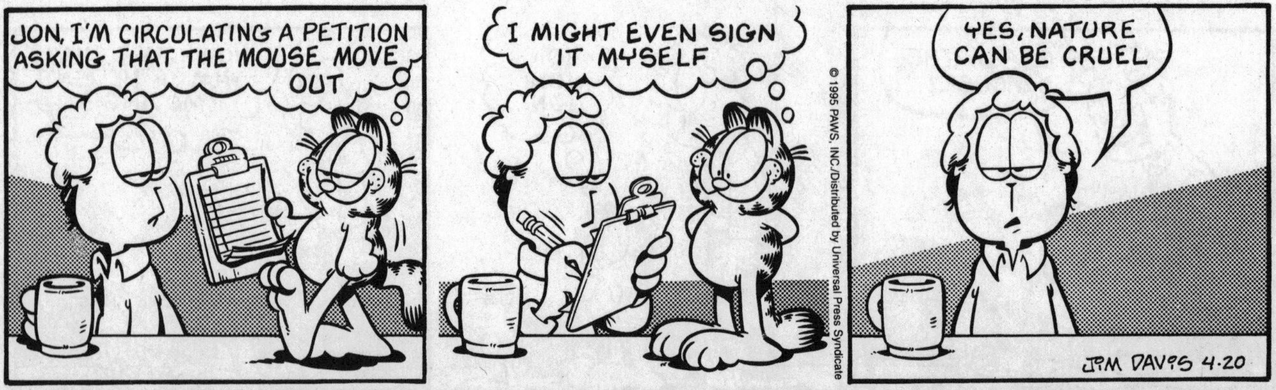
JON, I'M CIRCULATING A PETITION ASKING THAT THE MOUSE MOVE OUT
I MIGHT EVEN SIGN IT MYSELF
YES, NATURE CAN BE CRUEL
JIM DAVIS 4-20
© 1995 PAWS, INC./Distributed by Universal Press Syndicate

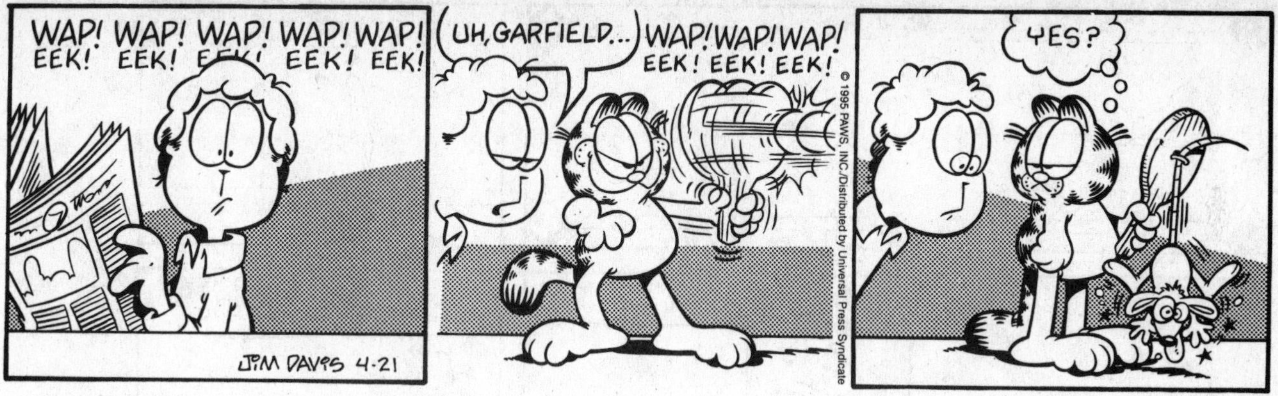
WAP! WAP! WAP! WAP! WAP!
EEK! EEK! EEK! EEK!
JIM DAVIS 4-21
UH, GARFIELD...
WAP! WAP! WAP!
EEK! EEK! EEK!
© 1995 PAWS, INC./Distributed by Universal Press Syndicate
YES?

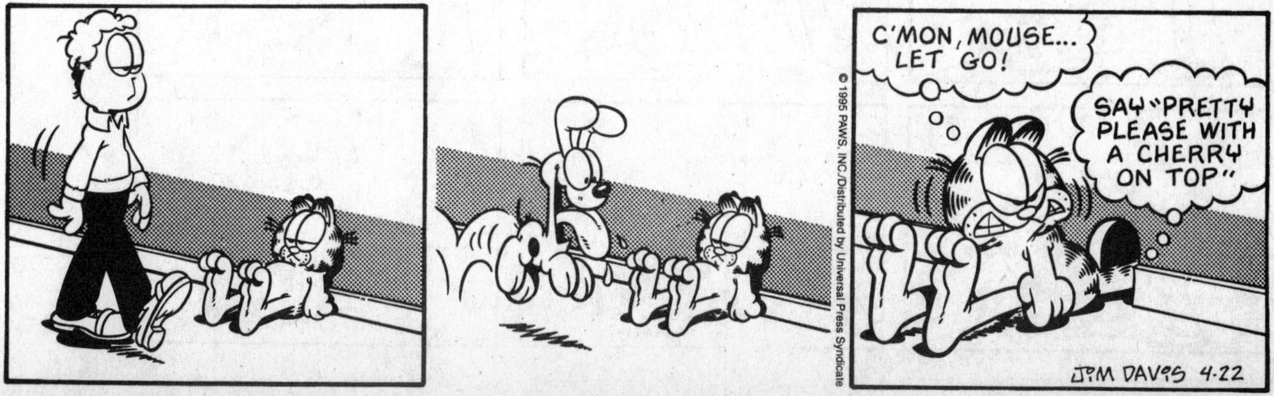
© 1995 PAWS, INC./Distributed by Universal Press Syndicate
C'MON, MOUSE... LET GO!
SAY "PRETTY PLEASE WITH A CHERRY ON TOP"
JIM DAVIS 4-22

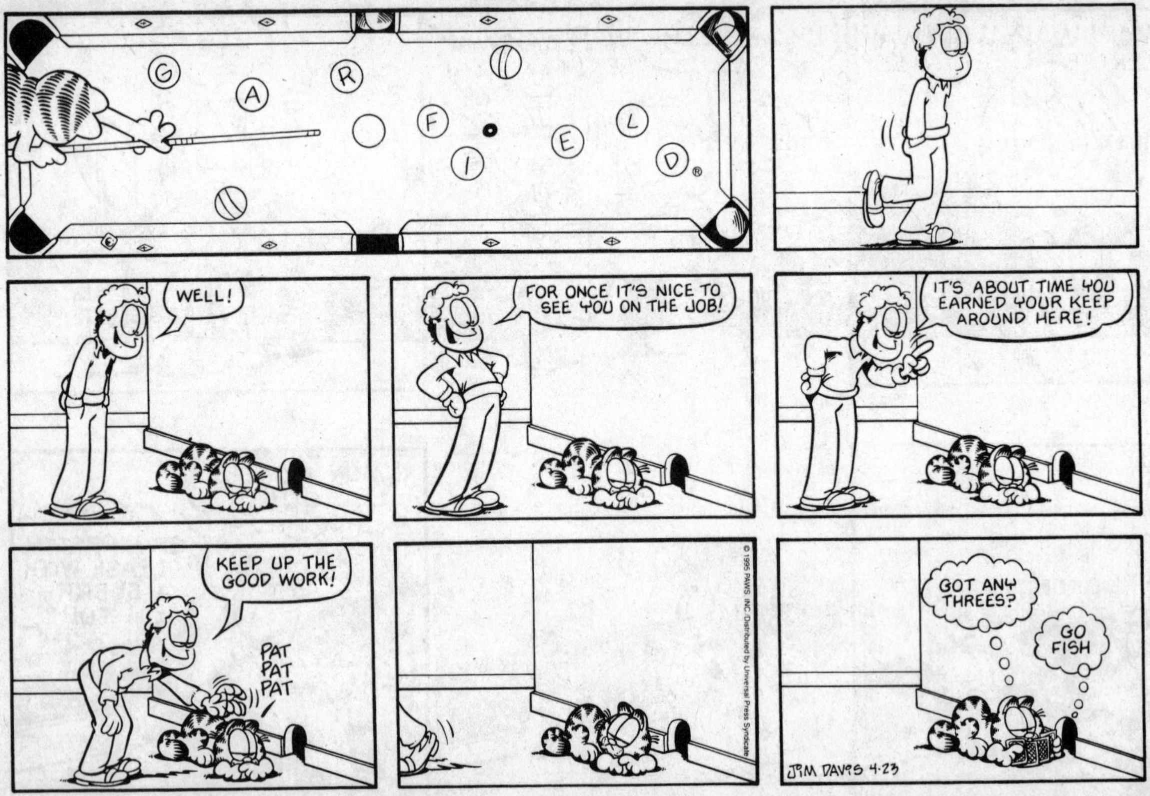
GARFIELD®
WELL!
FOR ONCE IT'S NICE TO SEE YOU ON THE JOB!
IT'S ABOUT TIME YOU EARNED YOUR KEEP AROUND HERE!
KEEP UP THE GOOD WORK!
PAT PAT PAT
© 1995 PAWS, INC./Distributed by Universal Press Syndicate
GOT ANY THREES?
GO FISH
JIM DAVIS 4-23

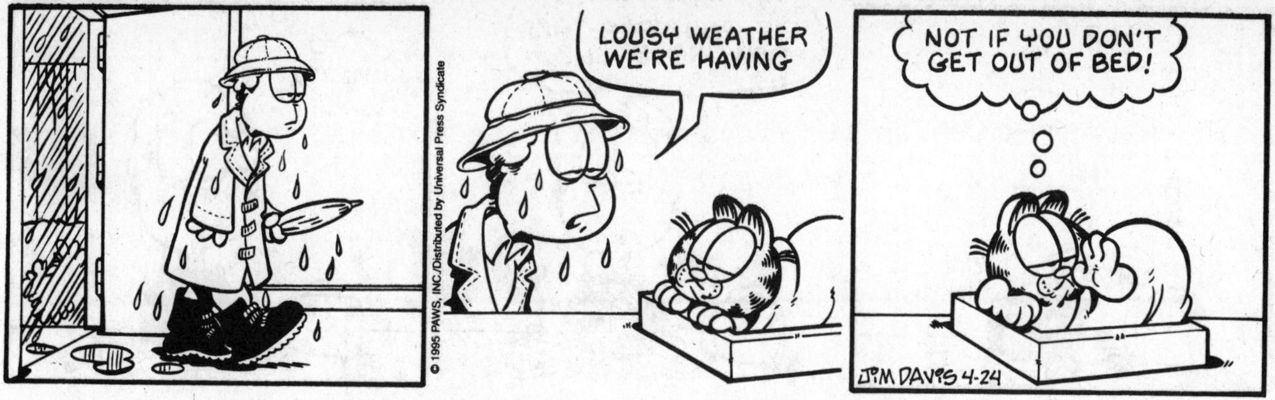
LOUSY WEATHER WE'RE HAVING
NOT IF YOU DON'T GET OUT OF BED!
JIM DAVIS 4-24
© 1995 PAWS, INC./Distributed by Universal Press Syndicate

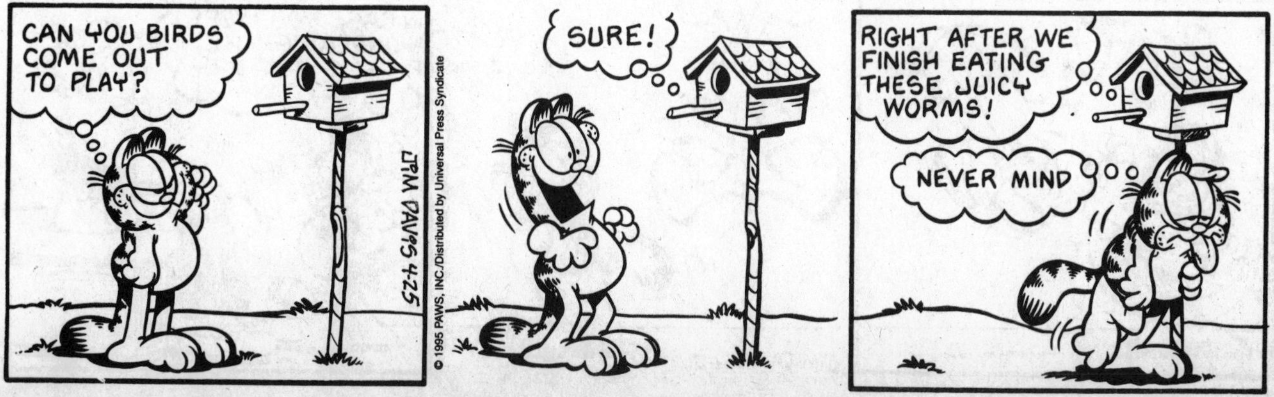
CAN YOU BIRDS COME OUT TO PLAY?
JIM DAVIS 4-25
SURE!
RIGHT AFTER WE FINISH EATING THESE JUICY WORMS!
NEVER MIND
© 1995 PAWS, INC./Distributed by Universal Press Syndicate

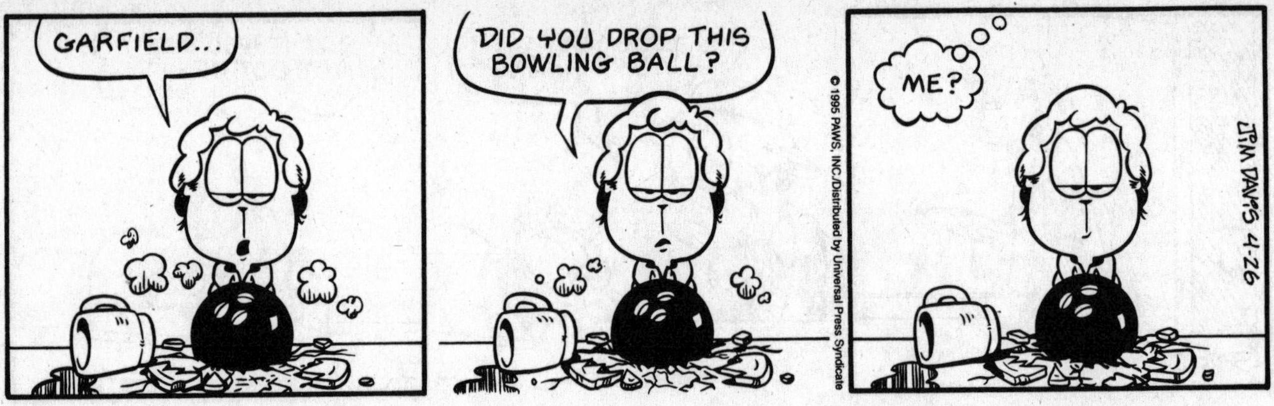
GARFIELD...
DID YOU DROP THIS BOWLING BALL?
© 1995 PAWS, INC./Distributed by Universal Press Syndicate
ME?
JIM DAVIS 4-26

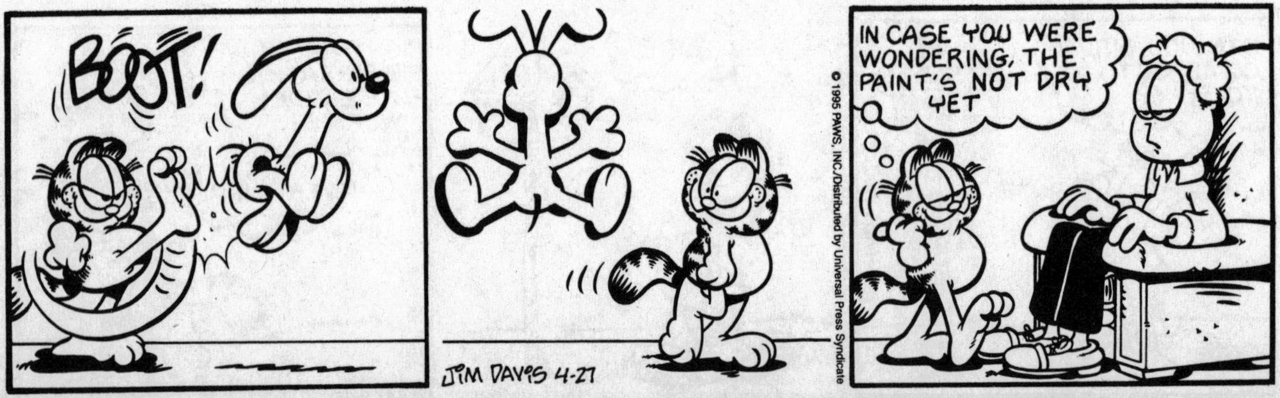
BOOT!
JIM DAVIS 4-27
© 1995 PAWS, INC./Distributed by Universal Press Syndicate
IN CASE YOU WERE WONDERING, THE PAINT'S NOT DRY YET

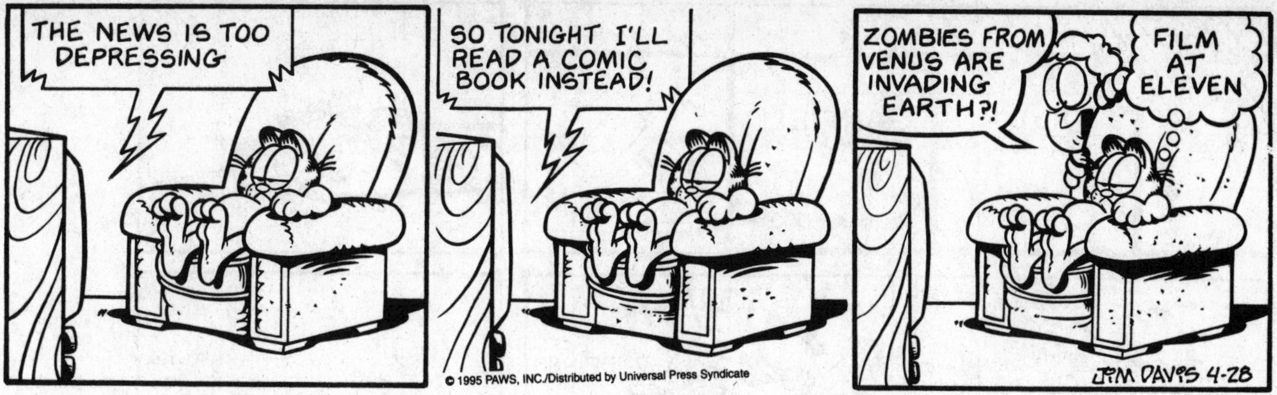
THE NEWS IS TOO DEPRESSING
SO TONIGHT I'LL READ A COMIC BOOK INSTEAD!
ZOMBIES FROM VENUS ARE INVADING EARTH?!
FILM AT ELEVEN
© 1995 PAWS, INC./Distributed by Universal Press Syndicate
JIM DAVIS 4-28

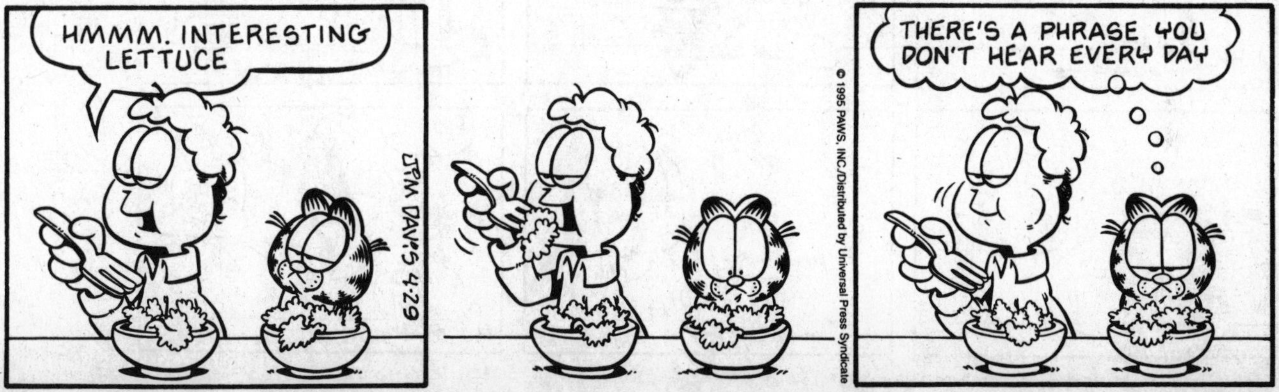
HMMM. INTERESTING LETTUCE
JIM DAVIS 4-29
THERE'S A PHRASE YOU DON'T HEAR EVERY DAY
© 1995 PAWS, INC./Distributed by Universal Press Syndicate

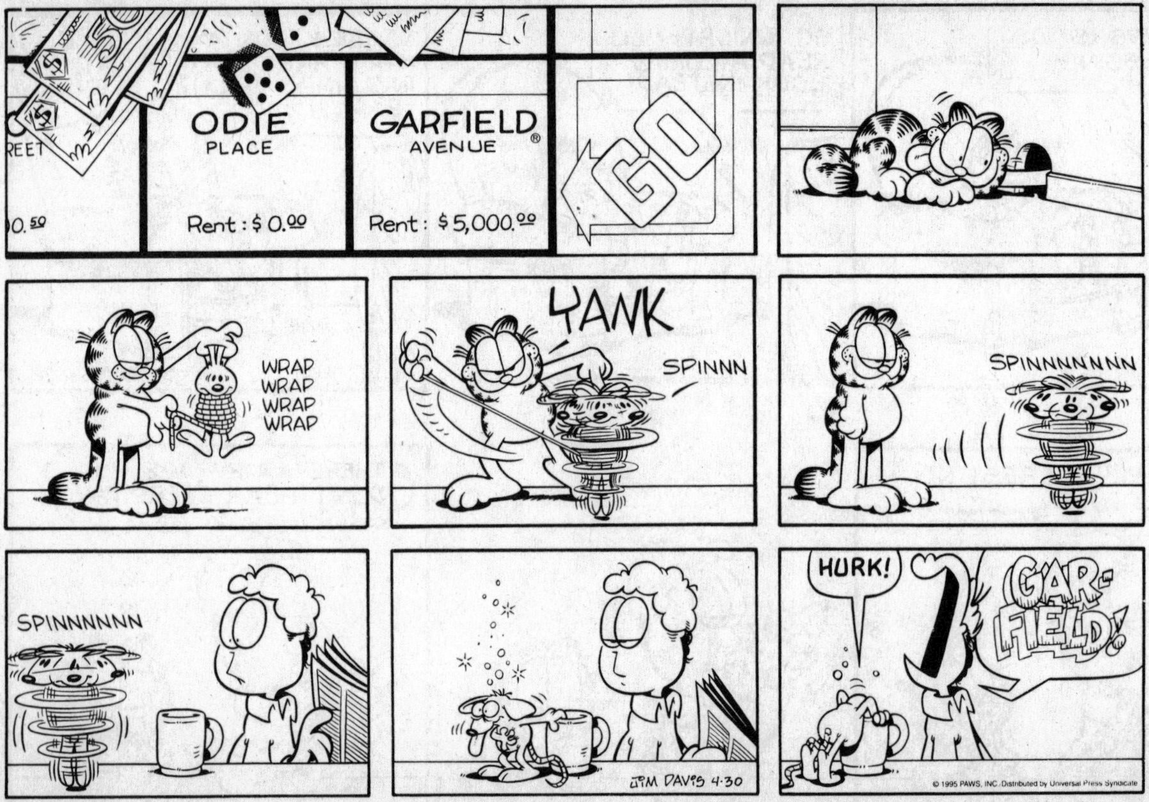

REET
0.50
ODIE
PLACE
Rent : $ 0.00
GARFIELD
AVENUE
Rent : $ 5,000.00
GO
WRAP
WRAP
WRAP
WRAP
YANK
SPINNN
SPINNNNNNNN
SPINNNNNNN
JIM DAVIS 4·30
HURK!
GAR-
FIELD!
© 1995 PAWS, INC. Distributed by Universal Press Syndicate

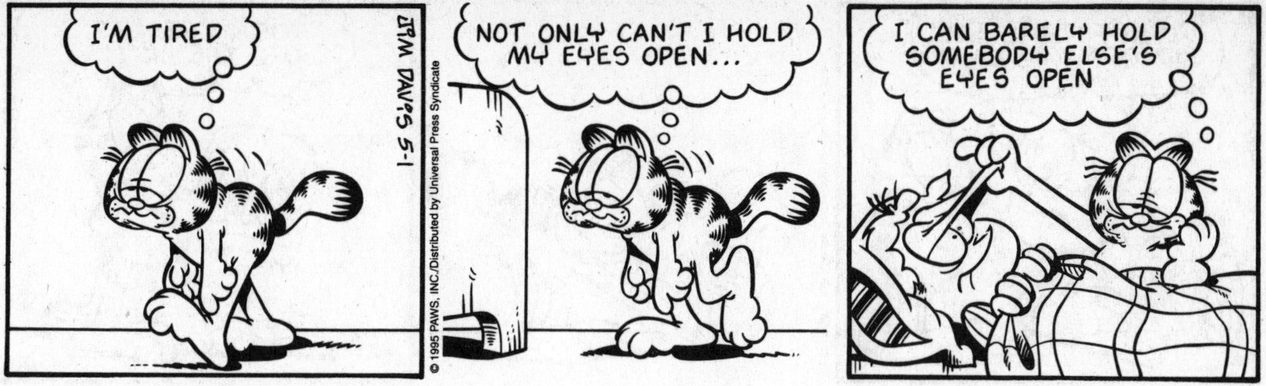
I'M TIRED
JIM DAVIS 5-1
© 1995 PAWS, INC./Distributed by Universal Press Syndicate
NOT ONLY CAN'T I HOLD MY EYES OPEN...
I CAN BARELY HOLD SOMEBODY ELSE'S EYES OPEN

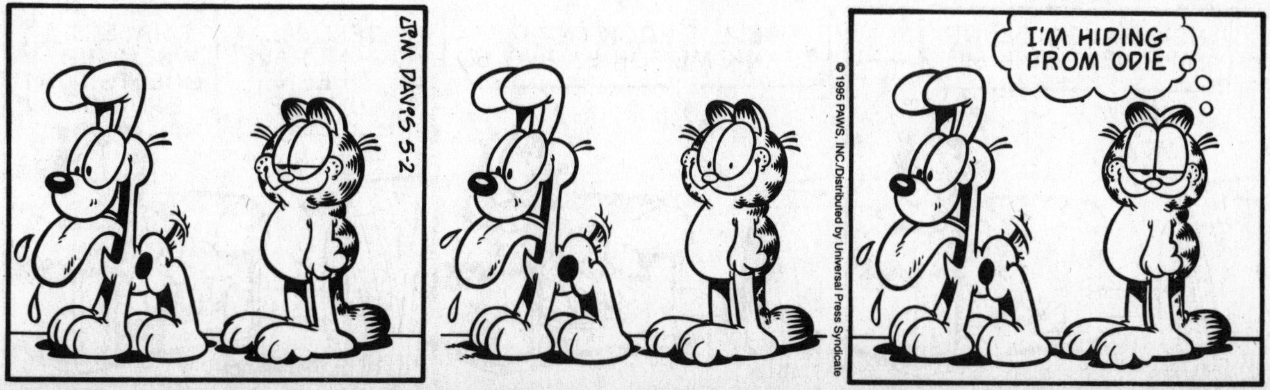
JIM DAVIS 5-2
© 1995 PAWS, INC./Distributed by Universal Press Syndicate
I'M HIDING FROM ODIE

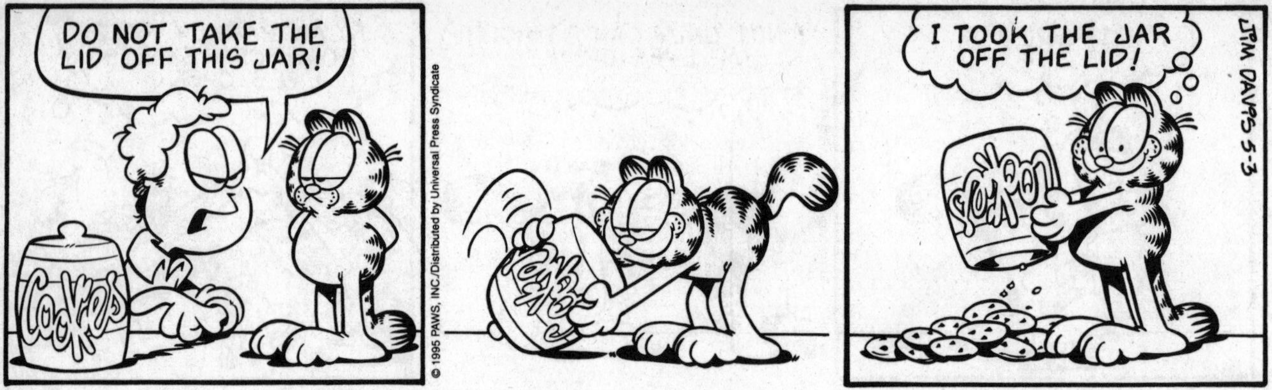
DO NOT TAKE THE LID OFF THIS JAR!
Cookies
© 1995 PAWS, INC./Distributed by Universal Press Syndicate
I TOOK THE JAR OFF THE LID!
JIM DAVIS 5-3

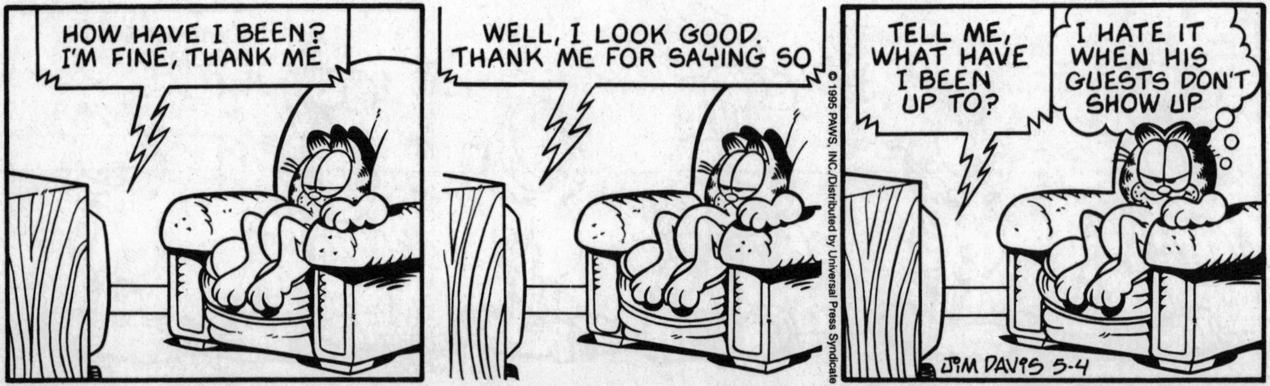
HOW HAVE I BEEN? I'M FINE, THANK ME
WELL, I LOOK GOOD. THANK ME FOR SAYING SO
© 1995 PAWS, INC./Distributed by Universal Press Syndicate
TELL ME, WHAT HAVE I BEEN UP TO?
I HATE IT WHEN HIS GUESTS DON'T SHOW UP
JIM DAVIS 5-4

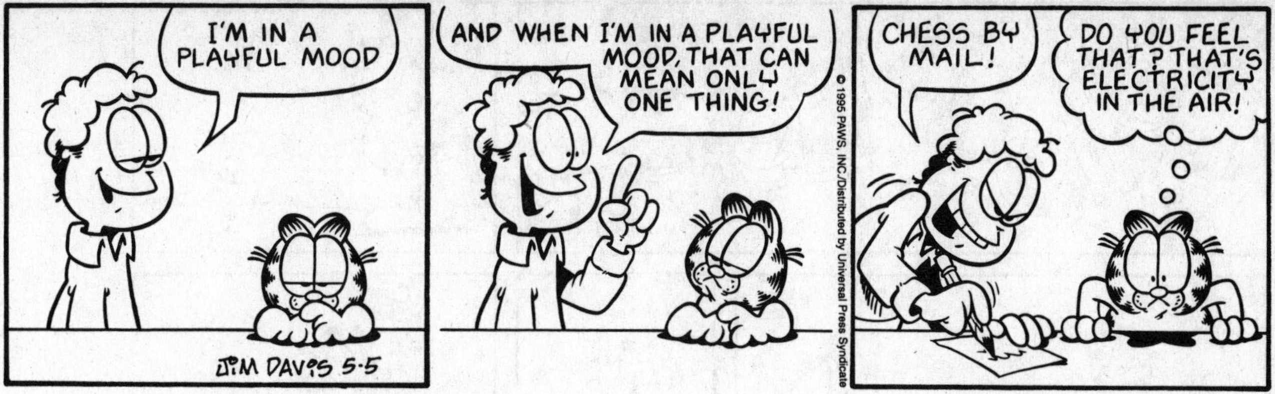
I'M IN A PLAYFUL MOOD
JIM DAVIS 5-5
AND WHEN I'M IN A PLAYFUL MOOD, THAT CAN MEAN ONLY ONE THING!
© 1995 PAWS, INC./Distributed by Universal Press Syndicate
CHESS BY MAIL!
DO YOU FEEL THAT? THAT'S ELECTRICITY IN THE AIR!

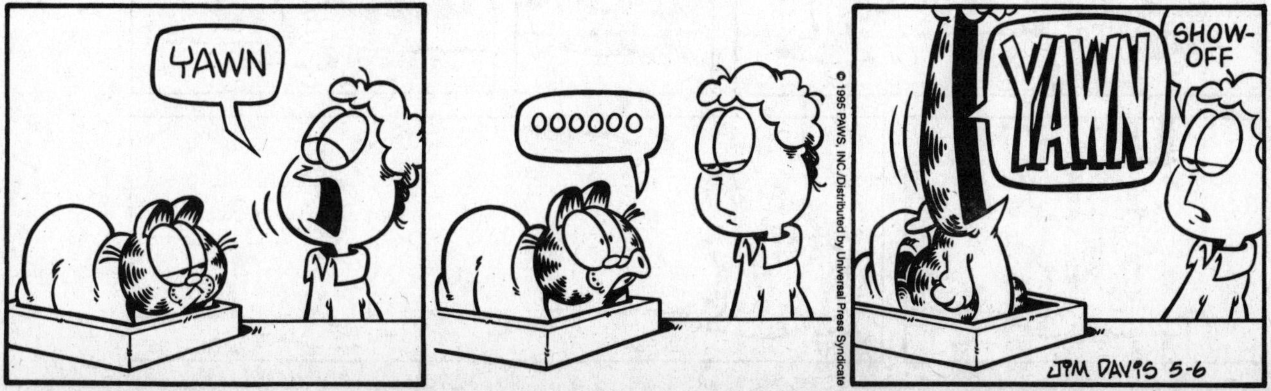
YAWN
OOOOOO
© 1995 PAWS, INC./Distributed by Universal Press Syndicate
YAWN
SHOW-OFF
JIM DAVIS 5-6

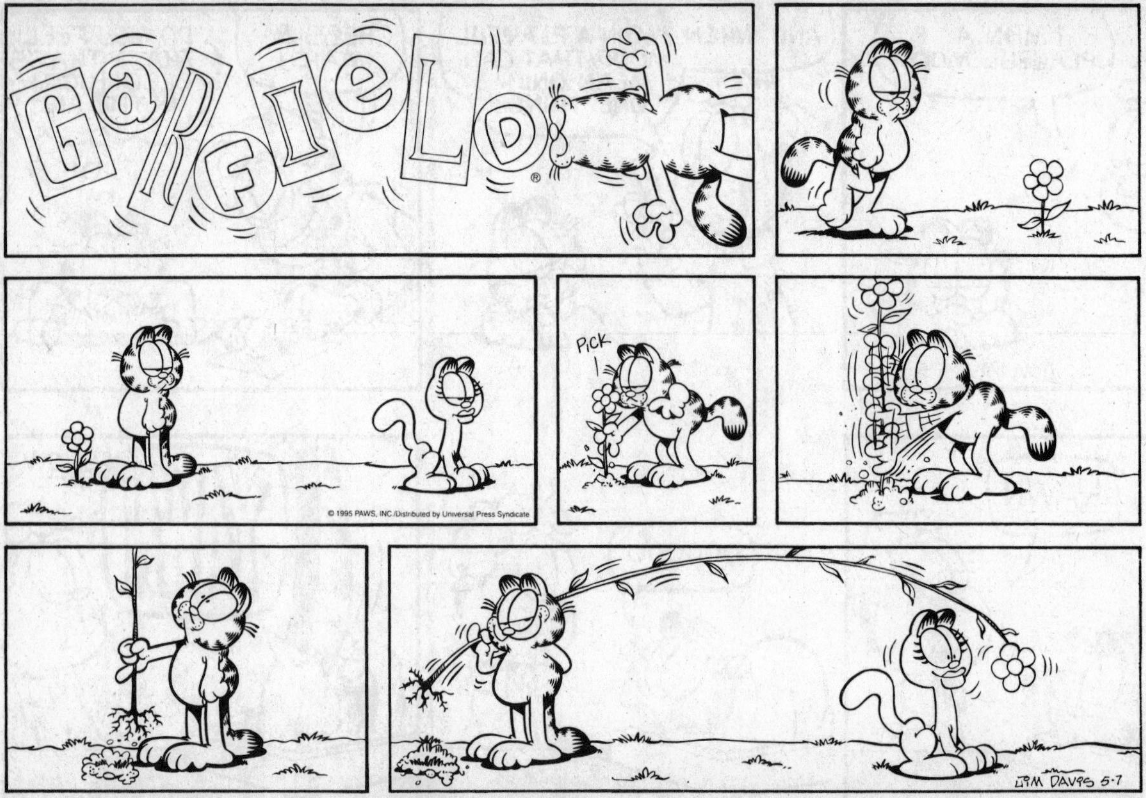
GARFIELD®
PICK
© 1995 PAWS, INC./Distributed by Universal Press Syndicate
JIM DAVIS 5-7

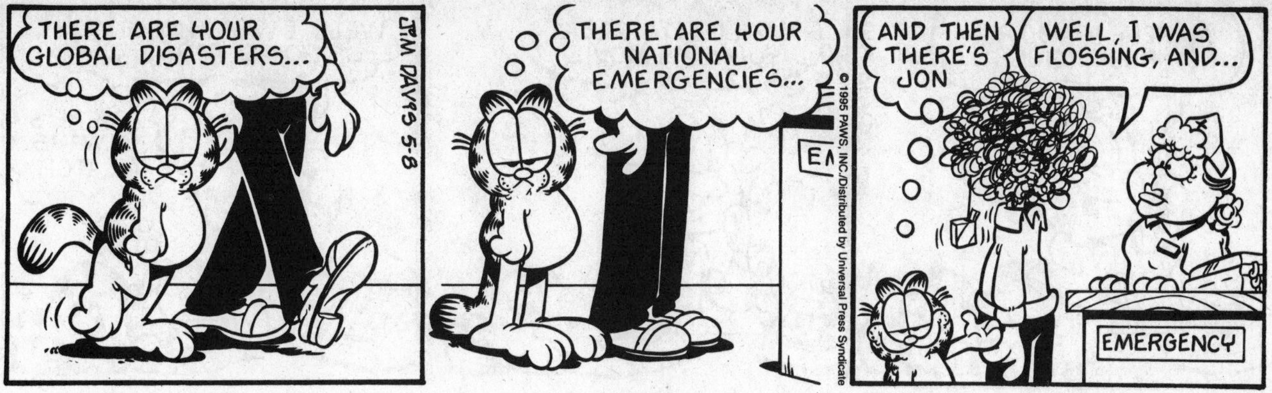
THERE ARE YOUR GLOBAL DISASTERS...
JIM DAVIS 5-8
THERE ARE YOUR NATIONAL EMERGENCIES...
© 1995 PAWS, INC./Distributed by Universal Press Syndicate
AND THEN THERE'S JON
WELL, I WAS FLOSSING, AND...
EMERGENCY

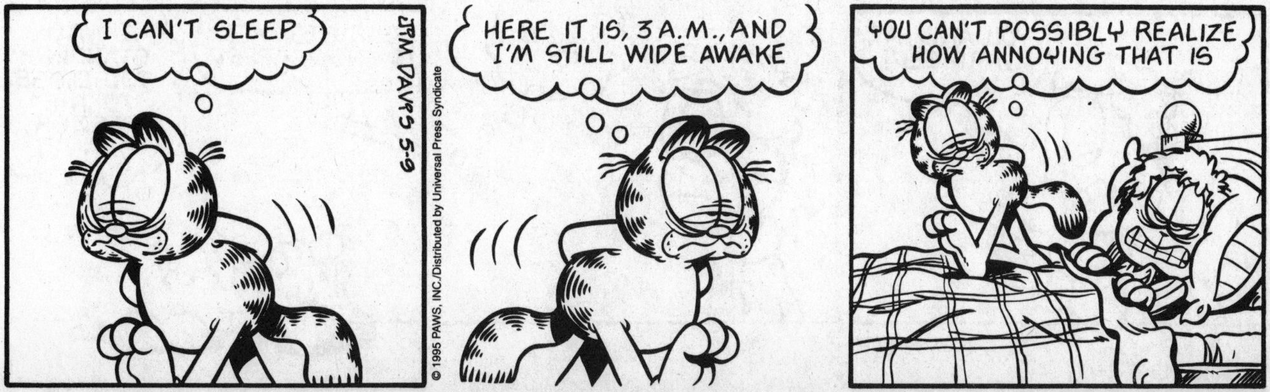
I CAN'T SLEEP
JIM DAVIS 5-9
© 1995 PAWS, INC./Distributed by Universal Press Syndicate
HERE IT IS, 3 A.M., AND I'M STILL WIDE AWAKE
YOU CAN'T POSSIBLY REALIZE HOW ANNOYING THAT IS

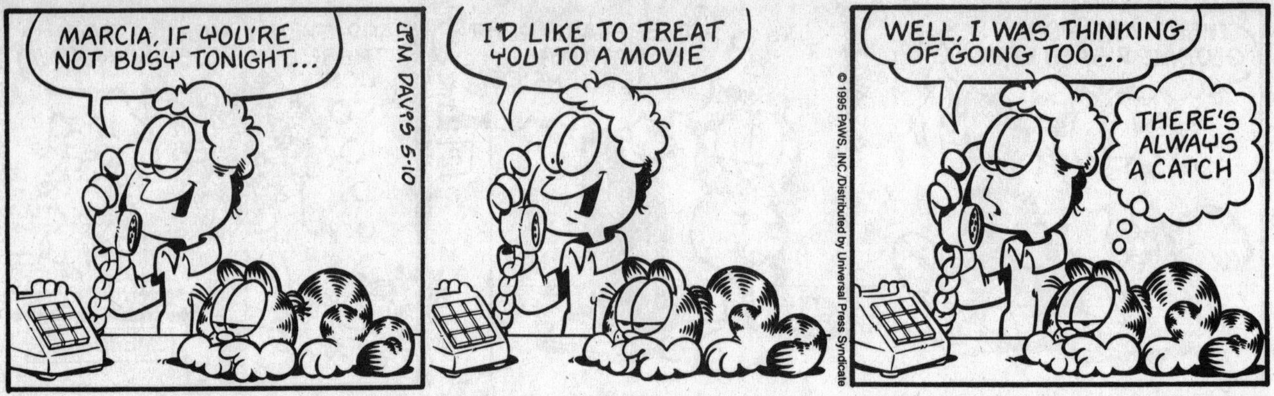
MARCIA, IF YOU'RE NOT BUSY TONIGHT...
JIM DAVIS 5-10
I'D LIKE TO TREAT YOU TO A MOVIE
© 1995 PAWS, INC./Distributed by Universal Press Syndicate
WELL, I WAS THINKING OF GOING TOO...
THERE'S ALWAYS A CATCH

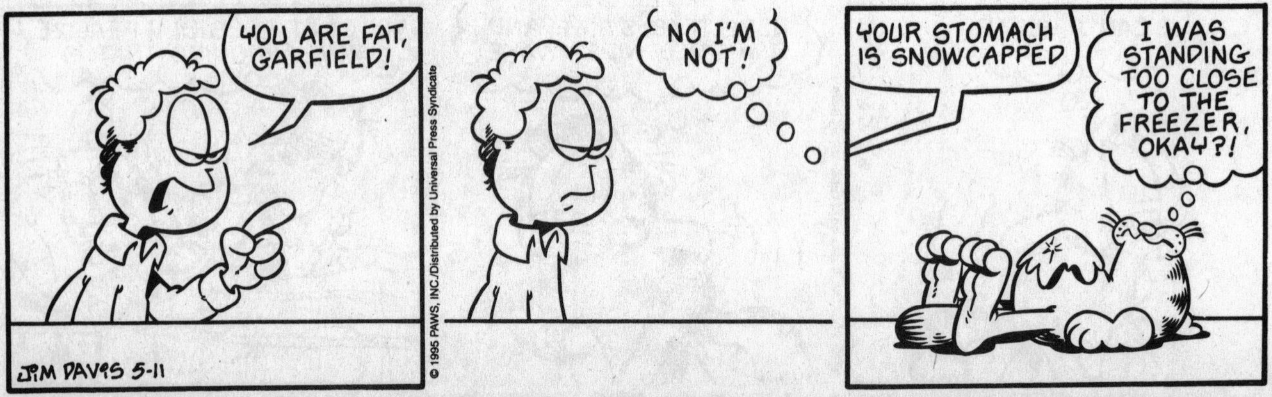
YOU ARE FAT, GARFIELD!
JIM DAVIS 5-11
© 1995 PAWS, INC./Distributed by Universal Press Syndicate
NO I'M NOT!
YOUR STOMACH IS SNOWCAPPED
I WAS STANDING TOO CLOSE TO THE FREEZER, OKAY?!

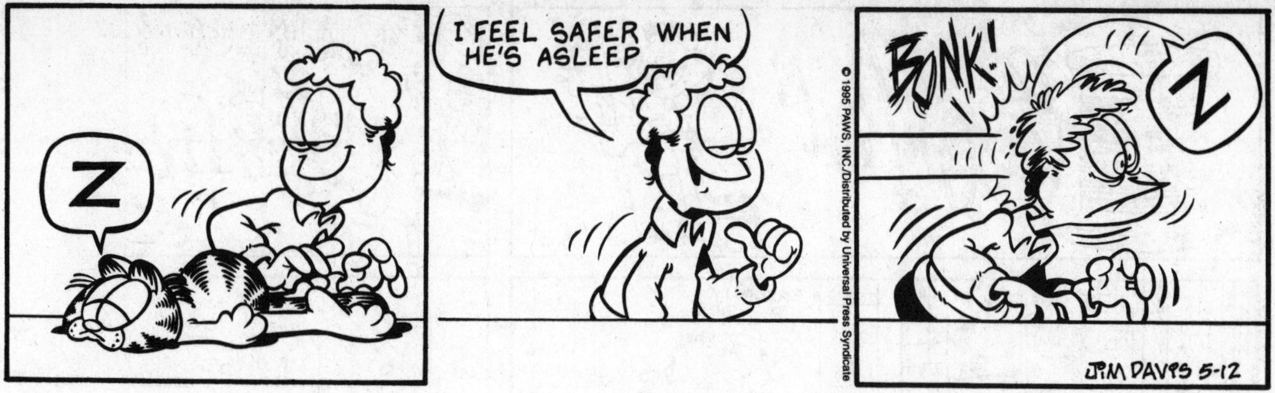

Z
I FEEL SAFER WHEN HE'S ASLEEP
BONK!
Z
JIM DAVIS 5-12

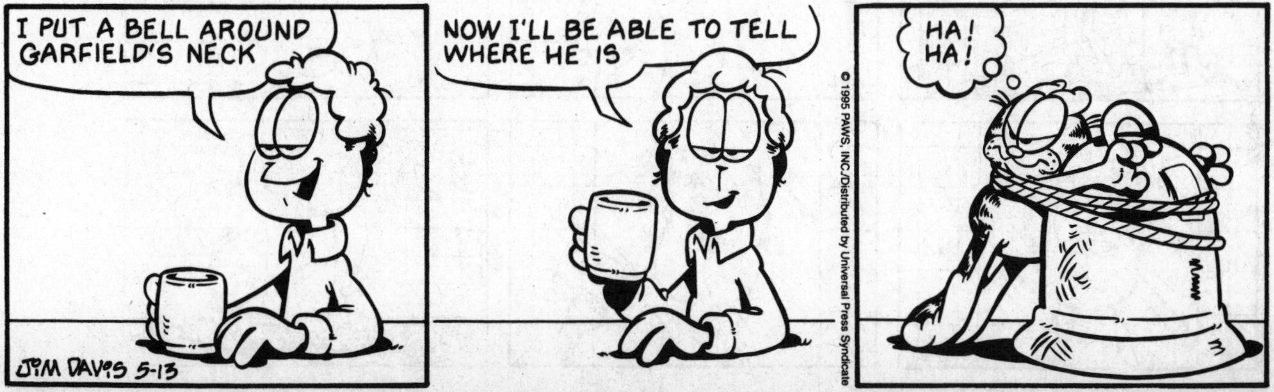

I PUT A BELL AROUND GARFIELD'S NECK
JIM DAVIS 5-13
NOW I'LL BE ABLE TO TELL WHERE HE IS
HA! HA!

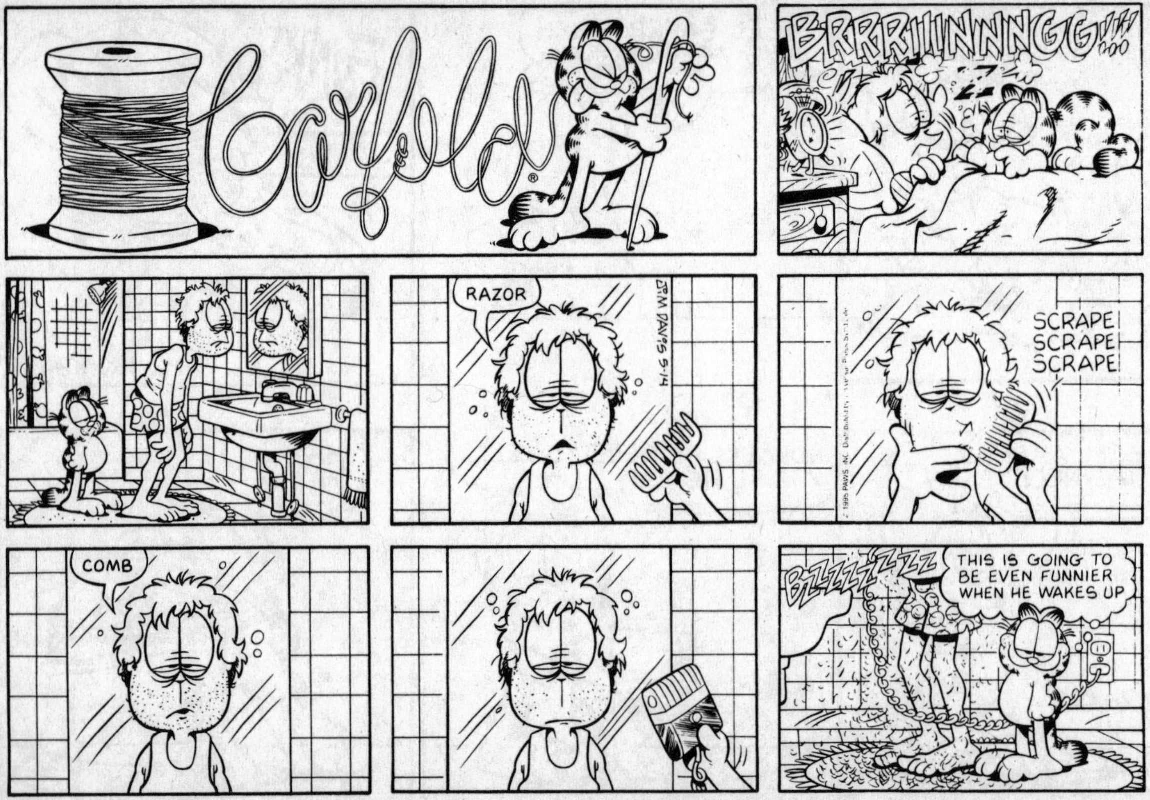
Garfield
BRRRIIINNNGG!!!!
RAZOR
SCRAPE
SCRAPE
SCRAPE
COMB
BZZZZZZZ
THIS IS GOING TO BE EVEN FUNNIER WHEN HE WAKES UP

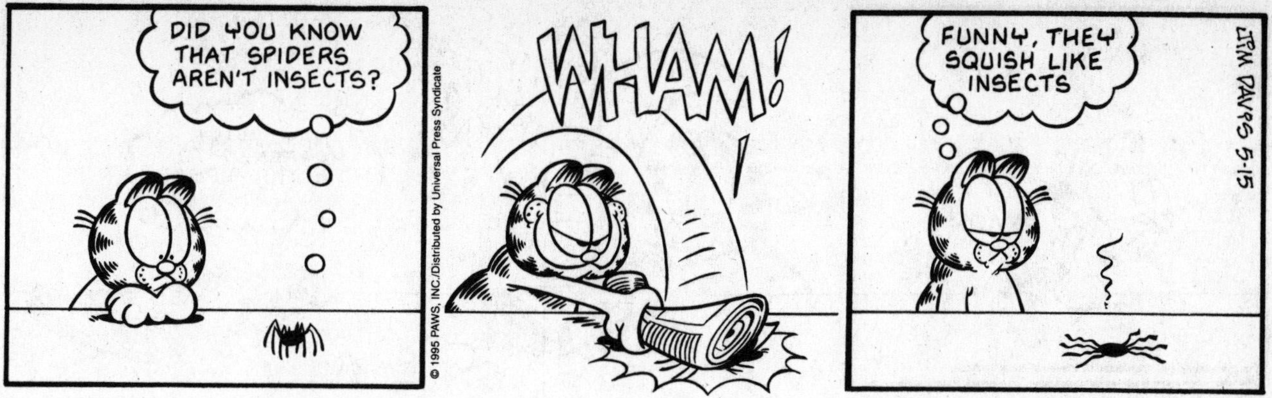
DID YOU KNOW THAT SPIDERS AREN'T INSECTS?
WHAM!
FUNNY, THEY SQUISH LIKE INSECTS
JIM DAVIS 5-15

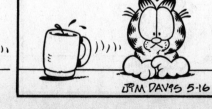

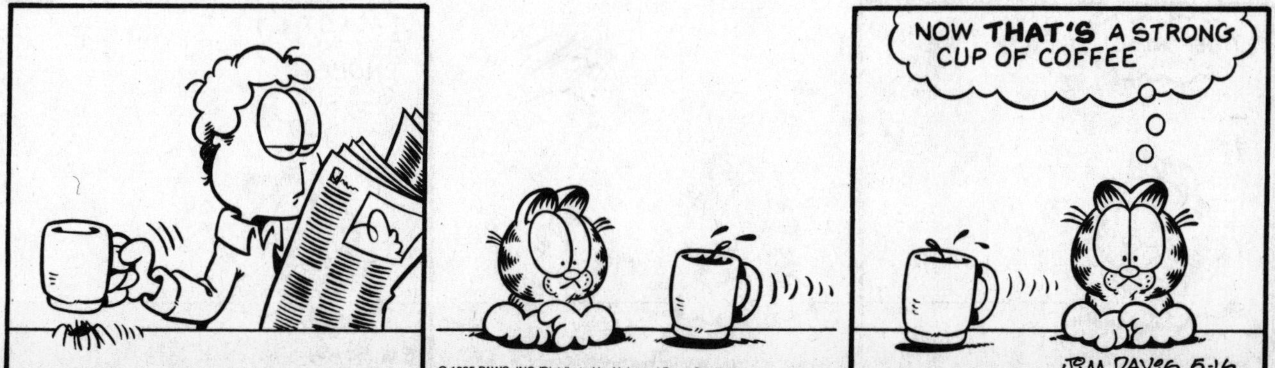
NOW **THAT'S** A STRONG CUP OF COFFEE
JIM DAVIS 5-16

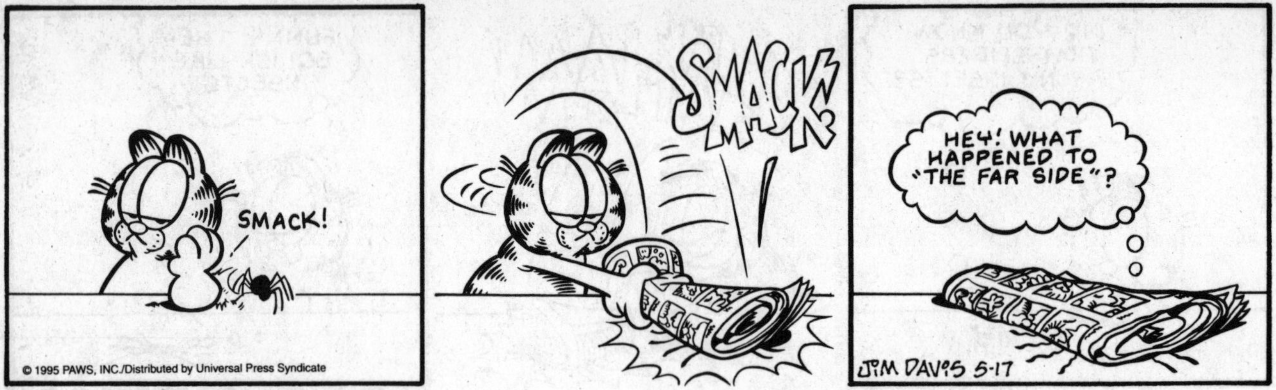
SMACK!
SMACK
HEY! WHAT HAPPENED TO "THE FAR SIDE"?
JIM DAVIS 5-17

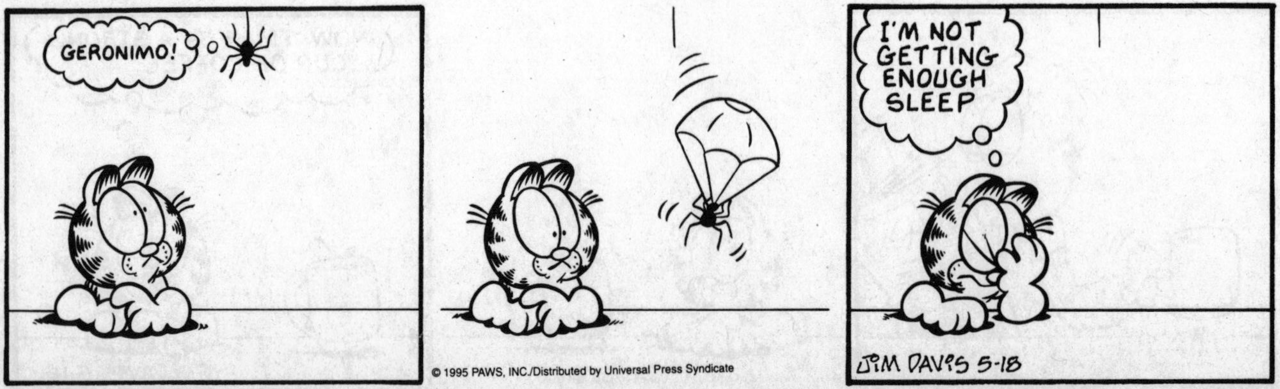
GERONIMO!
I'M NOT GETTING ENOUGH SLEEP
JIM DAVIS 5-18

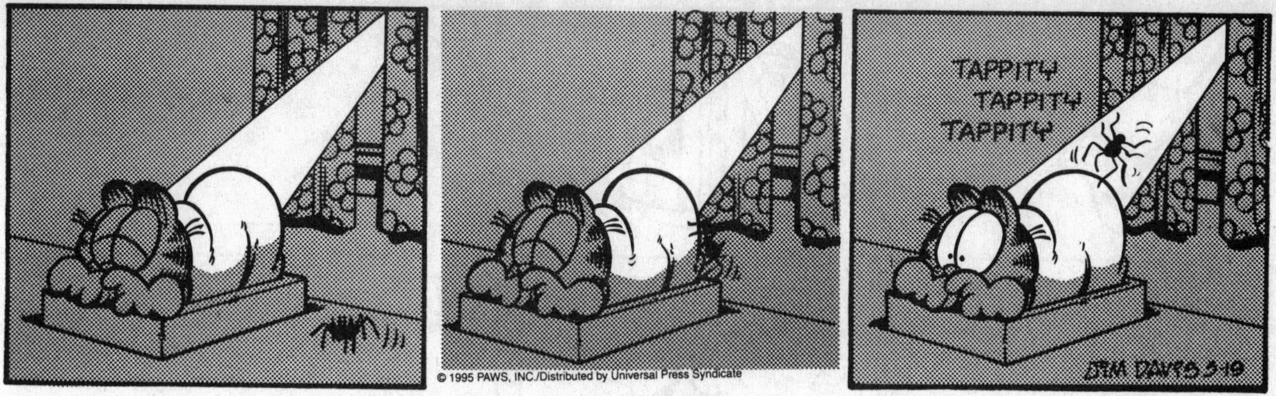
TAPPITY
TAPPITY
TAPPITY
JIM DAVIS 5-19

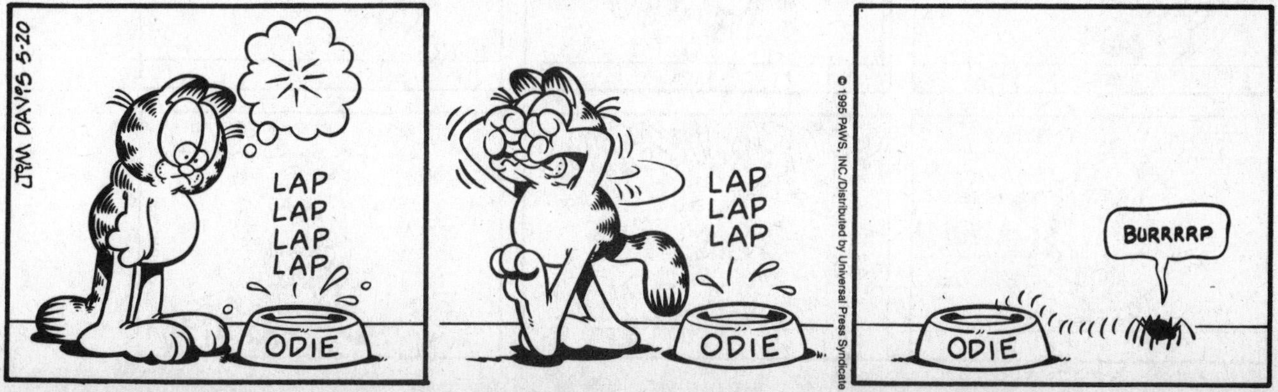
JIM DAVIS 5-20
LAP
LAP
LAP
LAP
ODIE
LAP
LAP
LAP
ODIE
ODIE
BURRRRP

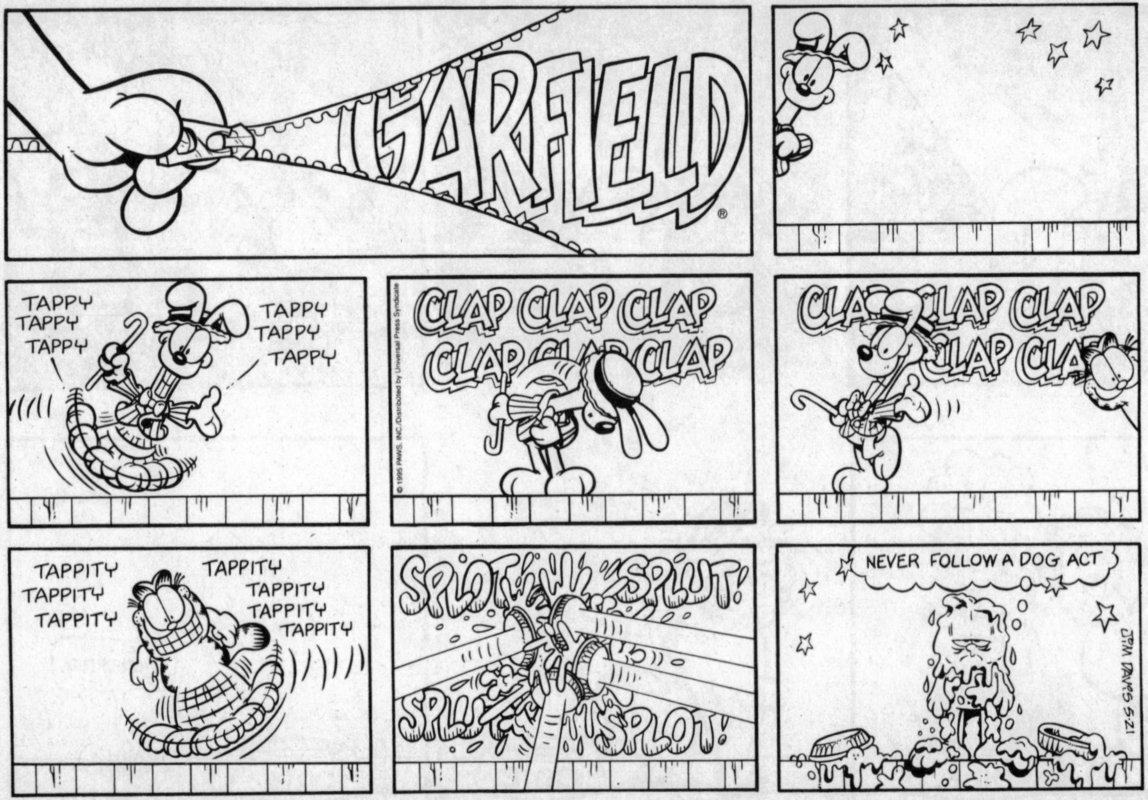
GARFIELD®
TAPPY TAPPY TAPPY
TAPPY TAPPY TAPPY
© 1995 PAWS, INC./Distributed by Universal Press Syndicate
CLAP CLAP CLAP CLAP CLAP CLAP
CLAP CLAP CLAP CLAP CLAP
TAPPITY TAPPITY TAPPITY
TAPPITY TAPPITY TAPPITY TAPPITY
SPLOT! SPLUT!
SPLUT! SPLOT!
NEVER FOLLOW A DOG ACT
JIM DAVIS 5-21

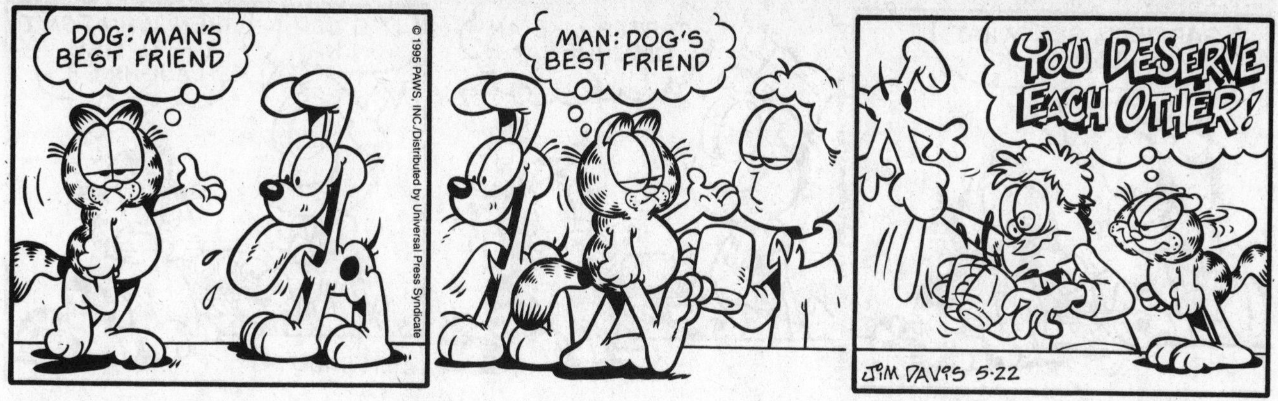
DOG: MAN'S BEST FRIEND
© 1995 PAWS, INC./Distributed by Universal Press Syndicate
MAN: DOG'S BEST FRIEND
YOU DESERVE EACH OTHER!
JIM DAVIS 5-22

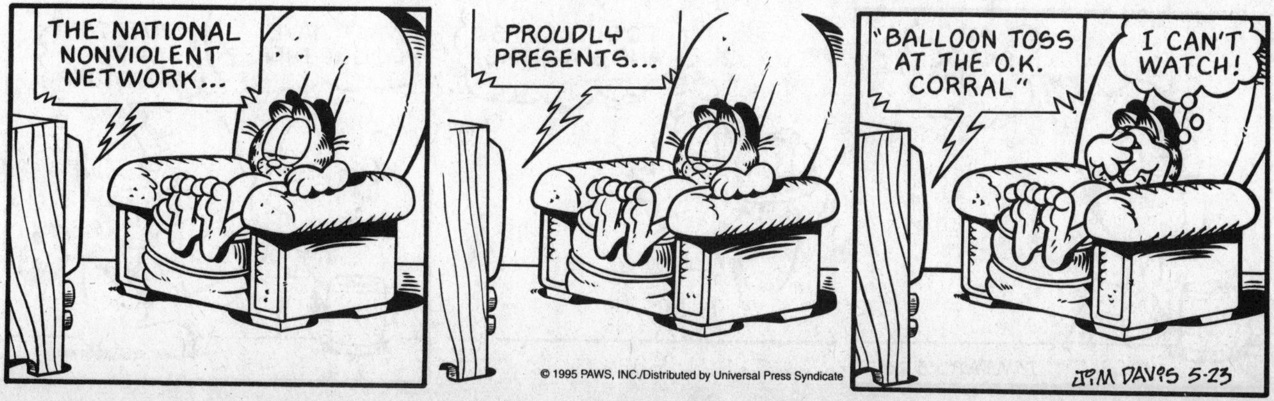
THE NATIONAL NONVIOLENT NETWORK...
PROUDLY PRESENTS...
"BALLOON TOSS AT THE O.K. CORRAL"
I CAN'T WATCH!
© 1995 PAWS, INC./Distributed by Universal Press Syndicate
JIM DAVIS 5-23

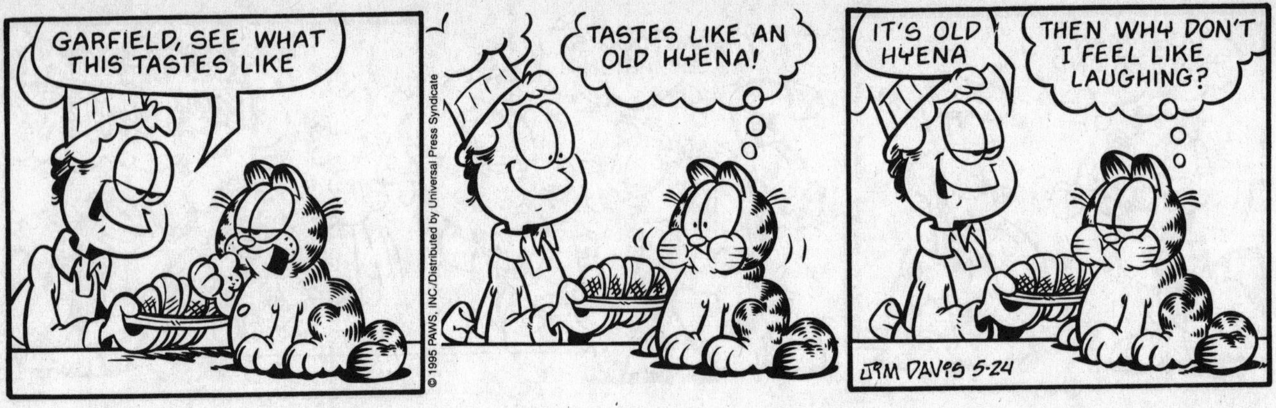
GARFIELD, SEE WHAT THIS TASTES LIKE
TASTES LIKE AN OLD HYENA!
IT'S OLD HYENA
THEN WHY DON'T I FEEL LIKE LAUGHING?
JIM DAVIS 5-24

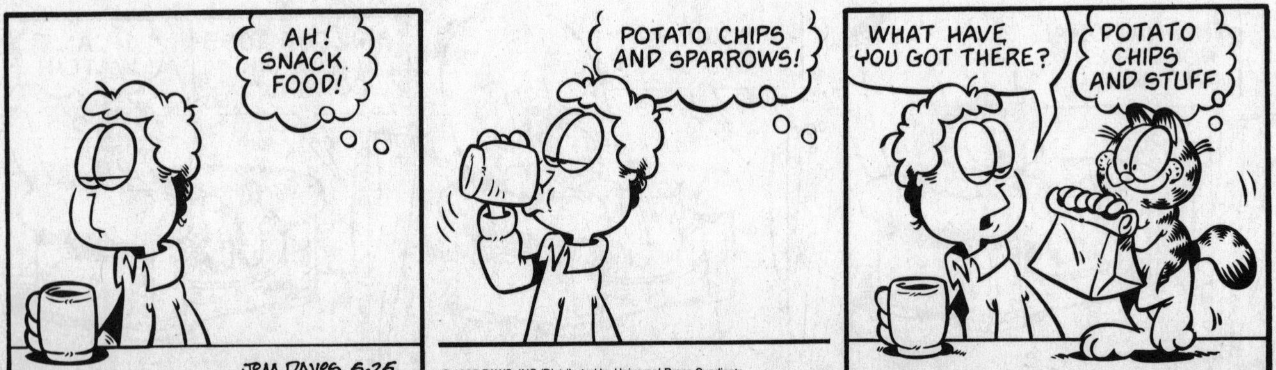
AH! SNACK FOOD!
JIM DAVIS 5-25
POTATO CHIPS AND SPARROWS!
WHAT HAVE YOU GOT THERE?
POTATO CHIPS AND STUFF

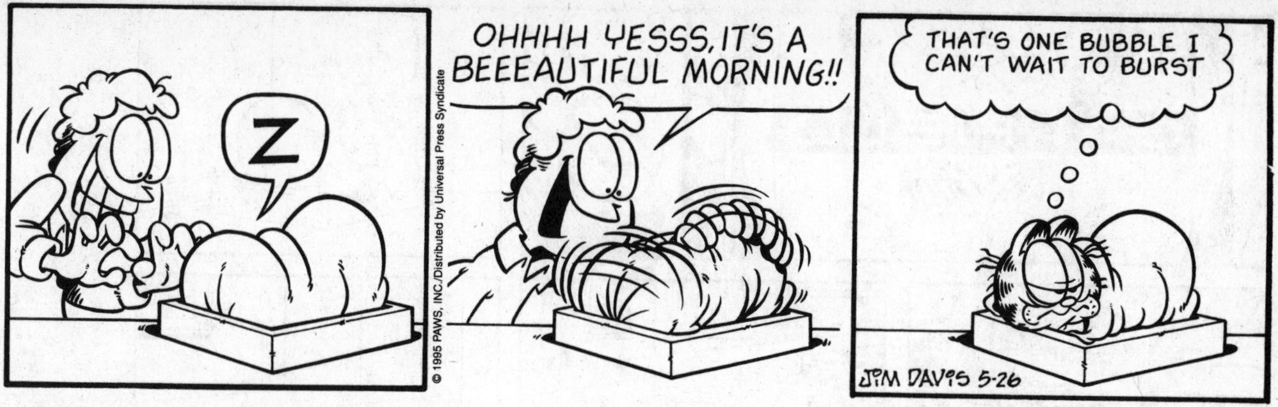
Z
© 1995 PAWS, INC./Distributed by Universal Press Syndicate
OHHHH YESSS, IT'S A BEEEAUTIFUL MORNING!!
THAT'S ONE BUBBLE I CAN'T WAIT TO BURST
JIM DAVIS 5-26

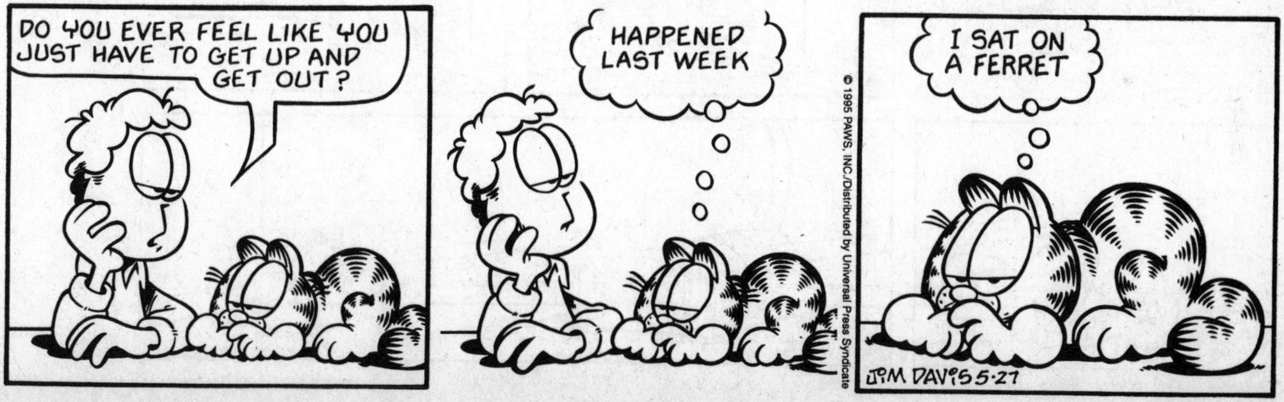
DO YOU EVER FEEL LIKE YOU JUST HAVE TO GET UP AND GET OUT?
HAPPENED LAST WEEK
© 1995 PAWS, INC./Distributed by Universal Press Syndicate
I SAT ON A FERRET
JIM DAVIS 5-27

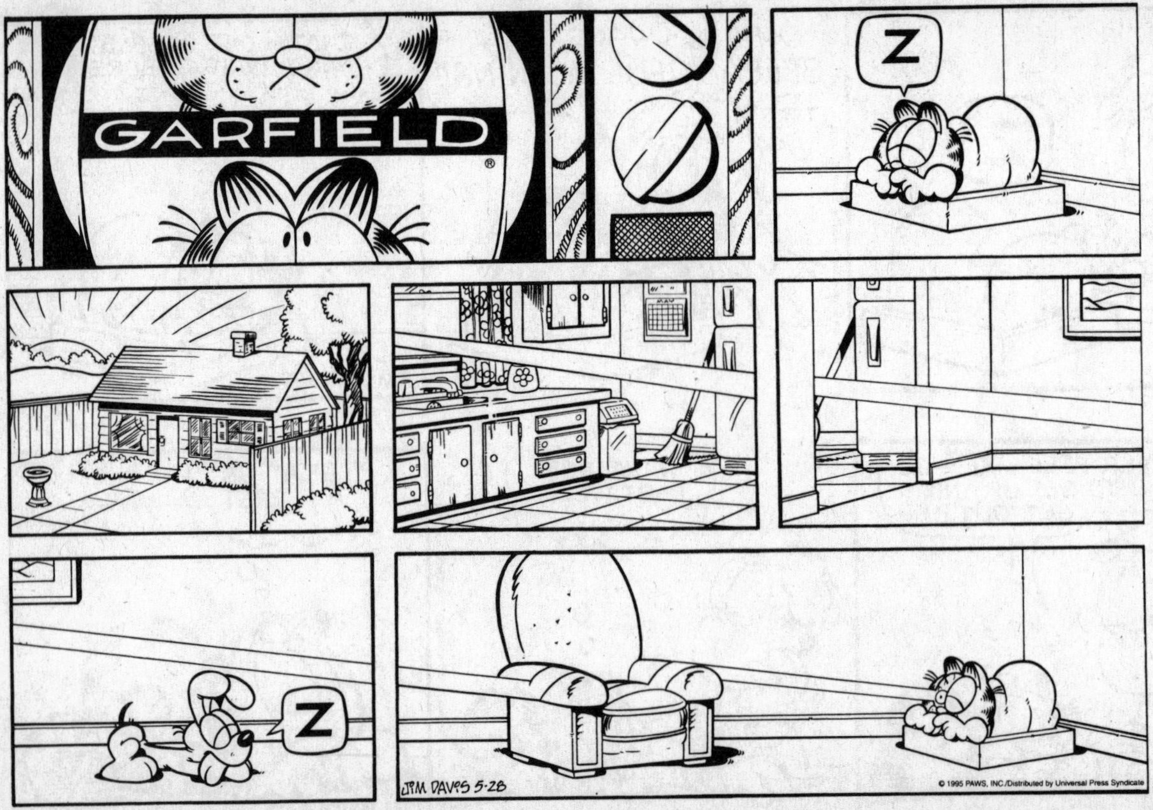
GARFIELD®
Z
Z
JIM DAVIS 5-28
© 1995 PAWS, INC./Distributed by Universal Press Syndicate

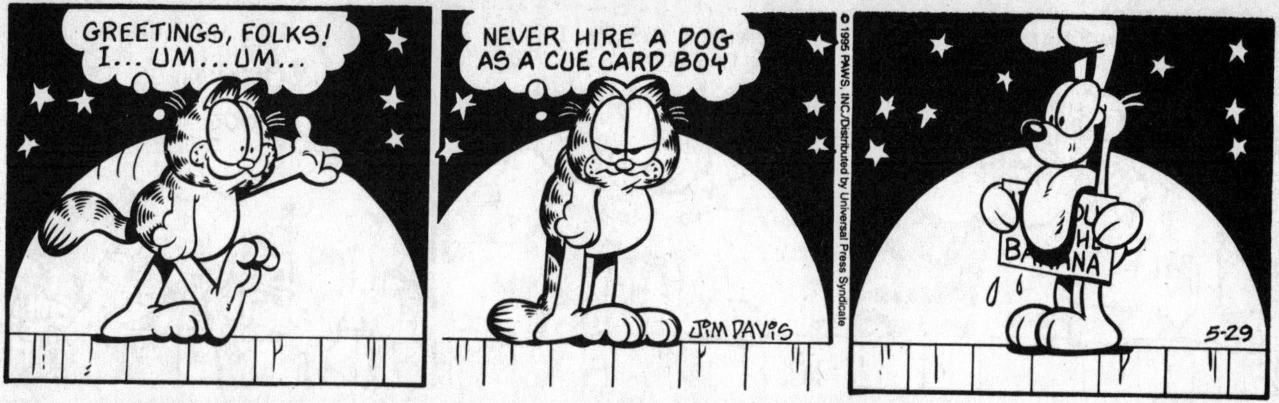

GREETINGS, FOLKS! I... UM... UM...
NEVER HIRE A DOG AS A CUE CARD BOY
JIM DAVIS
© 1995 PAWS, INC./Distributed by Universal Press Syndicate
5-29

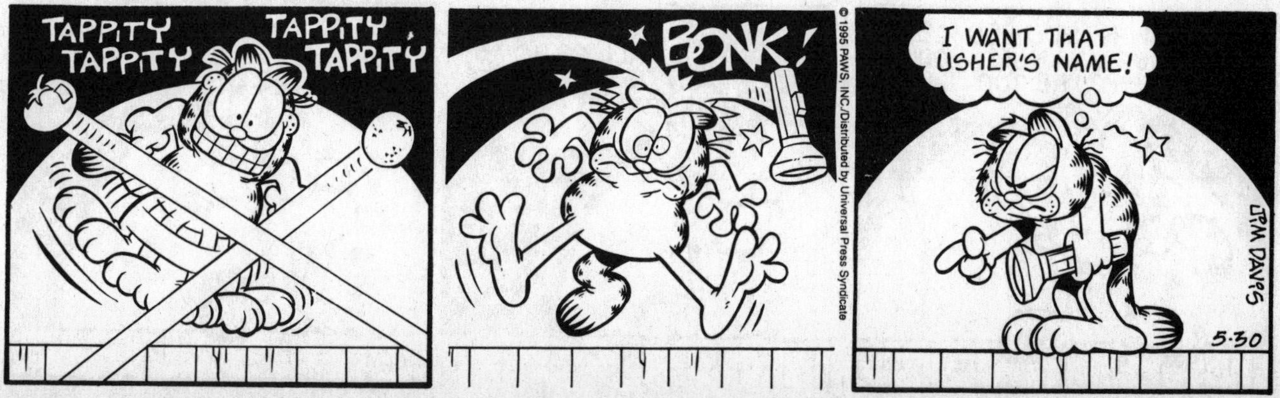

TAPPITY TAPPITY TAPPITY TAPPITY
BONK!
© 1995 PAWS, INC./Distributed by Universal Press Syndicate
I WANT THAT USHER'S NAME!
JIM DAVIS
5-30

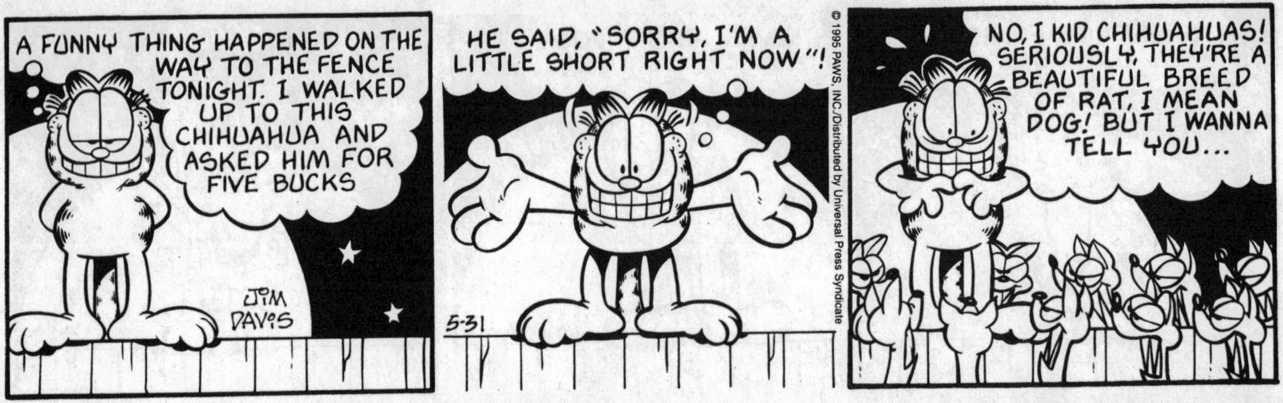
A FUNNY THING HAPPENED ON THE WAY TO THE FENCE TONIGHT. I WALKED UP TO THIS CHIHUAHUA AND ASKED HIM FOR FIVE BUCKS
JIM DAVIS
HE SAID, "SORRY, I'M A LITTLE SHORT RIGHT NOW"!
5-31
© 1995 PAWS, INC./Distributed by Universal Press Syndicate
NO, I KID CHIHUAHUAS! SERIOUSLY, THEY'RE A BEAUTIFUL BREED OF RAT, I MEAN DOG! BUT I WANNA TELL YOU...

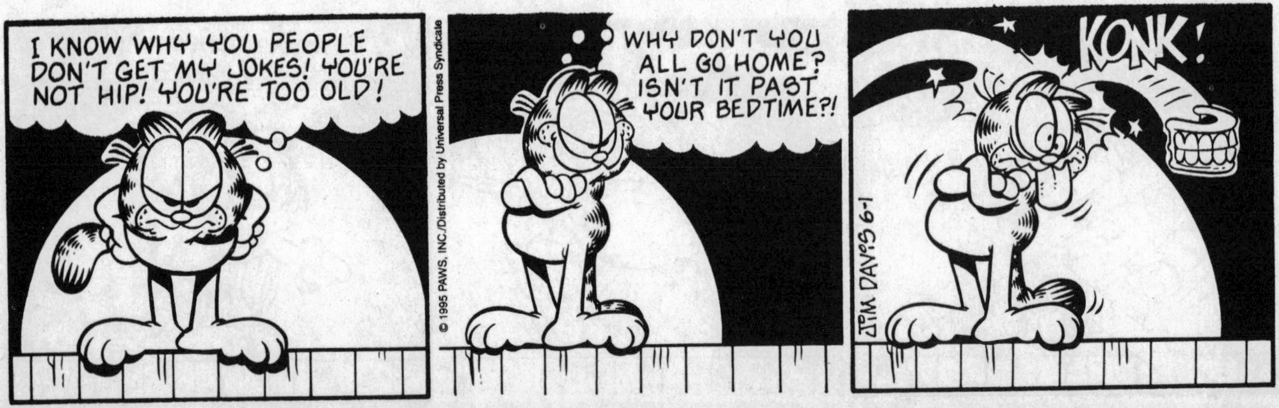
I KNOW WHY YOU PEOPLE DON'T GET MY JOKES! YOU'RE NOT HIP! YOU'RE TOO OLD!
© 1995 PAWS, INC./Distributed by Universal Press Syndicate
WHY DON'T YOU ALL GO HOME? ISN'T IT PAST YOUR BEDTIME?!
JIM DAVIS 6-1
KONK!

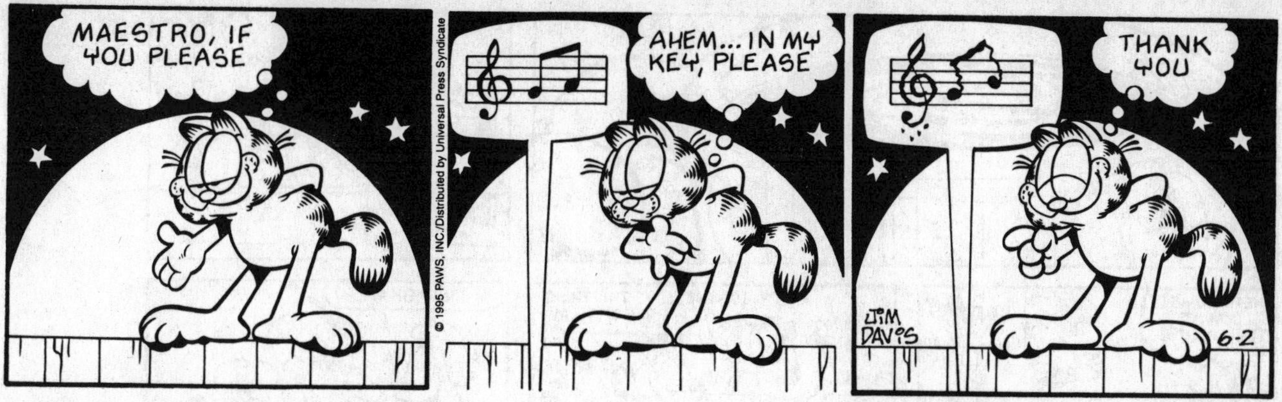
MAESTRO, IF YOU PLEASE
© 1995 PAWS, INC./Distributed by Universal Press Syndicate
AHEM... IN MY KEY, PLEASE
THANK YOU
JIM DAVIS
6-2

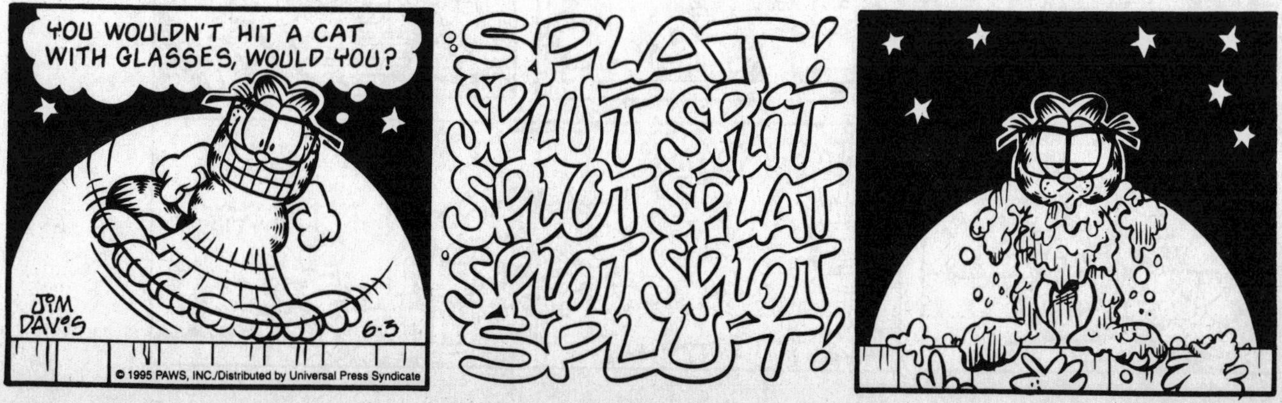
YOU WOULDN'T HIT A CAT WITH GLASSES, WOULD YOU?
JIM DAVIS
6-3
© 1995 PAWS, INC./Distributed by Universal Press Syndicate
SPLAT!
SPLUT SPLIT
SPLOT SPLAT
SPLIT SPLOT
SPLUT!

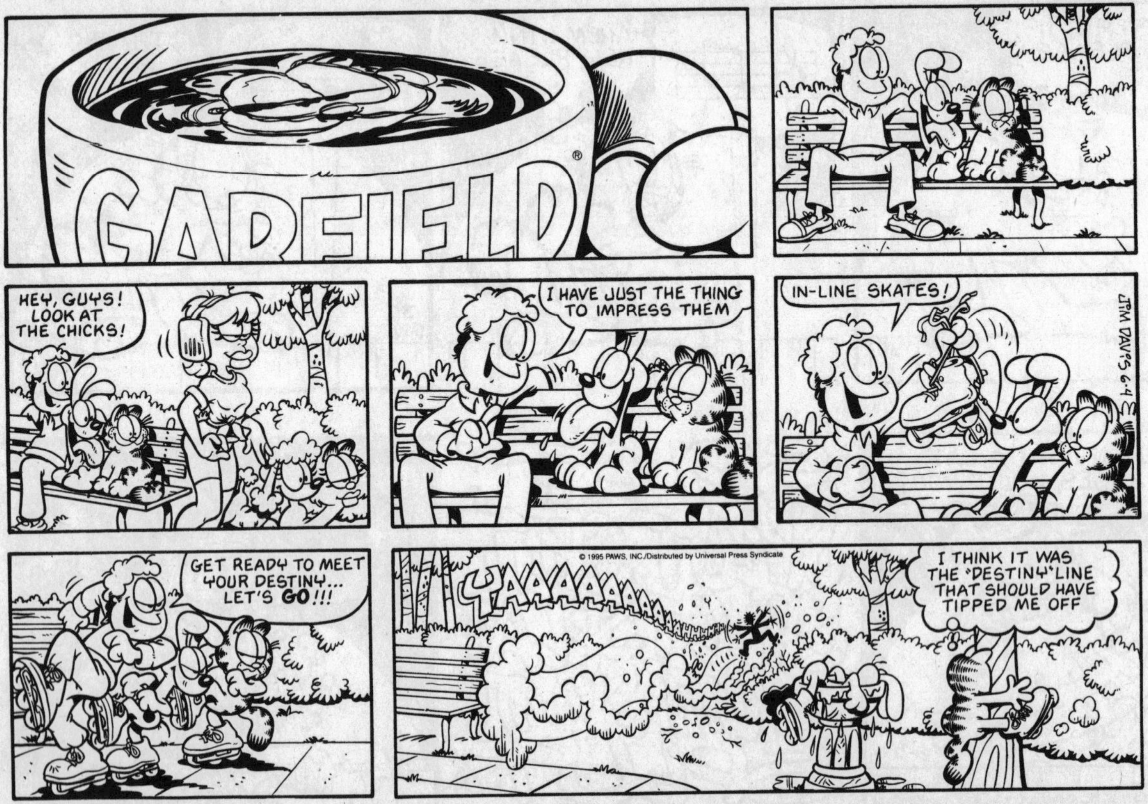
GARFIELD
HEY, GUYS! LOOK AT THE CHICKS!
I HAVE JUST THE THING TO IMPRESS THEM
IN-LINE SKATES!
JIM DAVIS 6-4
GET READY TO MEET YOUR DESTINY... LET'S GO!!!
© 1995 PAWS, INC./Distributed by Universal Press Syndicate
YAAAAAAAAAAAAHHHHH
I THINK IT WAS THE "DESTINY" LINE THAT SHOULD HAVE TIPPED ME OFF

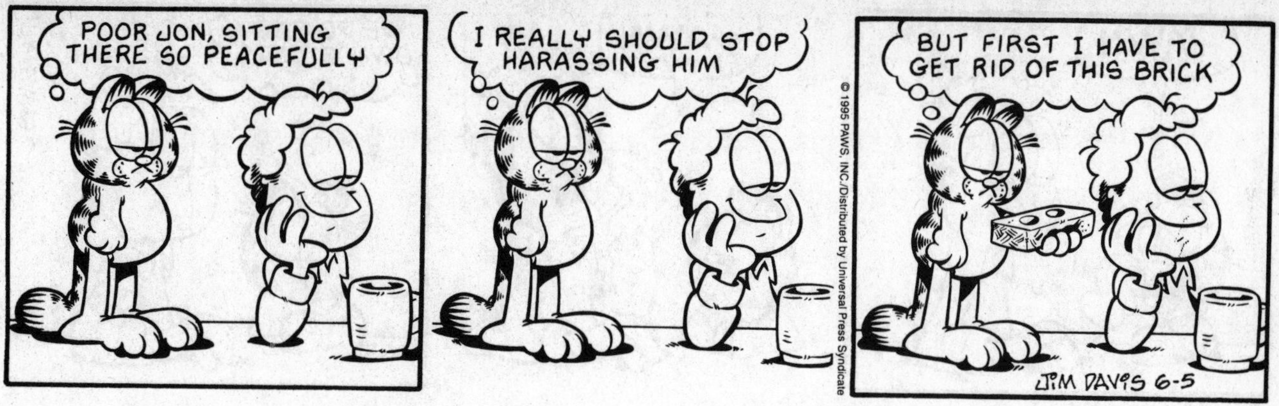
POOR JON, SITTING THERE SO PEACEFULLY
I REALLY SHOULD STOP HARASSING HIM
BUT FIRST I HAVE TO GET RID OF THIS BRICK
JIM DAVIS 6-5

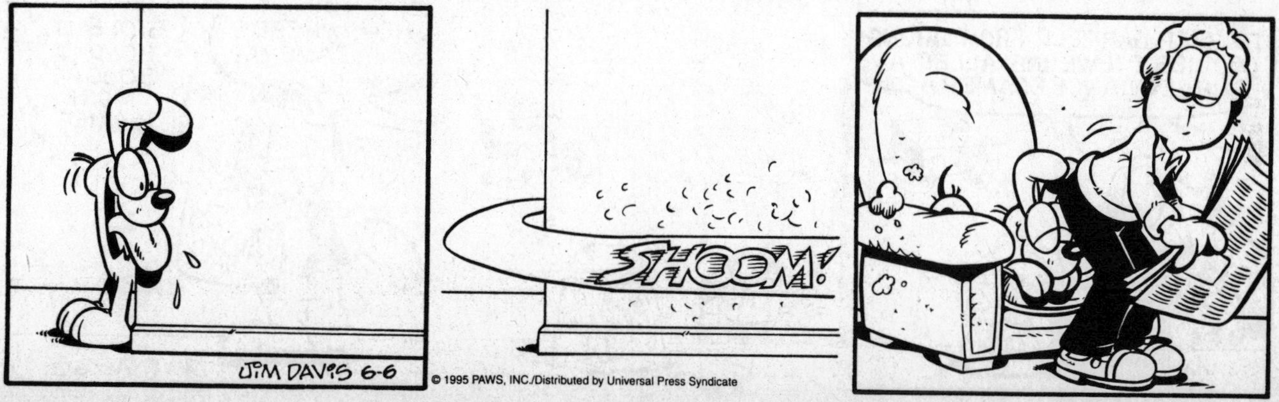
JIM DAVIS 6-6
SHOOM!

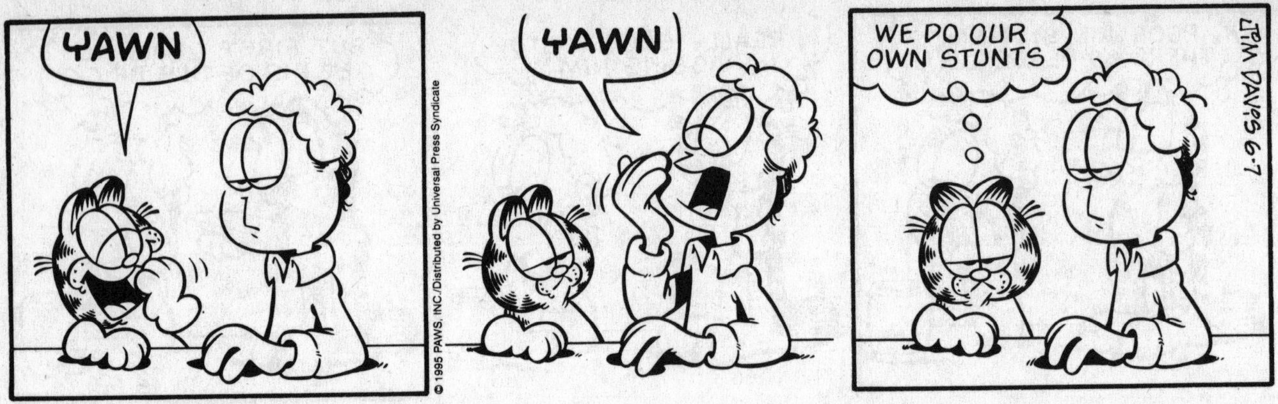
YAWN
YAWN
WE DO OUR OWN STUNTS
JIM DAVIS 6-7
© 1995 PAWS, INC./Distributed by Universal Press Syndicate

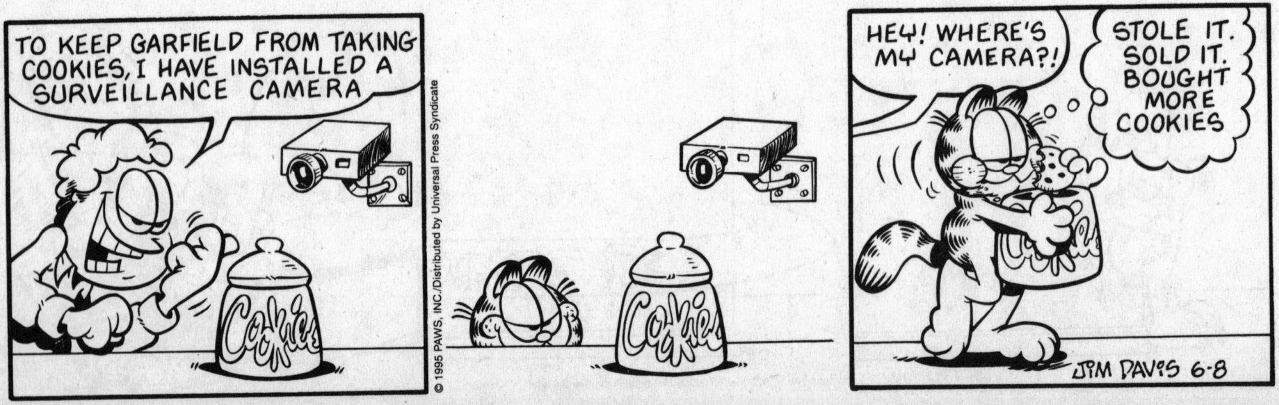
TO KEEP GARFIELD FROM TAKING COOKIES, I HAVE INSTALLED A SURVEILLANCE CAMERA
© 1995 PAWS, INC./Distributed by Universal Press Syndicate
HEY! WHERE'S MY CAMERA?!
STOLE IT. SOLD IT. BOUGHT MORE COOKIES
JIM DAVIS 6-8

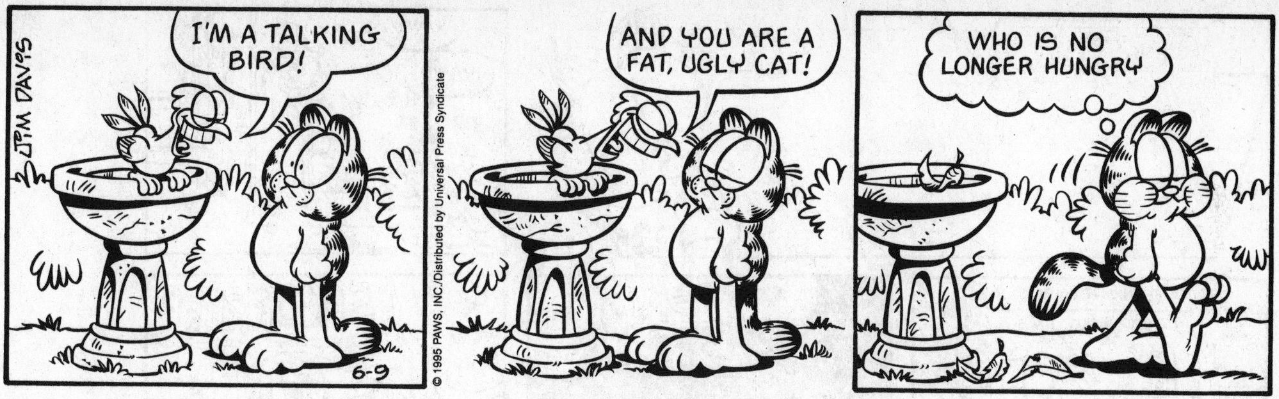
JIM DAVIS
I'M A TALKING BIRD!
6-9
© 1995 PAWS, INC./Distributed by Universal Press Syndicate
AND YOU ARE A FAT, UGLY CAT!
WHO IS NO LONGER HUNGRY

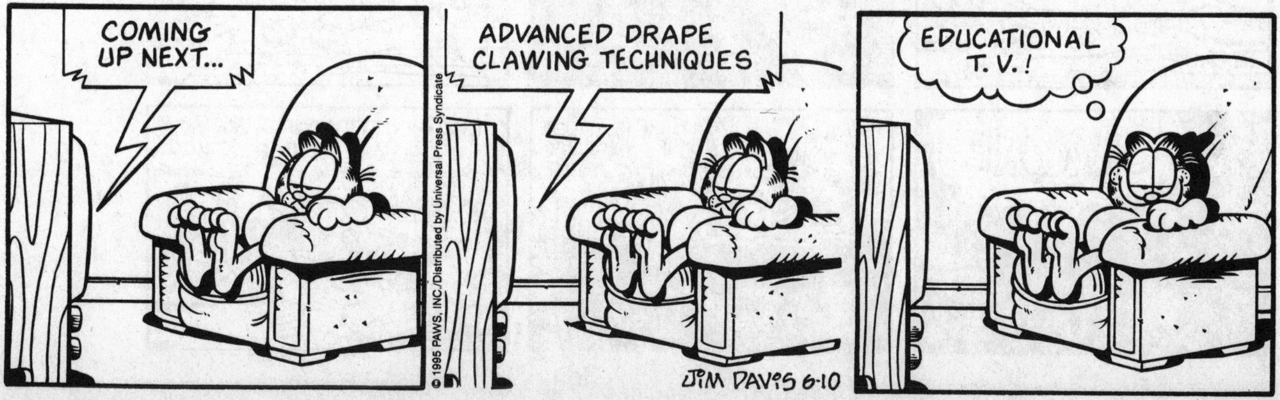
COMING UP NEXT...
© 1995 PAWS, INC./Distributed by Universal Press Syndicate
ADVANCED DRAPE CLAWING TECHNIQUES
JIM DAVIS 6-10
EDUCATIONAL T.V.!

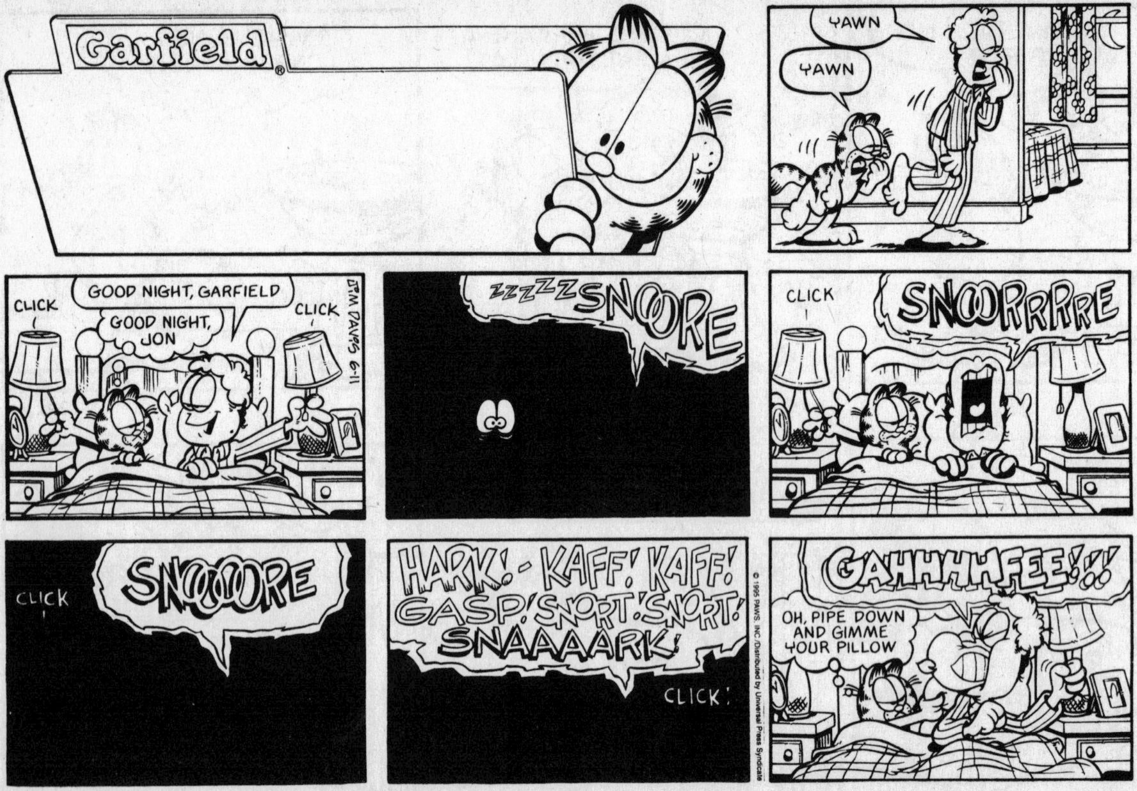
Garfield
YAWN
YAWN
CLICK
GOOD NIGHT, GARFIELD
GOOD NIGHT, JON
CLICK
JPM DAVPS 6-11
ZZZZZSNOORE
CLICK
SNOORRRRE
CLICK
SNOOOORE
HARK! - KAFF! KAFF!
GASP! SNORT! SNORT!
SNAAAARK!
CLICK!
© 1995 PAWS, INC./Distributed by Universal Press Syndicate
GAHHHHFEE!!!
OH, PIPE DOWN AND GIMME YOUR PILLOW

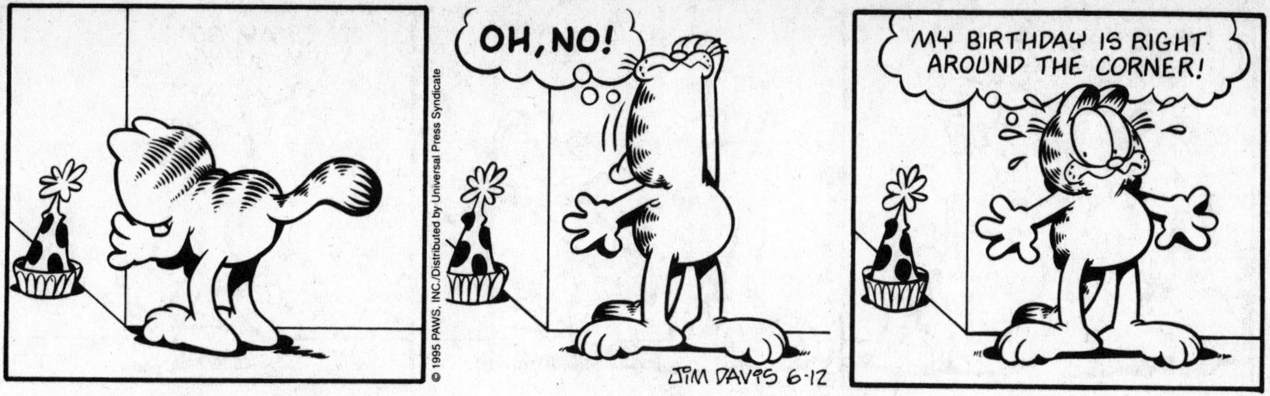
OH, NO!
MY BIRTHDAY IS RIGHT AROUND THE CORNER!
JIM DAVIS 6-12
© 1995 PAWS, INC./Distributed by Universal Press Syndicate

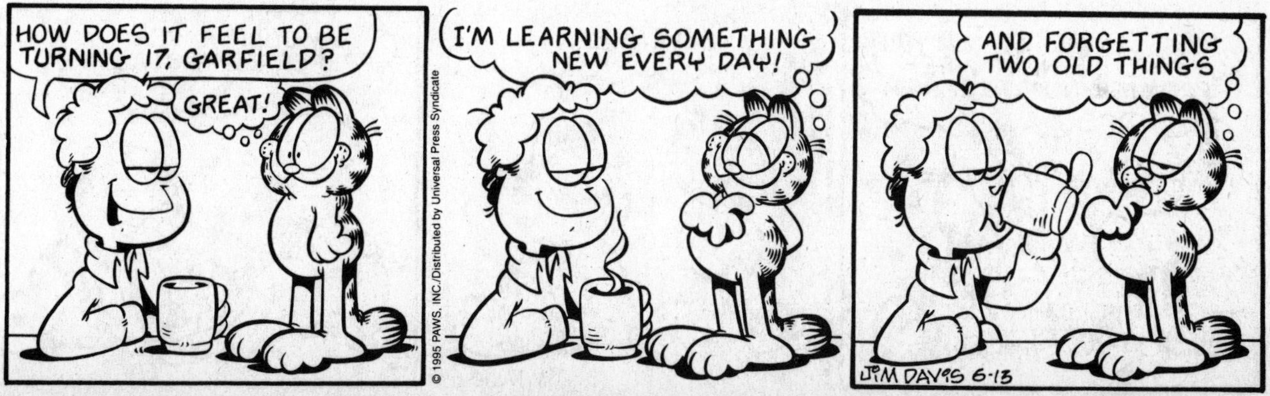
HOW DOES IT FEEL TO BE TURNING 17, GARFIELD?
GREAT!
I'M LEARNING SOMETHING NEW EVERY DAY!
AND FORGETTING TWO OLD THINGS
JIM DAVIS 6-13
© 1995 PAWS, INC./Distributed by Universal Press Syndicate

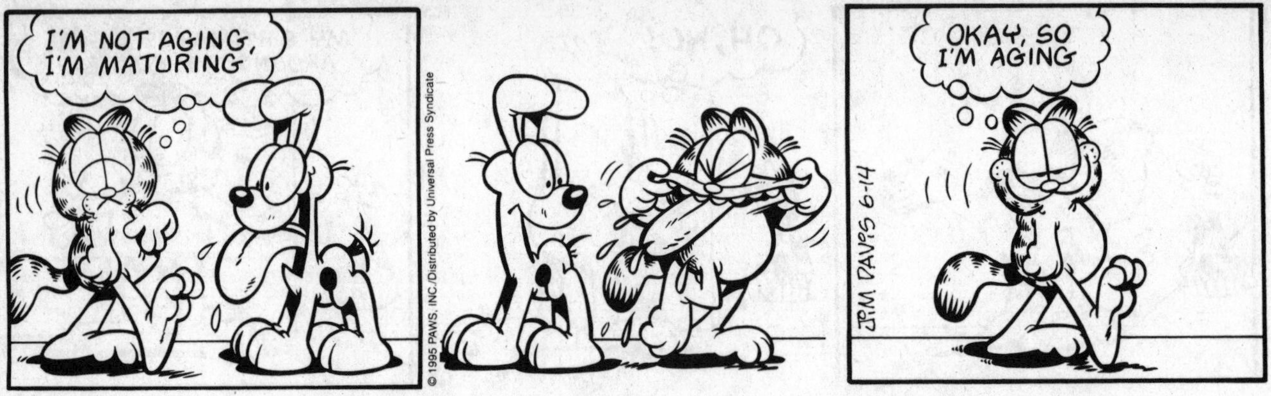
I'M NOT AGING, I'M MATURING
© 1995 PAWS, INC./Distributed by Universal Press Syndicate
JIM DAVIS 6-14
OKAY, SO I'M AGING

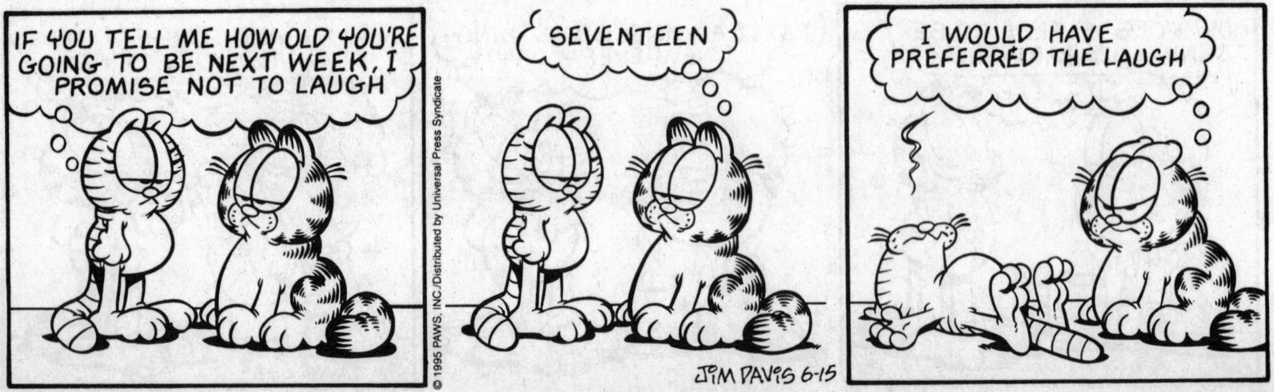
IF YOU TELL ME HOW OLD YOU'RE GOING TO BE NEXT WEEK, I PROMISE NOT TO LAUGH
© 1995 PAWS, INC./Distributed by Universal Press Syndicate
SEVENTEEN
I WOULD HAVE PREFERRED THE LAUGH
JIM DAVIS 6-15

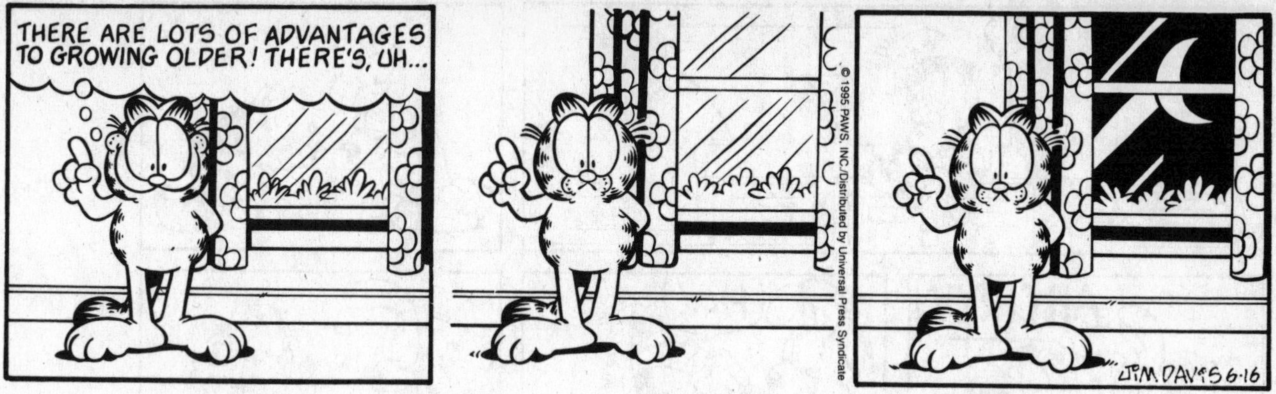
THERE ARE LOTS OF ADVANTAGES TO GROWING OLDER! THERE'S, UH...
JIM DAVIS 6·16

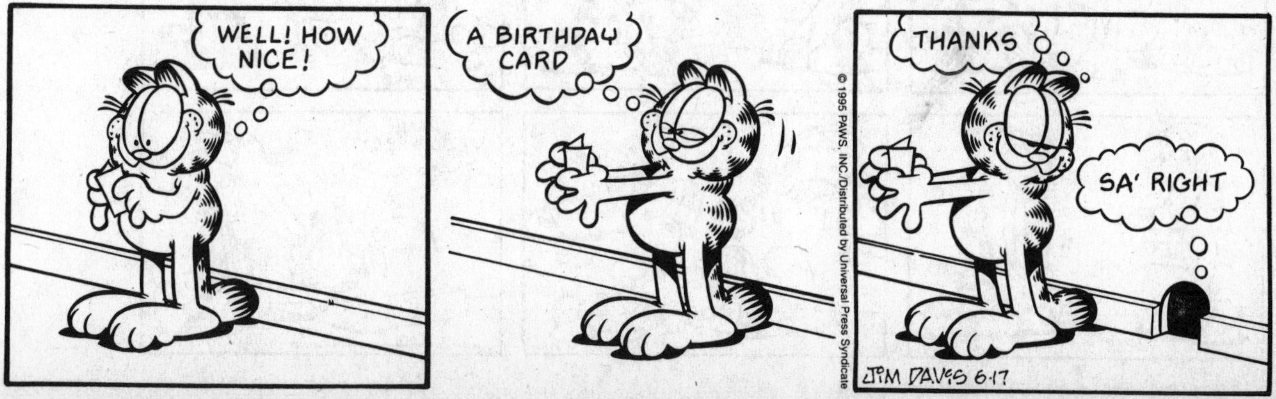
WELL! HOW NICE!
A BIRTHDAY CARD
THANKS
SA' RIGHT
JIM DAVIS 6·17

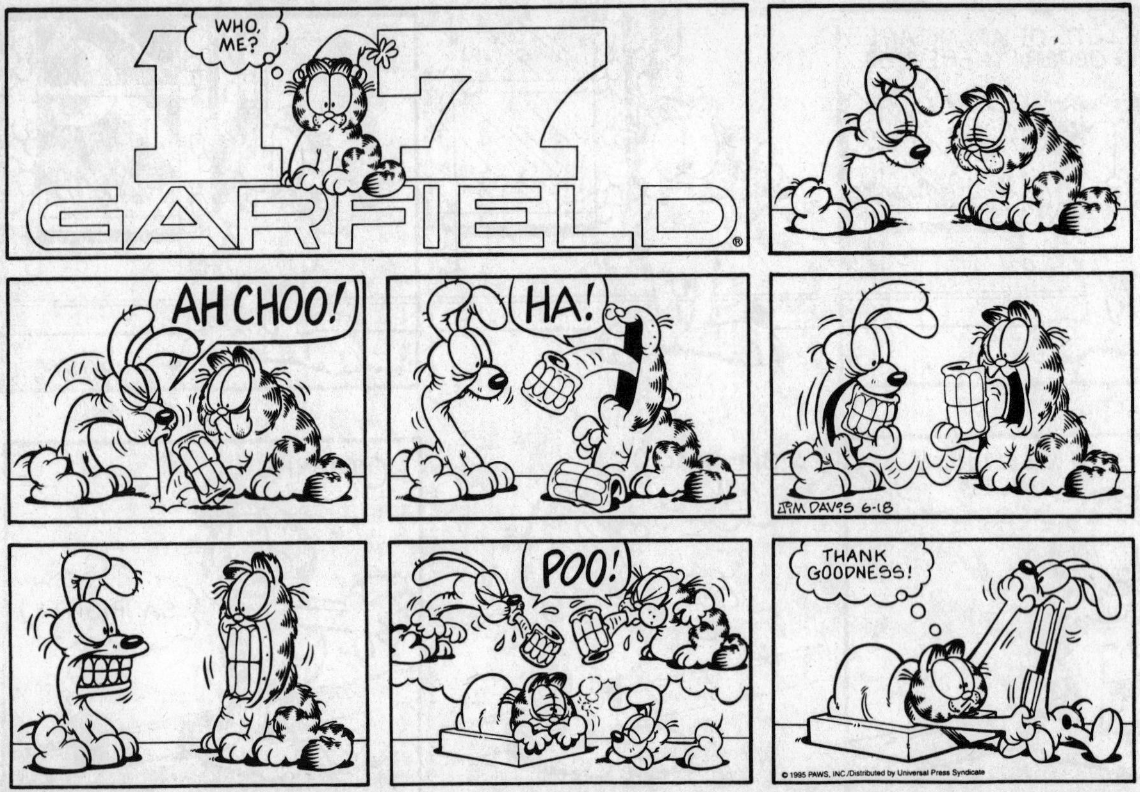
WHO, ME?
GARFIELD®
AH CHOO!
HA!
JIM DAVIS 6-18
POO!
THANK GOODNESS!
© 1995 PAWS, INC./Distributed by Universal Press Syndicate

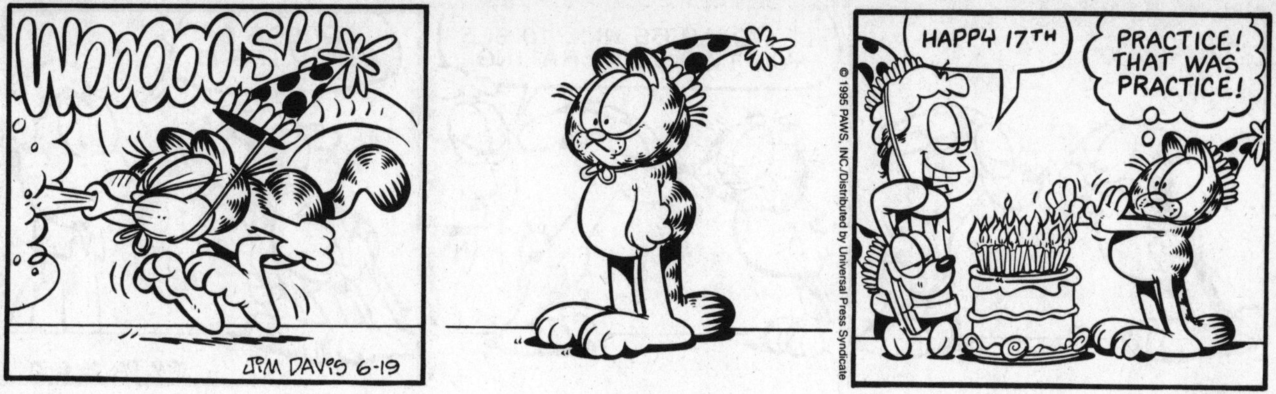
WOOOOOSH
JIM DAVIS 6-19
HAPPY 17TH
PRACTICE! THAT WAS PRACTICE!
© 1995 PAWS, INC./Distributed by Universal Press Syndicate

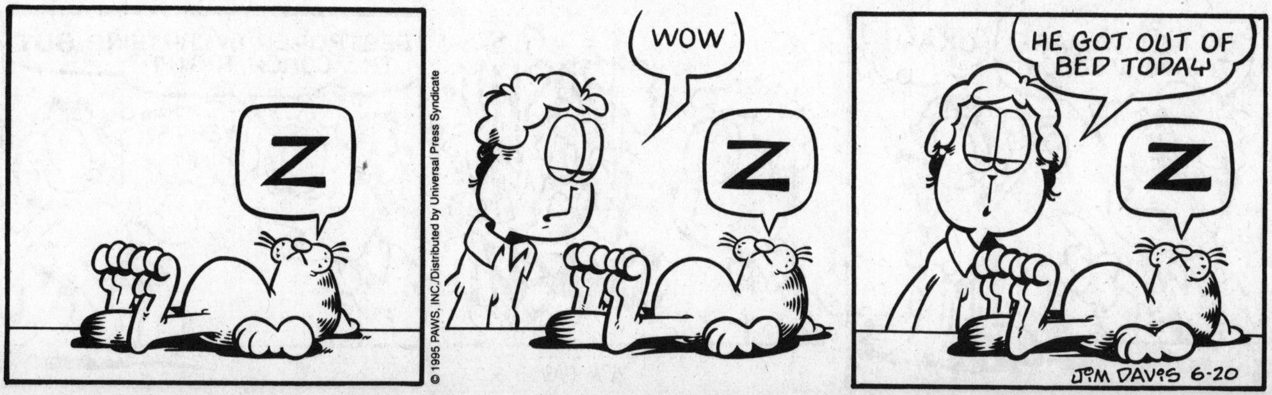
Z
© 1995 PAWS, INC./Distributed by Universal Press Syndicate
WOW
Z
HE GOT OUT OF BED TODAY
Z
JIM DAVIS 6-20

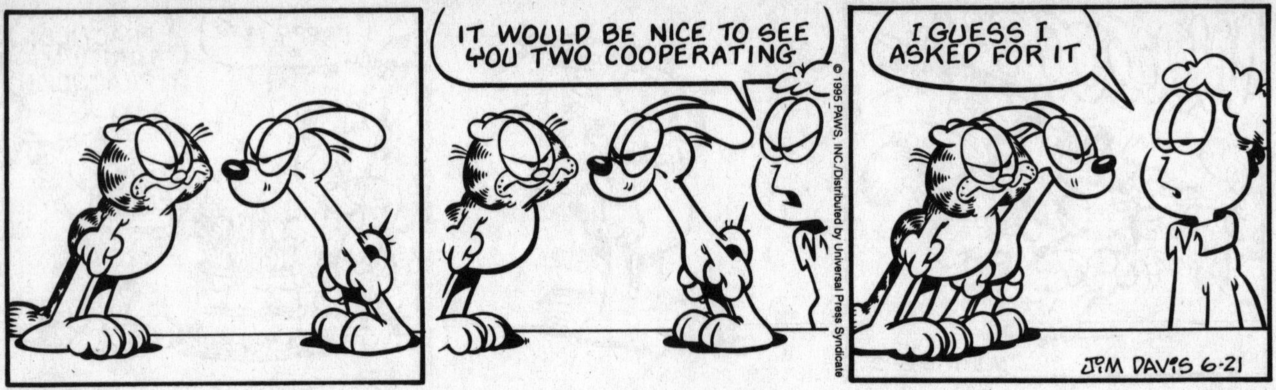
IT WOULD BE NICE TO SEE YOU TWO COOPERATING
I GUESS I ASKED FOR IT
JIM DAVIS 6-21
© 1995 PAWS, INC./Distributed by Universal Press Syndicate

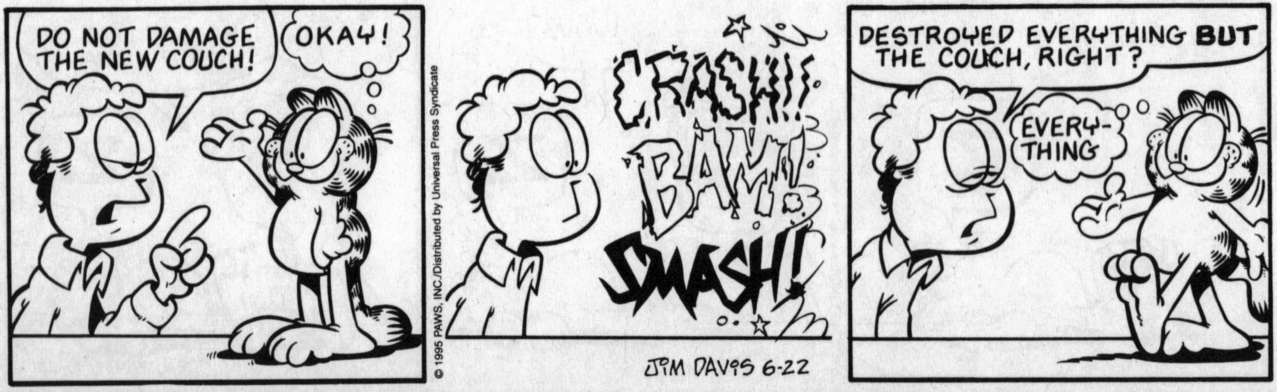
DO NOT DAMAGE THE NEW COUCH!
OKAY!
CRASH!
BAM!
SMASH!
DESTROYED EVERYTHING **BUT** THE COUCH, RIGHT?
EVERY-THING
JIM DAVIS 6-22
© 1995 PAWS, INC./Distributed by Universal Press Syndicate

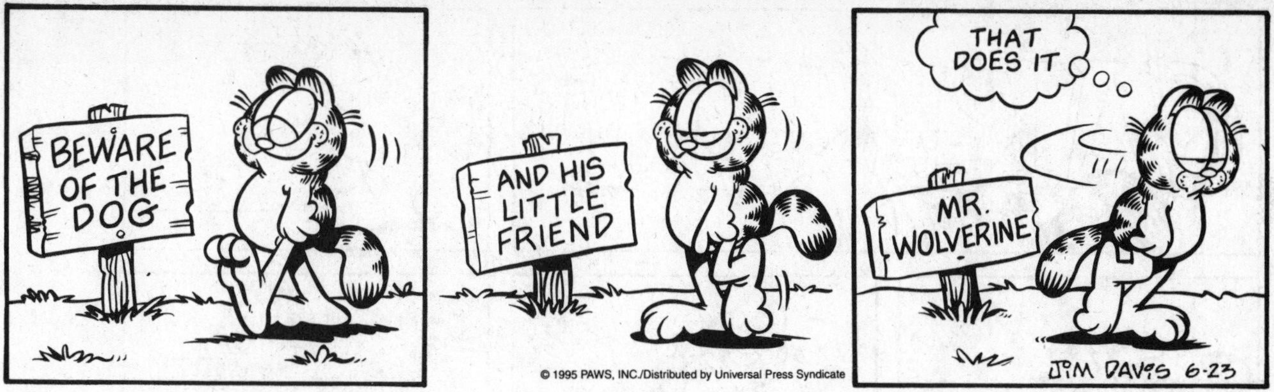

BEWARE OF THE DOG
AND HIS LITTLE FRIEND
MR. WOLVERINE
THAT DOES IT
© 1995 PAWS, INC./Distributed by Universal Press Syndicate
JIM DAVIS 6-23

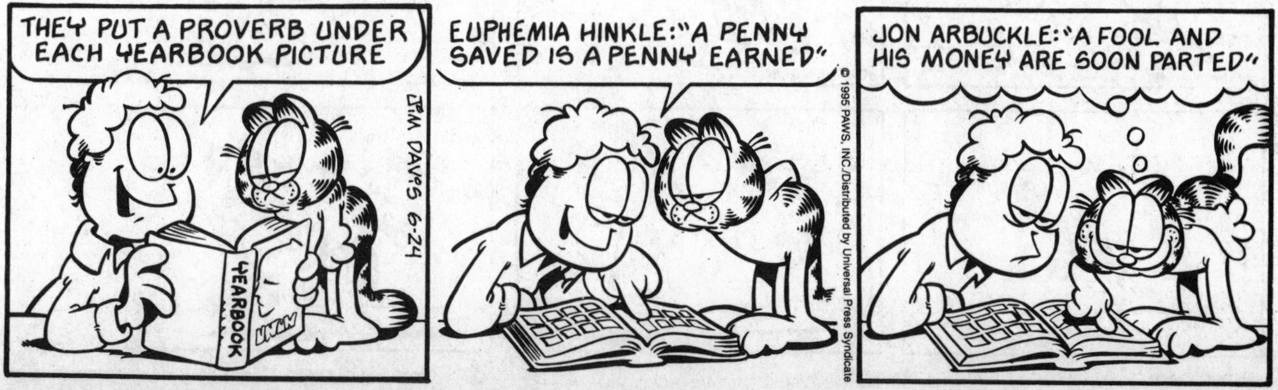

THEY PUT A PROVERB UNDER EACH YEARBOOK PICTURE
YEARBOOK
JIM DAVIS 6-24
EUPHEMIA HINKLE: "A PENNY SAVED IS A PENNY EARNED"
© 1995 PAWS, INC./Distributed by Universal Press Syndicate
JON ARBUCKLE: "A FOOL AND HIS MONEY ARE SOON PARTED"

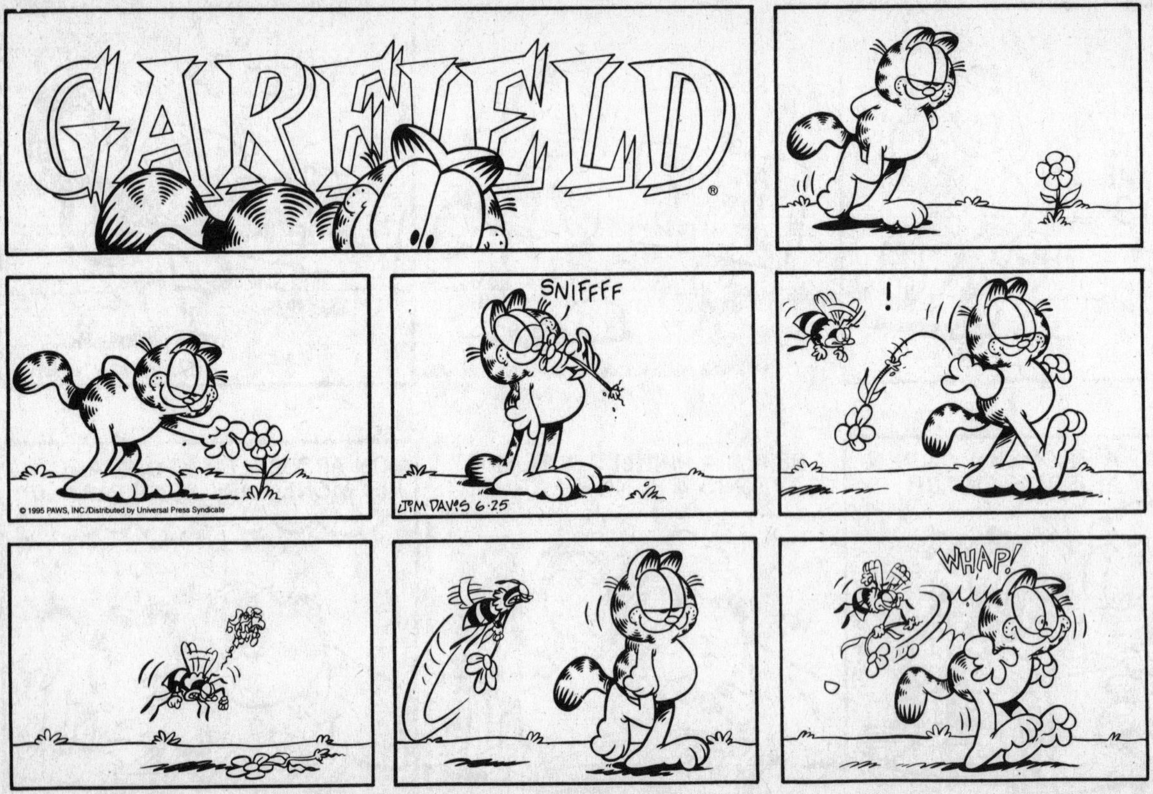
GARFIELD
SNIFFFF
!
WHAP!
© 1995 PAWS, INC./Distributed by Universal Press Syndicate
JIM DAVIS 6·25

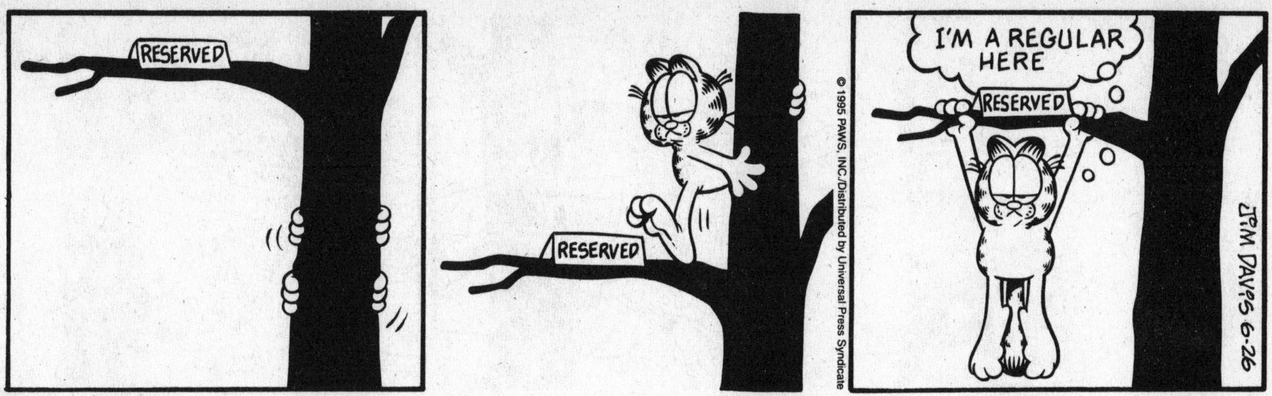
RESERVED
RESERVED
I'M A REGULAR HERE
RESERVED
JIM DAVIS 6-26
© 1995 PAWS, INC./Distributed by Universal Press Syndicate

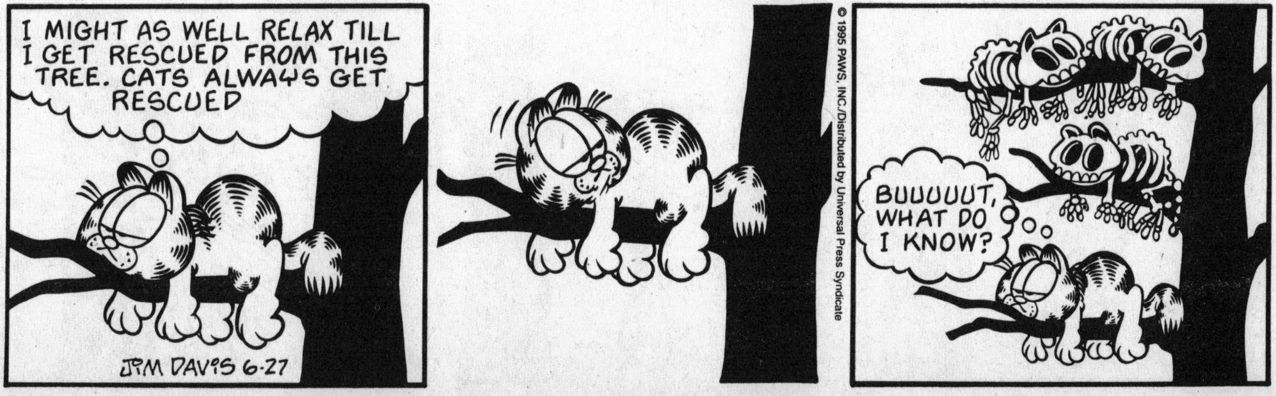
I MIGHT AS WELL RELAX TILL I GET RESCUED FROM THIS TREE. CATS ALWAYS GET RESCUED
JIM DAVIS 6-27
BUUUUUT, WHAT DO I KNOW?
© 1995 PAWS, INC./Distributed by Universal Press Syndicate

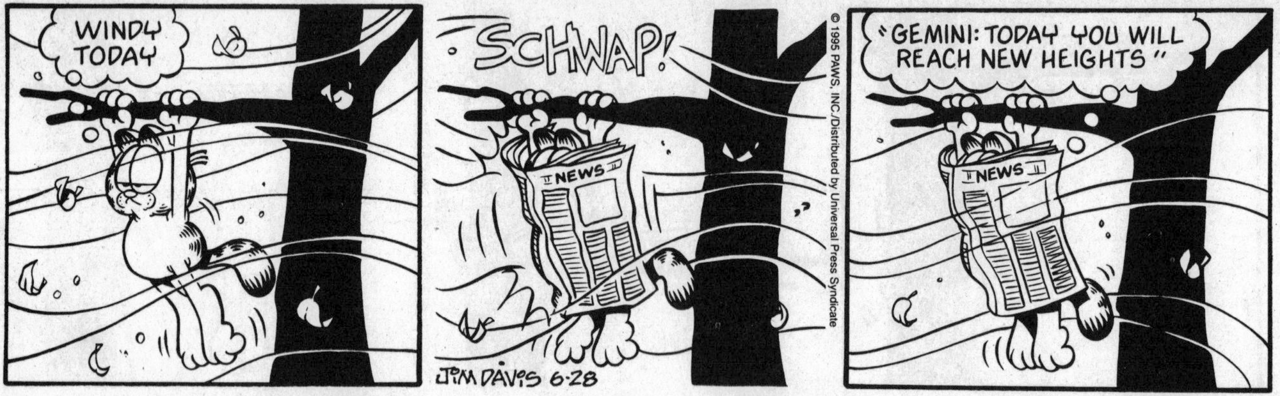
WINDY TODAY
SCHWAP!
NEWS
JIM DAVIS 6-28
© 1995 PAWS, INC./Distributed by Universal Press Syndicate
"GEMINI: TODAY YOU WILL REACH NEW HEIGHTS"

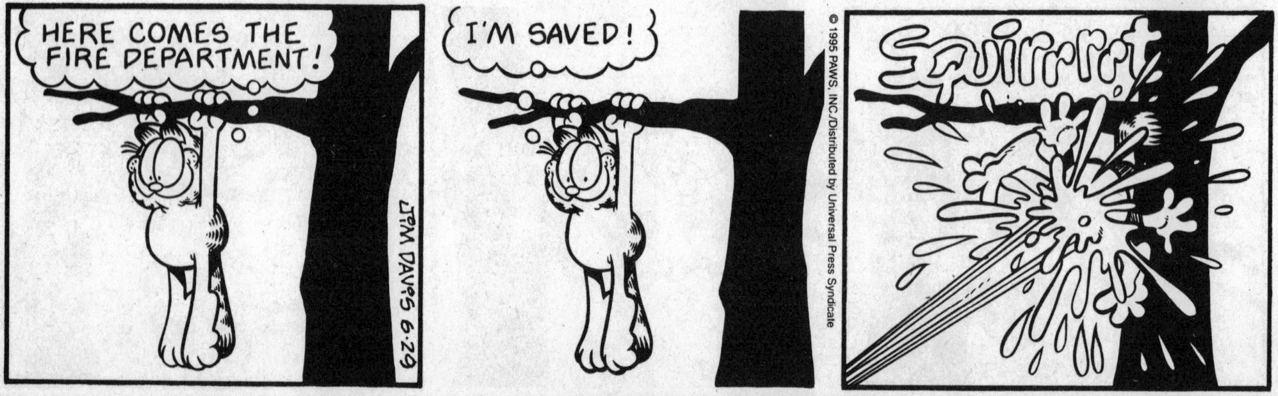
HERE COMES THE FIRE DEPARTMENT!
JIM DAVIS 6-29
I'M SAVED!
© 1995 PAWS, INC./Distributed by Universal Press Syndicate
Squirrrrt

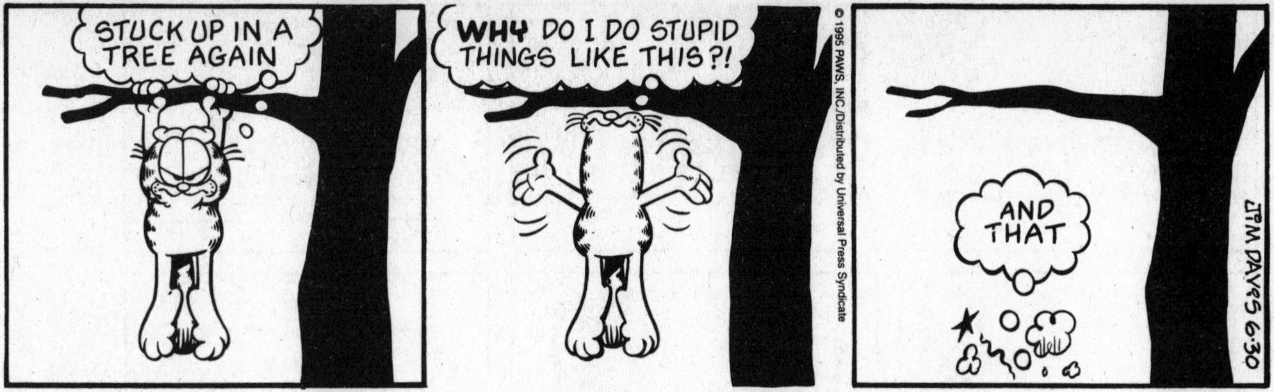
STUCK UP IN A TREE AGAIN
WHY DO I DO STUPID THINGS LIKE THIS?!
AND THAT
JIM DAVIS 6-30

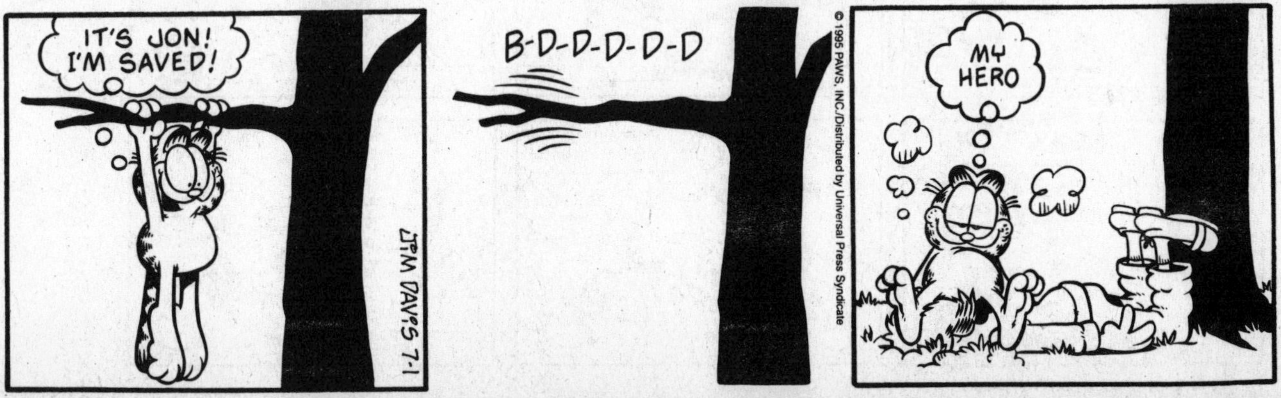
IT'S JON! I'M SAVED!
JIM DAVIS 7-1
B-D-D-D-D-D
MY HERO

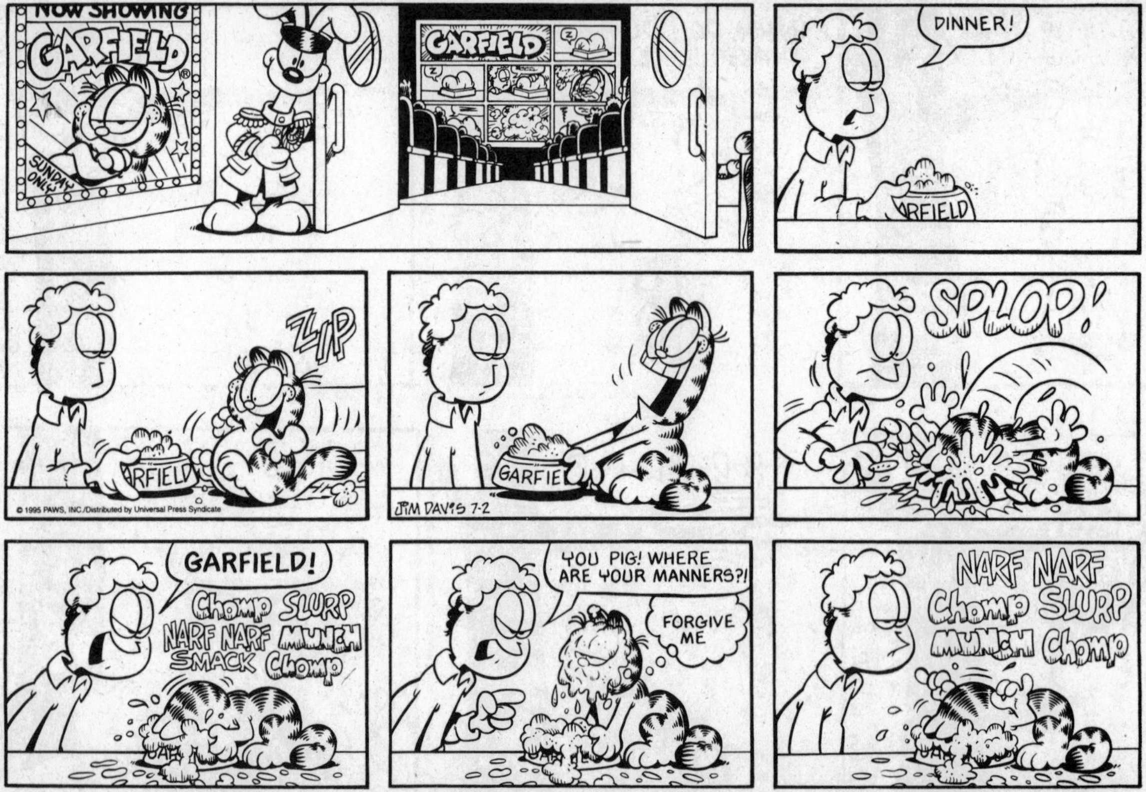
NOW SHOWING
GARFIELD
SUNDAY ONLY
GARFIELD
DINNER!
ZIP
© 1995 PAWS, INC./Distributed by Universal Press Syndicate
JIM DAVIS 7-2
SPLOP!
GARFIELD!
Chomp SLURP
NARF NARF MUNCH
SMACK Chomp
YOU PIG! WHERE ARE YOUR MANNERS?!
FORGIVE ME
NARF NARF
Chomp SLURP
MUNCH Chomp

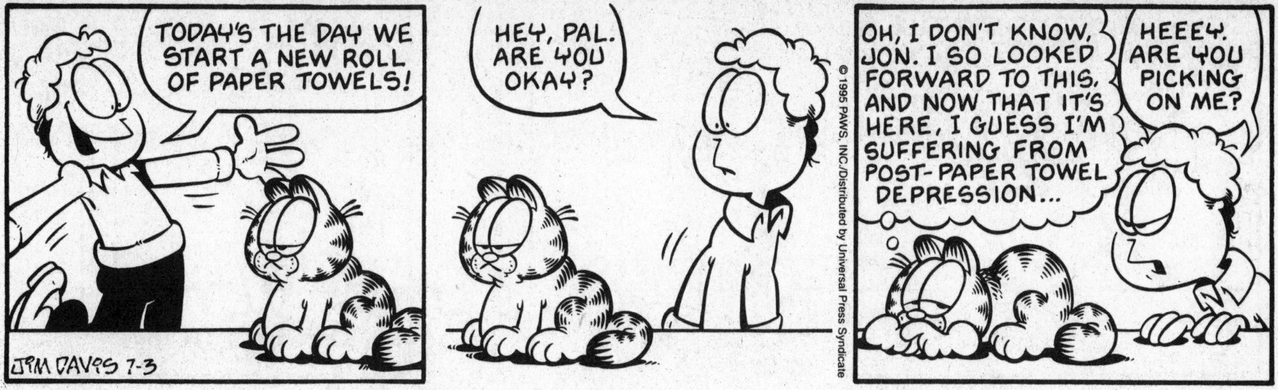
TODAY'S THE DAY WE START A NEW ROLL OF PAPER TOWELS!
JIM DAVIS 7-3
HEY, PAL. ARE YOU OKAY?
© 1995 PAWS, INC./Distributed by Universal Press Syndicate
OH, I DON'T KNOW, JON. I SO LOOKED FORWARD TO THIS, AND NOW THAT IT'S HERE, I GUESS I'M SUFFERING FROM POST-PAPER TOWEL DEPRESSION...
HEEEY. ARE YOU PICKING ON ME?

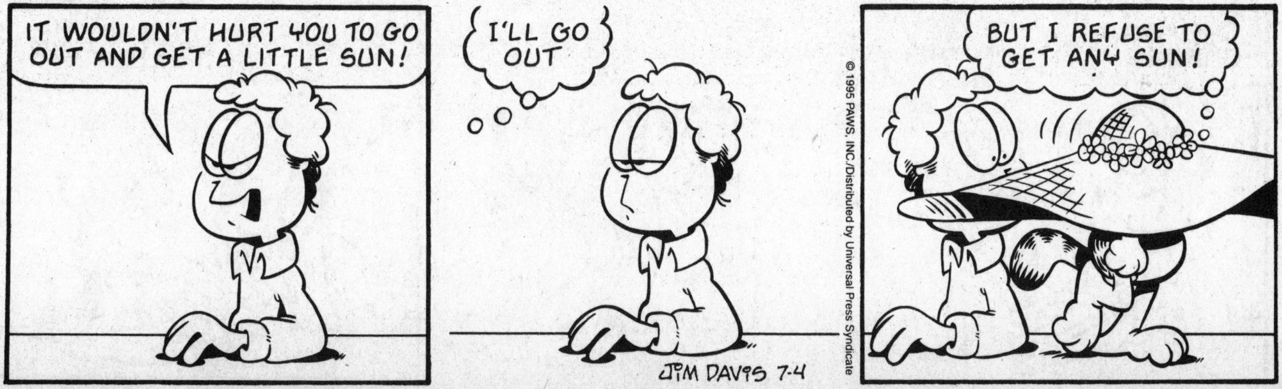
IT WOULDN'T HURT YOU TO GO OUT AND GET A LITTLE SUN!
I'LL GO OUT
JIM DAVIS 7-4
© 1995 PAWS, INC./Distributed by Universal Press Syndicate
BUT I REFUSE TO GET ANY SUN!

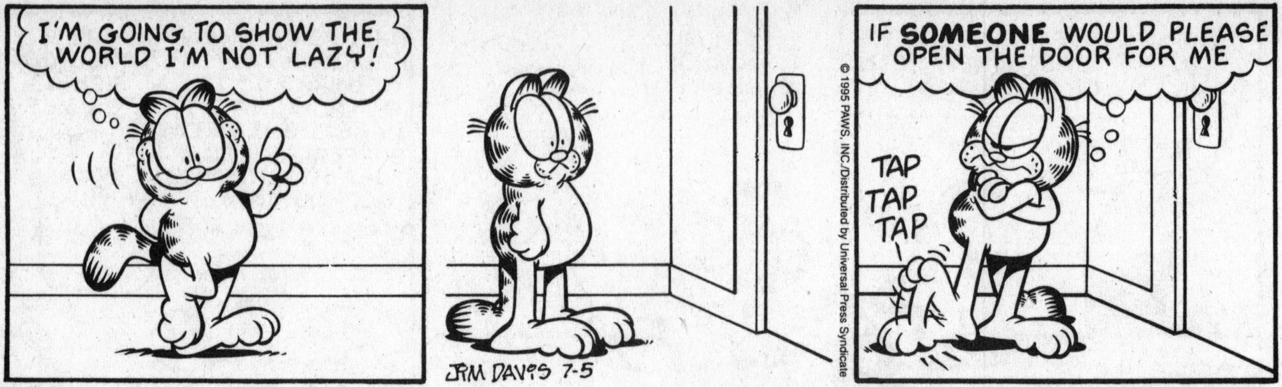
I'M GOING TO SHOW THE WORLD I'M NOT LAZY!
JIM DAVIS 7-5
IF SOMEONE WOULD PLEASE OPEN THE DOOR FOR ME
TAP
TAP
TAP
© 1995 PAWS, INC./Distributed by Universal Press Syndicate

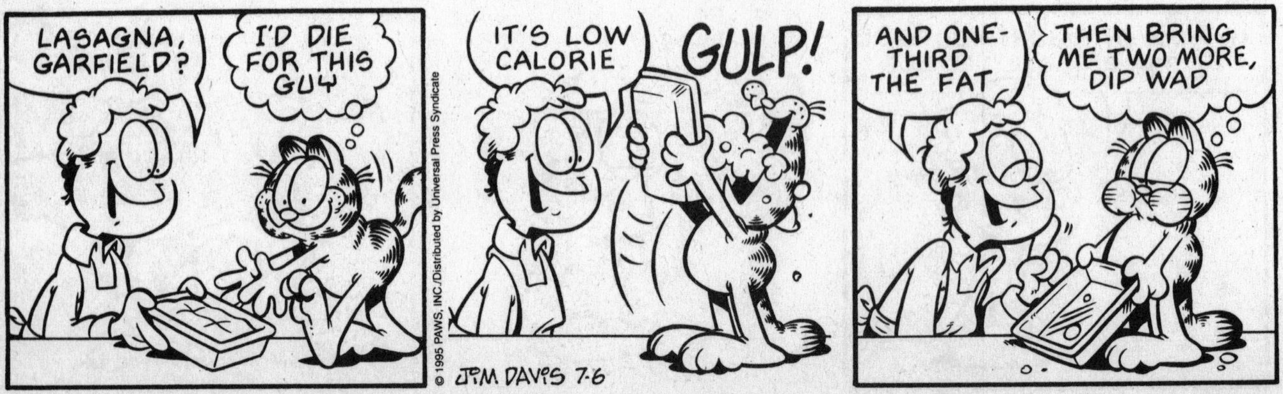
LASAGNA, GARFIELD?
I'D DIE FOR THIS GUY
© 1995 PAWS, INC./Distributed by Universal Press Syndicate
JIM DAVIS 7-6
IT'S LOW CALORIE
GULP!
AND ONE-THIRD THE FAT
THEN BRING ME TWO MORE, DIP WAD

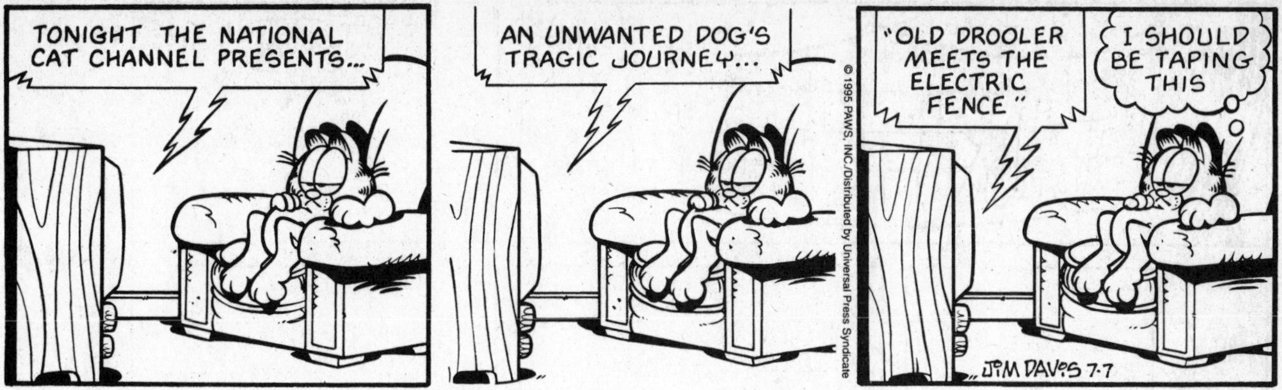
TONIGHT THE NATIONAL CAT CHANNEL PRESENTS...
AN UNWANTED DOG'S TRAGIC JOURNEY...
"OLD DROOLER MEETS THE ELECTRIC FENCE"
I SHOULD BE TAPING THIS
JIM DAVIS 7-7
© 1995 PAWS, INC./Distributed by Universal Press Syndicate

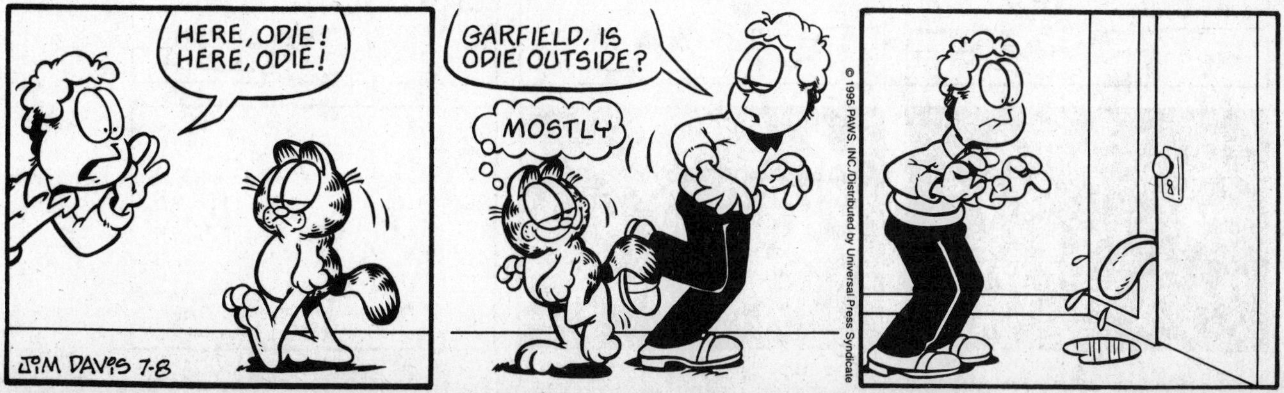
HERE, ODIE! HERE, ODIE!
JIM DAVIS 7-8
GARFIELD, IS ODIE OUTSIDE?
MOSTLY
© 1995 PAWS, INC./Distributed by Universal Press Syndicate

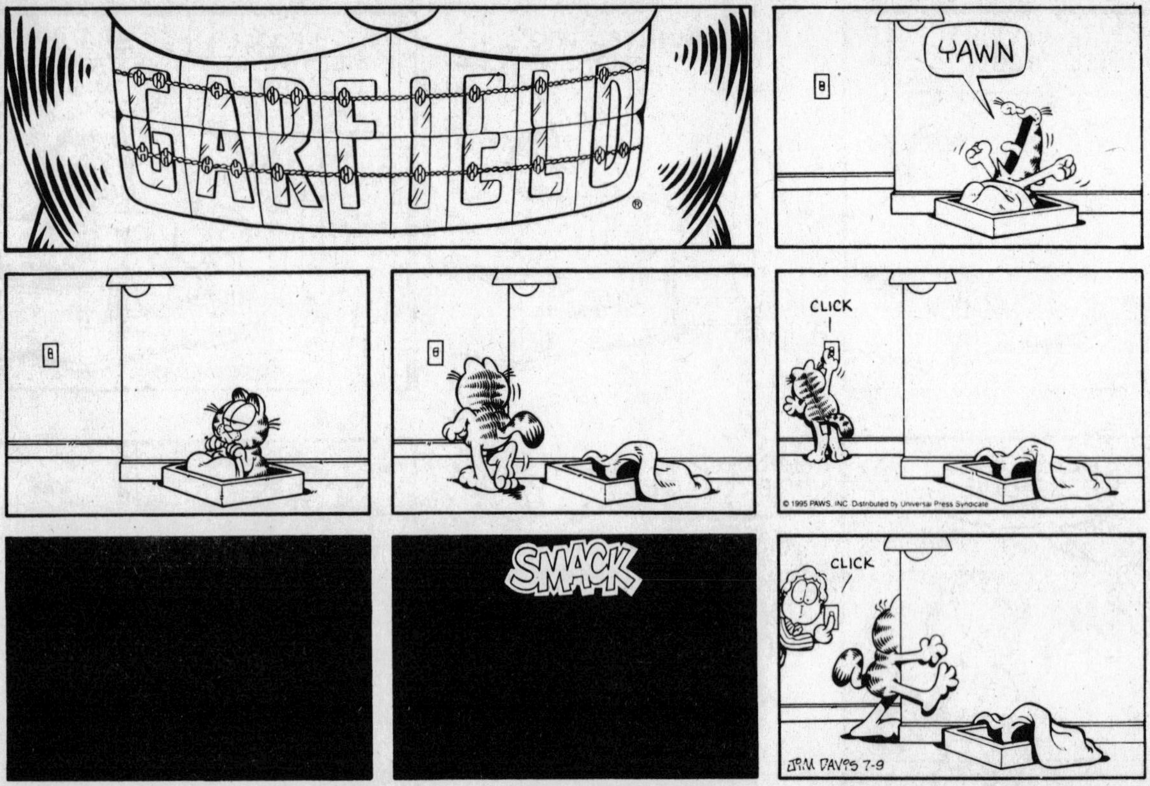
GARFIELD®
YAWN
CLICK
© 1995 PAWS, INC. Distributed by Universal Press Syndicate
SMACK
CLICK
JPM DAVPS 7-9

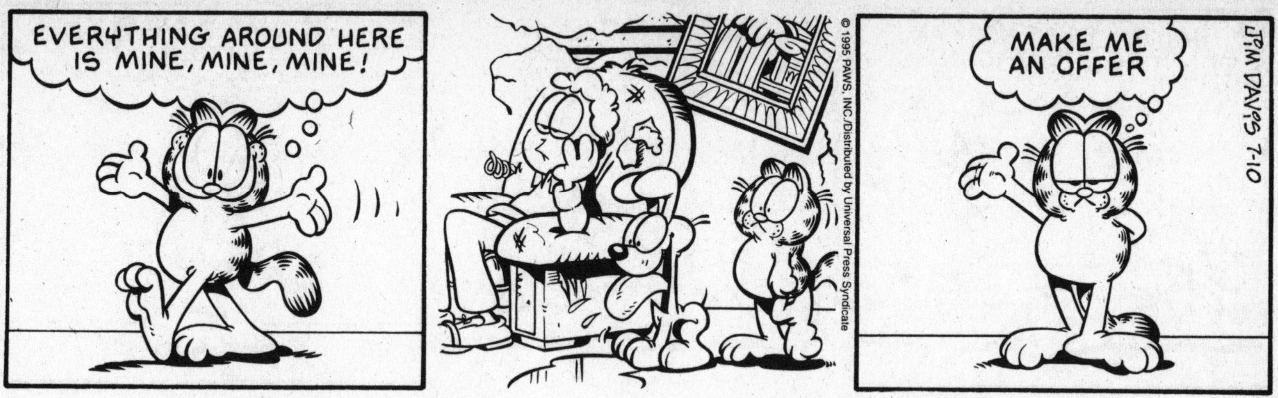
EVERYTHING AROUND HERE IS MINE, MINE, MINE!
MAKE ME AN OFFER
JIM DAVIS 7-10
© 1995 PAWS, INC./Distributed by Universal Press Syndicate

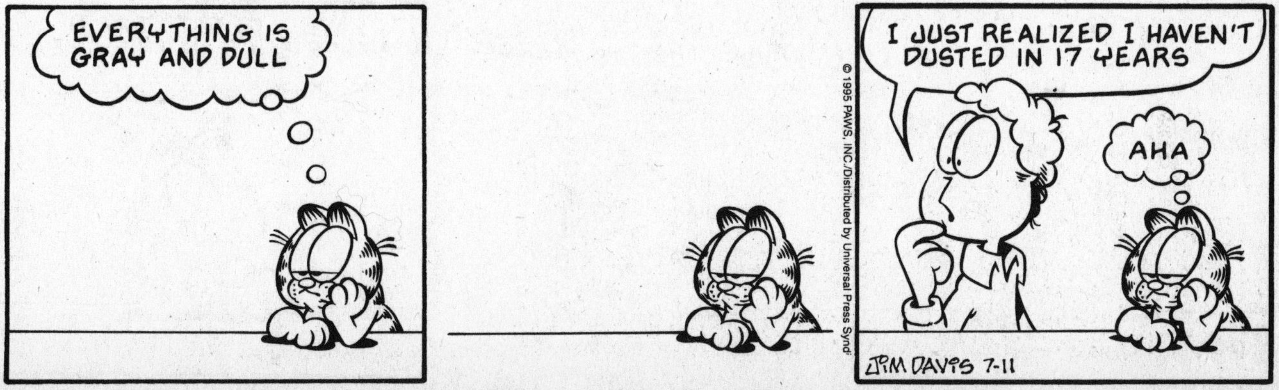
EVERYTHING IS GRAY AND DULL
I JUST REALIZED I HAVEN'T DUSTED IN 17 YEARS
AHA
JIM DAVIS 7-11
© 1995 PAWS, INC./Distributed by Universal Press Syndi

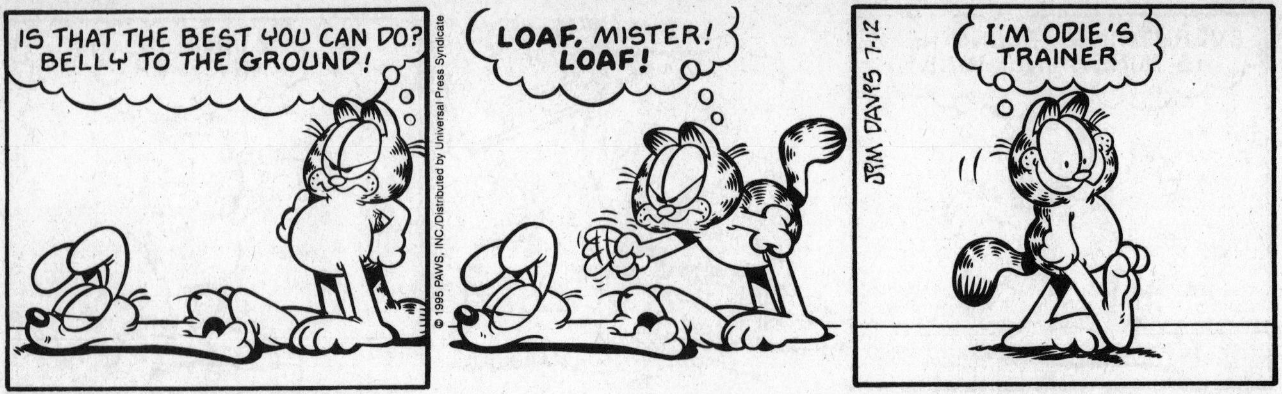
IS THAT THE BEST YOU CAN DO? BELLY TO THE GROUND!
© 1995 PAWS, INC./Distributed by Universal Press Syndicate
LOAF, MISTER! LOAF!
JIM DAVIS 7-12
I'M ODIE'S TRAINER

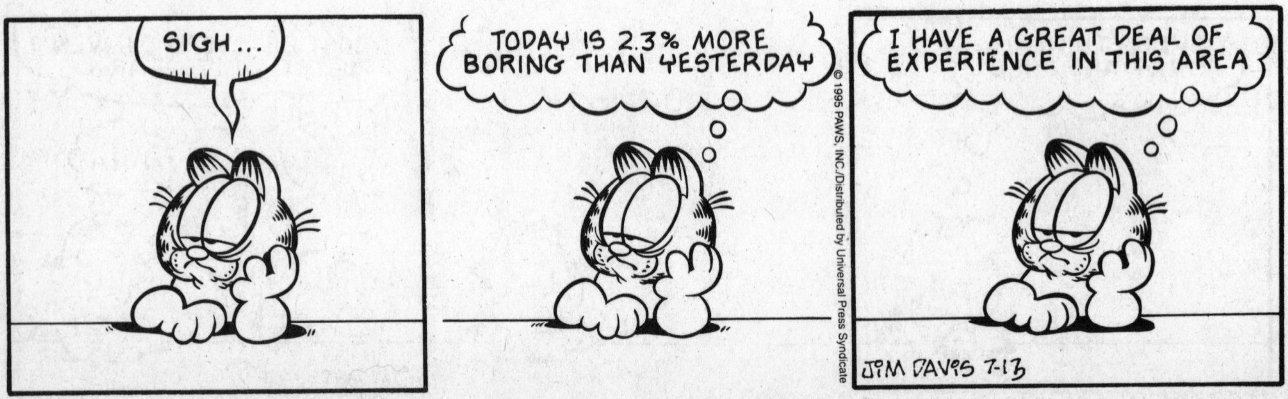
SIGH...
TODAY IS 2.3% MORE BORING THAN YESTERDAY
© 1995 PAWS, INC./Distributed by Universal Press Syndicate
I HAVE A GREAT DEAL OF EXPERIENCE IN THIS AREA
JIM DAVIS 7-13

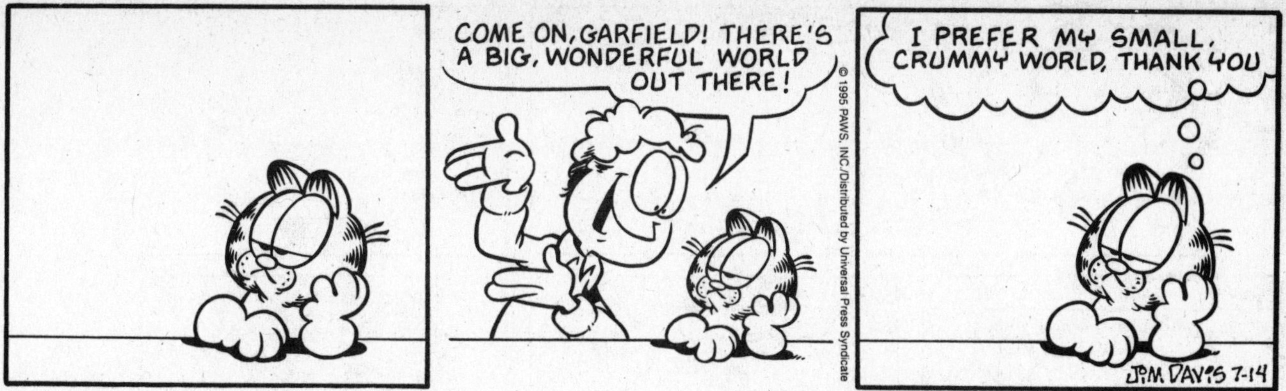
COME ON, GARFIELD! THERE'S A BIG, WONDERFUL WORLD OUT THERE!
I PREFER MY SMALL, CRUMMY WORLD, THANK YOU
JIM DAVIS 7-14

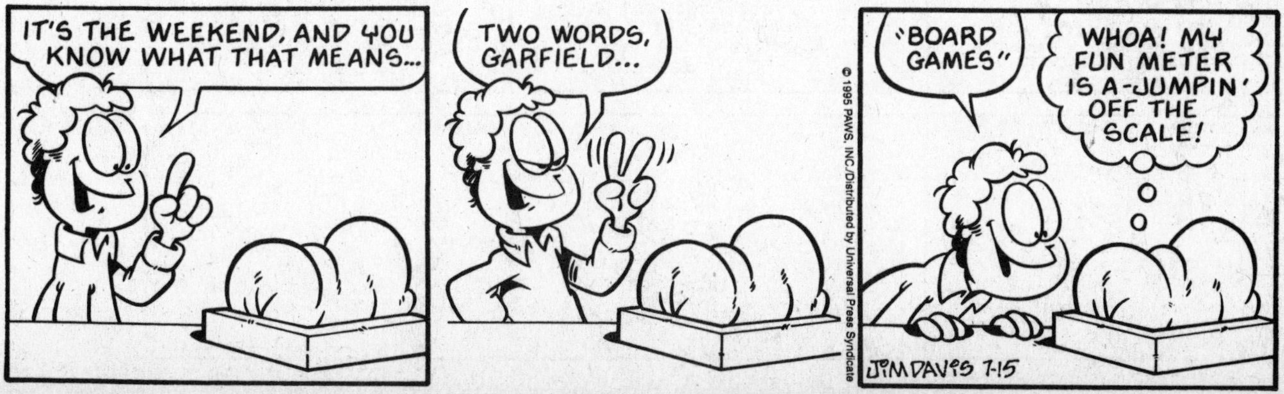
IT'S THE WEEKEND, AND YOU KNOW WHAT THAT MEANS...
TWO WORDS, GARFIELD...
"BOARD GAMES"
WHOA! MY FUN METER IS A-JUMPIN' OFF THE SCALE!
JIM DAVIS 7-15

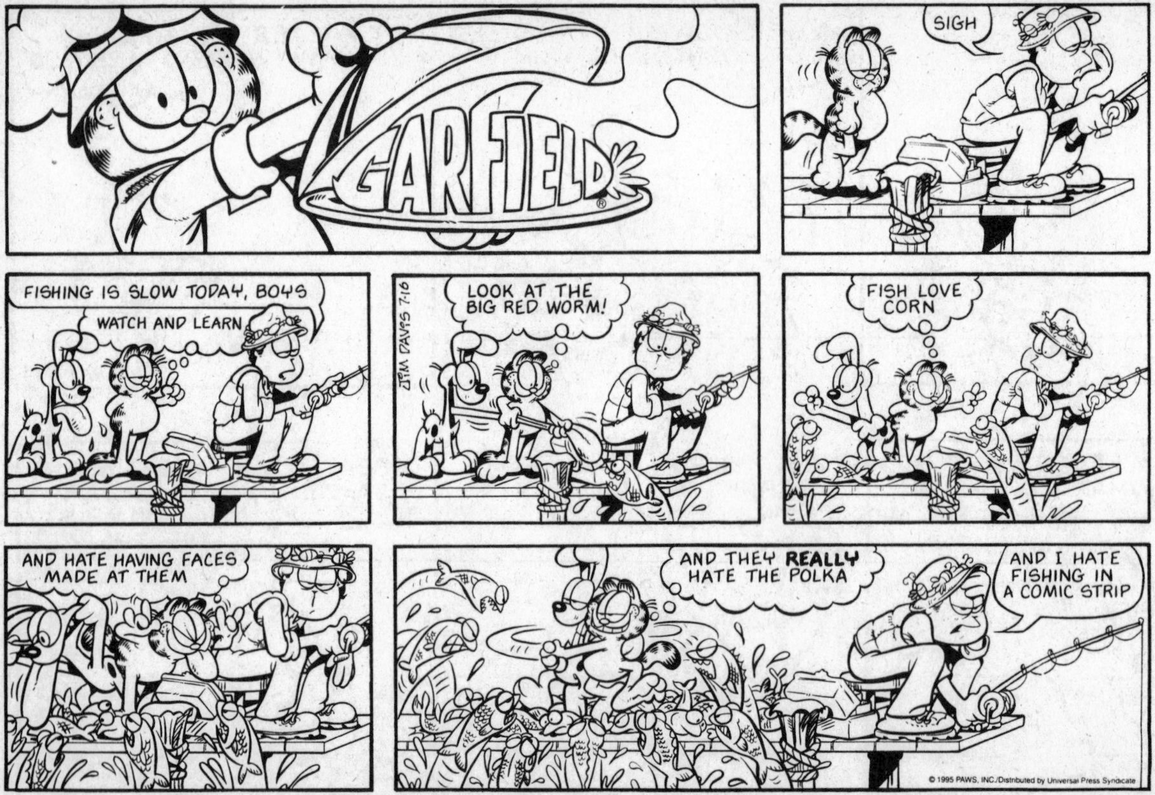
GARFIELD®
SIGH
FISHING IS SLOW TODAY, BOYS
WATCH AND LEARN
JIM DAVIS 7-16
LOOK AT THE BIG RED WORM!
FISH LOVE CORN
AND HATE HAVING FACES MADE AT THEM
AND THEY **REALLY** HATE THE POLKA
AND I HATE FISHING IN A COMIC STRIP
© 1995 PAWS, INC./Distributed by Universal Press Syndicate

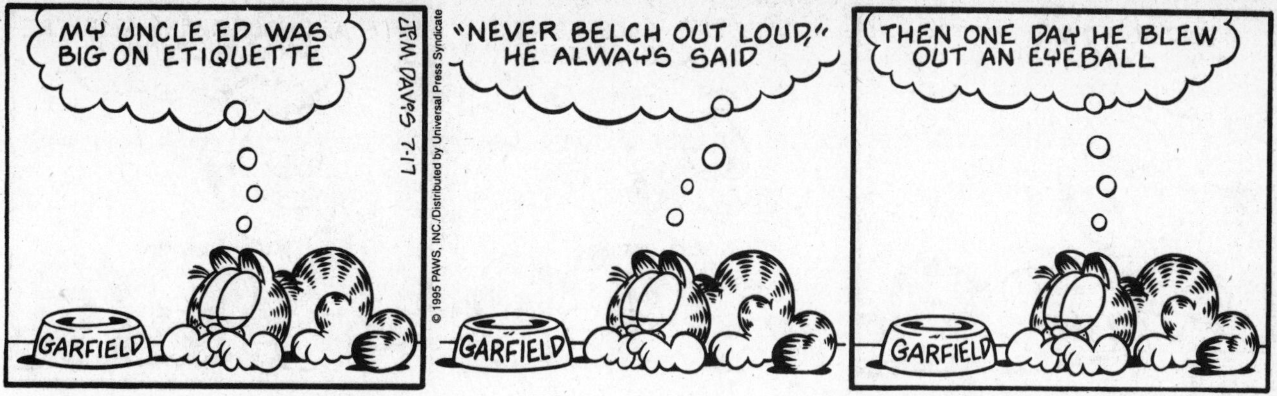
MY UNCLE ED WAS BIG ON ETIQUETTE
"NEVER BELCH OUT LOUD," HE ALWAYS SAID
THEN ONE DAY HE BLEW OUT AN EYEBALL
GARFIELD
JIM DAVIS 7-17
© 1995 PAWS, INC./Distributed by Universal Press Syndicate

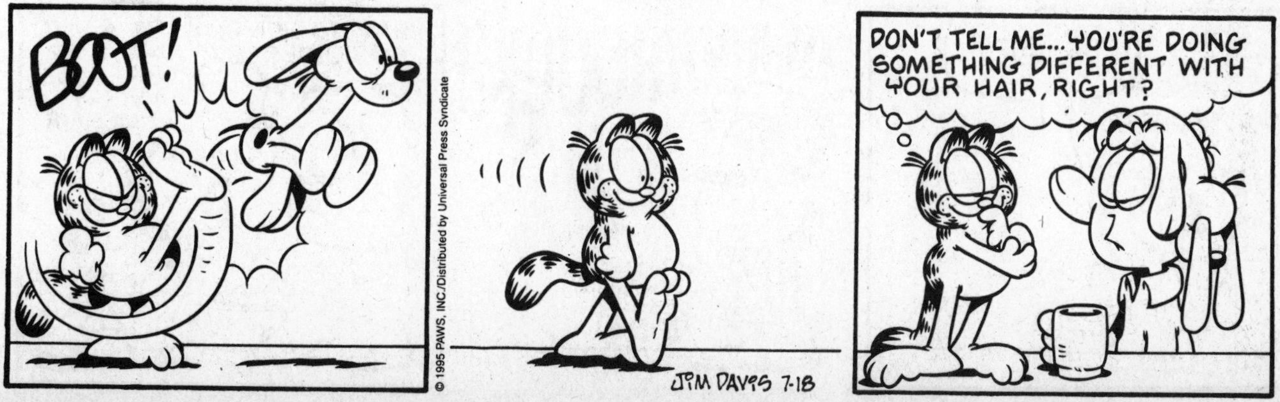
BOOT!
DON'T TELL ME... YOU'RE DOING SOMETHING DIFFERENT WITH YOUR HAIR, RIGHT?
JIM DAVIS 7-18
© 1995 PAWS, INC./Distributed by Universal Press Syndicate

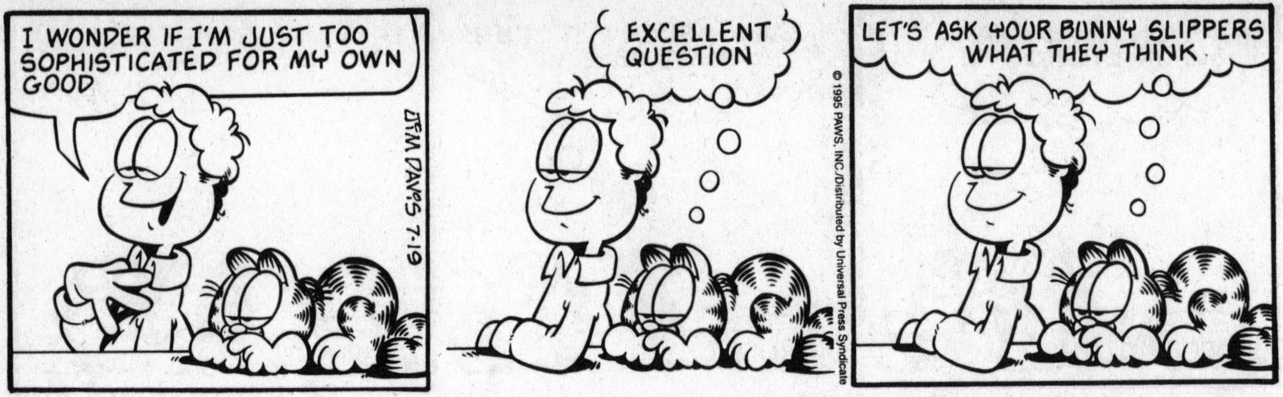
I WONDER IF I'M JUST TOO SOPHISTICATED FOR MY OWN GOOD
JIM DAVIS 7-19
EXCELLENT QUESTION
© 1995 PAWS, INC./Distributed by Universal Press Syndicate
LET'S ASK YOUR BUNNY SLIPPERS WHAT THEY THINK

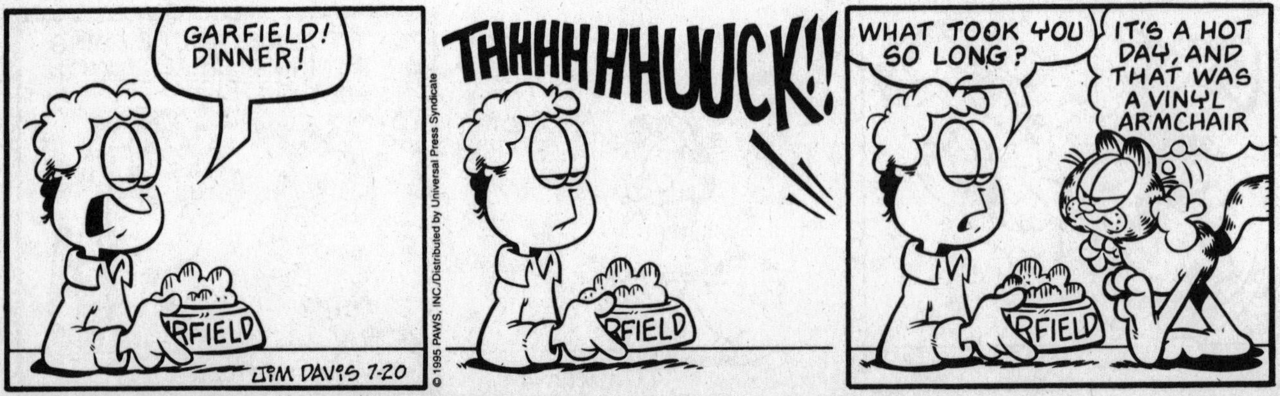
GARFIELD! DINNER!
RFIELD
JIM DAVIS 7-20
© 1995 PAWS, INC./Distributed by Universal Press Syndicate
THHHHHHUUCK!!
RFIELD
WHAT TOOK YOU SO LONG?
IT'S A HOT DAY, AND THAT WAS A VINYL ARMCHAIR
RFIELD

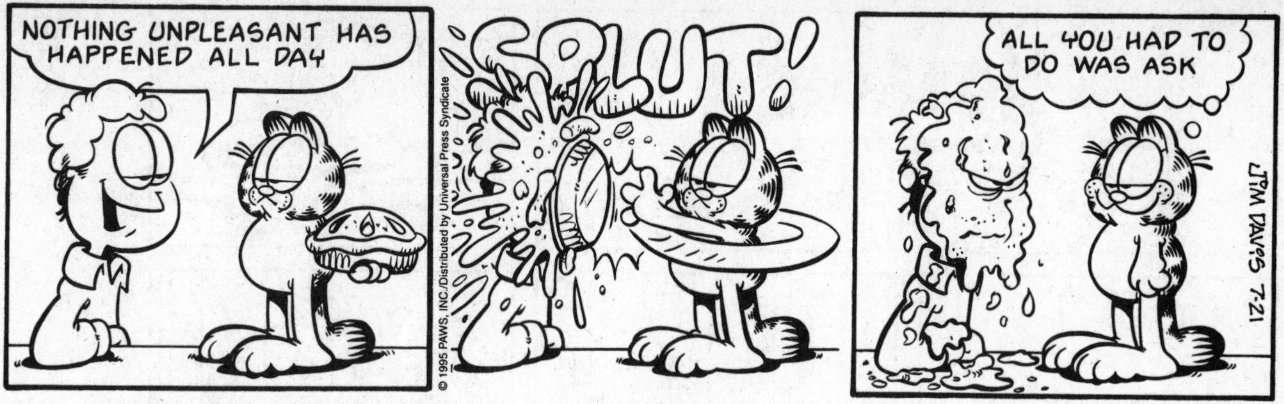
NOTHING UNPLEASANT HAS HAPPENED ALL DAY
SPLUT!
ALL YOU HAD TO DO WAS ASK
© 1995 PAWS, INC./Distributed by Universal Press Syndicate
JIM DAVIS 7·21

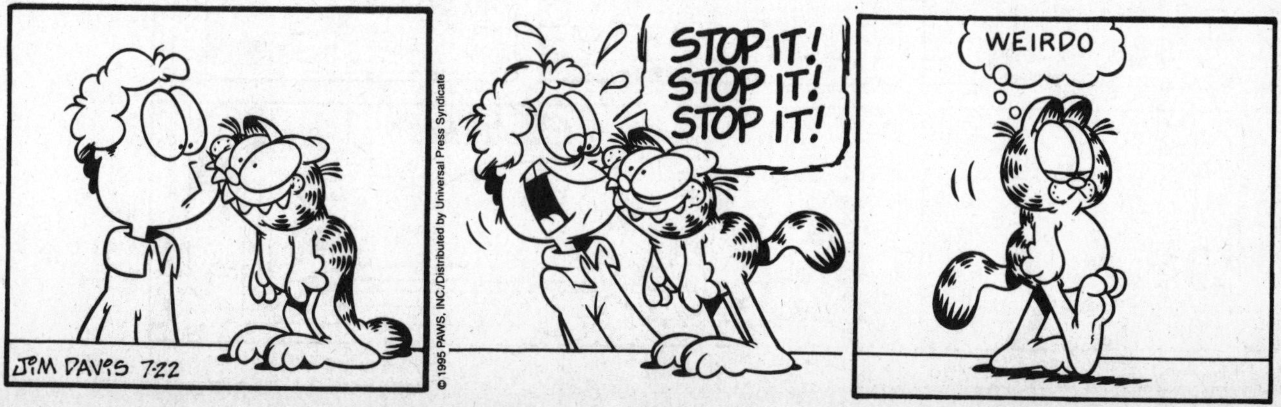
STOP IT! STOP IT! STOP IT!
WEIRDO
© 1995 PAWS, INC./Distributed by Universal Press Syndicate
JIM DAVIS 7·22

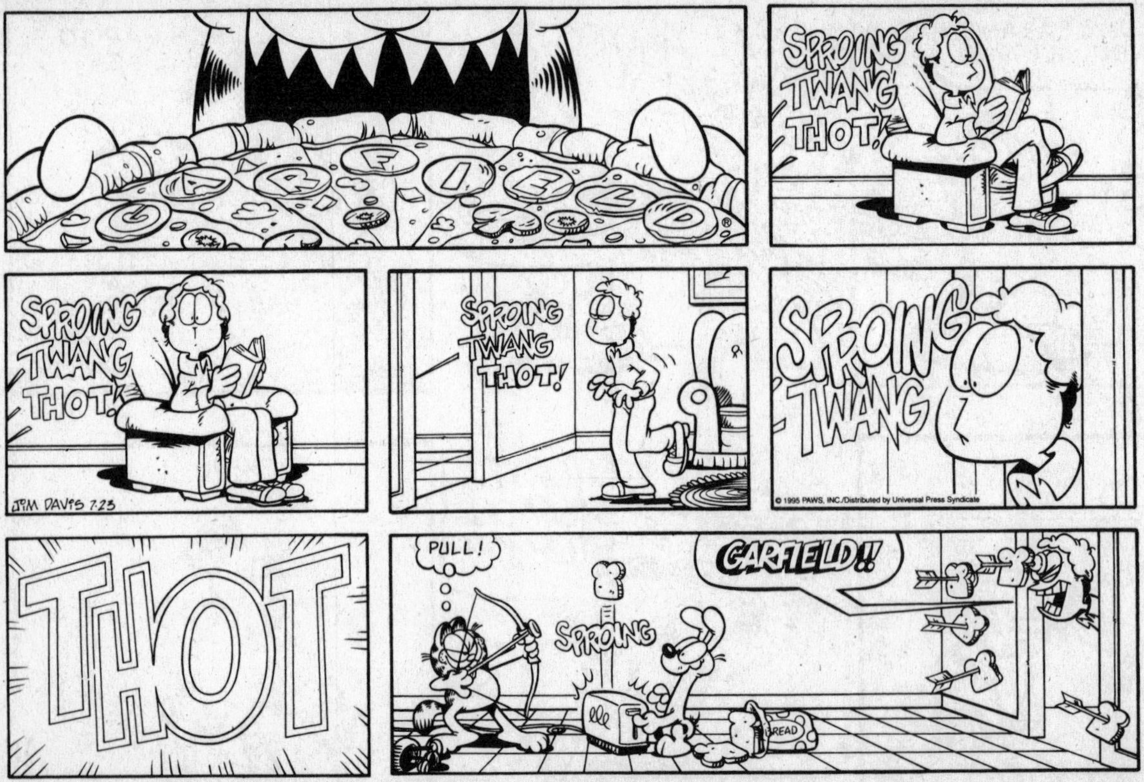
GARFIELD
SPROING
TWANG
THOT!
SPROING
TWANG
THOT!
JIM DAVIS 7-23
SPROING
TWANG
THOT!
SPROING
TWANG
© 1995 PAWS, INC./Distributed by Universal Press Syndicate
THOT
PULL!
GARFIELD!!
SPROING
BREAD

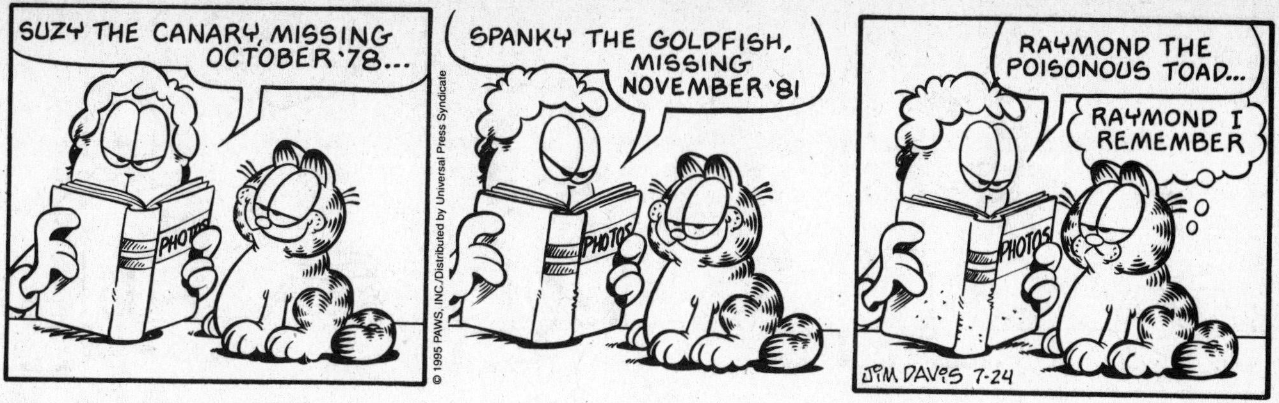
SUZY THE CANARY, MISSING OCTOBER '78...
PHOTOS
SPANKY THE GOLDFISH, MISSING NOVEMBER '81
PHOTOS
RAYMOND THE POISONOUS TOAD...
RAYMOND I REMEMBER
PHOTOS
JIM DAVIS 7-24

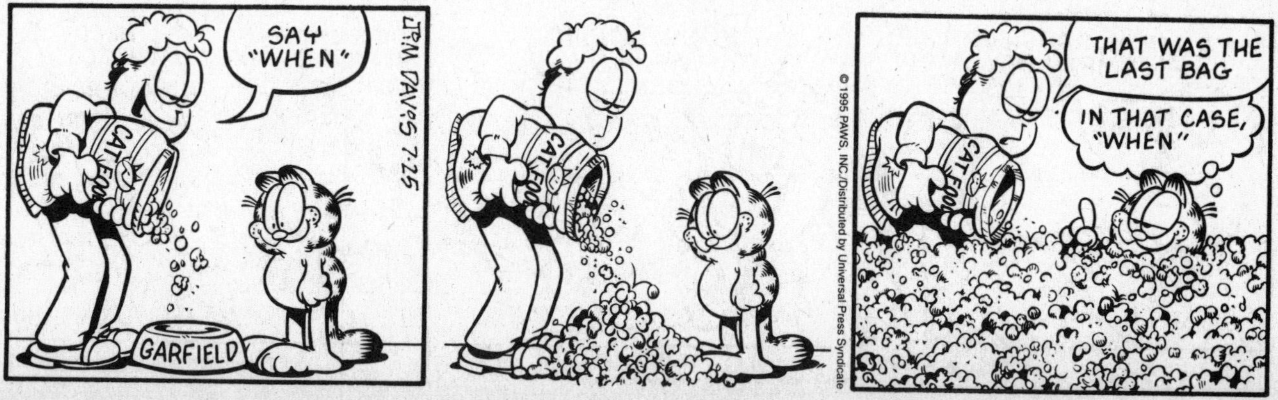
SAY "WHEN"
CAT FOOD
GARFIELD
JIM DAVIS 7-25
CAT FOOD
THAT WAS THE LAST BAG
IN THAT CASE, "WHEN"
CAT FOOD

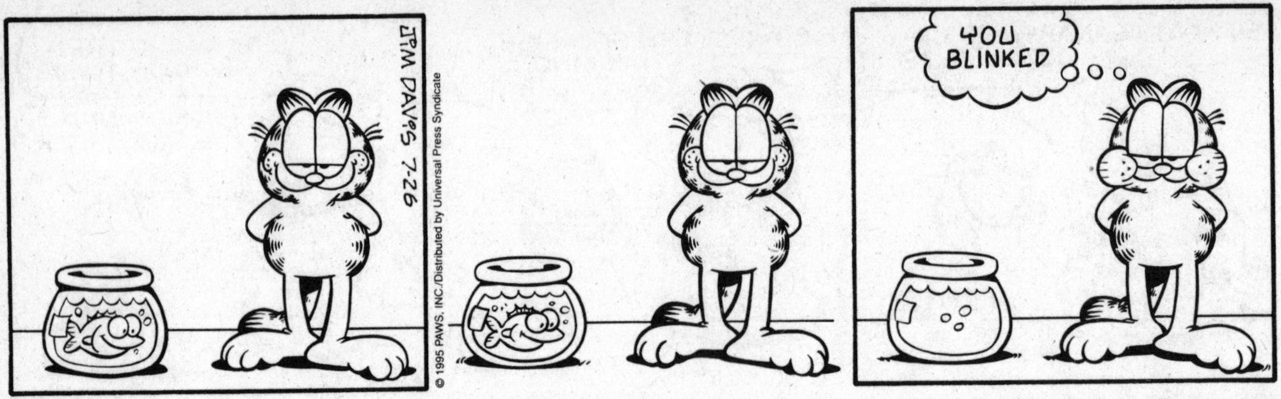
JIM DAVIS 7-26
YOU BLINKED

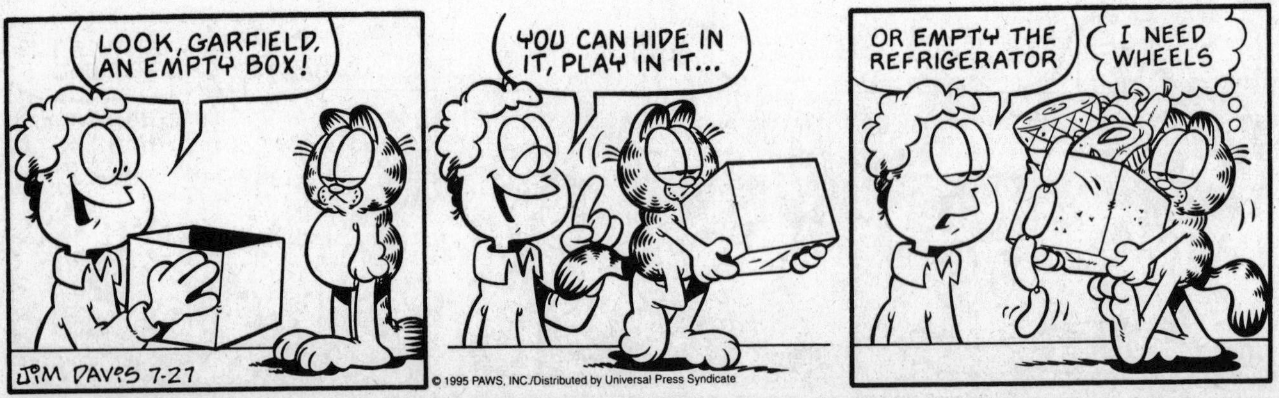
LOOK, GARFIELD, AN EMPTY BOX!
JIM DAVIS 7-27
YOU CAN HIDE IN IT, PLAY IN IT...
OR EMPTY THE REFRIGERATOR
I NEED WHEELS

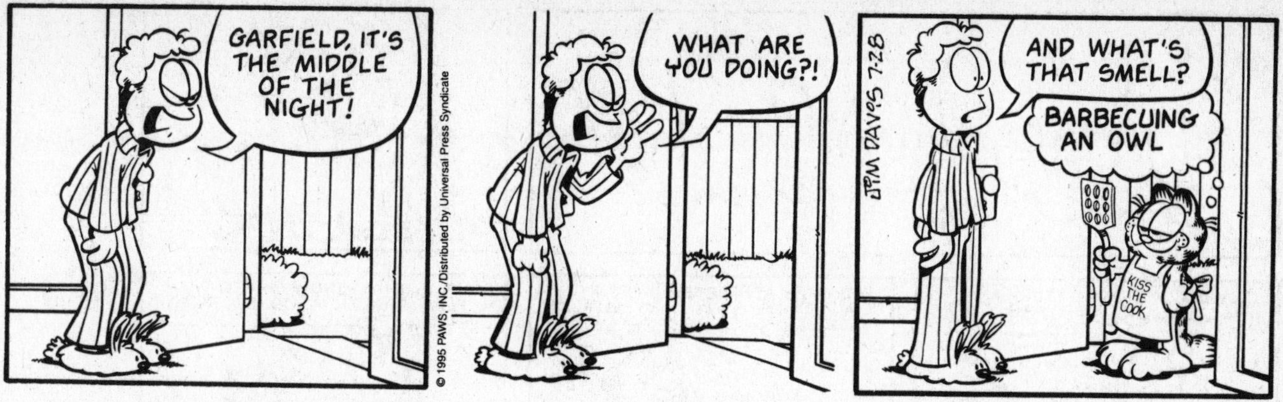
GARFIELD, IT'S THE MIDDLE OF THE NIGHT!
WHAT ARE YOU DOING?!
JIM DAVIS 7-28
AND WHAT'S THAT SMELL?
BARBECUING AN OWL
KISS THE COOK

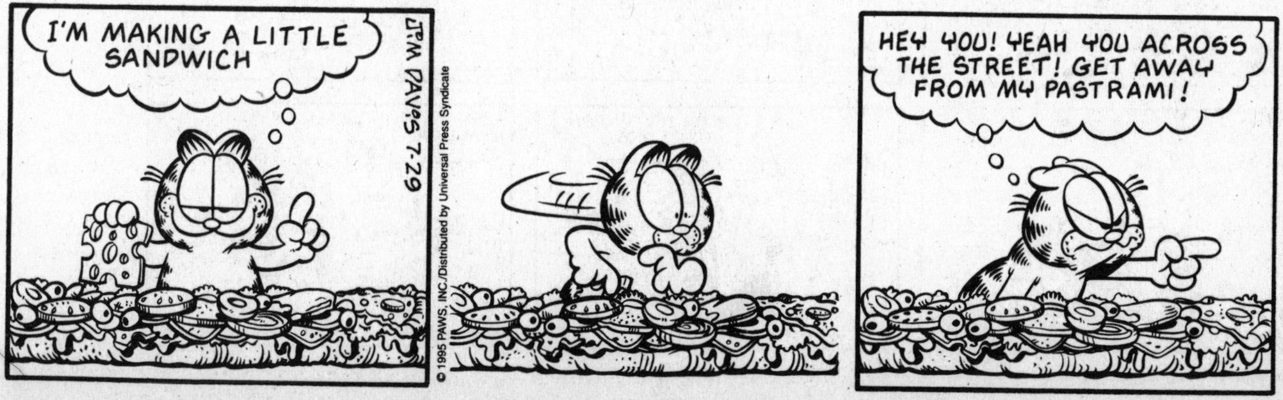
I'M MAKING A LITTLE SANDWICH
JIM DAVIS 7-29
HEY YOU! YEAH YOU ACROSS THE STREET! GET AWAY FROM MY PASTRAMI!

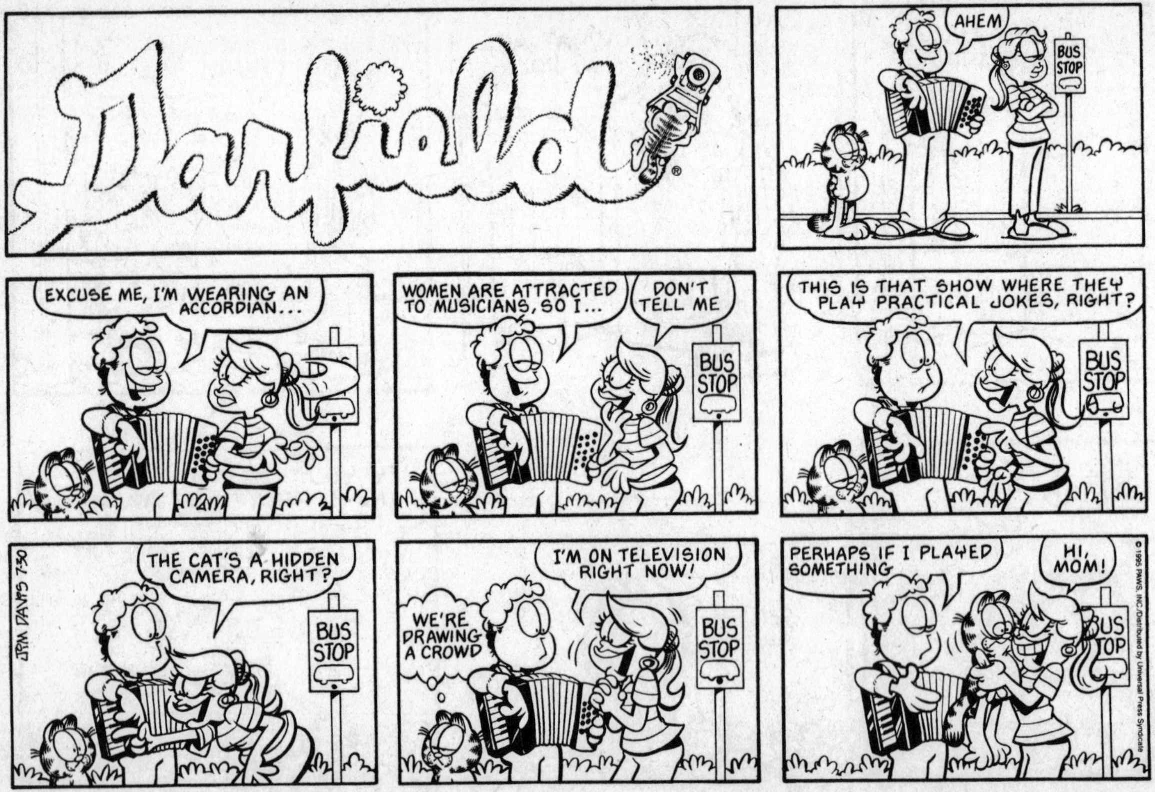
Garfield®
AHEM
BUS STOP
EXCUSE ME, I'M WEARING AN ACCORDIAN...
WOMEN ARE ATTRACTED TO MUSICIANS, SO I...
DON'T TELL ME
BUS STOP
THIS IS THAT SHOW WHERE THEY PLAY PRACTICAL JOKES, RIGHT?
BUS STOP
JIM DAVIS 7-30
THE CAT'S A HIDDEN CAMERA, RIGHT?
BUS STOP
I'M ON TELEVISION RIGHT NOW!
WE'RE DRAWING A CROWD
BUS STOP
PERHAPS IF I PLAYED SOMETHING
HI, MOM!
© 1995 PAWS, INC./Distributed by Universal Press Syndicate

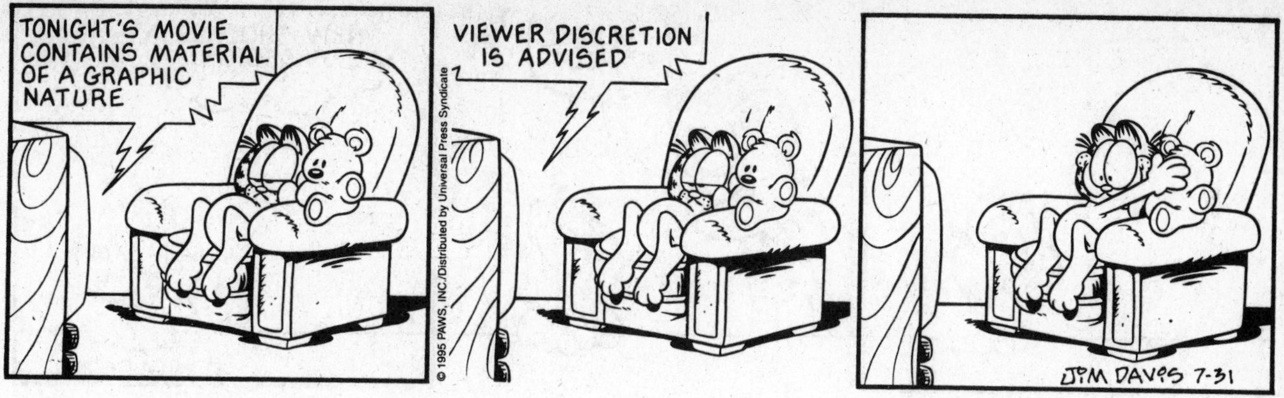
TONIGHT'S MOVIE CONTAINS MATERIAL OF A GRAPHIC NATURE
VIEWER DISCRETION IS ADVISED
© 1995 PAWS, INC./Distributed by Universal Press Syndicate
JIM DAVIS 7-31

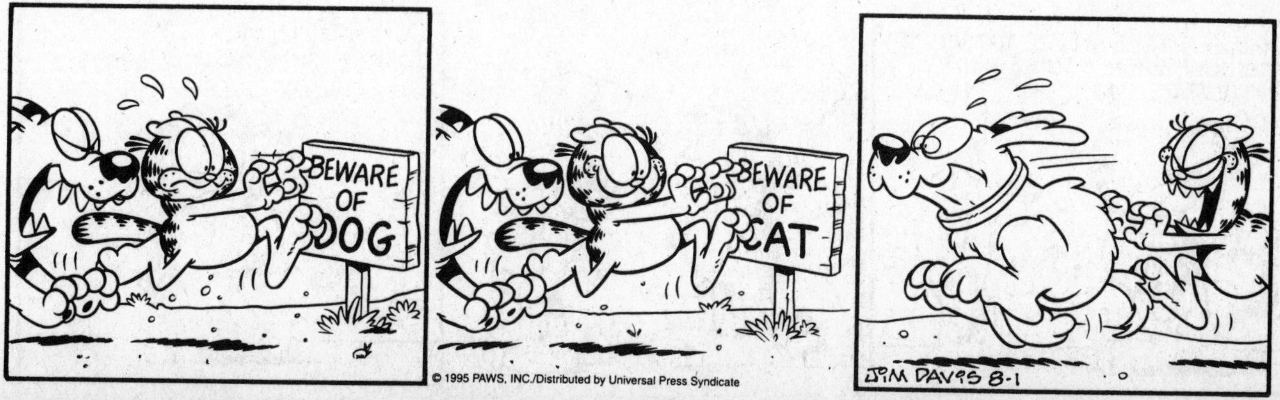
BEWARE OF DOG
BEWARE OF CAT
© 1995 PAWS, INC./Distributed by Universal Press Syndicate
JIM DAVIS 8-1

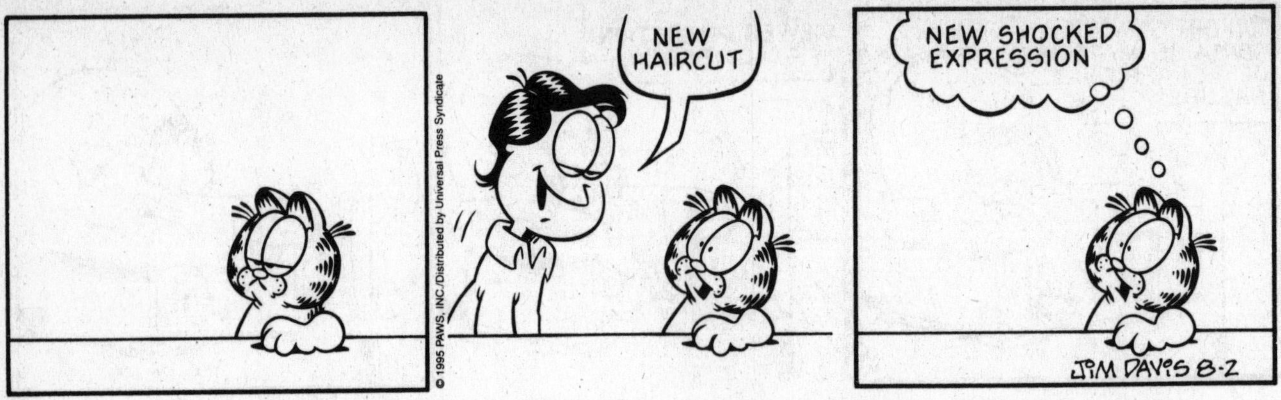
© 1995 PAWS, INC./Distributed by Universal Press Syndicate
NEW HAIRCUT
NEW SHOCKED EXPRESSION
JIM DAVIS 8-2

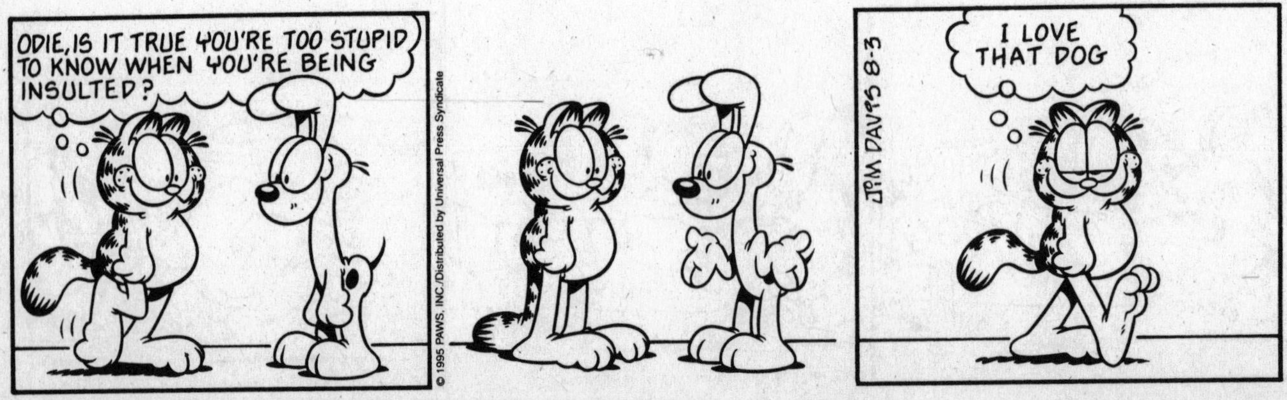
ODIE, IS IT TRUE YOU'RE TOO STUPID TO KNOW WHEN YOU'RE BEING INSULTED?
© 1995 PAWS, INC./Distributed by Universal Press Syndicate
JIM DAVIS 8-3
I LOVE THAT DOG

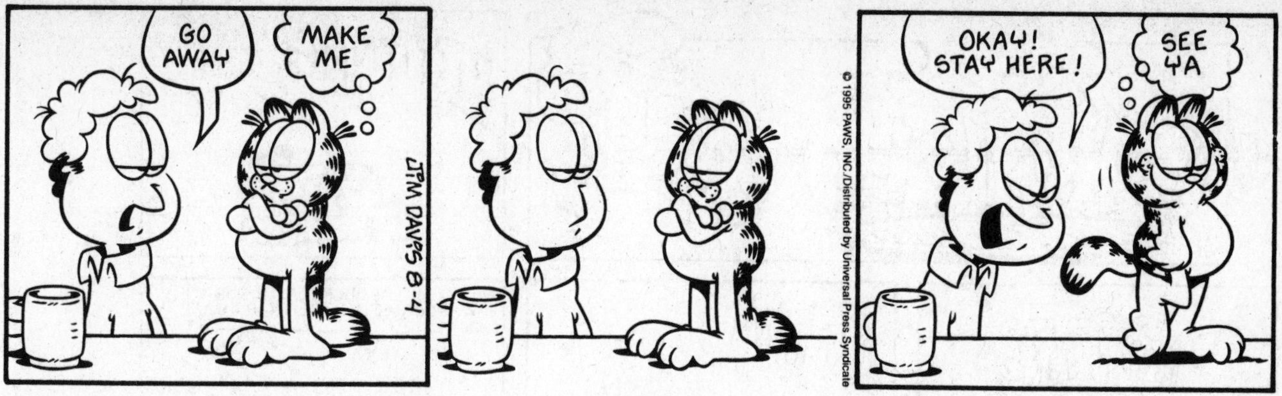
GO AWAY
MAKE ME
JIM DAVIS 8-4
OKAY! STAY HERE!
SEE YA
© 1995 PAWS, INC./Distributed by Universal Press Syndicate

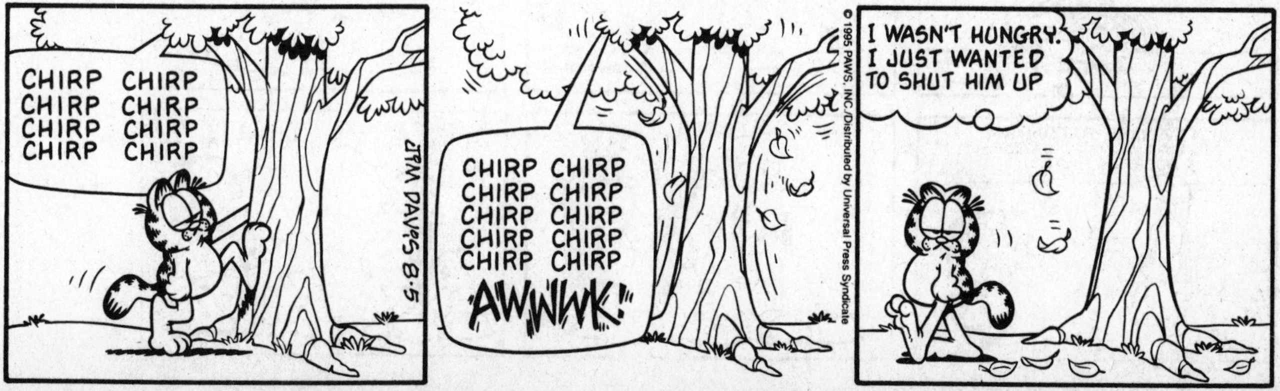
CHIRP CHIRP CHIRP CHIRP CHIRP CHIRP CHIRP CHIRP
JIM DAVIS 8-5
CHIRP CHIRP CHIRP CHIRP CHIRP CHIRP CHIRP CHIRP CHIRP CHIRP
AWWWK!
© 1995 PAWS, INC./Distributed by Universal Press Syndicate
I WASN'T HUNGRY. I JUST WANTED TO SHUT HIM UP

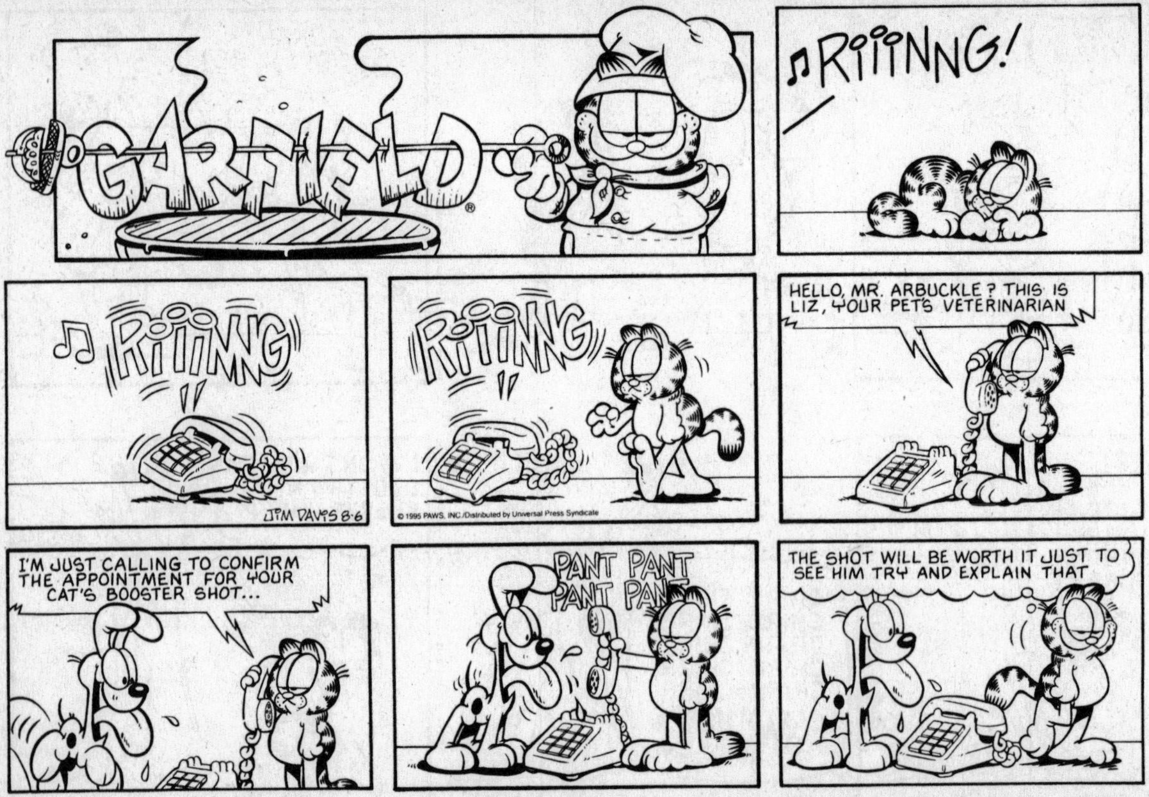
GARFIELD®
RIIINNG!
RIIINNG
RIIINNG
JIM DAVIS 8-6
© 1995 PAWS, INC./Distributed by Universal Press Syndicate
HELLO, MR. ARBUCKLE? THIS IS LIZ, YOUR PET'S VETERINARIAN
I'M JUST CALLING TO CONFIRM THE APPOINTMENT FOR YOUR CAT'S BOOSTER SHOT...
PANT PANT PANT PANT
THE SHOT WILL BE WORTH IT JUST TO SEE HIM TRY AND EXPLAIN THAT

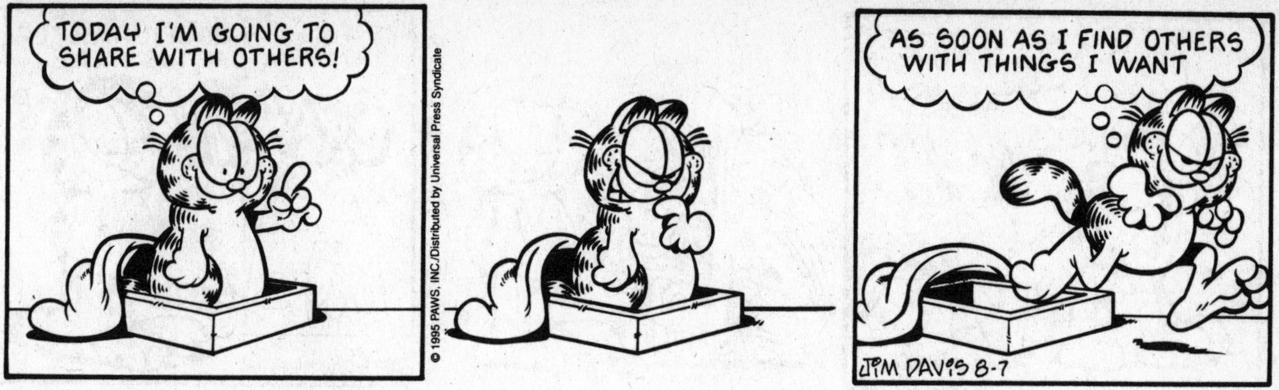
TODAY I'M GOING TO SHARE WITH OTHERS!
AS SOON AS I FIND OTHERS WITH THINGS I WANT
JIM DAVIS 8-7
© 1995 PAWS, INC./Distributed by Universal Press Syndicate

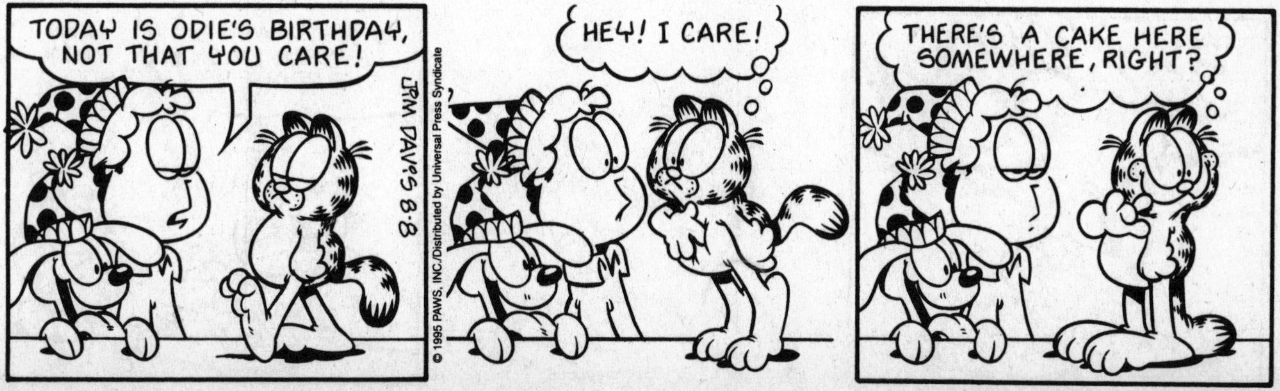
TODAY IS ODIE'S BIRTHDAY, NOT THAT YOU CARE!
JIM DAVIS 8-8
HEY! I CARE!
THERE'S A CAKE HERE SOMEWHERE, RIGHT?
© 1995 PAWS, INC./Distributed by Universal Press Syndicate

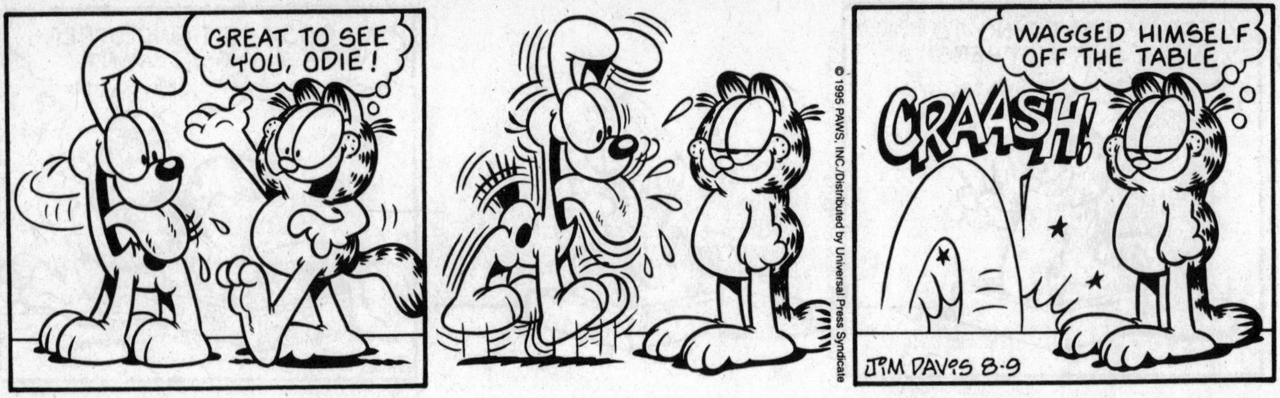
GREAT TO SEE YOU, ODIE!
CRAASH!
WAGGED HIMSELF OFF THE TABLE
© 1995 PAWS, INC./Distributed by Universal Press Syndicate
JIM DAVIS 8-9

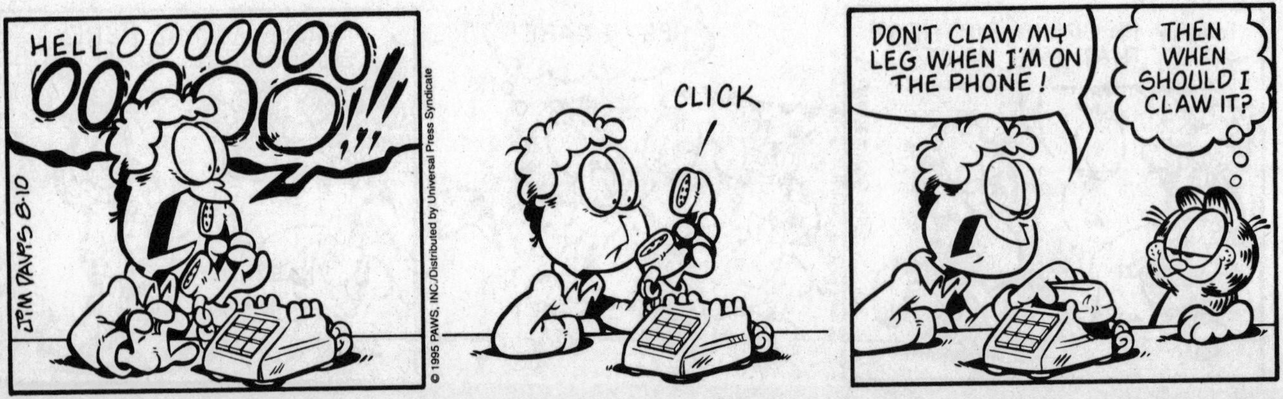
HELLOOOOOOOOOOOOO!!!
JIM DAVIS 8-10
© 1995 PAWS, INC./Distributed by Universal Press Syndicate
CLICK
DON'T CLAW MY LEG WHEN I'M ON THE PHONE!
THEN WHEN SHOULD I CLAW IT?

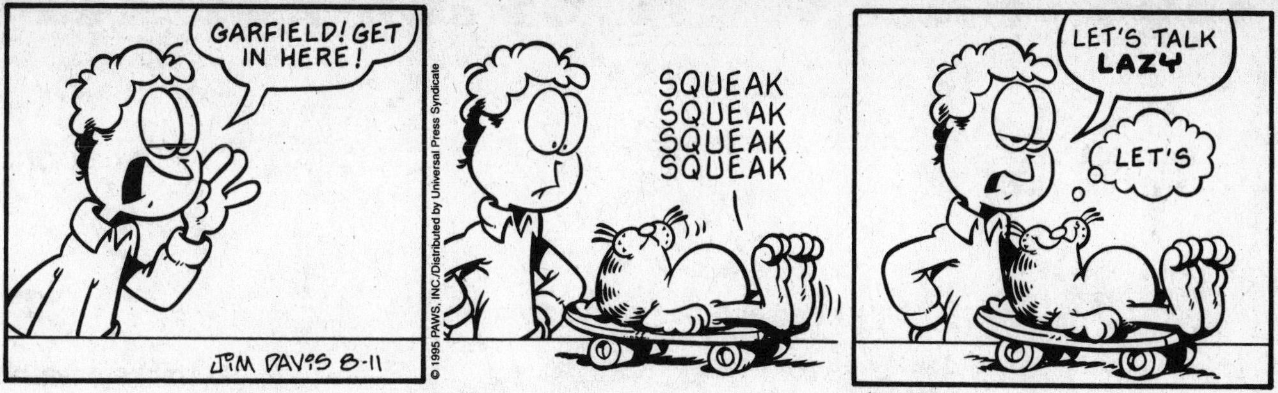
GARFIELD! GET IN HERE!
JIM DAVIS 8-11
© 1995 PAWS, INC./Distributed by Universal Press Syndicate
SQUEAK SQUEAK SQUEAK SQUEAK
LET'S TALK **LAZY**
LET'S

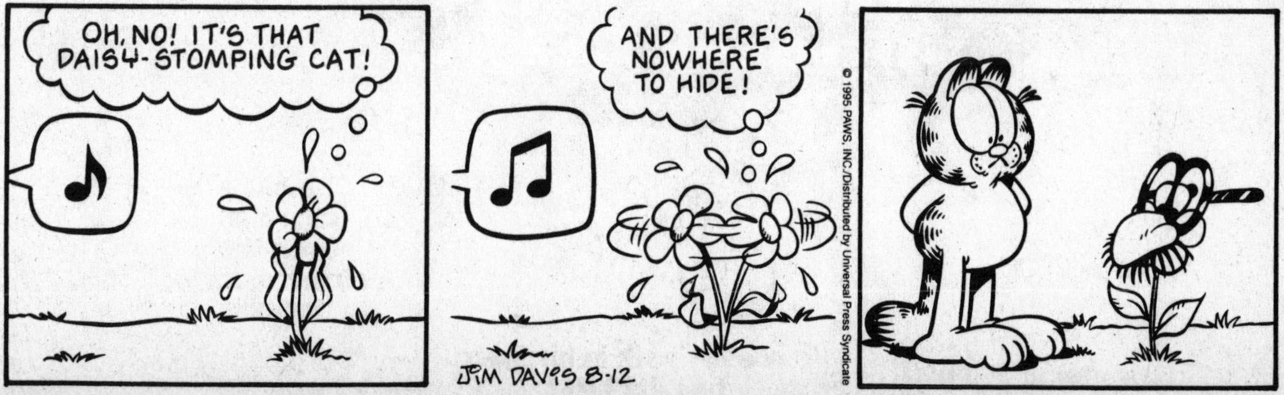
OH, NO! IT'S THAT DAISY-STOMPING CAT!
AND THERE'S NOWHERE TO HIDE!
JIM DAVIS 8-12
© 1995 PAWS, INC./Distributed by Universal Press Syndicate

How lazy is Garfield?

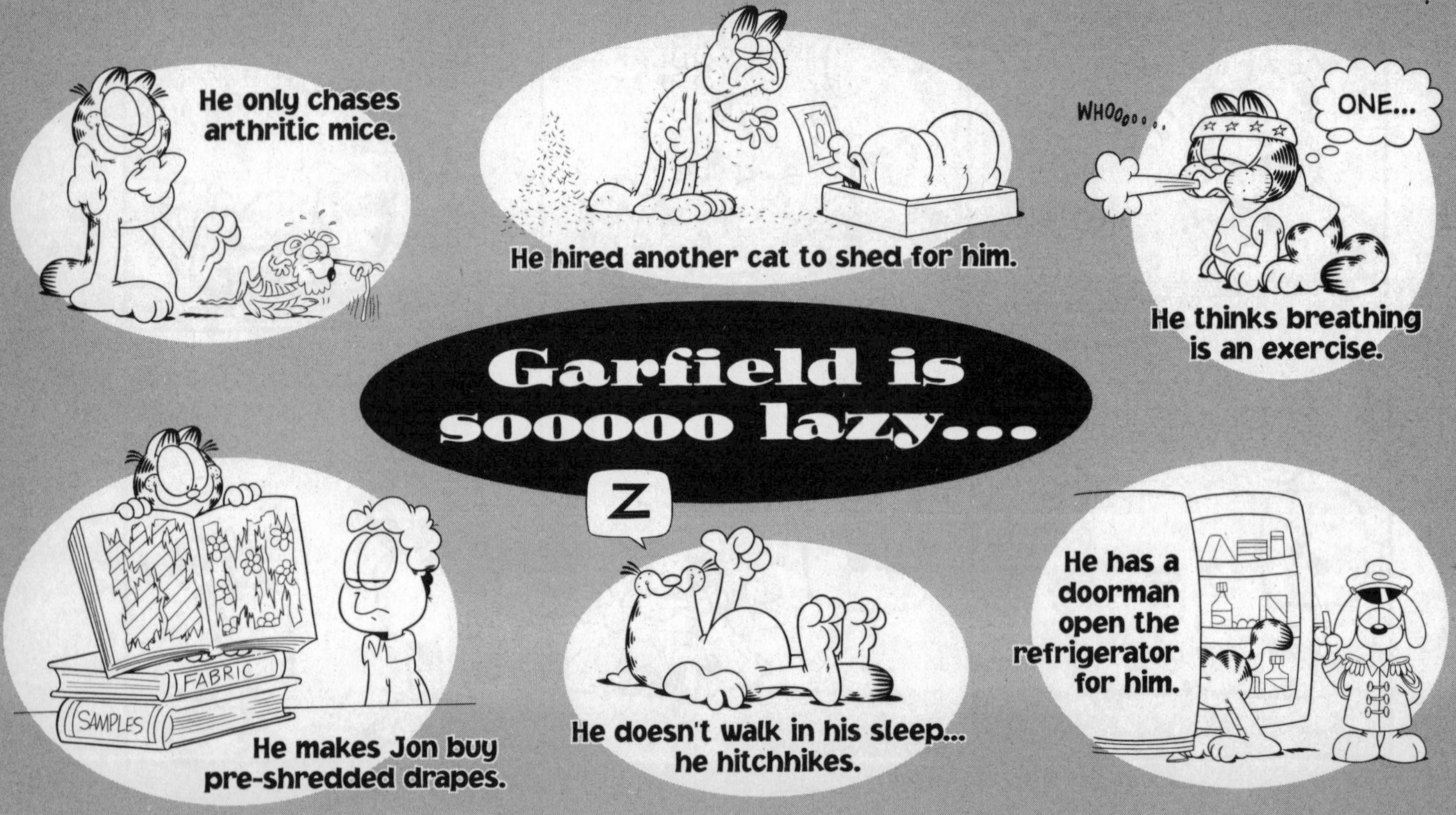
Garfield is sooooo lazy...
He only chases arthritic mice.
He hired another cat to shed for him.
WHOOooo...
ONE...
He thinks breathing is an exercise.
FABRIC
SAMPLES
He makes Jon buy pre-shredded drapes.
Z
He doesn't walk in his sleep... he hitchhikes.
He has a doorman open the refrigerator for him.

Garfield
bigger and better

BY: JIM DAVIS

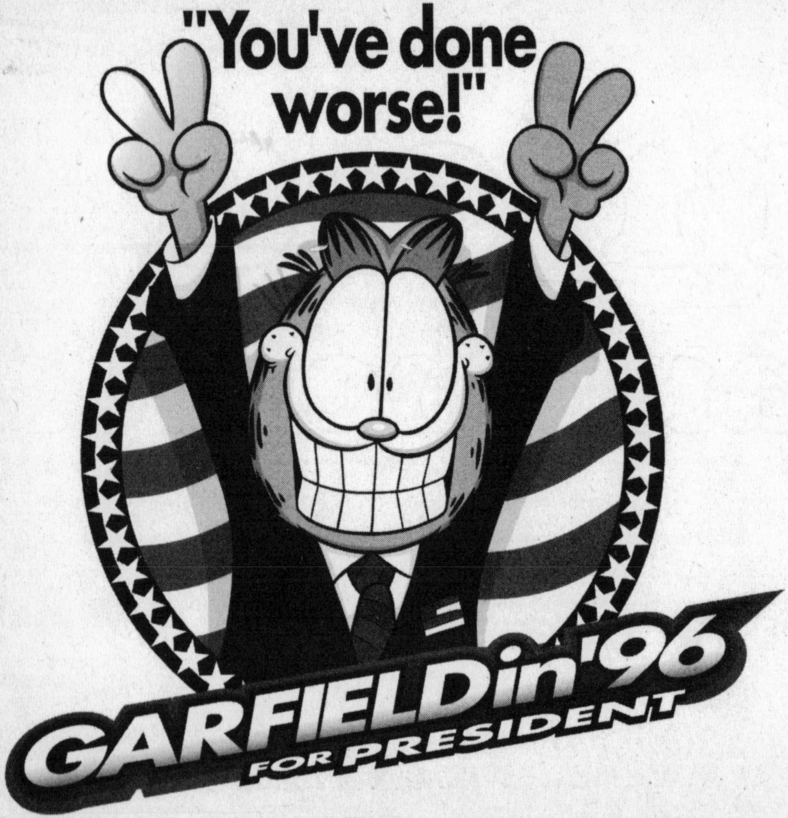
"You've done worse!"
GARFIELD in '96
FOR PRESIDENT

IF GARFIELD WERE PRESIDENT, HE WOULD...

- Abolish Mondays!
- Put a sweat tax on gyms and health clubs
- Give federal subsidies for napping
- Pour millions into the fight against dog breath
- Establish The President's Council on Snacking!
- Put a dessert bar in every school cafeteria!

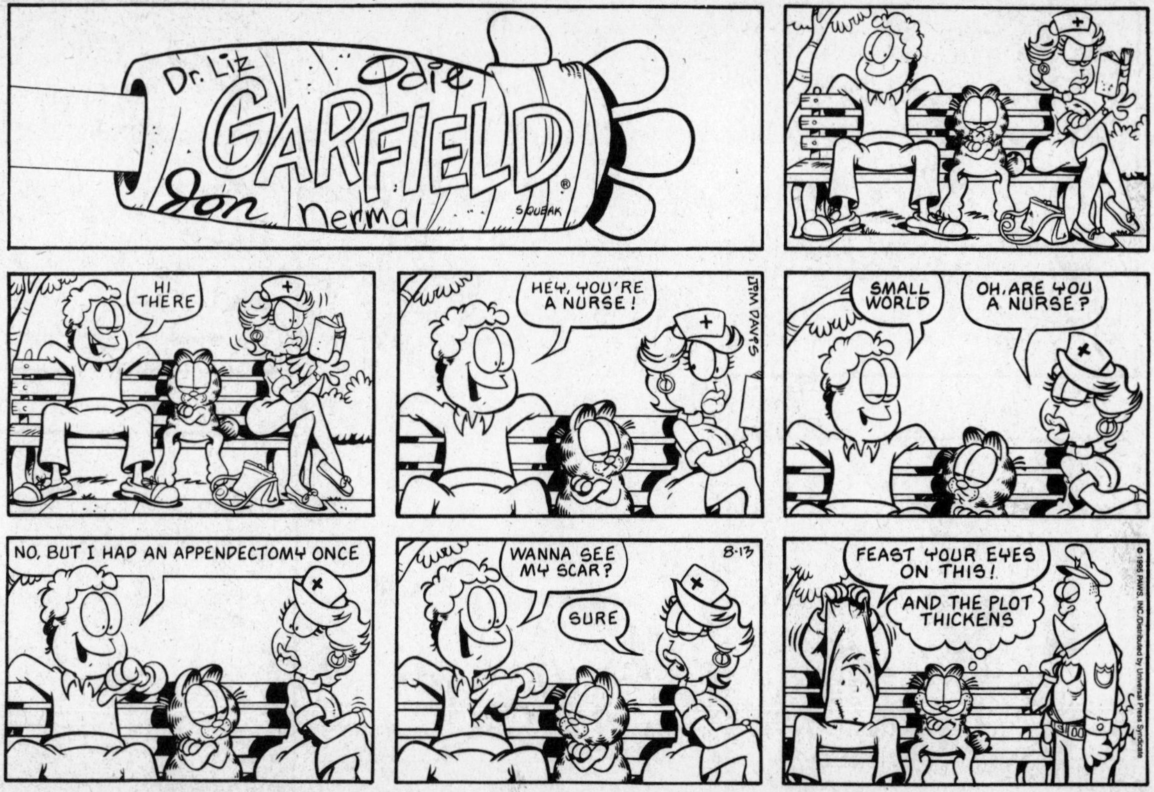
Dr. Liz
Odie
GARFIELD®
Jon
Nermal
SQUEAK
HI THERE
HEY, YOU'RE A NURSE!
JIM DAVIS
SMALL WORLD
OH, ARE YOU A NURSE?
NO, BUT I HAD AN APPENDECTOMY ONCE
8-13
WANNA SEE MY SCAR?
SURE
FEAST YOUR EYES ON THIS!
AND THE PLOT THICKENS
© 1995 PAWS, INC./Distributed by Universal Press Syndicate

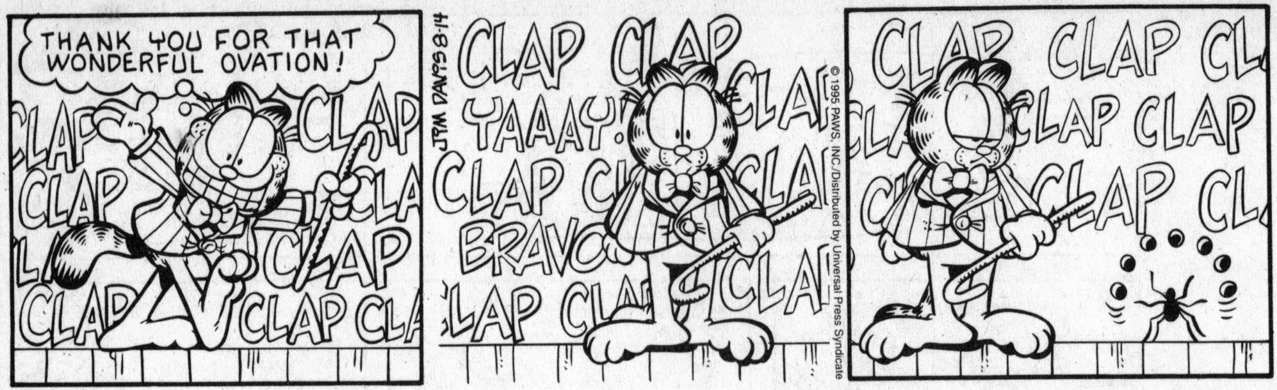
THANK YOU FOR THAT WONDERFUL OVATION!
CLAP CLAP CLAP CLAP
JIM DAVIS 8-14
CLAP CLAP
YAAAY!
CLAP
BRAVO
© 1995 PAWS, INC./Distributed by Universal Press Syndicate
CLAP CLAP
CLAP CLAP
CLAP

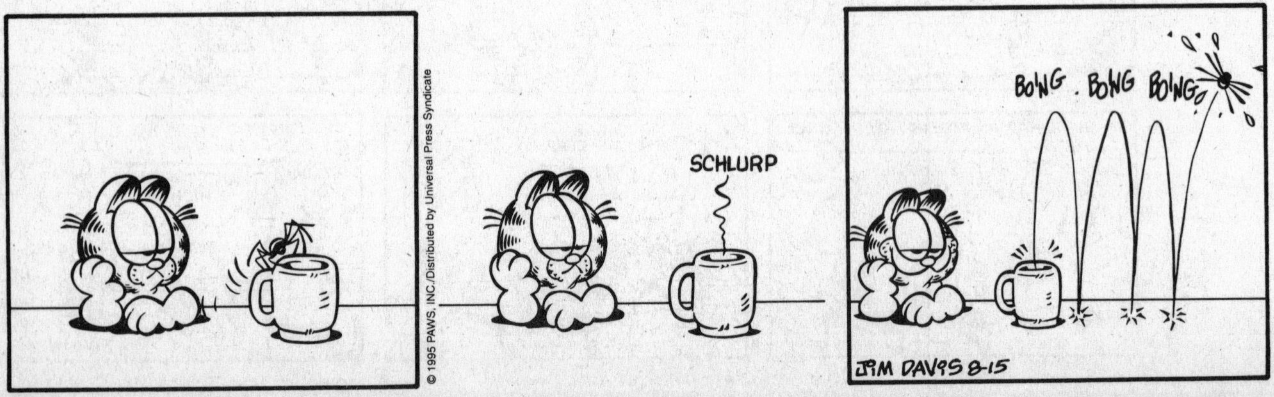
© 1995 PAWS, INC./Distributed by Universal Press Syndicate
SCHLURP
BOING BOING BOING
JIM DAVIS 8-15

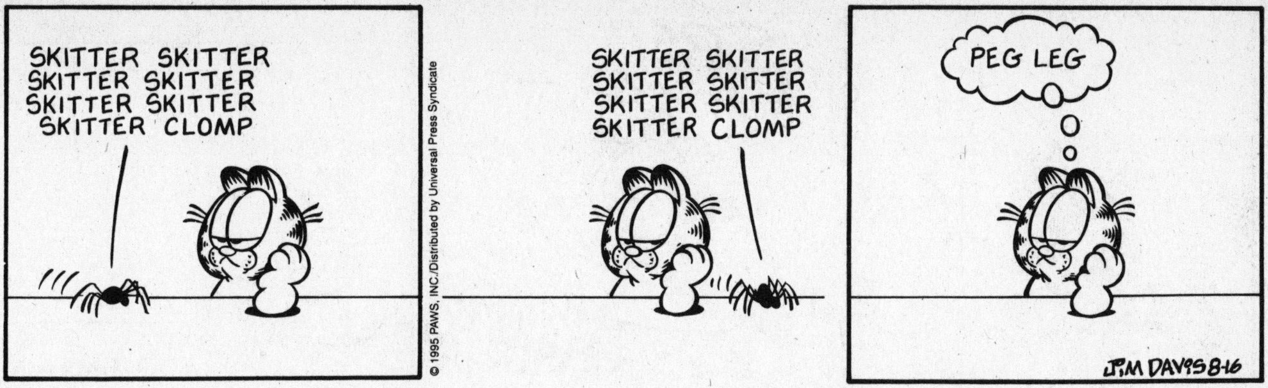
SKITTER SKITTER SKITTER SKITTER SKITTER SKITTER SKITTER CLOMP
© 1995 PAWS, INC./Distributed by Universal Press Syndicate
SKITTER SKITTER SKITTER SKITTER SKITTER SKITTER SKITTER CLOMP
PEG LEG
JIM DAVIS 8-16

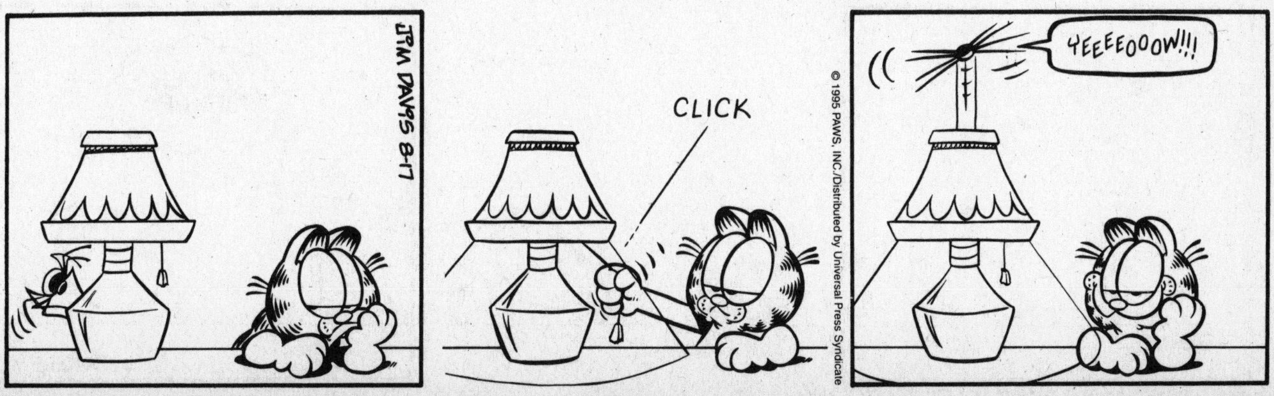
JIM DAVIS 8-17
CLICK
© 1995 PAWS, INC./Distributed by Universal Press Syndicate
YEEEEOOOW!!!

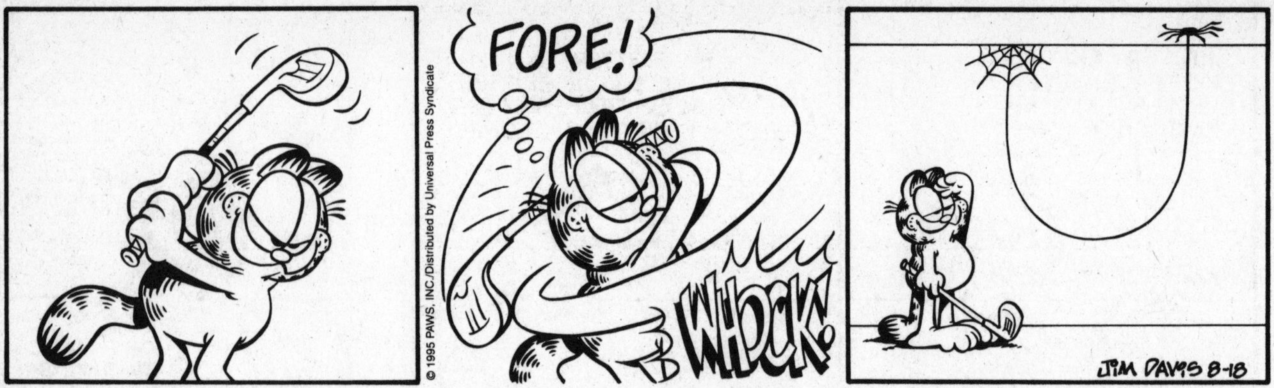
© 1995 PAWS, INC./Distributed by Universal Press Syndicate
FORE!
WHOCK!
JIM DAVIS 8-18

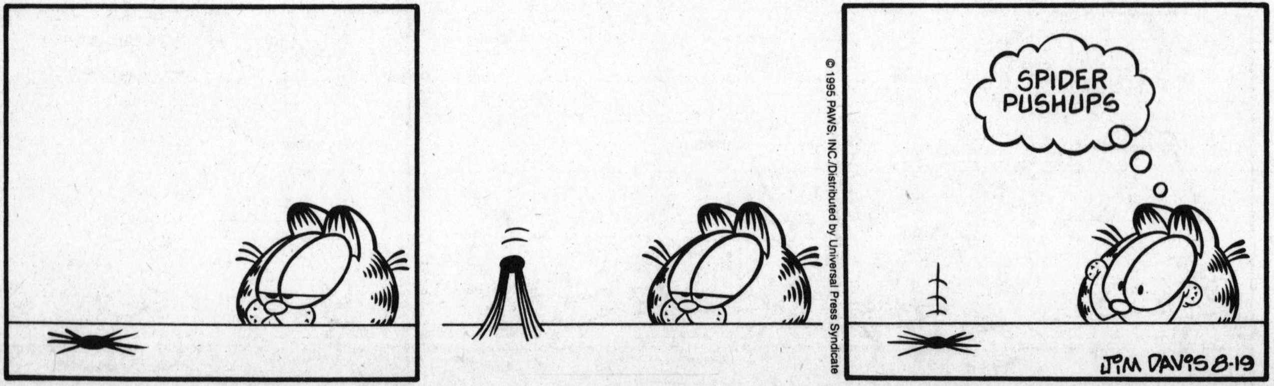
© 1995 PAWS, INC./Distributed by Universal Press Syndicate
SPIDER PUSHUPS
JIM DAVIS 8-19

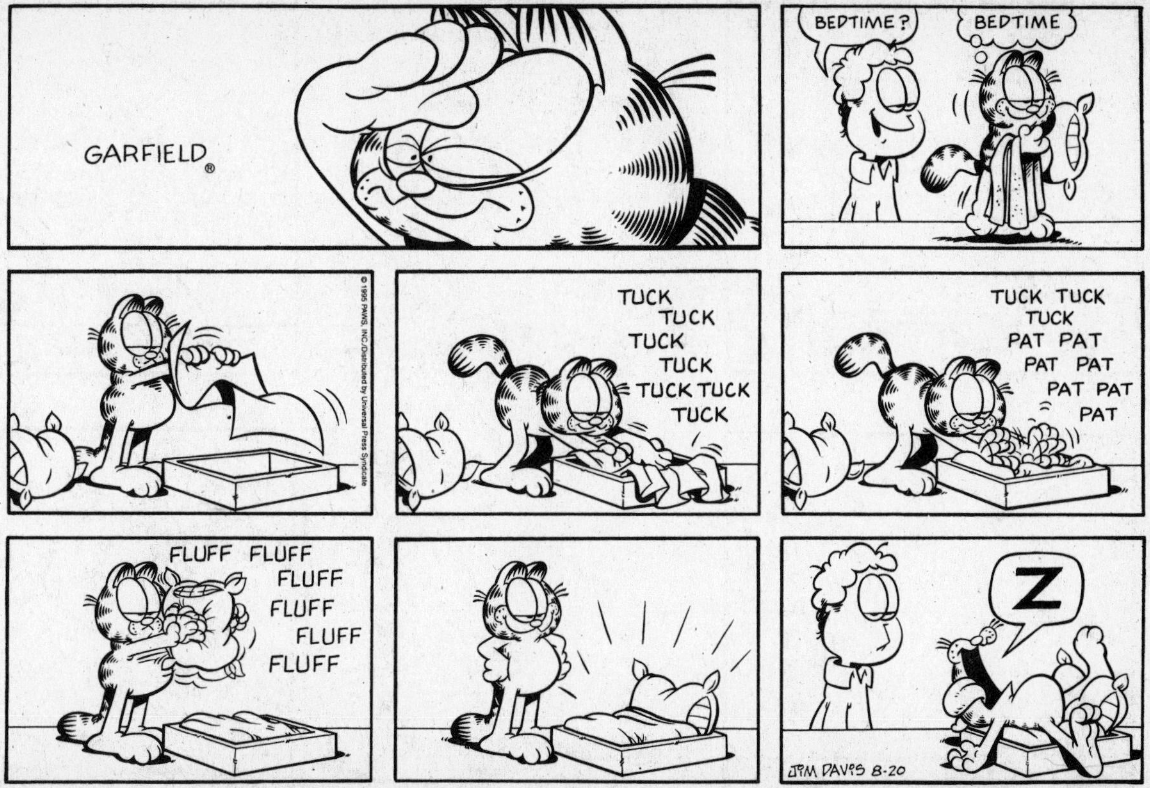
GARFIELD®
BEDTIME?
BEDTIME
© 1995 PAWS, INC./Distributed by Universal Press Syndicate
TUCK
TUCK
TUCK
TUCK
TUCK TUCK
TUCK
TUCK TUCK
TUCK
PAT PAT
PAT PAT
PAT PAT
PAT
FLUFF FLUFF
FLUFF
FLUFF
FLUFF
FLUFF
Z
JIM DAVIS 8-20

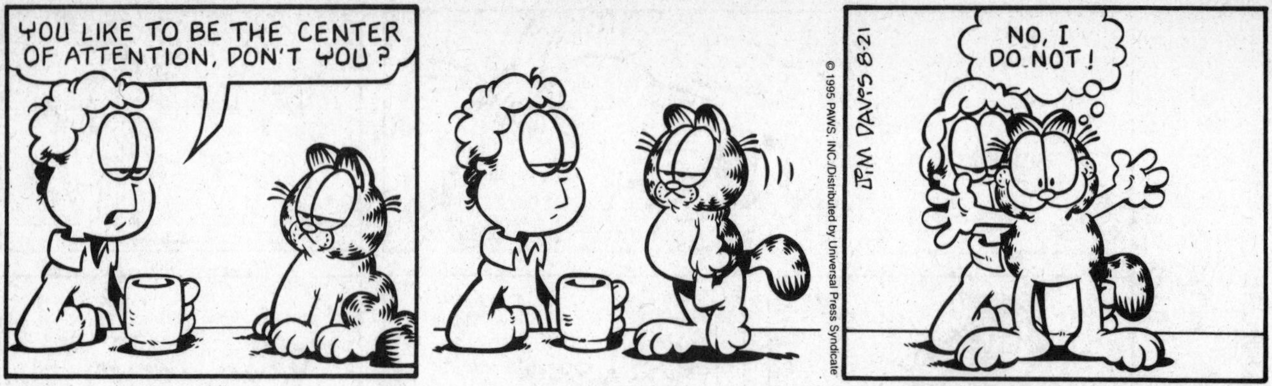
YOU LIKE TO BE THE CENTER OF ATTENTION, DON'T YOU?
© 1995 PAWS, INC./Distributed by Universal Press Syndicate
JIM DAVIS 8-21
NO, I DO NOT!

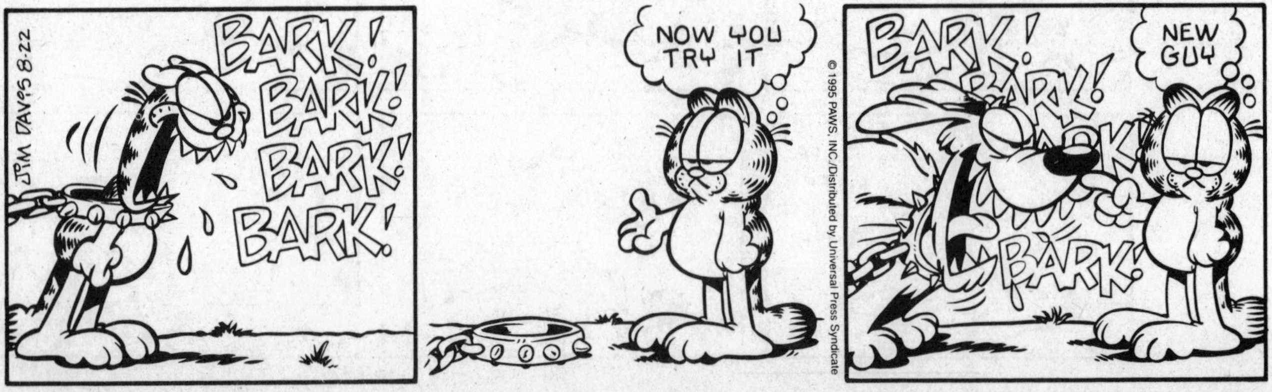
JIM DAVIS 8-22
BARK! BARK! BARK! BARK!
NOW YOU TRY IT
© 1995 PAWS, INC./Distributed by Universal Press Syndicate
BARK! BARK! BARK!
NEW GUY

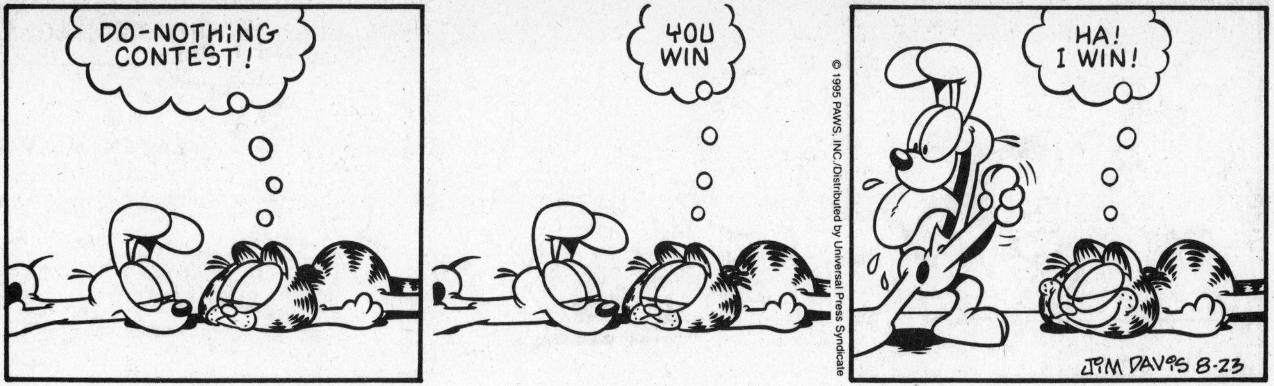
DO-NOTHING CONTEST!
YOU WIN
HA! I WIN!
JIM DAVIS 8-23
© 1995 PAWS, INC./Distributed by Universal Press Syndicate

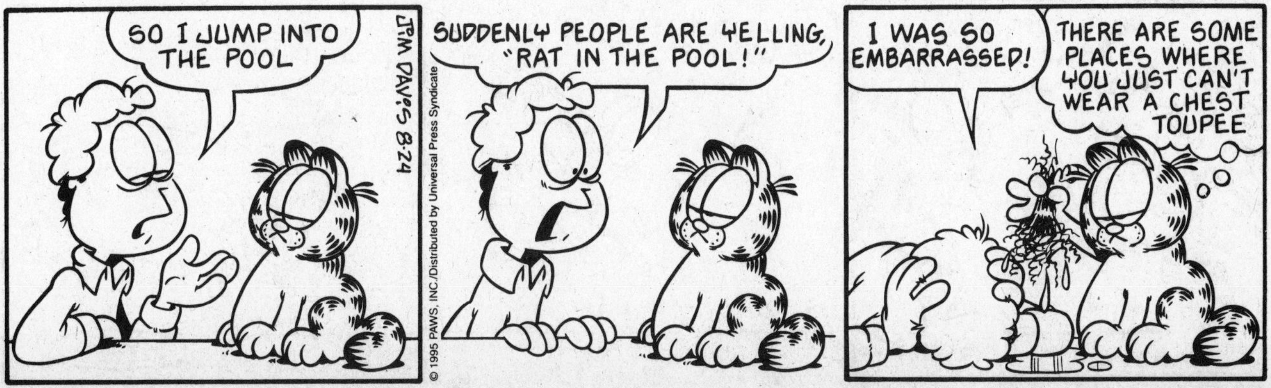
SO I JUMP INTO THE POOL
SUDDENLY PEOPLE ARE YELLING, "RAT IN THE POOL!"
I WAS SO EMBARRASSED!
THERE ARE SOME PLACES WHERE YOU JUST CAN'T WEAR A CHEST TOUPEE
JIM DAVIS 8-24
© 1995 PAWS, INC./Distributed by Universal Press Syndicate

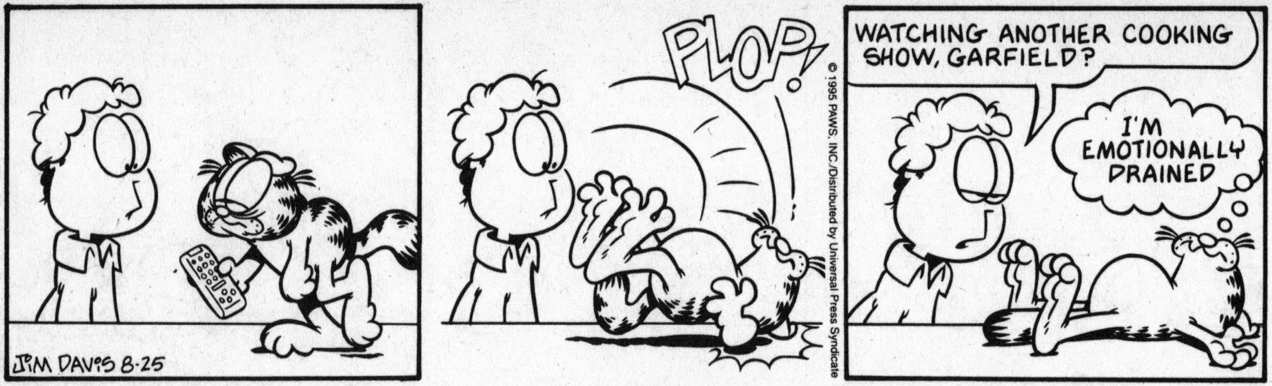
JIM DAVIS 8-25
PLOP!
WATCHING ANOTHER COOKING SHOW, GARFIELD?
I'M EMOTIONALLY DRAINED
© 1995 PAWS, INC./Distributed by Universal Press Syndicate

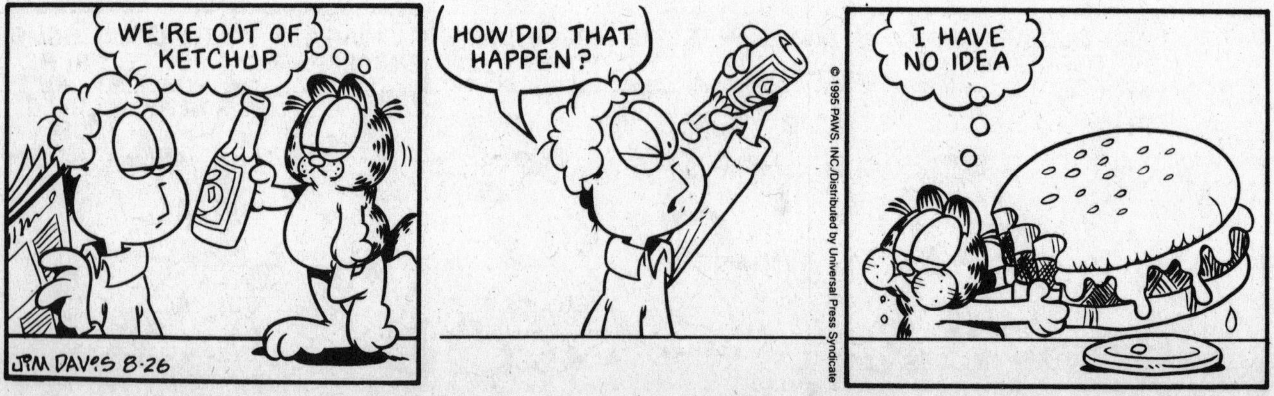
WE'RE OUT OF KETCHUP
JIM DAVIS 8-26
HOW DID THAT HAPPEN?
I HAVE NO IDEA
© 1995 PAWS, INC./Distributed by Universal Press Syndicate

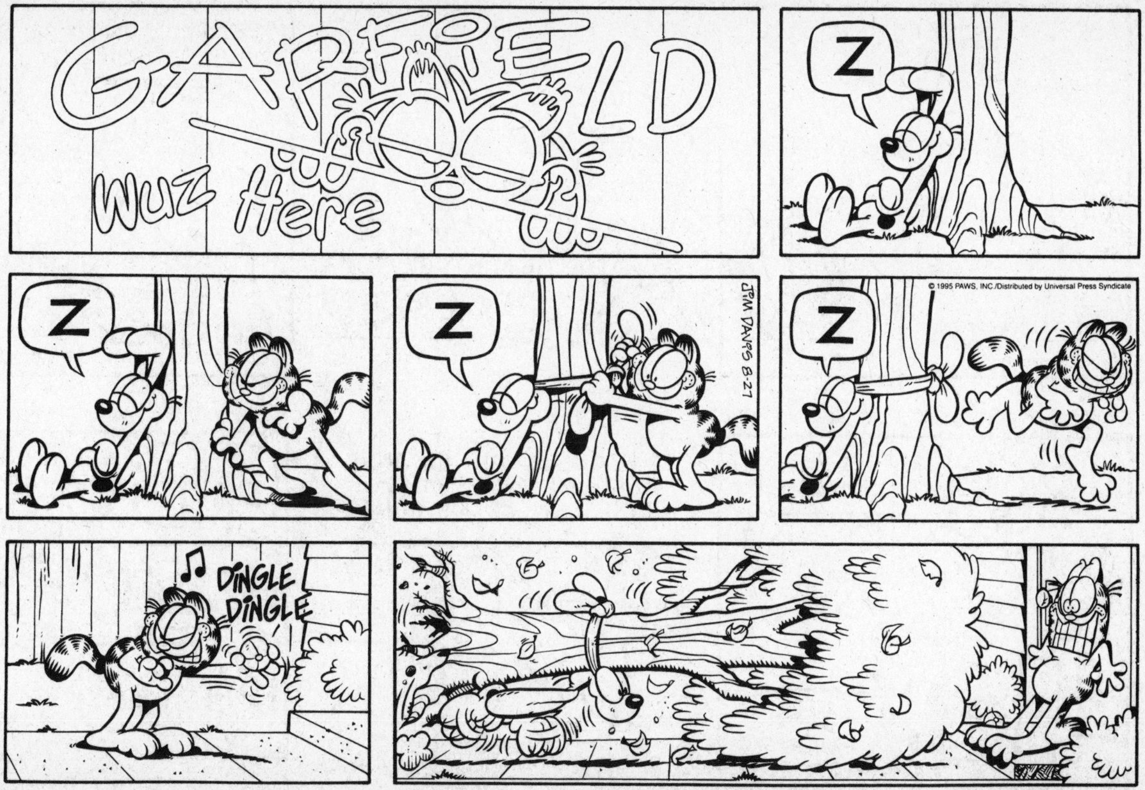
GARFIELD
WUZ HERE
Z
Z
Z
JIM DAVIS 8-27
© 1995 PAWS, INC./Distributed by Universal Press Syndicate
Z
DINGLE
DINGLE

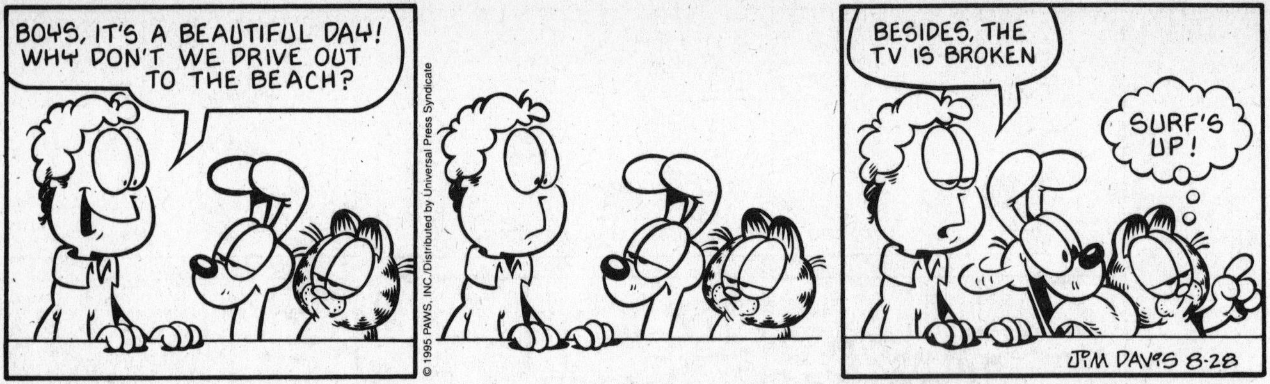
BOYS, IT'S A BEAUTIFUL DAY! WHY DON'T WE DRIVE OUT TO THE BEACH?
BESIDES, THE TV IS BROKEN
SURF'S UP!
JIM DAVIS 8-28
© 1995 PAWS, INC./Distributed by Universal Press Syndicate

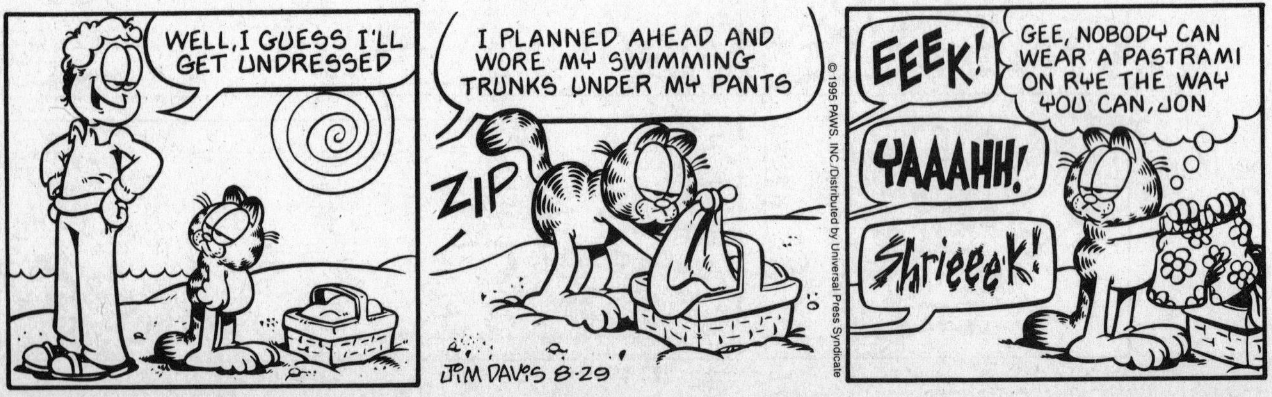
WELL, I GUESS I'LL GET UNDRESSED
I PLANNED AHEAD AND WORE MY SWIMMING TRUNKS UNDER MY PANTS
ZIP
JIM DAVIS 8-29
EEEK!
YAAAHH!
Shrieeek!
GEE, NOBODY CAN WEAR A PASTRAMI ON RYE THE WAY YOU CAN, JON
© 1995 PAWS, INC./Distributed by Universal Press Syndicate

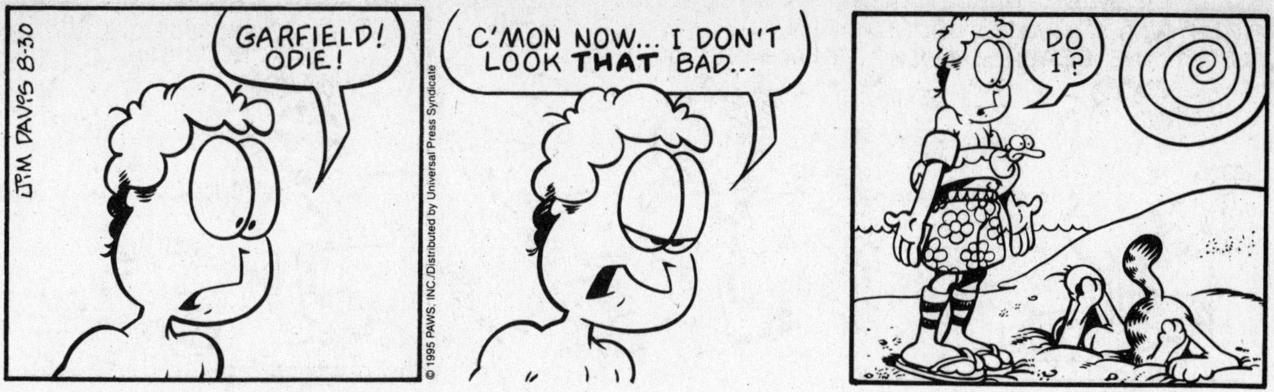
JIM DAVIS 8-30
GARFIELD! ODIE!
© 1995 PAWS, INC./Distributed by Universal Press Syndicate
C'MON NOW... I DON'T LOOK **THAT** BAD...
DO I?

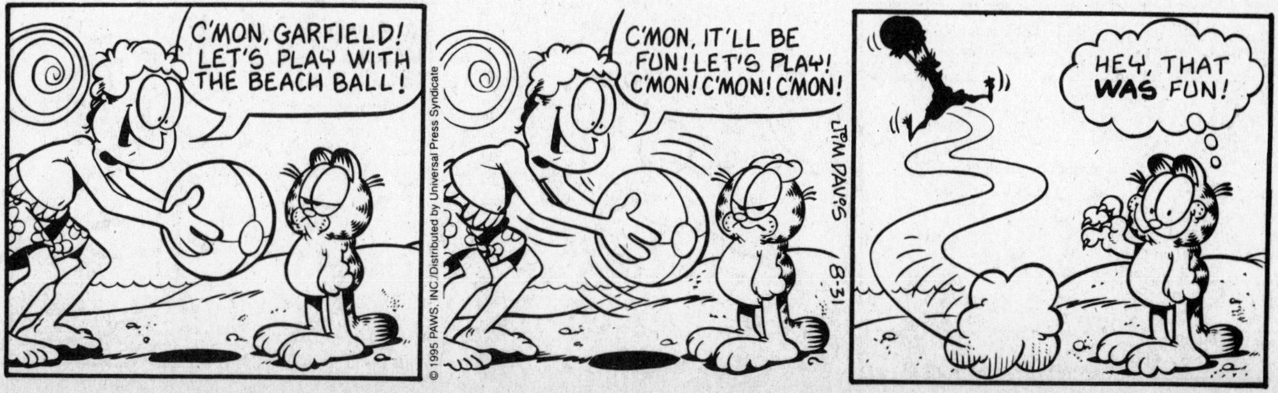
C'MON, GARFIELD! LET'S PLAY WITH THE BEACH BALL!
© 1995 PAWS, INC./Distributed by Universal Press Syndicate
C'MON, IT'LL BE FUN! LET'S PLAY! C'MON! C'MON! C'MON!
JIM DAVIS 8-31
HEY, THAT **WAS** FUN!

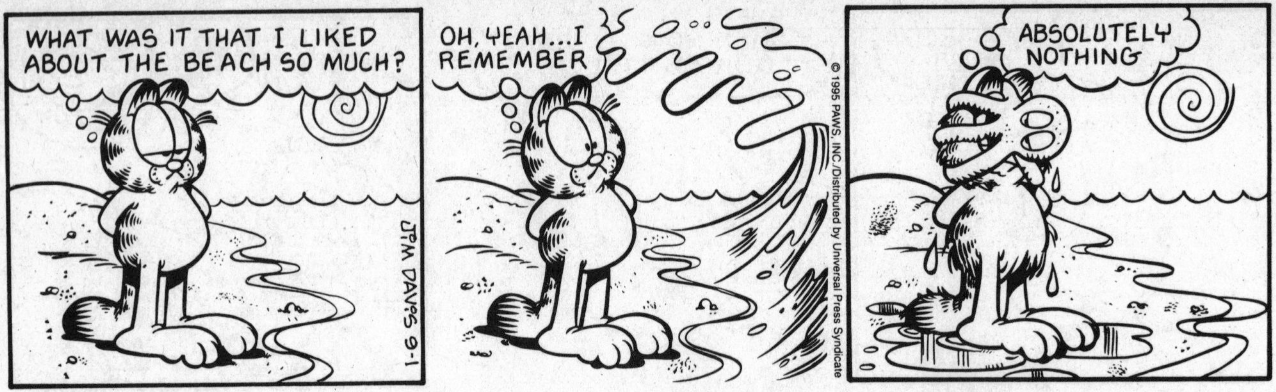
WHAT WAS IT THAT I LIKED ABOUT THE BEACH SO MUCH?
JIM DAVIS 9-1
OH, YEAH...I REMEMBER
© 1995 PAWS, INC./Distributed by Universal Press Syndicate
ABSOLUTELY NOTHING

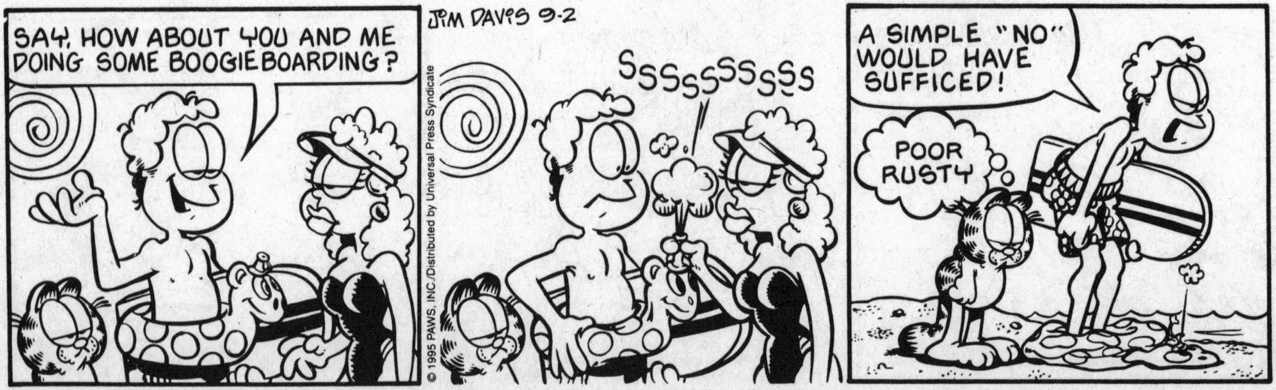
SAY, HOW ABOUT YOU AND ME DOING SOME BOOGIEBOARDING?
© 1995 PAWS, INC./Distributed by Universal Press Syndicate
JIM DAVIS 9-2
SSSSSSSSSSS
A SIMPLE "NO" WOULD HAVE SUFFICED!
POOR RUSTY

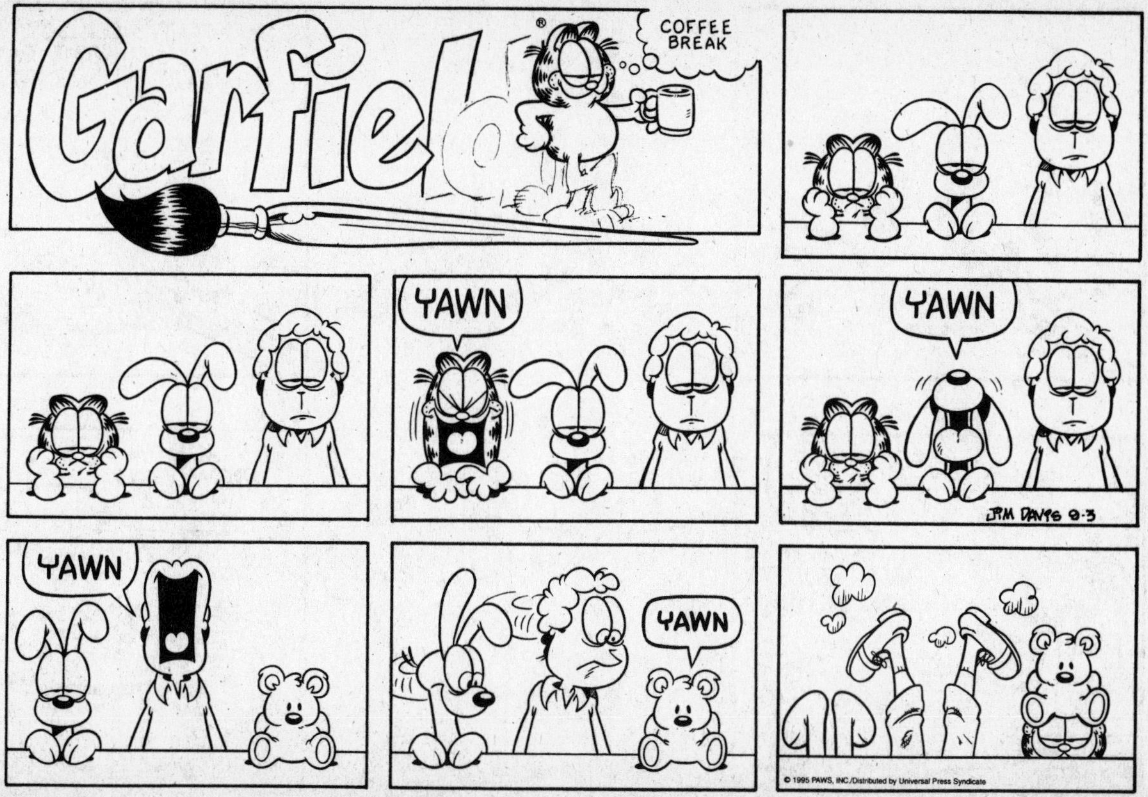
Garfield®
COFFEE BREAK
YAWN
YAWN
JIM DAVIS 9-3
YAWN
YAWN
© 1995 PAWS, INC./Distributed by Universal Press Syndicate

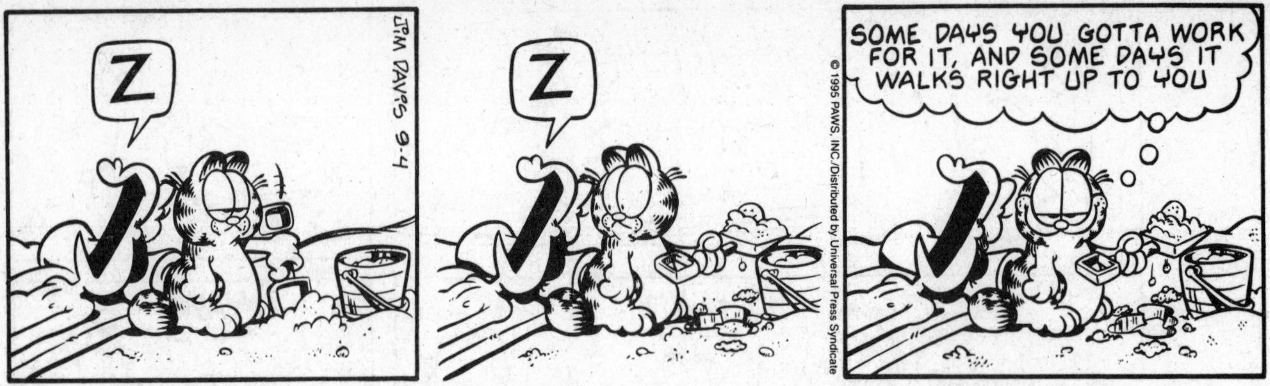
JIM DAVIS 9-4
Z
Z
SOME DAYS YOU GOTTA WORK FOR IT, AND SOME DAYS IT WALKS RIGHT UP TO YOU
© 1995 PAWS, INC./Distributed by Universal Press Syndicate

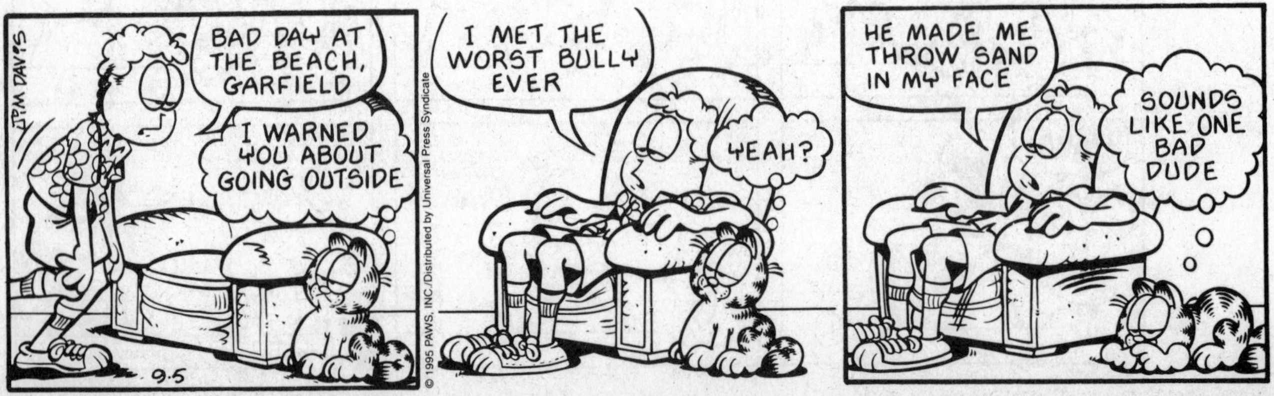
JIM DAVIS
BAD DAY AT THE BEACH, GARFIELD
I WARNED YOU ABOUT GOING OUTSIDE
9-5
© 1995 PAWS, INC./Distributed by Universal Press Syndicate
I MET THE WORST BULLY EVER
YEAH?
HE MADE ME THROW SAND IN MY FACE
SOUNDS LIKE ONE BAD DUDE

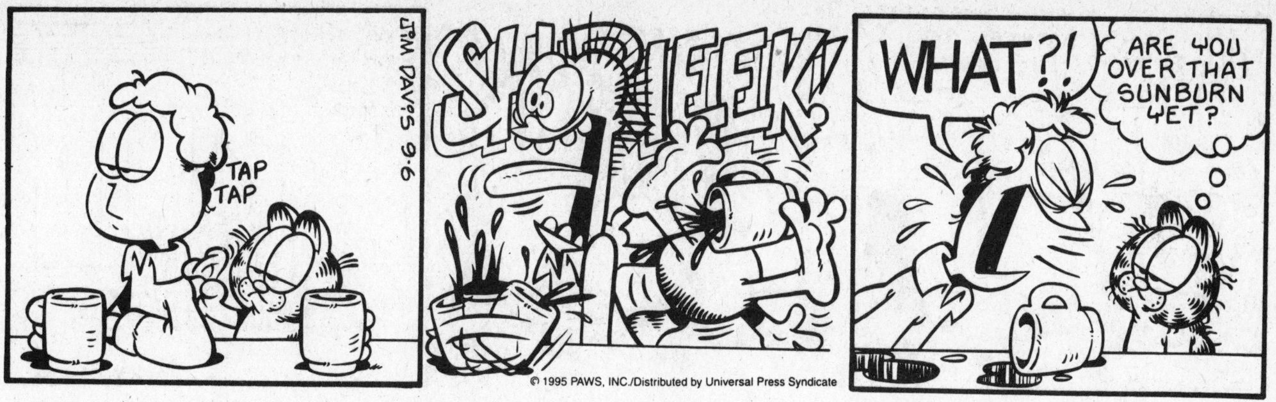
JIM DAVIS 9-6
TAP TAP
SHRIEEEK!
WHAT?!
ARE YOU OVER THAT SUNBURN YET?
© 1995 PAWS, INC./Distributed by Universal Press Syndicate

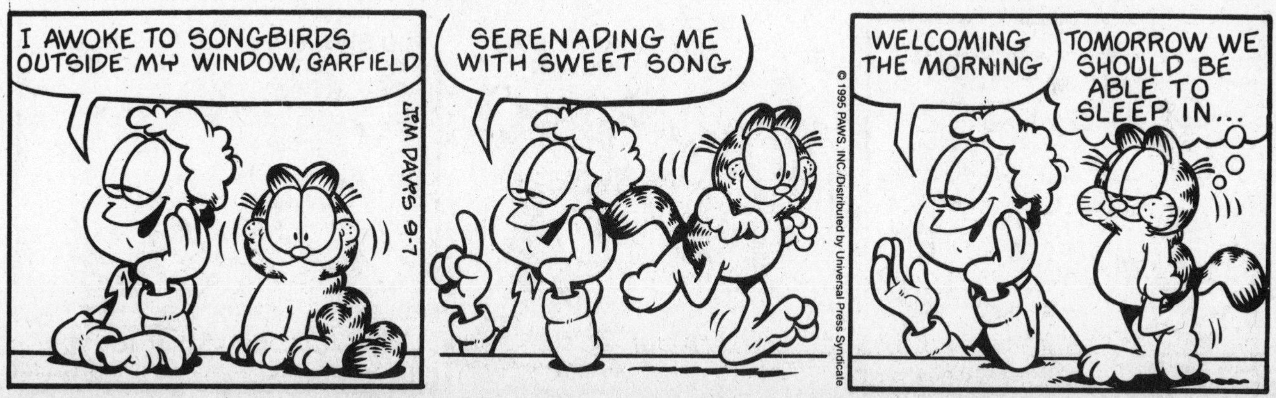
I AWOKE TO SONGBIRDS OUTSIDE MY WINDOW, GARFIELD
JIM DAVIS 9-7
SERENADING ME WITH SWEET SONG
© 1995 PAWS, INC./Distributed by Universal Press Syndicate
WELCOMING THE MORNING
TOMORROW WE SHOULD BE ABLE TO SLEEP IN...

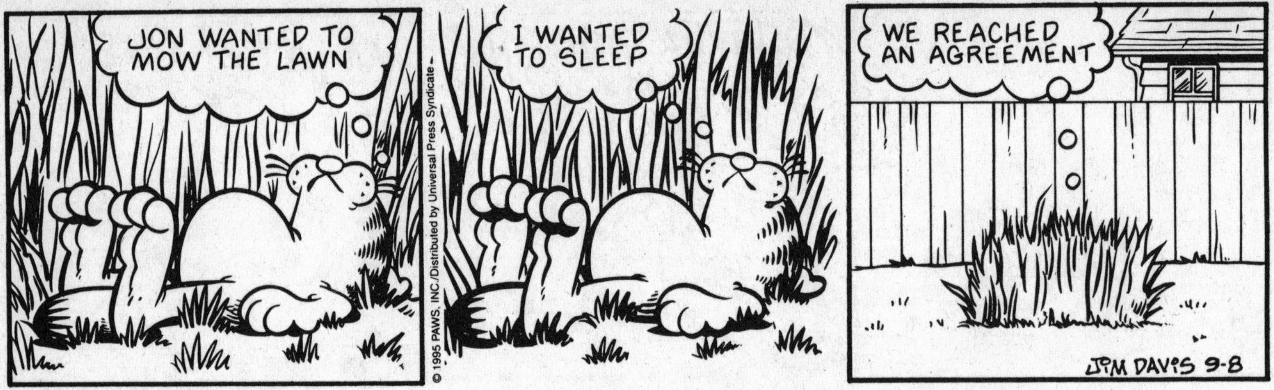
JON WANTED TO MOW THE LAWN
I WANTED TO SLEEP
WE REACHED AN AGREEMENT
JIM DAVIS 9-8
© 1995 PAWS, INC./Distributed by Universal Press Syndicate

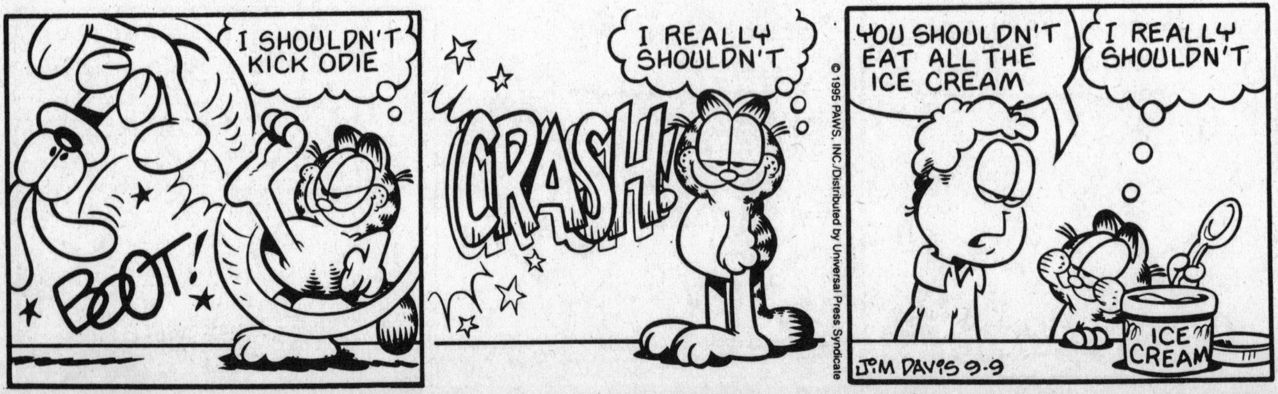
I SHOULDN'T KICK ODIE
BOOT!
CRASH!
I REALLY SHOULDN'T
YOU SHOULDN'T EAT ALL THE ICE CREAM
I REALLY SHOULDN'T
ICE CREAM
JIM DAVIS 9-9
© 1995 PAWS, INC./Distributed by Universal Press Syndicate

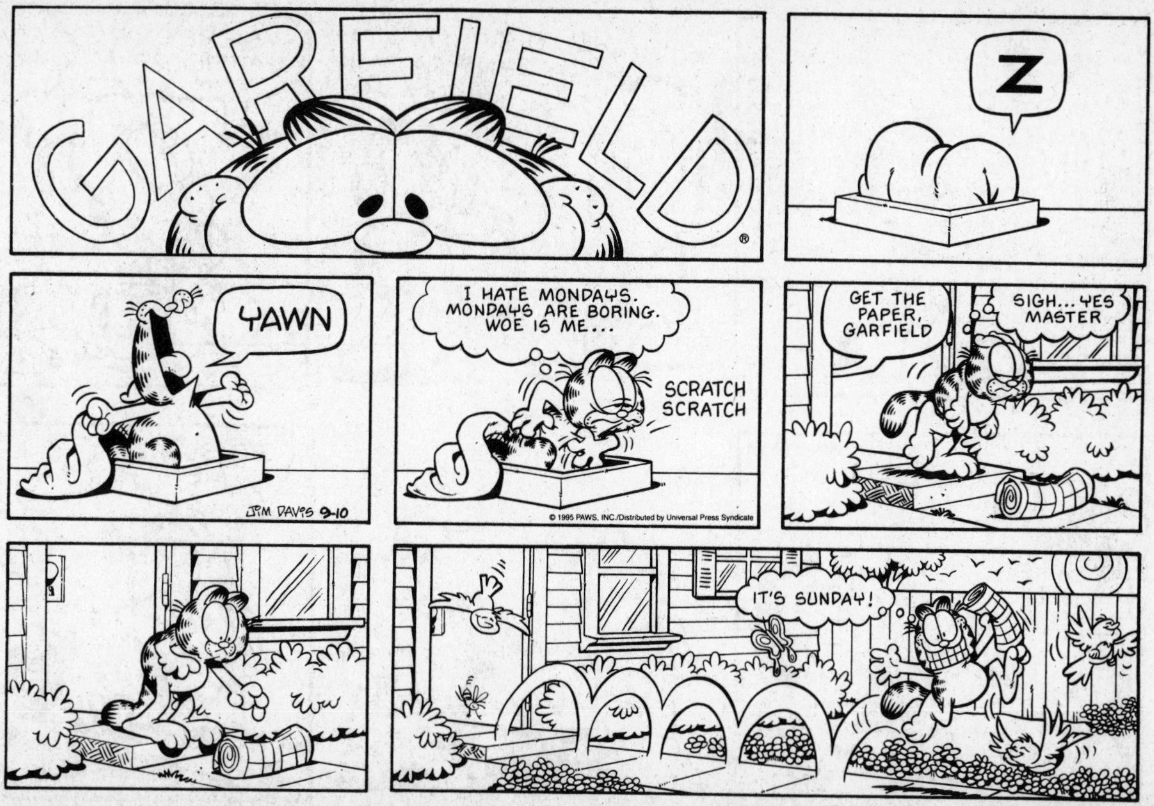
GARFIELD
Z
YAWN
JIM DAVIS 9-10
I HATE MONDAYS. MONDAYS ARE BORING. WOE IS ME...
SCRATCH SCRATCH
© 1995 PAWS, INC./Distributed by Universal Press Syndicate
GET THE PAPER, GARFIELD
SIGH... YES MASTER
IT'S SUNDAY!

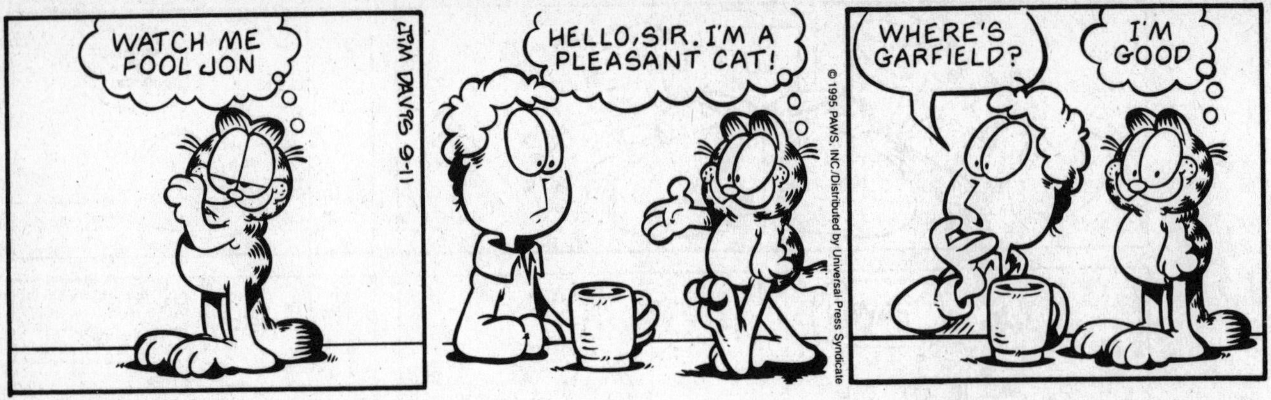
WATCH ME FOOL JON
JIM DAVIS 9-11
HELLO, SIR. I'M A PLEASANT CAT!
WHERE'S GARFIELD?
I'M GOOD

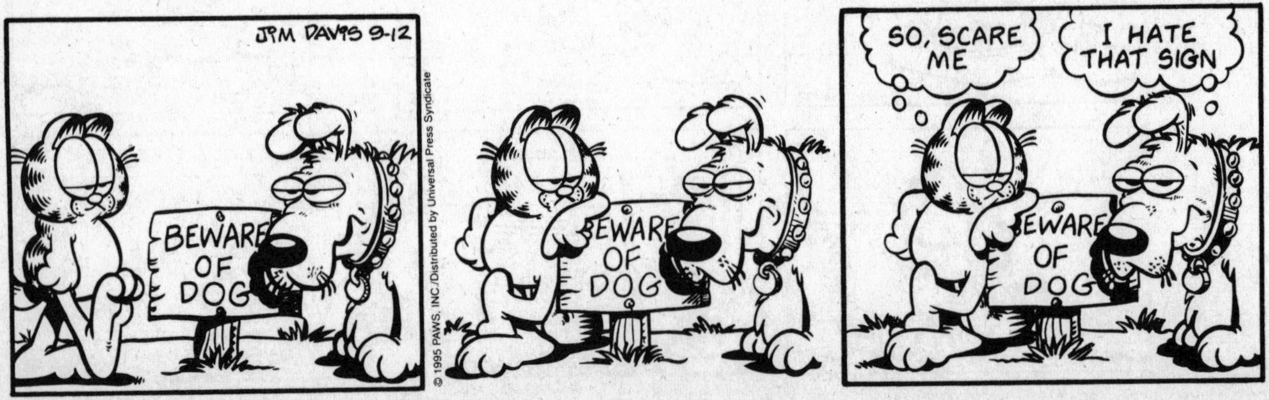
JIM DAVIS 9-12
BEWARE OF DOG
BEWARE OF DOG
SO, SCARE ME
I HATE THAT SIGN
BEWARE OF DOG

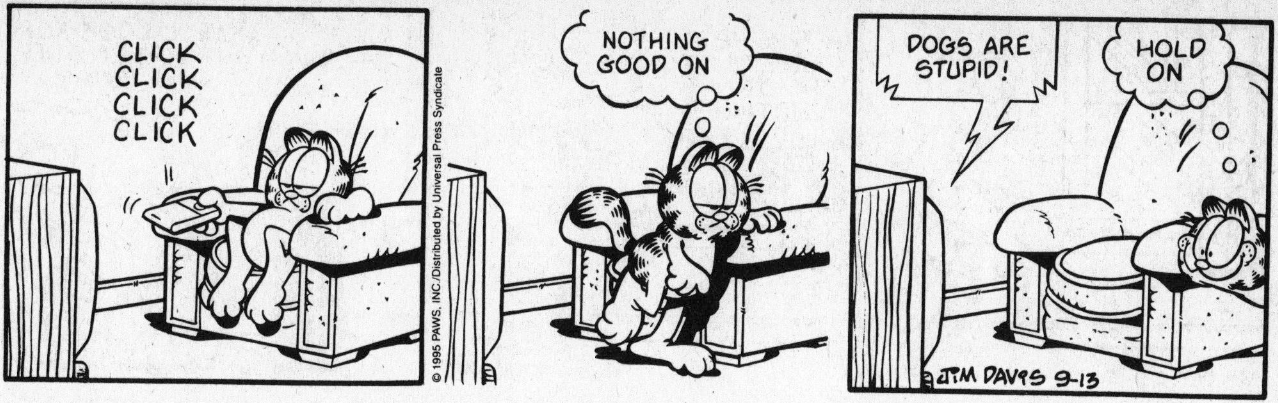
CLICK
CLICK
CLICK
CLICK
NOTHING GOOD ON
DOGS ARE STUPID!
HOLD ON
JIM DAVIS 9-13

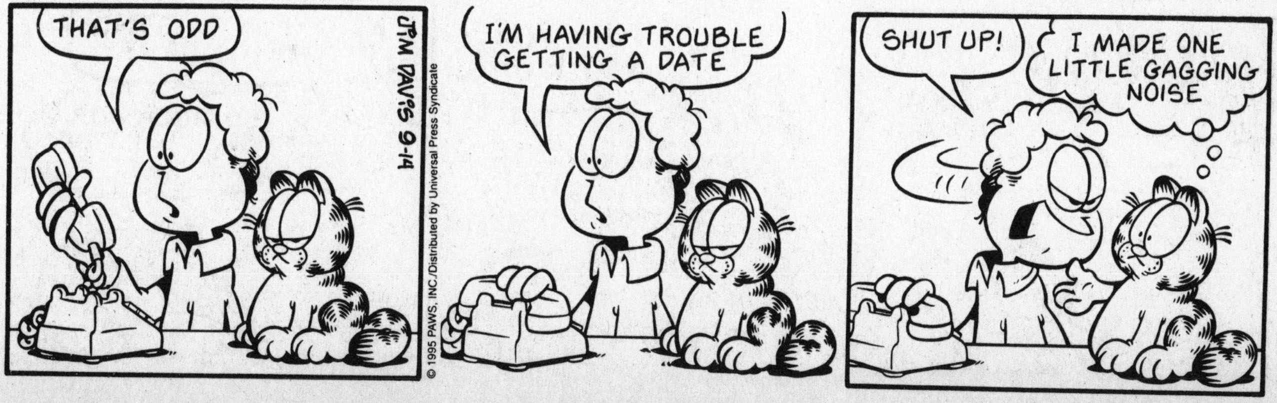
THAT'S ODD
JIM DAVIS 9-14
I'M HAVING TROUBLE GETTING A DATE
SHUT UP!
I MADE ONE LITTLE GAGGING NOISE

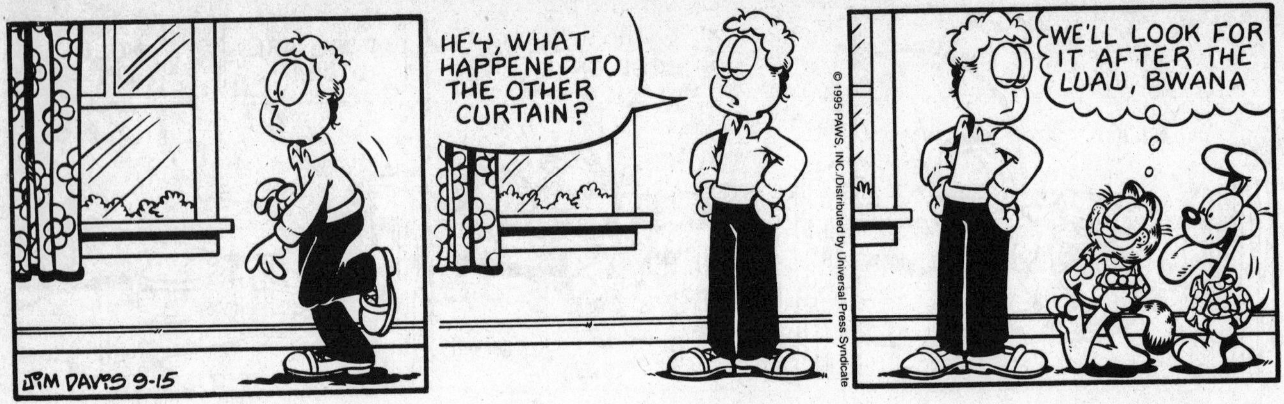
JIM DAVIS 9-15
HEY, WHAT HAPPENED TO THE OTHER CURTAIN?
© 1995 PAWS, INC./Distributed by Universal Press Syndicate
WE'LL LOOK FOR IT AFTER THE LUAU, BWANA

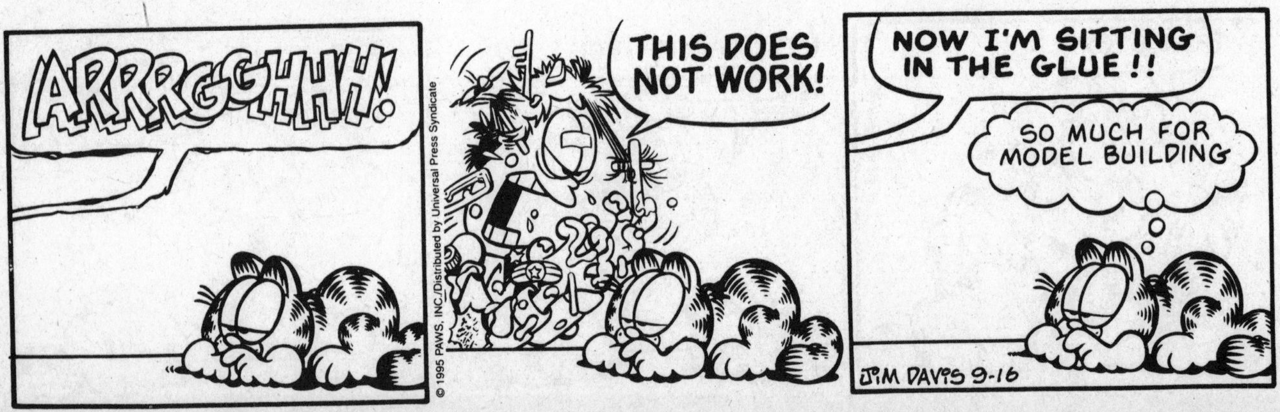
ARRRGGHHH!
© 1995 PAWS, INC./Distributed by Universal Press Syndicate
THIS DOES NOT WORK!
NOW I'M SITTING IN THE GLUE!!
SO MUCH FOR MODEL BUILDING
JIM DAVIS 9-16

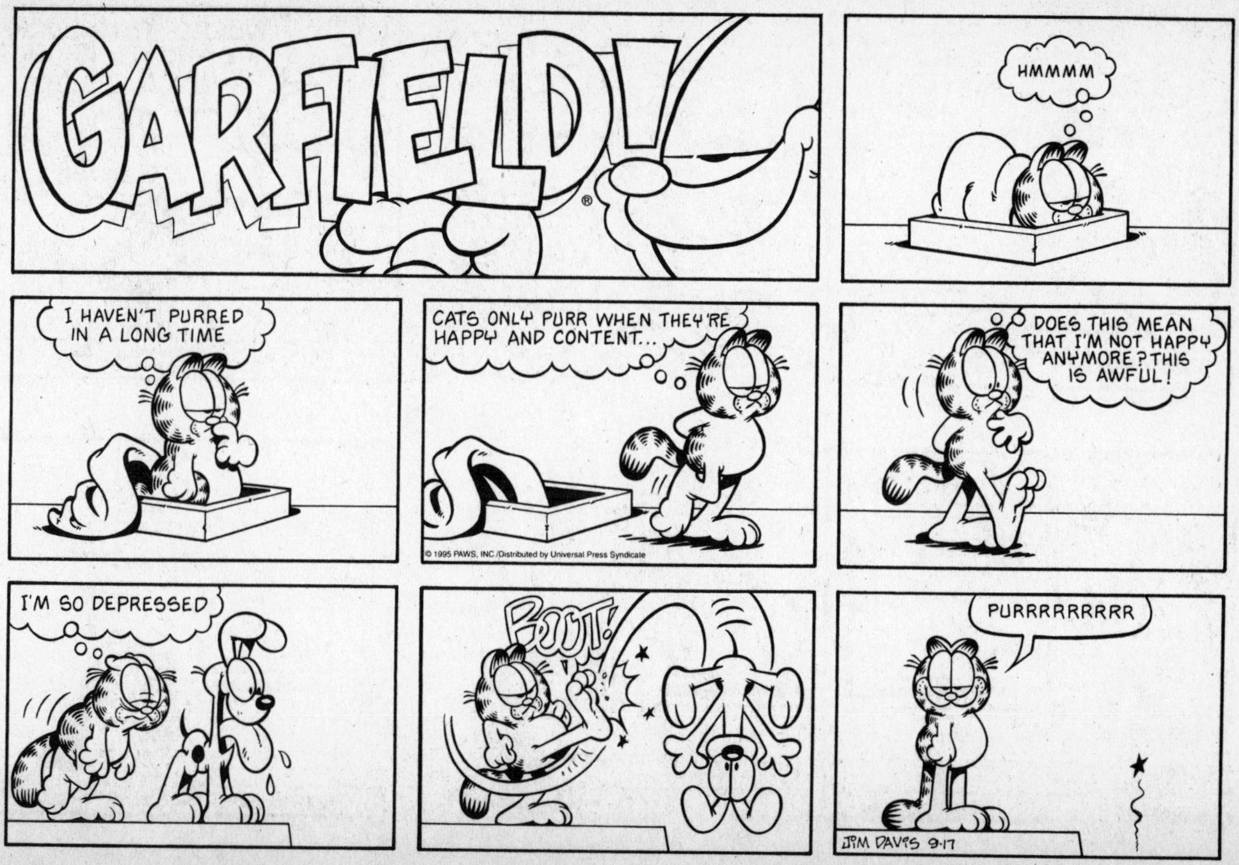
GARFIELD®
HMMMM
I HAVEN'T PURRED IN A LONG TIME
CATS ONLY PURR WHEN THEY'RE HAPPY AND CONTENT...
© 1995 PAWS, INC./Distributed by Universal Press Syndicate
DOES THIS MEAN THAT I'M NOT HAPPY ANYMORE? THIS IS AWFUL!
I'M SO DEPRESSED
BOOT!
PURRRRRRRRR
JIM DAVIS 9-17

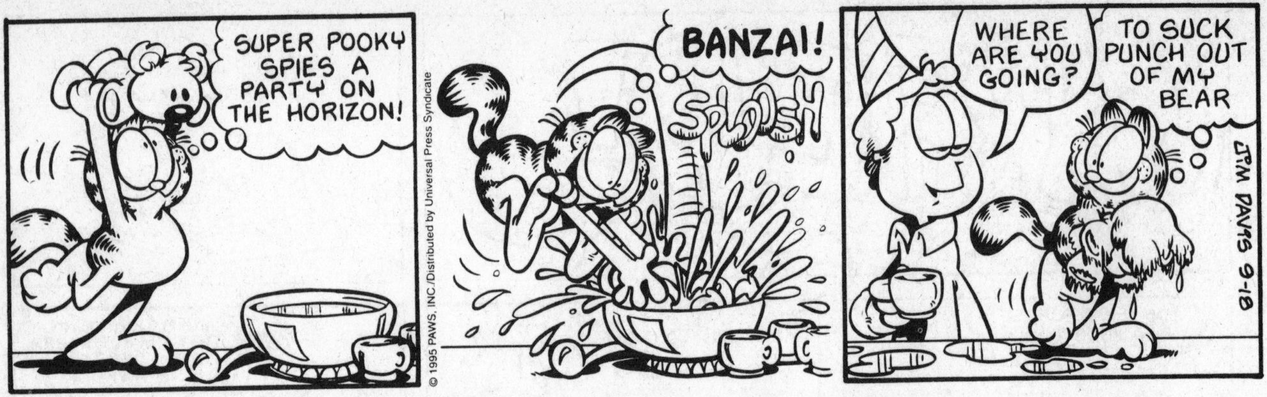
SUPER POOKY SPIES A PARTY ON THE HORIZON!
© 1995 PAWS, INC./Distributed by Universal Press Syndicate
BANZAI!
SPLOOSH
WHERE ARE YOU GOING?
TO SUCK PUNCH OUT OF MY BEAR
JIM DAVIS 9-18

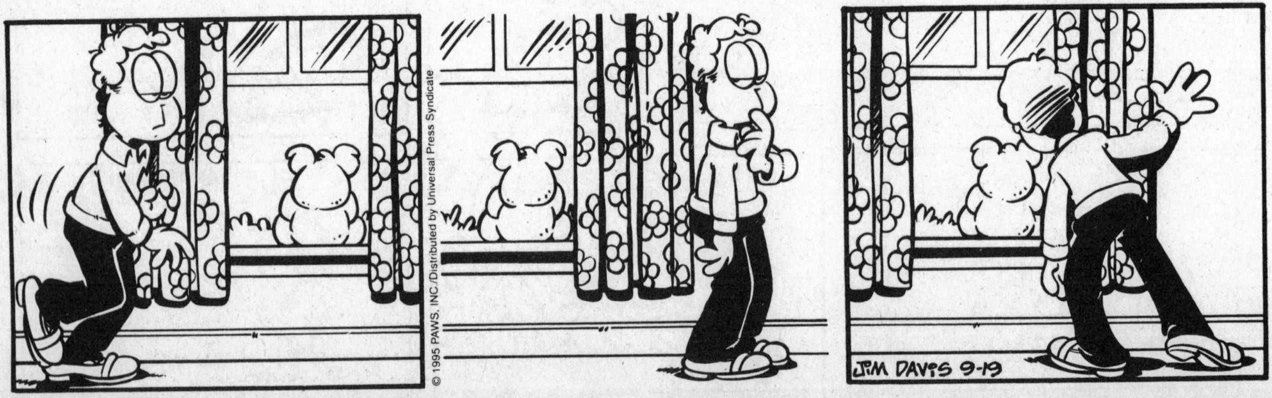
© 1995 PAWS, INC./Distributed by Universal Press Syndicate
JIM DAVIS 9-19

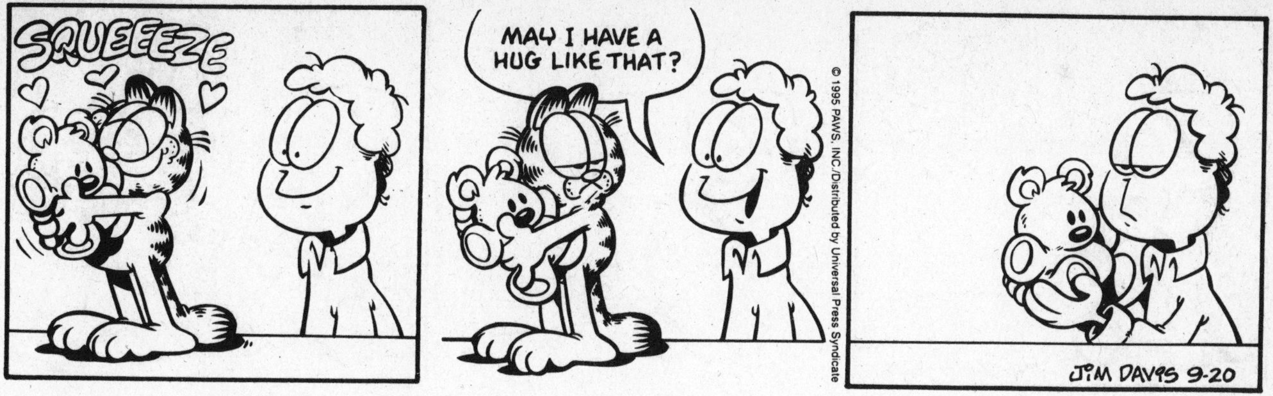
SQUEEEEZE
MAY I HAVE A HUG LIKE THAT?
JIM DAVIS 9-20

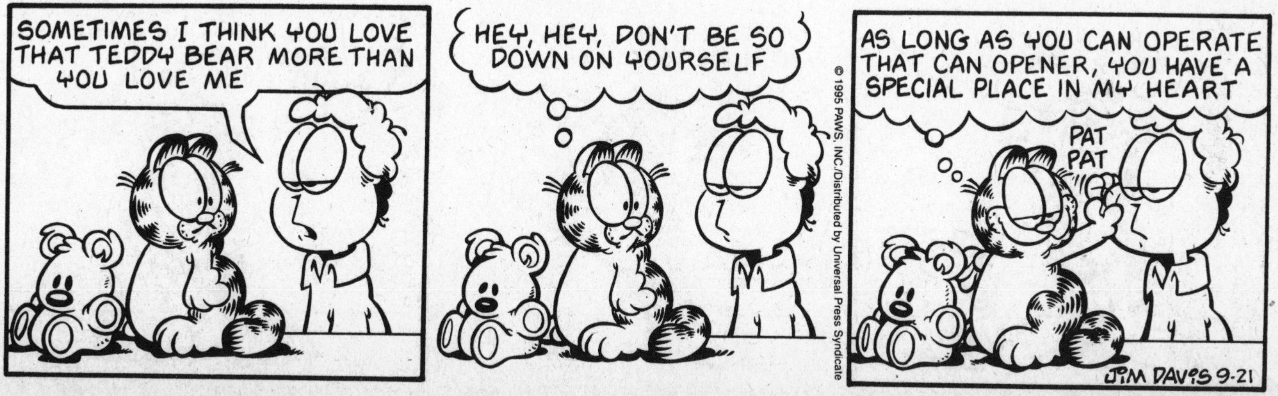
SOMETIMES I THINK YOU LOVE THAT TEDDY BEAR MORE THAN YOU LOVE ME
HEY, HEY, DON'T BE SO DOWN ON YOURSELF
AS LONG AS YOU CAN OPERATE THAT CAN OPENER, YOU HAVE A SPECIAL PLACE IN MY HEART
PAT PAT
JIM DAVIS 9-21

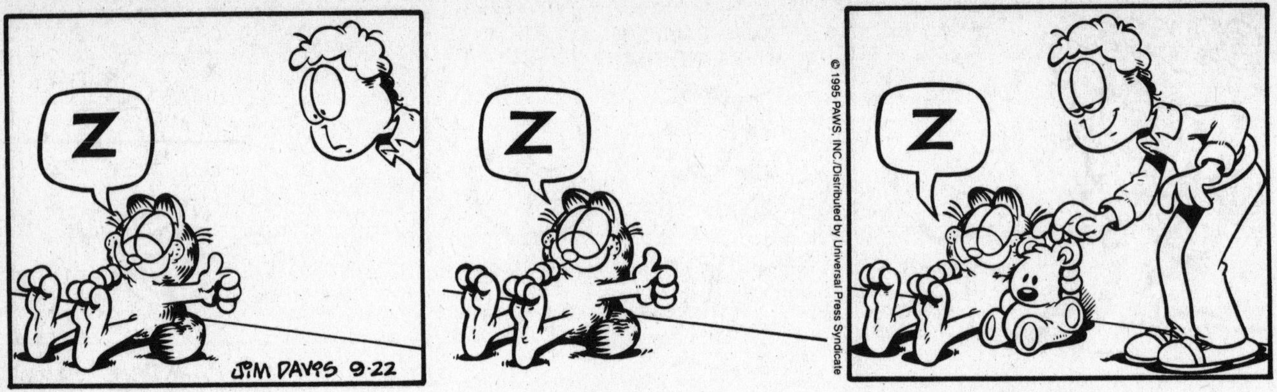
Z
Z
Z
JIM DAVIS 9·22
© 1995 PAWS, INC./Distributed by Universal Press Syndicate

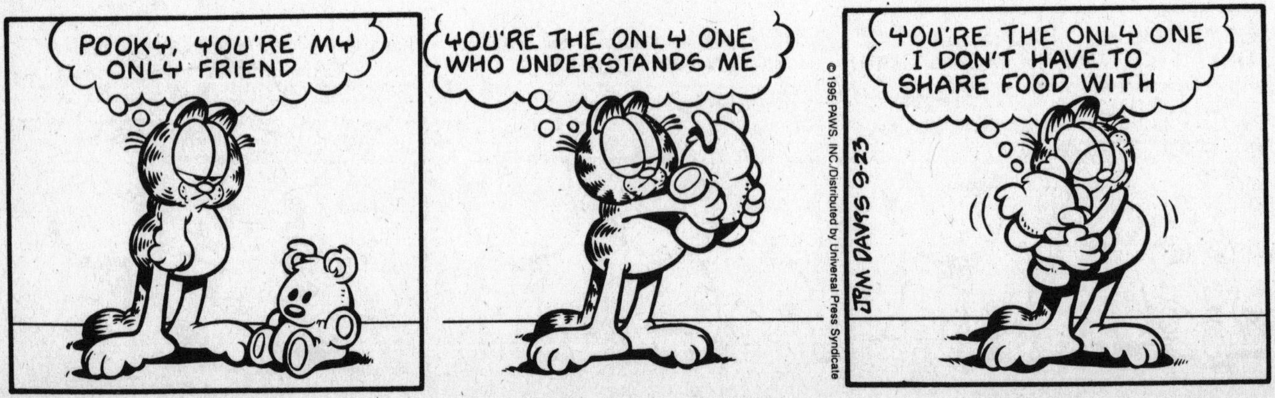
POOKY, YOU'RE MY ONLY FRIEND
YOU'RE THE ONLY ONE WHO UNDERSTANDS ME
YOU'RE THE ONLY ONE I DON'T HAVE TO SHARE FOOD WITH
JIM DAVIS 9-23
© 1995 PAWS, INC./Distributed by Universal Press Syndicate

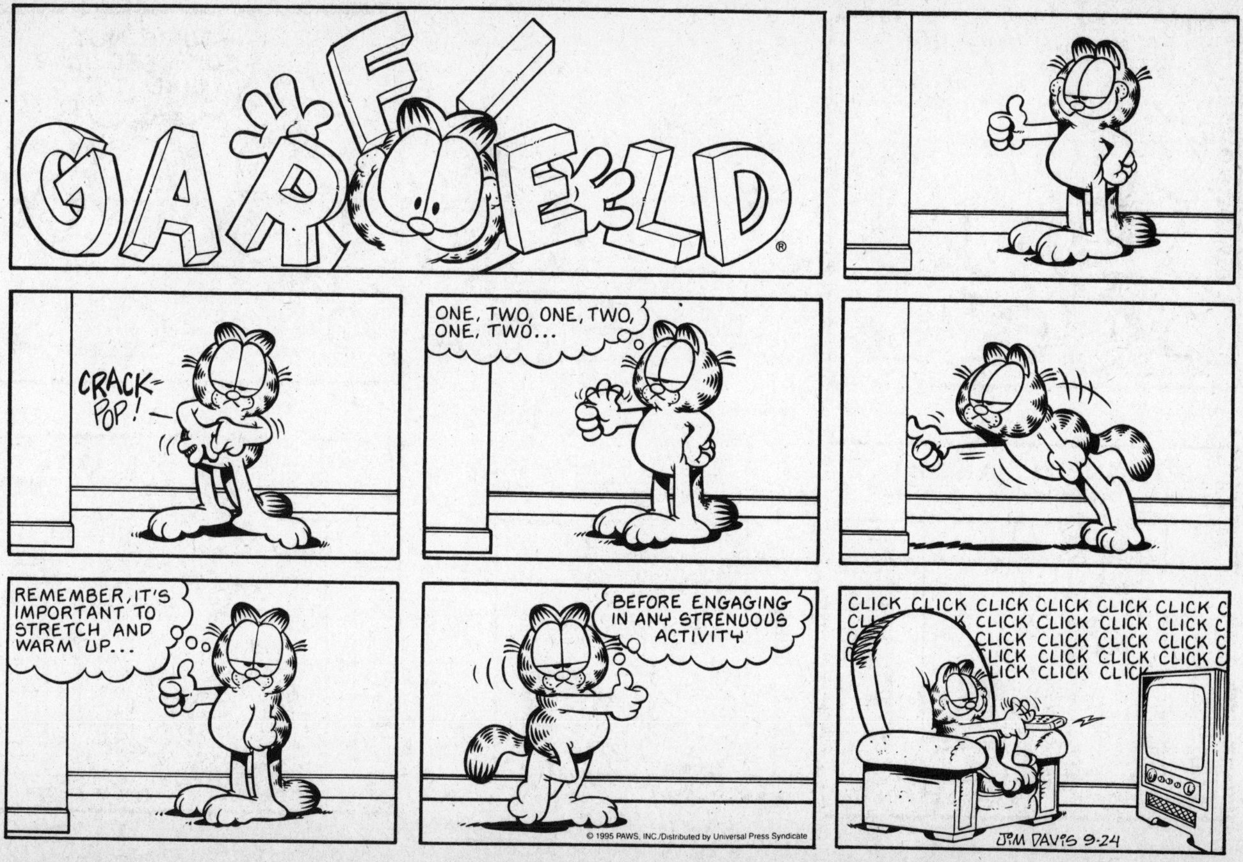
GARFIELD®
CRACK
POP!
ONE, TWO, ONE, TWO, ONE, TWO...
REMEMBER, IT'S IMPORTANT TO STRETCH AND WARM UP...
BEFORE ENGAGING IN ANY STRENUOUS ACTIVITY
CLICK CLICK CLICK CLICK CLICK CLICK
CLICK CLICK CLICK CLICK
CLICK CLICK CLICK CLICK
CLICK CLICK CLICK CLICK
CLICK CLICK CLICK
© 1995 PAWS, INC./Distributed by Universal Press Syndicate
JIM DAVIS 9-24

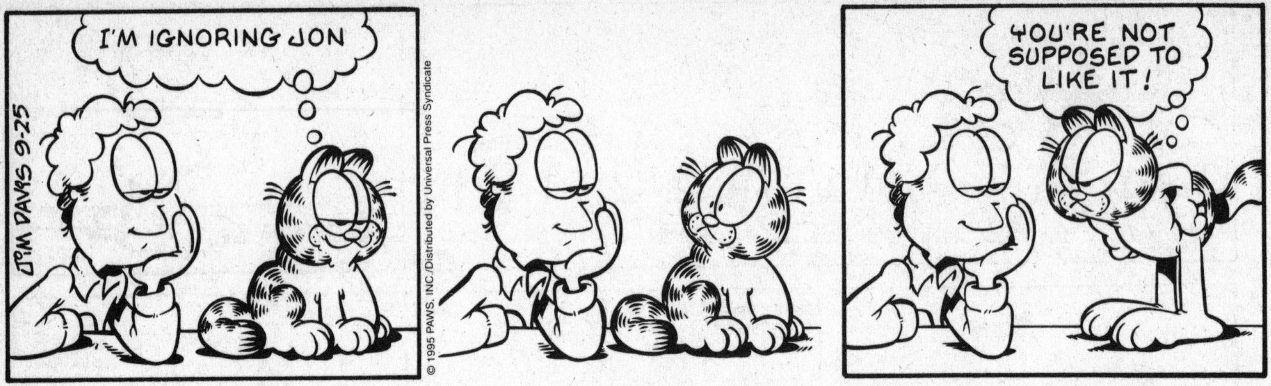
I'M IGNORING JON
YOU'RE NOT SUPPOSED TO LIKE IT!
© 1995 PAWS, INC./Distributed by Universal Press Syndicate

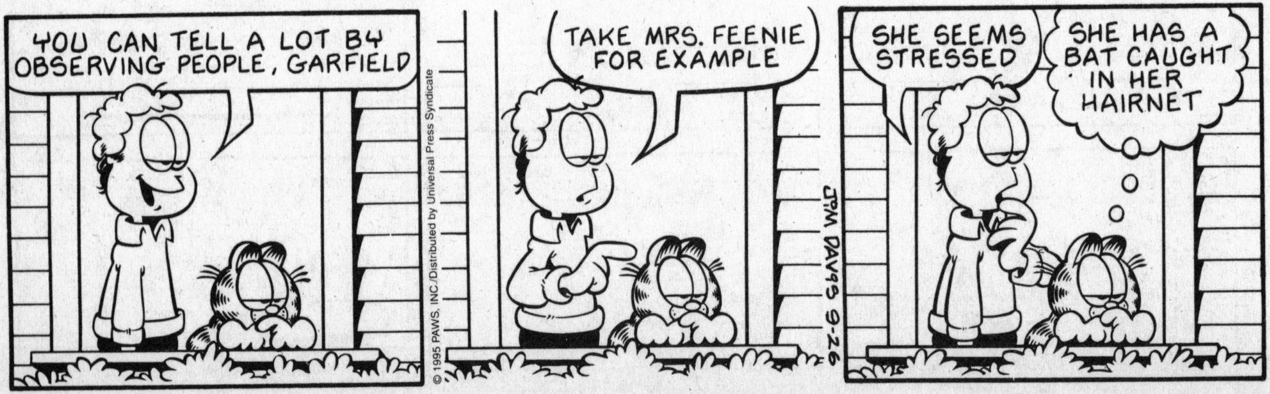
YOU CAN TELL A LOT BY OBSERVING PEOPLE, GARFIELD
TAKE MRS. FEENIE FOR EXAMPLE
SHE SEEMS STRESSED
SHE HAS A BAT CAUGHT IN HER HAIRNET
© 1995 PAWS, INC./Distributed by Universal Press Syndicate

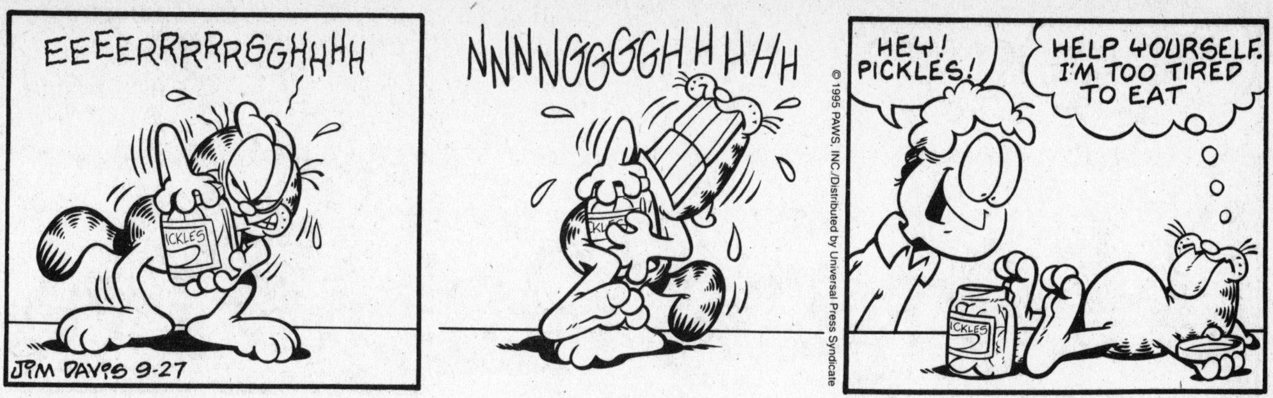
EEEERRRRRRGGHHHH
JIM DAVIS 9-27
NNNNGGGGGHHHHH
HEY! PICKLES!
HELP YOURSELF. I'M TOO TIRED TO EAT
PICKLES

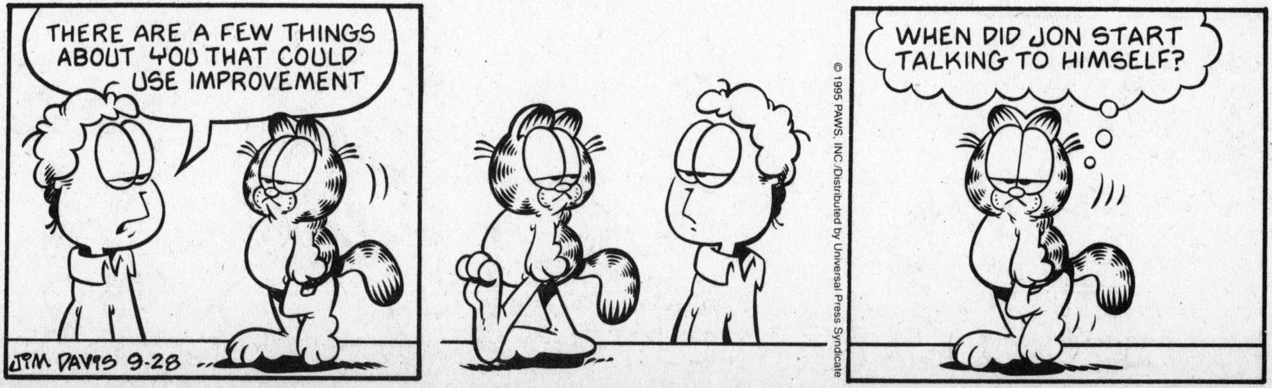
THERE ARE A FEW THINGS ABOUT YOU THAT COULD USE IMPROVEMENT
JIM DAVIS 9-28
WHEN DID JON START TALKING TO HIMSELF?

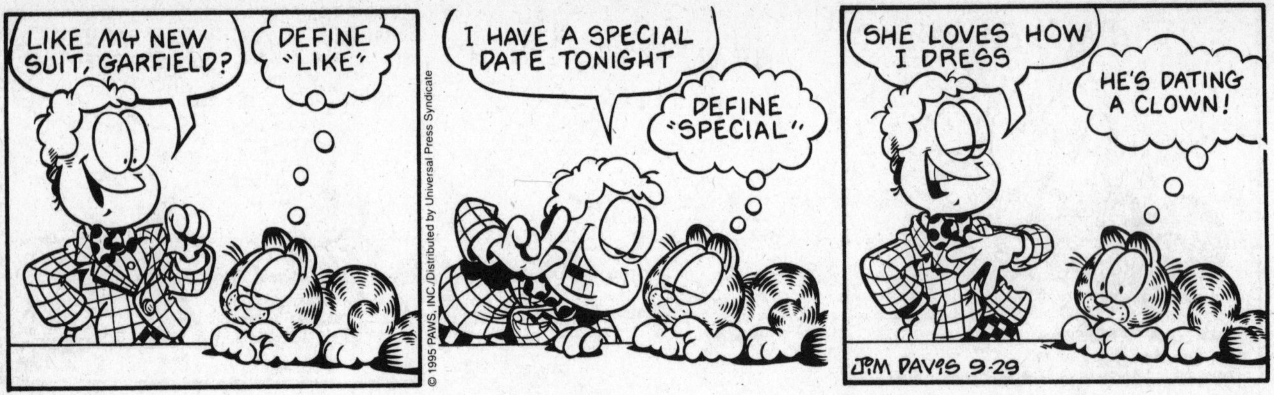
LIKE MY NEW SUIT, GARFIELD?
DEFINE "LIKE"
I HAVE A SPECIAL DATE TONIGHT
DEFINE "SPECIAL"
SHE LOVES HOW I DRESS
HE'S DATING A CLOWN!
JIM DAVIS 9-29

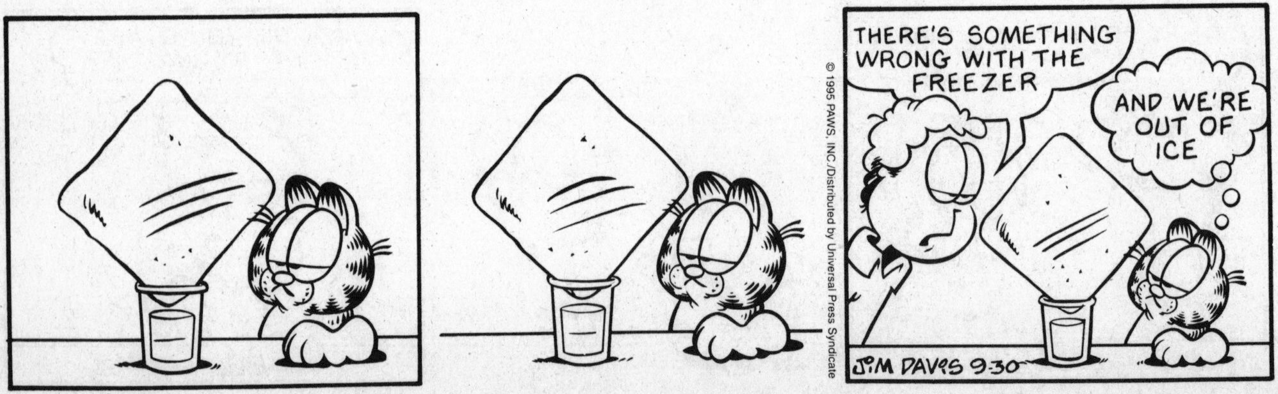
THERE'S SOMETHING WRONG WITH THE FREEZER
AND WE'RE OUT OF ICE
JIM DAVIS 9-30

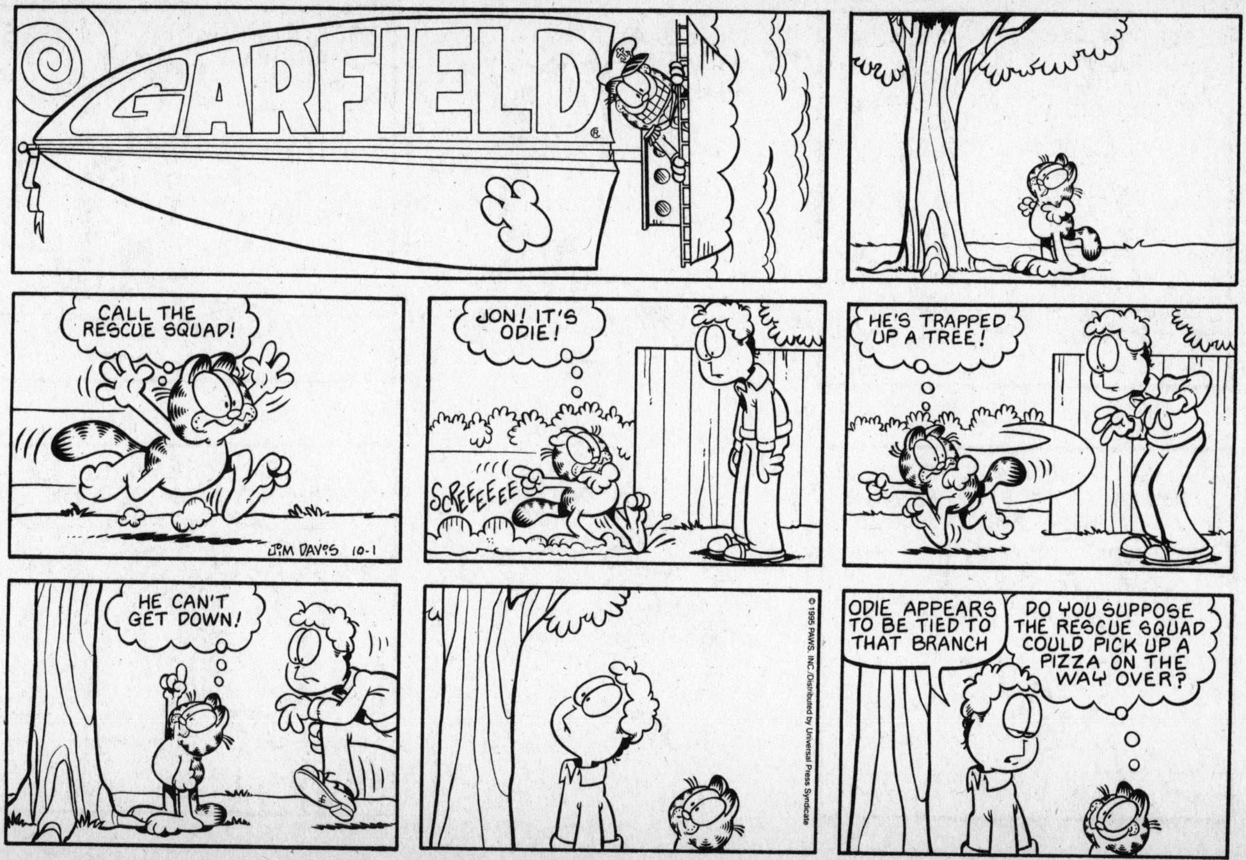
GARFIELD®
CALL THE RESCUE SQUAD!
JIM DAVIS 10-1
JON! IT'S ODIE!
SCREEEEEE
HE'S TRAPPED UP A TREE!
HE CAN'T GET DOWN!
© 1995 PAWS, INC./Distributed by Universal Press Syndicate
ODIE APPEARS TO BE TIED TO THAT BRANCH
DO YOU SUPPOSE THE RESCUE SQUAD COULD PICK UP A PIZZA ON THE WAY OVER?

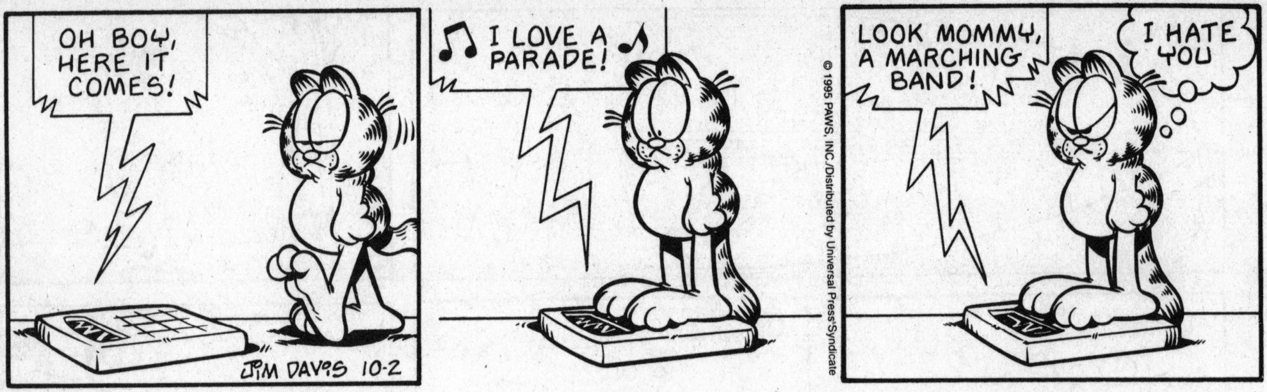
OH BOY, HERE IT COMES!
I LOVE A PARADE!
JIM DAVIS 10-2
LOOK MOMMY, A MARCHING BAND!
I HATE YOU

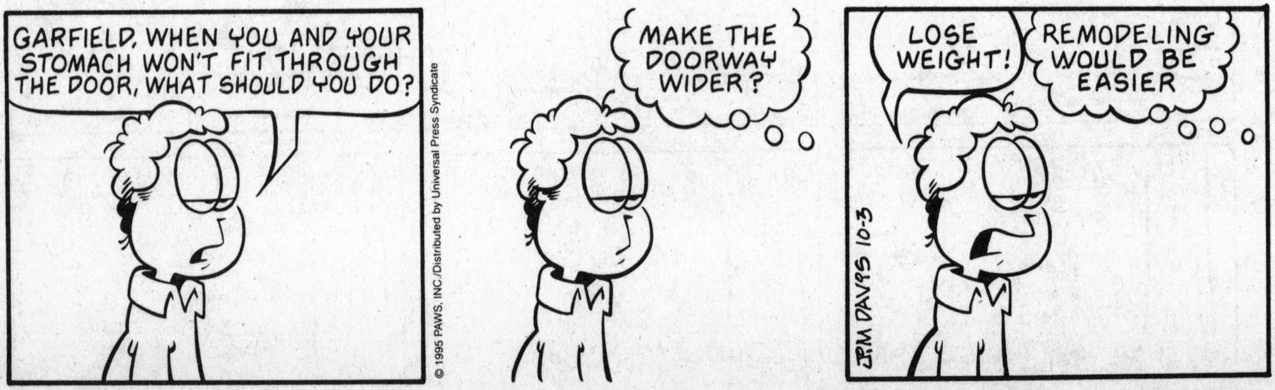
GARFIELD, WHEN YOU AND YOUR STOMACH WON'T FIT THROUGH THE DOOR, WHAT SHOULD YOU DO?
MAKE THE DOORWAY WIDER?
JIM DAVIS 10-3
LOSE WEIGHT!
REMODELING WOULD BE EASIER

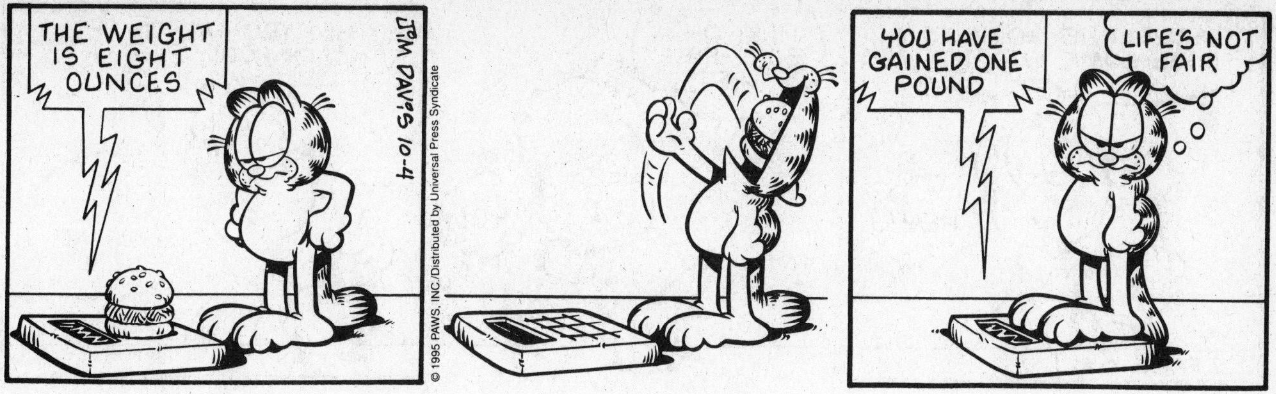
THE WEIGHT IS EIGHT OUNCES
JIM DAVIS 10-4
© 1995 PAWS, INC./Distributed by Universal Press Syndicate
YOU HAVE GAINED ONE POUND
LIFE'S NOT FAIR

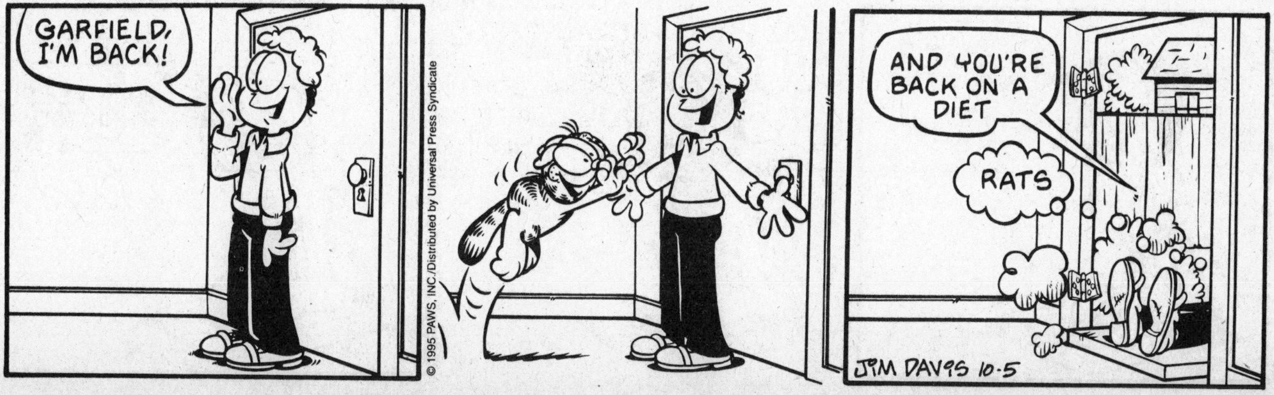
GARFIELD, I'M BACK!
© 1995 PAWS, INC./Distributed by Universal Press Syndicate
AND YOU'RE BACK ON A DIET
RATS
JIM DAVIS 10-5

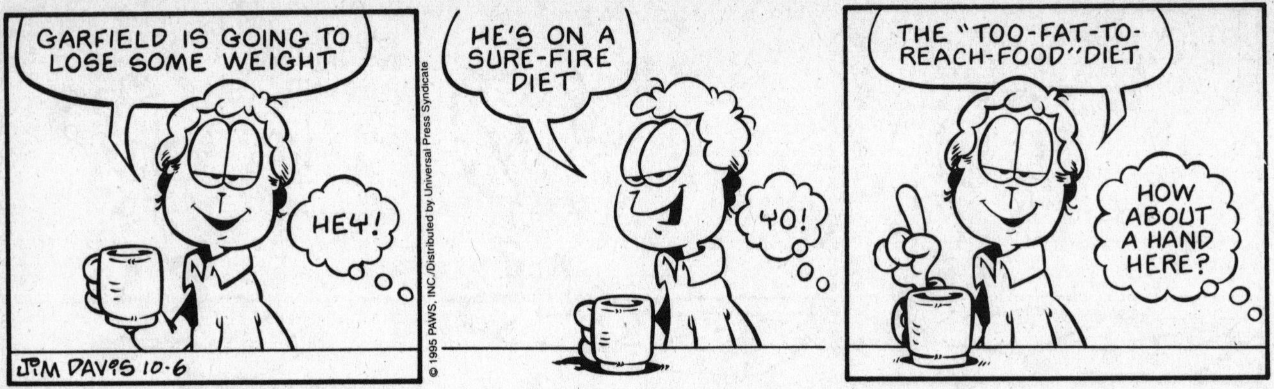
GARFIELD IS GOING TO LOSE SOME WEIGHT
HEY!
JIM DAVIS 10-6
© 1995 PAWS, INC./Distributed by Universal Press Syndicate
HE'S ON A SURE-FIRE DIET
YO!
THE "TOO-FAT-TO-REACH-FOOD" DIET
HOW ABOUT A HAND HERE?

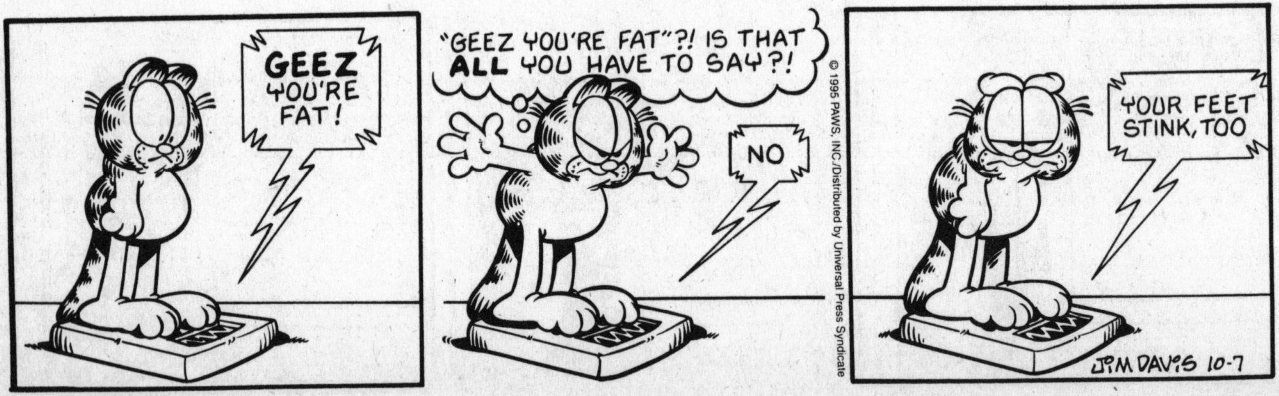
GEEZ YOU'RE FAT!
"GEEZ YOU'RE FAT"?! IS THAT **ALL** YOU HAVE TO SAY?!
NO
© 1995 PAWS, INC./Distributed by Universal Press Syndicate
YOUR FEET STINK, TOO
JIM DAVIS 10-7

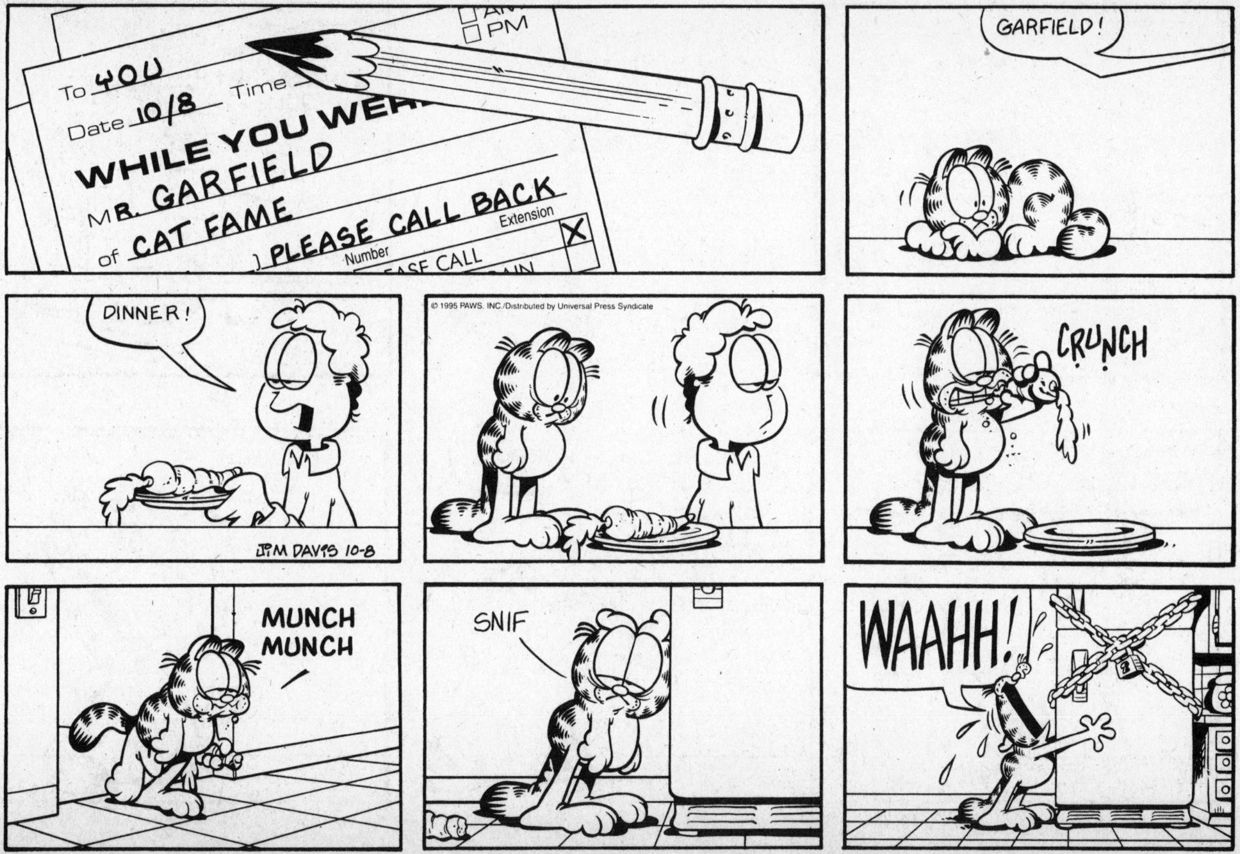
PM
To YOU
Time
Date 10/8
WHILE YOU WER
MR. GARFIELD
of CAT FAME
) PLEASE CALL BACK
Number
Extension
X
GARFIELD!
DINNER!
JIM DAVIS 10-8
© 1995 PAWS, INC./Distributed by Universal Press Syndicate
CRUNCH
MUNCH
MUNCH
SNIF
WAAHH!

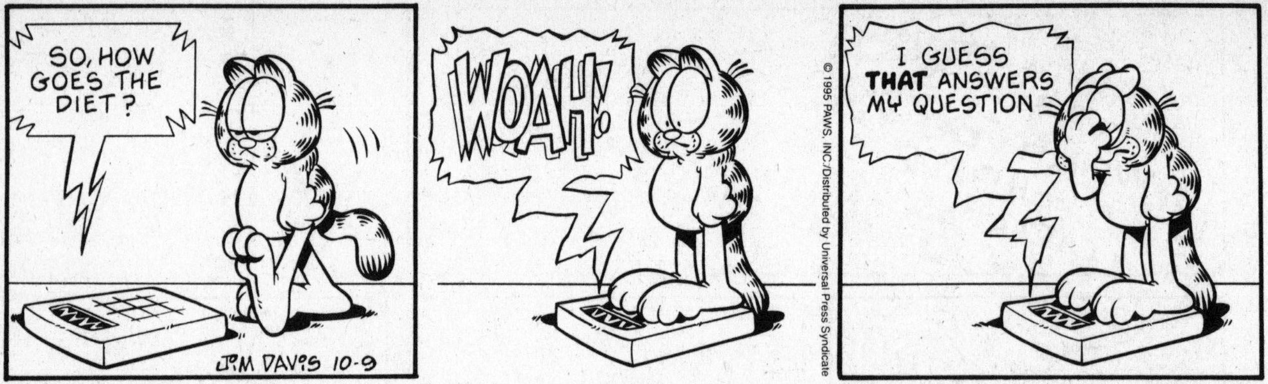
SO, HOW GOES THE DIET?
WOAH!
I GUESS **THAT** ANSWERS MY QUESTION
JIM DAVIS 10-9

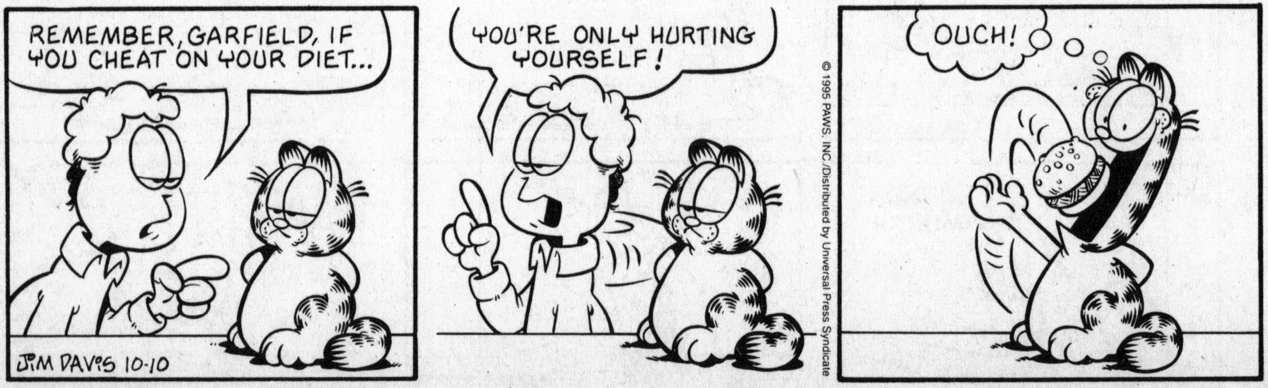
REMEMBER, GARFIELD, IF YOU CHEAT ON YOUR DIET...
YOU'RE ONLY HURTING YOURSELF!
OUCH!
JIM DAVIS 10-10

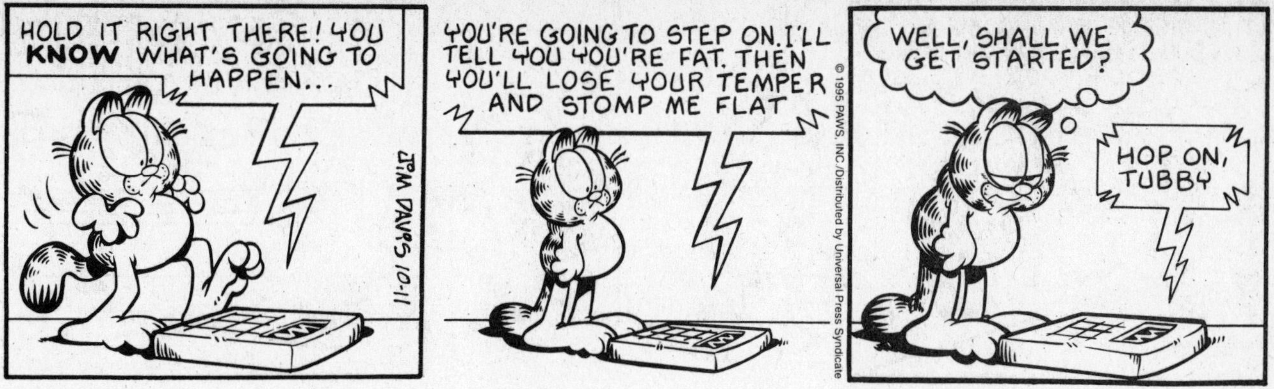
HOLD IT RIGHT THERE! YOU **KNOW** WHAT'S GOING TO HAPPEN...
JIM DAVIS 10-11
YOU'RE GOING TO STEP ON. I'LL TELL YOU YOU'RE FAT. THEN YOU'LL LOSE YOUR TEMPER AND STOMP ME FLAT
© 1995 PAWS, INC./Distributed by Universal Press Syndicate
WELL, SHALL WE GET STARTED?
HOP ON, TUBBY

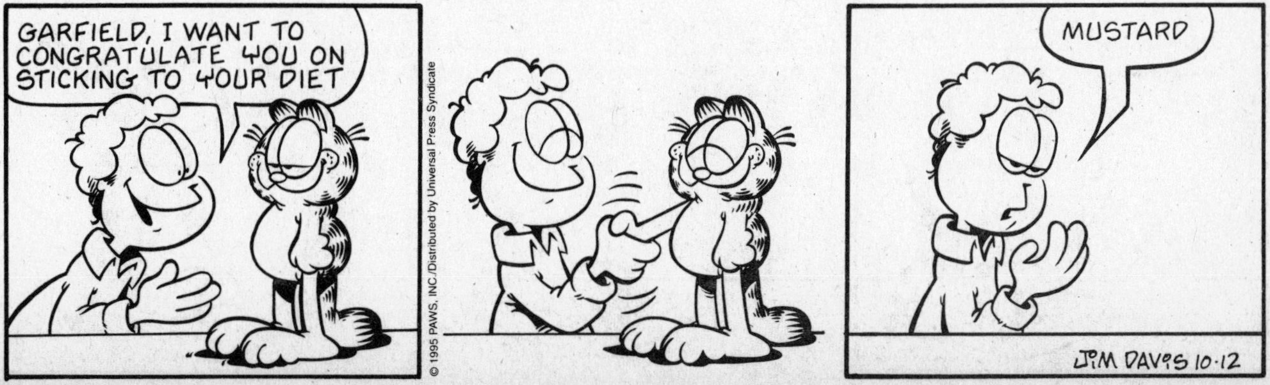
GARFIELD, I WANT TO CONGRATULATE YOU ON STICKING TO YOUR DIET
© 1995 PAWS, INC./Distributed by Universal Press Syndicate
MUSTARD
JIM DAVIS 10-12

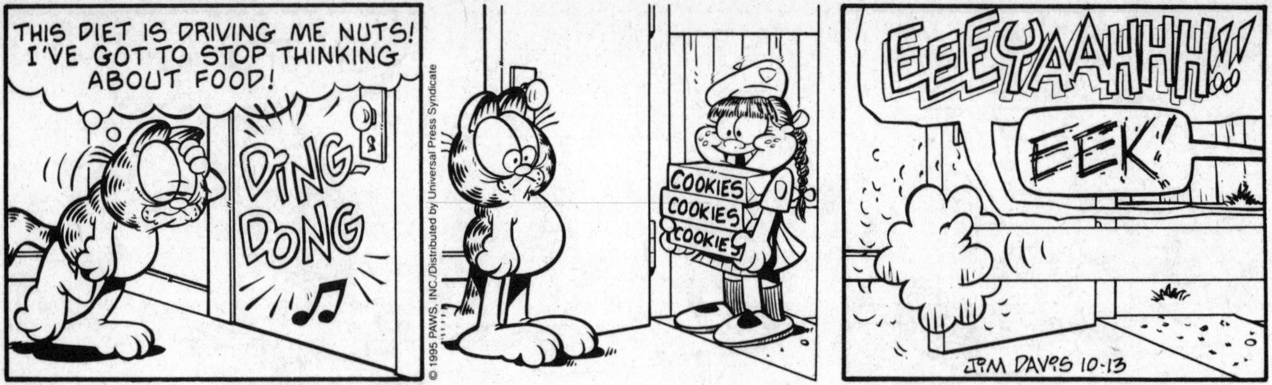
THIS DIET IS DRIVING ME NUTS! I'VE GOT TO STOP THINKING ABOUT FOOD!
DING DONG
COOKIES
COOKIES
COOKIES
EEEYAAHHH!!!
EEK!
JIM DAVIS 10-13

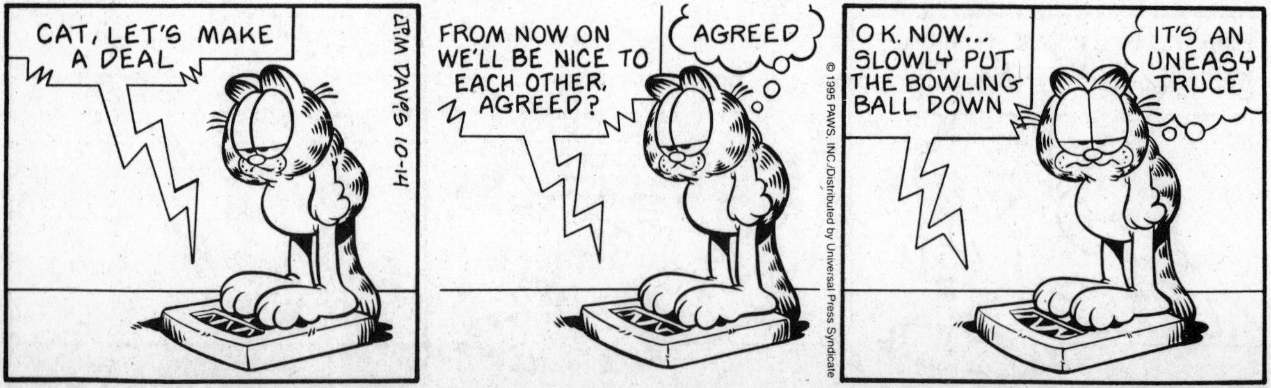
CAT, LET'S MAKE A DEAL
JIM DAVIS 10-14
FROM NOW ON WE'LL BE NICE TO EACH OTHER, AGREED?
AGREED
O.K. NOW... SLOWLY PUT THE BOWLING BALL DOWN
IT'S AN UNEASY TRUCE

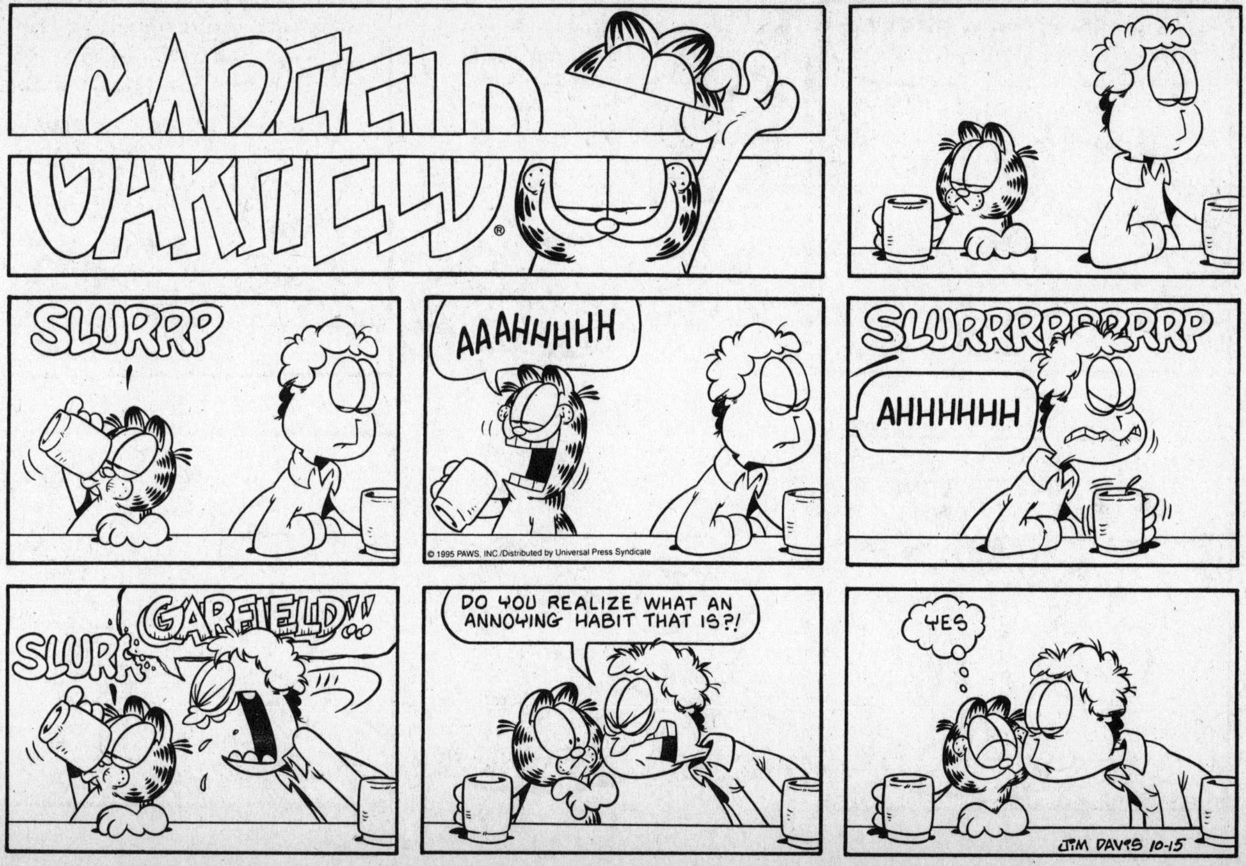
GARFIELD®
SLURRP
AAAHHHHH
SLURRRRRRRRP
AHHHHHH
SLURR
GARFIELD!!
DO YOU REALIZE WHAT AN ANNOYING HABIT THAT IS?!
YES
JIM DAVIS 10-15

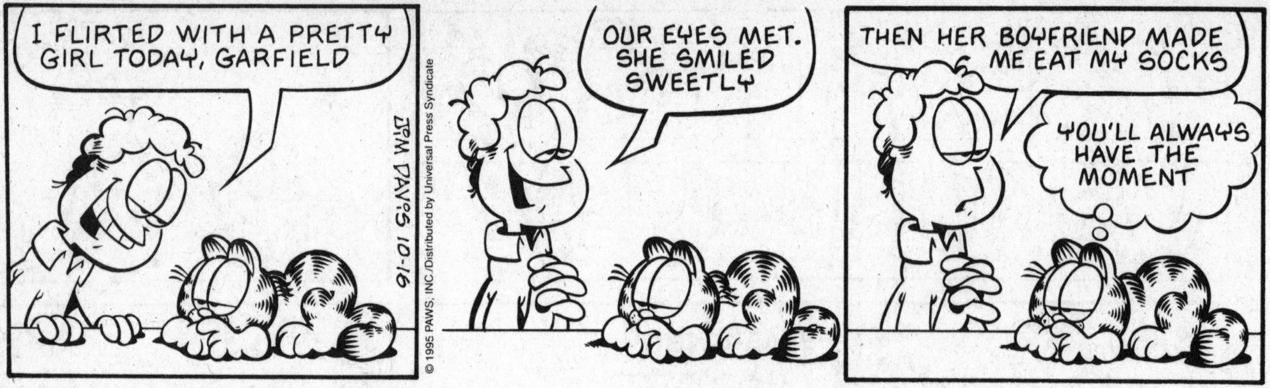
I FLIRTED WITH A PRETTY GIRL TODAY, GARFIELD
JIM DAVIS 10-16
© 1995 PAWS, INC./Distributed by Universal Press Syndicate
OUR EYES MET. SHE SMILED SWEETLY
THEN HER BOYFRIEND MADE ME EAT MY SOCKS
YOU'LL ALWAYS HAVE THE MOMENT

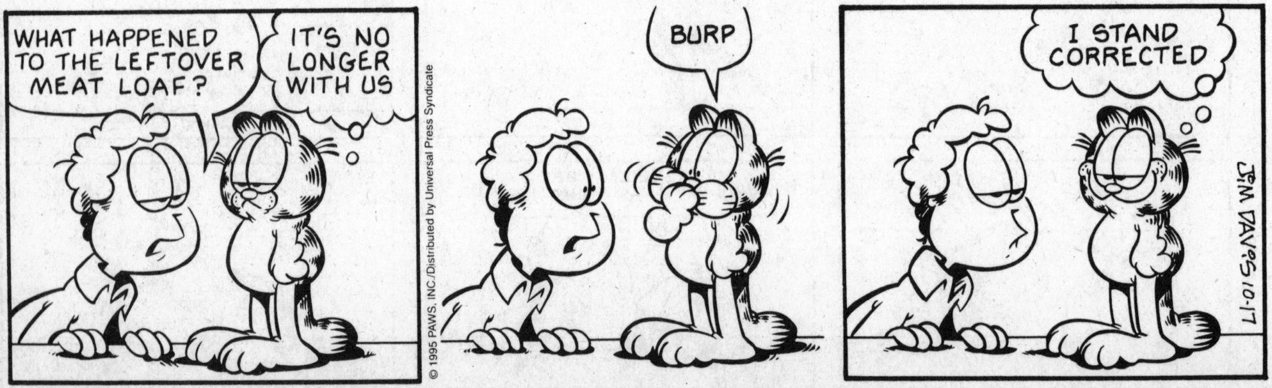
WHAT HAPPENED TO THE LEFTOVER MEAT LOAF?
IT'S NO LONGER WITH US
© 1995 PAWS, INC./Distributed by Universal Press Syndicate
BURP
I STAND CORRECTED
JIM DAVIS 10-17

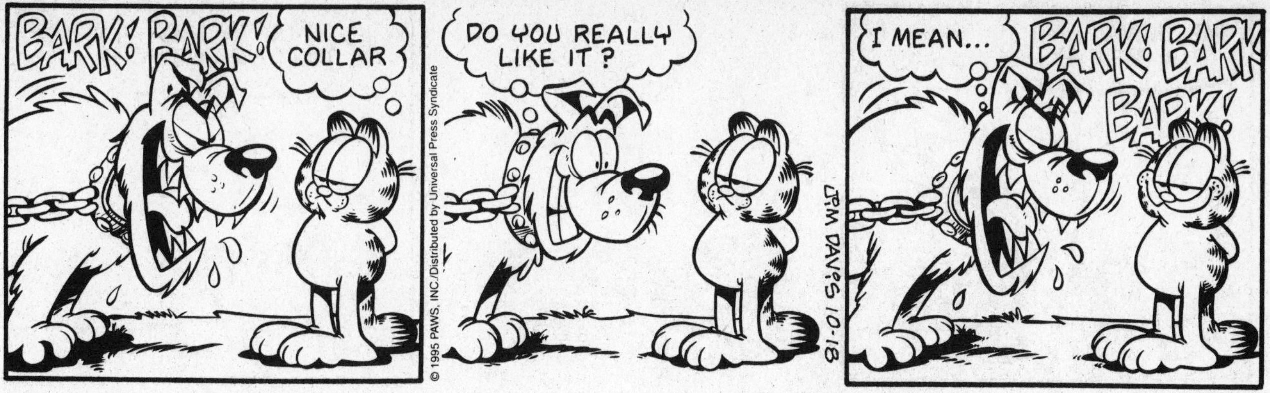
BARK! BARK!
NICE COLLAR
DO YOU REALLY LIKE IT ?
I MEAN...
BARK! BARK BARK!
© 1995 PAWS, INC./Distributed by Universal Press Syndicate
JIM DAVIS 10-18

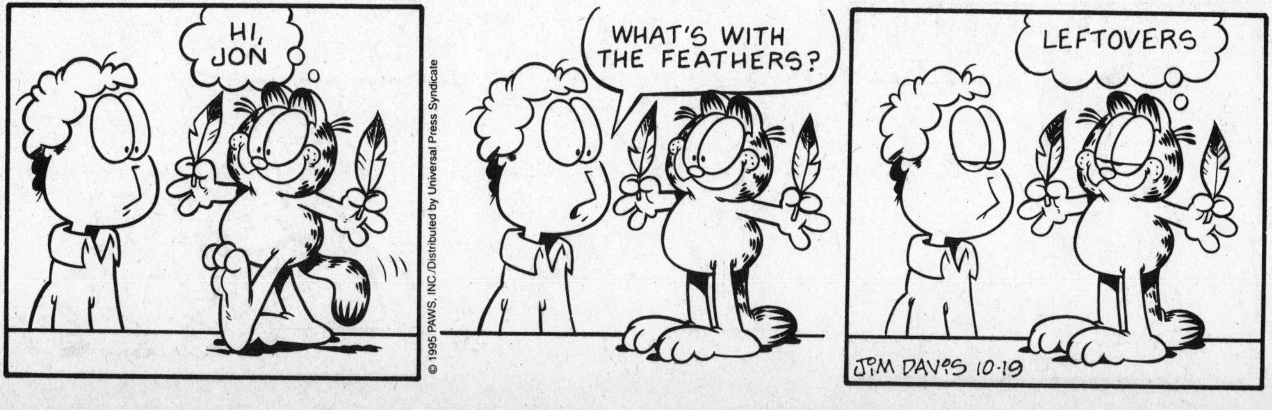
HI, JON
WHAT'S WITH THE FEATHERS?
LEFTOVERS
© 1995 PAWS, INC./Distributed by Universal Press Syndicate
JIM DAVIS 10-19

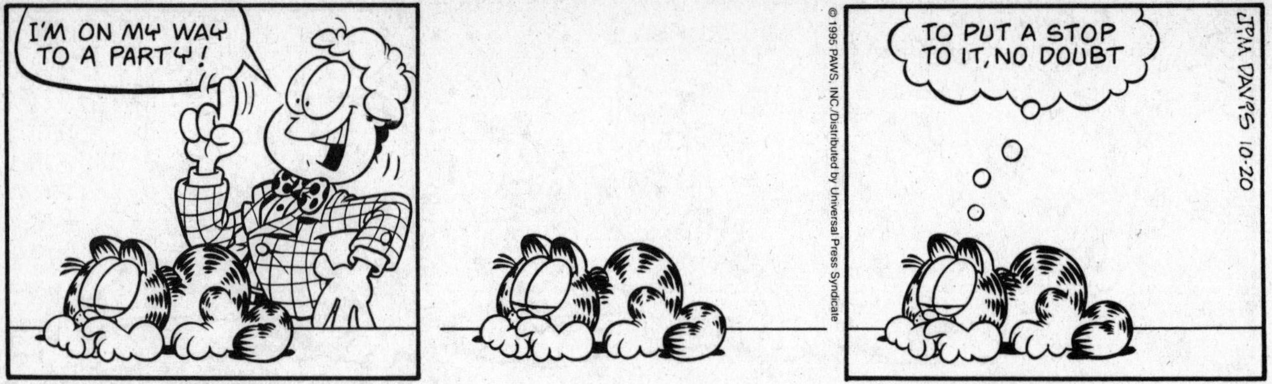
I'M ON MY WAY TO A PARTY!
TO PUT A STOP TO IT, NO DOUBT
JIM DAVIS 10-20
© 1995 PAWS, INC./Distributed by Universal Press Syndicate

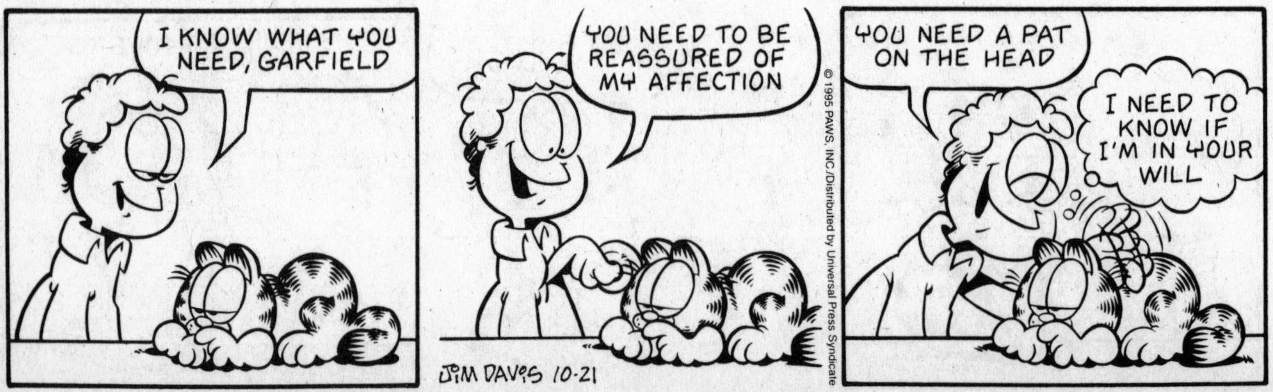
I KNOW WHAT YOU NEED, GARFIELD
YOU NEED TO BE REASSURED OF MY AFFECTION
YOU NEED A PAT ON THE HEAD
I NEED TO KNOW IF I'M IN YOUR WILL
JIM DAVIS 10-21
© 1995 PAWS, INC./Distributed by Universal Press Syndicate

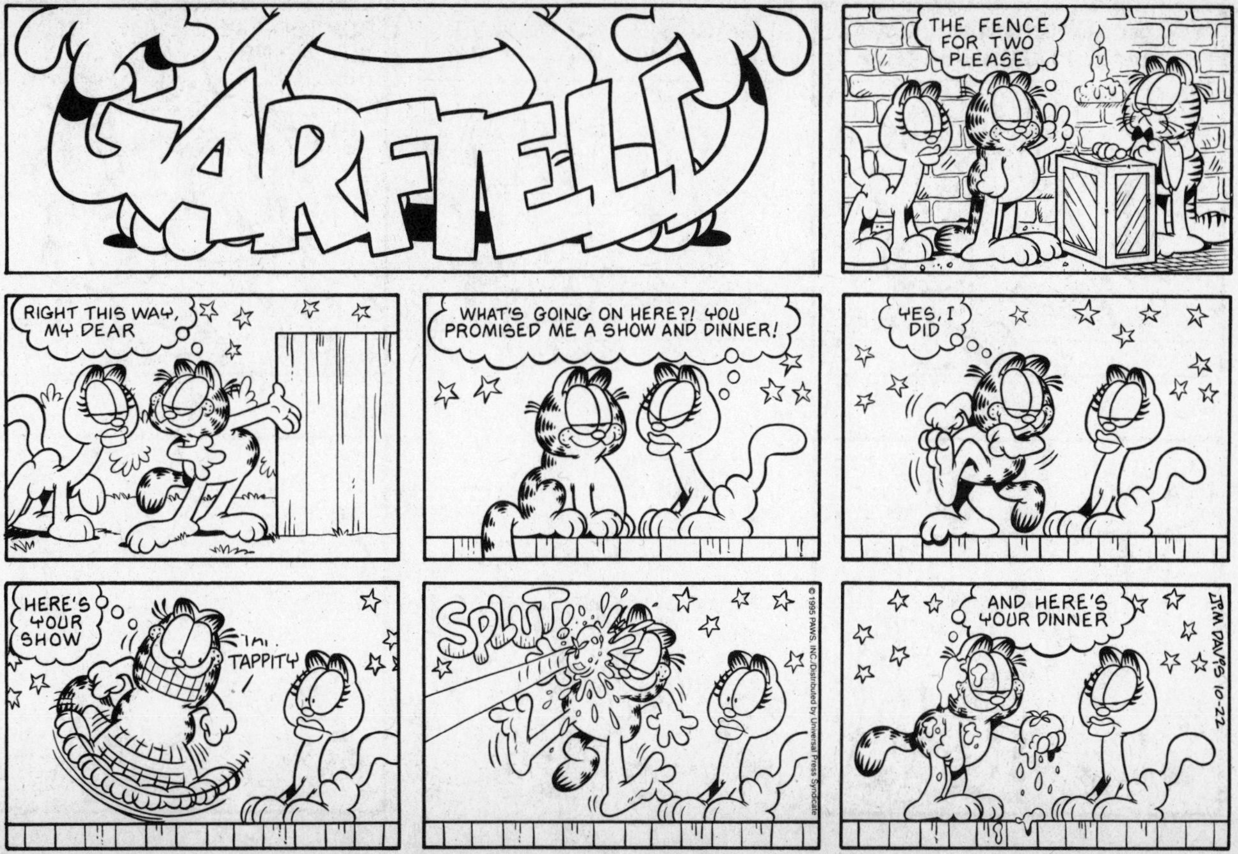
GARFIELD
THE FENCE FOR TWO PLEASE
RIGHT THIS WAY, MY DEAR
WHAT'S GOING ON HERE?! YOU PROMISED ME A SHOW AND DINNER!
YES, I DID
HERE'S YOUR SHOW
TAPPITY TAPPITY
SPLUT!
AND HERE'S YOUR DINNER
© 1995 PAWS, INC./Distributed by Universal Press Syndicate
JPM DAVIS 10-22

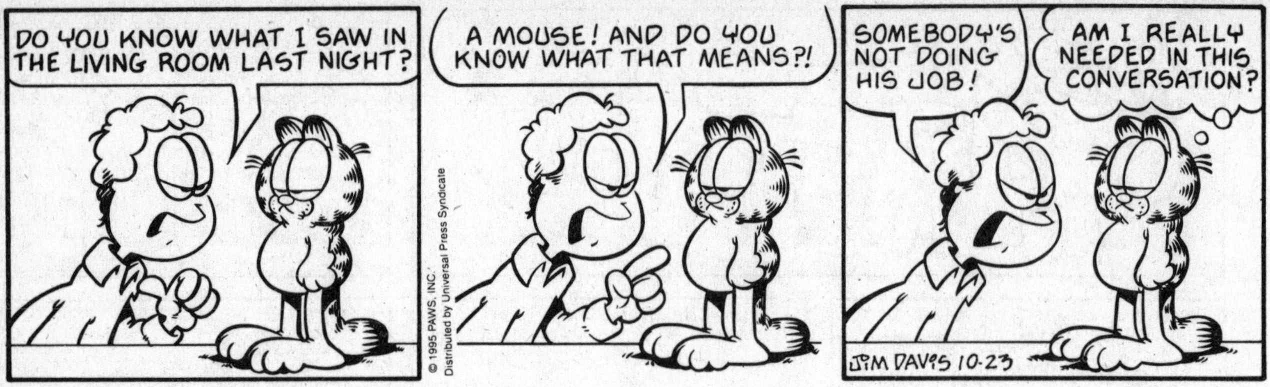
DO YOU KNOW WHAT I SAW IN THE LIVING ROOM LAST NIGHT?
A MOUSE! AND DO YOU KNOW WHAT THAT MEANS?!
SOMEBODY'S NOT DOING HIS JOB!
AM I REALLY NEEDED IN THIS CONVERSATION?
JIM DAVIS 10-23

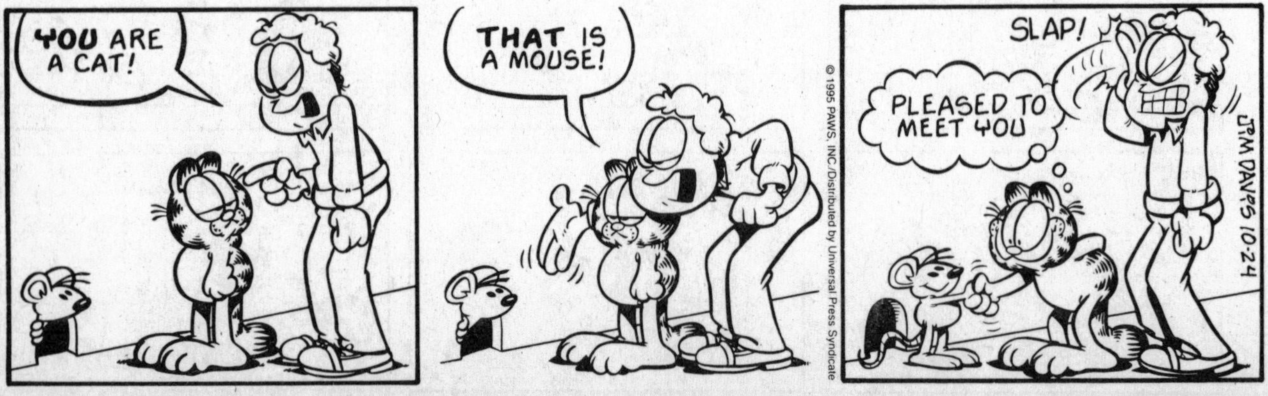
YOU ARE A CAT!
THAT IS A MOUSE!
SLAP!
PLEASED TO MEET YOU
JIM DAVIS 10-24

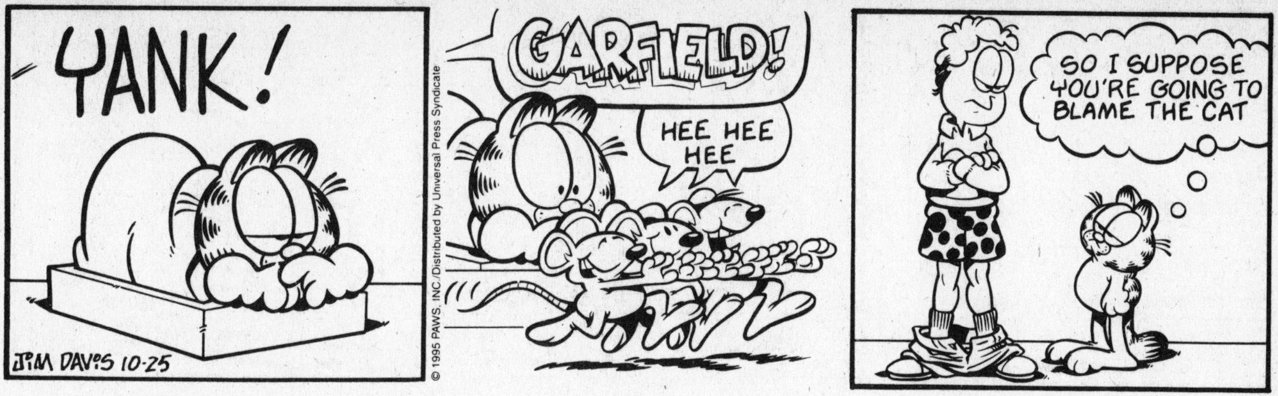
YANK!
JIM DAVIS 10-25
GARFIELD!
HEE HEE HEE
SO I SUPPOSE YOU'RE GOING TO BLAME THE CAT

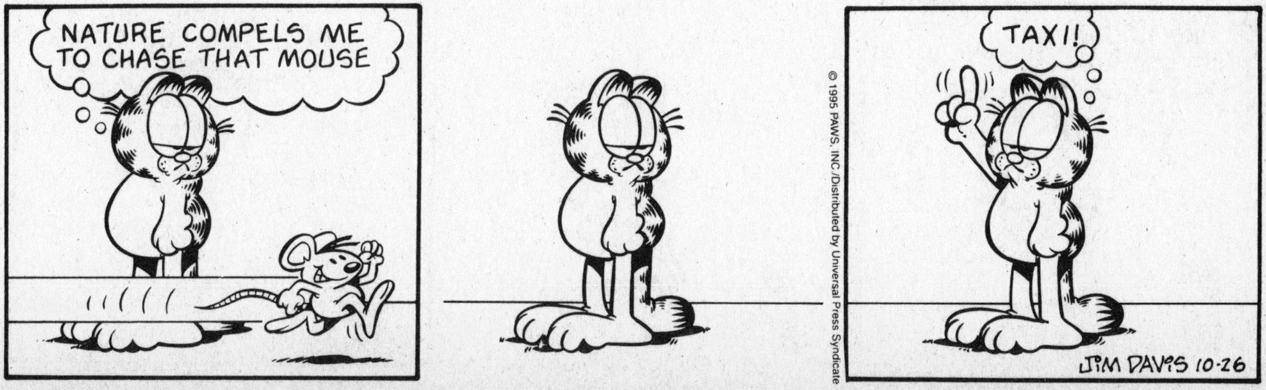
NATURE COMPELS ME TO CHASE THAT MOUSE
TAXI!
JIM DAVIS 10-26

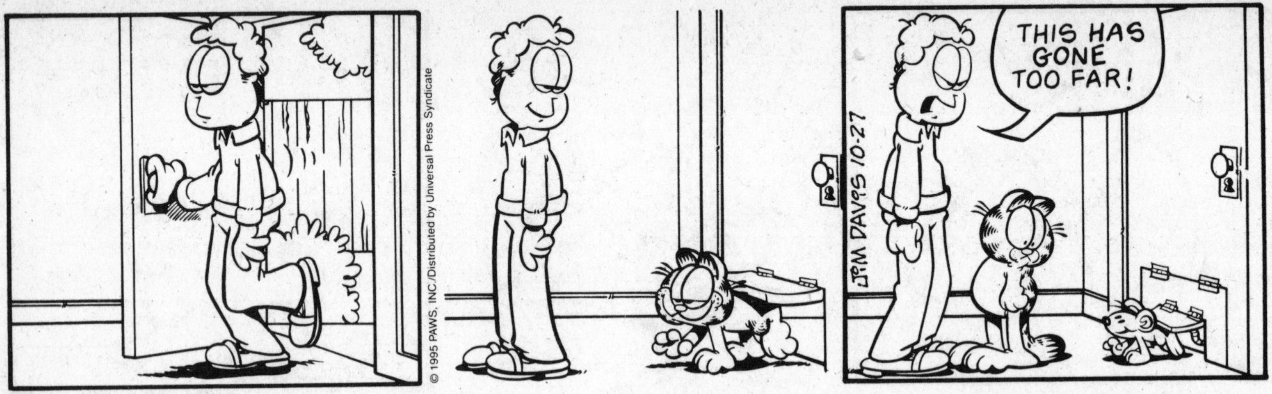
JIM DAVIS 10-27
THIS HAS GONE TOO FAR!

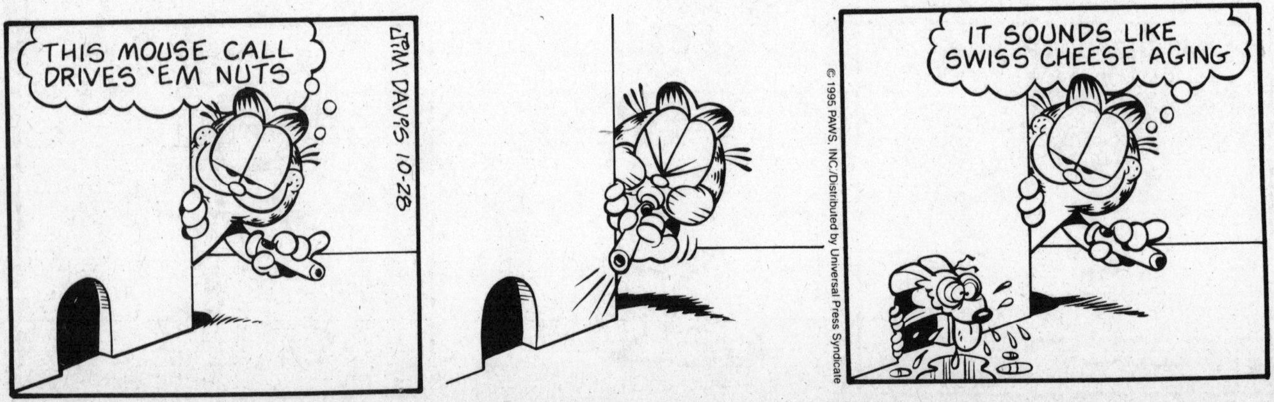
THIS MOUSE CALL DRIVES 'EM NUTS
JIM DAVIS 10-28
IT SOUNDS LIKE SWISS CHEESE AGING

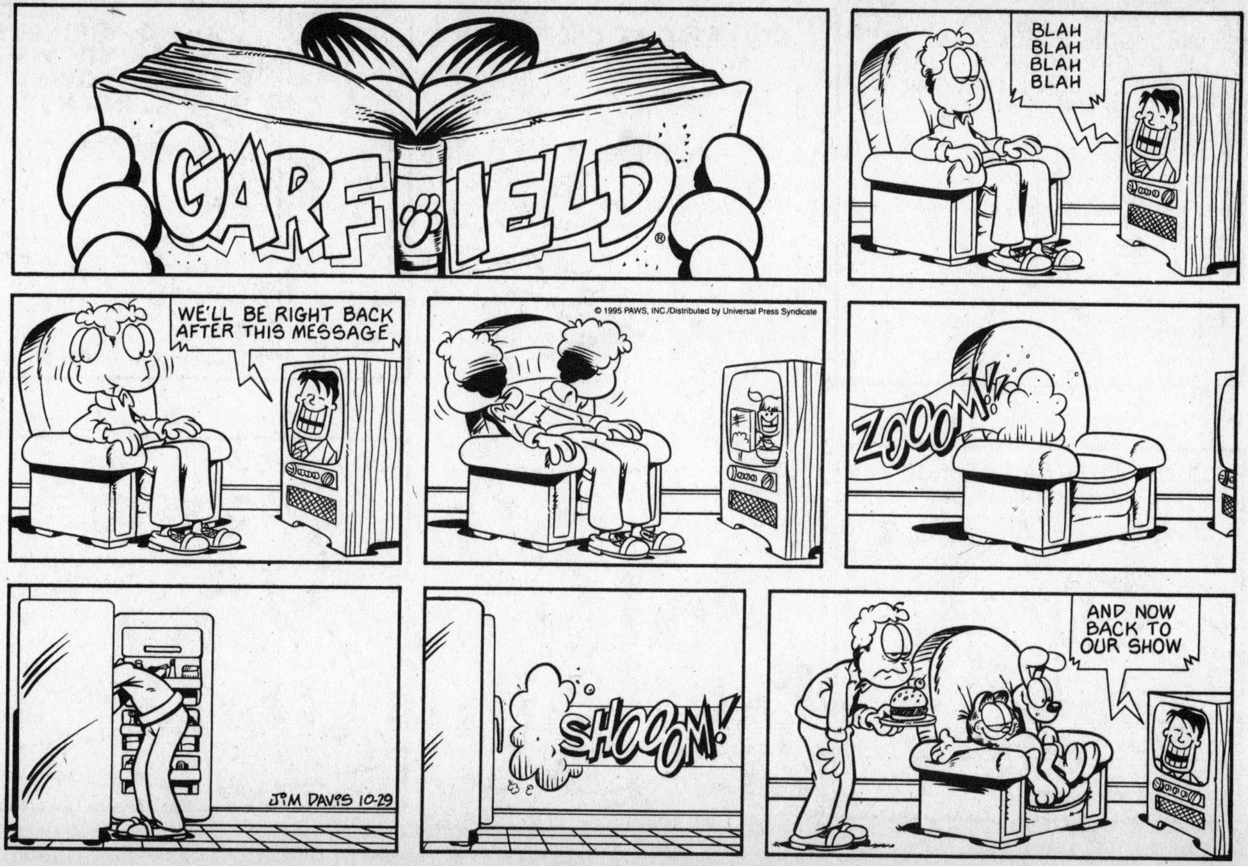

GARFIELD®
BLAH BLAH BLAH BLAH
WE'LL BE RIGHT BACK AFTER THIS MESSAGE
© 1995 PAWS, INC./Distributed by Universal Press Syndicate
ZOOOM!!
JIM DAVIS 10-29
SHOOOM!
AND NOW BACK TO OUR SHOW

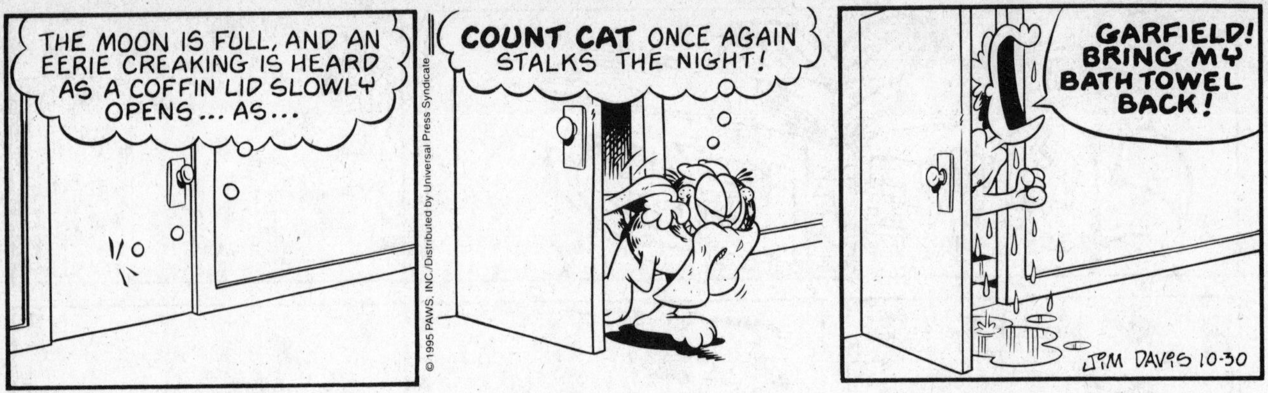
THE MOON IS FULL, AND AN EERIE CREAKING IS HEARD AS A COFFIN LID SLOWLY OPENS... AS...
COUNT CAT ONCE AGAIN STALKS THE NIGHT!
GARFIELD! BRING MY BATH TOWEL BACK!
© 1995 PAWS, INC./Distributed by Universal Press Syndicate
JIM DAVIS 10-30

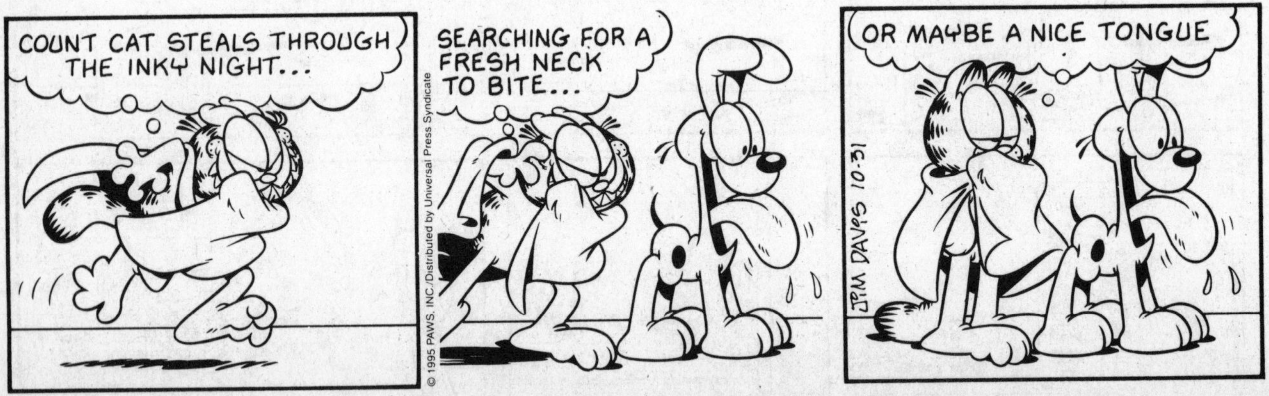
COUNT CAT STEALS THROUGH THE INKY NIGHT...
SEARCHING FOR A FRESH NECK TO BITE...
OR MAYBE A NICE TONGUE
© 1995 PAWS, INC./Distributed by Universal Press Syndicate
JIM DAVIS 10-31

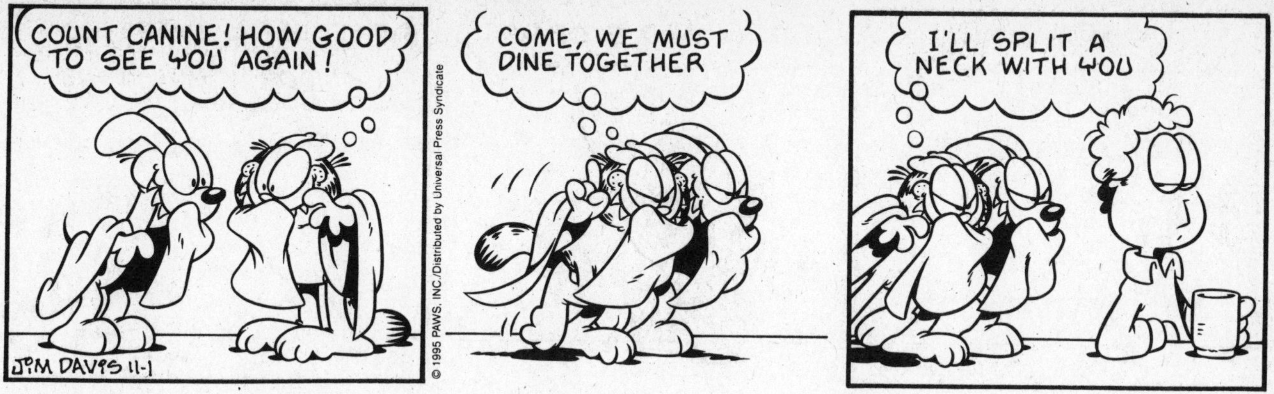
COUNT CANINE! HOW GOOD TO SEE YOU AGAIN!
JIM DAVIS 11-1
© 1995 PAWS, INC./Distributed by Universal Press Syndicate
COME, WE MUST DINE TOGETHER
I'LL SPLIT A NECK WITH YOU

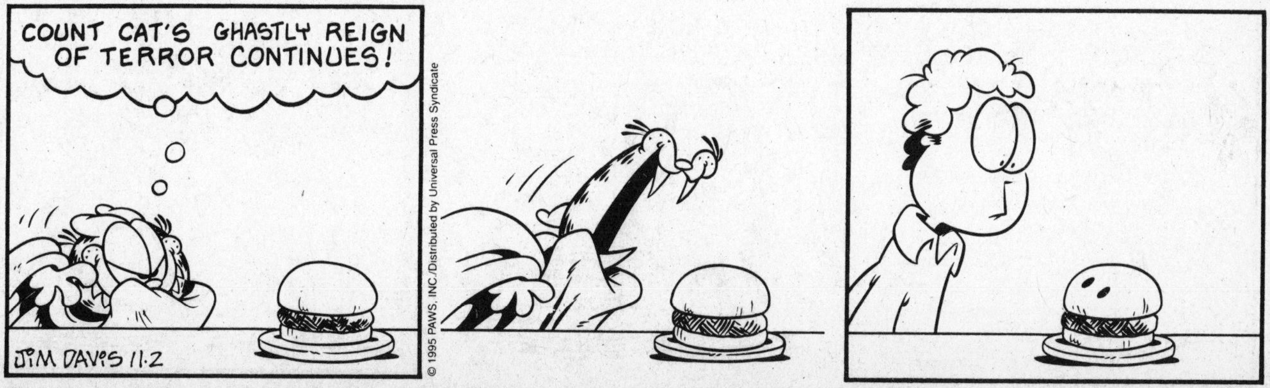
COUNT CAT'S GHASTLY REIGN OF TERROR CONTINUES!
JIM DAVIS 11.2
© 1995 PAWS, INC./Distributed by Universal Press Syndicate

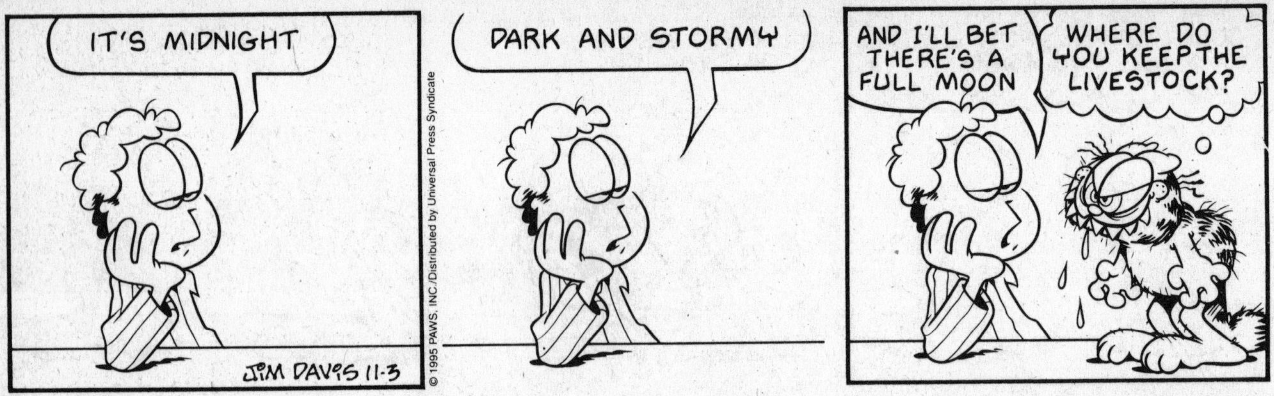
IT'S MIDNIGHT
JIM DAVIS 11-3
© 1995 PAWS, INC./Distributed by Universal Press Syndicate
DARK AND STORMY
AND I'LL BET THERE'S A FULL MOON
WHERE DO YOU KEEP THE LIVESTOCK?

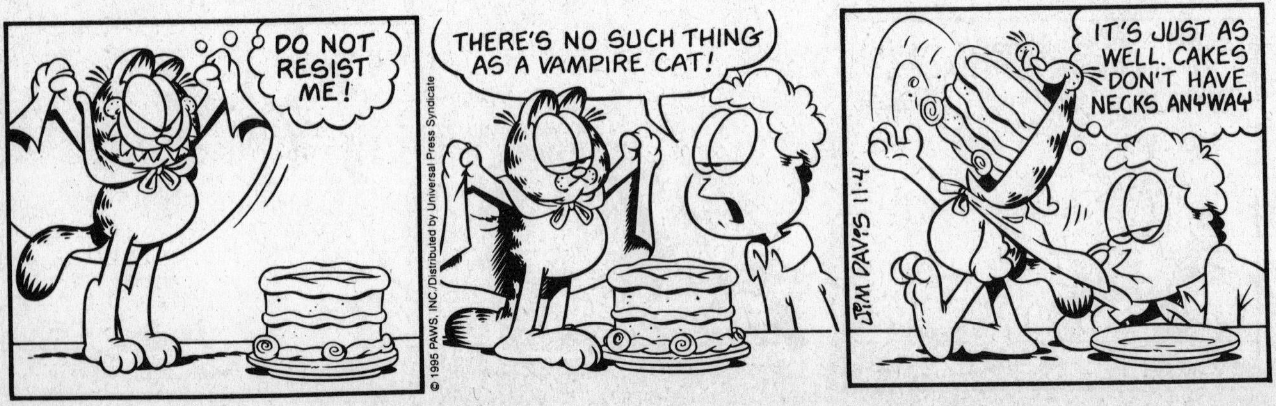
DO NOT RESIST ME!
© 1995 PAWS, INC./Distributed by Universal Press Syndicate
THERE'S NO SUCH THING AS A VAMPIRE CAT!
JIM DAVIS 11-4
IT'S JUST AS WELL. CAKES DON'T HAVE NECKS ANYWAY

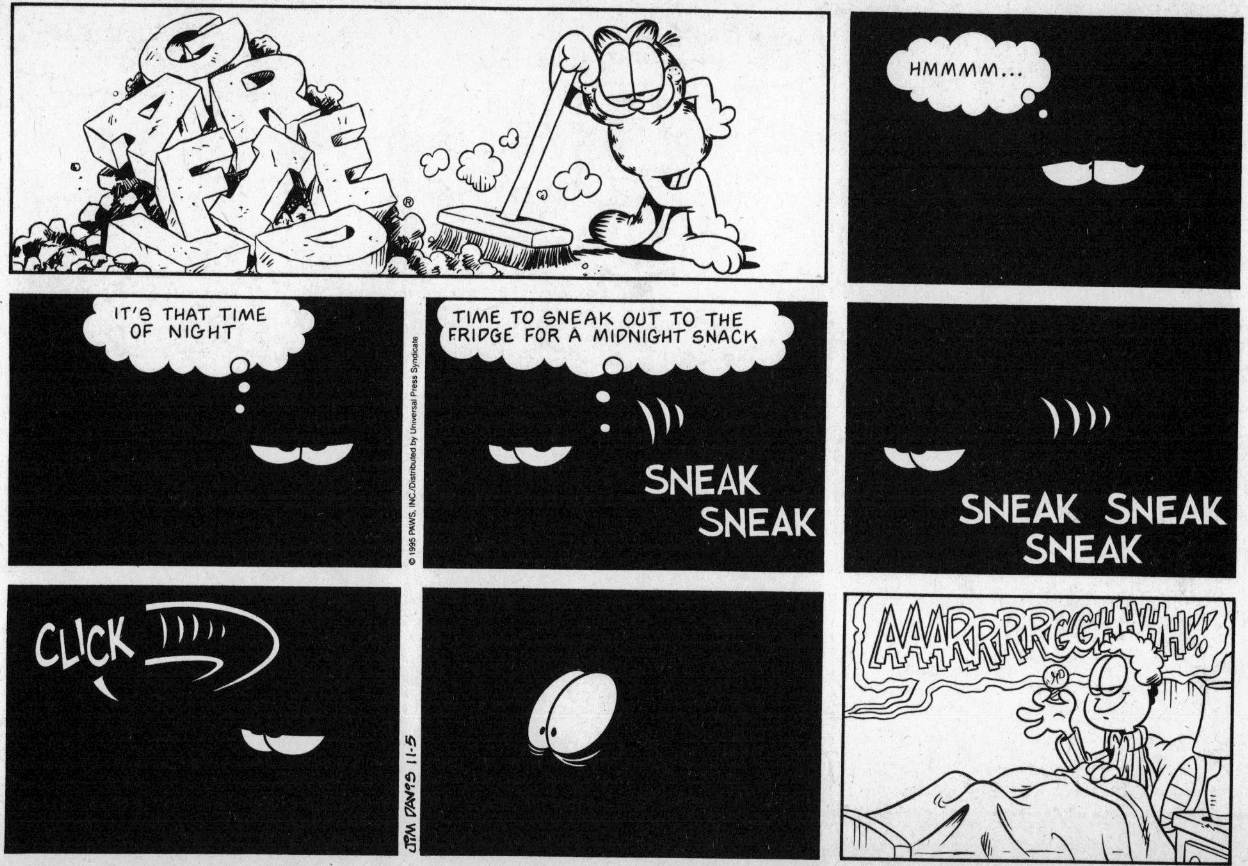
GARFIELD®
HMMMM...
IT'S THAT TIME OF NIGHT
TIME TO SNEAK OUT TO THE FRIDGE FOR A MIDNIGHT SNACK
SNEAK SNEAK
SNEAK SNEAK SNEAK
CLICK
AAARRRRGGHHHH!!
© 1995 PAWS, INC./Distributed by Universal Press Syndicate
JIM DAVIS 11-5

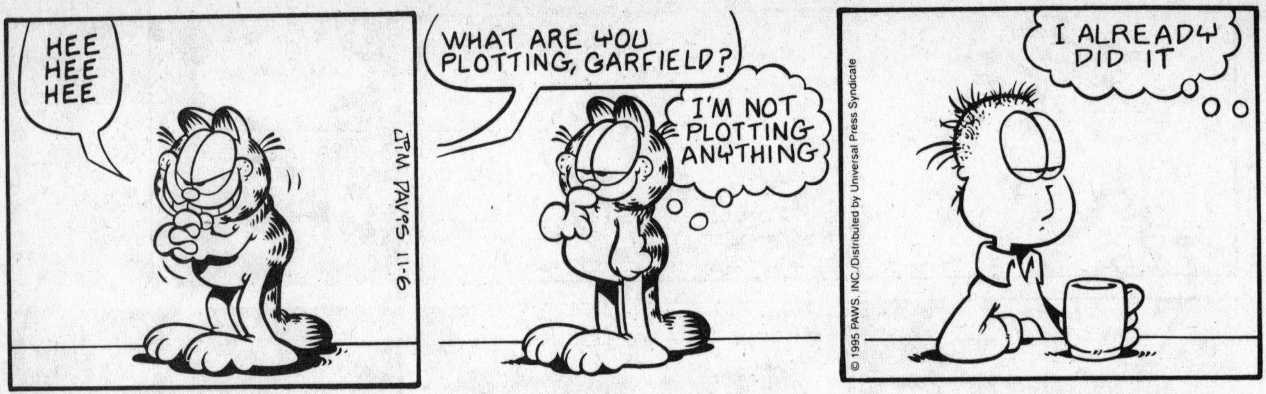
HEE HEE HEE
JIM DAVIS 11-6
WHAT ARE YOU PLOTTING, GARFIELD?
I'M NOT PLOTTING ANYTHING
© 1995 PAWS, INC./Distributed by Universal Press Syndicate
I ALREADY DID IT

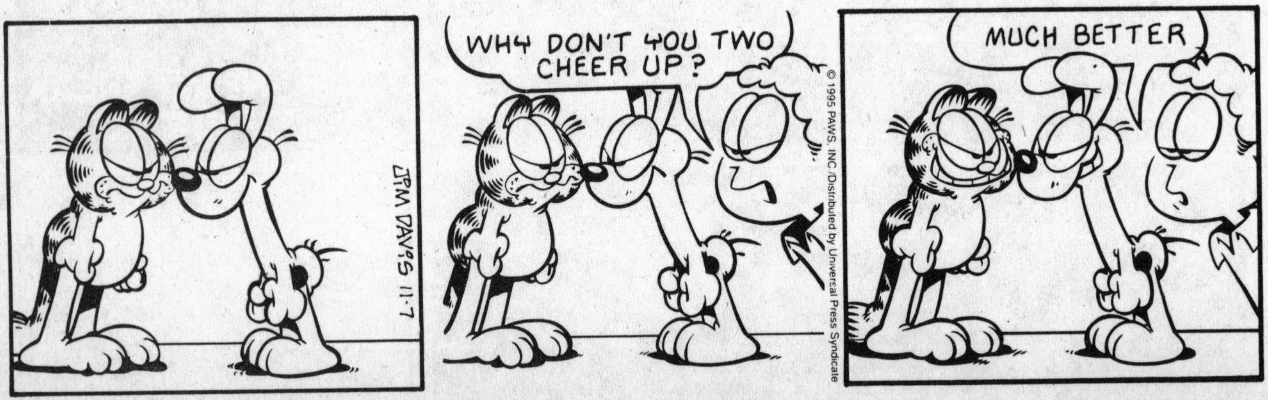
JIM DAVIS 11-7
WHY DON'T YOU TWO CHEER UP?
© 1995 PAWS, INC./Distributed by Universal Press Syndicate
MUCH BETTER

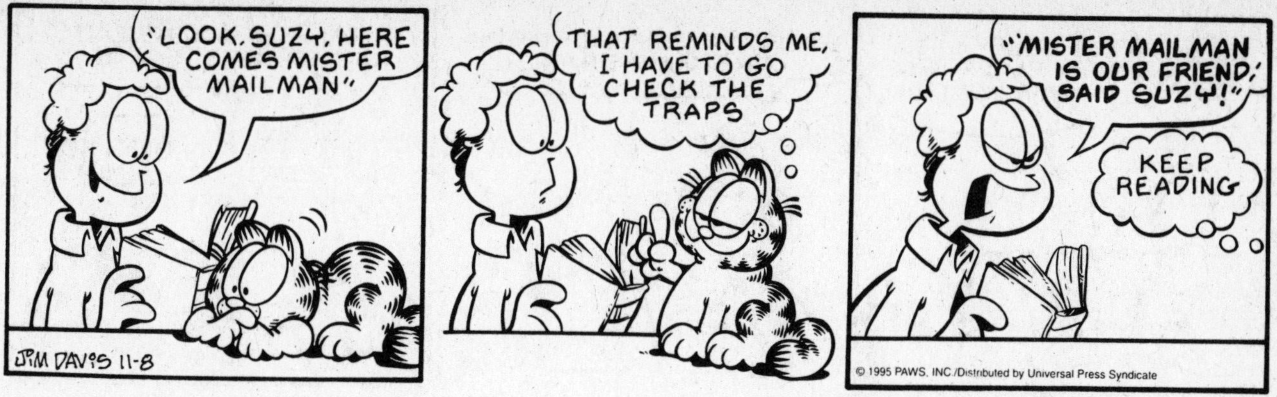
"LOOK, SUZY, HERE COMES MISTER MAILMAN"
JIM DAVIS 11-8
THAT REMINDS ME, I HAVE TO GO CHECK THE TRAPS
"MISTER MAILMAN IS OUR FRIEND,' SAID SUZY!"
KEEP READING
© 1995 PAWS, INC./Distributed by Universal Press Syndicate

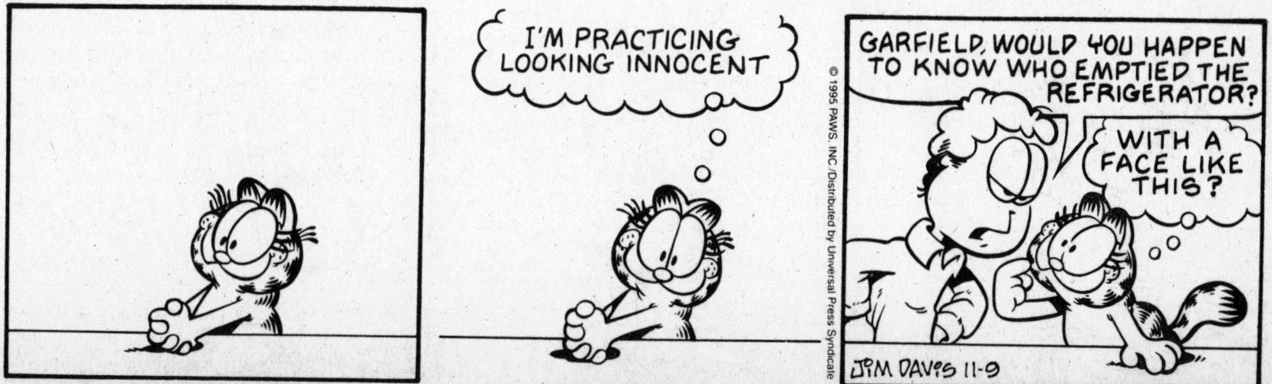
I'M PRACTICING LOOKING INNOCENT
© 1995 PAWS, INC./Distributed by Universal Press Syndicate
GARFIELD, WOULD YOU HAPPEN TO KNOW WHO EMPTIED THE REFRIGERATOR?
WITH A FACE LIKE THIS?
JIM DAVIS 11-9

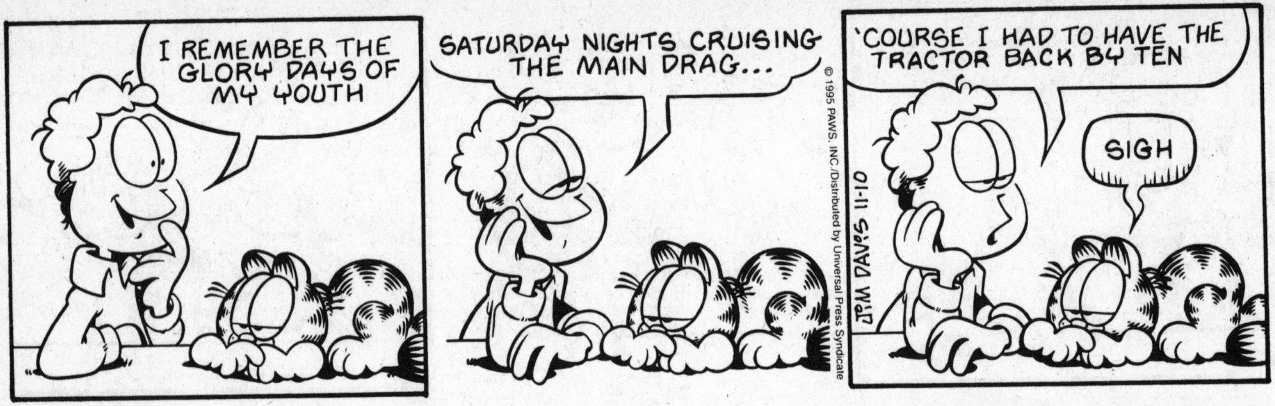
I REMEMBER THE GLORY DAYS OF MY YOUTH
SATURDAY NIGHTS CRUISING THE MAIN DRAG...
© 1995 PAWS, INC./Distributed by Universal Press Syndicate
JIM DAVIS 11-10
`COURSE I HAD TO HAVE THE TRACTOR BACK BY TEN
SIGH

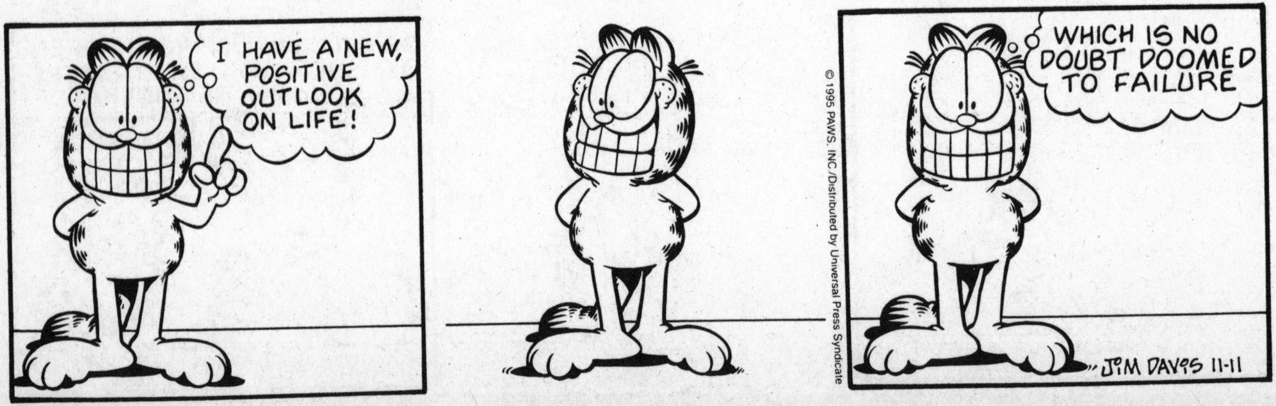
I HAVE A NEW, POSITIVE OUTLOOK ON LIFE!
© 1995 PAWS, INC./Distributed by Universal Press Syndicate
WHICH IS NO DOUBT DOOMED TO FAILURE
JIM DAVIS 11-11

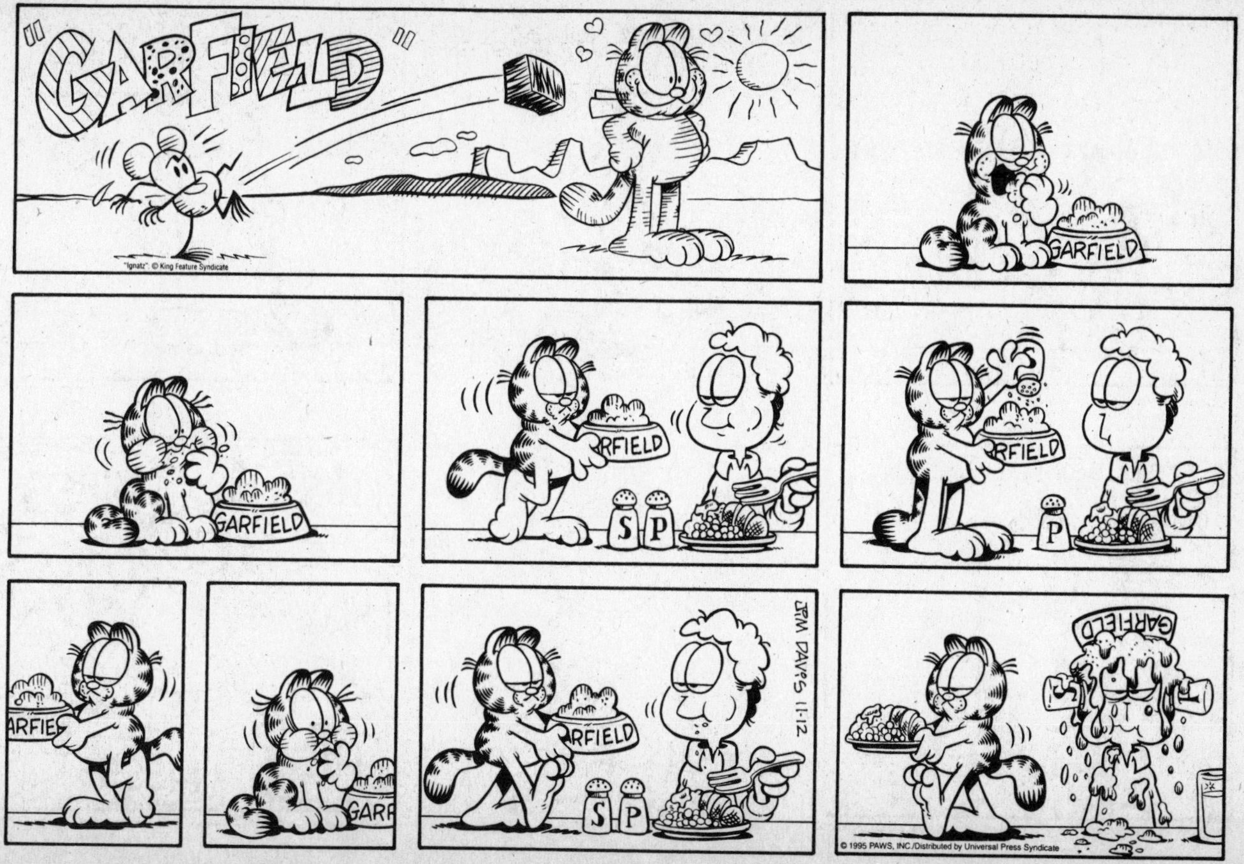
"GARFIELD"
"Ignatz": © King Feature Syndicate
GARFIELD
GARFIELD
RFIELD
S
P
RFIELD
P
ARFIE
GARF
JPM DAVPS 11-12
RFIELD
S
P
GARFIELD
© 1995 PAWS, INC./Distributed by Universal Press Syndicate

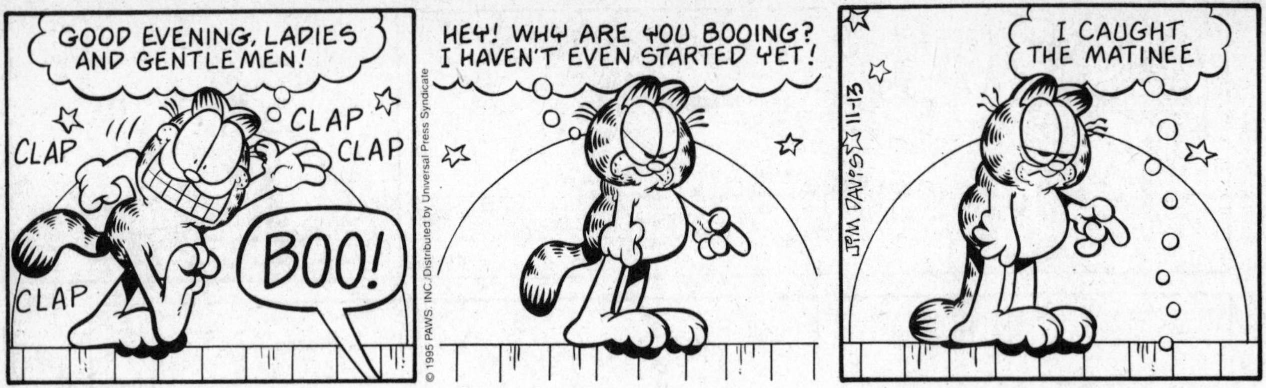
GOOD EVENING, LADIES AND GENTLEMEN!
CLAP
CLAP
CLAP
CLAP
BOO!
HEY! WHY ARE YOU BOOING? I HAVEN'T EVEN STARTED YET!
I CAUGHT THE MATINEE
JPM DAVPS 11-13
© 1995 PAWS. INC./Distributed by Universal Press Syndicate

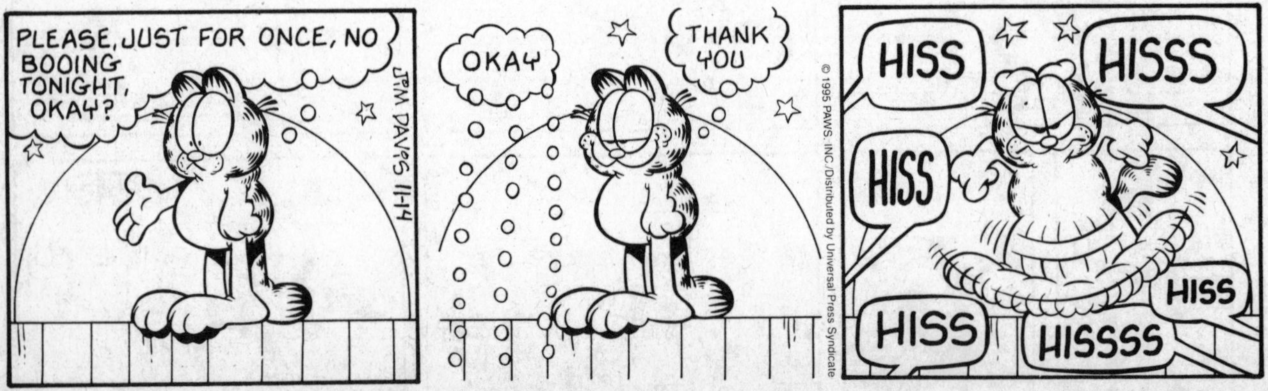
PLEASE, JUST FOR ONCE, NO BOOING TONIGHT, OKAY?
JPM DAVPS 11-14
OKAY
THANK YOU
HISS
HISSS
HISS
HISS
HISSSS
HISS
© 1995 PAWS. INC./Distributed by Universal Press Syndicate

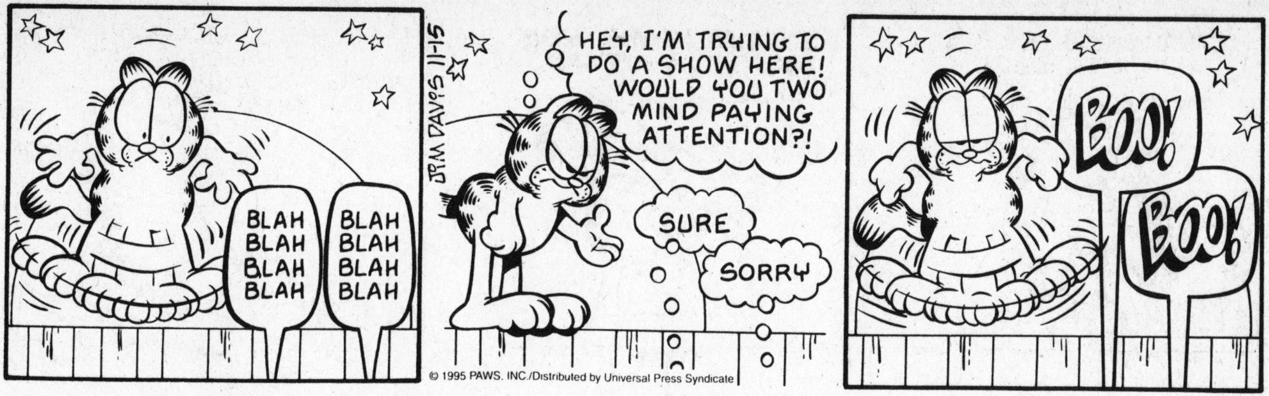

BLAH BLAH BLAH BLAH
BLAH BLAH BLAH BLAH
JIM DAVIS 11-15
HEY, I'M TRYING TO DO A SHOW HERE! WOULD YOU TWO MIND PAYING ATTENTION?!
SURE
SORRY
© 1995 PAWS, INC./Distributed by Universal Press Syndicate
BOO!
BOO!

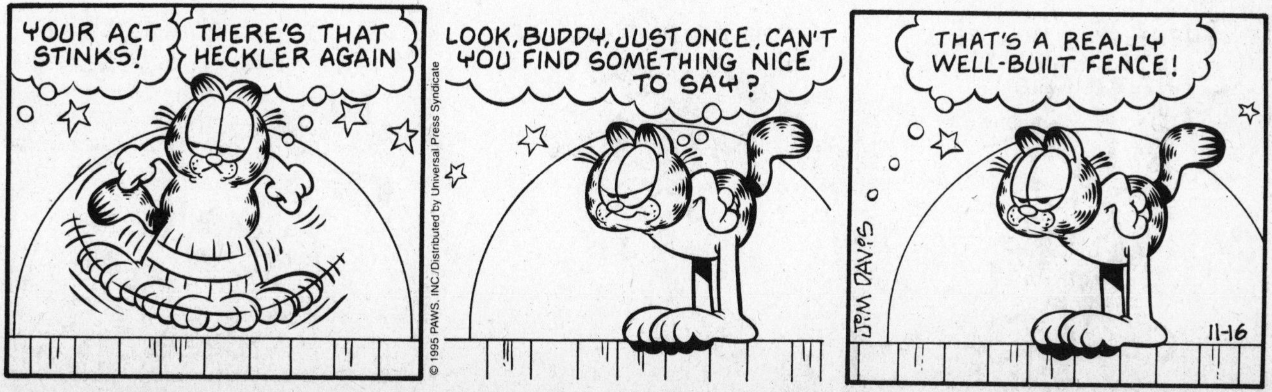

YOUR ACT STINKS!
THERE'S THAT HECKLER AGAIN
© 1995 PAWS, INC./Distributed by Universal Press Syndicate
LOOK, BUDDY, JUST ONCE, CAN'T YOU FIND SOMETHING NICE TO SAY?
THAT'S A REALLY WELL-BUILT FENCE!
JIM DAVIS
11-16

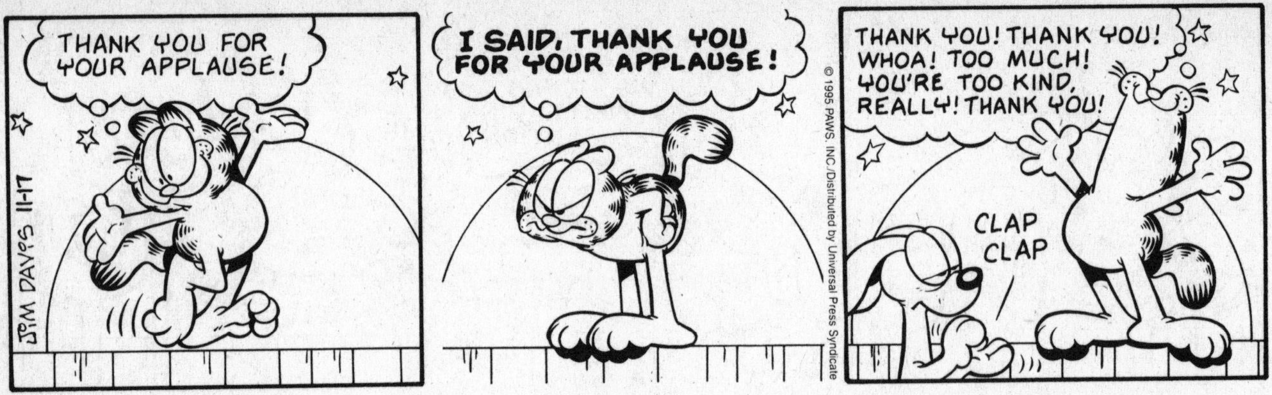
THANK YOU FOR YOUR APPLAUSE!
JIM DAVIS 11-17
I SAID, THANK YOU FOR YOUR APPLAUSE!
© 1995 PAWS, INC./Distributed by Universal Press Syndicate
THANK YOU! THANK YOU! WHOA! TOO MUCH! YOU'RE TOO KIND, REALLY! THANK YOU!
CLAP CLAP

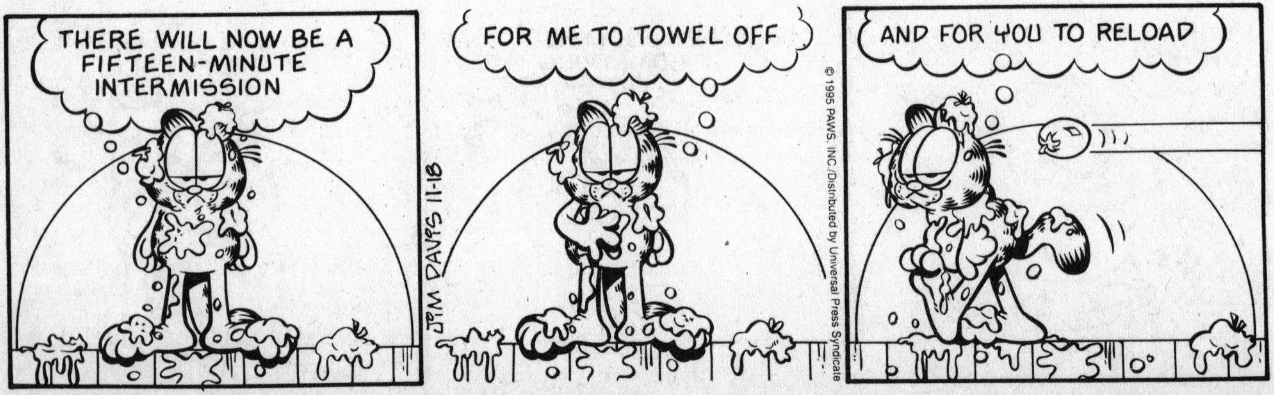
THERE WILL NOW BE A FIFTEEN-MINUTE INTERMISSION
JIM DAVIS 11-18
FOR ME TO TOWEL OFF
© 1995 PAWS, INC./Distributed by Universal Press Syndicate
AND FOR YOU TO RELOAD

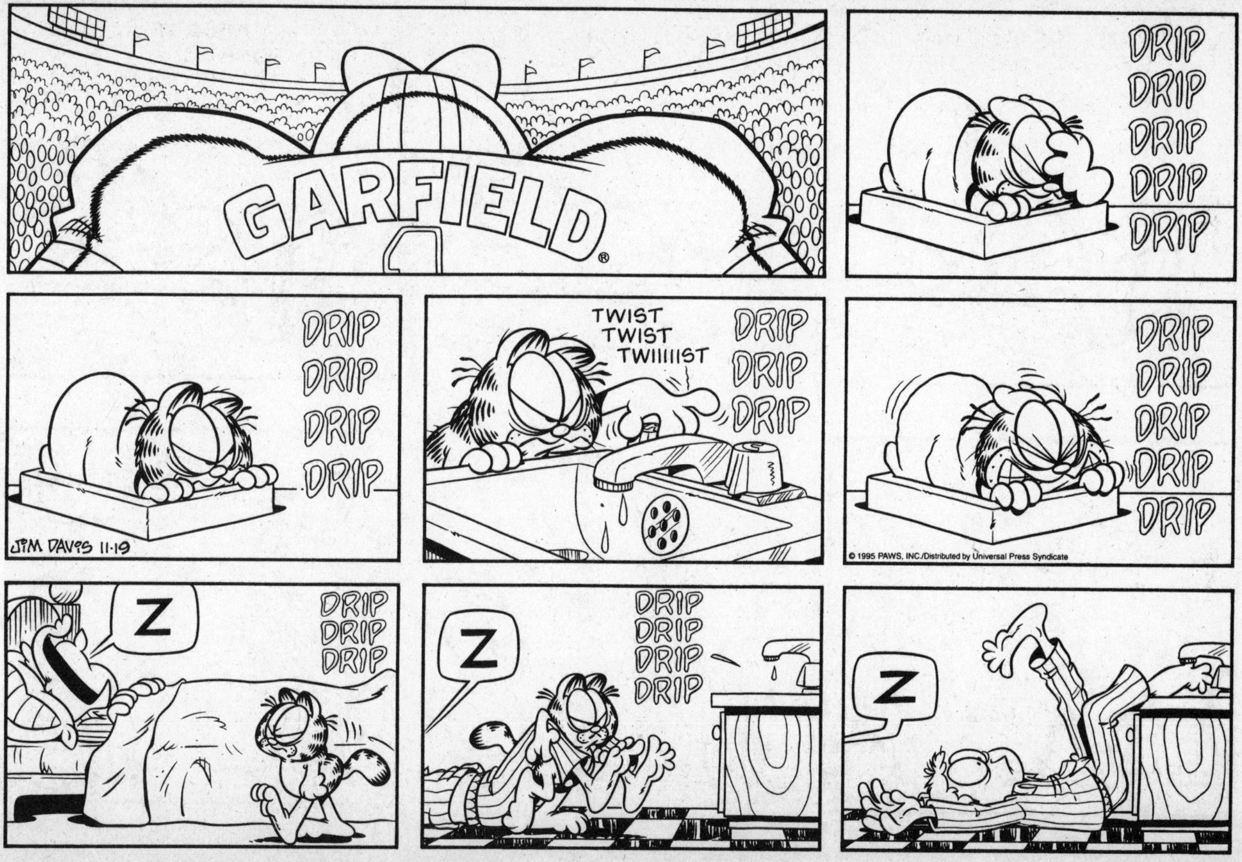
GARFIELD®
DRIP DRIP DRIP DRIP DRIP
DRIP DRIP DRIP DRIP
JIM DAVIS 11-19
TWIST TWIST TWIIIIIST
DRIP DRIP DRIP
DRIP DRIP DRIP DRIP DRIP
© 1995 PAWS, INC./Distributed by Universal Press Syndicate
Z
DRIP DRIP DRIP
Z
DRIP DRIP DRIP DRIP
Z

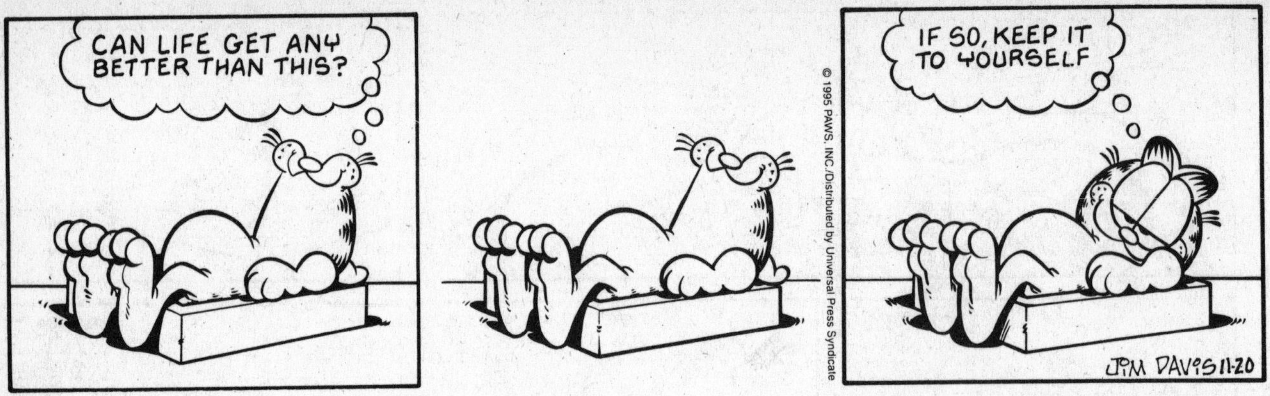
CAN LIFE GET ANY BETTER THAN THIS?
IF SO, KEEP IT TO YOURSELF
JIM DAVIS 11-20
© 1995 PAWS, INC./Distributed by Universal Press Syndicate

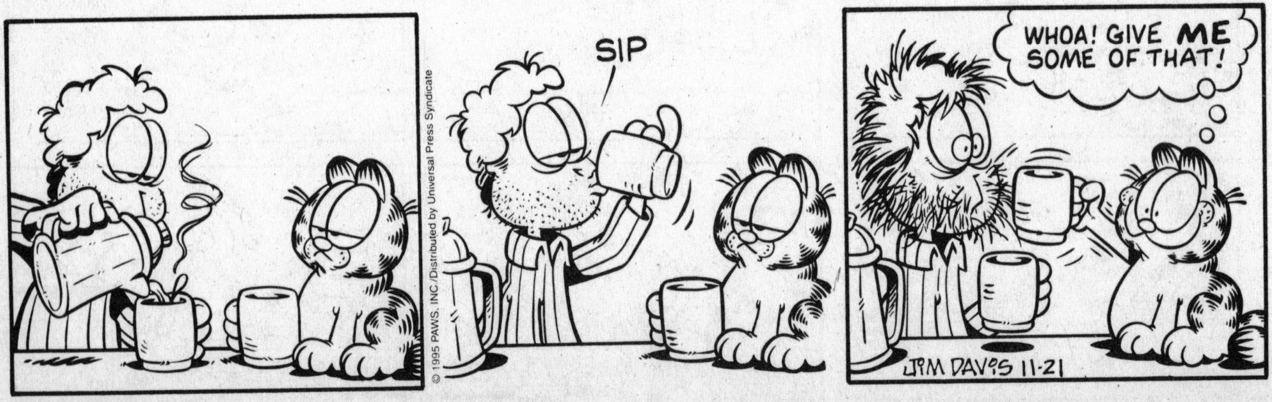
© 1995 PAWS, INC./Distributed by Universal Press Syndicate
SIP
WHOA! GIVE ME SOME OF THAT!
JIM DAVIS 11-21

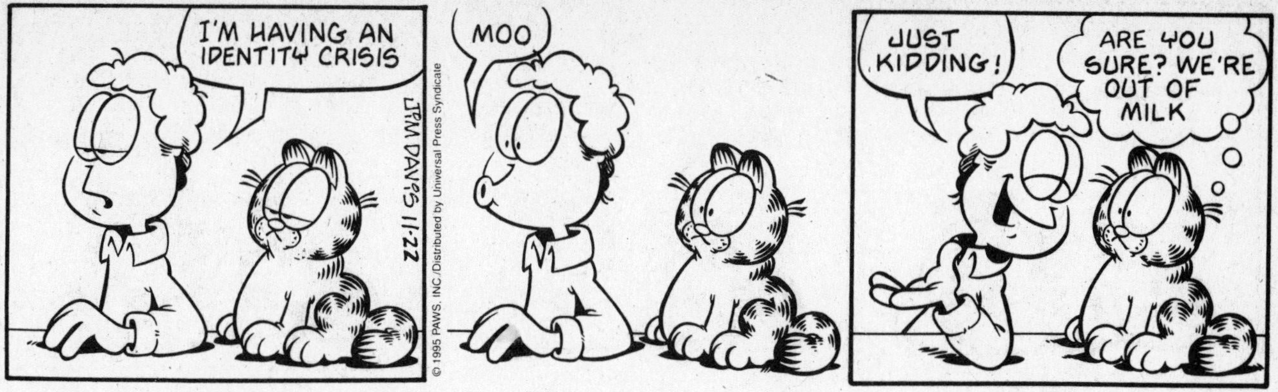
I'M HAVING AN IDENTITY CRISIS
JIM DAVIS 11-22
© 1995 PAWS, INC./Distributed by Universal Press Syndicate
MOO
JUST KIDDING!
ARE YOU SURE? WE'RE OUT OF MILK

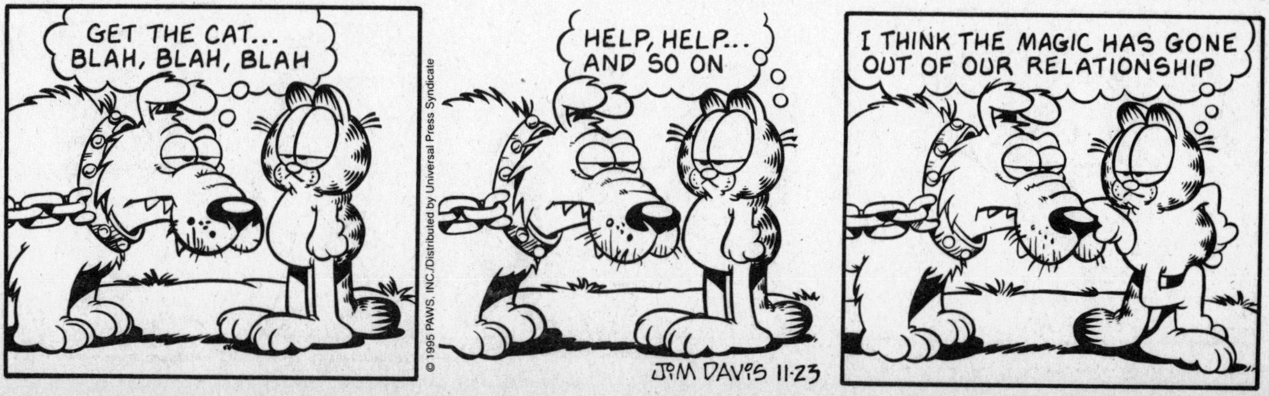
GET THE CAT... BLAH, BLAH, BLAH
© 1995 PAWS, INC./Distributed by Universal Press Syndicate
HELP, HELP... AND SO ON
JIM DAVIS 11-23
I THINK THE MAGIC HAS GONE OUT OF OUR RELATIONSHIP

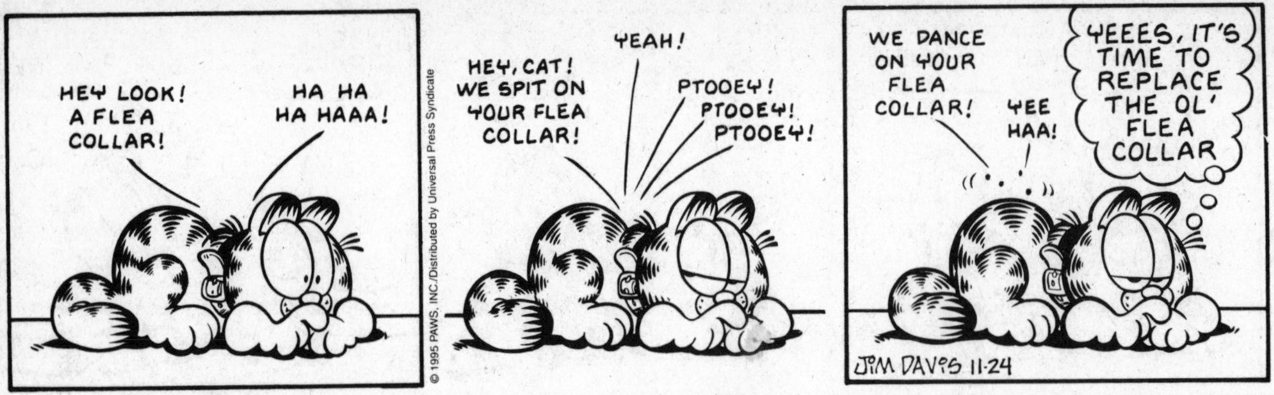
HEY LOOK! A FLEA COLLAR!
HA HA HA HAAA!
HEY, CAT! WE SPIT ON YOUR FLEA COLLAR!
YEAH!
PTOOEY! PTOOEY! PTOOEY!
WE DANCE ON YOUR FLEA COLLAR!
YEE HAA!
YEEES, IT'S TIME TO REPLACE THE OL' FLEA COLLAR
JIM DAVIS 11-24

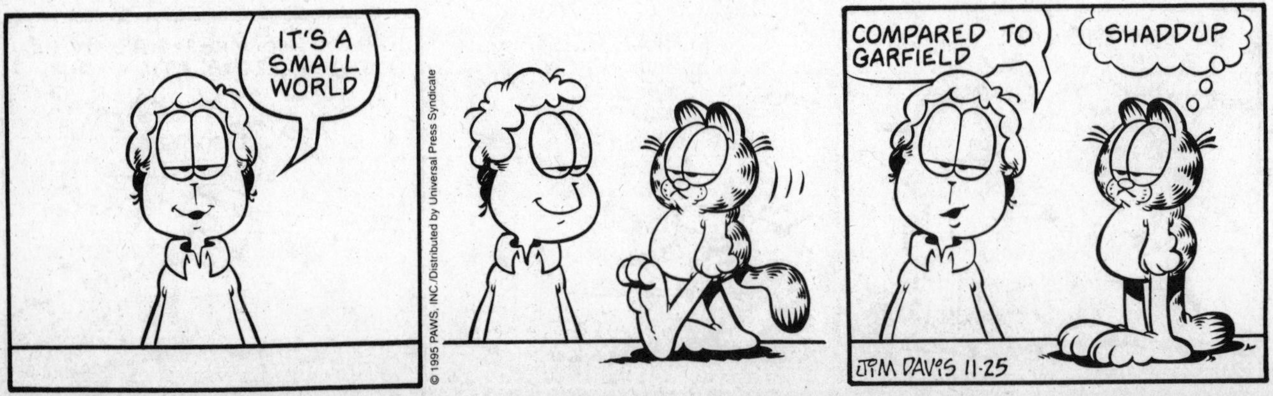
IT'S A SMALL WORLD
COMPARED TO GARFIELD
SHADDUP
JIM DAVIS 11-25

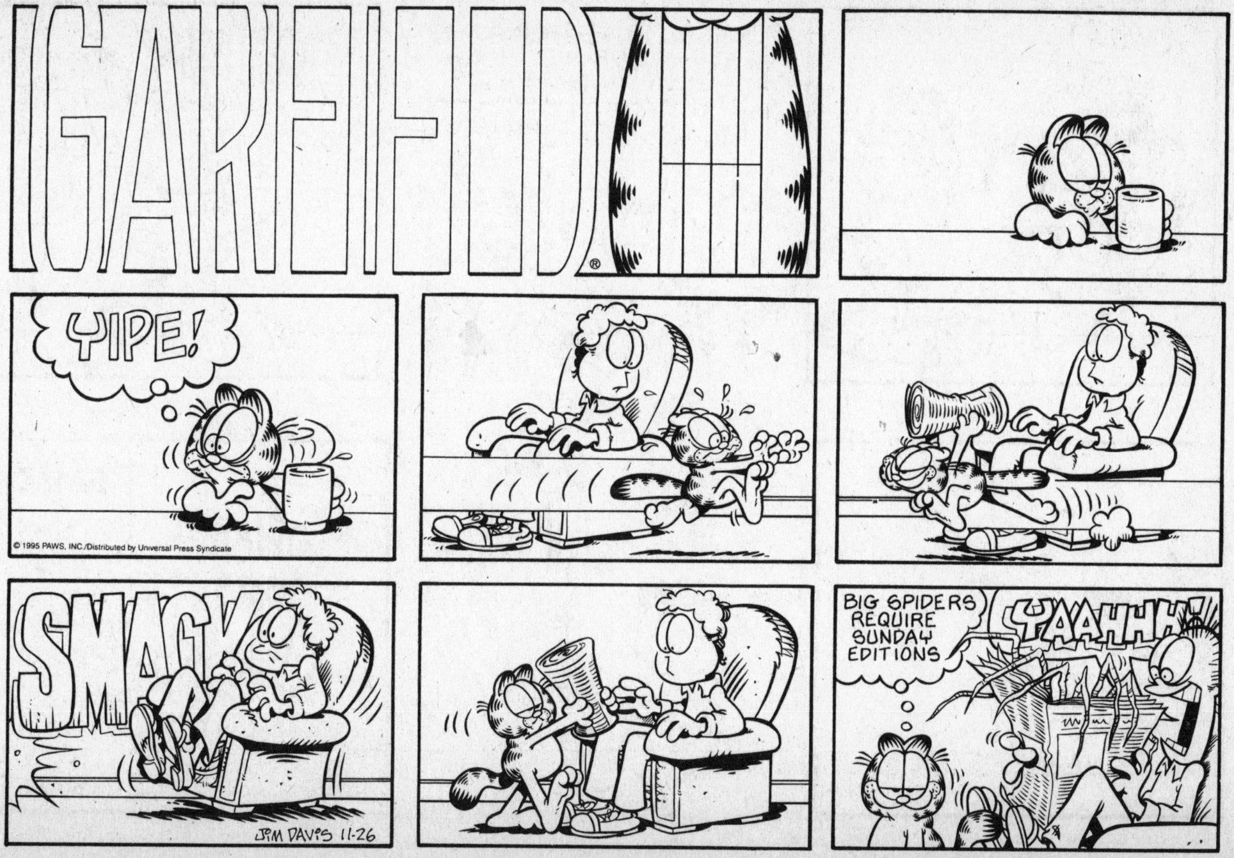
GARFIELD®
YIPE!
© 1995 PAWS, INC./Distributed by Universal Press Syndicate
SMACK
JIM DAVIS 11-26
BIG SPIDERS REQUIRE SUNDAY EDITIONS
YAAHHH!

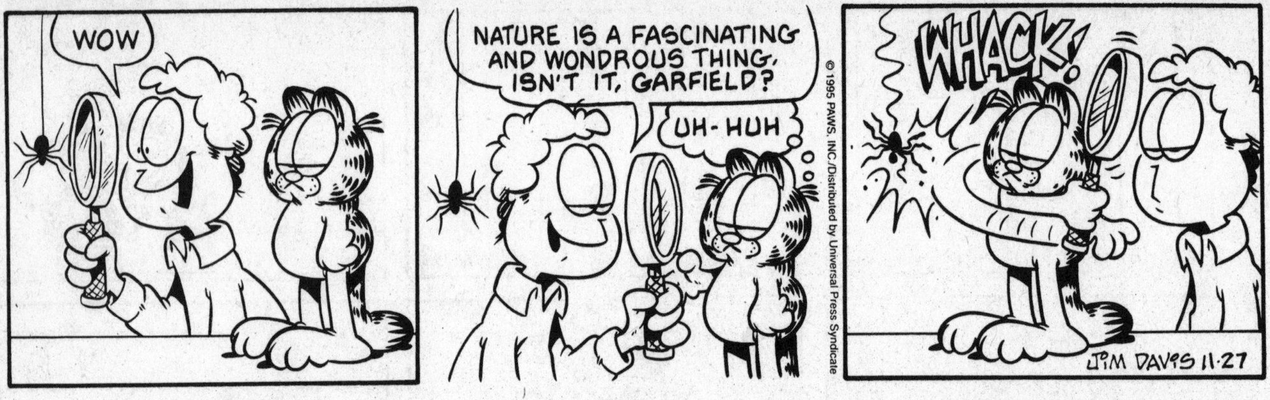
WOW
NATURE IS A FASCINATING AND WONDROUS THING, ISN'T IT, GARFIELD?
UH-HUH
WHACK!
JIM DAVIS 11·27

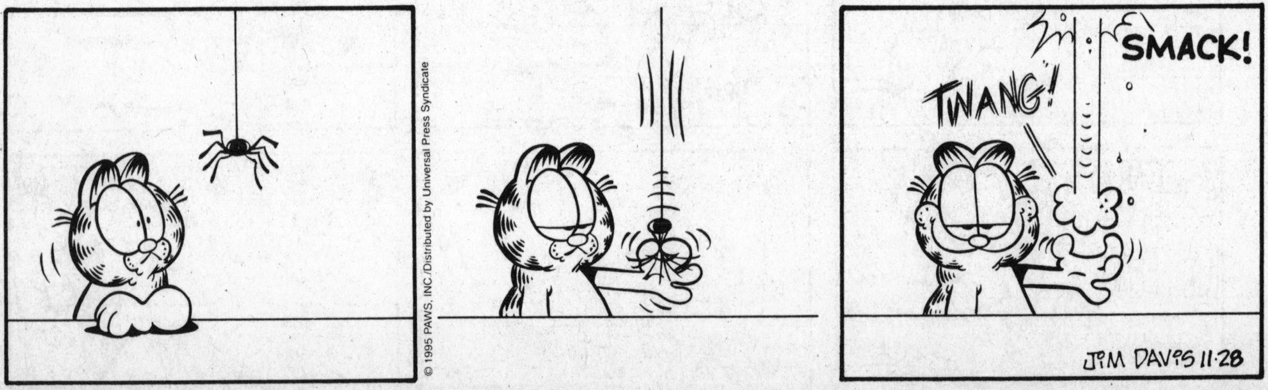
TWANG!
SMACK!
JIM DAVIS 11·28

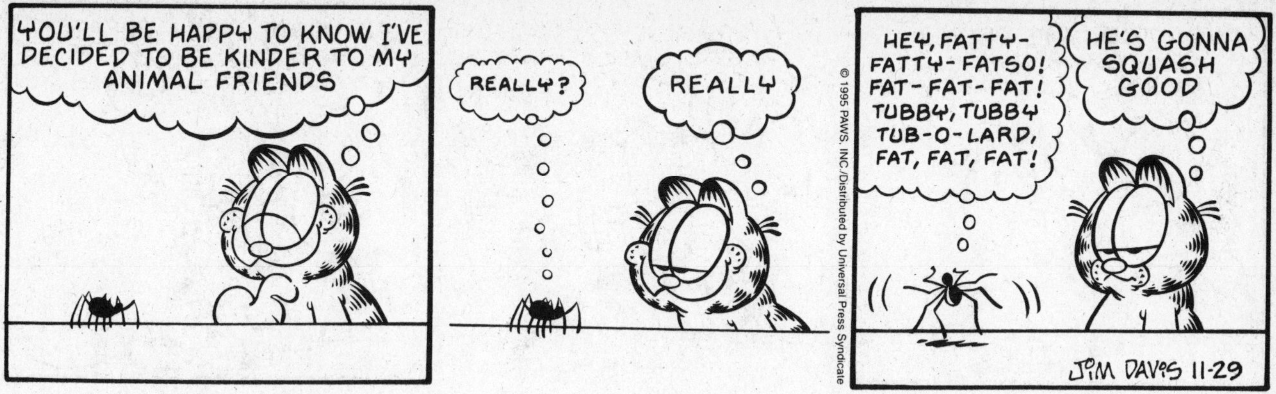
YOU'LL BE HAPPY TO KNOW I'VE DECIDED TO BE KINDER TO MY ANIMAL FRIENDS
REALLY?
REALLY
HEY, FATTY-FATTY-FATSO! FAT-FAT-FAT! TUBBY, TUBBY TUB-O-LARD, FAT, FAT, FAT!
HE'S GONNA SQUASH GOOD
JIM DAVIS 11-29

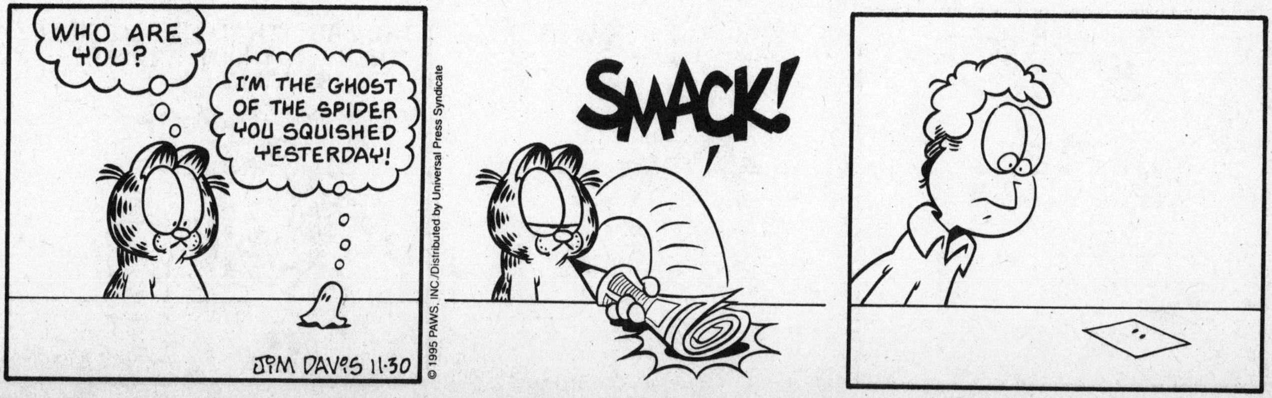
WHO ARE YOU?
I'M THE GHOST OF THE SPIDER YOU SQUISHED YESTERDAY!
JIM DAVIS 11-30
SMACK!

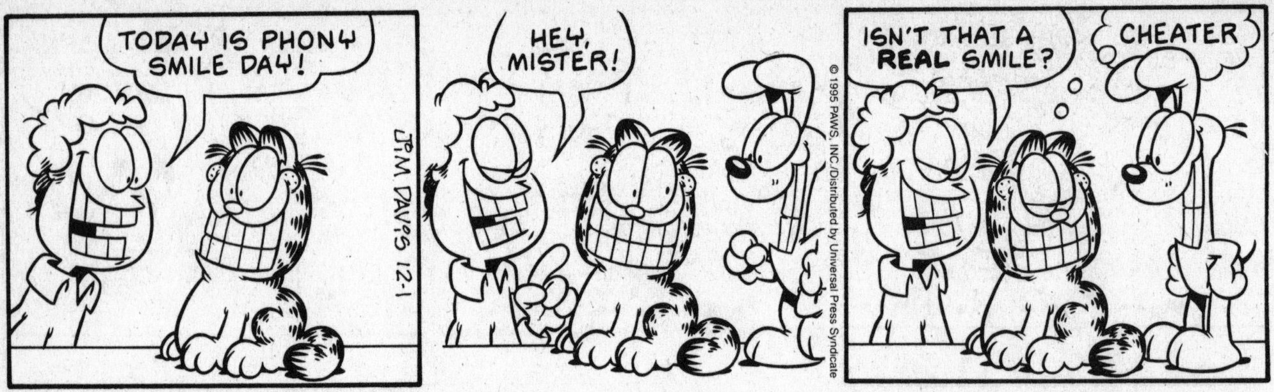
TODAY IS PHONY SMILE DAY!
JIM DAVIS 12-1
HEY, MISTER!
© 1995 PAWS, INC./Distributed by Universal Press Syndicate
ISN'T THAT A **REAL** SMILE?
CHEATER

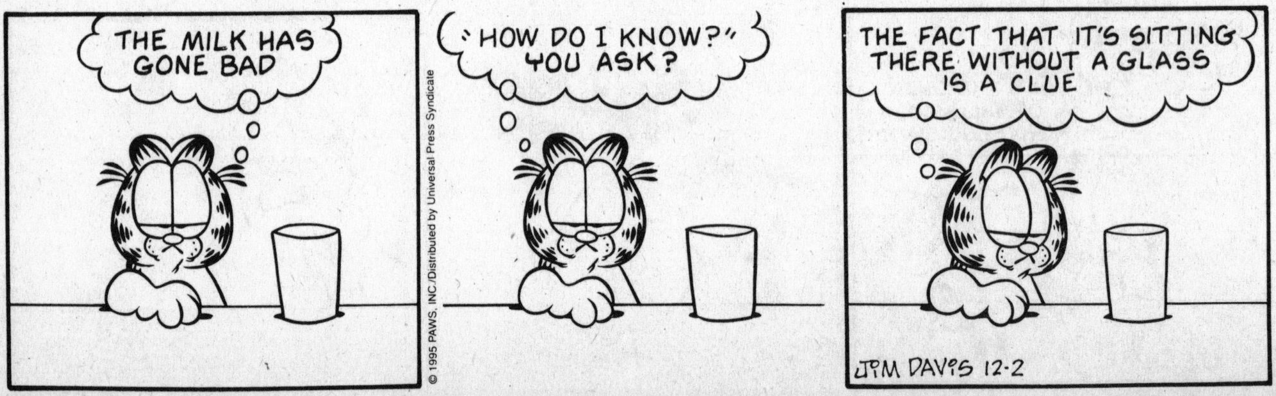
THE MILK HAS GONE BAD
© 1995 PAWS, INC./Distributed by Universal Press Syndicate
"HOW DO I KNOW?" YOU ASK?
THE FACT THAT IT'S SITTING THERE WITHOUT A GLASS IS A CLUE
JIM DAVIS 12-2

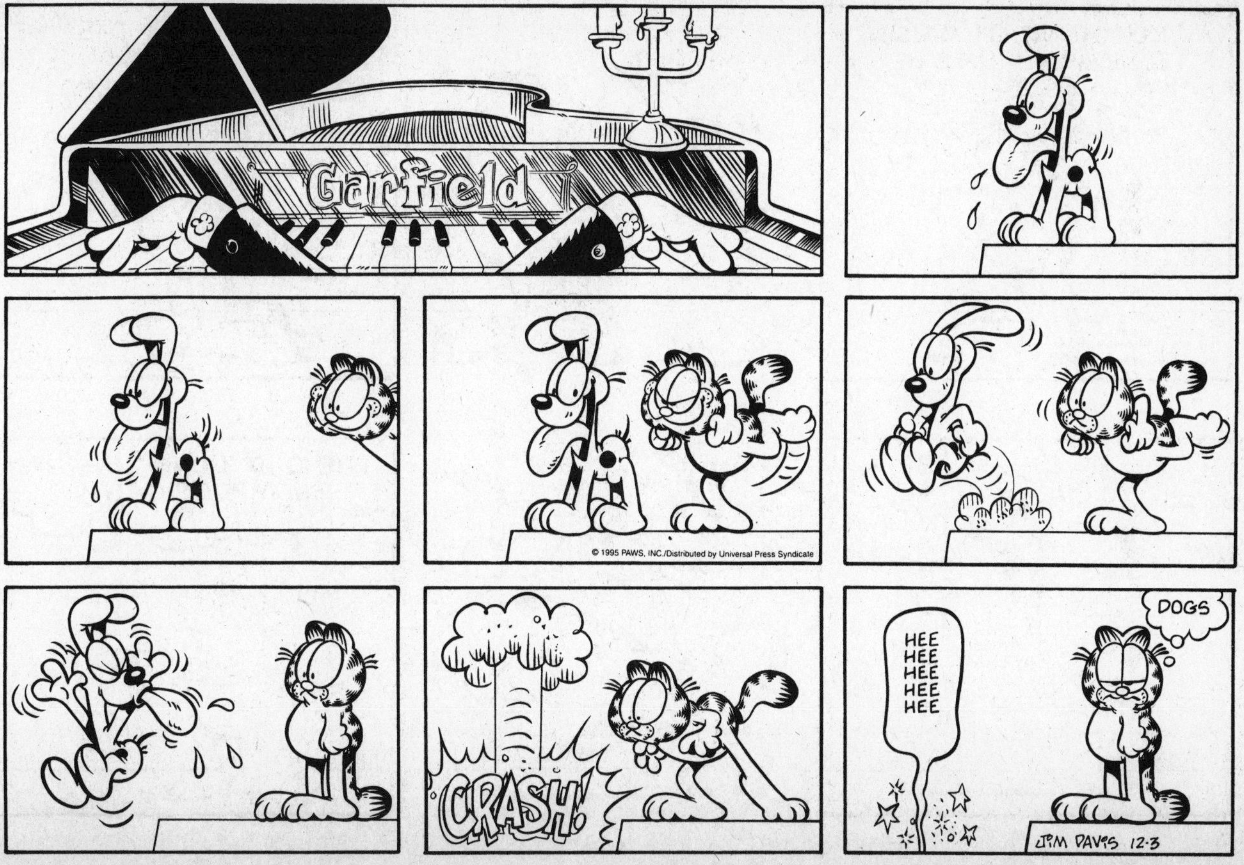
Garfield
© 1995 PAWS, INC./Distributed by Universal Press Syndicate
CRASH!
HEE HEE HEE HEE HEE
DOGS
JIM DAVIS 12-3

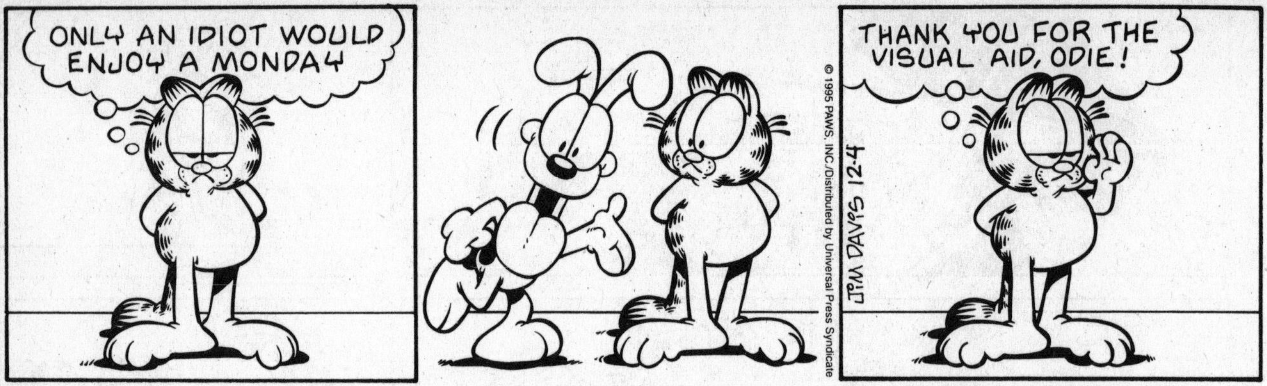
ONLY AN IDIOT WOULD ENJOY A MONDAY
JIM DAVIS 12-4
THANK YOU FOR THE VISUAL AID, ODIE!

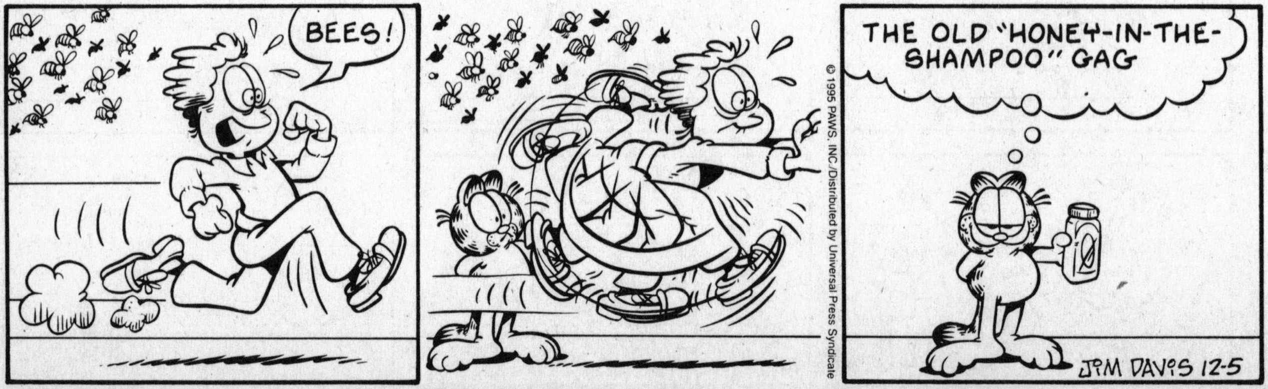
BEES!
THE OLD "HONEY-IN-THE-SHAMPOO" GAG
JIM DAVIS 12-5

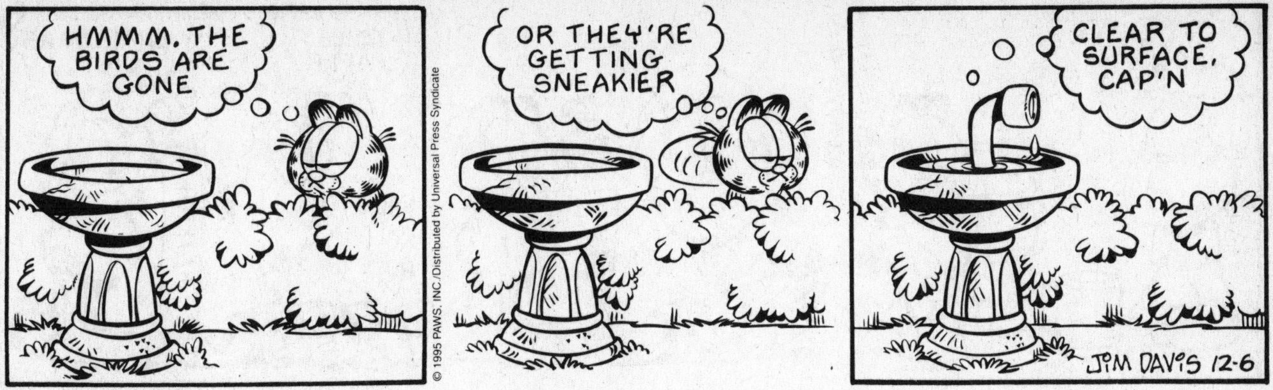
HMMM. THE BIRDS ARE GONE
OR THEY'RE GETTING SNEAKIER
CLEAR TO SURFACE, CAP'N
JIM DAVIS 12-6
© 1995 PAWS, INC./Distributed by Universal Press Syndicate

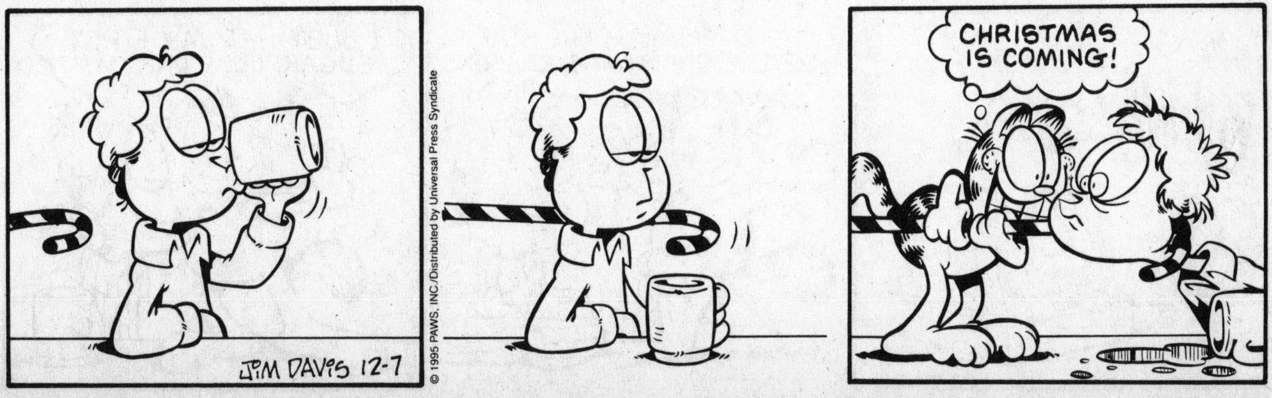
JIM DAVIS 12-7
CHRISTMAS IS COMING!
© 1995 PAWS, INC./Distributed by Universal Press Syndicate

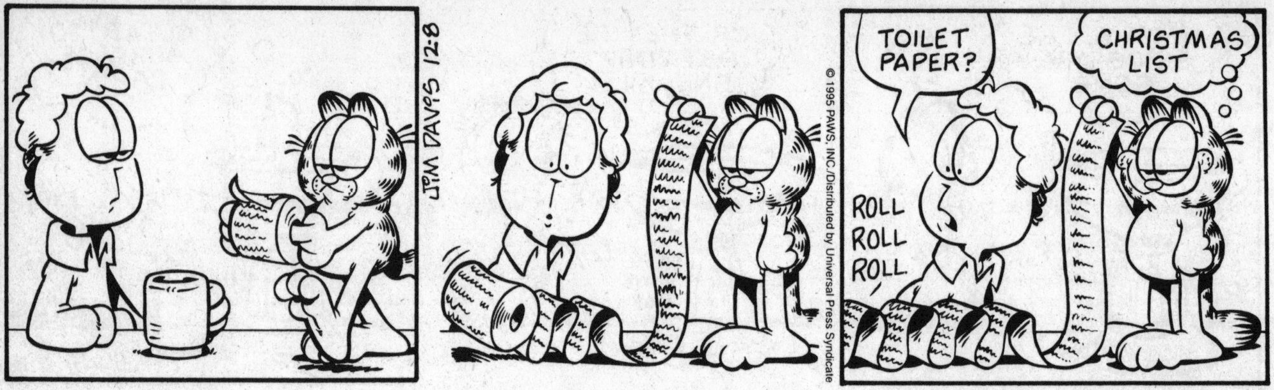
JIM DAVIS 12-8
© 1995 PAWS, INC./Distributed by Universal Press Syndicate
ROLL
ROLL
ROLL
TOILET PAPER?
CHRISTMAS LIST

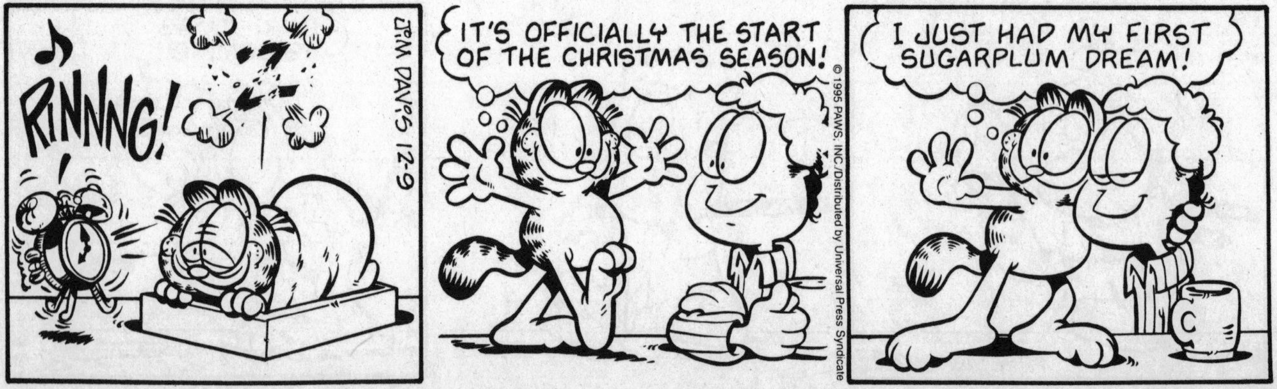
JIM DAVIS 12-9
RINNNG!
© 1995 PAWS, INC./Distributed by Universal Press Syndicate
IT'S OFFICIALLY THE START OF THE CHRISTMAS SEASON!
I JUST HAD MY FIRST SUGARPLUM DREAM!

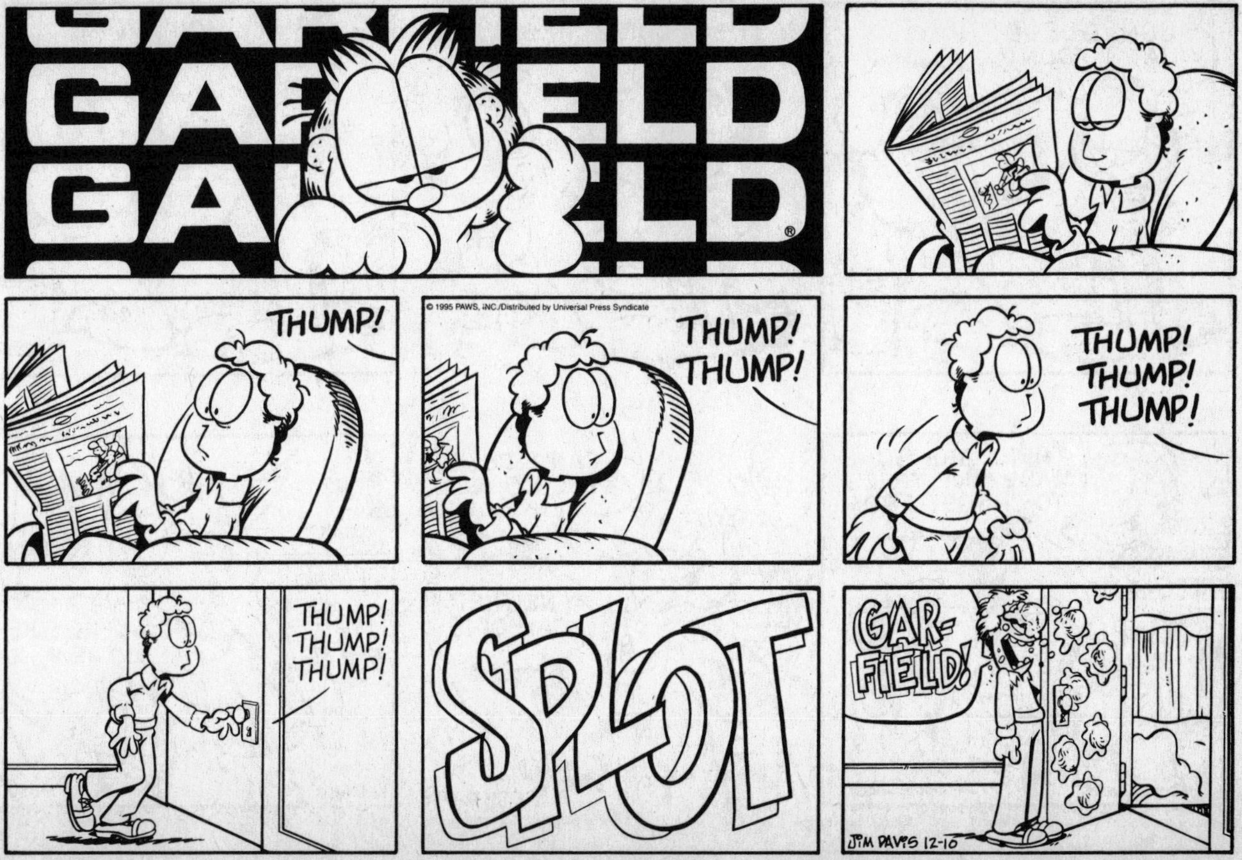
GARFIELD
GARFIELD
GARFIELD
THUMP!
© 1995 PAWS, INC./Distributed by Universal Press Syndicate
THUMP! THUMP!
THUMP! THUMP! THUMP!
THUMP! THUMP! THUMP!
SPLOT
GAR-FIELD!
JIM DAVIS 12-10

JON, GUESS WHAT I FOUND!

IT'S A CHRISTMAS STARTER KIT!

ALL YOU ADD IS THE TREE

JIM DAVIS 12-11

THERE ARE SO MANY NICE TREES TO CHOOSE FROM

STMAS TREES

I CAN'T DECIDE WHICH ONE I LIKE...

NEITHER CAN ODIE

STMAS TREES

JIM DAVIS

HE LIKES THEM ALL

STMAS TREES

12-12

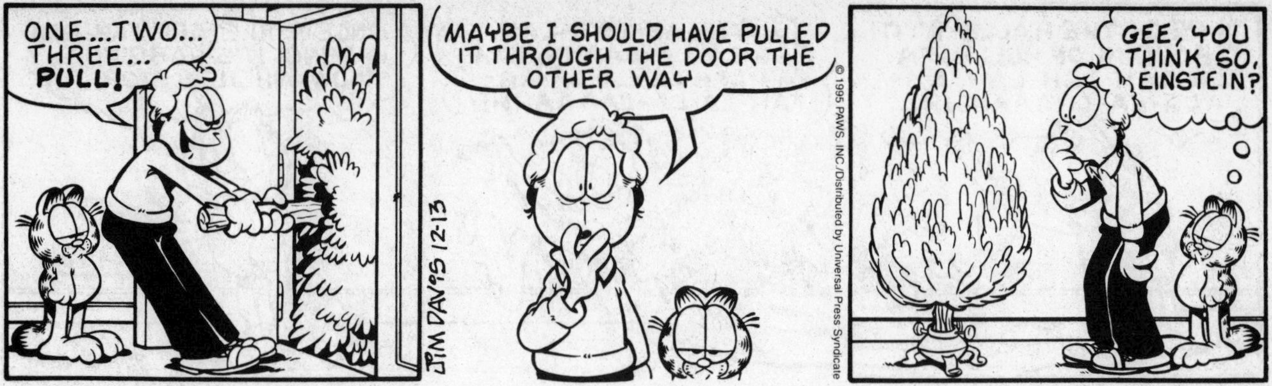
ONE...TWO... THREE... **PULL!**
JIM DAVIS 12-13
MAYBE I SHOULD HAVE PULLED IT THROUGH THE DOOR THE OTHER WAY
GEE, YOU THINK SO, EINSTEIN?

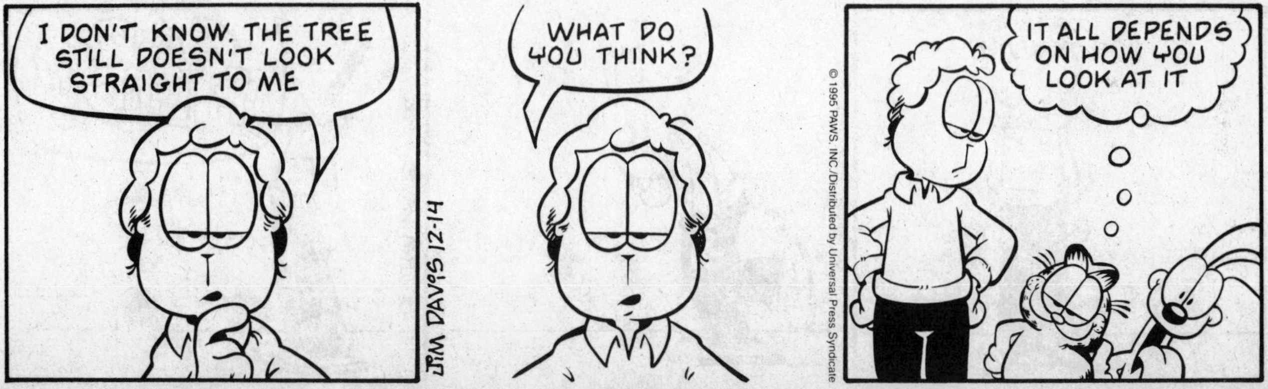
I DON'T KNOW. THE TREE STILL DOESN'T LOOK STRAIGHT TO ME
JIM DAVIS 12-14
WHAT DO YOU THINK?
IT ALL DEPENDS ON HOW YOU LOOK AT IT

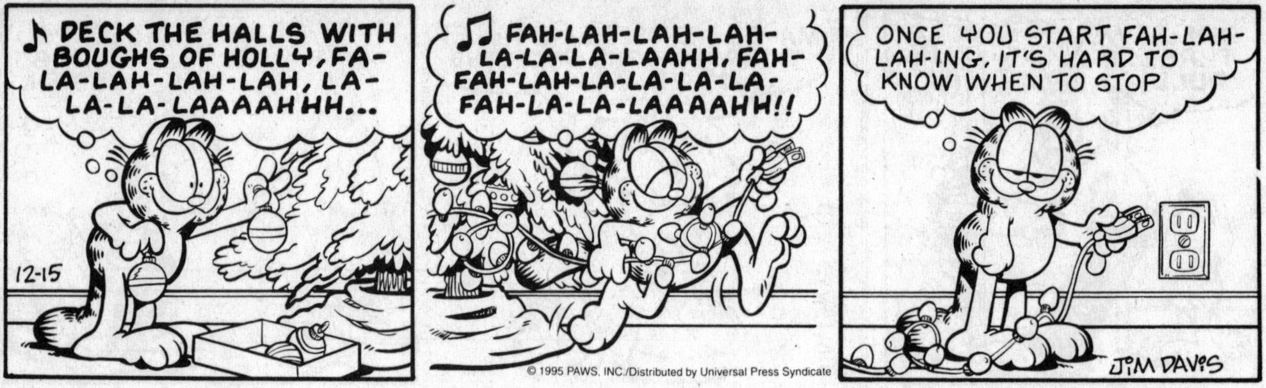
♪ DECK THE HALLS WITH BOUGHS OF HOLLY, FA-LA-LAH-LAH-LAH, LA-LA-LA-LAAAAHHH...
12-15
♫ FAH-LAH-LAH-LAH-LA-LA-LA-LAAHH, FAH-FAH-LAH-LA-LA-LA-LA-FAH-LA-LA-LAAAAHH!!
ONCE YOU START FAH-LAH-LAH-ING, IT'S HARD TO KNOW WHEN TO STOP
JIM DAVIS
© 1995 PAWS, INC./Distributed by Universal Press Syndicate

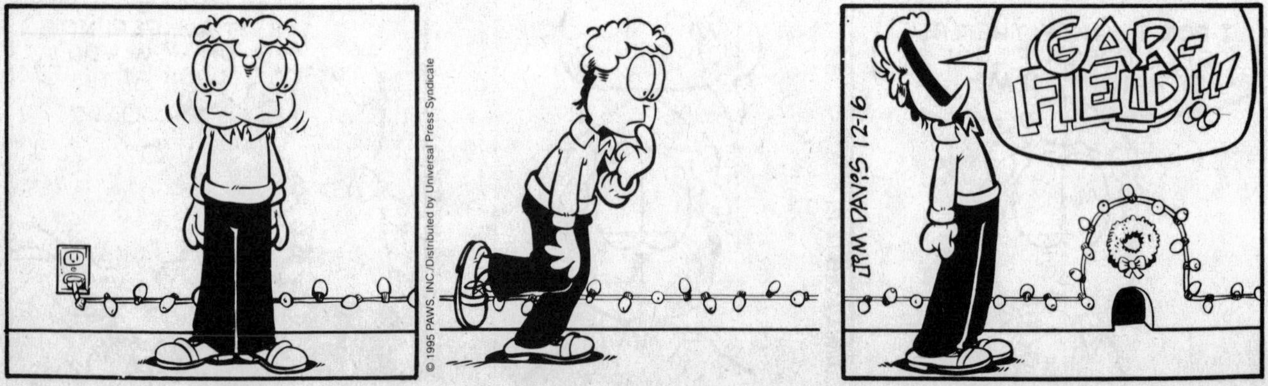
© 1995 PAWS, INC./Distributed by Universal Press Syndicate
JIM DAVIS 12-16
GAR-FIELD!!!

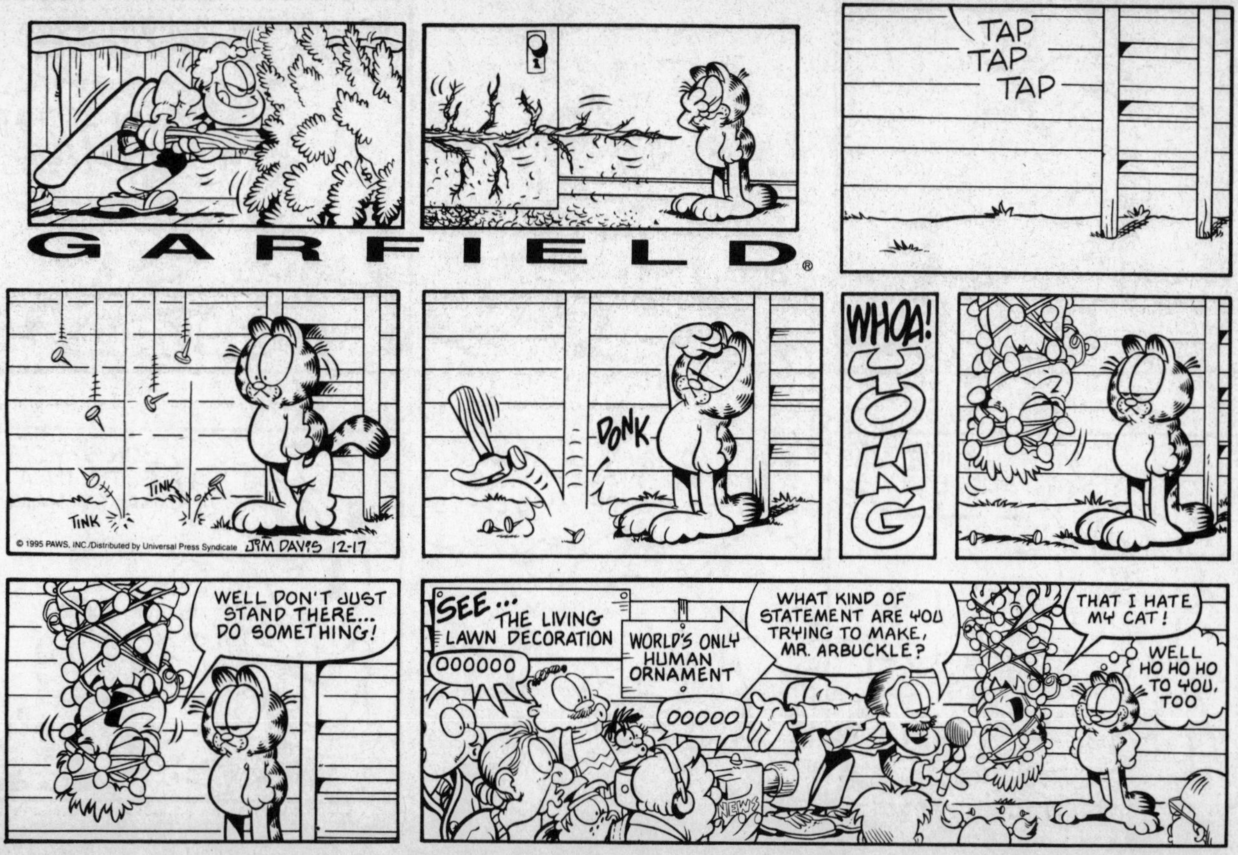
GARFIELD®
TAP TAP TAP
TINK
TINK
© 1995 PAWS, INC./Distributed by Universal Press Syndicate
JIM DAVIS 12-17
DONK
WHOA!
YOING
WELL DON'T JUST STAND THERE... DO SOMETHING!
SEE... THE LIVING LAWN DECORATION
WORLD'S ONLY HUMAN ORNAMENT
OOOOOO
OOOOO
WHAT KIND OF STATEMENT ARE YOU TRYING TO MAKE, MR. ARBUCKLE?
THAT I HATE MY CAT!
WELL HO HO HO TO YOU, TOO
NEWS

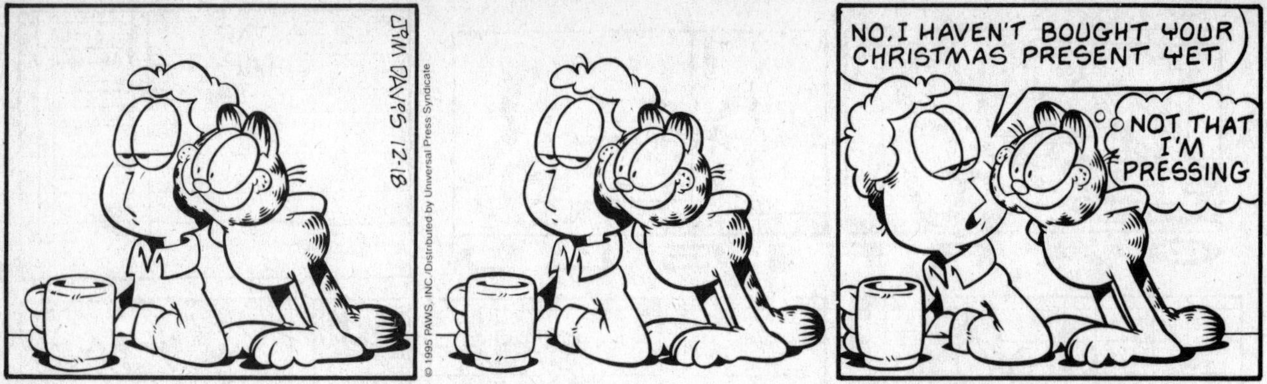
JIM DAVIS 12-18
© 1995 PAWS, INC./Distributed by Universal Press Syndicate
NO, I HAVEN'T BOUGHT YOUR CHRISTMAS PRESENT YET
NOT THAT I'M PRESSING

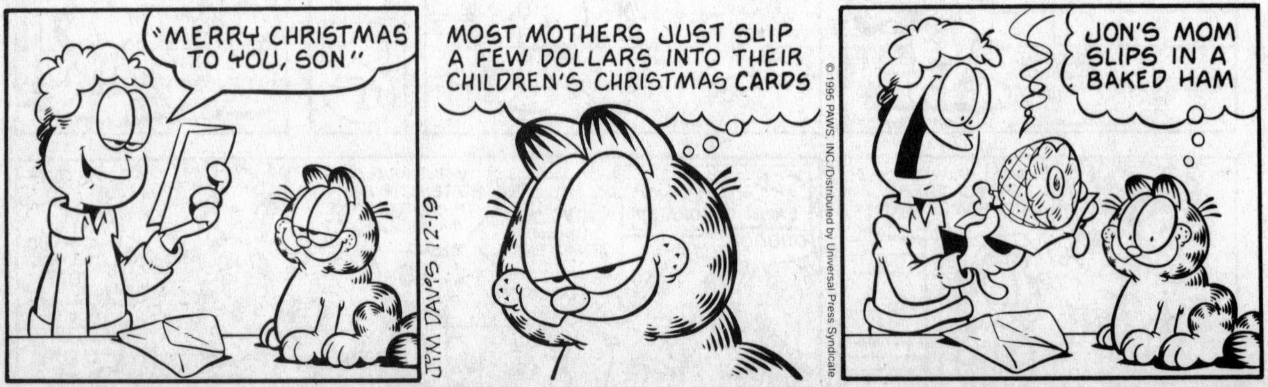
"MERRY CHRISTMAS TO YOU, SON"
JIM DAVIS 12-19
MOST MOTHERS JUST SLIP A FEW DOLLARS INTO THEIR CHILDREN'S CHRISTMAS CARDS
© 1995 PAWS, INC./Distributed by Universal Press Syndicate
JON'S MOM SLIPS IN A BAKED HAM

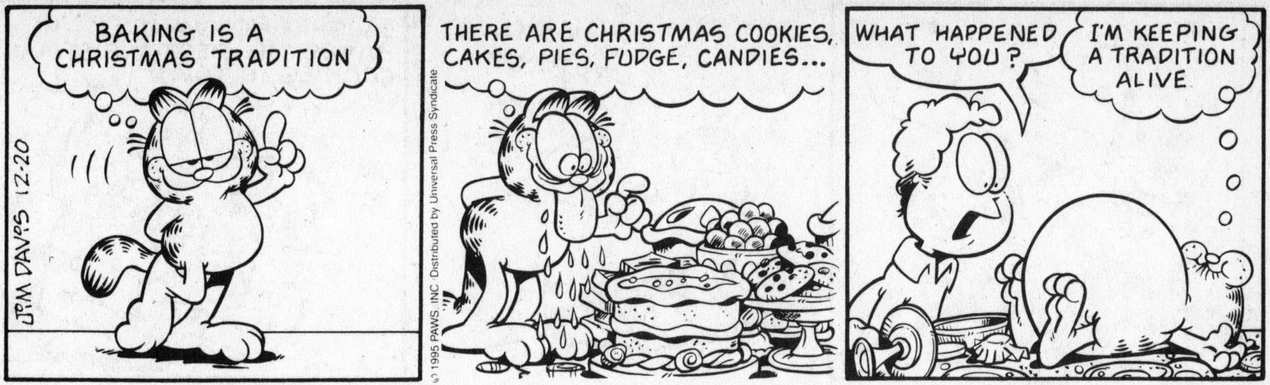
BAKING IS A CHRISTMAS TRADITION
JIM DAVIS 12-20
THERE ARE CHRISTMAS COOKIES, CAKES, PIES, FUDGE, CANDIES...
© 1995 PAWS, INC. Distributed by Universal Press Syndicate
WHAT HAPPENED TO YOU?
I'M KEEPING A TRADITION ALIVE

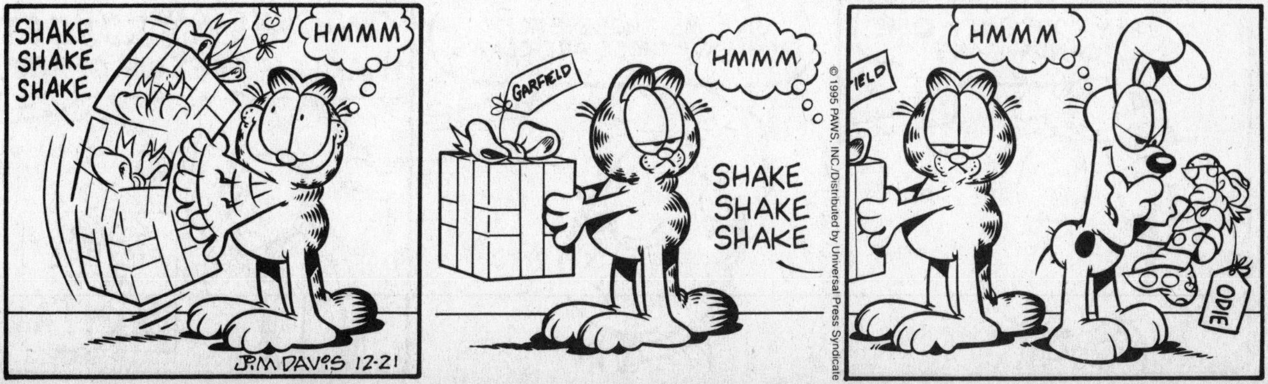
SHAKE SHAKE SHAKE
HMMM
JIM DAVIS 12-21
GARFIELD
HMMM
SHAKE SHAKE SHAKE
© 1995 PAWS, INC./Distributed by Universal Press Syndicate
HMMM
ODIE

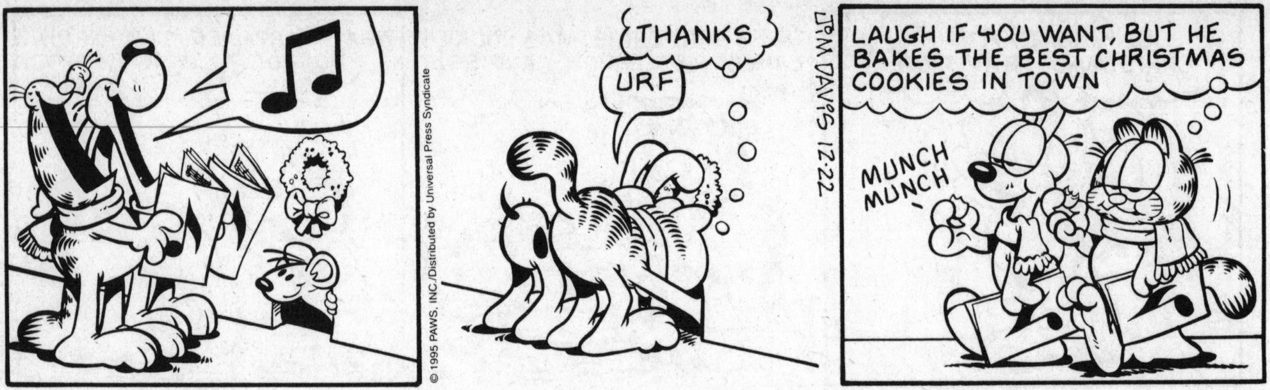
URF
THANKS
JIM DAVIS 12-22
LAUGH IF YOU WANT, BUT HE BAKES THE BEST CHRISTMAS COOKIES IN TOWN
MUNCH MUNCH

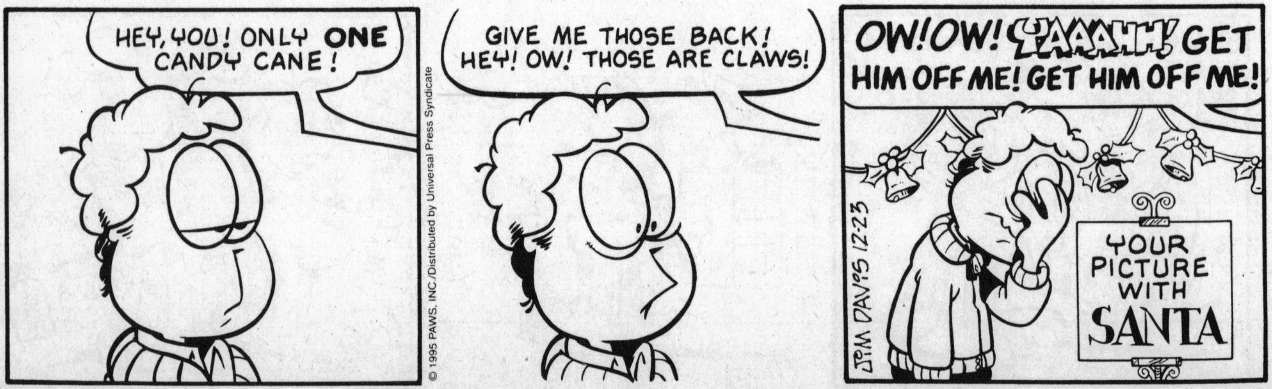
HEY, YOU! ONLY **ONE** CANDY CANE!
GIVE ME THOSE BACK! HEY! OW! THOSE ARE CLAWS!
OW! OW! YAAAHH! GET HIM OFF ME! GET HIM OFF ME!
JIM DAVIS 12-23
YOUR PICTURE WITH SANTA

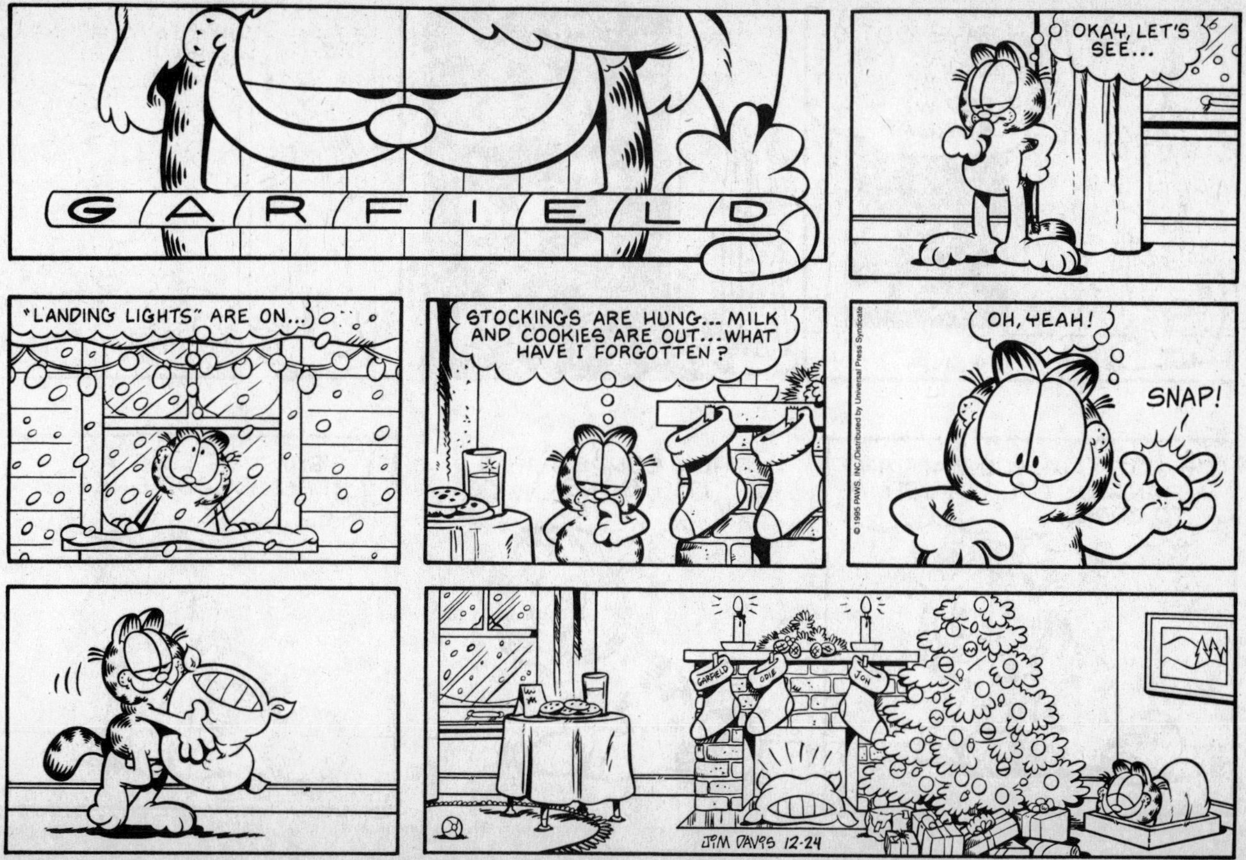
GARFIELD
OKAY, LET'S SEE...
"LANDING LIGHTS" ARE ON...
STOCKINGS ARE HUNG... MILK AND COOKIES ARE OUT... WHAT HAVE I FORGOTTEN?
OH, YEAH!
SNAP!
© 1995 PAWS, INC./Distributed by Universal Press Syndicate
GARFIELD
ODIE
JON
JIM DAVIS 12-24

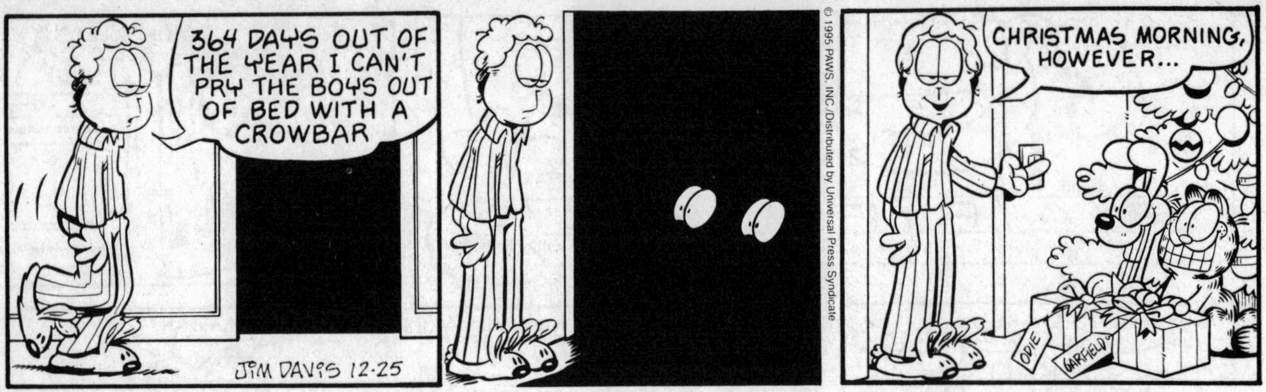
364 DAYS OUT OF THE YEAR I CAN'T PRY THE BOYS OUT OF BED WITH A CROWBAR
JIM DAVIS 12-25
© 1995 PAWS, INC./Distributed by Universal Press Syndicate
CHRISTMAS MORNING, HOWEVER...
ODIE
GARFIELD

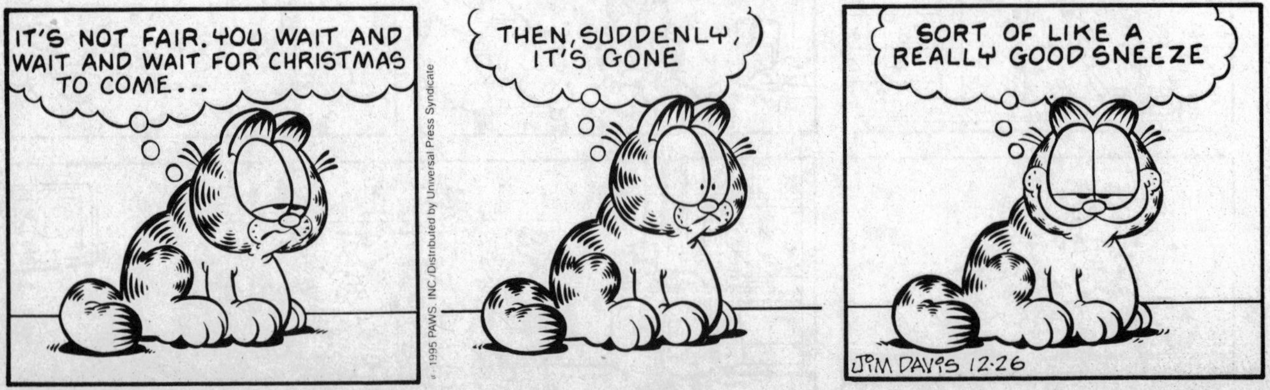
IT'S NOT FAIR. YOU WAIT AND WAIT AND WAIT FOR CHRISTMAS TO COME...
© 1995 PAWS, INC./Distributed by Universal Press Syndicate
THEN, SUDDENLY, IT'S GONE
SORT OF LIKE A REALLY GOOD SNEEZE
JIM DAVIS 12-26

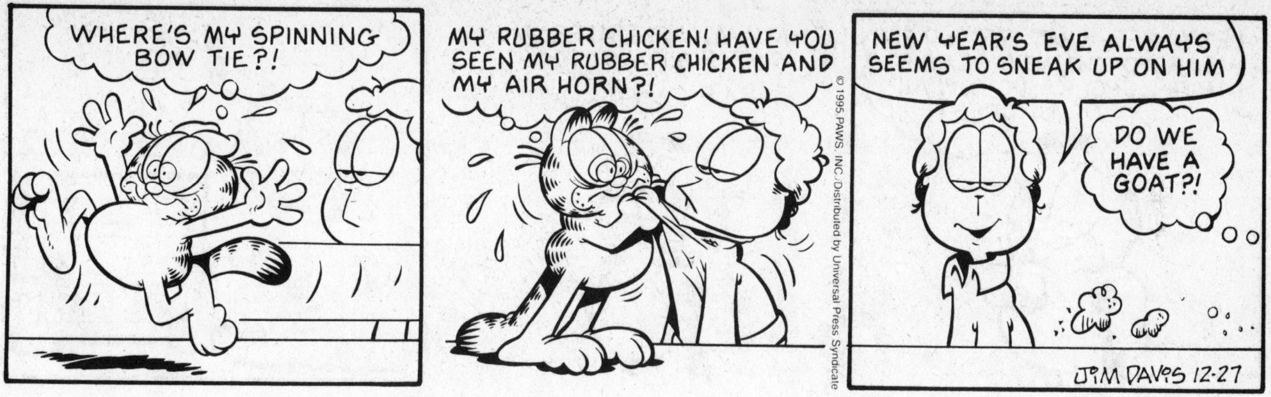
WHERE'S MY SPINNING BOW TIE?!
MY RUBBER CHICKEN! HAVE YOU SEEN MY RUBBER CHICKEN AND MY AIR HORN?!
NEW YEAR'S EVE ALWAYS SEEMS TO SNEAK UP ON HIM
DO WE HAVE A GOAT?!
JIM DAVIS 12-27
© 1995 PAWS, INC./Distributed by Universal Press Syndicate

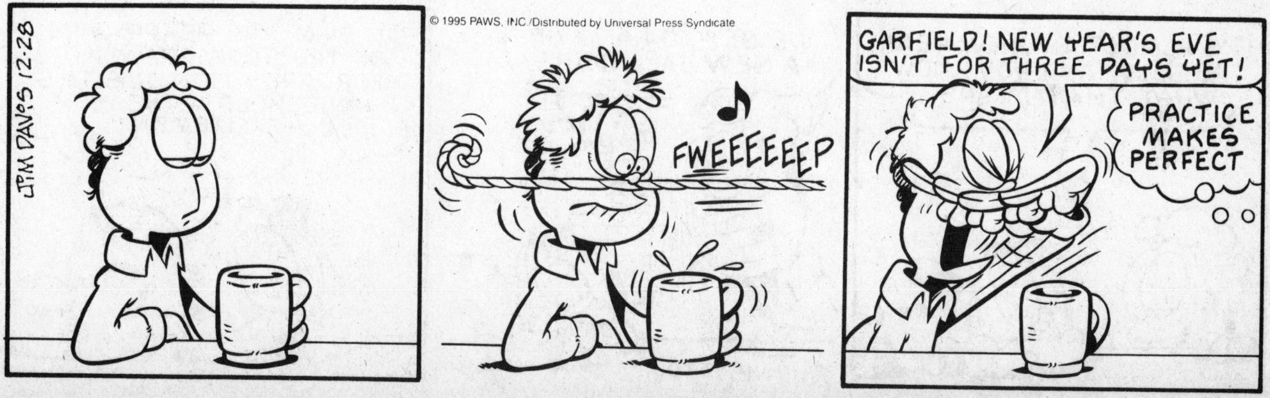
JIM DAVIS 12-28
© 1995 PAWS, INC./Distributed by Universal Press Syndicate
FWEEEEEEEP
GARFIELD! NEW YEAR'S EVE ISN'T FOR THREE DAYS YET!
PRACTICE MAKES PERFECT

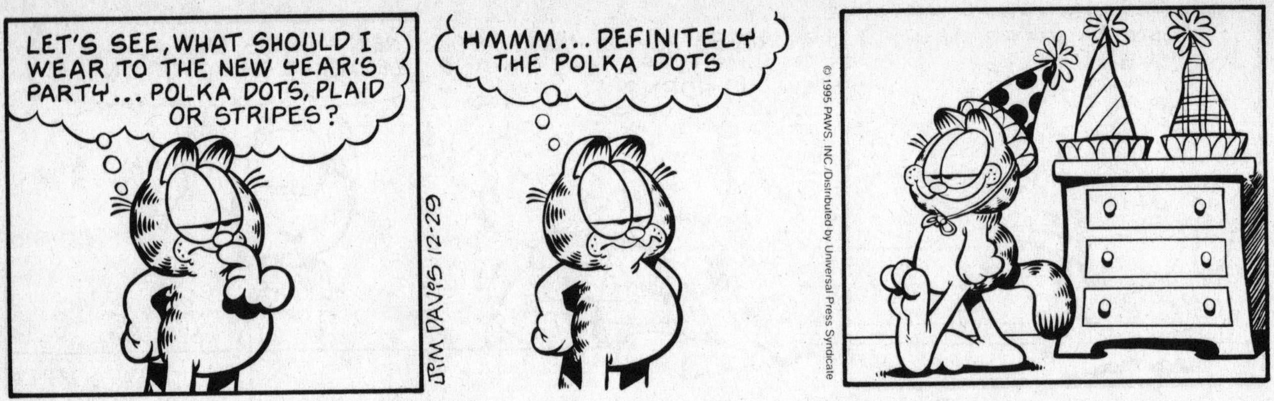
LET'S SEE, WHAT SHOULD I WEAR TO THE NEW YEAR'S PARTY... POLKA DOTS, PLAID OR STRIPES?
JIM DAVIS 12-29
HMMM... DEFINITELY THE POLKA DOTS
© 1995 PAWS, INC./Distributed by Universal Press Syndicate

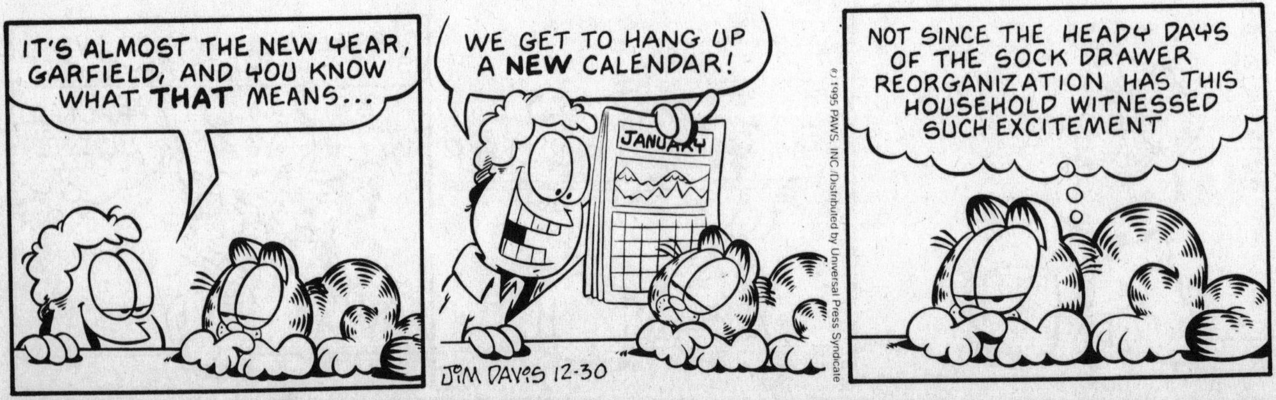
IT'S ALMOST THE NEW YEAR, GARFIELD, AND YOU KNOW WHAT **THAT** MEANS...
WE GET TO HANG UP A **NEW** CALENDAR!
JANUARY
JIM DAVIS 12-30
© 1995 PAWS, INC./Distributed by Universal Press Syndicate
NOT SINCE THE HEADY DAYS OF THE SOCK DRAWER REORGANIZATION HAS THIS HOUSEHOLD WITNESSED SUCH EXCITEMENT

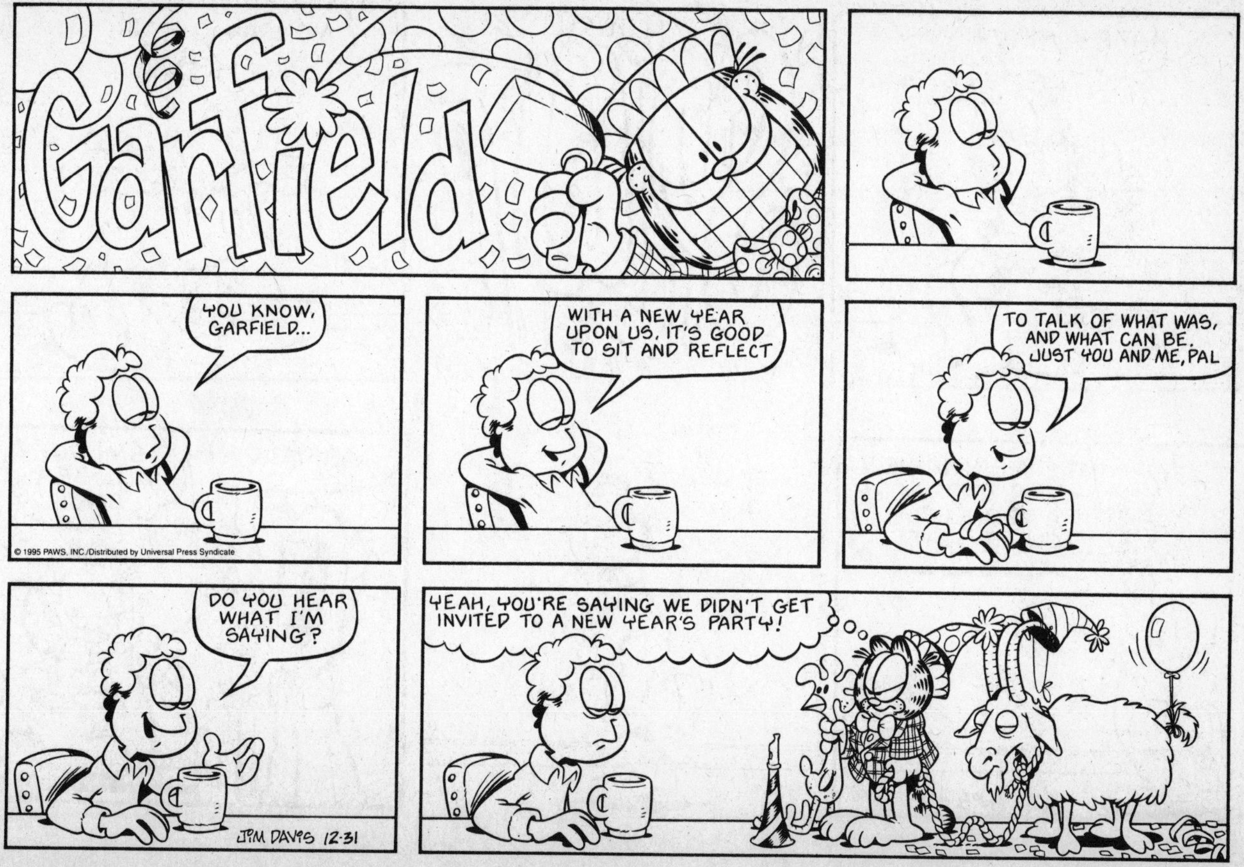
Garfield
YOU KNOW, GARFIELD...
WITH A NEW YEAR UPON US, IT'S GOOD TO SIT AND REFLECT
TO TALK OF WHAT WAS, AND WHAT CAN BE. JUST YOU AND ME, PAL
DO YOU HEAR WHAT I'M SAYING?
YEAH, YOU'RE SAYING WE DIDN'T GET INVITED TO A NEW YEAR'S PARTY!
JIM DAVIS 12-31
© 1995 PAWS, INC./Distributed by Universal Press Syndicate

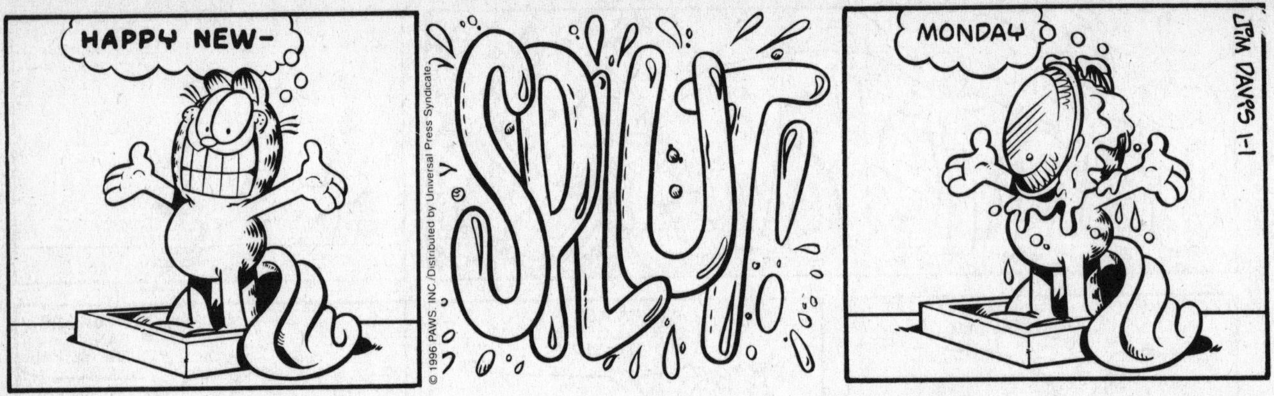
HAPPY NEW-
SPLUT!
MONDAY
JIM DAVIS 1-1
© 1996 PAWS, INC./Distributed by Universal Press Syndicate

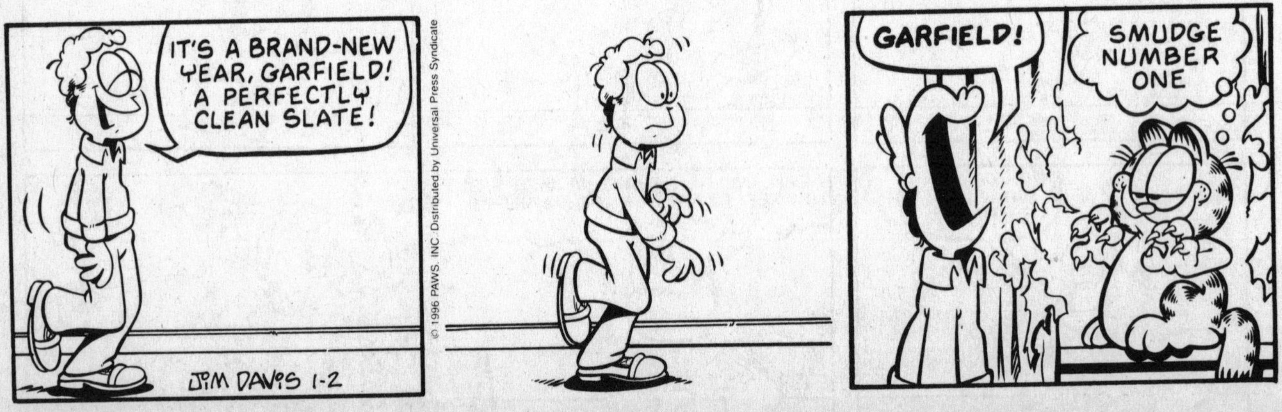
IT'S A BRAND-NEW YEAR, GARFIELD! A PERFECTLY CLEAN SLATE!
JIM DAVIS 1-2
GARFIELD!
SMUDGE NUMBER ONE
© 1996 PAWS, INC./Distributed by Universal Press Syndicate

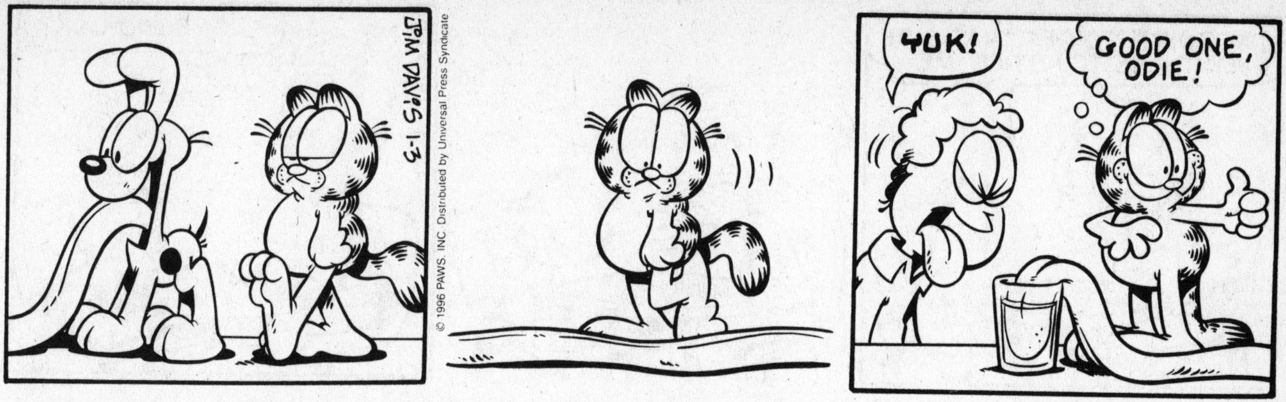
JIM DAVIS 1-3
© 1996 PAWS, INC. Distributed by Universal Press Syndicate
YUK!
GOOD ONE, ODIE!

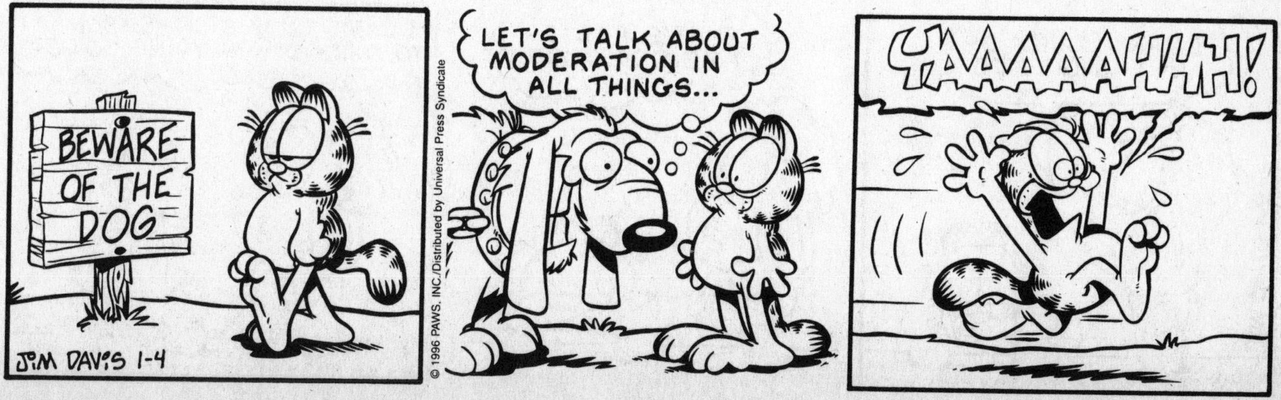
BEWARE OF THE DOG
JIM DAVIS 1-4
© 1996 PAWS, INC./Distributed by Universal Press Syndicate
LET'S TALK ABOUT MODERATION IN ALL THINGS...
YAAAAAHHH!

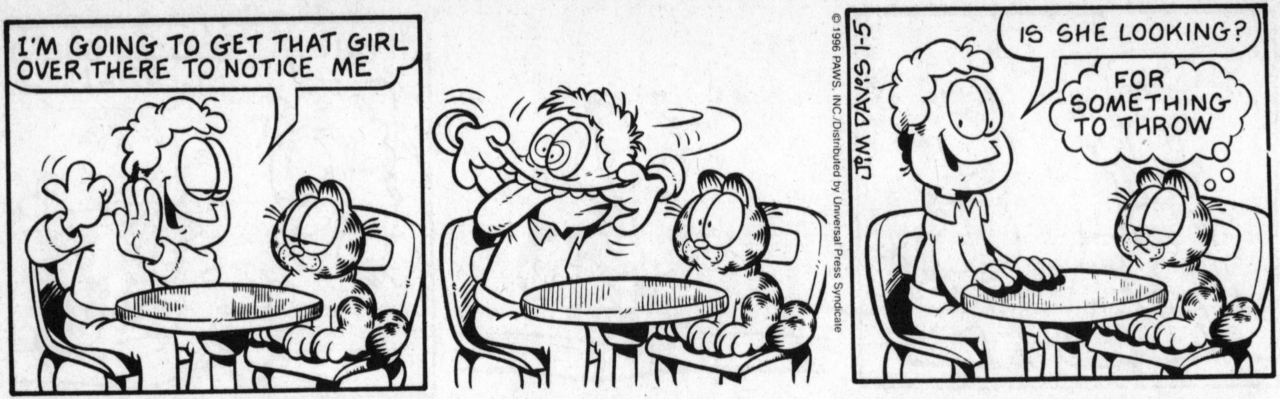
I'M GOING TO GET THAT GIRL OVER THERE TO NOTICE ME
IS SHE LOOKING?
FOR SOMETHING TO THROW
JIM DAVIS 1-5
© 1996 PAWS, INC./Distributed by Universal Press Syndicate

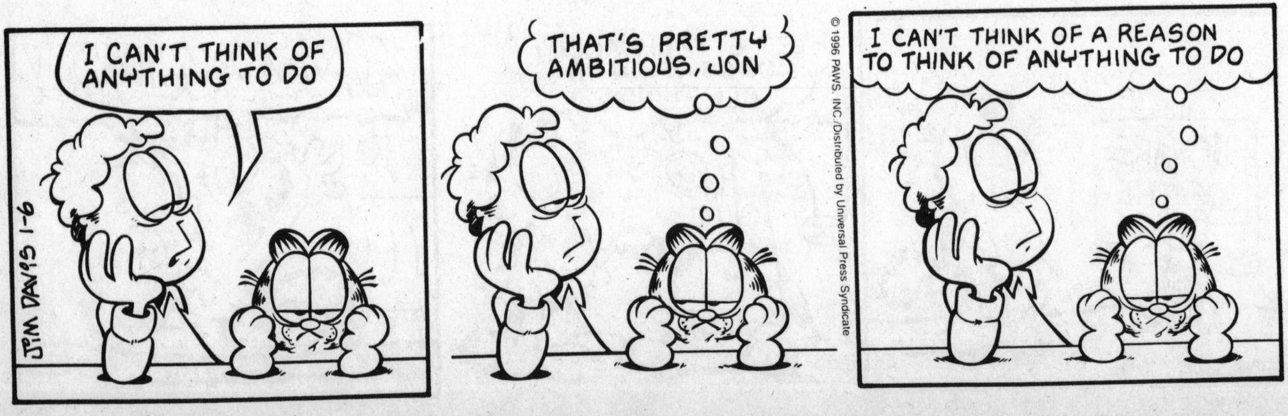
I CAN'T THINK OF ANYTHING TO DO
JIM DAVIS 1-6
THAT'S PRETTY AMBITIOUS, JON
I CAN'T THINK OF A REASON TO THINK OF ANYTHING TO DO
© 1996 PAWS, INC./Distributed by Universal Press Syndicate

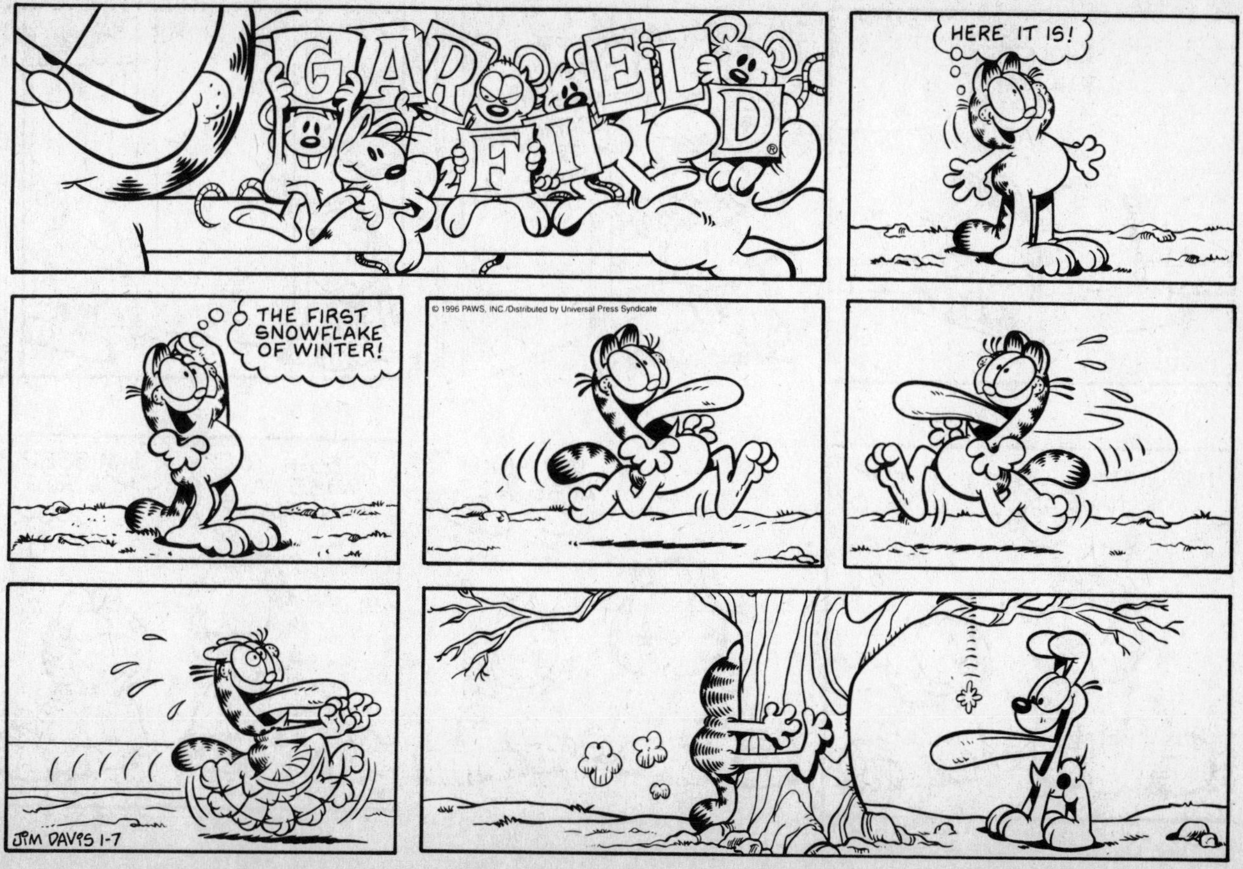
GARFIELD®
HERE IT IS!
THE FIRST SNOWFLAKE OF WINTER!
© 1996 PAWS, INC./Distributed by Universal Press Syndicate
JIM DAVIS 1-7

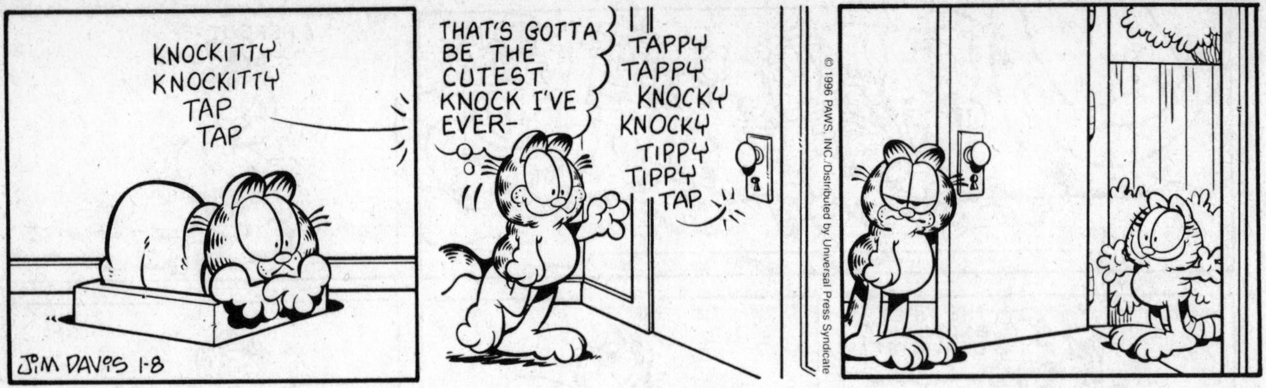
KNOCKITTY KNOCKITTY TAP TAP
JIM DAVIS 1-8
THAT'S GOTTA BE THE CUTEST KNOCK I'VE EVER-
TAPPY TAPPY KNOCKY KNOCKY TIPPY TIPPY TAP
© 1996 PAWS, INC./Distributed by Universal Press Syndicate

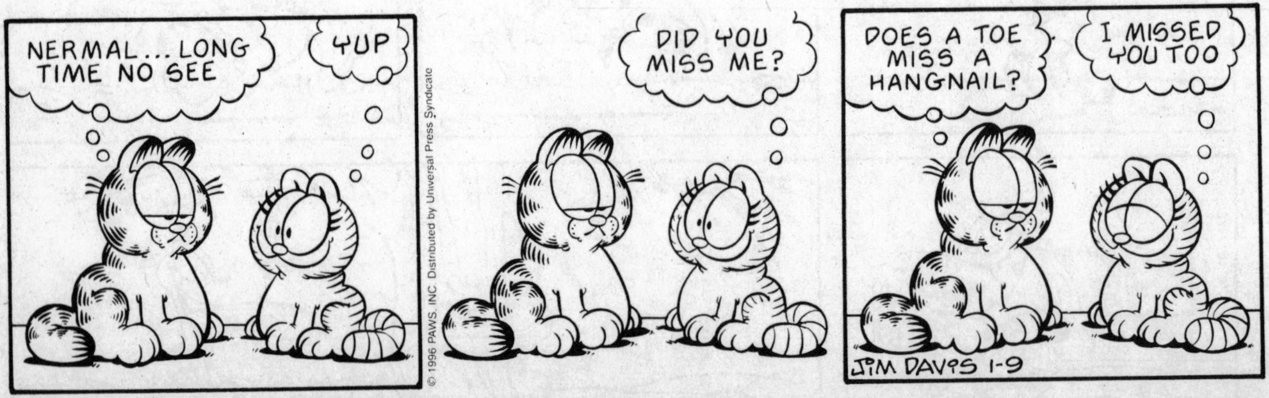
NERMAL... LONG TIME NO SEE
YUP
© 1996 PAWS, INC. Distributed by Universal Press Syndicate
DID YOU MISS ME?
DOES A TOE MISS A HANGNAIL?
I MISSED YOU TOO
JIM DAVIS 1-9

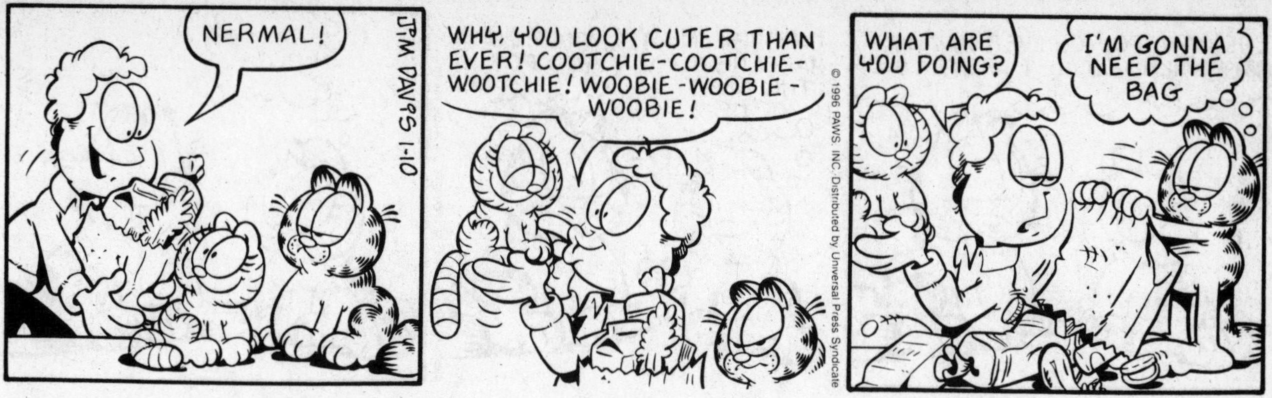

NERMAL!
JIM DAVIS 1-10
WHY, YOU LOOK CUTER THAN EVER! COOTCHIE-COOTCHIE-WOOTCHIE! WOOBIE-WOOBIE-WOOBIE!
© 1996 PAWS, INC./Distributed by Universal Press Syndicate
WHAT ARE YOU DOING?
I'M GONNA NEED THE BAG

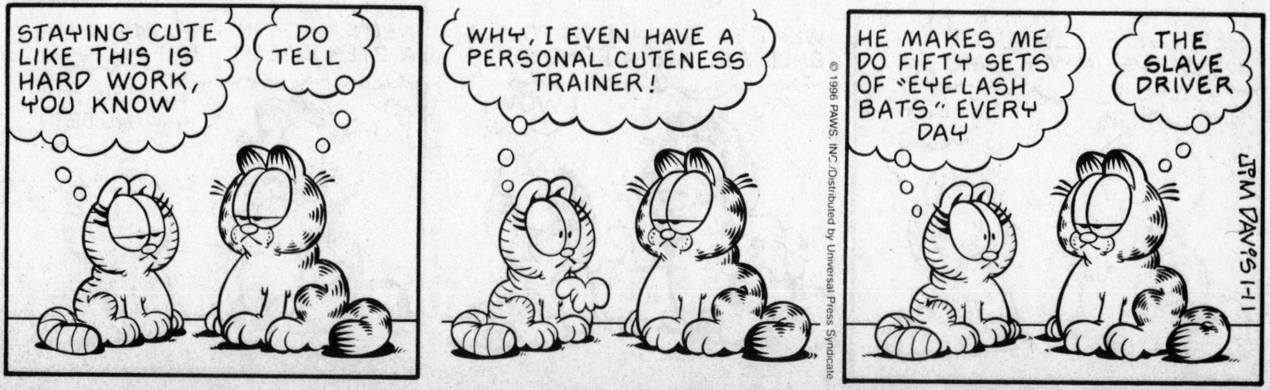

STAYING CUTE LIKE THIS IS HARD WORK, YOU KNOW
DO TELL
WHY, I EVEN HAVE A PERSONAL CUTENESS TRAINER!
© 1996 PAWS, INC./Distributed by Universal Press Syndicate
HE MAKES ME DO FIFTY SETS OF "EYELASH BATS" EVERY DAY
THE SLAVE DRIVER
JIM DAVIS 1-11

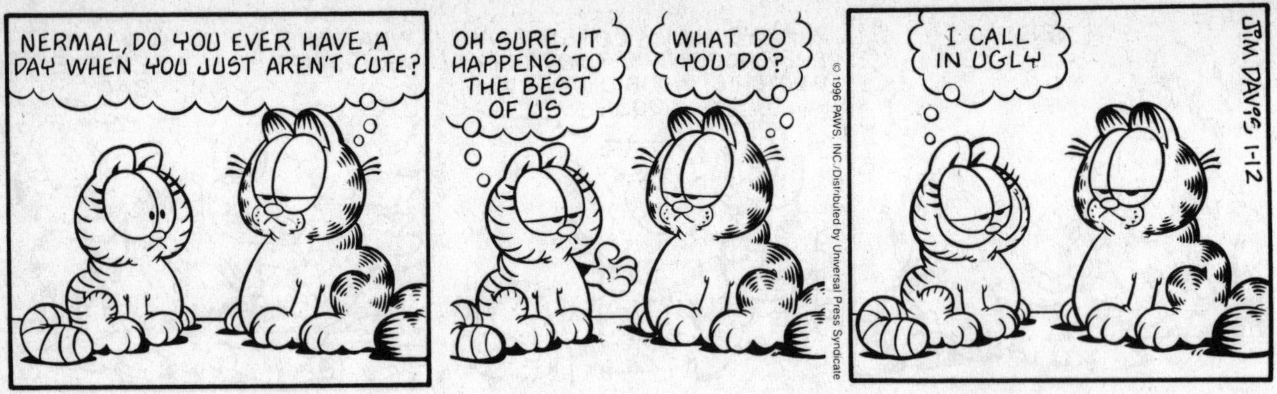
NERMAL, DO YOU EVER HAVE A DAY WHEN YOU JUST AREN'T CUTE?
OH SURE, IT HAPPENS TO THE BEST OF US
WHAT DO YOU DO?
I CALL IN UGLY
JIM DAVIS 1-12
© 1996 PAWS, INC./Distributed by Universal Press Syndicate

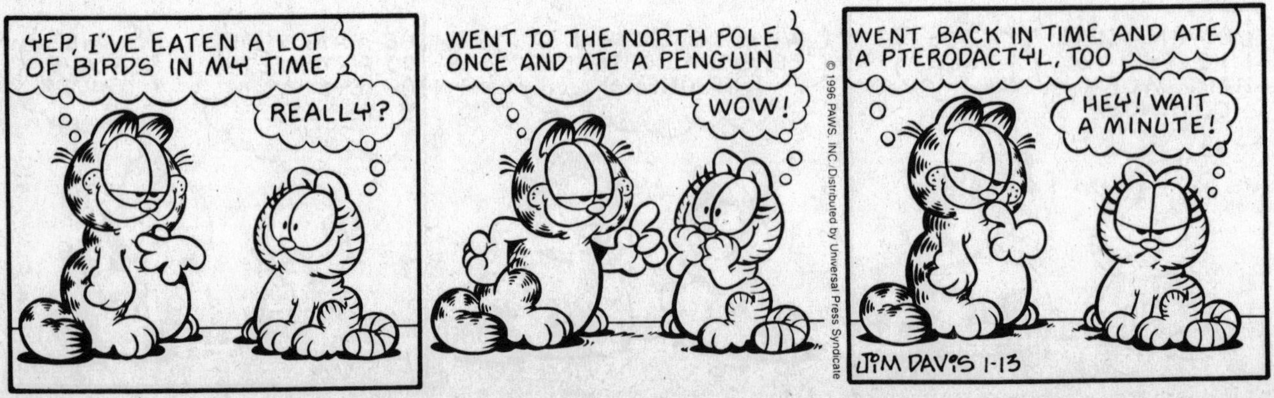
YEP, I'VE EATEN A LOT OF BIRDS IN MY TIME
REALLY?
WENT TO THE NORTH POLE ONCE AND ATE A PENGUIN
WOW!
WENT BACK IN TIME AND ATE A PTERODACTYL, TOO
HEY! WAIT A MINUTE!
JIM DAVIS 1-13
© 1996 PAWS, INC./Distributed by Universal Press Syndicate

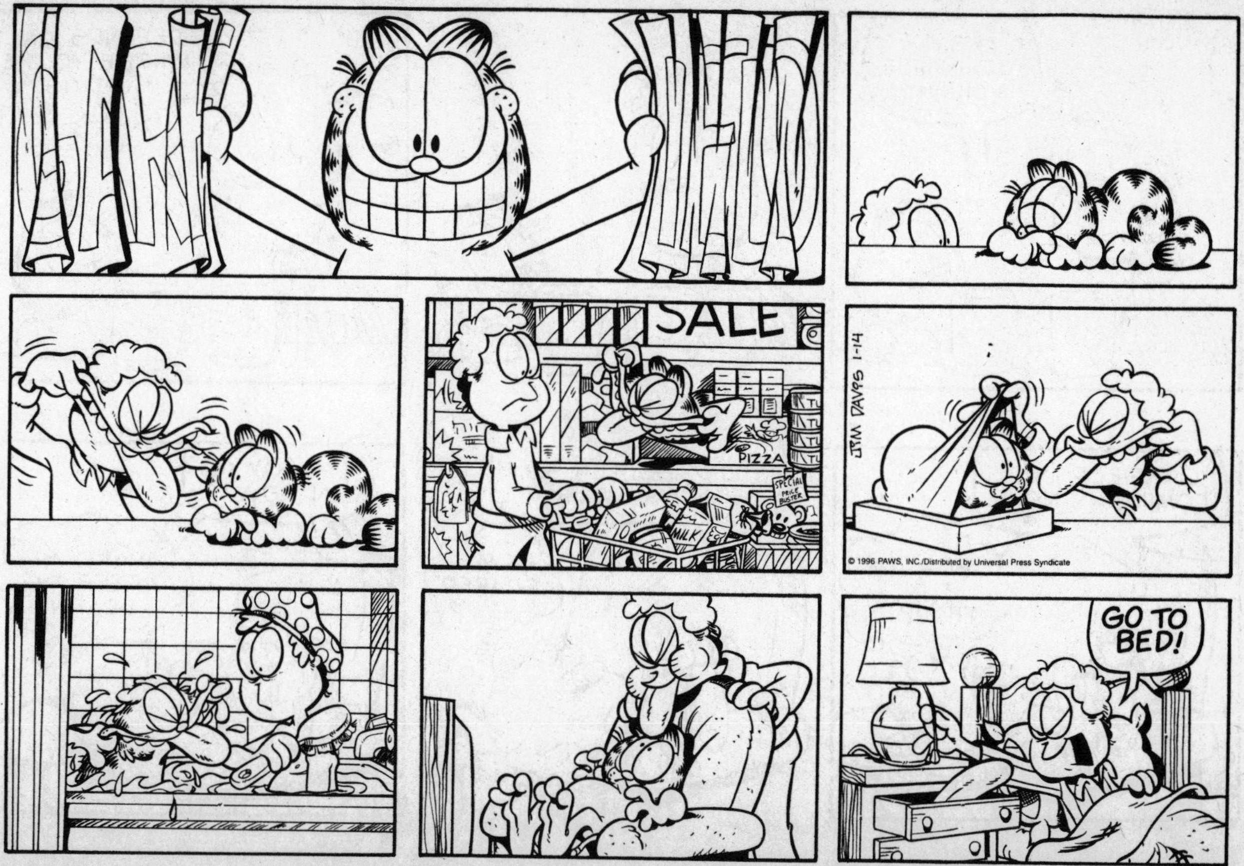
SALE
PIZZA
MILK
SPECIAL PRICE BUSTER
JPM DAVIS 1-14
© 1996 PAWS, INC./Distributed by Universal Press Syndicate
GO TO BED!

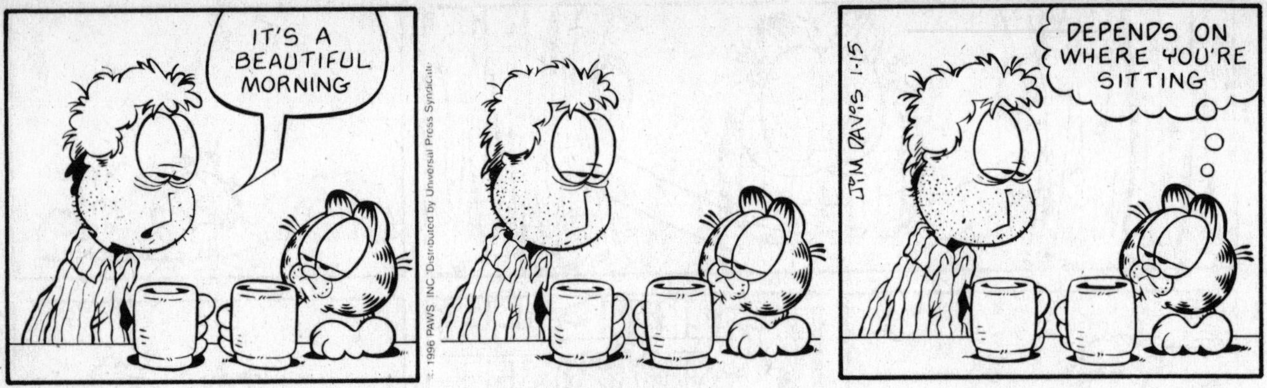
IT'S A BEAUTIFUL MORNING
© 1996 PAWS, INC. Distributed by Universal Press Syndicate
JIM DAVIS 1-15
DEPENDS ON WHERE YOU'RE SITTING

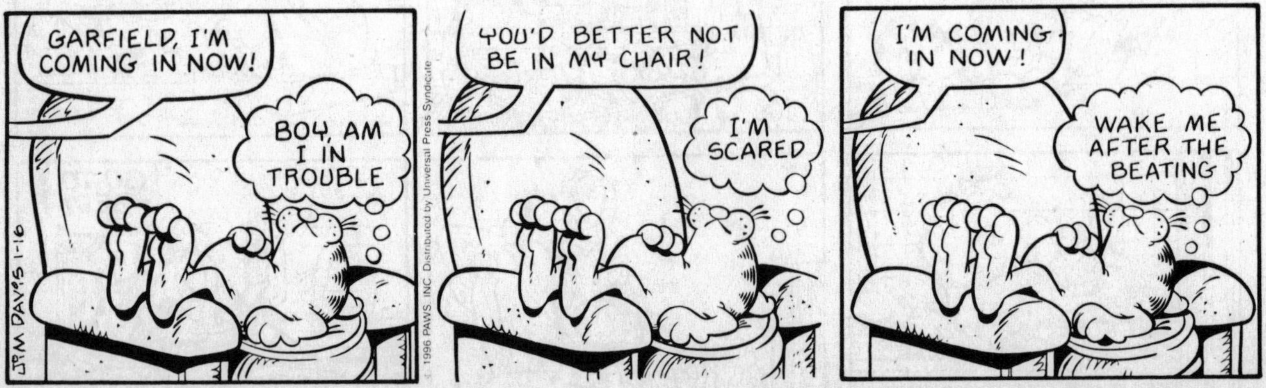
GARFIELD, I'M COMING IN NOW!
BOY, AM I IN TROUBLE
JIM DAVIS 1-16
© 1996 PAWS, INC. Distributed by Universal Press Syndicate
YOU'D BETTER NOT BE IN MY CHAIR!
I'M SCARED
I'M COMING IN NOW!
WAKE ME AFTER THE BEATING

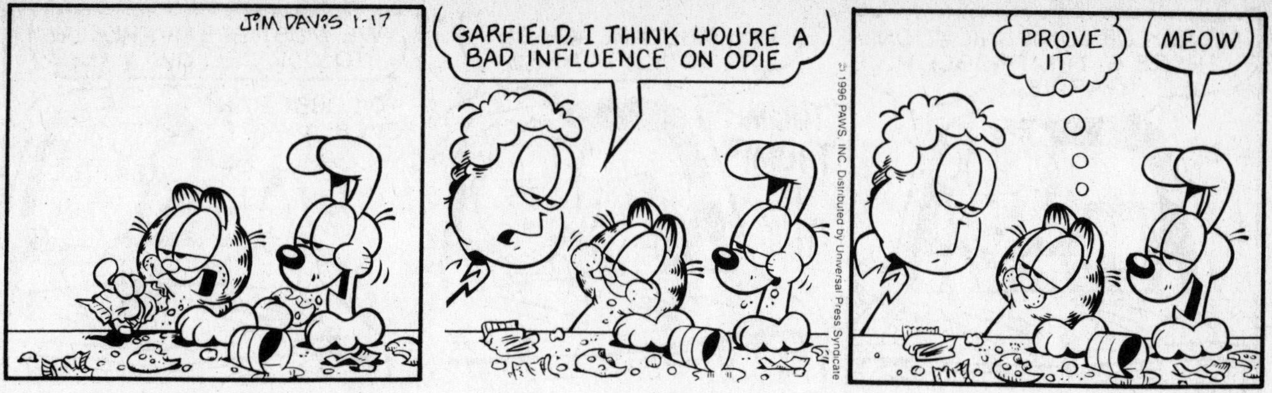
JIM DAVIS 1-17
GARFIELD, I THINK YOU'RE A BAD INFLUENCE ON ODIE
© 1996 PAWS, INC Distributed by Universal Press Syndicate
PROVE IT
MEOW

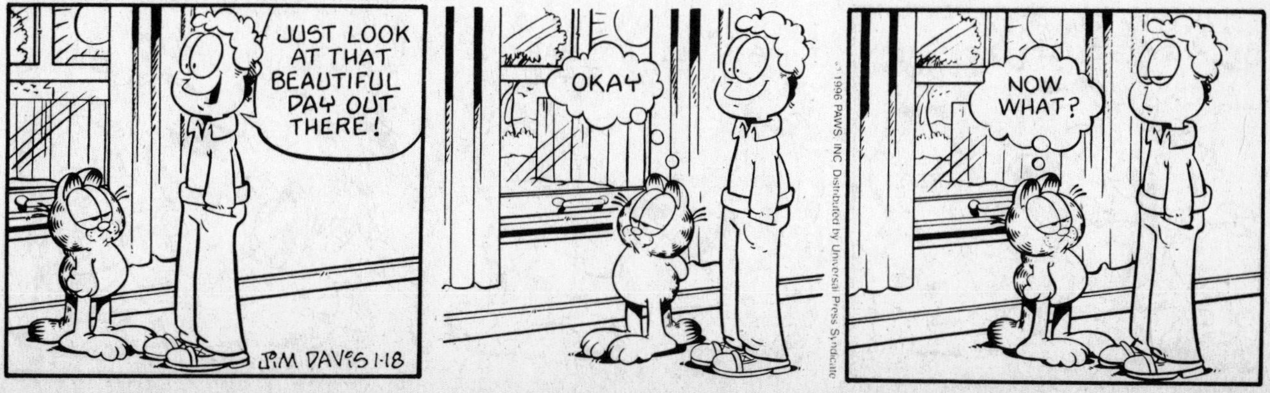
JUST LOOK AT THAT BEAUTIFUL DAY OUT THERE!
JIM DAVIS 1-18
OKAY
© 1996 PAWS, INC Distributed by Universal Press Syndicate
NOW WHAT?

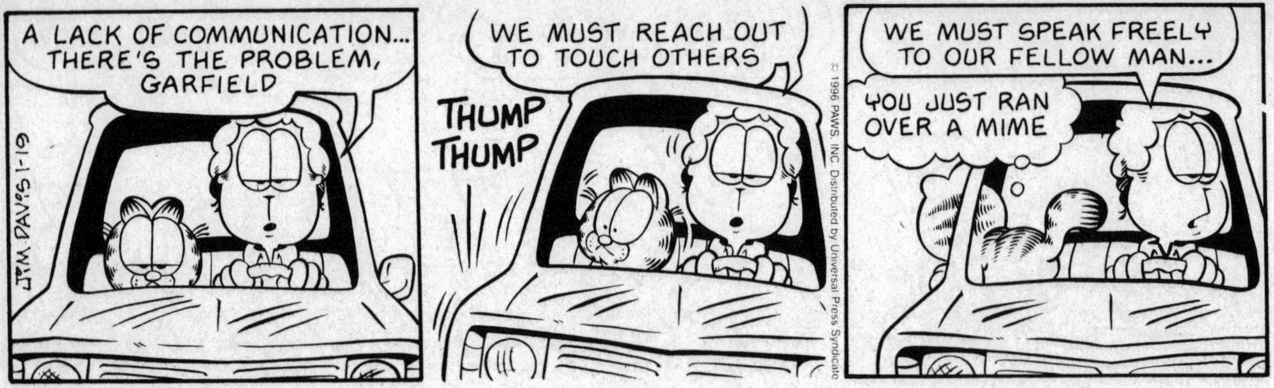
A LACK OF COMMUNICATION... THERE'S THE PROBLEM, GARFIELD
JIM DAVIS 1-19
WE MUST REACH OUT TO TOUCH OTHERS
THUMP THUMP
© 1996 PAWS, INC. Distributed by Universal Press Syndicate
WE MUST SPEAK FREELY TO OUR FELLOW MAN...
YOU JUST RAN OVER A MIME

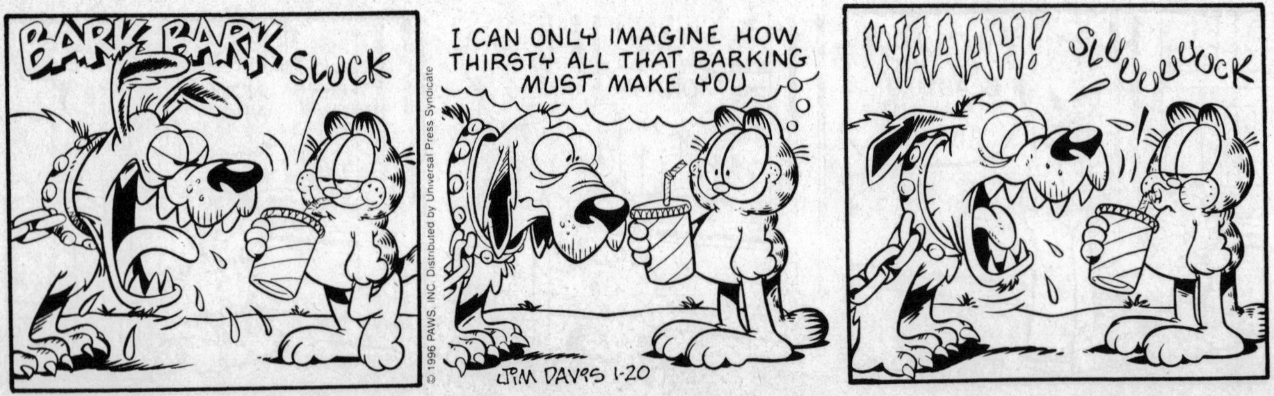
BARK BARK
SLUCK
© 1996 PAWS, INC. Distributed by Universal Press Syndicate
I CAN ONLY IMAGINE HOW THIRSTY ALL THAT BARKING MUST MAKE YOU
JIM DAVIS 1-20
WAAAH!
SLUUUUUUCK

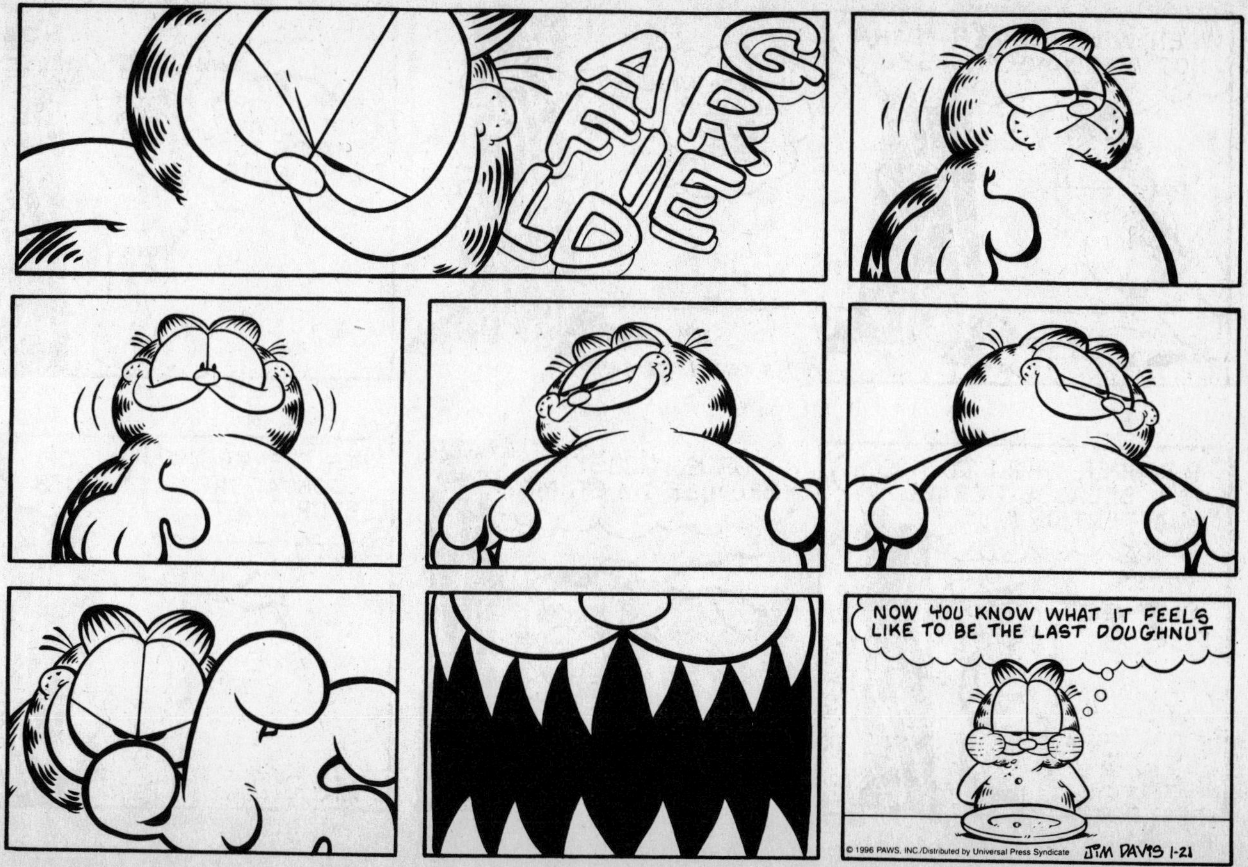
GARFIELD
NOW YOU KNOW WHAT IT FEELS LIKE TO BE THE LAST DOUGHNUT
© 1996 PAWS, INC./Distributed by Universal Press Syndicate
JIM DAVIS 1-21

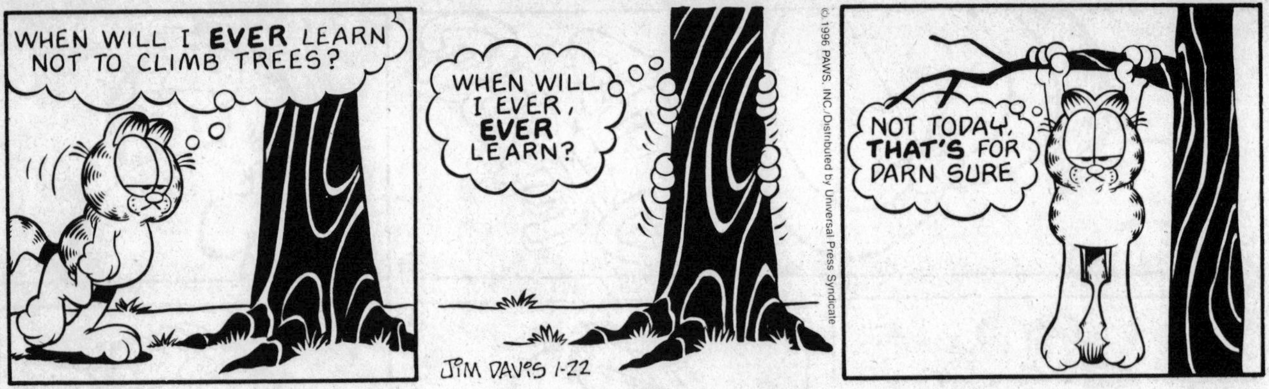
WHEN WILL I **EVER** LEARN NOT TO CLIMB TREES?
WHEN WILL I EVER, I EVER, **EVER** LEARN?
JIM DAVIS 1-22
© 1996 PAWS, INC./Distributed by Universal Press Syndicate
NOT TODAY, **THAT'S** FOR DARN SURE

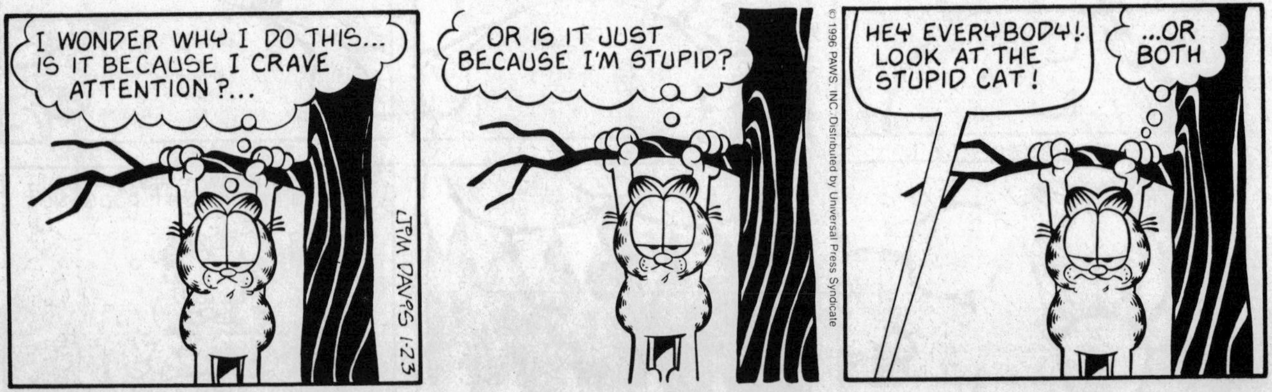
I WONDER WHY I DO THIS... IS IT BECAUSE I CRAVE ATTENTION?...
JIM DAVIS 1-23
OR IS IT JUST BECAUSE I'M STUPID?
© 1996 PAWS, INC./Distributed by Universal Press Syndicate
HEY EVERYBODY! LOOK AT THE STUPID CAT!
...OR BOTH

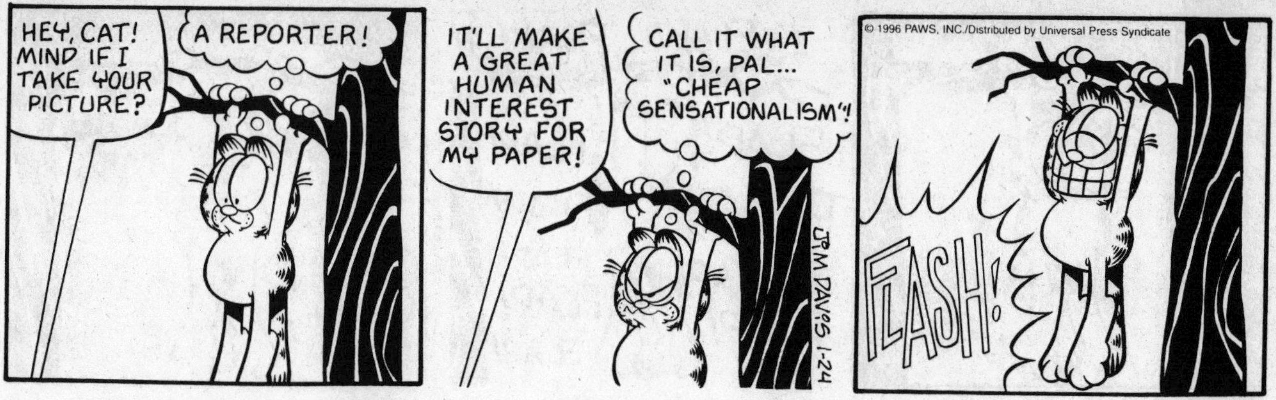
HEY, CAT! MIND IF I TAKE YOUR PICTURE?
A REPORTER!
IT'LL MAKE A GREAT HUMAN INTEREST STORY FOR MY PAPER!
CALL IT WHAT IT IS, PAL... "CHEAP SENSATIONALISM"!
JPM DAVIS 1-24
© 1996 PAWS, INC./Distributed by Universal Press Syndicate
FLASH!

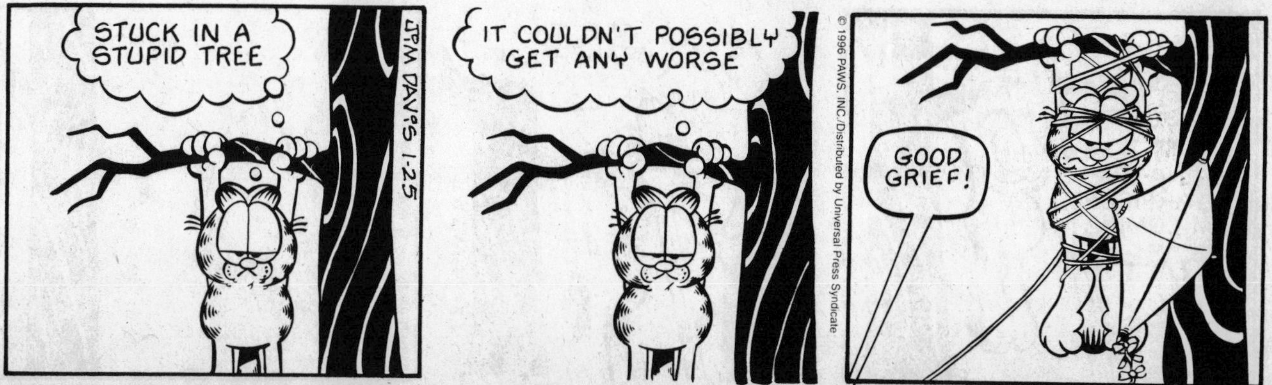
STUCK IN A STUPID TREE
JPM DAVIS 1-25
IT COULDN'T POSSIBLY GET ANY WORSE
© 1996 PAWS, INC./Distributed by Universal Press Syndicate
GOOD GRIEF!

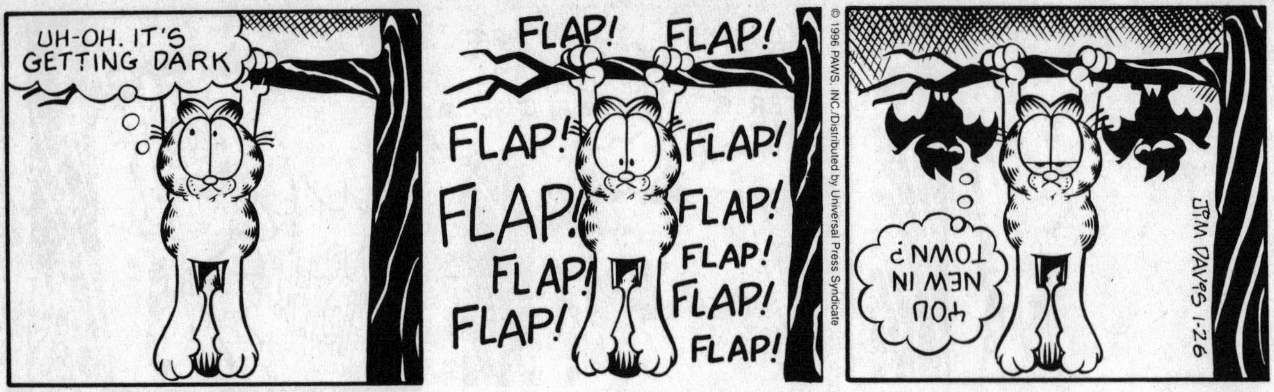
UH-OH. IT'S GETTING DARK
FLAP! FLAP!
FLAP! FLAP!
FLAP! FLAP!
FLAP! FLAP!
FLAP! FLAP!
FLAP!
YOU NEW IN TOWN?
JIM DAVIS 1-26
© 1996 PAWS, INC./Distributed by Universal Press Syndicate

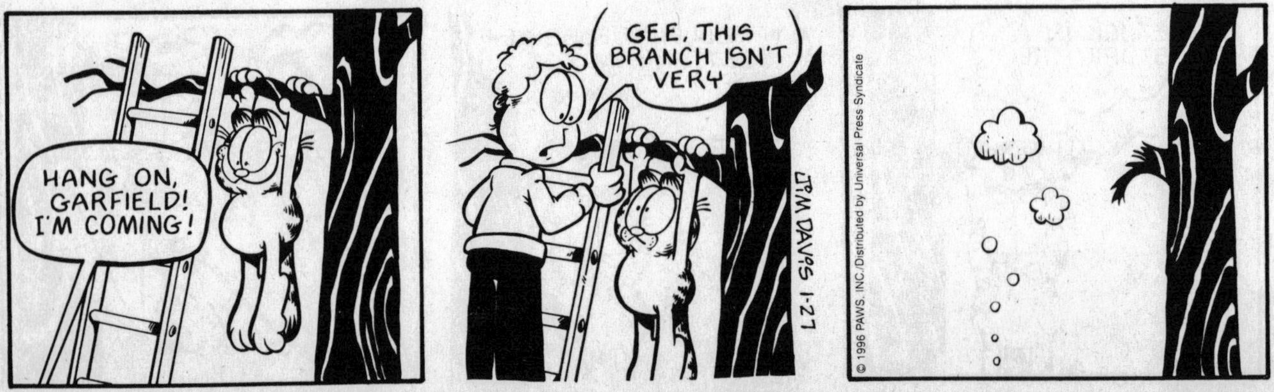
HANG ON, GARFIELD! I'M COMING!
GEE, THIS BRANCH ISN'T VERY
JIM DAVIS 1-27
© 1996 PAWS, INC./Distributed by Universal Press Syndicate

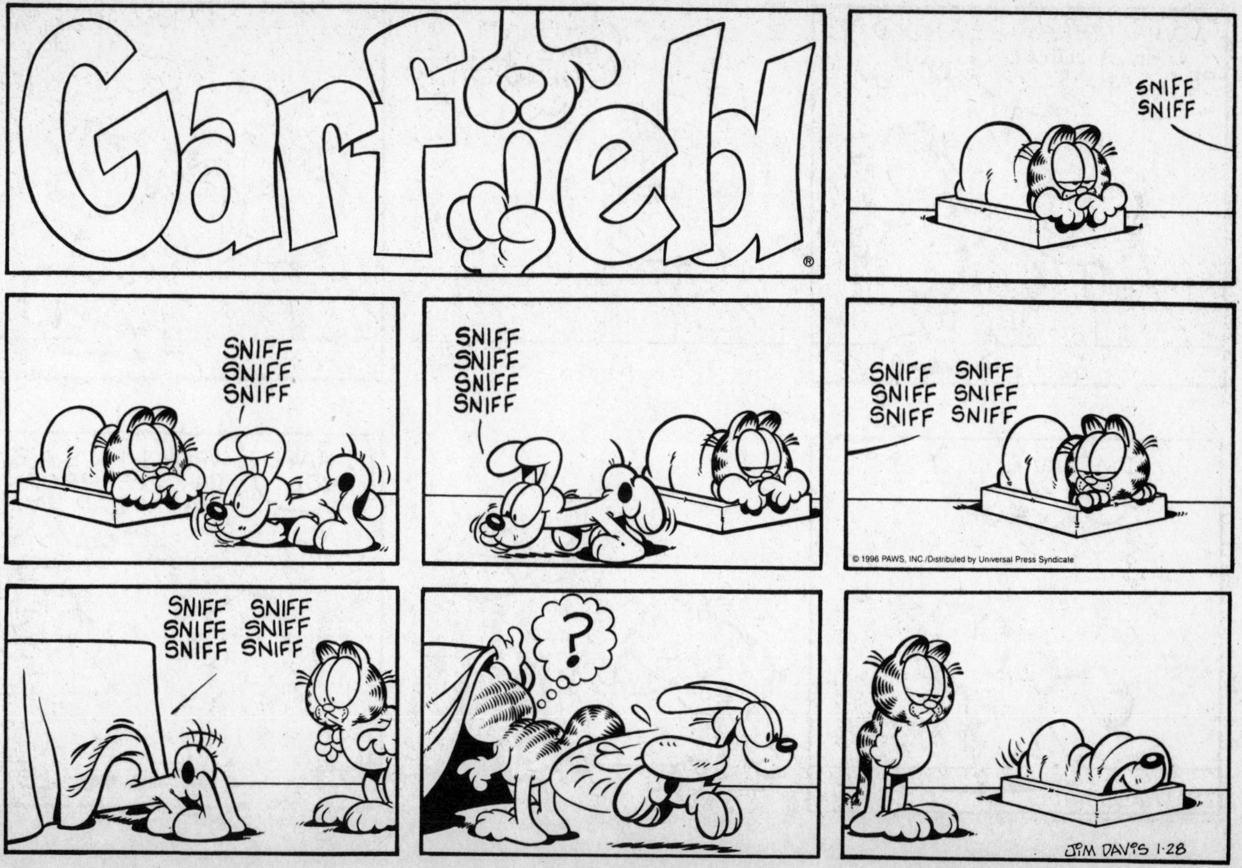
Garfield®
SNIFF SNIFF
SNIFF SNIFF SNIFF
SNIFF SNIFF SNIFF SNIFF
SNIFF SNIFF SNIFF SNIFF SNIFF SNIFF
© 1996 PAWS, INC./Distributed by Universal Press Syndicate
SNIFF SNIFF SNIFF SNIFF SNIFF SNIFF
?
JIM DAVIS 1·28

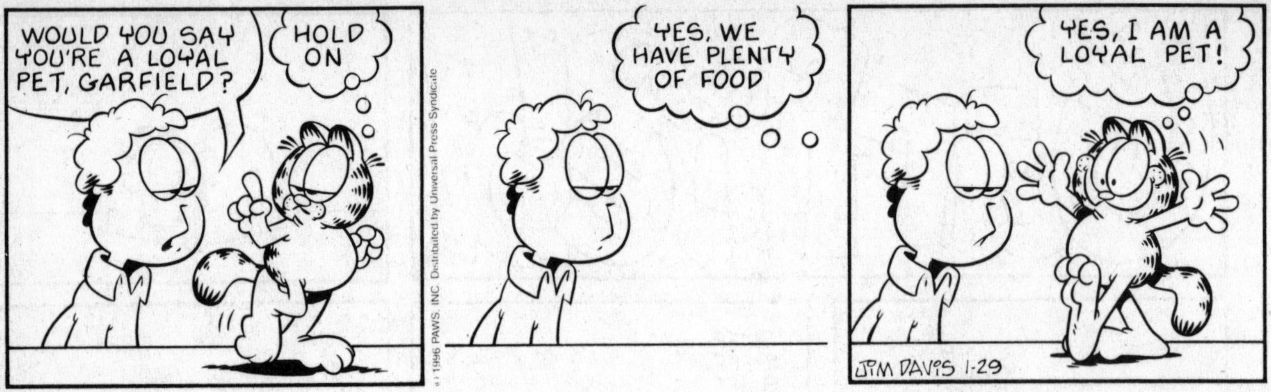
WOULD YOU SAY YOU'RE A LOYAL PET, GARFIELD?
HOLD ON
© 1996 PAWS, INC. Distributed by Universal Press Syndicate
YES, WE HAVE PLENTY OF FOOD
YES, I AM A LOYAL PET!
JIM DAVIS 1-29

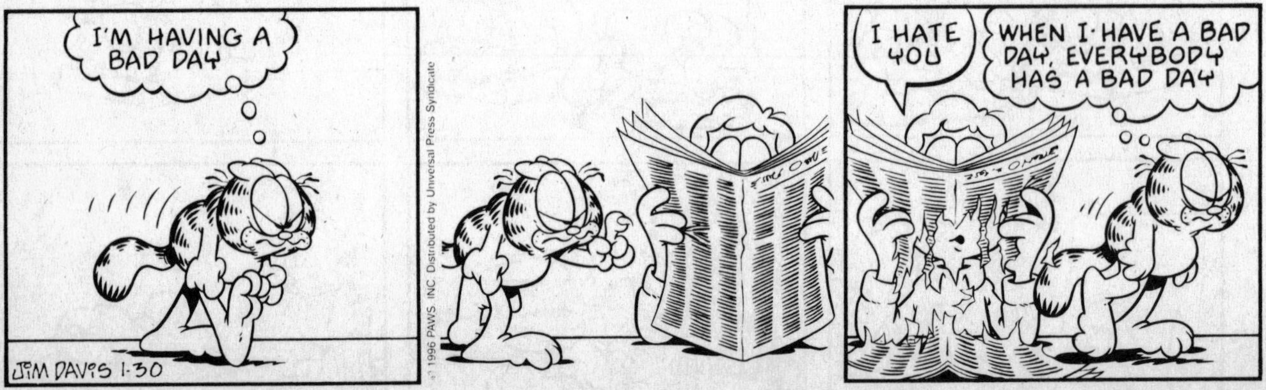
I'M HAVING A BAD DAY
JIM DAVIS 1-30
© 1996 PAWS, INC. Distributed by Universal Press Syndicate
I HATE YOU
WHEN I HAVE A BAD DAY, EVERYBODY HAS A BAD DAY

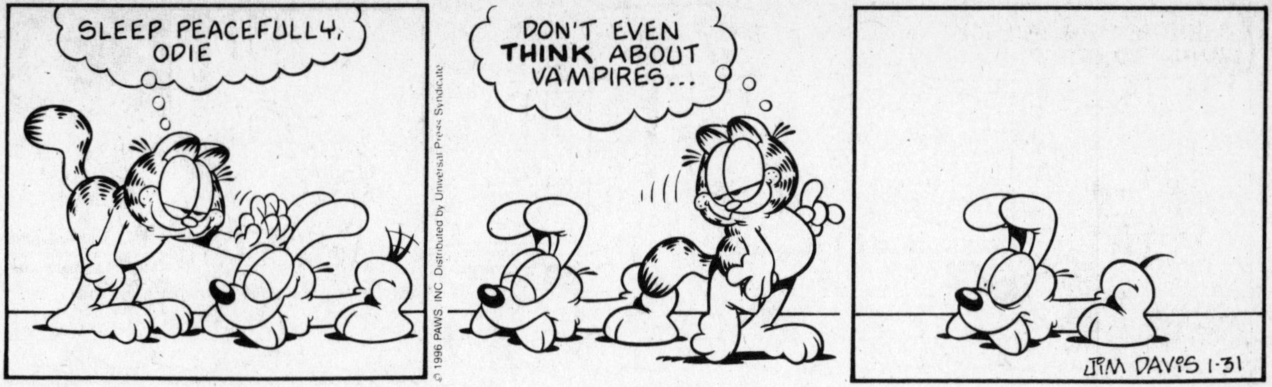
SLEEP PEACEFULLY, ODIE
DON'T EVEN **THINK** ABOUT VAMPIRES...
JIM DAVIS 1-31
© 1996 PAWS, INC. Distributed by Universal Press Syndicate

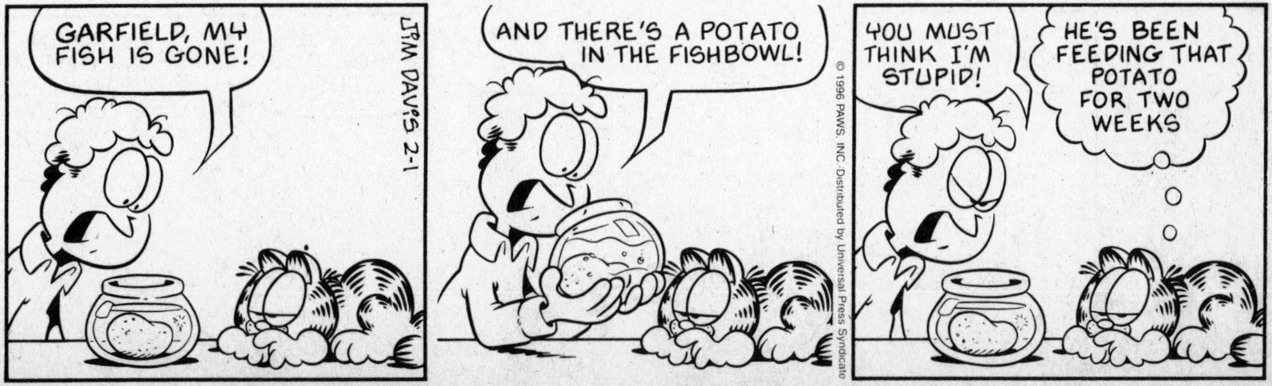
GARFIELD, MY FISH IS GONE!
JIM DAVIS 2-1
AND THERE'S A POTATO IN THE FISHBOWL!
© 1996 PAWS, INC. Distributed by Universal Press Syndicate
YOU MUST THINK I'M STUPID!
HE'S BEEN FEEDING THAT POTATO FOR TWO WEEKS

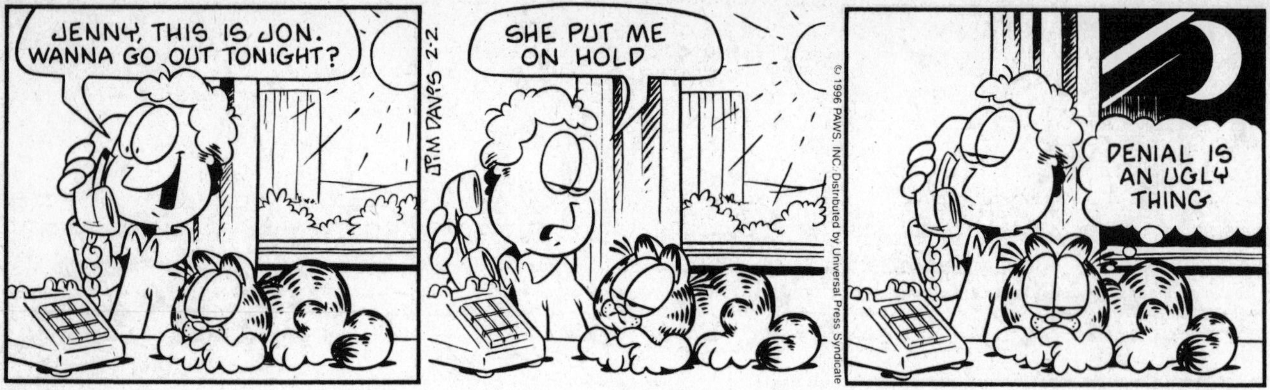
JENNY, THIS IS JON. WANNA GO OUT TONIGHT?
JIM DAVIS 2-2
SHE PUT ME ON HOLD
© 1996 PAWS, INC. Distributed by Universal Press Syndicate
DENIAL IS AN UGLY THING

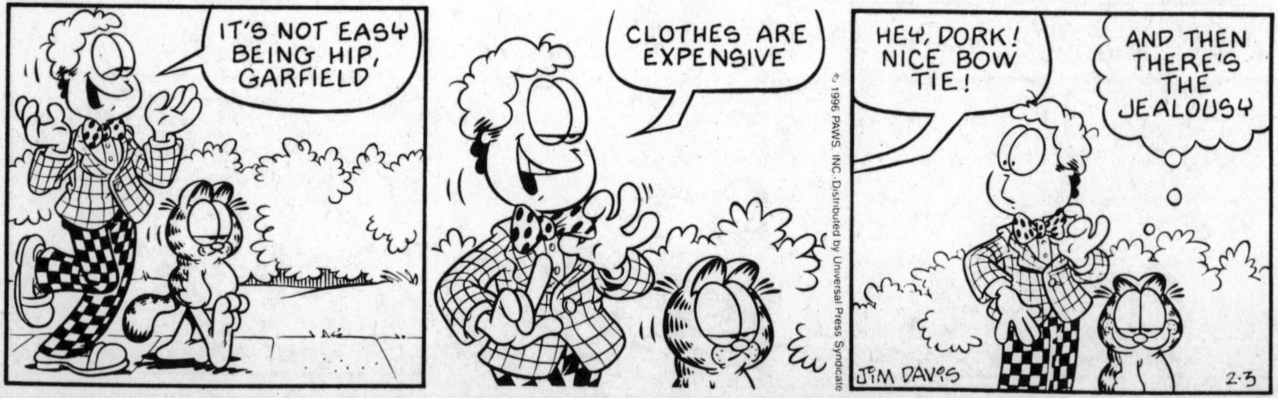
IT'S NOT EASY BEING HIP, GARFIELD
CLOTHES ARE EXPENSIVE
© 1996 PAWS, INC. Distributed by Universal Press Syndicate
HEY, DORK! NICE BOW TIE!
AND THEN THERE'S THE JEALOUSY
JIM DAVIS
2-3

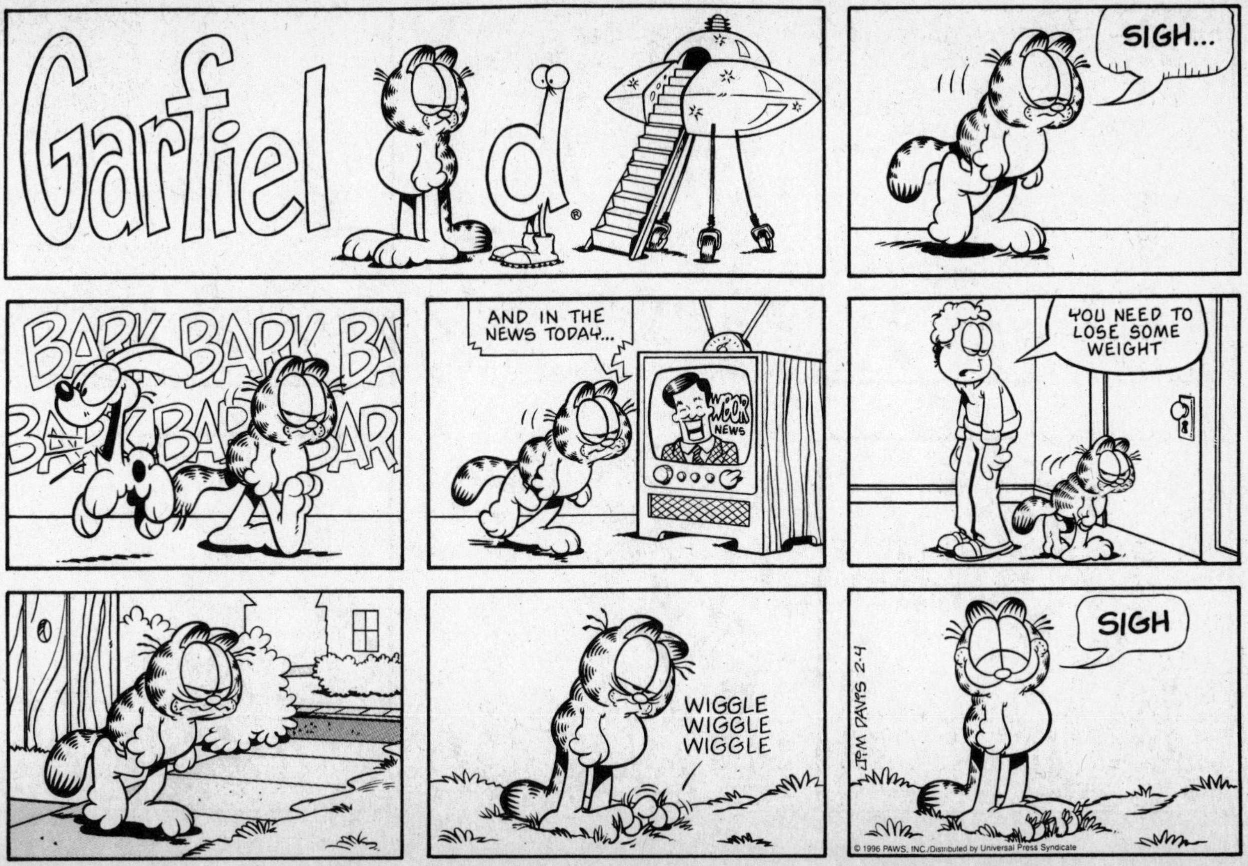
Garfield
SIGH...
BARK BARK BARK BARK BARK
AND IN THE NEWS TODAY...
WOOR NEWS
YOU NEED TO LOSE SOME WEIGHT
WIGGLE WIGGLE WIGGLE
JIM DAVIS 2-4
SIGH
© 1996 PAWS, INC./Distributed by Universal Press Syndicate

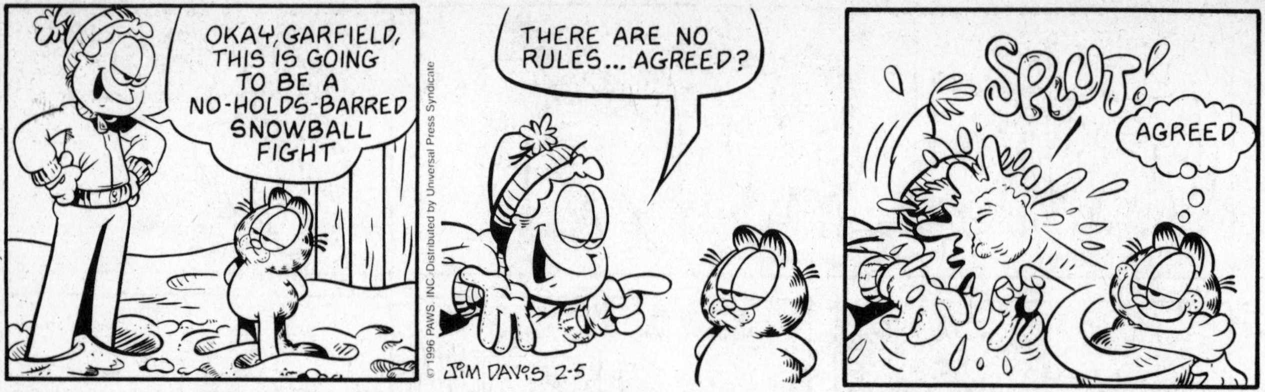
OKAY, GARFIELD, THIS IS GOING TO BE A NO-HOLDS-BARRED SNOWBALL FIGHT
THERE ARE NO RULES... AGREED?
SPLUT!
AGREED
JIM DAVIS 2-5
© 1996 PAWS, INC./Distributed by Universal Press Syndicate

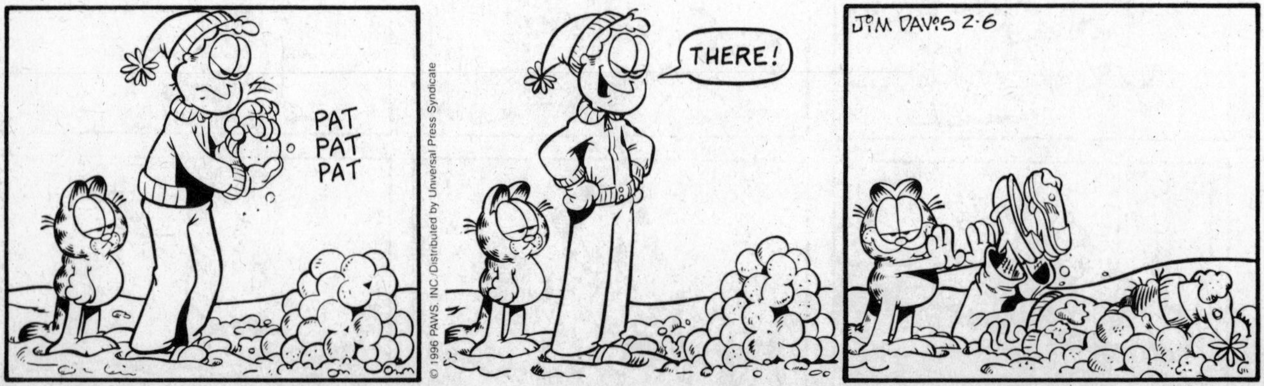
PAT PAT PAT
THERE!
JIM DAVIS 2-6
© 1996 PAWS, INC./Distributed by Universal Press Syndicate

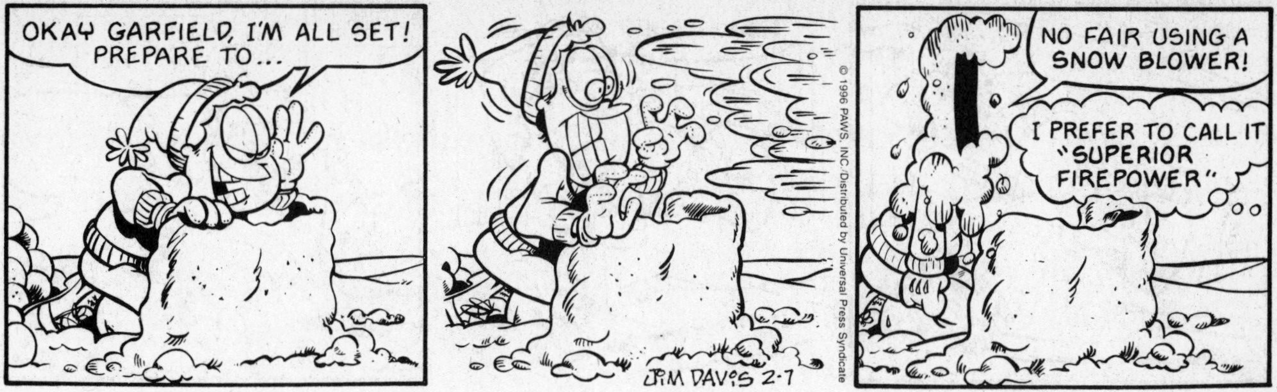
OKAY GARFIELD, I'M ALL SET! PREPARE TO...
JIM DAVIS 2-7
© 1996 PAWS, INC./Distributed by Universal Press Syndicate
NO FAIR USING A SNOW BLOWER!
I PREFER TO CALL IT "SUPERIOR FIREPOWER"

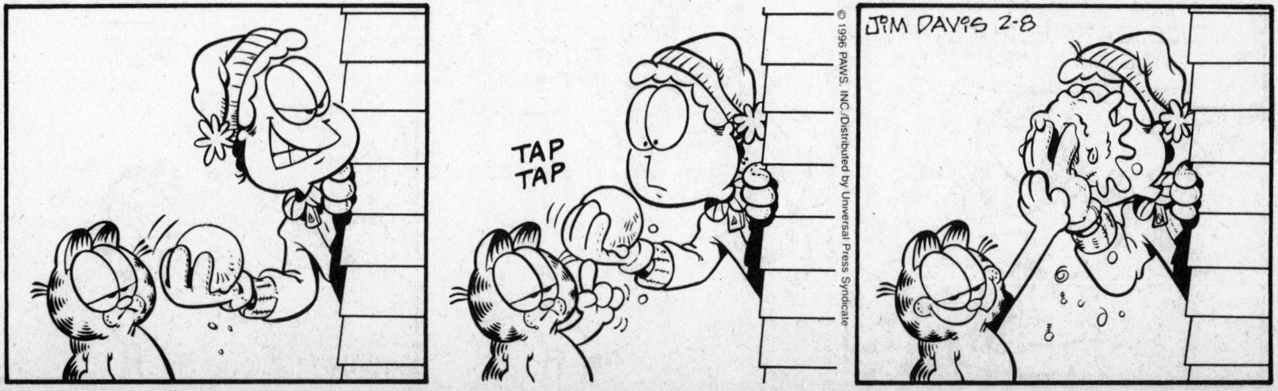
TAP
TAP
© 1996 PAWS, INC./Distributed by Universal Press Syndicate
JIM DAVIS 2-8

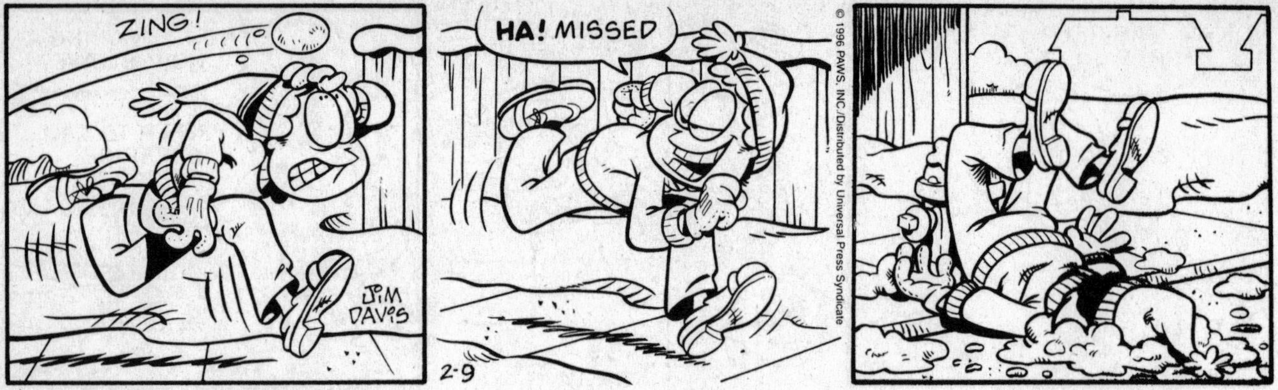
ZING!
HA! MISSED
JIM DAVIS
2-9
© 1996 PAWS, INC./Distributed by Universal Press Syndicate

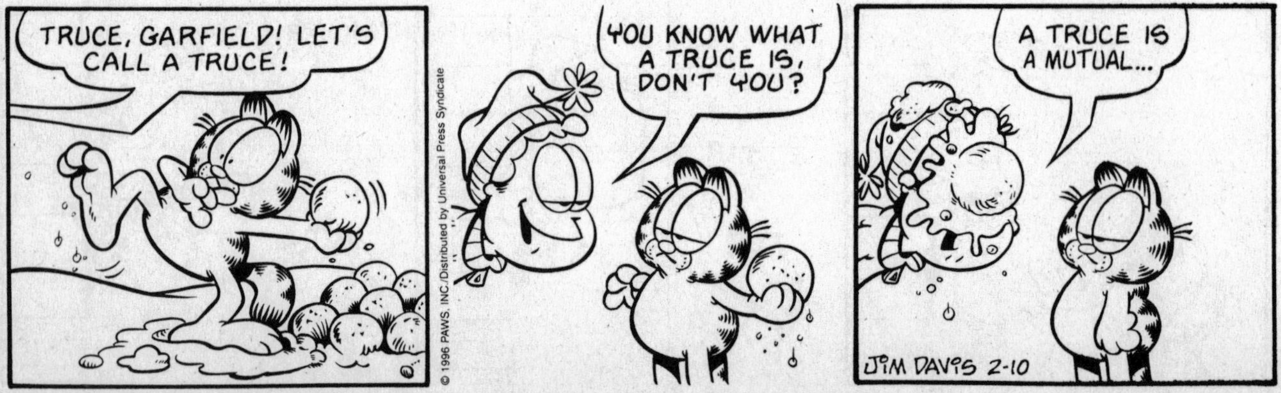
TRUCE, GARFIELD! LET'S CALL A TRUCE!
YOU KNOW WHAT A TRUCE IS, DON'T YOU?
A TRUCE IS A MUTUAL...
JIM DAVIS 2-10
© 1996 PAWS, INC./Distributed by Universal Press Syndicate

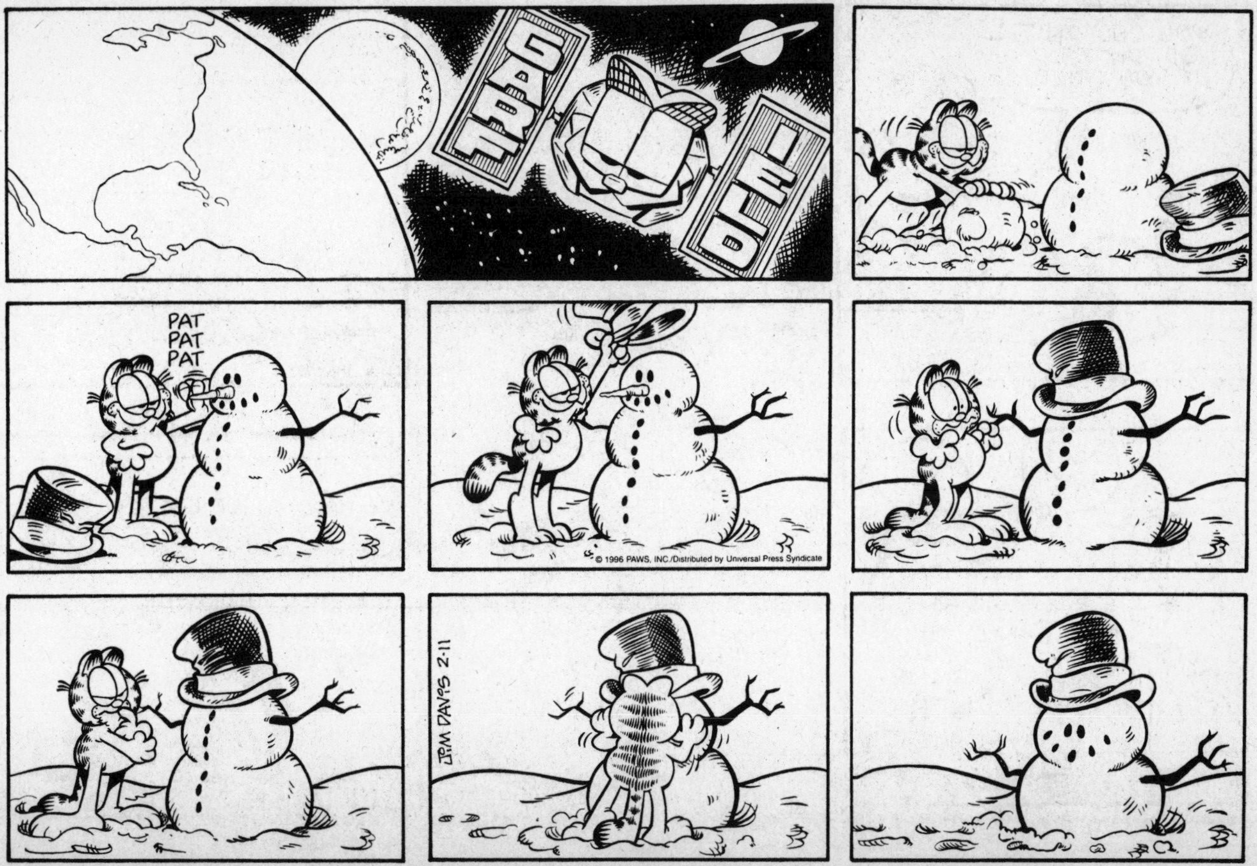
GARFIELD
PAT
PAT
PAT
© 1996 PAWS, INC./Distributed by Universal Press Syndicate
JIM DAVIS 2-11

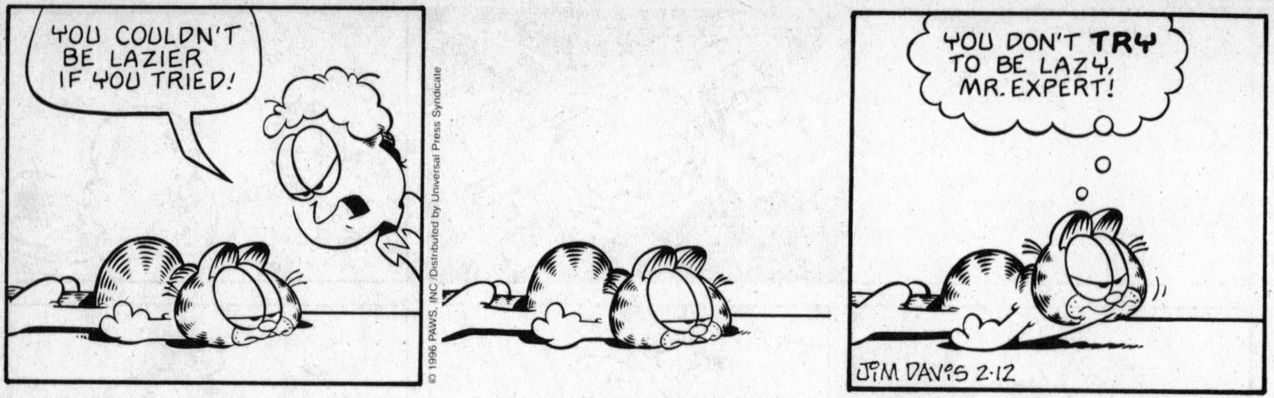
YOU COULDN'T BE LAZIER IF YOU TRIED!
YOU DON'T TRY TO BE LAZY, MR. EXPERT!
JIM DAVIS 2-12
© 1996 PAWS, INC./Distributed by Universal Press Syndicate

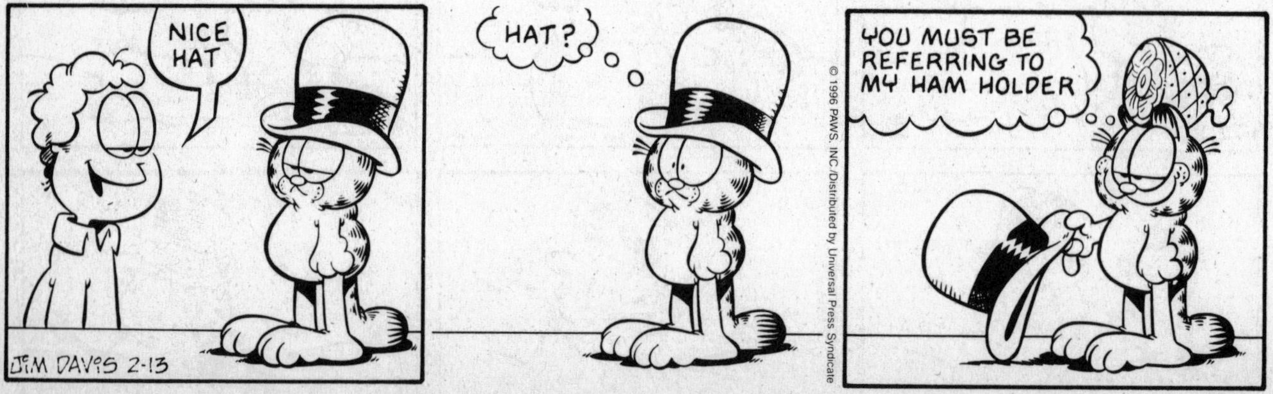
NICE HAT
HAT?
YOU MUST BE REFERRING TO MY HAM HOLDER
JIM DAVIS 2-13
© 1996 PAWS, INC./Distributed by Universal Press Syndicate

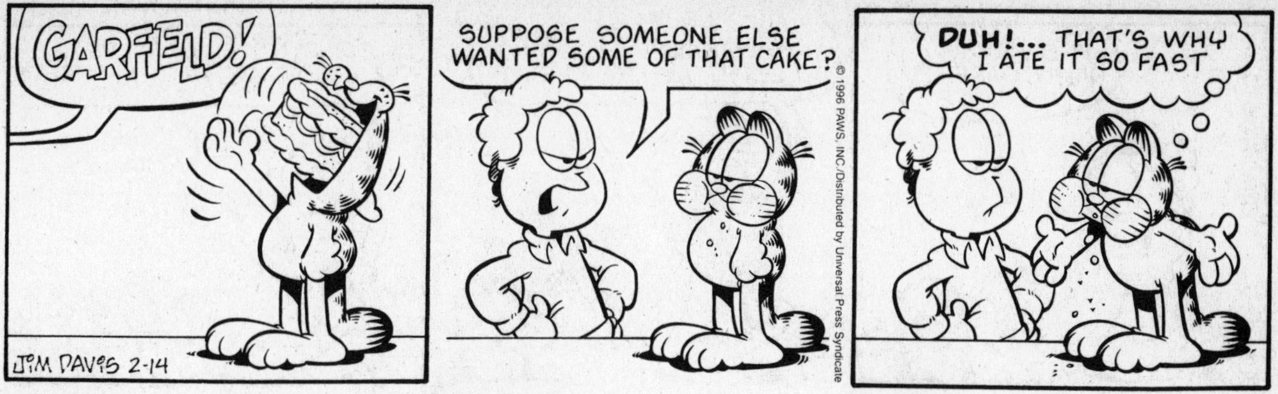
GARFIELD!
SUPPOSE SOMEONE ELSE WANTED SOME OF THAT CAKE?
DUH!... THAT'S WHY I ATE IT SO FAST
JIM DAVIS 2-14
© 1996 PAWS, INC./Distributed by Universal Press Syndicate

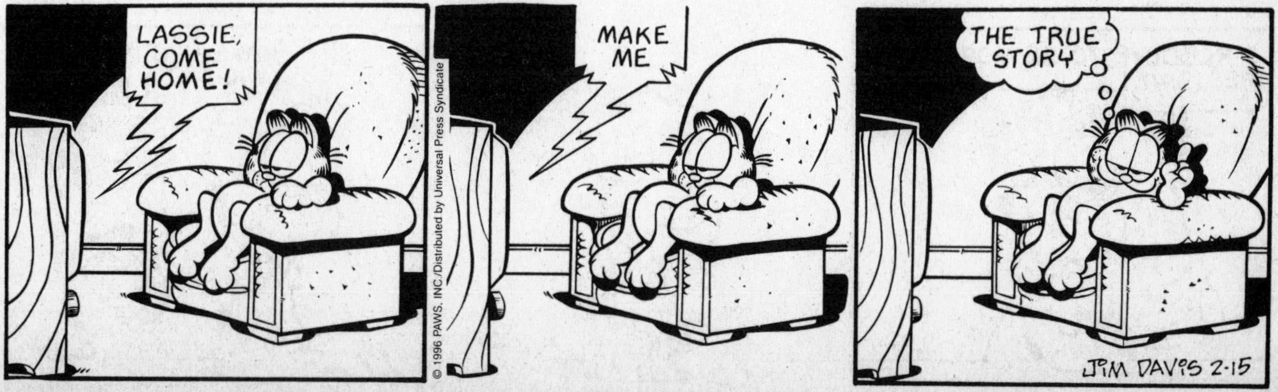
LASSIE, COME HOME!
MAKE ME
THE TRUE STORY
JIM DAVIS 2-15
© 1996 PAWS, INC./Distributed by Universal Press Syndicate

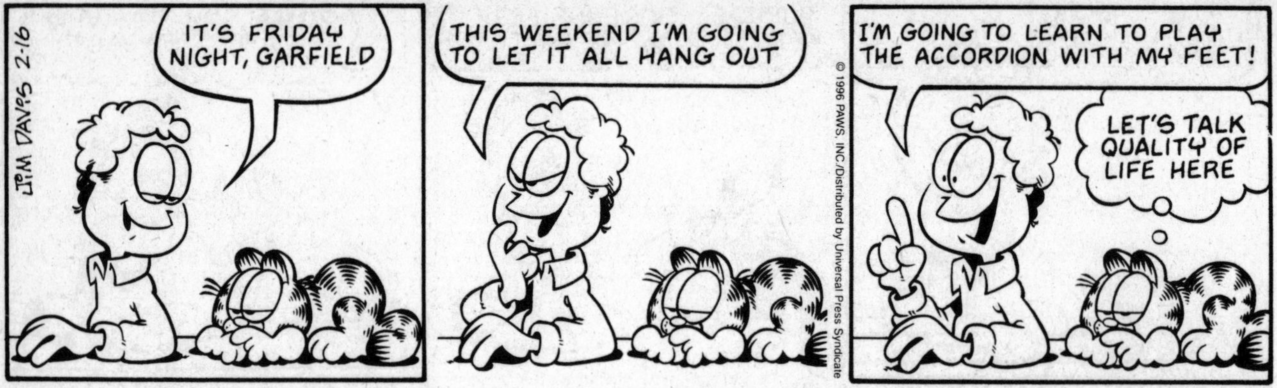
JIM DAVIS 2·16
IT'S FRIDAY NIGHT, GARFIELD
THIS WEEKEND I'M GOING TO LET IT ALL HANG OUT
I'M GOING TO LEARN TO PLAY THE ACCORDION WITH MY FEET!
LET'S TALK QUALITY OF LIFE HERE

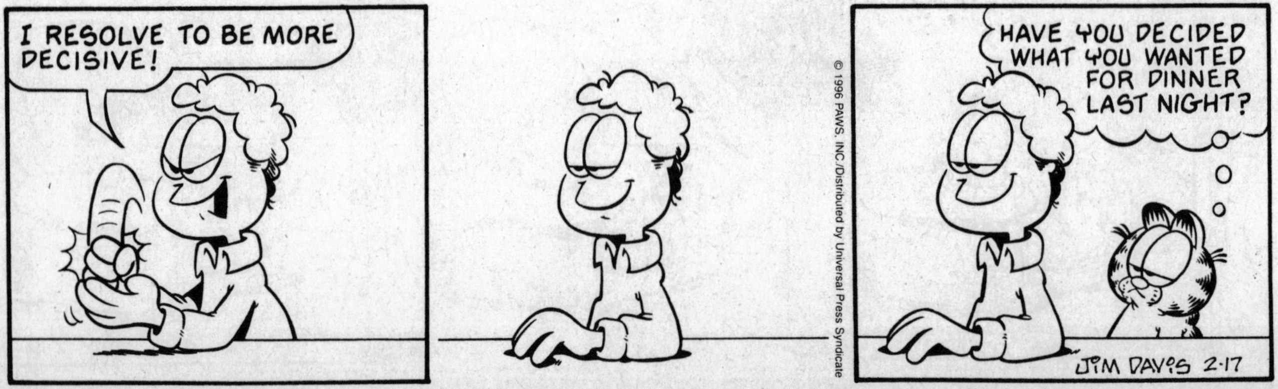
I RESOLVE TO BE MORE DECISIVE!
HAVE YOU DECIDED WHAT YOU WANTED FOR DINNER LAST NIGHT?
JIM DAVIS 2·17

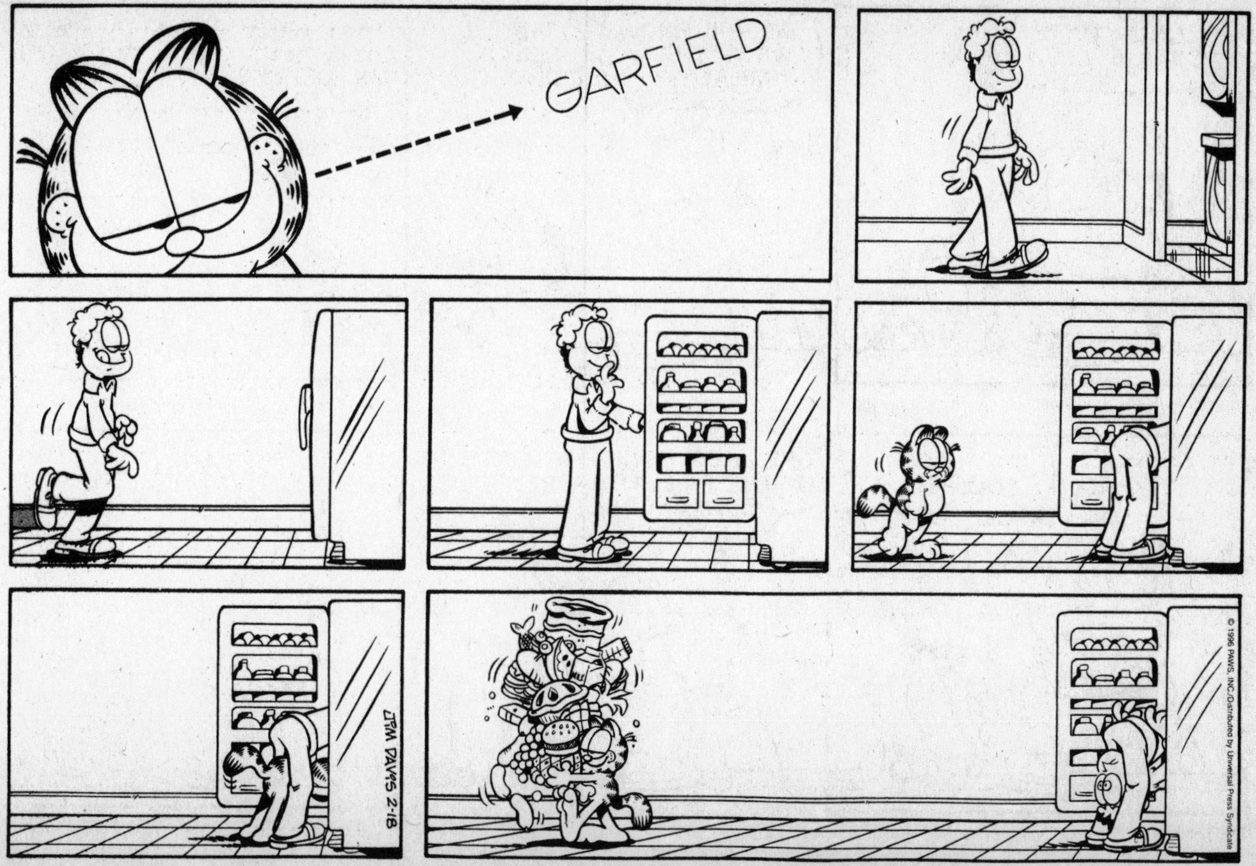
GARFIELD
JIM DAVIS 2-18
© 1996 PAWS, INC./Distributed by Universal Press Syndicate

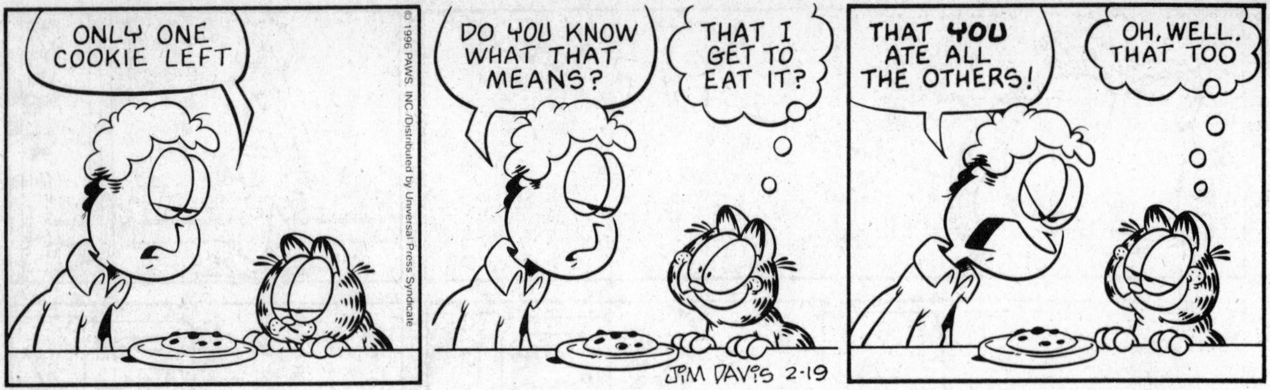
ONLY ONE COOKIE LEFT
© 1996 PAWS, INC./Distributed by Universal Press Syndicate
DO YOU KNOW WHAT THAT MEANS?
THAT I GET TO EAT IT?
JIM DAVIS 2-19
THAT YOU ATE ALL THE OTHERS!
OH, WELL. THAT TOO

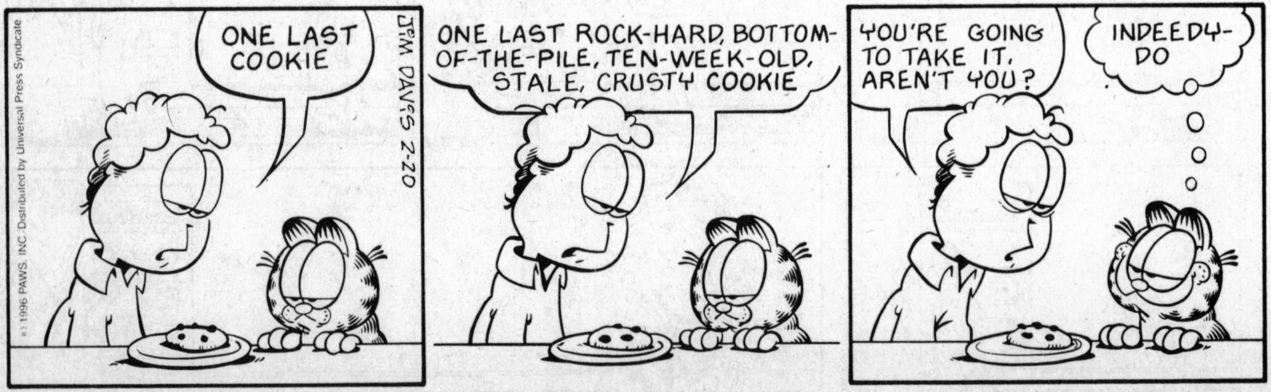
© 1996 PAWS, INC. Distributed by Universal Press Syndicate
ONE LAST COOKIE
JIM DAVIS 2-20
ONE LAST ROCK-HARD, BOTTOM-OF-THE-PILE, TEN-WEEK-OLD, STALE, CRUSTY COOKIE
YOU'RE GOING TO TAKE IT, AREN'T YOU?
INDEEDY-DO

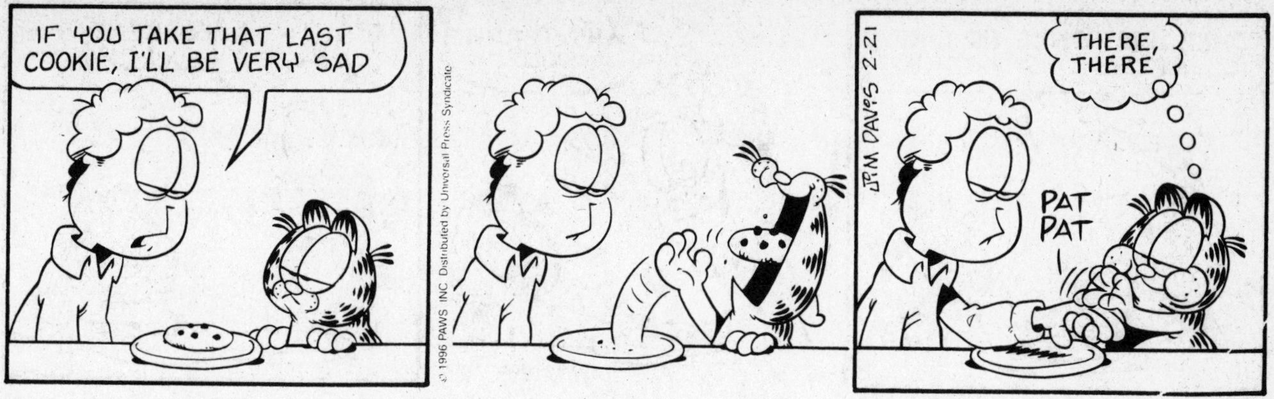
IF YOU TAKE THAT LAST COOKIE, I'LL BE VERY SAD
THERE, THERE
PAT PAT
JIM DAVIS 2-21

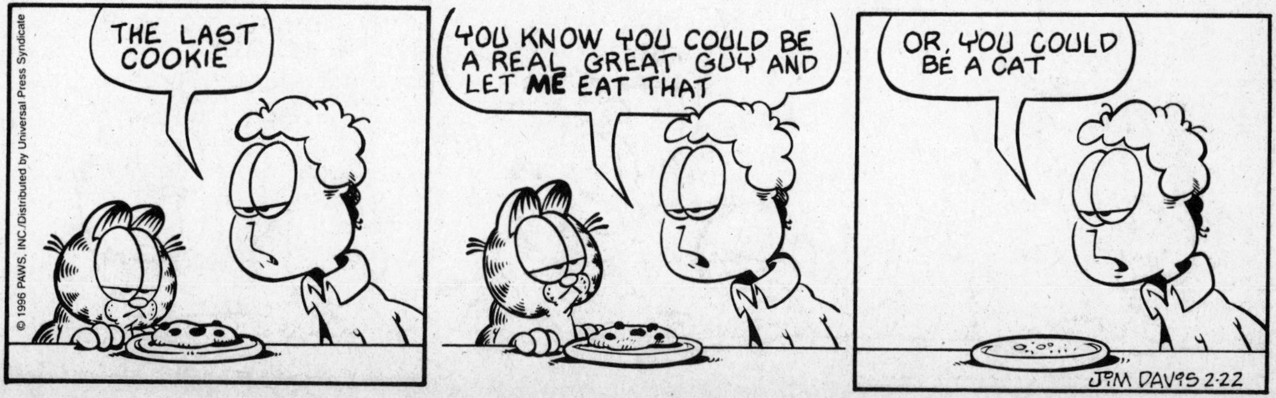
THE LAST COOKIE
YOU KNOW YOU COULD BE A REAL GREAT GUY AND LET **ME** EAT THAT
OR, YOU COULD BE A CAT
JIM DAVIS 2-22

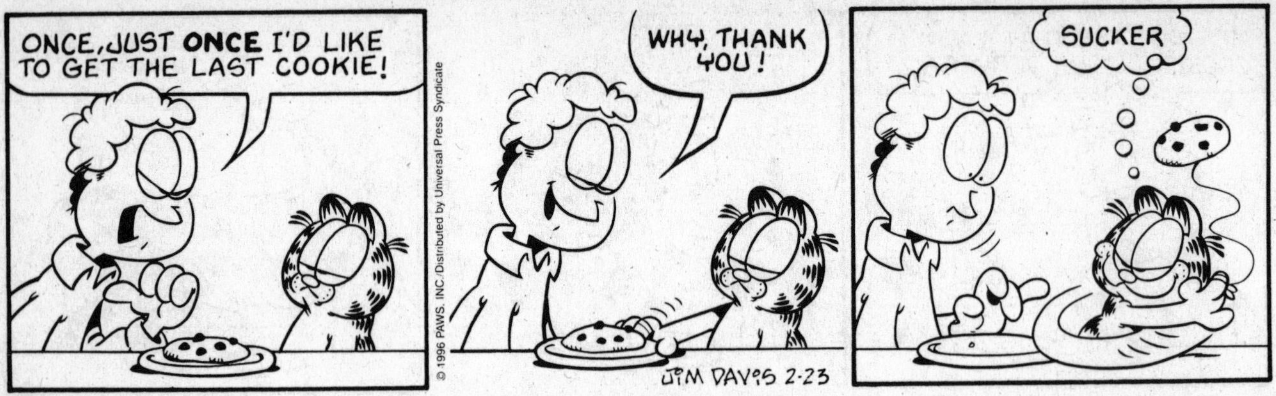
ONCE, JUST **ONCE** I'D LIKE TO GET THE LAST COOKIE!
WHY, THANK YOU!
SUCKER
JIM DAVIS 2-23

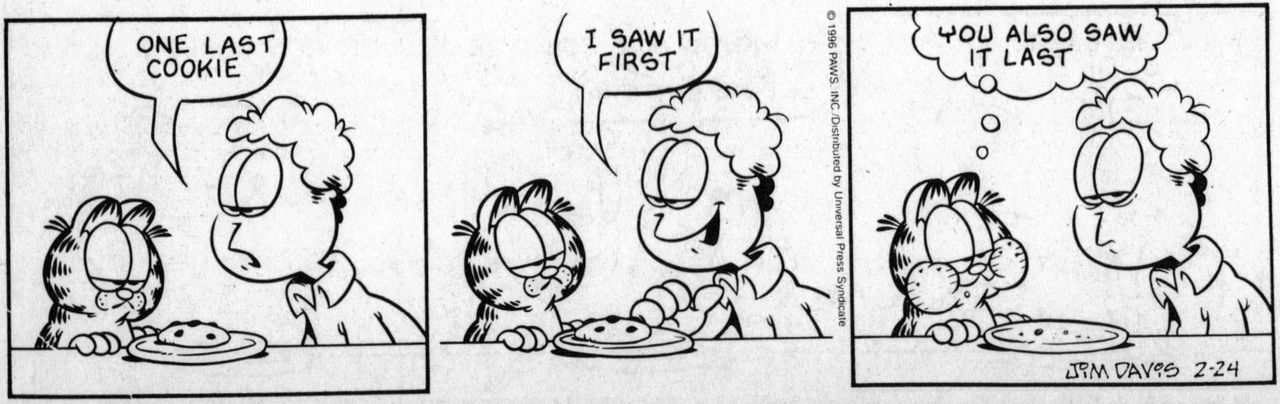
ONE LAST COOKIE
I SAW IT FIRST
YOU ALSO SAW IT LAST
JIM DAVIS 2-24

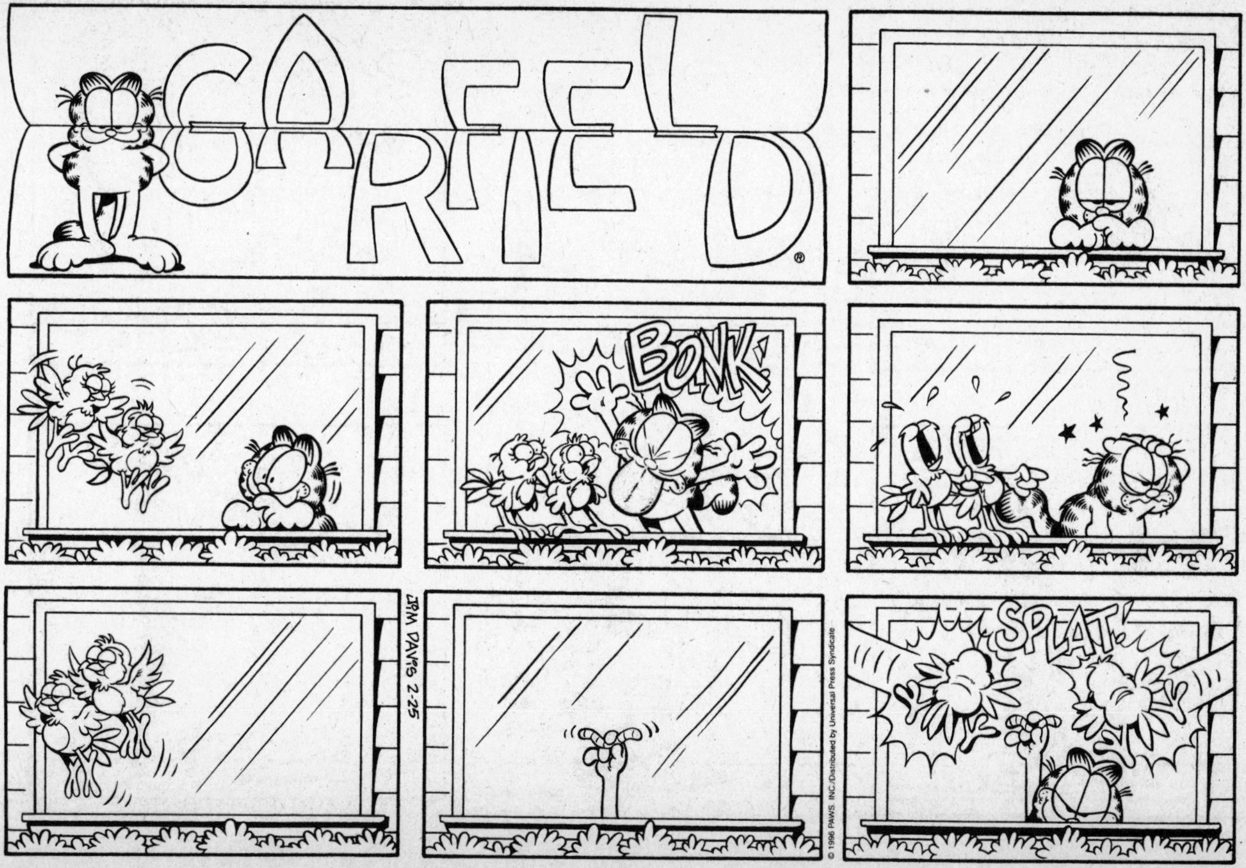
GARFIELD®
BONK
SPLAT!
JPM DAVIS 2-25

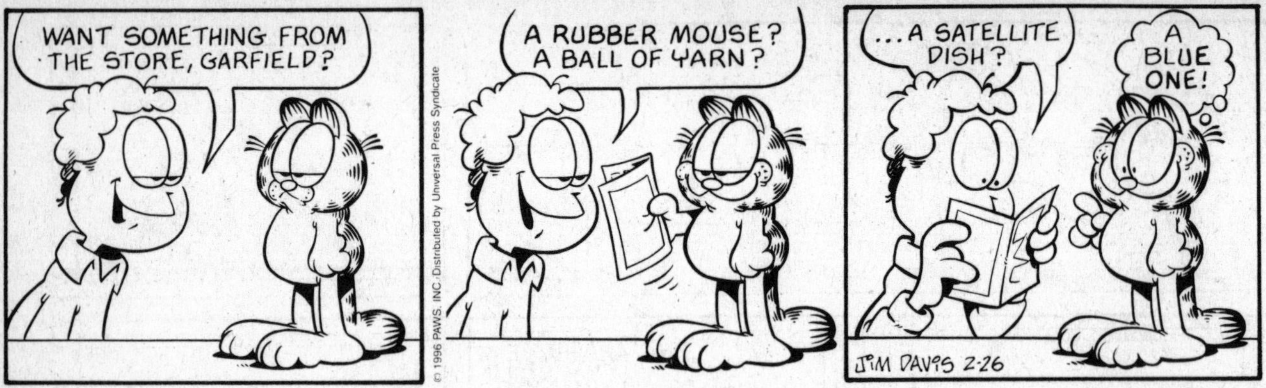
WANT SOMETHING FROM THE STORE, GARFIELD?
A RUBBER MOUSE? A BALL OF YARN?
...A SATELLITE DISH?
A BLUE ONE!
© 1996 PAWS, INC. Distributed by Universal Press Syndicate
JIM DAVIS 2-26

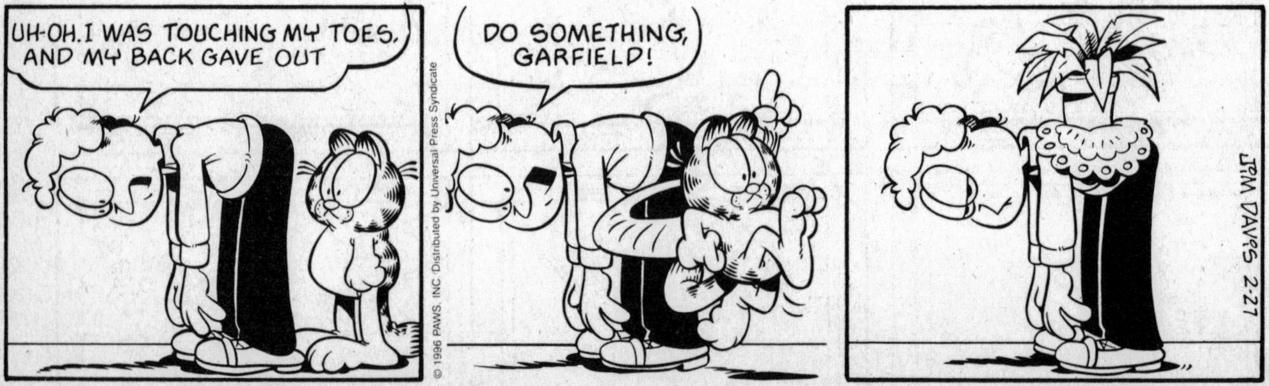
UH-OH. I WAS TOUCHING MY TOES, AND MY BACK GAVE OUT
DO SOMETHING, GARFIELD!
© 1996 PAWS, INC. Distributed by Universal Press Syndicate
JIM DAVIS 2-27

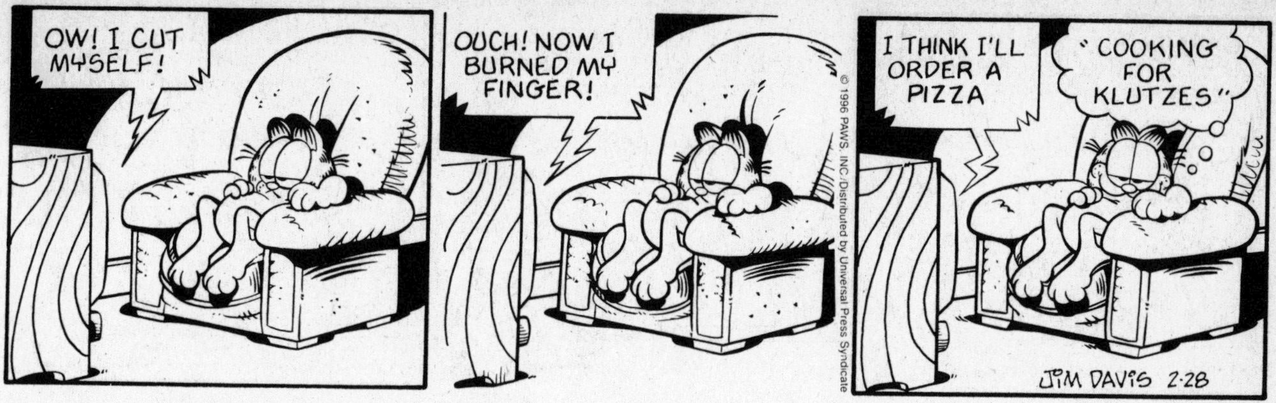
OW! I CUT MYSELF!
OUCH! NOW I BURNED MY FINGER!
I THINK I'LL ORDER A PIZZA
"COOKING FOR KLUTZES"
JIM DAVIS 2·28
© 1996 PAWS, INC./Distributed by Universal Press Syndicate

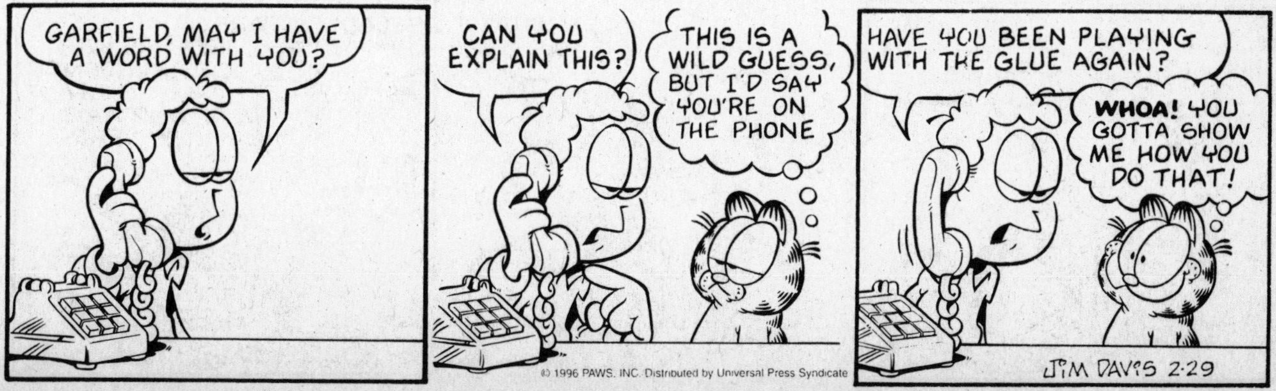
GARFIELD, MAY I HAVE A WORD WITH YOU?
CAN YOU EXPLAIN THIS?
THIS IS A WILD GUESS, BUT I'D SAY YOU'RE ON THE PHONE
HAVE YOU BEEN PLAYING WITH THE GLUE AGAIN?
WHOA! YOU GOTTA SHOW ME HOW YOU DO THAT!
JIM DAVIS 2·29
© 1996 PAWS, INC. Distributed by Universal Press Syndicate

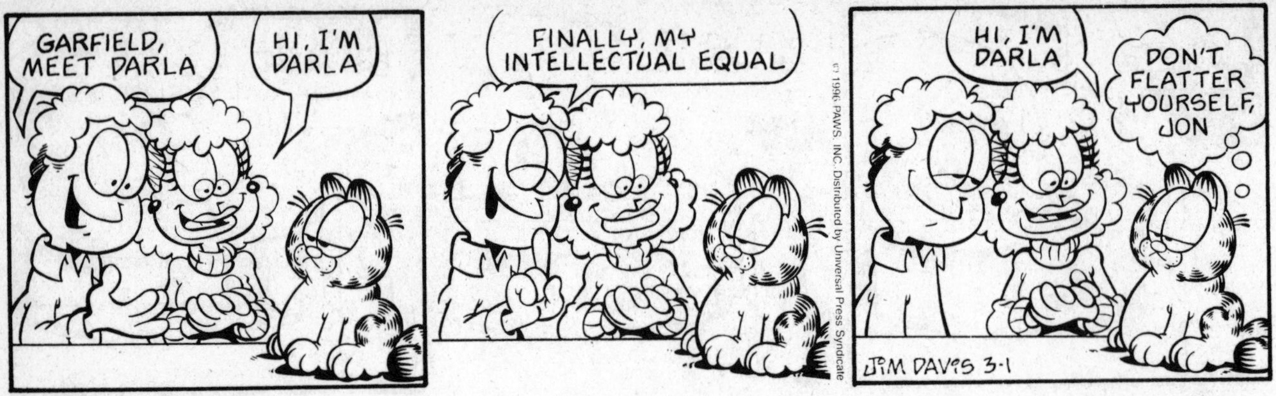
GARFIELD, MEET DARLA
HI, I'M DARLA
FINALLY, MY INTELLECTUAL EQUAL
HI, I'M DARLA
DON'T FLATTER YOURSELF, JON
JIM DAVIS 3-1

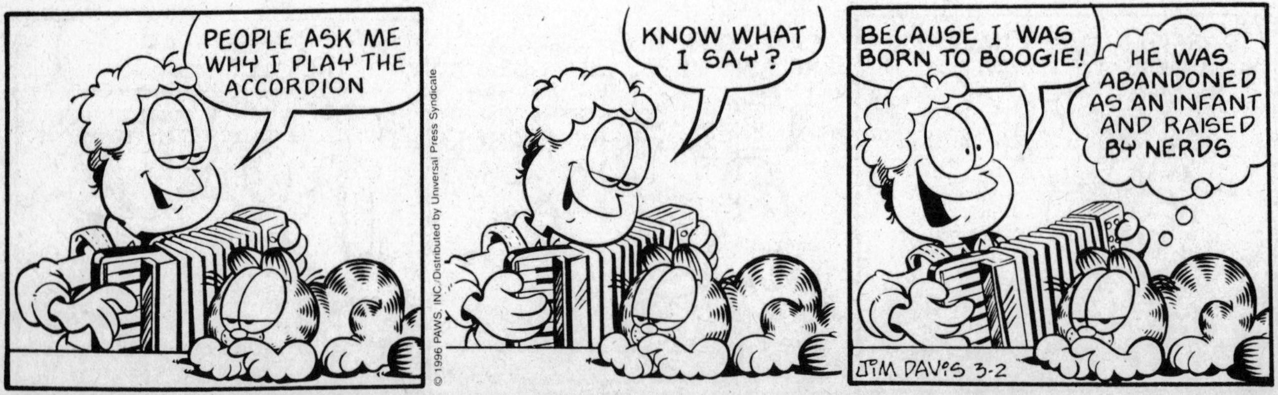
PEOPLE ASK ME WHY I PLAY THE ACCORDION
KNOW WHAT I SAY?
BECAUSE I WAS BORN TO BOOGIE!
HE WAS ABANDONED AS AN INFANT AND RAISED BY NERDS
JIM DAVIS 3-2

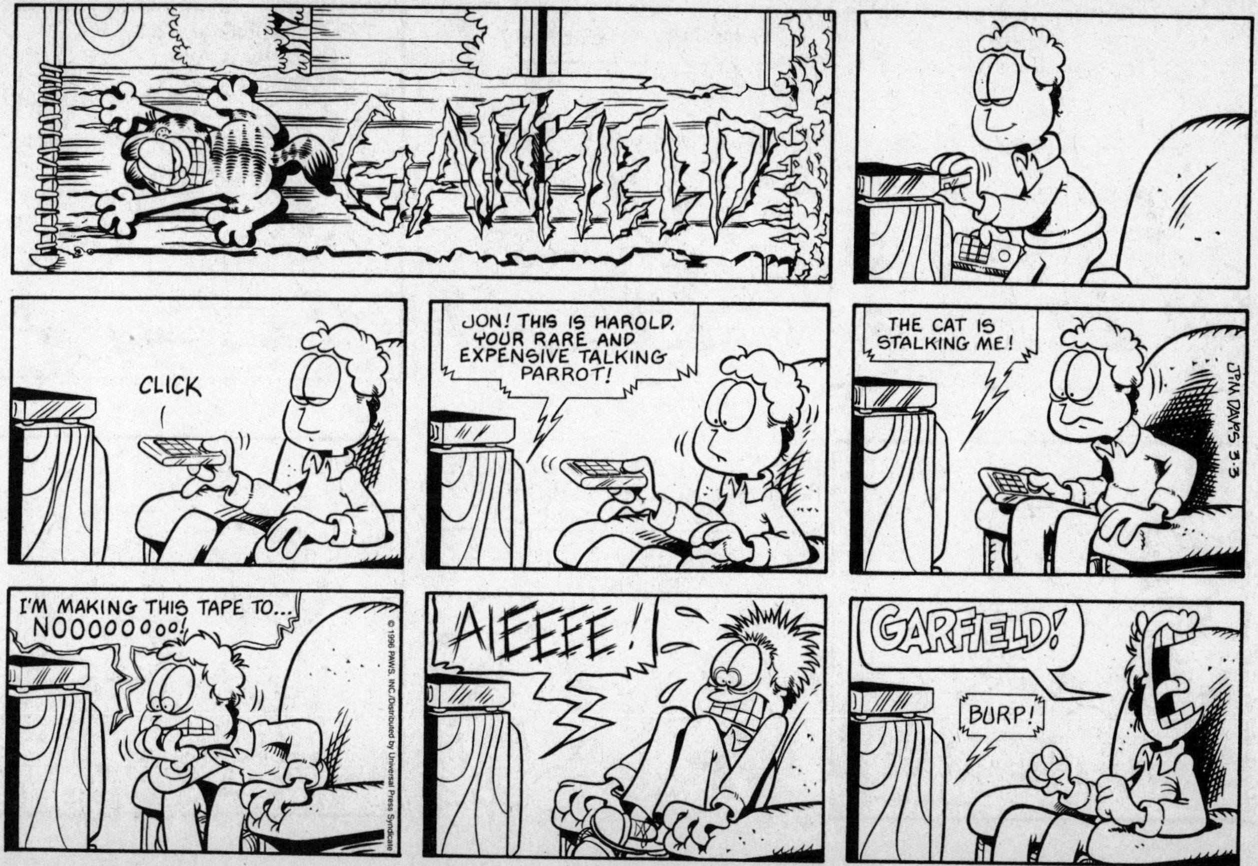
GARFIELD
CLICK
JON! THIS IS HAROLD, YOUR RARE AND EXPENSIVE TALKING PARROT!
THE CAT IS STALKING ME!
JIM DAVIS 3-3
I'M MAKING THIS TAPE TO... NOOOOOOoo!
© 1996 PAWS, INC./Distributed by Universal Press Syndicate
AEEEEE!
GARFIELD!
BURP!

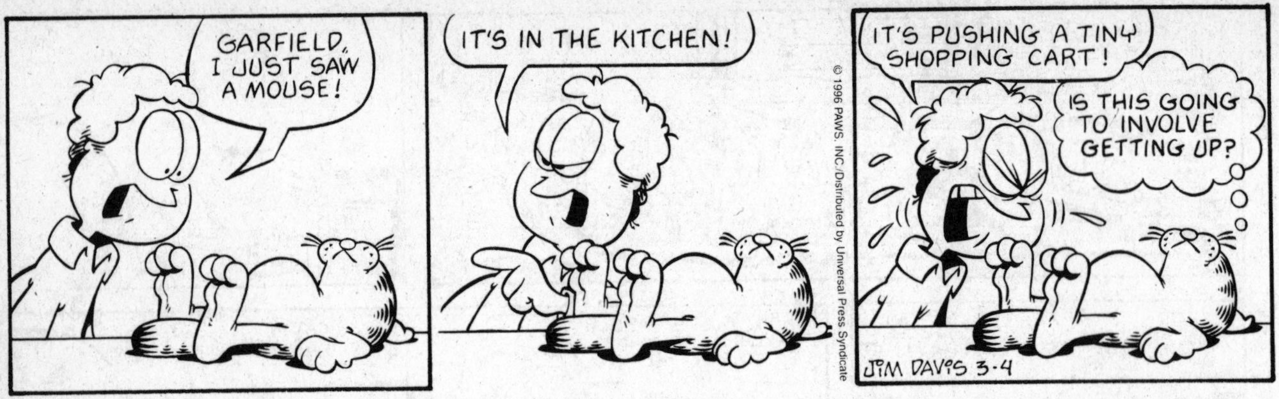
GARFIELD, I JUST SAW A MOUSE!
IT'S IN THE KITCHEN!
IT'S PUSHING A TINY SHOPPING CART!
IS THIS GOING TO INVOLVE GETTING UP?
JIM DAVIS 3-4

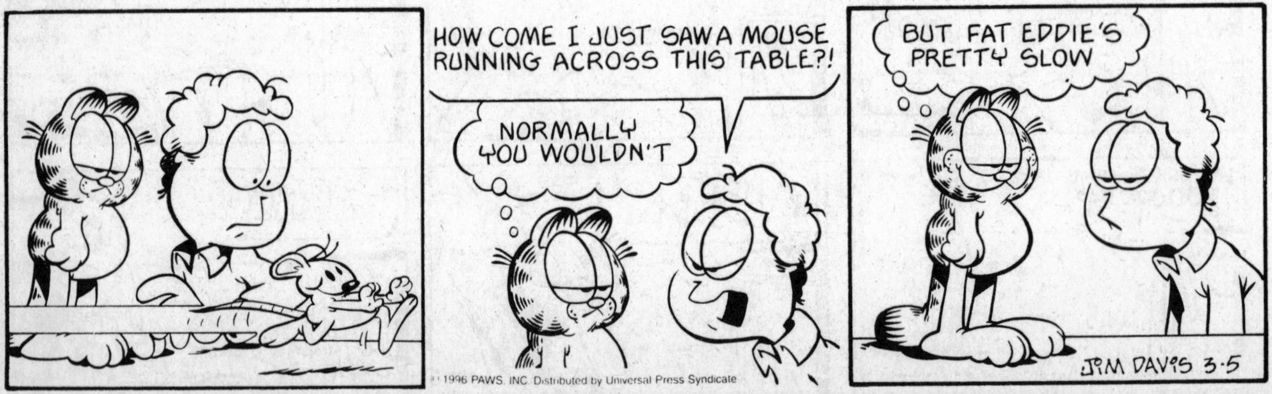
HOW COME I JUST SAW A MOUSE RUNNING ACROSS THIS TABLE?!
NORMALLY YOU WOULDN'T
BUT FAT EDDIE'S PRETTY SLOW
JIM DAVIS 3-5

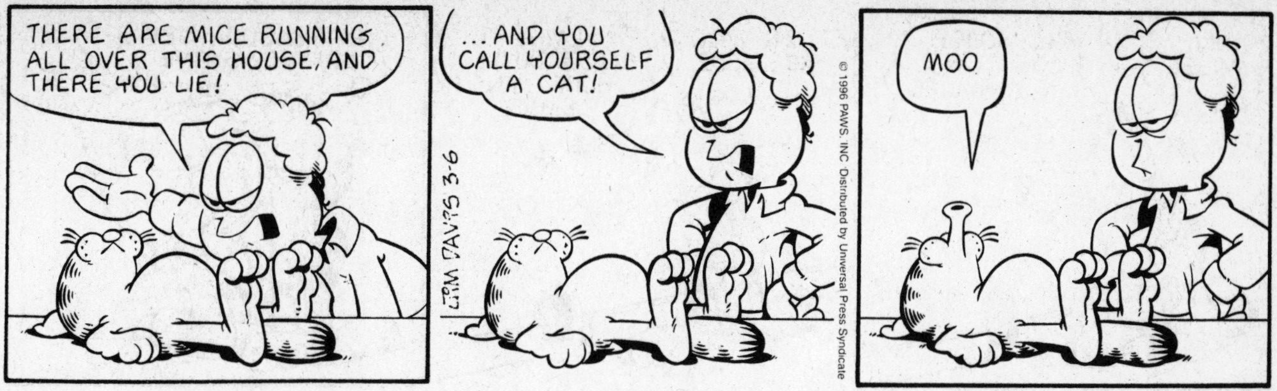
THERE ARE MICE RUNNING ALL OVER THIS HOUSE, AND THERE YOU LIE!
...AND YOU CALL YOURSELF A CAT!
MOO
JIM DAVIS 3-6
© 1996 PAWS, INC./Distributed by Universal Press Syndicate

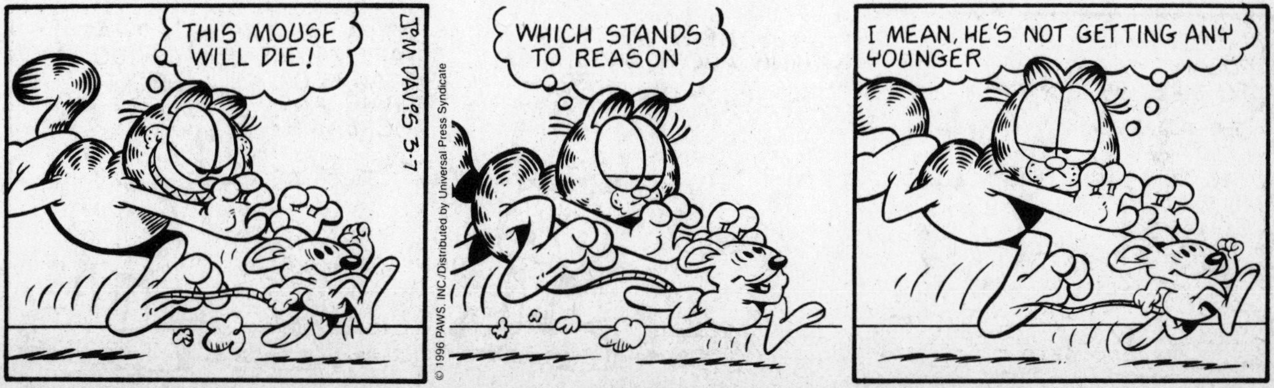
THIS MOUSE WILL DIE!
WHICH STANDS TO REASON
I MEAN, HE'S NOT GETTING ANY YOUNGER
JIM DAVIS 3-7
© 1996 PAWS, INC./Distributed by Universal Press Syndicate

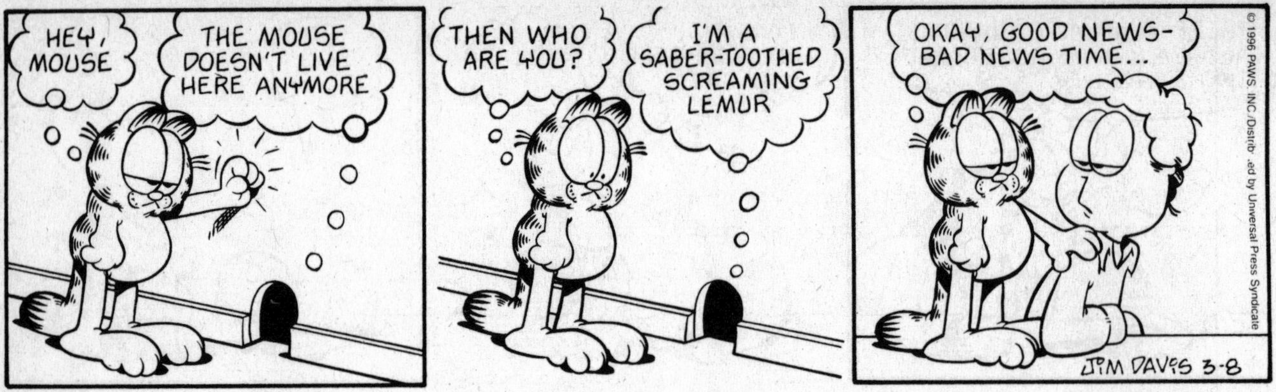
HEY, MOUSE
THE MOUSE DOESN'T LIVE HERE ANYMORE
THEN WHO ARE YOU?
I'M A SABER-TOOTHED SCREAMING LEMUR
OKAY, GOOD NEWS-BAD NEWS TIME...
JIM DAVIS 3-8
© 1996 PAWS, INC./Distrib .ed by Universal Press Syndicate

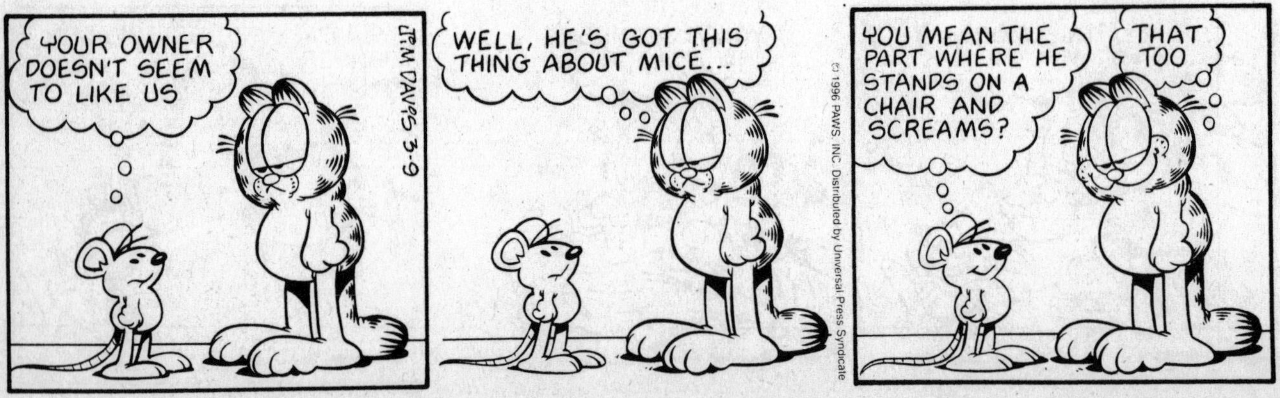
YOUR OWNER DOESN'T SEEM TO LIKE US
JIM DAVIS 3-9
WELL, HE'S GOT THIS THING ABOUT MICE...
(c) 1996 PAWS, INC. Distributed by Universal Press Syndicate
YOU MEAN THE PART WHERE HE STANDS ON A CHAIR AND SCREAMS?
THAT TOO

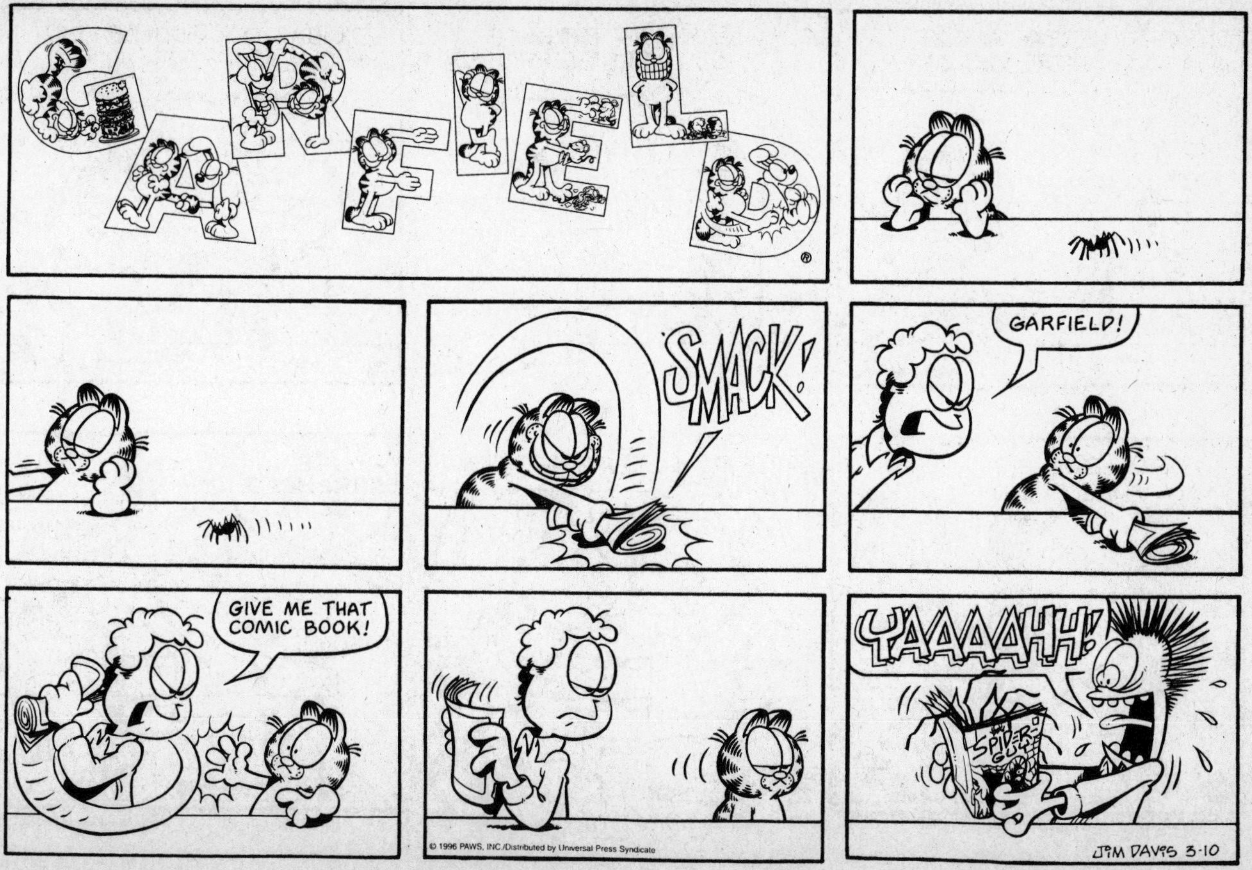
GARFIELD
SMACK!
GARFIELD!
GIVE ME THAT COMIC BOOK!
YAAAAHH!
SPIDER-GUY
© 1996 PAWS, INC./Distributed by Universal Press Syndicate
JIM DAVIS 3-10

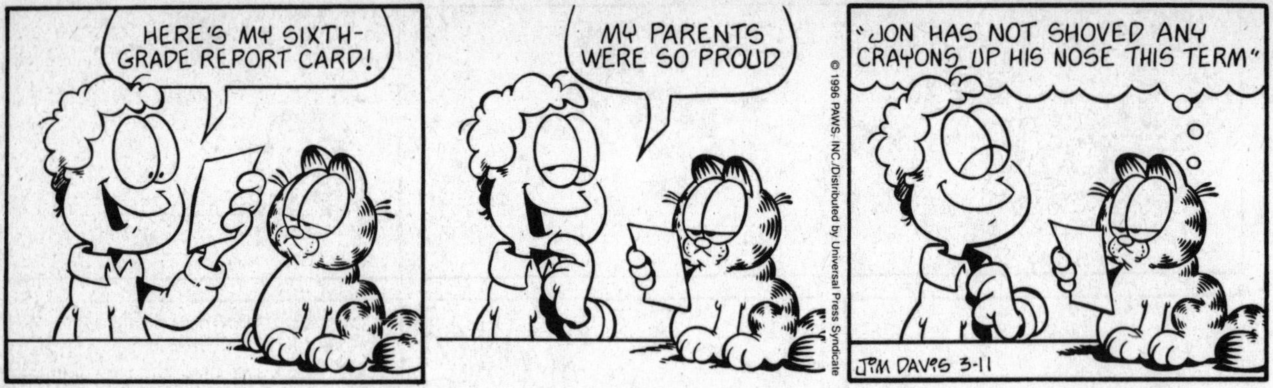
HERE'S MY SIXTH-GRADE REPORT CARD!
MY PARENTS WERE SO PROUD
"JON HAS NOT SHOVED ANY CRAYONS UP HIS NOSE THIS TERM"
JIM DAVIS 3-11
© 1996 PAWS, INC./Distributed by Universal Press Syndicate

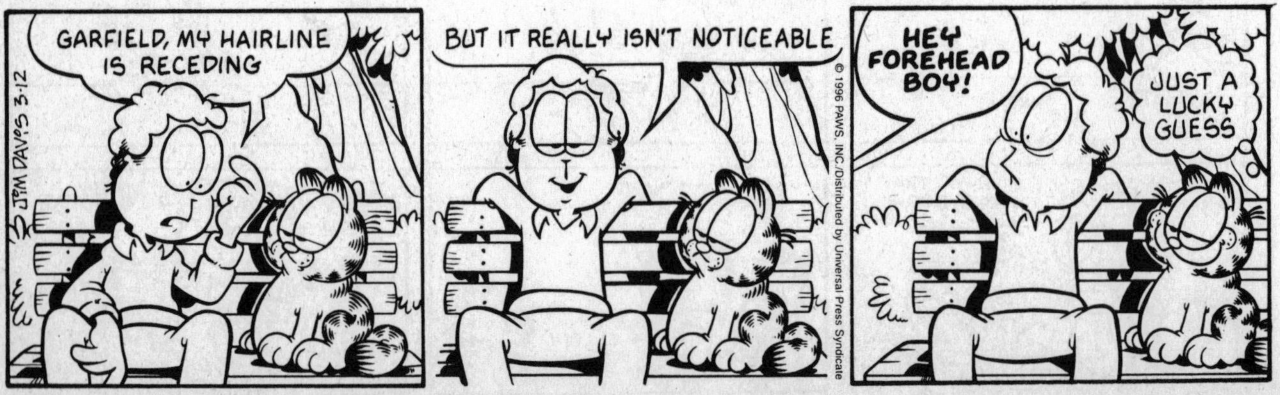
JIM DAVIS 3-12
GARFIELD, MY HAIRLINE IS RECEDING
BUT IT REALLY ISN'T NOTICEABLE
HEY FOREHEAD BOY!
JUST A LUCKY GUESS
© 1996 PAWS, INC./Distributed by Universal Press Syndicate

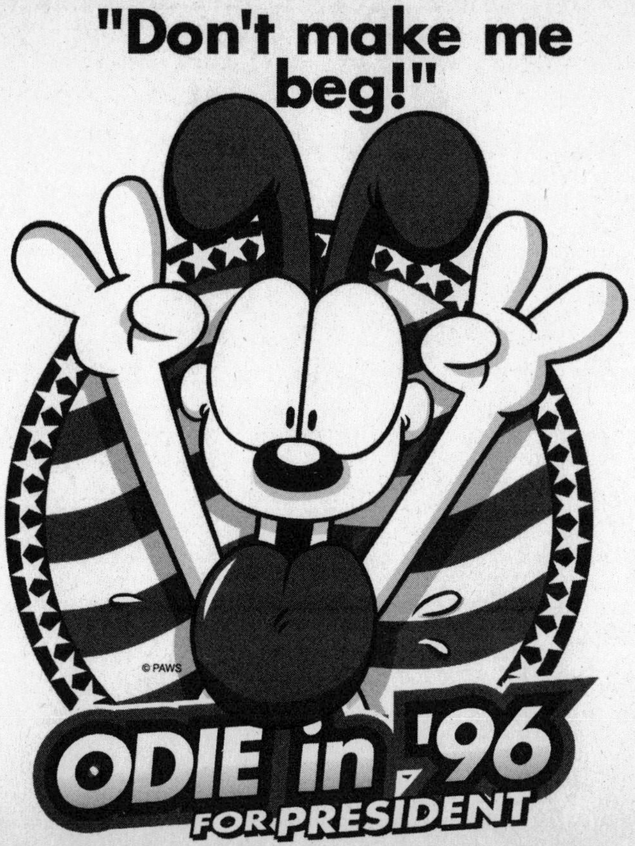
"Don't make me beg!"
© PAWS
ODIE in '96
FOR PRESIDENT

IF ODIE WERE PRESIDENT, HE WOULD...

- Replace Washington Monument with giant fire hydrant
- Start every press conference with an Underdog cartoon
- Repeal oppressive leash laws
- Have all cats de-clawed
- Require mailmen to wear short pants
- Be the first chief executive to lick himself in public!

STRIPS, SPECIALS, OR BESTSELLING BOOKS . . .
GARFIELD'S ON EVERYONE'S MENU
Don't miss even one episode in the Tubby Tabby's hilarious series!

__GARFIELD AT LARGE (#1) 32013/$6.95
__GARFIELD GAINS WEIGHT (#2) 32008/$6.95
__GARFIELD BIGGER THAN LIFE (#3) 32007/$6.95
__GARFIELD WEIGHS IN (#4) 32010/$6.95
__GARFIELD TAKES THE CAKE (#5) 32009/$6.95
__GARFIELD EATS HIS HEART OUT (#6) 32018/$6.95
__GARFIELD SITS AROUND THE HOUSE (#7) 32011/$6.95
__GARFIELD TIPS THE SCALES (#8) 33580/$6.95
__GARFIELD LOSES HIS FEET (#9) 31805/$6.95
__GARFIELD MAKES IT BIG (#10) 31928/$6.95
__GARFIELD ROLLS ON (#11) 32634/$6.95
__GARFIELD OUT TO LUNCH (#12) 33118/$6.95
__GARFIELD FOOD FOR THOUGHT (#13) 34129/$6.95
__GARFIELD SWALLOWS HIS PRIDE (#14) 34725/$6.95
__GARFIELD WORLDWIDE (#15) 35158/$6.95
__GARFIELD ROUNDS OUT (#16) 35388/$6.95
__GARFIELD CHEWS THE FAT (#17) 35956/$6.95
__GARFIELD GOES TO WAIST (#18) 36430/$6.95
__GARFIELD HANGS OUT (#19) 36835/$6.95
__GARFIELD TAKES UP SPACE (#20) 37029/$6.95
__GARFIELD SAYS A MOUTHFUL (#21) 37368/$6.95

__GARFIELD BY THE POUND (#22) 37579/$6.95
__GARFIELD KEEPS HIS CHINS UP (#23) 37959/$6.95
__GARFIELD TAKES HIS LICKS (#24) 38170/$6.95
__GARFIELD HITS THE BIG TIME (#25) 38332/$6.95
__GARFIELD PULLS HIS WEIGHT (#26) 38666/$6.95
__GARFIELD DISHES IT OUT (#27) 39287/$6.95
__GARFIELD LIFE IN THE FAT LANE (#28) 39776/$6.95
__GARFIELD TONS OF FUN (#29) 40386/$6.95
__GARFIELD BIGGER AND BETTER (#30) 40770/$6.95
__GARFIELD HAMS IT UP (#31) 41241/$6.95
__GARFIELD THINKS BIG (#32) 41671/$6.95
__GARFIELD THROWS HIS WEIGHT AROUND (#33) 42749/$6.95
__GARFIELD LIFE TO THE FULLEST (#34) 43239/$6.95

GARFIELD AT HIS SUNDAY BEST!
__GARFIELD TREASURY 32106/$11.95
__THE SECOND GARFIELD TREASURY 33276/$10.95
__THE THIRD GARFIELD TREASURY 32635/$11.00
__THE FOURTH GARFIELD TREASURY 34726/$10.95
__THE FIFTH GARFIELD TREASURY 36268/$12.00
__THE SIXTH GARFIELD TREASURY 37367/$10.95
__THE SEVENTH GARFIELD TREASURY 38427/$10.95
__THE EIGHTH GARFIELD TREASURY 39778/$12.00
__THE NINTH GARFIELD TREASURY 41670/$12.50

AND DON'T MISS...
__GARFIELD'S TWENTIETH ANNIVERSARY COLLECTION!
42126/$14.95

Please send me the BALLANTINE BOOKS I have checked above. I am enclosing $_____. (Please add $2.00 for the first book and $.50 for each additional book for postage and handling and include the appropriate state sales tax.) Send check or money order (no cash or C.O.D.'s) to Ballantine Mail Sales Dept. TA, 400 Hahn Road, Westminster, MD 21157.

To order by phone, call 1-800-733-3000 and use your major credit card.

Prices and numbers are subject to change without notice. Valid in the U.S. only. All orders are subject to availability.

Name_____

Address_____

City_____ State_____ Zip_____

BIRTHDAYS, HOLIDAYS, OR ANY DAY . . .

Keep GARFIELD on your calendar all year 'round!

GARFIELD TV SPECIALS
__GARFIELD GOES HOLLYWOOD   34580/$6.95
__GARFIELD'S HALLOWEEN ADVENTURE   33045/$6.95
(formerly GARFIELD IN DISGUISE)
__GARFIELD'S FELINE FANTASY   36902/$6.95
__GARFIELD IN PARADISE   33796/$6.95
__GARFIELD IN THE ROUGH   32242/$6.95
__GARFIELD ON THE TOWN   31542/$6.95
__GARFIELD'S THANKSGIVING   35650/$6.95
__HERE COMES GARFIELD   32012/$6.95
__GARFIELD GETS A LIFE   37375/$6.95

ALSO FROM GARFIELD:
__GARFIELD: HIS NINE LIVES   32061/$9.95
__THE GARFIELD BOOK OF CAT NAMES   35082/$5.95
__GARFIELD: THE ME BOOK   36545/$7.95
__GARFIELD'S JUDGMENT DAY   36755/$6.95
__THE TRUTH ABOUT CATS   37226/$6.95
__GARFIELD'S JOLLY HOLIDAY 3 PACK   42042-X/$10.95

30   Allow at least 4 weeks for delivery   7/93 TA-267

Like to get a **COOL CATalog** stuffed with great **GARFIELD** products? Then just write down the information below, stuff it in an envelope and mail it back to us...or you can fill in the card on our website - **HTTP://www.GARFIELD.com.** We'll get one out to you in two shakes of a cat's tail!

Name:
Address:
City:
State:
Zip:
Phone:
Date of Birth:
Sex:

Please mail your information to:

**Garfield Stuff Catalog
Dept.2BB38A
5804 Churchman By-Pass
Indianapolis, IN 46203-6109**

© PAWS